A HISTORY OF HUNGARIAN LITERATURE

Written by
István Nemeskürty, László Orosz,
Béla G. Németh and Attila Tamás

Edited by
Tibor Klaniczay

A HISTORY OF HUNGARIAN LITERATURE

Corvina Kiadó

The authors
István Nemeskürty — from the beginnings to 1770
László Orosz — from 1770 to 1840
Béla G. Németh — from 1840 to 1905
Attila Tamás — from 1905

Bibliography by Ildikó Tódor
Text translated by
István Farkas, Enikő Körtvélyessy, Catherine Lőwy, Erzsébet Perényi, Márta Rusznyák
Revised by Bertha Gaster
Poems translated by László András T., John Bátki, Michael Beevor, Keith Bosley, G. F. Cushing,
Emery George, Tony Connor, Thomas Kabdebo, Claire Lashley, Edwin Morgan, Kenneth
McRobbie, Peter Sherwood, W. D. Snodgrass, J. E. Sollosy, Vernon Watkins
Pictures selected by Éva B. Kiss
Photographs from the Archives of Petőfi Literary Museum
Cover design by István Mátrai

© Tibor Klaniczay 1982
ISBN 963 13 1542 8

Printed in Hungary 1983
Kner Printing House, Dürer Workshop

Contents

Preface

In order to carry any weight, a recommendatory preface to a *History of Hungarian Literature* must be honest, especially when it is written, as is the case here, by someone woefully deficient in his knowledge of Hungarian literature. But this handicap also has an advantage: it places the composer of the preface, very probably, into the same category as most of the readers of the work. For this *History* is, I believe, oriented less toward the expert than toward the comparatist curious about the literature and culture of this anomalous linguistic island called Hungary within a Germanic, Slavic, and Latin world, an island that has produced, as we all know, a share of world-renowned scientists and musicians (and beautiful women) far out of proportion with its population. What we know much less about, however, is its literature.

Had I been asked, when I was in high school, what Hungarian writer I knew, my answer would have consisted of one name only: Petőfi. That name would, however, have been pronounced with youthful enthusiasm, undiminished by the fact that I had to read him in translation. Even second-hand the thematic mixture of liberty, nature, and love, in youthful, unalloyed, stirring language that no translation could dim, fired the dreams of this *Gymnasiast*. Re-reading Petőfi recently, I found that advancing years have not reduced my fascination with him but have developed a greater sensitivity to the more problematic aspects of his life, thought, and works.

But Hungarian literature is, of course, not just Petőfi, nor Molnár, perhaps the most successful Hungarian writer ever, at least in the West. Hence I, personally, welcome the opportunity of being introduced by the present work to the broad spectrum of Hungarian literature. This *History* takes nothing for granted. It does not bury the reader under heaps of learned, esoteric references, but straightforwardly tells him or her the essential facts about the writer's life and times, the thrust of his thought, the nature of his works, and does not, fortunately, gloss over weaknesses either, for everything cannot be equally good.

I cannot, *faute de connaissance de cause,* assess the accuracy of the literary, philosophical, political, social, and other judgments and selections made in the book. What I can do is to state what it brought to me. Samples will have to do.

11

It conveyed to me such refreshing poems as Bálint Balassi's (1554–1594) "Celia's Bathing", such honest autobiographical writing as Miklós Bethlen's (1642–1716), and such characteristic epistolary literature as Kelemen Mikes's (1690–1761) *Letters from Turkey* reminding me of certain parts of Steen Steensen Blicher's *En Landsbydegns Dagbog* (1824) which also takes place in the first half of the 17th century. It calls attention to established or potential comparative influences or analogies such as Petrarca's impact on the work of Balassi or Sándor Kisfaludy (1772–1844), Balassi's affinities with Ronsard, Kochanowski, and Shakespeare's sonnets, Kazinczy's (1759–1831) debt to Cicero, Sallust, Horace, Plutarch, Winckelmann, Goethe, La Rochefoucauld, and Barthélemy, Csokonai's (1773–1805) reservations about Hervey and Young or his relatedness to Heine. It refers to the reception of European Romanticism (Herder, Byron, Alfieri, Mme de Staël, etc.) in the writings of István Széchenyi and gave me my first coherent introduction to such Romantic greats as Kölcsey, Vörösmarty (very inadequately appreciated abroad), János Arany, and Jókai. Nor had I knowledge of the Hungarian equivalent of *Faust* or *Moby Dick*, Madách's *Tragedy of Man* (1860).

On the 19th-century Realism side, I had never heard of Sándor Bölöni Farkas's influential *Travel in North America* (1834), nor of such novel and novella writers as Gyulai, Mikszáth (influenced by Dickens, Alphonse Daudet, and Bret Harte) nor of, around 1900, Petelei, Gozsdu, Bródy, Gárdonyi, Tömörkény, or Thury. And except for the facile Molnár, I had little substantive information on such 20th-century peaks as Ady, Móricz, Kosztolányi, Tóth, Margit Kaffka, József, and Radnóti. I was aware of Mihály Babits's remarkable *History of European Literature* (1936) but had no inkling of the overall importance of Babits in the literary life of his country, including his setting the highest standards for literary translation. Literary scholarship and criticism, such as the focal periodical, *Nyugat,* with which Babits and others were closely associated in the 1920s and 1930s, are well recognized in the present work.

Insights gained are not limited, however, to specific genres, movements, currents, titles, and names. Other cultural phenomena that elucidate literary evolution receive due attention, too. A few illustrations. Any reader of a history of Hungarian literature must note the signal role played by the Hungarian aristocracy in maintaining Hungarian identity in the many epochs of political dependence. Information provided explains this: about 80 per cent, it seems, of the aristocracy was ethnically Hungarian, whereas a significantly lower percentage held for the majority of the population in these periods. The slimness of the bourgeois class and the involvement of the high aristocracy with foreign culture and politics explains why such a consistent patriotic impetus came from the lower and middle aristocracy. The weakness of the bourgeoisie also accounts for the phenomenon that Romantic writings authored by aristocrats bypassed the bourgeoisie and romanticized the people. The connection between Free Masonry and literature in the 18th century, or the strong German cultural influence on the birth and evolution of Buda and Pest are just two random examples of much relevant socio-cultural information and explanation provided by this *History*.

No *History* can ever be definitive. But I dare say that for a generation of non-specialist readers of English this work will offer a lively, direct, clear, and rich introduction to the literary facet of a noteworthy culture.

Henry H. H. Remak
Indiana University

Editor's Preface

A history of Hungarian literature in a foreign language written by Hungarian authors came out in 1962; it was *Histoire abrégée de la littérature hongroise,* a joint undertaking by Tibor Klaniczay, József Szauder and Miklós Szabolcsi. The same year it was published in Russian, a German translation followed in 1963, an English translation in 1964, a Polish translation in 1966 and a Bulgarian translation in 1975. The book, long overdue, was, apart from a few critical remarks, well received abroad. The editors and publishers were not only aware of its merits, but also of the shortcomings, partly attributable to the book appearing shortly before the publication, in six volumes, of *History of Hungarian Literature* by the Institute of Literary History of the Hungarian Academy of Sciences. In this huge work, published from 1964 to 1966, sixty specialists summarized the more important scholarly work that had been devoted to the history of Hungarian literature. The authors of *Histoire abrégée* were naturally unable to take advantage of some of the ideas and insights in this important work. Hence the need to publish a new *History of Hungarian Literature* for foreign readers became more and more urgent. The present *History* is based on *Histoire abrégée* and the six volumes published by the Institute of Literary History; the editors have also taken criticism of the earlier work by Klaniczay, Szauder and Szabolcsi into account.

Tibor Klaniczay

The Middle Ages

From the Beginnings to the Early Sixteenth Century

1 The Origins and Ancient Poetry of the Magyars

The Settlement of the Magyars in Present-day Hungary

The Hungarians, or Magyars as they call themselves, who speak a Finno-Ugrian language, took possession of their present-day homeland in the Carpathian Basin at the end of the ninth century A.D. (896–900). A tribal federation of nomadic horsemen—referred to as "hungari" from Onogur, a name for a federation of tribes, subsequently applied to one group of them, the specifically Hungarian tribes, in several Latin chronicles, had pressed westwards from the grasslands between the Dnieper and Dniester rivers, in what is now the south-west European part of the USSR, in flight from the Petchenegs, another warlike race of the region.

The Magyars took the well-worn path westwards, which had previously been followed by the Huns in the fourth century A.D., the Avars in the seventh century, and a number of other peoples in the wave of migrations from East to West. All those powerful tribal federations, which had, one after another, threatened to conquer the whole of Europe, eventually fell largely due in the last resort to their outworn social structure in relation to the more advanced structure of contemporary Europe. The Hungarians alone found themselves capable of establishing an independent state by adopting a more advanced social and economic system based on a more settled way of life depending on agriculture and the private ownership of land, and consequently were in a position to foster and develop a national culture.

What enabled the Hungarian tribes to strike roots in the country must have been their knowledge of more advanced forms of organized statehood; for comparatively long periods they had formed a part of the Turkic empire and then of the Khazar empire that succeeded it, thus developing a social framework superior to that of the Huns. They were already familiar with elementary forms of agriculture, and had come into contact with Christianity through their connections with the Byzantine Empire. From the fifth century A.D., through the centuries of the Turkic and Khazar empires, the Hungarians inhabited the steppes bordering the Sea of Azov and developed from a group of totemistic clans into a tribal federation, reaching an advanced stage of nomadic feudalism.

Having conquered the Carpathian Basin, the Hungarians intermarried with the indigenous population of land-tilling Slavs and were thus introduced to more advanced forms of agriculture. They did not, however, entirely abandon their nomadic ways and, following the practice of other races in the time of the Great Migration, from time to time under the inspiration of their various rulers, would burst into the countries to the west of Hungary on marauding expeditions. About the same time that England was being harassed by the warlike Dane, the Normans making their appearance in the Mediterranean, and a host of Germanic tribes pushing the Slav population of the area eastwards along the river Oder, the Hungarians were plundering and laying waste the lands of present-day Austria, Bavaria, Switzerland, northern Italy and France. "The Hungarians came; and there was such a great multitude of them that people were moved to say, 'There is no power that can conquer the Magyars, save the earth cleaving open, and Heaven burying them,'" the Abbot Regino of Prüm in Germany recorded at the time.

The Magyars' raids were eventually brought to an end at the battle of Lechfeld near Augsburg, in A.D. 955 by the well-organized feudal army of Emperor Otto with its armoured cavalry and superior technique when the swift but comparatively ill-equipped Hungarian horsemen were routed. This débâcle was the moment of truth for the princely chiefs of the Hungarian tribal federation; they realized that if they were to retain their foothold in the Carpathian Basin—the territories watered by the rivers Danube and Tisza—they would have to adapt to their surroundings by adopting the economic and social system of feudalism prevailing in the West. Thus, in the last decade of the tenth century, Prince Géza, the paramount chief, and his son Vajk, who as Stephen the First was to become the first king of Hungary, became Christians embracing the Western Roman rite and not the Orthodox rite of Byzantium and forced on their people a similar conversion. A system of private ownership of land came into being and with it an organized sovereign Hungarian state.

Remains of the Poetry of Ancient Times

The culture and poetry of the Hungarians at the time of the Conquest was a folk culture handed down by word of mouth. Although they knew the art of writing (the Hungarian words for "to write" and "letter, character"—*ír* and *betű*—are part of the stock of ancient Hungarian words in the language) and did in fact possess a set of runic characters used for carving short inscriptions in wood or stone, it was not adapted for recording long or complex texts. Moreover, after some two hundred years of more or less continuous military and trading contact with Byzantium (a number of Hungarian chiefs had indeed been converted to Orthodox Christianity before the establishment of the Hungarian state), the Magyars must have acquired at least a notion of Greek characters. But there had been no demand for the recording of longer texts, for neither their previous social development nor their shamanistic beliefs of pagan times had needed it.

Not a single contemporary text of ancient Magyar poetry has survived, but a number of allusions to such poetry, and records of some later date, as well as ancient elements preserved in Hungarian folklore, bear witness to the wealth of that poetry. It was combined with music, dance and elementary drama, and its exponent was the priest or shaman. The chant of the shaman was an improvised incantation for the purposes of sorcery, prophesy, necromancy or healing. Fragments of these songs were first written down, out of scholarly curiosity, by men of the Renaissance, between 1488 and 1578. One much earlier piece of written evidence, however, indicates the existence of work songs. This record tells us how the Italian-born Bishop of Csanád, St. Gellért or Ghirardus while in Hungary on his way to the king's court, stayed overnight in a village where he heard a peasant woman singing an air as she ground her corn on the handmill. Turning to the priest Walter, who was his companion, the bishop, as the legend has it, remarked, "Do you hear the symphony of the Magyars?" And they both laughed at her song.

A number of Latin chronicles contain references indicating the existence of a body of heroic poetry—long poems or lays narrating the adventures of heroes. These would be recited at the banquets of chieftains or princes by men known as *regös (joculatores)*, former shamans who had become singers and minstrels. From various allusions and other stray bits of information it has proved possible to reconstruct two epic stories of the origin of the Magyars that had survived among the minstrels for many years. The better known of the two, that of *The Miraculous Stag*, recalls the fact that the stag was the totem of the Magyars. The *Lay of the White Steed* tells of the Magyars' conquest of their homeland. There were also a number of epic songs concerning the raids of the tenth century, especially the lay of *Lél* (Lehel) and that of *Botond*, being narratives of the adventures of two chiefs.

Reconstructing the original text of these lays in the absence of contemporary records presents considerable difficulties, because, as one might expect, they were remodelled and corrupted in the later medieval Latin sources which preserved them. We know little more than two lines preserved in a thirteenth-century *gesta* of a tale narrating the Transylvanian campaign of the Chief Töhötöm: *Omnes loca sibi aquireband, et nomen bonum accipiebant.* Several folk ballads contain traces of Hungarian epic poetry from the time of the Conquest, but the original story has generally been changed and associated with heroes of later periods, as in the *Ballad of Izsák Kerekes*. The versification is believed to have been similar to that of ancient European poetry; it is thought, for example, that the Hungarian minstrels did not employ rhyme, but relied rather on alliteration.

2 The Hungarian State and Hungarian Culture in the Middle Ages

Organization of the State and the Church

Following the conversion of the Magyars, the Kingdom of Hungary rapidly assimilated to the conditions of West European feudalism. Power was based on the vast lands owned by the king and the clergy. St. Stephen (*c.* 1001–1038), the first king of Hungary, was remarkable for the vigour and efficiency with which he organized the state, displaying what must be regarded as a strikingly modern mentality for his time. His kingdom extended beyond present-day Hungary, reaching as far as the heights of the Carpathians in the north-west, north, east and south-east, to the Sava and Drava rivers in the south, and stretching as far as the easternmost range of the Alps in the west. With the establishment of the Hungaro-Croatian Monarchy at the beginning of the twelfth century the writ of the King of Hungary ran down along the eastern shores of the Adriatic. These frontiers survived more or less unchanged until 1541, the beginning of the Turkish occupation. Stephen established ten bishoprics in his kingdom, and the great episcopal centres became the seats of learning. The first bishops—Bohemians, Italians, Frenchmen and Germans—were all members of the Benedictine order and adherents of the new and powerful reform movement centred on Cluny. It was a fortunate chance for Hungary that the conversion of the country to Christianity coincided with the peak of the Cluniac reform movement from 910 onwards. The first monastery built in Hungary, in A.D. 996, was Pannonhalma, north of Lake Balaton, which developed into a famous centre of learning in medieval Hungary. Several other monasteries were founded later during the eleventh century. A number of the bishops and abbots of the time were men of learning and writers, including the Bishop of Csanád, the Italian Gellért (d. 1046). In a letter, still in existence, the Bishop of Pécs, a Frenchman named Bonipertus, asked a friend in Chartres to send him some books; and King Stephen himself corresponded with the Abbot of Cluny. The influence of the French clerics increased in later years with the advent of the Cistercian monks who first arrived in Hungary in 1142. The churches and monasteries founded during this period were mostly built in the French Romanesque style, and this style maintained its dominant position until the arrival of the Dominicans and Franciscans in 1221 and 1232 respectively. For various other reasons the scene began to change from 1250 onwards.

Together with the growing links with the West, close relations were maintained with Byzantium and the Russian principality of Kiev. Hungary played a part in the attempts to reunify the Western and the Eastern Churches; Prince Géza was presented with a Byzantine crown by the Emperor Michael Ducas; cultural and trading links were strengthened through royal marriages; several of the heirs to the Hungarian throne were educated in Byzantium; and Andrew I and Béla I both spent their childhood and early youth in Kiev. As a result Hungarian kings and their chancellors adopted methods of administration and government learned during their years at the imperial court of Byzantium. Byzantine influence is apparent, too, in the murals of some of the eleventh-century churches, as for example at Feldebrő, once the seat of the Aba family, powerful in the reign of Ladislas IV (1272–1290).

The Culture of the Court and of the Chivalry

Cultural developments in Hungary in these early years received a marked stimulus in the reigns of Béla III (1172–1196) and his sons, Emeric and Andrew. The Provençal troubadour Peire Vidal visited the court of the King of Hungary during this period, presumably to entertain the Queen, Margaret Capet, of the French royal family. It was during this period as well that the cathedral and palace of Esztergom, then the seat of royalty, which had been destroyed by fire in 1188, began to be rebuilt: and the earliest surviving *gesta** was probably written about this time by one "Magister P", a cleric educated in France, long known, and still largely referred to, as Anonymus.

The first dynasty, the House of Árpád, sprung from the paramount chief of the Hungarian tribes at the time of the Conquest, came to an end in 1301. The fourteenth and fifteenth centuries were distinguished by the emergence of new social and economic conditions as well as by a succession of new dynasties: the new Angevin kings—of the Neapolitan line—brought with them the customs and the ethos of chivalry, which spread throughout the country during their reign in the fourteenth century, while the destiny of Hungary in the fifteenth century was shaped by the policies of Sigismund of Luxembourg, King of Hungary (1387–1437), later elected Holy Roman Emperor, his commander, János Hunyadi, and then by the latter's son, Matthias, who reigned on the Hungarian throne as Matthias Corvinus from 1458 to 1490. Their efforts to halt the northward thrust of the expansionist Ottoman empire, following the fall of Constantinople in 1453, were, at least for a time, successful.

Gesta in Hungarian literature means a chronicle which, as compared to German chronicles, does not present the events in chronological order.

In the early years of the fourteenth century the then powerful Dominican and Franciscan orders alone possessed some eighty monasteries in Hungary; nor were they alone. Churches began to be built in towns; and a new culture gradually began to develop, with its mainspring in the royal and baronial courts. The fine arts flowered: a statue of St. George and the Dragon, made in 1373 by Márton and György Kolozsvári and now in the Hradžin in Prague, is a remarkable early example of Gothic sculpture as distinct from Gothic architecture. Illuminated manuscripts from around this time by Hungarian miniaturists are treasured in a number of public and private collections in many countries: the library of the Vatican contains an ABC (1333) prepared for the children of Charles Robert I of Anjou; a Bible (*c.* 1338), once belonging to Chief Treasurer Dömötör Nekcsei, is in the Library of Congress in Washington and the *Illuminated Chronicle (Képes Krónika)* is in the National Széchényi Library in Budapest.

During the reigns of the Angevin kings and Sigismund the royal seats of Hungary were the scene of several meetings between heads of states and important dignitaries from home and abroad. Poets and scholars were also attracted to Buda and other Hungarian towns. Giovanni Serravalle dedicated his Latin translation of Dante's *Divine Comedy* to King Sigismund. Learning, which had been wholly theological until the 1350s, was slowly taking on a secular character; official posts in the chancelleries and elsewhere were thrown open to laymen, and the names of a number of lay scholars and lawyers appear among the chroniclers.

Universities were founded: at Pécs in 1367; in Buda in 1395, and in Pozsony (now Bratislava, Czechoslovakia) in 1467. None of them, however, functioned for long. Similarly, although printing from movable type reached Hungary in the century of its invention, it did not survive for long: András Hess owned and managed a printing-press in Buda in 1473, but only for a few years. In spite of some fine individual achievements, these two unsuccessful experiments, together with the slow development of the towns, were largely instrumental in the failure of Hungary to reach the level of the Western European countries in medieval learning.

3 Hungarian Literature in the Latin Tongue

Legends

The earliest extant specimens of the use of Latin in Hungary include deeds and other documents, laws and edicts, such as King Stephen's *Admonitions,* Bishop Gellért's essay in theology *Deliberatio supra hymnum trium puerorum,* and, more particularly, legends of the Hungarian saints. These early legends played an important part in forming the general picture of their history in the minds of Hungarians. A glance at the mounted statue of King Stephen beside the Matthias Church in Buda is indication enough that the influence exercised by *The Greater Legend of Stephen, King and Saint* (dating from about 1077) was still active at the end of the nineteenth century. While the first king of Hungary was in reality a gifted but ruthlessly iron-willed and iron-fisted statesman, the popular eye saw him as a benign and pious almsgiver, a holy and venerable old man, as presented by the legend that had begun to evolve from the moment of his canonization.

This, however, was not the earliest of Hungarian legends; it was preceded by *The Legend of the Hungarian Hermits Zoerard and Benedict* (1060), written by Mór, the Bishop of Pécs, a work that is of especial interest because the author was personally acquainted with the two saintly recluses. *The Legend of Saint Emeric,* Prince of Hungary, Stephen's son, is similar in concept to the *Greater Legend of Stephen:* the chaste life of the virgin prince enshrined in it was designed to propagate the ideal of priestly celibacy; it is believed to date from around 1115, subsequent to the synods of Esztergom which dealt precisely with this subject.

These three legends or "legenda" provided monastic reading after the manner of Cluny. There were, however, more "secular" legends; to be more precise, legends more directly designed for political ends, embodying the concept of a national state as presented by the now firmly established Kingdom of Hungary. One of these is the *Lesser Legend of Stephen, King and Saint* differing from the "greater" legend: the King in the "lesser" legend is a determined and purposeful politician, with a character approximating more closely to the contemporary idea of government and the realities of the day (it was written in the reign of Coloman Beauclerc, 1095–1116, who was an energetic ruler and a highly efficient administrator). Legends, believed to be more or less contemporary with the "lesser" legend are

The Greater Legend of Saint Ghirardus, Bishop of Csanád, a vivid romanticized picture of the age based on a number of written sources, much of it taken from various chronicles, and *The Legend of Saint Ladislas* (c. 1200), which contains a good deal of secular material. It extols the virtues of chivalry and is woven around the handsome and attractive person of its hero. These legends, probably substitutes for *gestae*, are full of historical allusions and references.

Religious Poetry

The Latin hymns of Hungarian writers are mostly written in praise of Hungarian saints and their subject-matter is generally taken from the legends of these saints; a fact which supports the suggestion that most of them date from the thirteenth century. Little more is known of their origins, as only late copies survive. Only one of these hymn-writers is known by name, *Antal Tatai*, a Pauline monk from Budaszentlőrinc, who wrote a hymn around 1476 to the patron saint of his order. Other hymns worth mentioning include those on St. Stephen (*Corde, voce, mente pura...*), St. Emeric (*Plaude parens Pannonia...*), and St. Ladislas (*Novae laudis attollamus...*).

One of the most important specimens of Latin poetry in the body of medieval Latin literature in Hungary is a lament over the rape of Hungary by the Mongols, entitled *Planctus destructionis Regni Hungariae per tartaros* (Lament for the Destruction of Hungary by the Tartars); it was written by an unknown author in 1242, immediately after the invasion of Hungary in 1241 and 1242 by the Mongol horde. It is not surprising that the shock of this appalling national disaster, in which it is estimated the great majority of the population were annihilated, inspired the finest piece of national writing to that date. The sudden, terrible blow broke through all the time-honoured conventions of the literature of the time; the poet was fired by the experience he had himself undergone to give it emotional expression. The wrath of God had fallen on the Hungarian nation, he cried, and those who aroused His anger were none other than the lords of the realm: they were proud liars and lechers pranking it in their glittering flamboyance, oppressing widows, persecuting the poor, plundering the sick, and dealing brutally with strangers. The Christian neighbour to the West—Frederick of Babenburg, Duke of Austria—also comes in for his share of execration; instead of coming to the aid of Hungary at the time of the pagan invasion, he seized the opportunity to fall upon the country and pillage the people.

Histories

The earliest surviving *gesta* is the *Gesta Ungarorum* written around 1200 by "Magister P", a man of gentle birth tentatively identified with Péter, Bishop of Győr. All that he reveals about himself, in the opening section of his work on the Hungarian Conquest, is that he was a notary (or head of the Chancellery) at the court of Béla III; hence the name under which he is generally known, *Anonymus*—from "Anonymus Belae Regis notarius"—"the anonymous scribe of King Béla". In his *Gesta Ungarorum* the author reveals that his sympathies lie with the newly emerging oligarchy of great nobles opposed to the royal house. Projecting his own times back into the past, as was the custom of the age, he portrays a "nobility" following the rules of chivalry, and even lists certain families among the Magyar clans of the Conquest whose ancestors had in fact settled in Hungary many years after the Conquest had taken place. The prose text occasionally includes rhyme, a device of the chroniclers, and also occasionally breaks into verse. His style is skilful and refined; he has a predilection for a play on words, for the mounting accumulation of nouns and adjectives as well as for the alliteration. The *gesta* of Anonymus was certainly preceded by several others, but the existence of these can only be inferred. The early *gestae* of 1060, 1100 and 1170 were always expressions of various dynastic interests, designed to justify the king's deeds and hold them up to admiration. These writers made little use of records and cited no foreign sources. Judging from the fragments incorporated in later works, these early *gestae* must have been deftly constructed, full of stirring events and tales all told with a definite end in view.

Carmen miserabile (1244), the reminiscences of Master *Rogerius,* the Italian-born Dean of Várad, is another account of the Mongol Invasion of 1241 and 1242. For a short time Rogerius himself had been held captive by the Mongols. He examined with great care the conditions and circumstances that allowed so great and rich a nation as Hungary to succumb to the sudden onslaught of the Tartars, his approach was scholarly, methodical and unsparingly honest which, combined with his gifts as a writer, make him one of the outstanding authors of the time.

The most important of all the thirteenth-century histories, and the one which had the most powerful impact, was the *Gesta Hungarorum,* written about 1280 by *Simon Kézai,* chaplain to King Ladislas IV the Cuman. Kézai, who had studied at Italian universities, relied on a number of sources: the chronicles of Jordanes and Godfrey of Viterbo, and even the *Nibelungenlied*. While Kézai is a superb story-teller, and there is a ring of truth about much of his narrative there are moments when fiction takes over, as for instance his identification, as imposing as it is absurd, of the Huns with the Hungarians. This "folk etymology" of Kézai's was immensely influential in shaping the Hungarian historical consciousness; its effect on literature was equally great, providing the inspiration for the poems and tales of many writers of the nineteenth century. A number of foreign historians had referred to Hungarians, somewhat disparagingly, as "Huns"; Kézai defiantly turned the slight on its head As the Huns were the ancestors of the Hungarians it had in fact been the Hungarians, he contended it, who had ridden victoriously across Europe, bringing fear and trembling even to the Pope himself. Compared with his vivid, absorbing and skilfully constructed story of the Huns, his account of the medieval history of Hungary reveals his small interest in the subject; Kézai simply makes use of Master Ákos's chronicle, written some decades earlier, only expanding it a little where the exploits of the king he served were concerned.

The chroniclers of the Angevin era occasionally gave accounts of contemporary events. One of these related the attempt made by a noble, Felicián Zách, on the king's life in 1330, and was so graphically told that it inspired the poet János Arany to write one of the greatest ballads of the nineteenth century. Other writers of the period attempted to summarize the various versions in earlier chronicles and weld them into a single whole. One such attempt resulted in the Hungarian *Illuminated Chronicle (Képes Krónika)* of 1358, the most remarkable of the compilations of medieval Hungarian history.

It was around this period that more sophisticated forms of historiography made their appearance. *János Küküllei,* the Archdeacon of Küküllő, made a study of written records for his biography of the Angevin king Louis I ("the Great") of Hungary, modelling the work on the life of Louis IX of France by Guillaume de Nangis. A century later, in 1487, *János Thuróczi* compiled a history of fifteenth-century Hungary. Practically all the earlier historians were bishops or clerics; Thuróczi, a judge of the royal court, was the first of the secular chroniclers. His sympathies lay with the class of the lesser nobility*, and made no bones about separating the history of the Hungarians as such from that of their ruling dynasties. Like his predecessor Simon Kézai, Thuróczi emphasizes the indivisibility of the noble class as whole *(una cademque nobilitas)*, without division into a greater nobility, that is the barons and the lesser nobility. He dwells on the importance of its mission and of presenting a united front and consequently the central characters of his history are the great general János Hunyadi and his son, who succedded to the throne as King Matthias Corvinus. (Thuróczi's literary model was Guido da Columna's *Roman de Troie*.) Thuróczi's chronicle owed its literary importance to his taste for irony, running like a silver

---

*The lesser nobility, a term which frequently confuses foreigners, were in fact the freeman class. Not the great barons or upper class, not the serfs, but those between, ranging from wealthy gentry and squires with landed estates down to poverty-stricken peasants, living near the economic level of the serfs, but with none of the obligations of serfs. In the political context, however, as here, it mostly referred to the wealthier and more influential gentry.

26

thread throughout the history: in Thuróczi we see the first traces of the wry humour that was to blossom in the writings of Gáspár Heltai in the sixteenth century and which became a characteristic of later Hungarian prose. Thuróczi also was the first to make use of some of the more graphic excerpts interpolated in the earlier *gesta,* presumably deriving from minstrel songs, as apt and effective "anecdotes". Thuróczi's chronicle was written after the invention of printing and was indeed published as a book, not in Hungary, however, but in Augsburg and Brünn (now Brno, Czechoslovakia; 1488).

Sermons

The favourite literary form of the Middle Ages, the sermon, was much cultivated in fourteenth-century Hungary. The sermons of the most eminent Hungarian exponent of that art, *Pelbárt (Privartus) Temesvári* (1440–1504), a Franciscan monk, were widely read both in his native country and abroad. His best-known works, *Stellarium coronae Mariae Virginis* (Strasbourg, 1496) and *Pomerium sermonum* (Hagenau, 1499) are models of pulpit discourses written in what is essentially the spirit of the Scholastics. They are marked by the strongly anti-Dominican attitude so prevalent among the Franciscans, usually expressed by contrasting the teachings of St. Thomas Aquinas with those of Duns Scotus. Temesvári exerted a great influence in his day, and contemporary manuscripts in the Hungarian language contain many of his sermons translated from Latin into the vernacular.

4 Literature in the Hungarian Tongue

The Earliest Records

The oldest continuous text in Hungarian that has come down to us is the *Funeral Oration* (Halotti Beszéd), written around 1150, a free version of the Latin original found in the same codex. The Oration is a powerful, dramatic piece of writing, sublimely simple, terse, yet eloquent. The longer, more complex sentences of the oration end with a short, sharply rhetorical question that calls the congregation back from the mist-shrouded past of the Fall to the frightening present, with the chastening reminder that they too must come to the same end as their brother laid out before them.

A hundred years after the *Funeral Oration,* at the end of the thirteenth century, an unknown priest was stimulated by the *Planctus Santae Mariae* of Geoffroy de Breteuil (d. 1196) to translate it into Hungarian. His *Old Hungarian Lament of Mary* (Ómagyar Mária-siralom) is a Hungarian transformation of the original liturgical hymn into a lay, pious song with mystic undercurrent. It was written in the ancient Hungarian line, consisting of eight syllables, with stress on the first and fifth syllable. The versification, the cadences and the use of this ancient line in the Hungarian *Lament* are so accomplished that the song must be assumed to have a background of several centuries of Hungarian literary practice behind it; unfortunately, no earlier specimens are extant. The song describes the grief-stricken Mother, exhausted to the point of collapse, standing beside the Cross and imploring her torture-racked son to comfort her; as the blood of Jesus flows from his body drop by drop, she feels her own life ebbing away. Here the economy of the *Funeral Oration* combines with the poetic and mystical union of these two suffering creatures.

The Poetry of Chivalry

The poetry of chivalry, both lyric and epic, which had flourished in Europe alongside religious poetry, had passed its golden age by the end of the thirteenth century and was on the decline. Although this style of poetry failed to take root in Hungary, there is nevertheless indirect evidence suggesting that both the lyric and the epic poetry, popular in other parts of Europe, were known in Hungary and that such poems were indeed written in Hungary. Certainly, well-known troubadours and Minnesingers of the early thirteenth century—Peire Vidal, Neidhart von Reuenthal and Tannhäuser, for instance—were not infrequent visitors to the Hungarian court, "while the mysterious Klingsor is often referred to in contemporary sources as Killingsor von Ungerland". No Hungarian poems, however, bearing traces of their influence have survived.

More is known about the lost epic poetry of Hungary. From the beginning of the twelfth century the unusual names of the heroes and heroines of romances appear as Christian names among the Hungarian greater nobility: Alexander, Achilles, Priam, Hector, Helen, Tristan and Roland are all found, which leads one to believe that they must have been acquainted with the *Roman d'Alexandre,* the *Roman de Troie,* the *Chanson de Roland,* and the stories of Tristan. Anonymus wrote in his preface to the *Gesta Ungarorum* that at the request of a friend he had written a history of Troy in Latin. This would support the theory that Hungarian versions of some of the romances and *chansons de geste* had once existed and certain features of South Slavonic versions of the *Roman de Troie* and the *Roman d'Alexandre* also suggest the existence of Hungarian variants.

Romances and troubadour songs with Hungarian themes are known to have been written in the fourteenth century. Towards the end of the century a kind of Hungarian *chanson de geste* was woven around the figure of Miklós Toldi (*c.* 1320–1370), a Hungarian noble who was a *condottiere* in Italy in 1365. Elements of this lost Toldi story passed into Hungarian folklore and his person and adventures formed the basis of many works of literature from the sixteenth century onwards, culminating in János Arany's masterpiece, an epic trilogy, in the nineteenth century. The fourteenth-century original was probably a late version of the French *chansons de geste,* and most probably contained some of its tales and adventures.

While there is a wealth of indirect evidence indicating the existence of troubadour and trouvère songs in Hungarian, nothing of this kind has survived. It is probable that these poems, chanted and sung, were only rarely transcribed, or found any place in the Hungarian literary culture of the Middle Ages.

Legends and Parables

On the other hand, some fine specimens of the Hungarian religious prose of the fourteenth and fifteenth centuries have come down to us. The oldest of these is *The Legend of Blessed Margaret* (Margit királylány legendája), written about 1310, but only known through a late copy telling the story of the princess who secluded herself in a convent on an island in the Danube, now named after her and situated in the middle of present-day Budapest. She sought and found fulfilment in the mystic ecstasy of religion, and was later canonized. The legend is a Hungarian version of the evidence presented at the canonization process written for the edification of the nuns of the Dominican order. Daily life in a medieval convent, with its small joys and cares, is here painted with a disarming naivety that omits none of the details so prized by posterity. An even more important feature of the work, though more lacking in purely literary merit, is the powerful account of the dramatic conflict between the realities of the outside world and the spiritual world of Margaret's aspirations. This strong-willed princess, who did not hesitate to remind her sisters in religion of her royal status on occasion, found especial pleasure in mystic ecstasy and self-mortification, and rejected nothing that would lead her to mystic union with her heavenly betrothed. The genuinely religious ecstasy she experienced was also the revolt of a strongly individual temperament against the outer world she despised. The legend traced this conflict back to its source in describing the seven-year-old Margaret's horror at the prospect of marriage (and sexual contact) with the Prince of Poland. Another vivid vignette showed Margaret, carrying a pail of dirty water, commanding Sister Csenge Bodoldi, the daughter of a great nobleman, to help her. She reluctantly obeyed but once they were outside the walls of the convent building in the garden, where they could not be seen, the humiliated Sister Csenge poured the dirty water over the princess. No example of medieval Hungarian prose still extant can compare with *The Legend of Blessed Margaret* in its abundance of carefully observed detail and its authentic picture of a given medieval environment.

The Legend of St. Francis (c. 1370, but known only from a fifteenth-century copy) is less valuable from a literary point of view. The *Jókai Codex* which contains the legend of St. Francis is the oldest known book in the Hungarian language, and the translators' struggles with Latin syntax are very much in evidence. It does not necessarily follow from its crudity that this was the first substantial Hungarian prose translation; it may well be that the good friar was simply not a very experienced writer.

Some hundred and fifty parables and legends in a number of Hungarian manuscripts dating from around 1500 are still in existence. Among the more important are the *Legend of St. Alexis,* a translation of a romance in the *Gesta Romanorum,* distinguished by its sensitive psychological interest, and the well-known *Legend of Josaphat.* Particularly important is the *Érdy Codex* (1524–27), consisting of 90 legends and 104 sermons, many obviously written under the influence of Pelbárt Temesvári, which was compiled by an unknown Carthusian monk. The dates are significant; the disastrous battle of Mohács, which opened the way for the Turkish occupation of the country, took place in 1526, and in several places in this sizable manuscript the writer expressed the fears of the lesser nobility over the imminent collapse of the Hungarian state.

Differing only in form from these works is the *Legend of St. Catherine of Alexandria.* In 4,067 lines of verse it expounded the involved and not very convincing theological disputations with this virgin martyr, so popular in the Middle Ages. Towards the end even the translator himself was so confused that he silenced the fifty philosophers confronting Catherine by introducing Plato as the ultimate authority.

Translations of the Bible

The first Hungarian translation of the Bible (*c.* 1430–40) was undertaken by the Hussites. The two translators, Tamás and Bálint, were both priests and had studied at Prague University. They set about their work in their native Szerémség but were forced to complete it in exile on the other side of the Hungarian border, on the eastern slopes of the Carpathian mountains, where they fled from persecution of the Church.

Szerémség, now Srem in Yugoslavia, then an area in southern Hungary at the confluence of the Danube, Tisza and Sava rivers, was one of the most socially advanced regions in medieval Hungary, and was the focal point for several of the heretical movements. Situated on the important trade route to Byzantium the towns of the region were peopled by lively and intelligent men whose cultural and other interests turned them towards Venice and northern Italy on the one hand and Prague on the other. This rich and beautiful country was reduced to stagnation, after revolts, by the persecution of the Franciscan friar, Jacobus de Marchia, sent by the Pope as Inquisitor to Hungary to stamp out the Hussite heresy, and had still not recovered by the second half of the fifteenth century.

This translation of the Bible is of extraordinary importance on account of its vast and diversified vocabulary, embracing practically the whole of contemporary learning, which the translators were forced to invent and adapt themselves, for medieval Hungarian was neither sophisticated nor rich enough to express the finer shades of meaning required by the language of the Bible. The contribution of these two priests to the Hungarian vocabulary was permanent; the words still form part of the Hungarian language. Their efforts to enrich it compare favourably with the language reform movement of the early nineteenth century led by the poet Ferenc Kazinczy and his associates, even though the effect of their innovations was less far-reaching. The two priests had to coin hundreds of abstract terms, and also had to attempt to standardize a more consistent orthography than those previously in use. Lacking, as far as one knows, the benefit of any earlier efforts to translate the Bible into Hungarian, they set about the task as pioneers. They were concerned to distinguish between words of a similar meaning, using each with a different connotation to express different shades of meaning. Through the translation can be felt the strong feeling of the two writers against the proud and mighty, the great barons and oligarchs as a class; where the sacred text permits, the Hungarian translation often burns with their righteous anger. It must not be forgotten in discussing medieval translations of the Bible into the vernacular that the very fact of translation indicated heresy; it was forbidden by the Church, for such translations would enable those unschooled in theology to understand and interpret the text themselves.

This Hussite translation of the Bible was followed in the late fifteenth and early sixteenth centuries by further versions, some of them incomplete. One of them is a magnificent translation of *The Song of Songs*.

Secular Poetry

As the Renaissance neared its peak in Italy towards the end of the fifteenth century, several types of secular poetry in the vernacular also began to emerge in Hungary. A considerable amount of epic poetry written by educated laymen made its appearance: the untutored singers and rhymesters were joined by increasing numbers of educated clerks and scribes or "scholars" who supplemented the epics of the bards with their own compositions, which included historical songs as well as social satire and love-songs.

A fascinating specimen of this historical poetry is the narrative poem entitled *The Siege of Szabács* (Szabács viadala, 1476), recounting an episode in King Matthias Corvinus's wars with the Turks. Scholars have been baffled by the contradictions in this poem; it lacks poetry, it is dull, it reads like a school composition. Yet it is distinguished by a strikingly modern vocabulary and impeccable versification; its use of decasyllabic rhymed couplets is without rival in contemporary Hungarian poetry.

This would seem to indicate the existence of a great variety of vernacular poetry; unfortunately, the general indifference towards literacy and the written word meant that many songs and poems were never recorded; considered unworthy of the attention of the learned, they remained on the outer periphery of the accepted culture of the time.

An interesting example of a genre that must have been much cultivated at this time is *Mihály Szabadkai's Cantio Petri Beriszló* (1515). Szabatkai was in the service of Péter Beriszló, Bishop of Veszprém and Ban of Croatia and Slavonia, one of whose encounters with the Turks is described in the song. The graphic description of the fighting in the open is full of unexpected twists and turns, both exciting and amusing, and the extraordinarily vivid visual power of the narrative already foreshadows the poems of Bálint Balassi. A memorable incident is that of the hussars dividing the spoils and measuring out lengths of cambric with their lances while the frightened Turks look on, hidden high in the branches of a nearby tree.

Another line of development also led to secular poetry from hymns and sacred poetry as seen in the *Song on Ladislas, King and Saint* (Ének Szent László királyról), which was an adaptation from a Latin original that displayed definite secular tendencies. The unknown author reveals an unerring sense of form in adapting the traditional techniques of hymn-writing; the metre imitates the Sapphic decasyllabic line. The influence of the Song on St. Ladislas can be seen in the fine *Song on the Death of King Matthias* (Emlékdal Mátyás király halálára) (who died in 1490), praising his conquests and acclaiming his policy in foreign affairs, even with so great a state as Venice, although Matthias always showed himself very cautious in such dealings. Only one of its nine stanzas dwelt on the internal affairs of Hungary, and it revealed the same typical attitude of the lesser nobility, on whose support Matthias largely depended, united in opposition to the political aspirations of the oligarchy.

The same views of the lesser nobility are reflected in an interesting *Cantilena* (c. 1523), a satire written by Ferenc Apáti in the agonizing years leading up to the effective destruction of the medieval Hungarian state at the Battle of Mohács (1526), when Suleiman's invading armies finally and decisively defeated the ill-equipped forces of King Louis II Jagiello.

This satire derided every class of contemporary Hungarian society, reserving its bitterest scorn for the clergy, the great barons and the peasants. Prejudiced in favour of the views of the lesser nobility, the Cantilena for all its bitter humour was yet imbued with a genuine fighting spirit, and Apáti's general outlook was an authentic reflection of the explosive contradictions of the age of peasant revolts and the Reformation, and made the Cantilena a faithful mirror of sixteenth-century Hungary. From then on, medieval literature gave way to the literature of the Renaissance, with its fresh colours and new ideals, which had developed alongside it from the late fifteenth century onwards.

Renaissance Literature

(From the Late Fifteenth to the Early Seventeenth Century)

5 The Hungarian Renaissance

The first signs of the Renaissance in Hungary appeared in the second half of the fifteenth century. It was to reach its zenith in the following century, one of the most bitter and tragic periods of Hungarian history.

The Renaissance Court of Matthias Corvinus

The first Renaissance court in Hungary was that of Matthias Corvinus (reigned 1458–1490), the younger son of János Hunyadi, the famous conqueror of the Turks. With the aid of the lesser nobility, who put him on the throne, Matthias assumed firm control of his kingdom through a strong army and an efficient administrative machine. He successfully resisted the repeated attacks of the Turks, and even extended his rule westwards, conquering Bohemia—he became King of Bohemia in 1469—and the eastern part of Austria; in 1485, indeed he transferred the royal seat to "Vienna Pannoniae" in Austria. The strongly centralized royal power and its corollary, an efficient administration, needed to curb the anarchical attitudes of the feudal barons, were well served by the cultured, humanist paid officials in his chancelleries. Educated in the universities of Italy and other countries, eminent European humanists well versed in the arts and sciences, such as the Italian Pier Paolo Vergerio or the Pole Gregory of Sanok, had already been at the head of the chancelleries before the accession of Matthias Corvinus. In ever-growing numbers Hungarian students studied at the universities of Padua and Bologna and the fashionable private colleges of Italy, Guarino da Verona's school in Ferrara being particularly favoured. Those unable to get to Italy went to the universities of Vienna or Cracow. One professor at Vienna University, Konrad Celtis (1459–1508), founded a learned society called *Sodalitas Litteraria Danubiana,* which held symposia in Vienna and Buda with the co-operation of Hungarian, Bohemian and German scholars.

The humanist learning of Italy made a particular impact in Hungary after 1476, the year of Matthias's marriage to Beatrix, daughter of Ferdinand I of Naples. Italian architects, masons, sculptors, painters and miniaturists, priests and scholars came to Hungary in large numbers. Mantegna, Filippino Lippi and Botticelli received commissions from Matthias; book-binders and illuminators from Florence and elsewhere supplied the king's library in Buda with illuminated manuscripts by the hundred. This library—the *Bibliotheca Corviniana*—was founded by Matthias; its stock of over one thousand volumes contained three thousand works embracing practically the whole body of contemporary learning.

After the death of Matthias Corvinus, this markedly Italianate aristocratic culture continued to flourish in the castles and mansions of Hungarian prelates, barons and high officials who had studied in that country. The red marble chapel constructed in 1507 for Cardinal Tamás Bakócz, Archbishop of Esztergom, is a fine piece of the architectural richness of this period which still survives, built into the nineteenth-century cathedral there. There were fine Hungarian artists painting during this period, as for instance the painter known simply as M. S. whose work, however, still shows the influence of Late Gothic.

The successors to Matthias, Wladislas II and his son, Louis II, of the Polish House of Jagiello, proved incapable of maintaining his strong, centralized power; the Hungarian state became a plaything of the great barons each struggling for supremacy. As a result of this sorry state of affairs, learning and the arts withered; the Hungarian economy passed largely into the hands of the great German trading families, especially the Fuggers, and exploitation of the serfs increased, preventing development of an indigenous middle class, and in turn strengthening the already strong position of the landowners. Under their oppression the peasants seethed with bitterness and in 1514 their desperation came to a head in the form of a mass uprising when large numbers of peasants joined a crusade against the Turks which rapidly turned to a revolt against the great barons. They were led by György Dózsa, a Transylvanian officer. The revolt was savagely repressed; the position of the serfs worsened; and twelve years later the nobility, already riven with feuds, found itself even more isolated than before and proved itself incapable of defending the country at the Battle of Mohács.

The Turkish Conquest

In August 1526, close to the town of Mohács, near the confluence of the Danube and the Drava, the invading forces of Suleiman the Great routed the badly organized army of King Louis II; the king himself was killed as he fled the battlefield. The defeat brought about the collapse of the centralized power. The Turkish army subsequently withdrew from Hungarian territory, and although substantial Hungarian forces still remained in the country, these were never committed to the war against the Turks but were used in the internecine strife of the claimants to the throne. The long-standing conflict between the great barons and the lesser nobility erupted into civil war, with each party crowning its own candidate; Ferdinand of Habsburg, the younger brother of Charles V, on the one hand and János Zápolya, Voivode of Transylvania on the other. In 1538, after twelve years of inconclusive fighting, the two claimants were reconciled through the joint mediation of the Pope, Francis I of France, Henry VIII of England and Emperor Charles V and pledged themselves to joint action against the Turks; but the struggle for power was renewed on the death of János I. In 1541 Suleiman II invaded the country again and occupied the castle of Buda in 1541 without a shot being fired.

Yet despite all the political anarchy, Renaissance art and learning, humanism in general and the Reformation in particular flourished during this fifteen year period from 1526 to 1541. The Lutheran Reformation, denounced as a national peril and as deepest heresy by the Diet of 1526, spread unchecked, and with it the growth of a vernacular literature. A new aristocracy arose, a Renaissance aristocracy of amateurs of art and lovers of learning who yet, in the Renaissance fashion, were unashamedly acquisitive and ambitious. It was this class that was to give the nation, in the second half of the century, the greatest Hungarian poet of the age in the person of Bálint Balassi. A number of splendid Renaissance castles were built in the better protected regions, such as Péter Perényi's castle at Sárospatak (1536–1542). The spread of the new learning and the new appreciation of the arts did not, however, lead to any reverence for the art of the past; relics of medieval learning and art, paintings, sculpture and manuscripts, as well as churches and finely wrought metalwork and church furniture and treasure, masterpieces of the goldsmith's craft, fell victim either to the plundering greed of the nobility or, as elsewhere, to the iconoclastic zeal of the Reformers. The Turks continued their advance, gradually occupying more and more of the country, setting the seal on the orgy of destruction conducted by the Hungarian nobility in the years of internecine strife. The lack of records, the scarcity of any remains of Hungarian medieval letters and art is the consequence of these tragic years.

Following the Turkish invasion of 1541, Hungary was split into three. The central, wedge-shaped area was occupied by the Turks. Its apex ended a little to the north of Buda; one side extended as far as Croatia in the south-west, and to the western fringes of Transylvania (the town of Temesvár, now Timişoara, Rumania) in the south-east. The Habsburgs of Austria, who were subsequently to reign over Hungary for nearly four hundred years, were in control of the western and northern regions of the country with Pozsony (now Bratislava, Czechoslovakia), a town lying conveniently near to Vienna, as its administrative centre. To the east lay the principality of Transylvania, an independent Hungarian state that was to be a bastion of Hungarian culture for the next hundred and fifty years. Due to this particular historical situation the further development of the Renaissance, after the initial period of vigorous expansion under Matthias Corvinus, slowly declined, but as in the other East European countries, continued to linger on well into the seventeenth century.

From 1541 onwards the Turkish occupation was to define and delimit the age. While outright war was comparatively rare, border warfare, skirmishes and armed warfare of one sort or another practically never ceased throughout the 150 years of occupation. Detachments from the Turkish garrisons would raid a village or un-defended town or fall upon caravans of merchants; and bands of German and Hun-garian soldiers, unpaid for months and out for money, food and arms, would harass and loot the population not only of the Turkish-occupied regions but also in the territories under Habsburg control. These same soldiers would nonetheless fight the Turk valiantly and successfully, with feats of heroism such as the siege of Eger, 1552, the sieges of Szigetvár, 1556 and 1566, the "Long War", 1593–1606, that inspired many poets, then and later. Transylvania and the Habsburg-controlled territories were also often at war with each other—wars that affected the north-eastern part of the country most of all. The plight of the people was worsened by the despotism of the nobility and excessive demands for feudal rent and the fulfilment of other onerous feudal obligations, with the result that the population of many a village fled to the Turks as the lesser evil.

The Reformation

Due to the constant fighting, the internecine political strife, and the grave social tensions that followed, the Reformation spread rapidly. Protestantism gave the great barons a pretext for seizing church land; the lesser nobility saw it as justifying their national aspirations, and as an instrument of resistance to the Catholic Habsburgs, and the masses adopted it as a means of class warfare. The great variety of motives and interests that went to the spread of the new religion was reflected in the number of different Protestant sects that struck root in Hungary, and were often locked in fierce internecine fighting themselves. Dominant among them, eclipsing even the Lutherans, was the theology of Geneva, which was to give birth to the Hungarian Reformed (Calvinist) Church. The Unitarians, who gained the upper hand in Transylvania in the 1560s, for many years posed a serious threat to the Calvinists; but by the early seventeenth century the supremacy of the Calvinist Church was undisputed throughout the Hungarian-speaking lands, even including the area under Turkish occupation. Calvinism was to remain firmly entrenched until the Counter-Reformation.

It was specifically due to the Reformation that general standards of culture and education rose appreciably. Literacy, earlier the monopoly of the clergy and a privilege of the prosperous lesser nobility and the middle class, now became accessible to the broad masses of the people. Protestant preachers set up hundreds of schools, some of them in small villages and hamlets. The spread of literacy brought into being a far wider reading public than ever before and consequently gave rise to an unprecedented demand for reading matter. A number of famous schools, such as the schools in Debrecen, Sárospatak and Kolozsvár (now Cluj-Napoca, Rumania) were founded around this time through the patronage of merchants or nobles; and over the succeeding centuries these schools were to become important centres of Hungarian letters and cultural development. There were still no universities in Hungary, and Hungarian students went to Vienna, Cracow, Padua and, especially, Wittenberg for their university education. It was owing to the Reformation and the munificence of a number of noble benefactors that printing-presses were established from the 1530s onwards at Brassó (now Braşov, Rumania), Sárvár, Kolozsvár, Magyaróvár, Debrecen and other places. Some of the presses were founded by leading personalities of the Reformation to further the cause of religious reform; others were set up by noble patrons of science and letters to support a literary venture or movement. As a result of the extension of education and the spread of printing, the sixteenth century saw a new vitality, a new rebirth in Hungarian—and now this meant primarily in the Hungarian language—literature in spite of the unpropitious circumstances of the time.

Renaissance Literature in Full Bloom

The Latin literature of the humanists continued to dominate the literary scene through the end of the fifteenth to the beginning of the sixteenth century; but Hungarian, as a literary language, which developed principally under the spur of the Reformation, had gained the ascendancy around the middle of the century, and the next fifty years saw the rise of a secular literature in Hungarian. This development was closely connected with the transformation of the contemporary political, social and economic scene.

The end of the sixteenth century was a critical period for agriculture: the great landowners did their utmost to make sure of a continuous supply of unpaid labour by attempts to impose a state of permanent serfdom on the peasants and the semi-independent agricultural towns of the plains, agricultural in that the inhabitants gained their living from their land, being in fact farming communities, something like very large villages. A strong, centralized royal government might have curbed the power of the great lords, but it did not exist, and in so far as the Habsburgs took any steps in that direction, it represented a threat to Hungarian independence.

The Turkish conquest of Hungary moreover, which around 1550 was still regarded by many as merely temporary, was later in the century being recognized as an occupation that would continue for many years to come. The middle years of the sixteenth century were marked by fervour and bravery; by heroic resistance to the Turks; by a simultaneous intensification of the class war by the forces of anti-feudalism embodied in the Reformation, and by bloodthirsty competition for wealth and power by the members of the new nobility that had first emerged under King Matthias. There were all conflicting aspirations and goals, but all were undertakings that sought to bring about real changes. In the last thirty years of the century, this fighting spirit had all but disappeared: in the surface things had settled down to a fixed pattern, but dangerous currents, as yet barely discernible, were nevertheless gathering force beneath the calm waters. The pattern of confrontation of the earlier years became hopelessly confused, with the result that these years were marked by an absence of progressive social and political movements. The literature of the period therefore differs from the literature both preceding and succeeding it in lack of any expression of social or political developments. Despite the Renaissance hedonism that prevailed towards the end of the century, the best minds of the time were conscious of the evils of the time: they rejected the burdensome present and offered the ideal of a better future. But lacking clear notions of what or whom they rebelled against, and of the goal to which they aspired, their portrayal of social reality failed to reach the level even of the writers of the Reformation, and in formulating both their criticisms and their ideals, they fell into the snare of being either too moralistic or too idealistic.

Writers attempting to express the latent conflicts and general malaise of the age, as well as the finest ideals and aspirations of the Renaissance, found in the theme and emotional range of love their most congenial means of expression. The literature of the Hungarian Renaissance reached its peak in the literature of love, and it was Renaissance love poetry that gave Hungarian literature its first classic poet.

The love poetry that marked this apex of the Renaissance in the late sixteenth century was followed by the abundant and varied literature of the first half of the seventeenth century that in fact brought it to an end. This Late Renaissance literature was predominantly Protestant and marked by mannerism. It ran concurrently, moreover, with the beginnings of the Counter-Reformation, and this in turn brought in its wake the new Baroque culture which was to permeate the literature of the remainder of the century.

6 Humanism in the Latin Tongue

Janus Pannonius (1434-1472)

In August 1469 the Italian humanist Marsilio Ficino published a commentary on Plato's *Symposium,* which he admiringly dedicated to a 35-year-old Hungarian bishop. It was not the bishop that was being honoured but the fellow poet, one of the most important of the Latin poets of the fifteenth century, János Csezmicei, known as Janus Pannonius. Bishop, diplomat and poet, Janus Pannonius is the first writer of stature in the history of Hungarian literature. He was a Hungarian humanist scholar, born in Croatia and carried off at the early age of 38 by consumption, heightened by the strain and tensions of a plot against King Matthias in which he took part. He spent the most important years of his life in Italy, where he had been sent to complete his education by his maternal uncle, the humanist Bishop János Vitéz, tutor and later chancellor of King Matthias. For eleven years, from 1447 to 1458, interrupted only when he returned for a brief visit to his country in 1451, Pannonius lived in northern Italy. He went there first when he was thirteen, and returned to his homeland at the age of 24, and consequently all his formative years were spent in Italy. He first went to Guarino da Verona's private school in Ferrara, where he was at school with Galeotto Marzio, the historian who later came to Matthias's court upon his friend's recommendation to write a royal history of the king's deeds; Mantegna painted a joint portrait of them.

Pannonius completed his studies at Padua University, with frequent visits to Venice. Following his return to Hungary, Pannonius was installed as Bishop of Pécs, and then returned to Italy, as a diplomat accredited to the Papal court. The favour of the king was, however, soon withdrawn; when his uncle fell, he fell with him. For several years of his short life Pannonius was encumbered with the cares of office and in terms of culture showed much concern over the shortcomings of Hungarian learning and standards of taste, then far short of Italian civilisation, and he finished his short life in isolation. Ironically, by the time that Italy indeed came to Hungary in the person of Beatrix of Aragon, the second queen of King Matthias, Janus Pannonius was dead.

His epigrams and elegies, together with two panegyrics, take first place in his poetry. In 1450, at the age of sixteen, he wrote a cycle of caustic epigrams on the

43

profitable business enjoyed by Rome and its Pontiff from the pilgrims flocking to the Eternal City for the jubilee year. A year later he wrote of himself on his seventeenth birthday in a strikingly modern poem *(De sua aetate)* in which he described the spiritual and physical perturbations of an adolescent boy in his intellectual and sexual desires. This short poem—unparalleled in world literature if we consider the youth of the poet—shows the influence of Beccadelli's *Hermaphroditus* and of Martial.

The finest, and still the most popular of his elegies, is his *Farewell to Várad* *(Abiens valere jubet sanctos reges, Varadini*—Going away He Says Good-bye to Várad, Town of Saintly Kings). In seven stanzas he bade farewell to the town, the episcopal see of his uncle where he had spent a brief holiday and incidentally been given a benefice of some sort. He described the country in winter, conveying through the cadences of his verses the joyous impatience shared by both the departing traveller and the horses drawing his sled. His choice of subjects strike one as a good deal less academic than those of many of his contemporaries. Experience at first hand inspired him: camping out; an almond-tree unexpectedly budding in early spring; travelling; departing; his mother's death. Direct experience of the flooding of the river Danube provided the inspiration for his longest poem, *De inundatione* *(The Flood, 1468)*. One might say that Leonardo da Vinci's compelling drawings of flood water came to life in this poem: the poet's imagination transmitted the natural disaster into the Biblical Flood. The breadth and depth of his outlook on the world, his erudition, his philosophical interests reveal themselves most clearly in his elegies, especially in *Ad animam suam (To his Soul, 1466)*. In this poem Janus reflected upon the transcience of all mortal things, yearning for the release of his soul from the prison of his sick body in order to soar freely to the stars. All the problems of being and non-being were considered in the neo-Platonic terms of age.

In addition to his epigrams and elegies, two of his panegyrics deserve particular attention, though more as perfectly polished specimens of the fashionable Humanist versification of the time than as genuine lyric poetry. One of them, written in 1456-58, praised Giacomo Antonio Marcello, mayor of Padua, a man who had displayed affection for the young poet and gave him encouragement. His other panegyric—on which he worked, on and off, throughout his life—was addressed to his master, Guarino, and through him to all Italy, seen as the cradle of Humanism. In this panegyric to Guarino there is a suggestion that Janus intended to write a poem on János Hunyadi. Unfortunately this work, if it was ever written, has been lost. On the other hand, a fine epigram, *Laus Pannoniae (In Praise of Pannonia)* has come down to us, in which he proudly announced that it was his mission to make Hungary a part of the literary community of Europe.

Quod legerent omnes quondam dabat Itala tellus,
Nunc e Pannonia carmina missa legit.
Magna quidem nobis haec gloria: sed tibi major,
Nobilis ingenio Patria facta meo.

The land of Italy was once the source of all my songs;
To you, my fair Pannonia, that honour now belongs.
Great glory have I won, indeed, but more on you be poured,
My homeland, whose illustrious fame my spirit sheds abroad.

(Translated by G. F. Cushing)

The successors of Janus Pannonius followed in his footsteps, and humanist poetry became firmly established in Hungary, every Hungarian poet who wrote in Latin taking Pannonius as his model. There were several eminent poets in Hungary among his contemporaries; Italian humanists praised poems written by some of them, but the majority of these works are lost. There were volumes of works by several other poets from the early sixteenth century onwards, made up by a number of people speaking different languages. Latin was an excellent means of communication between both the Hungarian and non-Hungarian-speaking men of letters in the kingdom of Hungary. One of these latter was *Jakab Piso* (1470?–1527), a Transylvanian Saxon diplomat, tutor to King Louis II, friend of Erasmus, and poet laureate of the Emperor Maximilian. A selection of his poems *(Schedia)* shows him at his satirical best in *Dum-Alba Regalis caperetur.* Another German humanist, Stephan Stieröxel (*c.* 1480–1519), under the *nom de plume* of *Taurinus,* gave an account of the peasant rebellion of 1514 led by György Dózsa and its bloody suppression (*Stauromachia,* Vienna, 1519). Having lived in Hungary as a cleric from 1511 until his death, he experienced the events he describes at first hand; not unexpectedly, his sympathies lie with the ruling feudal class, and he speaks of Hungarian peasant fighters in contemptuous terms. By contrast, Márton Nagyszombati, a Benedictine monk writing as *Martinus Tyrnavinus,* was spurred on by the news that Belgrade had fallen to the Turks in 1521 to remind the nobles of their obligation to defend the homeland (*Opusculum ad regni Hungariae proceres,* Vienna, 1523). While holding the same conservative views as the nobility, he nonetheless urged the ruling class to follow the courageous example of its ancestors by fighting the Turks.

In the course of the sixteenth century practically every humanist writing in the Latin tongue composed poems, though these were for the most part occasional verses addressed to friends. Pre-eminent among these writers was *Christian Schaeseus* (d. 1585), a Saxon from Transylvania whose epic poem *Ruinae Pannonicae* reveals the influence of Virgil. But the writer with the greatest reputation after Janus Pannonius was the historian and philologist *Iohannes Sambucus* or János Zsámboki (1531–1584). His volumes of poetry *Poemata* (Padua, 1555) and *Emblemata* (Antwerp,

1564) were very popular; the latter was even translated into Flemish and French. Shakespeare is believed to have known his *Emblemata,* and have used some of them. Sambucus edited a number of Greek and Roman authors (Horace, 1564; Plautus, 1566), as well as the poems of Janus Pannonius (Vienna, 1569) and Bonfini's *History of Hungary* (Basel, 1568).

Early Humanist Historians

The court of Matthias Corvinus saw the rise of a school of Hungarian humanist historians who, both by virtue of their choice of subjects and their high literary standards, remained one of the mainsprings of inspiration of Hungarian writers for many centuries to come.

Among the many Italian scholars, poets and artists attracted to the court of Matthias Corvinus were *Galeotto Marzio,* a good-humoured man and a shrewd observer, and the historian Antonio Bonfini both of whom gained important positions for themselves in the history of Hungarian literature. In the course of a varied and adventurous life Galeotto (1427–1497) visited the Hungarian court several times. On one occasion the Hungarian monarch obtained his release from a prison of the Inquisition, where his free-thinking, materialist writings had landed him. He wrote an extremely vivid account of King Matthias, closely observed and very detailed, which is greatly valued by students of social and cultural history (*De egregie, sapienter, jocose dictis ac factis regis Matthiae,* 1485).

Antonio Bonfini (1427–1503) is a less colourful and less gifted writer than Galeotto, but his historical works nevertheless make him more important to students of Hungarian history. This schoolmaster from Recanati in Italy arrived in Hungary at the age of sixty, in the last years of Matthias's reign, having spent many years trying to gain the favour of Queen Beatrix. In 1486 he was finally appointed "reader" and a kind of personal secretary to the queen, and in this position was encouraged to write a history of Hungary in the new spirit of humanism. While however Matthias was alive Bonfini spent more time in Italy than at the royal court (which had been situated in Vienna since 1485), and only settled in Hungary as royal historian in 1491, the year after the king's death. He was given a patent of nobility for his work, *Hungaricarum rerum decades.* Although of little value as source material except for those passages where the author deals with developments he knew at first hand or which were contemporary occurrences, this work exercised an extraordinary influence on the Hungarian people. It was translated into German as early as the mid-sixteenth century, and a Hungarian version, revised by Gáspár Heltai, was published in 1575.

Memoirs of the National Catastrophe

The generation of Hungarian humanists after the death of Matthias Corvinus were all obsessed by the national tragedy of the fateful Battle of Mohács (1526) which gave victory to the Turks. Like their predecessors, these humanists were at once high dignitaries of the church, diplomats and statesmen. Unlike their predecessors, however, they were neither protected nor harassed by a strong, centralized royal power: very often they were left to take decisions of national importance on their own responsibility; and this burden only increased their sense of guilt, shared by the best minds of the ruling class, over the ease with which the Ottoman empire had penetrated the Hungarian kingdom which in the days of great King Matthias had stood firm as a rock against them. It is consequently no coincidence that, regardless of age or position all their best work was written within years after Mohács, and that all of it is closely linked with the conditions prevailing in the Hungarian state at that time.

The oldest member of this group, *István Brodarics* (1470–1539) took his degree as a doctor of law in Padua in 1506 and was appointed chancellor and bishop in the spring of 1526. He was present at the Battle of Mohács in that year, and published his account of it in 1527, entitled *De conflictu hungarorum cum turcis ad Mohatz verissima descriptio*. What gives this description of the battle a personal flavour that still captivates us over the years is the conflict between the inevitable bias of the eyewitness and the objectivity of the reporter. The author is conscious of the fact that the vividness of his eyewitness account prejudices his attempt to give a true overall picture of the event; for after all he could not have been present at all the important incidents in the battle, which in any case had been brought to a dramatically abrupt close by torrential rain.

Although the career of *Miklós Oláh* (1493–1568) did not truly begin until after 1542, by 1562 he had become Archbishop of Esztergom and in that capacity governor of the areas of Hungary under Habsburg control. But his works on history and geography breathe the nostalgia of a young man longing for the land of his birth, for he wrote them in the Low Countries as secretary to Mary of Hungary, the widow of Louis II killed at the Battle of Mohács, and younger sister of Charles V who was Governor of the Low Countries at the time. In these books—*Hungaria* and *Attila* (1536–37)—he described his native country, dwelling lovingly on the natural beauty of the countryside, its treasures of art and architecture as well as its customs and manner of living. He gave an account of the ancient history of Hungary, and as if to redeem the present sad plight of his nation, related the glorious deeds of Attila the Hun, very much as Simon Kézai before him had drawn a glowing picture of the glorious Hun victories when the public administration of the country had stood on the brink of anarchy.

Sixteenth-century Humanist Historians

Ferenc Forgách and Miklós Istvánffy were two entirely different personalities. They were the most original and gifted Hungarian humanist historians of the generation born after the Battle of Mohács. They never achieved high positions in the government or the Church, like their predecessors who followed János Vitéz; their private lives were troubled by worldly vicissitudes and by conflicts of conscience, by defiant rebellions and by compromises. For them, the glory of a great single Hungarian empire was irrevocably a thing of the past; with this bitter fact always in their mind they poured envenomed scorn on their own class—the nobility—for its failings and for its responsibility for the present condition of Hungary. *Ferenc Forgách* (1535–1577) came from a long line of great barons and while still a young man became Bishop of Várad and a royal counsellor to Ferdinand I, but on the king's death, disenchanted with the refusal of the Habsburgs to take any active steps to drive the Turks out of Hungary, he entered the service of the Prince of Transylvania. In 1575 he went to Padua for medical treatment, but this voyage was also a form of escape from the irremediable realities of the age, and he died there two years later. His work, *De statu reipublicae Hungaricae... commentarii* (1568–1573), in which he recounted the history of Hungary from 1540 onwards, relying on personal experience for the period after 1556, is the most remarkable, if also the most passionately prejudiced, history of Hungary produced in his time. With bitter indignation he attacked his own class, the oligarchy, for failing to preserve the independence of Hungary. He entertained no hope of any change for the better, for he was personally too well acquainted with those in power to put any faith in them; his anger spared none, but he never permitted his passion to blind him to his political aims which seem to contain the seeds of Miklós Zrínyi's later conclusions: the Hungarian nation should cease to look for foreign help and should rely on itself and its own resources in the task of establishment and reorganization. He was adept at sketching characters with a few deft strokes; and he had a trick of describing individual destinies, conflicts and unexpected twists of fate as if parts of some carefully constructed tragedy—without in any way impairing the historical authenticity of his account.

Miklós Istvánffy (1538–1615), though a contemporary of Forgách's, worked in a much later period; he knew and made use of Forgách's work. The later date of Istvánffy's work is evident both in the spirit in which it was written and the actual history of its publication. Istvánffy was a staunch supporter of the Counter-Reformation and a great admirer of its leading figure in Hungary, Cardinal Péter Pázmány. Just as Forgách, he harked back with longing to the great Matthias Corvinus; but for him "civic discipline" was as much a condition of national progress as religion—by which he meant Catholicism. With such views Istvánffy's book (*Historiarium de rebus*

Ungaricis, Cologne, 1622), unlike Forgách's, met with no obstacles in its publication, and with Pázmány's support, was widely read.

The work of *István Szamosközy* (1565?–1612) only survives in fragments. Educated at Heidelberg and Padua, he was keeper of the archives of Gyulafehérvár (now Alba Iulia, Rumania), the first historian to look for the mainsprings of history in economic, social and geographic factors as well as in important personalities. Here he seems to follow—whether consciously or not—the method adopted by the French social and political philosopher Jean Bodin (1530–1596). His prose is less refined than that of his predecessors, but he was more outspoken, a more merciless critic of his time. For it was his own age more than any other that engaged Szamosközy's attention as a historian; his narrative began at around the date of his own birth; the later chapters, dealing with the end of the sixteenth century, were mainly devoted to the history of Transylvania; he was the first historian to emphasize the separate existence of the Principality of Transylvania.

These historians, still writing in the Latin tongue, prepared the ground for the literary memoirs of the seventeenth century. The golden age of historiography, which enjoyed great popularity not only among scholars, stretched from Bonfini, the Italian at the court of King Matthias, to Szamosközy, the historian of independent Transylvania. Without the Latin histories of such men as Forgách or Istvánffy, the Hungarian prose of Miklós Zrínyi or Miklós Bethlen might never have seen the light.

7 Humanism and the Reformation in the Hungarian Tongue

Prose

Printing made a relatively early appearance in Hungary: in Buda, András Hess produced the first book printed in Hungary in 1472, five years before William Caxton brought out the first dated book printed in England. But Hess's incunabulum was a Latin-language chronicle, and some sixty years were to pass before the earliest printed books in the Hungarian language appeared. The belated appearance of the first printed books in the Hungarian tongue should be seen in the light of two peculiar circumstances: on the one hand, when they first appeared in between 1500 and 1550 monks in Hungarian monasteries were still busy copying manuscripts from earlier centuries, thus preserving for posterity medieval codices written in Hungarian. Because of the civil war in Hungary that raged after the Turkish occupation of Buda in 1541 the first works printed in Hungarian were published in Cracow and Vienna. The first was an edition of *The Epistles of St. Paul,* translated by Benedek Komjáti (1533), and the second the first Hungarian collection of Aesop's fables (1536), translated by Gábor Pesti. As befits a humanist brought up on Erasmus, Pesti wrote in his native tongue to prove that Hungarian was in no way inferior to Latin as a vehicle of learning and culture. In adopting the principles of Erasmus Pesti regarded himself as a pioneer: "The nations of the world have produced a prodigious number of translations," he wrote, and for that reason he was anxious to give the language of his country great splendour with "the wisdom of the ancient sages". In translating these brief fables he wasted no words, giving his version a wholly delightful crispness and concision.

János Sylvester (c. 1504–after 1551), another follower of Erasmus, was even more single-minded than Pesti in his devotion to the Hungarian language and in the cultivation of a fitting style. Sylvester produced works on his native language at fairly regular intervals beginning with a manual of Latin–Hungarian conversation and grammar for beginners, which he compiled while still a student at Cracow University (1527). His unhappy private life, a broken marriage and the loss of his inheritance through fraud was counterbalanced by an academic career of distinction: as a protégé of the wealthy noble and politician Tamás Nádasdy, Sylvester found on his patron's estate at Sárvár in western Hungary the peace and tranquillity that enabled him to devote himself to his scholarly studies. During his last years he lectured at Vienna University. Sylvester wrote the first outline of Hungarian grammar in his *Grammatica Hungarolatina* (1539); comparing the two languages he proudly praised the beauties of his mother tongue. "If we only overcome our reluctance to use our native tongue, this treasure hitherto hidden from us but which we have now uncovered," he wrote, "...we poor ones may... before long become immensely rich." The teachings of Erasmus led Sylvester from Latin to an appreciation of his own vernacular language; indeed, Sylvester took his own advice and translated the *New Testament* into Hungarian (1541), and as a result the New Testament appeared in print in Hungarian only a few years after Luther's German Bible. With pedantic precision, Sylvester produced a periphrastic and heavy-handed Hungarian version which was far from the simplicity and dramatic force of Luther's work. But it is equally true that his summaries in verse at the end of each Gospel and Dedication are the first rhymed distichs ever written in Hungarian—and with astonishing success. He was in fact the first writer ever to attempt poetry based on metre rather than the traditional accentual rhythm in Hungarian.

The early writers of the Reformation made their first appearance in print at about the same time as Sylvester; students of theology, even beyond the borders of Hungary, are acquainted with some of them and some have earned a place for themselves in the history of Hungarian literature. Here, however, it will be enough to mention their names, for their work was rather more important in terms of theology than in the creative and aesthetic world of literature. Three names stand out among the Protestant writers of the period: *Mátyás Dévai Bíró* (d. 1545), Luther's first and most important Hungarian disciple, who was active between 1530 and 1540; *Péter Méliusz Juhász* (1536–1572), a Debrecen theologian and one of the leaders of the Calvinist (Reformed) Church of Hungary; and his most formidable opponent, *Ferenc Dávid* (d. 1579), a Transylvanian, a religious philosopher and one of the founders and leading theologians of the Unitarian faith. By this time most works of theology were being written in Hungarian, and religious treatises in Hungarian were being published in such vast numbers that merely to list them would cover several pages. The name of *Gáspár Károlyi* (1530–1591) was made immortal by his translation and publication of the first complete Hungarian Bible (Gönc, 1590), a Bible which had an incalculable influence in shaping the Hungarian literary language.

Of all the didactic works of the Reformation writers those with historical or ethical themes, where individual literary qualities are most in evidence, are the most important in a literary context. The Protestant concept of history was first extended to universal history—in Hungarian—by István Székely, who wrote the *Chronicle of Notable Events of the World* (Chronica ez világnak jeles dolgairól) in 1559. It was in fact a moralizing treatise disguised as a work of history, an apologia presenting the Reformation as inevitable and justified. Gáspár Károlyi, the translator of the Bible, expounded a complete philosophy of history in a work entitled *On the Causes of the Good and Ill Fate of All Countries and Kings* (Minden országoknak és királyoknak jó és gonosz szerencséjeknek okairól, 1563). This work collected and summed up the arguments against feudalism and the great lords of the realm which were widely disseminated in the popular songs of the Reformation. Károli's beliefs were taken further some forty years later by another preacher and writer, *István Magyari* (d. 1605), in a polemical treatise entitled *On the Causes of the Numerous Corruptions in the Nations* (Az országokban való sok romlásoknak okairól, 1602). Magyari did more than merely bewail sinful behaviour and note failings and errors; he also proposed a political programme of action. Besides attacking the "idolatry" of the Catholic ritual and emphasizing the need to abolish social injustices, he also advocated reforms in warfare and military discipline.

Dramatists of the Reformation

Hungarian drama originated as a tool of religious reform. Earlier occasional medieval forays into drama—*Tractus stellae*, 1490; *Three Christian Maidens* (Három köröszténly leány), 1500, now lost—preceded the first Hungarian plays, still extant, of *Mihály Sztárai* (d. 1575), a preacher who was active in Turkish-occupied Hungary. He wrote two plays, both examples of Lutheran religious propaganda: *On the Marriage of Priests* (A papok házasságáról) championing the priests' right to marry, and *A Mirror of True Priesthood* (Az igaz papságnak tüköre), 1559, a general vindication of the Reformation, setting out more particularly to prove the superiority of Protestant pastors over "papist" priests, pictured as illiterate and rigidly bound to all the liturgical trappings of their religion. The play contains several lively, popular characters, shrewd and quick-witted, who soon demolish their opponents. The play ends with the worsted disputants being sent off to work in the fields.

The influence of Sztárai's plays is evident in the anti-Trinitarian *Debrecen Dispute* (Debreceni disputa), 1572. Here, the conflict was not the familiar one between Protestant and Catholic, but between two types of Protestantism. The play was based on actual historical events, the protagonists being Péter Méliusz Juhász, a leading Calvinist, thinly and derisively disguised as "Pope Péter," and the Unitarian Ferenc Dávid. Lively turns of speech and vivid powers of satire are evidence of the literary competence of the unknown author, and presaged encouraging developments in Hungarian drama.

Even more successful as drama was an anonymous satirical morality play, *The Comedy of the Treachery of Menyhárt Balassi* (Comoedia Balassi Menyhárt árultatásáról), published in 1569. The playwright gave a convincing picture of one of the famous ruthless barons of the time, who was at the same time a very able military commander.

The subject of the comedy was no longer the clash of religious beliefs but a wholly secular and political conflict: the exposure of the treacheries and other wicked deeds committed by Balassi. The dialogue, often masterly in style, indicates a theatrical tradition which is already well-developed, as well as the popularity of satirical plays on political themes.

The finest examples of Hungarian prose and drama written in the spirit of humanism, and closely associated with the Reformation, are connected with the names of two Protestant preachers of greater importance than those dealt with so far, Gáspár Heltai and Péter Bornemisza.

Gáspár Heltai (c. 1500-1574)

Gáspár Heltai was a Transylvanian German who is in himself evidence of the crucial part played by the Reformation in the rise of vernacular literature. But for the Reformation, the German-speaking Heltai might never have learnt Hungarian. But he took to heart the teaching of Luther that the Gospel should be preached in the language of the people; and since he lived in Kolozsvár where the majority of the population spoke Hungarian, at the age of 36 he made it his business to learn to read, write and speak the language. And consequently, under Luther's influence, this German-speaking Lutheran minister came to write in Hungarian. For a cleric, Heltai had an astute business sense: in Kolozsvár, where he held a living, he was engaged in a number of small undertakings, including a printing-press which he used for his own paper as well as his own books and pamphlets. The purpose of his works was always the improvement of the spiritual state of the people: he set about it in fables, the *Dialogue* on the evils of drink (Dialogus, 1552), in a Hungarian chronicle, a catechism, a book of prayers, and a pamphlet exposing the criminal record of the Inquisition (*The Net—* Háló, 1570). These were not original works from his pen; as was common at the time, he adapted original works written in other languages. An interesting and important aspect of his numerous activities was that he was the first to translate from contemporary German, skilfully weaving many scenes of contemporary Hungarian life into his Hungarian adaptations of the German writers of the time. His versions of foreign authors are by no means word for word translations; he was not bound by any "sacred" Latin text, and unlike the Erasmian Gábor Pesti, Heltai provided Hungarian readers with the thoughts and themes of the original authors rather than the actual text of the original, re-shaping and remoulding as he thought best. This is well shown in *Hundred Fables* (Száz fabula), 1566, a series of colourful and romantic tales of great diversity, which grew out of one of the editions of Sebastian Brant's collection of children's tales. His tales flow as smoothly as honey, his penchant for the anecdote is aided by the robust humour he gave his characters. Here can be seen the beginnings of the type of fiction, based on the anecdote, which was to reach its highest point of development in the works of Kálmán Mikszáth at the end of the nineteenth century. The animal characters of his fables represent the citizens of his time: they are sly and astute, cowardly and submissive, or prone to lament their misfortunes. His gifts as a story-teller, and his sharp criticism of society are nowhere more evident than in his original fable on a well-known theme *The Nobleman and the Devil* (Egy nemes emberről és az ördögről). The avarice of a noble leads him to employ the Devil as his bailiff. The Devil only asks in return that the wish of the first person to meet the noble in the street be granted. As the Devil is a ruthless taskmaster who oppresses the peasants on behalf of their lord, the wish of the first person the noble meets—a little girl who sees him coming her way—is "may the devil take him!" Which the Devil promptly does, taking with him his wife and other nobles as well.

Heltai was a contemporary of Rabelais, the kind of Renaissance writer so fondly remembered by Anatole France: a man with a robust appreciation of life, a man of business acumen appalled by the institution of serfdom, not on emotional grounds, but because he regarded it as sheer folly, an unprofitable proposition. Rabelaisian mirth informs another of the masterpieces of Heltai's, a Hungarian version of the famous medieval cycle *The Seven Sages of Rome,* under the title *The History of Pontian* (Ponciánus históriája). And even his translation or adaptation of Bonfini's *Chronicle* is filled with the splendid interpolations so typical of his pen. He cared little for historical research, made little attempt to check facts against documents and records. Happy to take a snippet of information here, an anecdote there, he was only concerned to fashion his tale in order to draw from it as many morals as possible.

Of the many tales in the *Hungarian Chronicle* (Chronica az magyaroknak dolgairól, 1575), the most important is his account of the family background of János Hunyadi. Allowing for the fact that, as usual, he presents unconfirmed tales as historical fact, the story is told with such spontaneity and imagination that it has to be regarded as one of the earliest short stories written in Hungarian. His rich vocabulary and bold imagination, his able characterizations and shrewd observations, his careful turns of phrase and the uninhibited flow of his narrative rightly make Heltai an important writer who can be read with much enjoyment even today.

Péter Bornemisza (1535-1584)

While Heltai's strength lay in the tale told with philosophical detachment, Bornemisza excelled in the extremely pointed drama and the brief and incisive short story. Very much a child of his turbulent time, Bornemisza had an adventurous youth, travelling extensively in Germany and Italy. While a student in Vienna he was encouraged by his professor, Georg Tanner, to produce a Hungarian version of Sophocles' *Electra* (1558). During the 1560s he held a post in the royal chancellery and was subsequently tutor to Bálint Balassi, the future poet, on the territory of today's Slovakia. A sudden determination led him to take holy orders and he became a tireless preacher on the domains of Count Julius Salm, first at Galgóc (now Hlohovec, Czechoslovakia) and then at Sempte (now Lintava, Czechoslovakia). *The Temptations of the Devil* (Ördögi kísértetek, 1578), was a collection of sermons containing a considerable amount of history and many tales as well as matter for sermons. He attacked the ruling class with such vehemence that he was tried by his own church for heresy; fleeing to Vienna, he was there convicted of lèse majesté in 1579 and imprisoned. He escaped from prison and spent the remainder of his life in hiding at István Balassi's castle at Detrekő (now Podhrad, Czechoslovakia) and in the neighbourhood. At the time of his sudden death he was working on a translation of the Bible and planning to compile a Universal Chronicle.

Bornemisza, writing in Hungarian, tried his hand at practically every literary form: perhaps he was impelled by literary ambition, perhaps by evangelistic zeal, possibly both. He wrote religious songs, at least one splendid song of farewell (*It is Lamentable for me...* —Siralmas énnéköm..., 1553), and a tragedy as well as eleven thousand pages of sermons and a textbook for religious instruction. His version of *Electra, A Tragedy in the Hungarian Language from Sophocles' Electra* (Tragédia magyar nyelven a Sophocles Electrájából, 1558), is the earliest known Hungarian tragedy. This synthesis of the Reformation and humanism bore on its title-page a quotation from the Bible threatening despotic princes; and in an epilogue Bornemisza interpreted Sophocles' play as involving openly political issues: "Is it right to oppose a tyrant when the nation lies in cruel bondage?" he asked. He divided the Greek original into acts, added new characters (such as Parasitus, a turncoat courtier), and violated the three unities of classical drama. The text was adapted to the codnitions of sixteenth-century Hungary. In translating *Electra* Bornemisza showed that he was aware of the tasks lying ahead: "Some years ago a beginning was made in producing works in the Hungarian language," Bornemisza wrote. "We must follow the example of Cicero and all civilized nations and cultivate and develop our vernacular tongue."

His sermons *A Book of Sermons in Five Volumes* (Ötkötetes prédikációskönyv, 1573–1579); *Foliopostilla,* 1584, were full of personal observations and revealed a great deal about himself, often in the form of personal statements, but he also observed and described the world around him, painting the bustling daily life of contemporary Hungarian towns and castles, manors and markets. His urge to reveal all about himself was so powerful that he devoted a book to his mental and spiritual conflicts, laying bare the problems, new and unusual as compared with preceding centuries, which preyed on him and his contemporaries. *The Temptations of the Devil* (Ördögi kísértetek, 1578) marked a milestone in Hungarian fiction. Inspired by St. Augustine's *Confessions*, he recorded his mental anguish and his sins in painstaking detail and with ruthless sincerity, with the design of aiding and comforting his readers.

The importance of Bornemisza's work is best summed up in his own words: "The purpose of the many stories I have recorded, the inclination of the many words I have written, all tend towards this point: what, in actual fact, is human nature?" It is the curiosity and excitement with which he searched for an answer to this question that makes Bornemisza an author of consequence, whose works are the final word in the achievements of Hungarian literature up to his time presaging the Baroque era to come. In his examination of the newly realized inner world of Renaissance man Bornemisza recognized the contradictions and complexities of that world. He was on the point of crossing the threshold of a new era, nostalgically aware that he was yearning in vain for the peace of mind once provided by religion. Although he drew freely on works of Melanchton *(Vitae patrum)* and his circle, his bold conclusions extended beyond contemporary German "Devil literature", and there are passages akin to those in Montaigne's essays. Another new feature in his work is the frequent reference to contemporaries. He followed the careers of fellow preachers and writers, recommending their works to his readers' attention; behind his lines can be sensed a full and active literary life. Bornemisza also produced a collection of songs (Song-book—Énekeskönyv, 1582), rescuing many valuable works from oblivion.

He took the first steps along the road that the following century was to tread.

8 Songs Written in the Hungarian Tongue

Poetry for Singing in the Sixteenth Century

It was in the sixteenth century that Hungarian poetry began first to develop, then flower. The extraordinary large number of poems surviving from this period indicates that a considerable body of Hungarian poetry already existed in the Middle Ages, although through indifference and a number of other reasons relatively few of these were preserved. But from the mid-sixteenth century onwards the Reformation attitude to education and the advent of printing provided for the survival of works of literature, and a number of collections of poems and songs from this period are still in existence, both in manuscript and in print.

This substantial body of sixteenth-century Hungarian poetry was still inseparably linked to music. Hungarian poetry was not to emerge as an art in its own right until the advent of Bálint Balassi at the end of the century. Until then poems continued to be composed to be sung rather than read. This determined the form of the verse, with lyric as well as narrative poetry tending to be somewhat verbose, and their excellent rhythm marred by crude rhymes, since rhyme was regarded as taking second place to the all-important tune. Repetitions and stereotyped phrases are frequent; one can recognize still lingering in them the vestiges of a centuries-old oral tradition. Nonetheless the authors of these songs were not the simple, uneducated poets of the people. On the contrary, they were cultured preachers, schoolmasters and professional bards who took great pains to dissociate themselves from the ordinary, uneducated wandering minstrel.

The subjects of sixteenth-century Hungarian songs are many and varied. The greater part of them propagate the ideas of the Reformation and are of a religious nature, drawing their inspiration from the Bible. Others are rhymed versions of Boccaccio's tales and other works of Renaissance literature. Many of them record events in Hungarian history. The sixteenth-century Hungarian bards were also inspired by important or interesting events in other countries of Europe, such as the wars of the Protestant Schmalkaldic League against Charles V or the burning of Thomas Cranmer, Archbishop of Canterbury, which provided the theme for a narrative poem written a year after his death by the dramatist Sztárai. Songs were part of the daily life of the citizen and often took on the form of greetings or personal exchanges in verse, didactic poems and so forth.

The borderline between religious and secular poetry was becoming increasingly lost. Songs written in the spirit of the Reformation were full of social and political references; secular songs and histories were, on the other hand, deeply religious in inspiration. Songs adapted from biblical stories served both as religious instruction and secular entertainment. Some song-writers saw the Psalms as a means of expressing completely secular sentiments, while writers of secular lyrics would as a matter of course turn to the Psalms for their inspiration. During this period most songs still circulated in manuscript, but the number of printed books of verse was growing rapidly, particularly during the last forty years of the century. As the different religious sects of the Reformation were stabilized by the establishment of the various Protestant churches, each of them discovered the need to supply their members with hymnals. The first of these, so far as is known, was printed in 1560 in Kassa (now Košice, Czechoslovakia) by Gál Huszár, a preacher and printer; many other hymnals followed. Collections of narrative and didactic songs had been made even earlier; Sebestyén Tinódi's collected historical songs, for example, together with the tunes he had composed for them (*Cronica*, Kolozsvár, 1554). Others, including Péter Bornemisza, gathered and published not only collections of hymns, but also the "propaganda" songs of the Reformation, together with biblical histories.

The Verse Propaganda of the Reformation

The poets of the Hungarian Reformation expressed their ideas within a biblical framework and in the language of the Old Testament. They regarded the Bible as a genuine history of mankind and thought they could discern an analogy between the destiny of the Jewish people in the Bible and that of the Hungarian people. They felt that the fate of these two long-suffering and persecuted peoples was identical: they maintained that God was punishing the Hungarians through the Turks for much the same reason that he had punished the Jews with the Babylonian captivity, for they had both sinned by abandoning the true faith and turning to idolatry. The earliest expression of this view is found in *András Farkas's* verse chronicle, *On the Jewish and Hungarian Nations* (Az zsidó és magyar nemzetről, 1538).

This theme was expanded and popularized by a number of eminent Protestant song-writers. One of the earliest of them was *András Batizi,* a learned preacher who between 1540 and 1545 took several Old Testament stories as subjects of his epic songs and tried to draw morals from them which would be applicable to the Hungary of his time, such as *On the Beloved and Godfearing Valiant Knight Gideon* (Az drága és istenfélő vitéz Gedeonról, 1540), or *A History of the Prophet Jonah* (Jónás prófétának históriája, 1541). His Bible-centred verse chronicle on world history, *A History of Things Past and Present* (Meglött és megleendő dolgoknak históriája, 1544) made a significant contribution towards the Reformation view of history. Batizi was also responsible for innovation in metrical form, being the first poet consciously and systematically to use the twelve-syllable line which was to become a characteristic epic form.

A poet of greater importance than Batizi was *András Szkhárosi Horváth,* an inveterate enemy of feudalism. His poetry combines the burning bitterness of Ferenc Forgách with the blunt and straightforward reactions of the common people. A former Franciscan monk turned Protestant preacher, he helped to spread the Lutheran faith in north-eastern Hungary, a region which, although unaffected by the Turkish invasion, was torn by internecine strife. He is known by only ten poems, written between 1540 and 1550, that is, when the Turkish occupation of the better part of the kingdom had just become an accomplished fact. Szkhárosi placed the blame for the débâcle squarely on the shoulders of the nobility and on the Roman Church. His major poems are: *On Princedom* (Az fejedelemségről, 1545); *On Avarice* (Az fösvény-ségről, 1545); and *On Anathema* (Az átokról, 1547). Princes and nobles, priests and prelates were all castigated as evil-doers, serving Antichrist; men who were the cause of the disaster that had befallen the nation. There was but one way out, only one road to salvation: the Lutheran creed, through intensive study of the Scriptures, and secession from the Church of Rome which had distorted the ancient Christian faith. Szkhárosi spoke for a middle class based on agriculture, which had risen rapidly in the first half of the century and was being increasingly harassed by the nobility. The intensity of feeling permeating Szkhárosi's poetry, his unerring sense of proportion and outstanding talents raise every poem to the highest level of poetry without detracting from his reforming zeal and passion on behalf of the masses. The use of nine different stanza schemes in the ten songs is evidence of a thorough grounding in music; and he displays a remarkable sense of rhythm in the formal perfection of his lines. His style represents a happy blend of medieval hymns, Goliardic songs, and is strongly influenced by the Bible.

Batizi and Szkhárosi began what turned into a spate of Bible histories in verse. As these stories were, in some sort, substitutes for sermons, as well as instruments of propaganda, nearly every minister felt duty-bound to compose a few, as for instance, *On the Prodigal Son* (Az tékozló fiúról, 1545) by *Pál Baranyai; The Story of Judas Maccabeus* (Judás Makkabeus története, 1549) by *András Dézsi; Joseph* (József, 1556) by *Mátyás Nagybáncsai.* Many of these Old Testament stories are remarkable not only for their topical applications but also for the skill with which the narrative is composed. These verse translations of the stories of the Bible paved the way for later epic poetry.

History Songs

The secular historical epic—the "history song" as it was called at the time—developed alongside the religious poetry of the Reformation. Often the authors of biblical narrative poems also wrote historical epics; Mátyás Nagybáncsai, author, we repeat, of the biblical story of Joseph, also wrote a "history song" *On the Valiant Voivode János Hunyadi* (Az vitéz Hunyadi János vajdáról, 1560), dedicated to the "soldiers of the marches". Many narrative poems about great commanders such as this one, and the glorious events of early Hungarian history, were composed at this time. Although most of these poems also appeared in print, it was still very much the custom to sing them at the banquets of the higher nobility. The great Elizabethan Sir Philip Sidney, who visited Hungary in the 1570s, also mentioned this in his *Apologie for Poetry*.

Contemporary events as well as historical subjects attracted the attention of the writers of these songs. These minstrels swiftly composed songs on various incidents in the war against the Turks, serving as national chroniclers and at the same time as "trumpets that sing to battle". The most famous of these national chroniclers was *Sebestyén Tinódi* (1510?–1556). In his early years Tinódi put Bible stories into verse and wrote songs on the memorable exploits of his master, Bálint Török; but after the Turkish victories of 1541 he spoke for the whole people when he chronicled the common sorrows of the nation. The events he recorded in his songs included the capture of Buda by the Turks in *On the Fall of Buda*, (Buda veszéséről..., 1541), and great incidents in the long border warfare against the invaders, as in *The Engagement on Szalka Field* (Az szalkai mezőn való viadal, 1544), and the successful defence of Eger fortress in *On the Siege of the Fortress of Eger* (Egervár viadaljáról, 1553). His reports are so reliable in fact that they can be regarded as historical source material. During his last years Tinódi enjoyed the patronage of Tamás Nádasdy, a confidant of Ferdinand of Habsburg, earlier mentioned as Sylvester's patron, who influenced his political thinking. Tinódi was granted a patent of nobility in 1553 and his collected songs were printed by Heltai at Kolozsvár in 1554. There are sudden lines, flashes, a number of turns, certain stanzas in Tinódi's poems—particularly when he deals with military events and adventures and the joys of a soldiering life—which seem to anticipate Bálint Balassi.

Among Tinódi's contemporaries *Péter Ilosvai Selymes* is remembered not for any particular quality in his poetry, but as the man whose major work on a well-known medieval Hungarian theme provided the literary raw material for a nineteenth-century masterpiece: János Arany's epic poem, the *Toldi Trilogy*, is based on Ilosvai Selymes's *History of the Distinguished Deeds and Jousts of the Far-famed Miklós Tholdi* (Az híres neves Tholdi Miklósnak jeles cselekedetiről és bajnokságáról való históriája, 1574).

One of the finest of these many "history songs" is the anonymous *Cantio de militibus pulchra* (*c.* 1560). It is the tale of a daring exploit by the ill-paid soldiers of László Kerecsényi, the avaricious and ruthless Constable of Gyula Castle. Burning with rancour and bitterness the defenders make a desperate sortie against a besieging Turkish army of vastly superior numbers. Their almost suicidal venture is told with the brevity of a ballad in this fine example of sixteenth-century Hungarian poetry.

The form of these verse chronicles shows the emergence of the stanza patterns which came to be favoured by Hungarian epic; of 23 verse chronicles 12 were written in four-line stanzas, eleven syllables to the line, already popular with Tinódi, and seven in four-line stanzas, twelve syllables to the line.

Narrative Love Poems

Narrative poems dealing with love deserve special attention for they were the vehicle through which a freer social ethic was widely disseminated, again foreshadowing Balassi. The first Hungarian adaptation of a Boccaccio story, *Historia regis Volter* was written for the wedding of János I in 1539 by Pál Istvánffy, a distinguished noble who had travelled in Italy, and father of the historian Miklós Istvánffy. It held up to praise the medieval ideal of the wife's unquestioning obedience and loyalty to her husband. By contrast, the Italian-educated Unitarian minister György Enyedi's *Historia elegantissima Gismundae, regis Tancredi filiae* (1577), also based on a story from Boccaccio, advocated woman's right to love and, more importantly, even placed nobility of intellect acquired through education above nobility of birth.

Craftsmanship of a strikingly high standard and sympathetically modern social thinking mark a number of other songs, adapted by the authors from oral tradition or from other languages. The anonymous *Historia continens verissimam excidii Troiani causam* (1576) is one; it ignores the historical narrative to concentrate on the story of Paris and Helen and "the mighty flames of the fire of love". The anonymous *Story of Eurialus and Lucretia* (Eurialusnak és Lukréciának szép históriája, 1577), based on the famous Latin novella of Aeneas Sylvius Piccolomini (later Pope Pius II), written in 1544, is so well told that many now attribute it to Bálint Balassi. *Eurialus and Lucretia* represents the first attempt in the Hungarian language to produce a psychological analysis of a woman's soul. It described a woman's conflicts and torments in love; Lucretia, after long consideration, finally chose the bold initiative, an act symbolizing a woman's right to choose her partner.

> *She who holds her quainted name too dear*
> *Lacks o' mettle and o' fortitude;*
> *'This but common knowledge; as I hear*
> *Such things have oft ensued.*

One of the finest love poems is the *Story of a Prince Named Argirus and a Fairy Maiden* (História egy Árgirus nevű királyfiról és egy tündér szűzleányról) by *Albert Gergei,* of whom nothing is known beyond his name. Gergei found the tale "in an Italian chronicle" and translated it into Hungarian. It was the love story of the "youngest prince", who went in search of happiness and perfect love and found the fairy maiden—not surprisingly—in the imaginary world of Fairyland. In *Argirus* Hungarian poetic language comes of age: the poem deals with love, the daily life of the community, and ways of contemporary thinking and feeling in all their complexity, and the poet now possessed a technique which allowed him to express whatever he wished with ease and elegance. Gone was the crudeness of style that once so hampered communication. The Hungarian language had become a polished and flexible tool for the use of poets and writers.

Lyric Genres

In the mid-sixteenth century the Psalms emerged as the leading type of lyric poetry. Following the devotion to the Old Testament manifested by the Hungarian Reformation, the spiritual world of the Psalms was placed at the heart of Protestant church-singing. But instead of producing word for word translations of the biblical texts, they re-fashioned them by adding contemporary allusions of a political or social nature. The dramatist Mihály Sztárai was a pioneer in this field, producing very forceful translations of many of the songs of David in a variety of metres, in which he hints broadly at such contemporary happenings as the devastation wrought by the Turks and the persecutors of the Reformation. Versions of psalms by even such minor poets as Benedek Tordai or Benedek Pap still capture the reader by their great emotional force and graphic imagery. *Mihály Kecskeméti Vég's* version of *Psalm 55* (1561) is famous as the text used in Zoltán Kodály's choral piece *Psalmus Hungaricus;* in this powerful song of biblical passion the man who was the chief magistrate of Kecskemét inveighs against his treacherous friends; it remains a much appreciated piece of Hungarian poetry to this day. It is, however, the version of the Psalm produced by *Gergely Szegedi* (d. 1566), a preacher who worked in Debrecen and later in Eger, which display the finest craftsmanship of all the Hungarian versions of the Psalms. In Szegedi's poems, Sztárai's anger against the enemy is replaced by a confident, warm lyric quality, a more profoundly religious tone. These Protestant poets laid the foundations of a school of Hungarian hymn-writing that includes some of the greatest poets of Hungary, ranging in time from Bálint Balassi up to that early twentieth-century giant, Endre Ady.

The "school poetry", that is, the poems and songs, and indeed plays as well, that were written in the great schools of Hungary, and form a genre of their own, kept the tradition and practice of poetry alive, and its influence was to endure through succeeding centuries; it helped pave the way, for example, for the courtly Renaissance poetry. A few examples of this genre survive: satirical poems, epithalamia and the occasional autobiographical poem of an ironical songster. One such poem is the *Song of Mihály Moldovai* (Moldovai Mihály éneke); the author was a Hungarian Villon of sorts and the poem recounts the story of his life with all its vicissitudes and his adventures and experiences with his fellow thieves.

Very few love lyrics dating before 1570 still survive, and in most cases they are merely fragments. Yet earlier than that in the 1540s János Sylvester, the grammarian and the translator of the New Testament, praised the linguistic richness and finely polished style of these poems even though he, like the other Reformation writers condemned their subject-matter. The repugnance felt over the lack of morality in the poems largely explains why the early Hungarian love lyrics no longer survive. That such poetry had existed and indeed reached a fairly high level is also convincingly proved by the fact that it was chiefly in this genre that the earliest great Hungarian poet, Bálint Balassi, produced the first true classics of Hungarian poetry.

9 Bálint Balassi (1554–1594)

His Life and Character

All the finest achievements of Hungarian Renaissance letters, from the love poetry to the play, are united in the poetry of Bálint Balassi. He was the eldest son of a rich Protestant noble of northern Hungary and was given an excellent education: as a child he was taught by no less a man than Péter Bornemisza, continued his education at Nuremberg and completed his studies in Germany and then probably at Padua. The future for this wealthy and cultured young noble would have appeared to be sunny and carefree; but the political twists and turns of fate so typical of the times intervened. His father, Baron János Balassi, was arrested on falsified charges on the orders of Emperor Maximilian II who was also the king of Hungary; he escaped from prison and fled with his family to Poland. Although the baron was eventually cleared of these charges and allowed to return from exile with his family, the shadow of political suspicion continued to hang over the Balassi family. In an attempt to retrieve his position with the Habsburgs, János Balassi sent his son with a sizeable armed force of men to fight against the principality of Transylvania, with which the Habsburgs, and therefore Habsburg-controlled northwestern Hungary, were at war. Young Bálint was taken prisoner in the course of an engagement, but was treated with great courtesy as a guest at the court of Prince István Báthory of Transylvania. After a few pleasant months at the Prince's court he accompanied him to Poland when the Polish nobles elected Báthory King of Poland. When in 1577 word reached him of his father's illness, together with other family troubles, Balassi left Poland to return to Hungary. But upon his return he found his father dead and most of his estates and property seized by kinsmen.

The year 1578 found the 24-year-old young man almost totally penniless and politically suspect; his marriage plans had miscarried, and he was in no position to profit from either his military skill, his education or his remarkable command of languages (in addition to his native Hungarian he was proficient in eight languages: Latin, Italian, German, Polish, Turkish, Slovak, Croatian and Rumanian). It was at this juncture that he met Anna Losonczi, wife of Kristóf Ungnád, a high-ranking government official and officer in the Imperial army. The mother of several children and several years older than Balassi, Anna was a pleasure-loving woman who found time hanging heavy on her hands; for years on end she saw very little of her husband, frequently away on official business. She fell passionately in love with young Bálint and their love gave the first impetus to his budding talent in the "Anna poems". The problem of a livelihood, however, still remained; he applied to serve in the army at Eger, a town famous in Hungarian history for its resistance to a protracted Turkish siege. He remained in Eger until 1582, when his wild and riotous zest for life led to his dismissal from the service, despite the fact that he was a good soldier famous for his courage. He lost Anna's favours as well; and the scandal of Balassi's love affairs were even causing concern in Vienna. In an attempt to regulate his life, Balassi now conceived a plan which he doubtless considered a masterstroke: at Christmas 1584, he marched into the castle at Sárospatak and married Krisztina Dobó, his cousin and the widowed daughter of István Dobó, the hero of the legendary siege of Eger, and as her dowry apparently included the castle, he took it by force. This exploit, however, aroused a widespread sense of outrage: on the one hand Sárospatak was a royal castle and on the other their marriage fell within the prohibited degrees of kinship, and it was therefore declared invalid. Around the same time, Balassi was finally and irrevocably deprived of his property by his uncle and guardian, András Balassi.

It was around this time that Balassi was converted to Catholicism. But following his divorce he returned to the deautiful Anna Losonczi, now a widow. He began plying her with marriage proposals and with expressions of his undying passion—a love siege, that produced in the "Júlia poems" the finest love lyrics Hungarian poetry was to know for centuries. But the widow—who, incidentally, displayed considerable skill in the protection of her property—rejected the inconstant suitor. And so in September, 1589, Balassi mounted his horse and set off alone for Poland, in the belief that the Poles were planning a campaign against the Turks in which he hoped to take part. The war, however, never broke out. On his way, Balassi stopped at the castle of Dębno, where he fell in love with Anna Szárkándy, the wife of the castle's owner, Ferenc Wesselényi, and lived blissfully with her for about six months. This affair in turn produced the "Celia poems". He then proceeded on his way to the Baltic coast, spending some time in the local Jesuit college of Braunsberg (Braniewo). From Braunsberg, he returned to Hungary in 1591. He earned his living trading in horses and wine and settled down to try to straighten out his financial affairs. But when the fifteen-year Turkish war broke out in 1593 Balassi took up arms against the Turks and fought with great valour against them. He even recaptured his inheritance from the Turks. But on May 19, 1594 he met his death at the siege of Esztergom. His legs were crushed by a cannon ball and he died after a painful operation and much suffering.

It was a strange, extraordinary life. He lived "in storm and strife", in continuous conflict with those around him, with the authorities and with the society of the day. In terms of wealth and social situation his fortune steadily declined. Every attempt he made to retrieve his position failed; and the greater his fall the more audacious—and unsuccessful—was every attempt to reverse his lot. It was this perennial tension and disharmony that released the great lyric poet in him, it was this that made him dream of a concord that he was never to achieve in his lifetime. Love and courage, the beauty of nature and, on occasion, God, were for him the vision and the enchantment of another better world distilled in his poetry in a quintessence of the Hungarian Renaissance.

Love and Courage

His earliest known poems were written around 1575 when he was 20 years old. These are poems of courtship and love addressed to women or girls of the nobility, many of whom are known by name; he set theme to the music of various love songs written in Latin, Italian, Polish, German, Croatian, Turkish or Rumanian; some of the poems were in fact adaptations of songs in these languages. Some ten years later, around 1583, his love poetry came under the influence of some of the highly cultivated humanist poets; he chanced upon a volume of poems by Michael Marullus, Hieronymus Angerianus and Janus Secundus (*Poetae tres elegantissimi,* 1582) and learned from them the technical skills and vocabulary of Renaissance poetry. But the intensity of personal experience of the soldier's life makes itself felt through the conscious refinement of these love poems. He expressed his pleasure in "good horses, swift hounds, sharp sabres and the company of young men and brave soldiers", translating a Latin poem he tells us while resting between forays, as he reclined, in the green grass beside his faithful horse *"Do you not see this land around resplendent with glorious flowers?"* (Széjjel tündökleni nem ládd-é ez földet gyönyörű virágokkal?) He enjoyed the splendid Whitsunday, but then his gaze fell on horsemen galloping across the field and on soldiers:

> *One on fair grass his good horse now will tend*
> *one gaily takes his ease with a brave friend*
> *one gives his bloody weapon to be cleaned.*
>
> (For *Wine-drinkers*— Borivóknak való;
> translated by Keith Bosley and Peter Sherwood)

His most perfectly composed and most frequently quoted poem is also a *cantio militaris* or soldier's song, *In Praise of the Marches* (A végek dicsérete, 1589). This picture of soldiers preparing for battle opens with a paean to life on the marches, and to the beauty of nature, and ends with a moving blessing and farewell. Between them, like a golden section, comes his praise of the virtue of soldiers:

> *To win a good name*
> *and excellent fame*
> *they leave all things behind:*
> *their humanity*
> *and their bravery*
> *all men should bear in mind...*

> (Translated by Keith Bosley
> and Peter Sherwood)

This balanced Renaissance composition with its carefully organized counterpoint maintains a brilliant equipoise between the faithful, shrewdly objective description of military life and its elevation on to a higher, more idealistic plane. Within the space of a few lines Balassi vividly recreates movement in a camp, the startled horses prancing restlessly at trumpet calls, the heavy steps of the horsemen trudging to their quarters in the night, and the stillness of the short slumbers.

> *Good Arab horses*
> *prance in their courses*
> *and when the bugle blared*
> *some stood guard, others*
> *dismounted to doze*
> *at morning where they'd heard*
> *the cock crow, for night*
> *after night in fight*
> *all are weary and tired.*

> (Translated by Keith Bosley
> and Peter Sherwood)

Religious Poetry

Balassi's cultivated and accomplished love poetry, carefully fashioned on the model of Marullus, was often interrupted by the forays and battles that were part of life in the marches. But this love poetry eventually died away under the pressures of his life, the failure of his marriage and the troubles besetting him. Like other poets before him, Balassi now turned to God, finding solace in the Psalms. His desire for spiritual comfort was coupled with the pride of the Renaissance man in a dawning consciousness of his own stature as a man. He disputes with God, argues with Him as a partner on equal terms, as one who knows that he and God assume each other to be equals. "What would you have to forgive if the faithful did not sin against you?" he asks. Balassi reached the final form of these poems, addressed to God by way of translations of the Psalms. He translated George Buchanan (*My Gracious God*—Az én jó istenem) as well as Théodore Béza (*Heavenly Hosts, Blissful, Pure Souls*—Mennyei seregek, boldog, tiszta lelkei) and Jan Kochanowski. And even his last poem *Psalm 51: All-merciful...* (Végtelen irgalmú...), written as he lay fatally wounded, is a paraphrase, one of Béza's. This poem conveys every last shudder of the poet as he lay on his deathbed in the camp at Esztergom, with such poignancy that every line comes home unbearably to the reader:

> *Here, unbandaged, behold, even as I unfold,*
> *This my poxed wound to thee.*

Balassi's genuinely religious poetry breathes a spirit of contention, of confrontation. These poems are deeply emotional, the anguished outpourings of an unquiet spirit, caught and held in inner conflict. The craftsmanship born of long years of careful translations of Marullus is here thrown to the winds; but the poems are all the finer for it, profoundly personal poems that defy all conventions and indeed truly "storm the gates of heaven".

The last group of Balassi's religious poems have death as their central theme. It was this theme which was first voiced in his poems in the months of despair during the summer of 1589, at the time the wrote his brief but moving supplication to God beginning *I Have Nowhere to Go* (Nincs már hová lennem...). Two years later, in 1591, a mood of acceptance of death found expression in two small masterpieces: *Merciful Lord* (Kegyelmes Isten) and *Give me Peace* (Adj már csendességet). Both are religious poems, the prayers of an outlaw in lonely exile far from family and friends. In these poems a man in exile, possessed of the most consummate poetic mastery and preparing himself for his last and final rest, longs for the final absolution of a death that will expiate his sins.

The Júlia Cycle

Balassi's love poetry entered on its second phase in 1587, when he returned to the mistress he had abandoned in 1584 with a major poem, recalling with elemental force the memory of past happiness. This poem *Fine Words and Joyful Kisses Sweeter than Honey* (Méznél édesb szép szók, örvendetes csókok), written for himself rather than anyone else, became the opening poem in his splendid cycle of love lyrics, the "Júlia poems". As they were designed to win again the heart of Anna Losonczi, they return to the Petrarchan style. Following in the footsteps of Janus Secundus, he gave his mistress the name of Júlia, and in imitation of Petrarchan poetry as he knew it, made the maximum use he could of the twists and turns of this type of humanist poetry. Ten of these poems drew their inspiration from Angerianus's "poetic inventions"; another two poems were influenced by Marullus and Regnart, respectively, and three by Turkish songs. His great technical skill and craftsmanship can be seen in the accomplished verse form he evolved for himself, with its many advantages over others, named after him: the Balassi stanza with a rhythm of 6/6/7-6/6/7-6/6/7 and an AAB-CCB-DDB rhyme pattern.

Each of the Júlia poems is a work of art in its own right; but together they grow in value and significance as units in a greater composition of which they form the elements. For Balassi was the first Hungarian poet to realize that the love lyrics which expressed his innermost feelings and desires had to be appreciated exclusively on the strength of their intrinsic literary worth. While the Júlia poems failed in their immediate aim to win Anna, they served to mature his awareness of himself as a poet to the point where he thought of committing them to print. And this was something a poet skilled in the Petrarchan mode could never have envisaged except in the superior form of a cycle of poems.

Balassi was certainly acquainted with Petrarch's *Canzoniere*, the greatest and most widely imitated model for Renaissance poem-cycles; but it is more likely that the Júlia cycle of Janus Secundus was his immediate model, and *Amarilli*, Castelletti's pastoral play in Italian, which Balassi read and adapted into Hungarian in 1588—at the very time he was writing his Júlia poems—was the direct source of the narrative framework linking the series of poems into one. But the story of the fugitive lover in the pastoral play could only have made Balassi more conscious of his instinctive predilection for the cycle of poems as a form, already apparent in his earlier poems. All that was then needed was a deliberate effort on the part of the poet for the Júlia poems—lyrics addressed to his lost and vainly sought mistress as yet far away—to take shape in what became, in the spring of 1589, the earliest cycle of lyrics ever written in the Hungarian language.

For the first time in Hungarian poetry we meet a real flesh-and-blood figure of a woman: she saunters, wanders and dances her way through a string of poems, now smiling, now petulant, and now again all sweetness; she is coquettish, she is distant, now gracious and now cruel. A hundred and one moments of daily life—hitherto unrecorded in Hungarian poetry — are captured, truly, precisely, in these poems. In one *When he Chanced upon Júlia* (Hogy Júliára talála, így köszöne néki), Júlia is pictured smiling at the poet as he appears before her.

> *Dawn of my sunlight*
> *your eyebrows' black fire*
> *my two eyes' bright light:*
> *live, live, my life's hope!*
> . . . .

Thus Julia I
greeted, seeing her:
I bowed knee, bowed head
and she merely smiled.

(Translated by Keith Bosley
and Peter Sherwood)

The essential aspiration of the poet was to record the stirrings of his soul, and paint a portrait of the "immortal mistress".

Any land I roam through, any deed I may do,
My mind must bear evermore
Julia's tender features, wonder-soft words of hers;
Julia alone I adore.
Should I glance left or right, radiant still on my sight,
She moves before me once more.

(*You, the Heaven's Domed Height* – Ó nagy kerek kék ég;
translated by W. D. Snodgrass)

It seems incredible that Balassi was able to maintain this "high tension" after his breach with "Júlia" Anna Losonczi. In his poems to Celia, the other Anna, Anna Szárkándy, his passion appears less explosive, yet his descriptions of Celia are more sensual, even livelier, and charged with an erotic quality.

Amazed at a bath
giving of its breath
in great puffs of vapour
he explains: This is
nothing to amaze
for Celia sits there
at whose naked form
love grows wild and warm
and as smoke fills the air.

(*In which he Describes the Manner*
of Celia's Bathing – Kiben az Célia feredésének módját
írja meg; translated by Keith Bosley
and Peter Sherwood)

Balassi must also be remembered as a pioneer in the development of Hungarian drama. In 1588–89, in what was the most fertile period of his career as a writer, he translated and adapted two Italian plays into Hungarian. One of them was an adaptation (1589) of *Amarilli* (1587), the Italian pastoral play by Cristoforo Castelletti.

Balassi was perfectly aware of the experimental nature of his undertaking. In the dedication "To the Gentle and Noble Ladies of Transylvania," and in his personal Prologue to the play, he explained his motive for the translation, his love for Julia, while at the same time propounding his literary views and principles, and what he was trying to do. He meant "to approach the writing of comedy as a new form," he explained in the Prologue, that is, he intended to naturalize the Renaissance love comedy as a new genre of literature in Hungary.

Balassi's work is not only a unique synthesis of all the achievements of Hungarian letters up to his time; it is also a great and bold advance on these achievements. Virtually single-handed he elevated the Hungarian poem from the level of the itinerant minstrel's song to that of the cultivated Renaissance poem. The poetry he thus created can be ranked with the work of such great contemporaries as Ronsard and Kochanowski, or the sonnets of Shakespeare. A *poeta doctus* in the truest sense of the phrase, he was at the same time a spontaneous poet of genius whose temperament and extraordinary personality made him a pioneer in lyrical writing of an excellence unmatched for many years in Hungarian lyric poetry.

10 The Literature of the Late Renaissance; Mannerism*

The years that followed Balassi saw the consciously cultivated poetry of the Hungarian Renaissance reach its peak. Though it failed to produce great poets of anything like Balassi's stature, the literary scene during this period was nevertheless alive with a host of important, learned and well-known poets and scholars; the lively literary activities of the age took shape in new genres and new schools, the majority of writers feeling themselves constrained to set forth the views and principles upon which their particular poetic creeds rested. János Rimay and Albert Szenci Molnár together were the leaders and the guiding spirits of hundreds of writers and even those lacking any poetic gifts at all felt it *de rigeur* to use the Balassi stanza when courting their ladies or trying to play the wit.

János Rimay (1570-1631)

The last poet of the Hungarian Renaissance was Balassi's favourite disciple. Perhaps even more cultivated and more deliberate in his craftsmanship than his master, he took great pains and devoted considerable time in chiselling and polishing his poems to the required degree of perfection: probably for this very reason he is a less original and less important artist than Balassi. But for all that, his work is significant in being the first in which the Late Renaissance trend towards Mannerism was tinged with the first signs of the Baroque. Rimay was the last humanist writer educated on Cicero and Erasmus, but his translation of Cicero was already influenced by the new contemporary style, with its taste for ornate embellishment. An assiduous collector and editor of Balassi's poems, his country house in North Hungary became a literary centre where his many poet friends could indulge their passion for Balassi and poetry in general. As might be expected, he followed his master in composing a cycle of love poems; but for him it was more a scholarly exercise than an expression of pro-

---

* Although in England the term "Mannerism" is confined to a period or style of fine arts, on the Continent the word is also used to designate a period or style of literature.

foundly felt sentiments and emotions. For him, poetry was something to be enjoyed by the intellect; it meant the painstaking polishing of lines and stanzas and the fastidious selection of words more elegant than those used in colloquial speech. Rimay's is the first body of poetry to be "patriotic" in the modern sense of the word, coupling a sense of national pride with very definite political views. He lamented the unhappy plight of the Hungarian people in a moving, beautiful poem—*In which he Laments the Ruin and Ravage of the Hungarian Nation* (Kiben kesereg a magyar nemzetnek romlásán s fogyásán)—and played an active political part in Prince István Bocskay's armed rising (1604–6).

Lyrics of a philosophical and religious nature form the most important part of his output; his meditative poems express anguish over the transcience of human affairs and behind this anguish a sense of guilt hides tempered by the comfort of religion and by his stoic constancy, if not into harmony, at least into fine poetry. Rimay's poems are full of strikingly modern associations of ideas and full of sensuous imagery. Yet what can only be described as a sort of Mannerist exaggeration, concerned to make the maximum effect, is liable to divert the reader's attention from the ideas embodied in the poem.

Albert Szenci Molnár (1574-1634)

The life of Albert Szenci Molnár, a wandering scholar who travelled over much of Europe, was very different from that of Rimay, the country gentleman; but however different, their ways in their literary career reveal them as kindred spirits: both were the leaders of literary groups, and both were highly skilled in the art of versification.

All the learning and scholarly prose of Hungarian humanism, all the theological activity and religious poetry of the Hungarian Protestant Reformation came together in the work of Albert Szenci Molnár. From the age of sixteen until he was thirty-eight (with the exception of a year spent partly in his native land and partly in travel in Italy and Switzerland) Szenci Molnár lived in Germany, where he first studied and later worked. The liberalism and active intellectual life existing in the German towns made a profound and enduring impression on him. Supported by Prince Maurice of Hesse he lived for five years in Marburg and, subsequently in Oppenheim. He married in Germany and never really took root in Hungary, although there were many who were glad to welcome him home and indeed begged him to stay. As he wrote later, he found he "could not accommodate himself to the conditions in that country". Nor could his family adjust to their new surroundings, and in addition they were frightened of war with the Turks. Consequently, after spending a few years in Hungary, Szenci Molnár returned to Germany in 1615.

Ironically, however, war caught up with him in Germany: in the course of the Thirty Years' War he was robbed and ruthlessly tortured by Catholic mercenaries in Heidelberg in 1622. A number of recorded remarks allow us to infer that jealous colleagues and the more conservative-minded Protestant circles often made life difficult for the much-travelled scholar. His nationwide influence as a scholar and author nonetheless continued undiminished until his death.

Szenci Molnár was the first writer to give scholars of other nations the key to an understanding of the Hungarian language, and so make Hungarian culture more accessible; his Latin-Hungarian dictionary (*Dictionarium Latino-Ungaricum et Ungarico-Latinum*, Nuremberg, 1604) and his *Nova grammatica Ungarica* (Hanza, 1610) fulfilled the need engendered by the usually lively interest in Hungarian displayed by European linguists at the time. He also produced a Hungarian Psalter (*Psalterium Ungaricum*, Herborn, 1607). He studied with great care a German version of the French edition of the Geneva Psalms by Clément Marot and Théodore Béza, and was particularly impressed by the tremendous poetic strength of Marot's translations. Szenci Molnár was not content to furnish merely matter for congregational singing at church service; he took pains to give his Hungarian version an intrinsically poetic and aesthetic value. He set his psalms to a total of about 130 different melodies, using nearly as many types of verse form and stanza pattern. He produced a Hungarian translation of Calvin's *Institutio religionis Christianae* and published in Germany a number of works in Latin on the political and social situation of the Hungary of his time. These books, with a number of anthologies of poetry, were very popular in seventeenth-century Germany and earned their author wide acclaim as a humanist scholar.

Prose Writers

Márton Szepsi Csombor (1595–1622), a young teacher who travelled in a number of European countries, wrote a book on his travels, *Europica varietas* (1620) which, though very popular at the time, is perhaps even more appreciated by contemporary literary historians. The book is a mine of invaluable information on the social and cultural history of the time; the Holland of Frans Hals, the France of Louis XIII and the England of James I and Ben Jonson are here depicted with fascinating liveliness, in a disarmingly cheerful account that is as sparkling as a newly-restored Brueghel painting. Here is Szepsi Csombor reporting on the seventeenth-century English enthusiasm for sport: "As you go up towards the Royal Palaces, coming from Westminster, you pass through a Gate made of two fine carved stones and adorned with fine statuary. Having entered, on the left you will behold a House built in the shape of a Cathedral: it contains many diverse playing Courts and Alleys, some of which are given over to ball games, some to skittles, others to hoops, and others again to bowls. And when you enter the Garden you will be amazed at the appearance of the garden, but chiefly you will marvel at the fine order of players therein, some of whom are pitching stones or poles, while other wrestle or jump..."

Of the many high-born humanists and middle-class Protestant preachers of the late Renaissance one figure stands out, *Simon Péchi* (*c.* 1570–1642), who as the heir of his landowner patron rose from a poor clerk to be the wealthiest noble in Transylvania, combined the learning of the humanists with an almost mystically contemplative religious faith. He investigated the life of the Jewish communities expelled from Spain, and they made so strong an impression on him that he was induced to learn Hebrew. He translated parts of the Old Testament into Hungarian, displays a poetic vigour and spirit which was combined with a delicate sense of style. He became one of the leading theologians of the Sabbatarian sect. The crowded ebullience and the feverish and visionary quality of his style foreshadows the Baroque, as do a number of Rimay's poems and Szepsi Csombor's account of his travels.

Baroque Literature

(From the Early Seventeenth Century to c. 1770)

11 History and Culture in the Baroque Period

Hungary under Habsburg Rule

The seventeenth century—the age of Cervantes and Lope de Vega, Racine and Molière, Milton, Louis XIV, Rembrandt and Monteverdi—was a critical and tragic period in Hungarian history. Hungary was still divided into three, the part under Habsburg control, the Turkish-occupied territories, and semi-independent Transylvania, with an even larger area under Turkish occupation than in the previous century. The Counter-Reformation of the Jesuits was in full swing throughout the territories under Habsburg control: the nobility, and especially the great barons, had recovered their former power, serfdom was consolidated, the system continuing for many years to come. Successive Hungarian princes of Transylvania, anxious for a share of European power politics, strengthened their military and political power in a number of victorious campaigns, but after the defeat of György Rákóczi II, Prince of Transylvania, in Poland in 1657, that country's prestige and power declined until the Transylvanian principality became little more than a vassal state of the Turkish empire. Miklós Zrínyi, a brilliant military commander and politician, to whom we shall return later, recognized the tragic inadequacies of the Habsburg Turkish policy and made plans for an independent, centralized kingdom of Hungary, and above all, for the organization of a strong army. There was nothing Utopian about the idea of an independent Hungarian national state, even at the time of the Turkish occupation; on the one hand Turkish power was in decline from the middle of the seventeenth century; and on the other the Habsburg monarchy was involved in problems of succession and a whole series of other political troubles. Zrínyi sought to establish contact with the government of Venice and France, but his sudden and tragic death in 1664 (he is thought to have been fatally gored by a wild boar while out hunting) prevented their fulfilment, and his inexperienced fellow conspirators were easily discovered and executed (1670–71). The government of Emperor Leopold made use of this conspiracy to tighten the military occupation of that part of Hungary under its control and intensified the oppression and persecution of Protestants. A large number of Hungarian pastors were sent to the galleys; their story is told in *Narratio brevis de oppressione libertatis Ecclesiarum Hungaricarum* (1646), written by Bálint Kocsi Csergő, the headmaster of a school at Pápa.

At the same time the whole of Hungarian foreign trade was made into a monopoly and given into the hands of a German–Austrian trading company. Discontent flared up in a series of anti-Habsburg uprisings, known as the "kuruc" revolts. Imre Thököly, a young noble brought up in Transylvania, led a series of "kuruc" uprisings in northeastern Hungary, and after a successful campaign forced the Emperor to restore the feudal constitution at a meeting of the Hungarian Diet in Sopron in 1681, thus appeasing the majority of "kuruc" leaders drawn from the lesser nobility, but providing little for the rank and file.

The late seventeenth century saw the end of one hundred and fifty years of Turkish occupation, a momentous change in the political fortunes of the nation. After the failure of the last great expansionist surge of the Turks—the siege of Vienna in 1683—the Christian armies of Europe, with Austria at their head, joined in a united effort to drive the Turks from Hungarian soil. Buda was recaptured on September 2, 1686, and the last of the Turks driven from Hungary in 1697. In the course of this campaign, Transylvania came under Habsburg control, though still as a separate political entity. The war to free Hungary from the Turks created the conditions for the reunification of Hungary, but brought in its wake economic disaster. The Imperial troops looted and pillaged the country at their pleasure, as if on a marauding campaign, with the result that the little that remained of Hungary's former greatness and wealth after a hundred and fifty years of Turkish occupation was now finally destroyed in the sixteen years of war from the defeat of the Turks before Vienna to the Treaty of Karlowicz in 1699, which finally freed Hungary from the Turks. Huge areas were depopulated and were subsequently settled by Germans, Slovaks and Serbians, an immigration that significantly altered the ethnic pattern of the country. Economically it was official Austrian policy to make of Hungary the granary of Austria; Chancellor Hörnigk of Austria, a supporter of Colbert's mercantilist principles, assigned to Hungary the role of providing the raw material for Austria's developing industries. In such circumstances it is not surprising that a few years after Hungary was freed from the Turkish yoke a great anti-Habsburg uprising should take place, led by Ferenc Rákóczi II, the wealthiest landowner in Hungary. Rákóczi's battle for freedom had the whole-hearted support of the oppressed classes and continued, with varying degrees of success, from 1703 to 1711. With the support of Louis XIV and Peter the Great of Russia, Rákóczi achieved important military successes in the early stages of the war and sought to consolidate them by introducing sweeping measures of reform in the lands he controlled. But the conflict between the interests of the noble classes and the serfs, who made up the bulk of Rákóczi's army, and the additions to the Imperial forces in the form of troops redeployed from the west after Austria's successes in the War of the Spanish Succession, sealed his fate, and with him the cause of Hungarian independence. Rákóczi and other insurgent *kuruc* leaders fled to exile in Poland, France and Turkey, but the Peace of Szatmár (1711) made with the Habsburgs confirmed the rights of the Hungarian estates and checked the power of Austrian absolutism.

The war left Hungary in a disastrous condition, but the relatively peaceful years of the eighteenth century brought slow but steady reconstruction, and the national administration, based on a balance of power between the Hungarian nobility and Viennese absolutism, was gradually established on a firm basis. But the influence of Vienna steadily increased and with all the consequences flowing from it, both advantageous and disadvantageous, with quiet determination the Counter-Reformation pressed ahead, with the result that the majority of the population were converted back to Catholicism. German, French and Italian social and intellectual influence gradually imposed themselves, to the detriment of native Hungarian traditions and cultural development, especially among the nobility, and even the Hungarian language took third place to Latin and German. The period therefore was often called in the 19th century, somewhat inaccurately, "the age of non-nationalism". At the same time, definite signs of progress could be observed; education, albeit along old-fashioned lines, improved; towns and castles were rebuilt; and the foundations were laid for subsequent progress towards a more refined standard of civilization. Controls from Vienna hampered the growth of industry and commerce, but agricultural output rose considerably and agricultural methods were modernized; and the Imperial court was even forced to take certain measures to protect the serfs, against the opposition of the nobility. The Habsburgs reached the peak of their prosperity in the reign of Maria Theresa (1740–1780); Hungarian life under the Empress was not quite a rococo idyll, but her reign formed the stepping-stone towards a period of greater advance marked by the spread of the Enlightenment and the growth of a bourgeois ideology.

The Counter-Reformation and Protestantism

Late Renaissance culture was still flourishing in Hungary when the Counter-Reformation began its work, moving from success to success. The movement was headed by the Jesuits, who had made several earlier abortive attempts to gain a foothold in Hungary, before finally succeeding around the first decade of the seventeenth century. Their principal centre was the Jesuit College at Nagyszombat (now Trnava, Czechoslovakia), which was transformed into a university in 1635. That northern town had been the seat of the Archbishop of Esztergom, the head of the Roman Catholic Church in Hungary since Esztergom itself had been occupied by the Turks in 1543. The Jesuits soon found themselves in a position to exert a decisive influence upon the Roman Catholic Church, particularly after one of their order, the eminent writer Péter Pázmány, became Archbishop of Esztergom in 1616. Pázmány and his

81

fellow Jesuits strengthened the position of the Catholic Church and waged a deter-mined campaign to win over to Catholicism the most influential families of the nobility. They succeeded, partly through the effectiveness of their arguments and their vigorous propaganda activities, and partly because the nobility was anxious to establish closer relations with the Habsburg ruler, only possible if they reverted to Catholicism. The conversion of the most powerful landowners led, in its turn, on the principle of *cuius regio, eius religio,* to large areas of the country being re-con-verted to Catholicism by the first half of the seventeenth century.

The Jesuit-led Counter-Reformation paved the way for the Baroque. The Jesuit colleges with their printing presses, and the accomplished theatrical perform-ances of their scholars, were powerful centres for dissemination of a Baroque culture. Although in the early seventeenth century teaching in the Jesuit schools contained a number of progressive features, by the eighteenth century, when it reached its greatest expansion, its teaching methods were old-fashioned and out of date, and formed an obstacle to the spread of modern learning. The exclusive use of Latin in the Jesuit schools was detrimental to the spread of Hungarian scholarship and letters, one of the causes of the temporary eclipse of literature in the vernacular tongue.

The gains of the Counter-Reformation considerably weakened Protestantism in Hungary; yet in the seventeenth century the majority of Hungarians were still of the Calvinist faith. And in Transylvania Calvinism became the state religion (a position, let it be said, only achieved by crushing Unitarianism) and successive Princes of Transylvania gave effective support to fellow religionists in Habsburg Hungary. Seventeenth-century Hungarian Calvinists maintained close links with scholarly and religious centres abroad; in the early part of the century, most Hunga-rian Calvinist students studied at the Calvinist university of Heidelberg, and following its destruction by fire in 1622, at universities in Holland and England. Here, they were in position to acquaint themselves with new trends in religion, such as Puritan-ism and Presbyterianism, and very soon embraced the philosophies of progressive thinkers like Descartes or Cocceius.

The most famous Calvinist colleges in Hungary owed their prosperity to sup-port from some powerful patron—such as the support given by the Prince of Transylvania to the college at Gyulafehérvár or by a great lord to Sárospatak or by a municipal council to the college at Debrecen. Prince Gábor Bethlen of Transyl-vania (ruled 1613–1629) filled the chairs of the college in his capital Gyulafehérvár with renowned teachers from abroad—Martin Opitz, Heinrich Alsted, Heinrich Bisterfeld and others all taught there. János Apácai Csere, an influential Hungarian propagator of Cartesian ideas (to whom we shall return in greater detail later) also taught there. In the 1640s János Tolnai Dali, one of the leaders of the Puritan movement was rector of Sárospatak College, a boarding-school, which enjoyed the patronage of the wealthy Rákóczi family, and between 1650 and 1654, the college was headed by the leading educationalist of the time, the Bohemian J. A. Comenius who wrote several of his major works there. Another leading personality of the Puritan movement, Pál Medgyesi, taught at the Debrecen college in the 1630s; while in the second half of the century this school, the centre of Calvinism in Eastern Hungary, was headed by György Komáromi Csipkés, an English-educated Bible translator and theologian, author of an English grammar. These flourishing academic institutions suffered a number of serious setbacks at the end of the seventeenth century, partly through war and partly as a result of the advance of the Counter-Reformation. The Transylvanian college at Gyulafehérvár was destroyed by the Tartar troops of the Turks in 1658. The college of neighbouring Nagyenyed (now Aiud, Rumania) succeeded it as the main Transylvanian seat of learning. In the middle of the eighteenth century likewise the colleges of Sárospatak and Debrecen took on a new lease on life and came to play a major role as the institutions which produced the generation that ushered in the Hungarian age of Enlightenment.

The Baroque Culture of the Nobility

The culture of the Baroque first appeared and then took root in the seventeenth century in Hungary at the seats of the wealthiest nobility of the country: little by little the lesser nobles followed suit and eventually it dominated the life-patterns of the whole of the nobility. The state of war that prevailed during much of the seventeenth century was scarcely conductive to building, few Baroque mansions and churches were built in the early years of its influence, and those for the most part in the western part of the country (now the Burgenland in Austria). The family which undertook the most extensive and grandiose building activities was the Esterházys, Counts and Princes of the Holy Roman Empire from 1712. The foundations of the wealth and political power of this leading family of the Baroque period were laid by the Palatine Miklós Esterházy (1582–1645) who, around 1635, contributed generously to the building of the first Baroque church in Hungary, the Jesuit university church at Nagyszombat (*c.* 1635), while his son, Pál, built the first Baroque château at Kismarton (now Eisenstadt, Austria) between 1663 and 1673. The first Transylvanian Baroque château was both designed and built by Miklós Bethlen, the noted writer, at Betlenszentmiklós (now Sânmiclăuş, Rumania). Many more were built after the Turkish occupation had ended, and were carried out with the help of famous master builders from abroad. Prince Eugene of Savoy, who had led the Christian armies to final victory over the Turks, invited Lucas von Hildenbrandt to build his château at Ráckeve in the neighbourhood of present-day

Budapest. Even noblemen with more modest resources rebuilt their mansions and country homes in the Baroque style; by the middle of the eighteenth century the Hungarian countryside was dotted with Baroque country houses with finely designed parks, the residences of nobles who were beginning to collect pictures for their galleries and books for their libraries and which became centres of elegant and polished living. Gothic churches destroyed during the Turkish wars, mainly in the country west of the Danube, were also rebuilt in the Baroque style.

The intellectual climate of the Baroque period favoured the arts, particularly from the end of the seventeenth century onwards. It stimulated the art of painting in particular, an art which had been found reprehensible by the Reformation. The portraitist Ádám Mányoki (1673–1756) became Prince Ferenc Rákóczi's court painter; Jakab Bogdány (1660–1724) attained the same position at the court of St. James's; his still-life paintings are greatly appreciated today. While these Hungarian artists lived the better part of their life abroad, many Austrian artists were at work in Hungary. Franz Anton Maulbertsch painted altarpieces in western Hungary (at Sümeg, Győr, Székesfehérvár and Pápa) and Rafael Donner was responsible for the statue of St. Martin, in Hungarian hussar uniform, in the Coronation Church in Pozsony.

The first newspapers came into being around this time; Ferenc Rákóczi II published military reports under the title *Mercurius Veridicus ex Hungaria* (1705–10); and Mátyás Bél edited *Nova Posoniensia* (1721–22) at Pozsony. The first modern geographical surveys were carried out, leading to the production of the first printed modern maps of Hungary. More and more foreign travellers visited Hungary, which had a touch of the exotic about it as a country recently freed from 150 years of Turkish occupation. About the middle of the eighteenth century, the level of development in literature, the arts, the sciences, education and the cultural level of the nation as a whole heralded the beginning of a new era.

12 Religious Literature

Péter Pázmány (1570-1637)

The famous writer greatly admired for his style, Cardinal Péter Pázmány, Archbishop of Esztergom, towers above all the religious authors of the Baroque period. A Jesuit from the age of 17, he had a brilliant career: he was Archbishop of Esztergom and Lord Chancellor from the autumn of 1616, and became a cardinal in 1629. His years in Baroque Rome (1593-1597) left an indelible impression on his life and thought. On purely logical grounds he became convinced that the future of his country was linked inseparably to the destiny of the Habsburg monarchy, and that it was the beliefs and the thinking of the Catholic Counter-Reformation, directed from Rome, which would provide the means of uniting his strife-torn nation. These ideas, fallacious as they were, yet sincerely held, guided his every step: a ruthless missionary of Catholicism, he served the Habsburg dynasty, but at the same time was concerned to further his country's interests, often opposing the Imperial court in Vienna and even the Austrian Jesuits. He also founded several important cultural institutions, a university at Nagyszombat, schools, printing-presses and libraries.

Of his literary works, his *Christian Book of Prayers* (Keresztényi imádságos könyv, 1606), is still used by Catholics, and was the book of his that had the most powerful impact. His finest work was his *Book of Sermons* (A Római Anyaszentegyház szokásából minden vasárnapokra és egy-nehány innepekre rendelt evangeliumokrul prédikációk, 1636), but it was *A Guide to Divine Truth* (Isteni igazságra vezérlő kalauz, 1613), a work of apologetics that for many years ranked above all the others. While unquestionably deserving attention as the first original formulation of theological theory and dogma in the history of Hungarian literature, and an important milestone in the development of a Hungarian theological and philosophical language, this book is nevertheless too specialized to be considered part of general Hungarian literature. The same is true of his polemical writings on religion, with the difference that the latter, with their impassioned arguments cast in the form of logical propositions, despite their emotionally charged contents, were for many years regarded as models of Hungarian polemical literature. These writings are also of importance as the beginnings of effervescence, a ferment in the intellectual life of the country. Pázmány's first controversial tract was his *Reply* (Felelet, 1603) to the Protestant historical and philosophical work already mentioned, *On the Cause of the Numerous Corruptions in the Nations,* (1602) by István Magyari. From that time onwards Pázmány was quick to react to every book on political issues or religious controversies. The same thinking led him to attack Péter Alvinczi, a preacher of Kassa and an adherent of the Protestant princes Bocskay and Bethlen of Transylvania, *Five Kind Letters to the Worthy Péter Alvinczi* (Alvinczi Péter uramhoz íratott öt szép levél, 1609).

As a literary craftsman his chief talent lay in his ability to raise the Hungarian vernacular to the plane of literary rhetoric. An outstanding feature of his style was the use of carefully proportioned and well-balanced periodic sentences. At times this symmetry lapsed into overloaded Baroque ornamentation, but in no case did Pázmány lose the logical thread of his thought. An effective, outspoken, bluff naturalism occasionally broke through his elaborately built sentences, but this method of writing was handled with caution. Still more characteristic was his constant use of biblical imagery and the biblical vocabulary and the originality and variety of his methods of attack as when, for example, he addressed his audience directly. He also had a keen ear for the music of a phrase.

Pázmány's robust and racy style not only reveals his realistic outlook on the world, but is more finished as a work of art than that of any of his Protestant adversaries, even though Magyari, Alvinczi and Szenci Molnár were no mean stylists themselves. His *Book of Sermons* is still a pleasure to read: compared with the speeches and writings of his European contemporaries—Bossuet or Fénelon, both of them younger than he, or Bellarmine, older,—his language is more rustic, more colourful, even perhaps a little more rough-hewn; his tone is livelier, his phrasing more passionate. In terms of painting Pázmány, the literary Jesuit educated at Rome, is more akin to the Flemish painters of the time, with their bold colours and hearty rombustious laughter, than to the restrained Baroque of Guido Reni and his fellows. But purely as a literary craftsman he can unquestionably be seen as the contemporary and opposite number of the Protestant Márton Szepsi Csombor or of the Hungarian encyclopaedist János Apácai Csere.

Baroque Religious Prose

In the heyday of Catholic religious writing in the early seventeenth century, devotional pieces and polemical pamphlets poured from the pens of countless authors. Notable among them were a Jesuit monk *György Káldi* (1572–1634) and a fellow Jesuit *Mátyás Hajnal* (1578–1644). Káldi was responsible for the first Catholic translation of the Bible into Hungarian (1626). Hajnal produced a Sacred Heart prayer-book (1629), reminiscent of the ecstatic and mystic writings of St. John of the Cross and

St. Teresa of Ávila; the book was written for women and dedicated to the wife of the Palatine, Count Miklós Esterházy, initiating the reader into the self-hypnosis of mystic ecstasy bordering on erotic pleasure, and written in a sophisticated style with subtle sentence rhythms, capable of expressing a thousand emotional nuances.

Outstanding among the Protestant mentors driven on to the defensive by the Counter-Reformation was *Péter Alvinczi* (1570–1634), a pastor in Kassa and a valued adviser of the Princes of Transylvania, who made energetic efforts to remove the differences dividing Calvinist and Lutheran. His Latin tract *Querela Hungariae* (1620) is an exposition of grievances afflicting the country, and describes with passion and anger the crimes perpetrated under the military and political terror of the Habsburg Counter-Reformation.

The Hungarian followers of the English Puritan movement are also worthy of attention. Most notable among them as writer is *Pál Medgyesi* (1605–1663), a pastor at Debrecen who later became preacher at the Transylvanian court. He made Hungarian translation of Lewis Bayly's *Praxis pietatis* (1636). He was a writer with a fine feeling for words; his Mannerist style was used to present consistently logical arguments expressed in fine, pliant yet concise sentences; in this respect he ranks with Pázmány whose views on translation he happened to share.

The Hungarian Puritans, and the religious doctrines they adopted, introduced to Hungary the social and political views which accompanied Puritanism in England; they advocated with impatience the development of a middle class as were concerned to raise the cultural level of the nation.

This outline of the religious literature of the period is by no means exhaustive. The age produced a spate of prayer-books, devotional, polemical and other theological writings so immense as to almost defy description. Some of these theologians were still active in the eighteenth century, as for instance *Zsigmond Csúzy* (1670–1729), a Pauline friar whose books of sermons, written in a popular style, reveal considerable concern for the sufferings of the common people, at the same time making no secret of his distaste for the polemical rhetoric of the Jesuits.

Religious Poetry

The output of religious poetry in the Baroque period like religious prose, was enormous; hundreds of hymns and hymnals were produced, mainly by Catholics.

The first religious poet of the Baroque of any importance was a Catholic, *Mátyás Nyéki Vörös* (1575–1654), an official in the Chancellery, later a canon at Győr in western Hungary. His early poetry showed the influence of Balassi and Rimay in the poetical forms he used, but his subject-matter was as far removed from Balassi's *leitmotif* of love and joyous living as the Baroque was from the

Renaissance. In the course of a long and peaceful life, secure in the possession of a carefully amassed fortune, Nyéki Vörös was immersed in meditations on the mystic other world of the soul, viewing life as a play acted out on the stage of a transient universe, which was no more than "winter sunshine, a sepulchral bubble" —and taking a morbid pleasure in envisaging the torments of hell after death. Yet the subject-matter of his poems, echoing the *danses macabres* of medieval times, is clothed somewhat incongruously in the melodious verse and the tuneful rhythms of Mannerist poetry:

> *Worms will haste to make foray*
> *Into the freshness of the grave*
> *So they might gnaw, devour and prey*
> *On your pampered, tender flesh.*
>
> > (Lament upon Mortality —
> > Siralom, az halandoságrol)

The music of Baroque poetry is heard in the two collections of church hymns of the period: the *Cantus Catholici* (1651) edited by the Catholic *Benedek Szőlősy* and the *Chanting Celestial Choir* (Zöngedező mennyei kar, 1696) by the Lutheran *Mihály Ács* together with the verses of a number of minor religious poets; but for all their polished craftsmanship and the virtuosity of their style, these poems cannot approach the masterpieces of Bálint Balassi or Miklós Zrínyi.

13 Miklós Zrínyi (1620-1664)

His Life and Character

While the age of the Baroque does not lack splendid epic poems, from the great Tasso's *Gerusalemme liberata* through Marino's *Strage degli innocenti* to Milton's *Paradise Lost,* none of the authors of cause had only first-hand knowledge of the wars and fighting they described. But Miklós Zrínyi, the greatest Hungarian commander of his time, was an eye-witness of the battles he described; he took an active part in the combats and engagements of the Turkish wars and described one of its early sieges in his epic poem, *The Siege of Sziget* (1646). This is more than merely a fact in his life; it exerted an important influence on his work: his epic is alive with the events of the age. For Zrínyi both the subject and the actual writing of his epic was a tragic reality; he was a soldier who took up his pen in winter quarters, when fighting ceased, to relate for the edifications and enjoyment of himself and others the heroic exploit of his great grandfather, of the same name.

> *Nor do I seek glory only with the quill,*
> *But also with my deadly sabre;*
> *I'll fight the Turk as long as I breathe,*
> *And cover him with earth forever.*

Zrínyi came from a wealthy and influential noble family of Croatian origin. He was orphaned at an early age, and was brought up under the spell of his great-grandfather's legendary feat of arms which has passed into Hungarian history. The elder Miklós Zrínyi, Ban (Governor) of Croatia, defended Szigetvár against the army of Suleiman the Great in 1566. When he saw that the fortress he had defended with such single-minded determination could no longer be held, he led his men out in a suicidal sortie and was killed. According to legend he stuffed his pockets with gold before breaking out to ensure that the Turkish soldier who finally cut him down received a due reward for his daring and bravery. This defiant gesture on the part of a man who was a proud and grasping noble and outstanding commander was also intended for the Habsburg ruler who had looked on passively, failing to send help and allowing the Turks to destroy one of his ablest commanders. His posthumous reward was the great reputation he earned, greater than that accorded to any person at the time: poem after poem chanted his praises, and a special anthology, *De Sigetho Hungariae propugnaculo,* dedicated to his heroism, was published at Wittenberg in 1587. His great-grandson, the poet, inherited his name and at the age of sixteen, after the customary grand tour—Venice, Florence, Rome, and Naples—returned home to settle at Csáktornya, the focal point of the family estates. His possessions bordered on Turkish-occupied Hungary, and as a result Zrínyi acquired great skill in the handling of weapons, and had plenty of opportunity to master the art of warfare.

In 1646, at the early age of twenty-six his military skill and prowess earned him promotion to the rank of general, and a year later he was appointed Ban of Croatia and commander-in-chief of Southern Hungary. Both as a soldier and a politician, Zrínyi came to recognize that the dynasty was failing to serve the best interests of his country; and consequently, with great caution and circumspection, and with constant regard to the prevailing political situation, he began to plot against the Empire with the aim of organizing the election of György Rákóczi II as King of Hungary. His design was frustrated by Rákóczi's ill-considered Polish campaign of 1657. Renewed attacks by the Turks recalled his attention to the old enemy on the frontier, and he waged a number of successful military campaigns, partly on his own initiative, along the southern marches (1663). The intrigues, however, of his jealous rival, General Montecuccoli, commander-in-chief of the Imperial forces, led to Zrínyi's dismissal from the leadership, and on the 18th November, 1664, he died suddenly while out hunting. He is said to have been gored by a wounded wild boar and to have bled to death before the wound could be stanched. His sudden death stunned Hungary, and as his dissident political views and aims were well known, it was rumoured that he had in fact been assassinated by order of the Habsburg ruler—a rumour that has not been dispelled to this day.

The Siege of Sziget

Zrínyi's principal work was *The Siege of Sziget* (Szigeti veszedelem). An account, translated into art, which faithfully mirrored long years of fighting against the Turkish invaders, this epic reached back to Tinódi's verse chronicles and the epic works of Virgil, Tasso and Marino; it is an enduring testimony to the Hungarian-Turkish wars and the century and a half of Turkish rule in Hungary. There is an authentic ring to the description of contemporary warfare, military usages and the soldier's way of life which in itself is of value apart from the merit of the work as poetry. The combination of the two—its intrinsic value as poetry and its contemporary realism—makes *The Siege* one of the finest of European epics. The epic of Tasso, Marino and their contemporaries do indeed contain glimpses of the life and customs of their own period, transposing the Crusades of Herod's Massacre of the Innocents into their own time as contemporary painters projected the biblical themes of their frescoes and panel paintings into their own word, yet their themes were events of the long-distant past; Zrínyi, on the contrary, impelled by the hard facts of Hungarian history, found his epic theme in his own time and made excellent use of it. Even the celestial opening obligatory in such poems—the war council of the gods—and the other various trappings of myth and fantasy have an authentic, realistic air in the reading: after all, the whole nation firmly believed that God had sent the Turks into Hungary to punish the Hungarians for their sins. Added to this was the political application of the work: into it Zrínyi wove the general features of his political attitude and views, and consequently invested it with a current relevance, much the same as Milton, a fervent partisan of the English Revolution, invested his biblical and mythological poetry with his own beliefs.

After Bornemisza's impassioned self-revelations, Heltai's sharp, satirical tales, and the love lyrics of Bálint Balassi, a new, colourful note was introduced into Hungarian literature. This note was explicit and fervent political commitment, a quality rarely lacking in Hungarian poetry from that time on. True, it had its disadvantages; Zrínyi's intellectual and moral preoccupation with national issues acted to the detriment of his love poetry; in the introductory verses of his great epic he proudly declared that in earlier years he had dallied with the sweet song of love, but such of his love lyrics as have survived are in no way comparable to those of Balassi.

The solidly wrought, graphic stanzas of *The Siege of Sziget* foreshadow the epic poetry of János Arany, two centuries later. It is not surprising that it was Arany who rediscovered Zrínyi for modern Hungarian literature; the following stanza could well have come from Arany's *Death of Buda*:

> *Lackaday! Wither these mighty great clouds of squall,*
> *Which corner of the earth are they going to fall?*
> *As they come bearing down, everyone they appal:*
> *They are the Wrath of Him that holds sway over all.*

Not surprisingly, Zrínyi's graphic powers are seen at their best in the battle scenes. Pieter Bruegel's 1562 *Suicide of Saul*, with its immense forest of gleaming lances, comes to mind in reading Zrínyi's vivid description of battle.

> *A thicket of pikes and spears behind and afore,*
> *Throngs engulfed the earth with terror, awe and fear.*
> *They seemed to walk in a forest that swerved and veered,*
> *Like a swarm of ants the Turkish troops appeared.*

When this forest of lances moves forward and the battle begins, Zrínyi, in a dramatic picture unrivalled in world literature, with all the power and dynamic sweep of a film, hurls himself into the thick of the fighting, carrying the reader with him:

> *Here weapons with weapons tumultuously clash;*
> *Fighters with fighters close, break, and start afresh.*
> *Cries of pain mount up high mingled with blood and ash,*
> *Spears splinter, pikes break and swords on scimitars crash.*
>
> *Here standards and banners topple by the scores,*
> *Heaps of Turkish horsemen lie in dense concourse.*
> *There a soldier, half-dead, falls on another's corpse;*
> *Some die in the saddle, some choke beneath their horse.*
>
> *Some, on their last leg, still claw and clutch the foe,*
> *Others like bloodsuckers gloat on blood's gushing flow,*
> *Some through gaping wounds give up their ghost in throe,*
> *Choked to death by the throng, some leave the life below.*

Prose

Zrínyi's prose writings mark the beginning of Hungarian military–political literature, and for many years they were its finest exemplars. Yet they are more than purely specialized military writing, as Pascal's inexorable logic is more than Jansenist theology. Zrínyi's powers of logical thought and his furious intellectual pursuit of socio-historical truth combined to produce no dry or pedantic treatise, but writing which is at once vivid and lively, written with an air of astonishing ease. Two of his books deserve special attention: *Reflections on the Life of King Matthias* (Mátyás király életéről való elmélkedések, 1656) and *Remedy against the Turkish Opium* (Az török áfium ellen való orvosság, 1660). The highly coloured image of Matthias, constantly invoked as a prosperous, unconquered king in "the good old days of peace", and exaggerated to near-mythological heights, was examined objectively in *Reflections,* but at the same time the author idealized all that in the seventeenth century could be idealized of his achievements. There are several reasons why this book should be seen as the first analytical historical study in Hungarian literature. It is remarkable to see Zrínyi going out of his way to emphasize the fact that Matthias's accession to the throne was no impeccably legal and constitutional act but one engineered by force; it is clear that here he meant to indicate his own concept of national kingship. Although he does indeed idealize the great ruler, he is not uncritical; he pronounces his strictures on the king's conduct with all the bluntness of a modern essayist; "One fault of yours, good King, my pen cannot conceal; it was one that was particularly great, it was ingratitude." Another observation reveals his enlightened tolerance: "This world of today (to name no princes' names), whenever it wishes to give its warrings some complexion of right, pretends to religion. But where in all the canons of Christendom, or in the teachings of Christ our Lord, do ye find any command that we must convert heretics or Turks to our faith by force of arms?" Here is a military commander who has defeated the Turks, objecting to wars waged under the pretext of religious conversion, the Thirty Years' War clearly included. Zrínyi was widely read in the military and political literature of his time. In his writings, in methods of thought and argument the direct and indirect influence of Machiavelli is clearly discernible. Though he condemns treachery and clandestine intrigue, he regards coercion as useful, a certain amount of deceit as prudent, and a strong centralized government as of fundamental importance.

His last great work, *Remedy Against the Turkish Opium*, was a kind of testament. As the title of the work makes clear, he has a recommendation, a cure to propose for the poison of the Turkish occupation and, in general, the ills besetting the nation. One by one he surveys the greater and lesser powers of Europe, from whom different Hungarian factions were seeking assistance and concludes that for a variety of geographical and other reasons the Hungarian nation could not expect enduring and effective aid from any of them. And if the Hungarian nobility continued to remain passive and faction-ridden, they too would prove a force on which the nation could not depend. This observation, in turn, le dhim to the conclusion that a state without the support of the common people, the peasants, could not stand. His counsel was to recruit the armed force of the nation from the peasantry. He went even further, declaring desirable to arm the people as a whole in the event of war, a step which, had it been taken by John I of Hungary, would have saved the country from the Turks. Zrínyi speaks with contempt and scorn of the army of the nobility assembled for the battle of Mohács in 1526, describing them as a ragged mob. Even at the present time, he said, a greater part of the nobility were without military discipline and lacked fighting experience: "Our sons either idle away their time at home with their parents, or, if they are brave enough to want to see and learn the ways of the world, they enter the service of a Hungarian noble as members of his retinue. And what do they learn there? They learn to drink. What else? To make a show of themselves, strutting in fur-lined and gold-braided pelisses, showing off spangled bridles and sporting plumes and embroidered gunpowder-pouches; in a word—to swear falsely, lie, and follow nothing that is good."

Zrínyi must have been a notable orator: he has a flair for employing proverbs and adages, popular phrases, graphic imagery and effective turns of speech precisely where needed. "For although I have truly depicted this our nation as it is at the present time, nevertheless if you ask me what is my wish and desire, which nation do I desire to protect me, I answer thus: the Magyar nation." At this point in his essay these remarks are made in no vainglorious or braggart manner; they are a sober realization of the fact that no matter what qualities it possesses, in the end a nation can trust only itself; moreover, "Hungary has been fighting the Turk for close on two hundred years"—hence, it was the nation that had the most experience in that struggle. Zrínyi's keen sense of national pride blends in a practical manner with his respect for neighbouring peoples. He regarded himself as both a Hungarian and a Croat; in his epic Magyars and Croats live together and fight shoulder to shoulder as brothers.

Zrínyi's ideas for Hungary as are set out in *Turkish Opium* greatly influenced Prince Ferenc Rákóczi and, much later, the finest minds of the early nineteenth century in the Reform Era: each phase of struggle for progress and independence saw in him its model, a poet and statesman—from Kazinczy and his friends, who embraced the ideas of the French Revolution in the late 1790s, to members of the Anti-Fascist People's Front during the Second World War.

His Place in Literature

When one considers his literary activities as a whole and attempts to appraise their influence, one must recognize Zrínyi as one of the greatest creative writers in early Hungarian literature. The poetry of the Hungarian Renaissance and Italian Baroque literature combined to form the major influence which shaped his early work. In the course of time he left these initial enthusiasms behind him, boldly breaking new ground both in his political thinking and his writing. His life and work, despite their diversity, form a single whole. He was quick to adapt to circumstances, would set himself different immediate objectives and employ different means of achieving them—yet they were all subordinate to the pursuit of a single final design or goal. The great task he set himself was to work for the advancement of the Hungarian nation. With Zrínyi began a long line of poets, authors and politicians who worked for the same final goal of a Hungarian national awakening.

Zrínyi, the great noble, gradually drifted away from the other barons, his peers in the Catholic Establishment, to become the leader of the lesser nobility, thus marking the transition to the prose and verse written by the nobles of the Baroque period. He came under the influence of the Protestant lesser nobility and their opposition, absolutism, and his later work may be seen as the political and intellectual forerunner of the rebel "kuruc" movements towards the end of the seventeenth century, also led by the lesser nobility.

14 Baroque Court Poetry

István Gyöngyösi (1629–1704)

The type of epic poetry begun by Zrínyi was continued by a courtier and county administrator who stayed a safe distance from weapons of any kind throughout his life. The heroes of István Gyöngyösi were also genuine nobles and ladies whose love secrets he reveals to his readers in great style, and with evident relish. Gyöngyösi's epic poems, however, are like the Baroque murals in which cherubim frolic above and among worldly courtiers and their buxom mistresses. His principal work, *The Venus of Murány in Converse with Mars* (Márssal társalkodó Murányi Vénus, 1664), recounts the amorous adventures and eventual marriage of a noble couple. Written in the very year of Zrínyi's death this is a far cry from the sombre political attitude of the commander whose life had been spent in active warfare. There is, however, no denying the skill and great craftsmanship Gyöngyösi displayed in everything he touched. The passages describing the countryside presage the poems of Sándor Petőfi and also those of János Arany who incidentally devoted an essay to Gyöngyösi. Some of his imagery—as for example, when he described darkness put to flight by the rising sun, and the light of day, "having cast off its mourning," is greeted "with yawning gaze" by the herdsmen, the lowing of cattle and the singing of birds—recall the pictures of nature in such Petőfi works as the folk epic *John the Hero* (János vitéz) and the poems *The Tisza* or *Kiskunság*. There is something comforting in the thought that even in that harsh and cruel age a note of quiet happiness and gaiety could still be sounded. And as Hungarian poetry progressed the reflection of the activity and animation of the Baroque world was an important step forward: the sense of movement, of restlessness, the continual change of scene echoes the age of Guido Reni, mirrors the dynamism of Bernini's Faun.

> Twice your dear letter from the grip I dropped,
> The reading on't did old with new cares compound;
> I pray now and my tears come rolling to the ground,
> Now do I see we are no more as lovers bound.

Though in my bosom hid, yet fell it from there,
A rush of wind arose and swept it far away,
Fluttering in the clouds it heightened my despair,
But like a frisky bird it turned back from the air.

Twice it flew round me as I ran after it,
Then turning once more it on my lap alit,
Returning to the place it had so lightly quit,
Which left my heart amazed and much perplexed my wit.

Gyöngyösi was a typical poet-follower of some great lord or other, but he was the finest example of that class of poets. He adapted his politics to the "great family" he happened to be serving at the time; for, after all, most of his works are no more than family or society histories, even if unquestionably competent and accomplished.

Another work of his, the narrative poem *The Phoenix Risen from its Ashes* (Porábul megéledett Phonix, 1665–1670), also deserves attention, if only for its subject. It was written to commemorate the tragic fate of Prince János Kemény of Transylvania, and the purpose of the poem was no less than a survey of five stormy years (1657–1662) of Hungarian history, spiced with moral and political lessons. Politically speaking, however, the poem fails to live up to expectations, since the author failed to draw the correct conclusions, although at heart he supported the nobles hostile to Vienna. *Phoenix* is the tale of the attempt made by Prince János Kemény to withstand Turkish pressure and the failure of the Imperial army to come to his help.

Deceitful Cupid (Csalárd Cupido, 1695) is an erotic poem, and at the time was the most widely read of all Gyöngyösi's work; it was in fact added to throughout the eighteenth century in noble circles. In this poem, the writer ostensibly desires to warn young people against the allurements and excesses of sex by detailing the temptations lying in wait for the young man wandering in the labyrinth of love; but he does so with such obvious relish and delight that he achieves the opposite effect; and this indeed appears to be his real intention. The erotic pleasures of adultery are here dwelt on openly and at length and with a certain amount of literary inventiveness.

Noble Poets

Gyöngyösi was not the only courtly noble poet: country houses alive with music and literary activity were plentiful in seventeenth-century Baroque Hungary; there were a number of nobles who wrote poetry themselves, most of it variations on Balassi. But in fact the seventeenth century had its own Balassi. Count *Bálint Balassa* (1626–1684) was a descendant of the poet's uncle. A soldier and landowner, he hardly measured up to his predecessor and namesake in his literary activities. Baron *László Liszti* (1628–1663), whose chequered career of crime ended when he was executed for counterfeiting, wrote a narrative poem *Hungarian Mars* (Magyar Márs, 1653) on the defeat of the Hungarian army by the Turks at Mohács in 1526. *Pál Kőszeghy*, a wealthy noble, borrowed a leaf from Gyöngyösi's book and put into verse the story of Count Miklós Bercsényi's marriage (1695). Of more importance than any of these were Pál Esterházy and István Koháry. The Palatine, Prince *Pál Esterházy* (1635–1712), was the most powerful as well as wealthiest noble in Hungary, and a great connoisseur of music—he was himself an accomplished player on the virginal—wrote nature poems with titles like *A Song of Summer* (Az nyárról való ének), *A Song of Autumn* (Az őszről való ének), *A Song of Winter* (A télről való ének), *Lines on Birds of the Sky* (Égi madarakról való versek). *István Koháry* (1649–1731), doctor of philosophy, a high-ranking soldier, a Lord Lieutenant and the Lord Chief Justice, wrote long meditative poems in which the intellectual world of Jesuit culture is mirrored with the accuracy of an inventory; his work is typical of the visionary, allegorizing poetry and dream-literature of the time. (*Poems Composed as a Diversion* — Üdő mulatás közben szerzett versek, 1687.) In a development that was typical of the new fashion for writing poetry, even high-born ladies, Erzsébet Rákóczi, Magdolna Esterházy, Miklós Bercsényi's wife Krisztina Csáky, and Mária Széchy took their pens in their hands and produced their poems. The only woman poet of any importance was *Kata Szidónia Petrőczi* (1662–1708), an ardent supporter of Prince Ferenc Rákóczi in his struggle for independence. Most of her fifty-odd poems are in the form of religious supplications; but the few love poems she wrote are very personal expressions of apprehension over an unfaithful husband and the emotions of a jealous yet lovingly loyal wife. In her poems on the fate of Hungary, she gives passionate utterance to her detestations of Habsburg oppression; one of them contains motifs which are reminiscent of the well-known Rákóczi Song.

Rococo Poetry

Baron *László Amade*'s life was very different from those of the poets of noble birth who preceded him. Amade (1703–1764), a dashing officer of the Hussars, first served in Italy, then distinguished himself in the War of the Austrian Succession and finally as a Knight of the Golden Spurs and one of Maria Theresa's councillors, settled down to live the life of a happy hedonist. A poet with remarkable command of form, he gallantly wrote a few poems for his friends under their names, in the manner of Rostand's *Cyrano de Bergerac*, but in far gayer vein. Amade played an important part in the development of the modern Hungarian poetic idiom. His recruiting song *The Gilded Life of a Soldier* (A szép fényes katonának arany-gyöngy

élete) was later set to music by Zoltán Kodály and incorporated in his comic opera
Háry János. With Faludi, whom we shall come to later, Amade can be regarded
as the archetypal "Rococo" poet, their melodious and elegant verse exalting the
sophisticated enjoyments of life.

There was a Hungarian father confessor at St. Peter's Basilica, Rome, in the
early 1740s, who spent his spare time translating handbooks of etiquette from Spanish, English and Italian into Hungarian. Little did these works suggest the great
poet that *Ferenc Faludi* (1704–1779) was later to become. On returning to his native
Hungary, the Jesuit abbot published these translations *The Noble Man Instructed in
Godly Charity and a Fortunate and Happy Life* (Istenes jóságra és szerencsés boldog
életre oktatott nemes ember, 1748) and they achieved an immediate success with
the public, particularly as manuals on etiquette and social behaviour were greatly
in demand in those days. Prompted by this initial success Faludi collected and
published some of his short stories under the title *Winter Nights* (Téli éjszakák,
1778). These were largely based on a 1666 German edition of a 1609 Spanish work,
Noches de invierno by Antonio de Eslava. Faludi also produced a Hungarian version
of Baltasar Gracián's *El oráculo manual* (1647). Since Gáspár Heltai's time, fiction
of this kind had remained on the periphery of Hungarian literature. But such
compilations were not his chief activity. The increased flexibility and polish of his
prose style opened the way to a growing interest in poetry. After Joseph II expelled
the Jesuit order from the Empire in 1773, Faludi found himself freed from monastic
life; and spent the rest of his days as a genial sage in the castles of nobles in western
Hungary, writing lyric poetry on secular subjects. His lyrics were the earliest
examples of truly modern poetry: the less experienced reader might well find
nothing in these poems to indicate they were written earlier than the present century.
Faludy's inspiration was so firmly grounded in reality that his earthy realism shows
through the obligatory affectation of the Rococo style. His shepherds are not like
Watteau's elegant ladies and lords: they wear country boots and peasant clothes,
they wield axes, they are in fact ordinary country folk. Faludi also experimented
with new prosody, his lines are captivatingly melodious. His free-wheeling poetry
was much imitated by poets and song-writers up to the time of Sándor Petőfi.

15 Memoirs

Mihály Veresmarti (1572-1645)

In 1604, as the Catholic Counter-Reformation gathered momentum, the Bishop of Nyitra in northern Hungary ordered a certain Calvinist pastor to be detained. The name of the pastor was Mihály Veresmarti, who had fled with the people of his village from Turkish-occupied territory and had settled in the Austrian-controlled part of Hungary—refugees from the renewed fighting with the Turks known as the Fifteen Years' War between 1591 and 1606. Veresmarti was arrested after a mêlée between Protestants and Catholics that the unruly anbd rawny preacher had unleashed in resisting the forced conversion of Protestants by Catholic priests. While he was in prison, pastor Veresmarti was given what the priests considered suitable reading matter to while away his days: Catholic proselytizing literature. Veresmarti studied these books, dan the arguments in them, presented with much wit and intelligence, and by the time he was released they had begun to make their effect. By then Calvinist-Lutheran thought and faithd ha lost its vigour, but these Catholic tracts used the same persuasive reasoning and the same critical ploys that the partisans of the Reformation had once so effectively employed in their assault on the Catholic creed. Veresmarti pondered what he had read: he was torn by mental conflict, and he ended by converting to Catholicism living for many years as a respected Catholic priest.

Veresmarti collected hids letters, his diary and other writingsdealing with his conflict of conscience and used them as the raw material for his *History of his Conversion* (Megtérése históriája), the most important of the autobiographical writings produced in Hungary, a genre first introduced by Bornemisza in the preceding century and which continued in popularity to the time of Miklós Bethlen. Veresmarti's *Conversion* was the first wholly original piece of literary Hungarian and also the first example of the pure Baroque style in Hungarian prose. His mental anguish was not medieval in type; it was that of Baroque man. He was only too well aware that the "Satanical temptations" he faced were the result of a psychological disease; but, like Bornemisza, he was impelled by an irresistible urge to communicate, to open his heart to his fellow men. His book is full of detailed descriptions of the endless friendly discussions that took place, of innumerable conversations, conten-

99

tious, conciliatory, sullen, forgiving, depressed and confident in turn. He describes in vivid, delicate detail the friendly arguments that gradually took on hostile, personal overtones and ended in scowling silences, generating lifelong hatred and rancour. Veresmarti draws a splendid picture of vociferous preachers shouting each other down, each intent on his own exposition totally, ignoring the other. The religious argument has lost its importance. What holds us is the shrewd observation of human behaviour.

Hungarian Memoirs

In the seventeenth century literary memoirs became the second most important genre in Hungarian literature and their influence can still be felt in our times. For writers desirous of expressing themselves, the writing of memoirs proved the simplest way to discard the fetters of religion, politics and social convention. In the memoir there is room for the poetic outpouring of the heart, for observations that might seem irrelevant in a sermon, for conversation pieces and short tales as well as for more uplifting messages addressed to a whole nation or generation. A long, unbroken line of memoirs—long enough to fill a bookshelf—flowed from the pens of the seventeenth and eigtheenth-century writers.

There were many politicians who were also writers in Transylvania. One of the most important was *János Kemény* (1607–1662) whose *Autobiography* (Önéletírás, 1658) deserves particular attention. He was held prisoner in Bakhchisarai by the Tartars when he wrote what was primarily a political and historical balance sheet, drawing lessons from his life, as it were, for himself and for posterity.

Miklós Bethlen (1642-1716)

Miklós Zrínyi's tragic death was witnessed by a 22-year-old young noble from Transylvania, who happened to be staying as a guest at Zrínyi's castle. Miklós Bethlen recorded the incident in his autobiography, written while he was held in the Imperial prison of Vienna. Bethlen's autobiography is an important continuation of the political, public writing that Zrínyi had produced. Bethlen studied at various universities in Holland and travelled to England, where he went on a trip to Oxford and also visited the court of Charles II. He travelled home through Paris, where he met Colbert. Back in Transylvania, he was invested with high government office. He frequently entertained visitors from abroad at his castle at Betlenszentmiklós. One of his guests, the Abbé Dominique Révérend, a French diplomat, wrote a biography of Bethlen. The *Mémoires historiques du Comte*

Betlem-Niklos contenant l'histoire des derniers trobles de Transylvanie (Amsterdam, 1736), were written twenty years after Bethlen's death. When an anti-Habsburg conspiracy headed by Péter Zrínyi, the Ban of Croatia, the brother of Miklós Zrínyi, and the Palatine, Ferenc Wesselényi, was discovered, Bethlen was arrested in 1704 on charges of treason and lèse majesté. He died shortly after his release after years of imprisonment.

Bethlen's autobiography is strikingly modern in its approach, not so much on account of its frankness as on his unwavering focus on himself. Bethlen found himself the most absorbing of subjects to study, as a human being whom he had an opportunity of observing much longer and more closely than any other person. This interest gave him the strength to overcome his reserve and saved him from mere exhibitionism. He describes in detail his physique, his character, his impulses, relates the sexual problems of his adolescence and his marital relations in every emotion and every thought. As he approaches the sombre present—the hopeless gloom of his twelve years' solitude in prison—his style becomes edged with bitterness, his words rougher. He looked on the world as a stage peopled by former foes and friends—all actors in a great drama, making their entrances and their exits at a nod from the great director—Destiny. This "theatrical" mode of viewing life is something that marks the memoir of the Baroque period. For Bethlen, his own life passed from tragedy to tragedy. He had a taste for theatrical terms in his description of events: a fatal event in Transylvanian history, for example, was a "tragedy" preceded by a "prologue", and the "actors" played their parts in different "scenes", for he saw events automatically metamorphosed into stage plays. The chief protagonist of the drama was Bethlen himself; and he made use of the latest innovations in seventeenth-century memoir-writing—in giving his work the *couleur d'un document psychologique*. He was also well-read in contemporary philosophical literature: he was strongly influenced by Descartes, and shows evidence, for instance, of having read Gassendi's treatise on the circulation of the blood. He was in fact as educated a man of letters as any French memoir-writer of his time, though he never flaunts his learning putting it with ease and dexterity.

Ferenc Rákóczi (1676-1735)

The famous leader of a nine-year struggle for freedom against the Austrians (1703–1711), Ferenc Rákóczi II, Prince of Transylvania, was also a writer. He left innumerable writings behind him—on politics, the sciences, the art of warfare, public administration, as well as speeches and prayers and a number of poems of debatable authenticity. His principal work is his *Confessiones* (1716–1719), which he wrote in Latin. In these confessions, and in the *Mémoires* appended to it (1717), he wrote with fascinating fire and passion of the failings of the Hungarian nobility and clergy, their lack of responsibility, and of the conditions that eventually led him to lead the uprising. It was true to say of Zrínyi and equally true of Rákóczi that in them Hungary possessed Saint-Simons who had in addition first-hand experience of war. Rákóczi was the leader in a campaign which lasted almost ten years, and he had acquired insight and penetration into the minds, interests and passions of his adherents and his subjects. What Saint-Simon saw from the palace, Rákóczi saw from the saddle. Rákóczi's autobiography is mixed in its motives and its attitudes—the head of state writing for a practical purpose—to justify his actions to the world, the deeply religious man making his confession before God. Some of Rákóczi's works were written in Latin, others in French. The *Mémoires* appeared as Volume V of the *Histoire des révolutions de Hongrie* (The Hague, 1739).

Rákóczi was the first Hungarian writer to write in French as well as in Latin or his native Hungarian. His education was basically French: the authors he read in his youth included Rabelais, Fénelon and Bruyère. His *Confessions* and *Mémoires* were written in France, where he took refuge following his final defeat in the War of Independence. He lived in France for five years, from the autumn of 1712 to the autumn of 1717, first as a guest of Louis XIV, later as a secular guest in a monastery at Grosbois. He saw plays by Racine and Molière; visited the various collections of paintings in the possession of private owners; met Saint-Simon who preserved a portrait of Rákóczi for posterity in his memoirs. Madame de Maintenon and the Marquis Dangeau also recorded their meetings with Rákóczi. But once he took up residence in the Grosbois Camaldule monastery, Rákóczi broke off links with the royal court. He became a confirmed Jansenist, his library was filled with Jansenist literature, and it was in Grosbois that he began to write his confessions. He had once been a pleasure-loving prince, then a general who displayed outstanding qualities as a military commander, a statesman fired by the political aims of his ancestors—his mother was Ilona Zrínyi, daughter of Miklós Zrínyi; and his father's line, the Rákóczis, had been Princes of Transylvania. By 1715 he had become a stoic, a religious writer free from all ecclesiastical conventions and denominational feuds. To say this is not to suggest that his political acumen and analytical powers had lessened; they had not. A careful analysis of the causes of his defeat led him to the conclusion that the principal cause of the débâcle had been the selfish interests of the nobility taken as a whole—that the Hungarian noble and the Hungarian common man were separated by an unbridgeable chasm. He made no attempt to exonerate himself, but supported statements by citations from the documents in his archives. At the same time, however, he saw and conducted himself throughout as a Prince. Again and again, the man who had turned his back on all things secular finds himself confronted by the ghost of his all-too-worldly personality. His conversion, never Augustinian in depth, was not enough to extirpate his desire for sovereignty and power; hence the tension between Christian humility and princely ambition that runs through his work, with the memoir-writer's recalling in tranquillity conflicting with the princely author and his turbulent emotions.

Kelemen Mikes (1690-1761)

From France Rákóczi went into exile in Turkey, at Rodosto (Tekirdag) on the European coast of the Sea of Marmora, where he lived from 1720 until his death. The chamberlain of his modest establishment at Rodosto was the finest Hungarian writer of the eighteenth century, Kelemen Mikes. Mikes joined the Prince as a young page and followed him into exile. He was little more than twenty years old when he left his native land for good, and only 27 when he wrote the first of the famous 207 letters with which his name is associated; the last was written in 1758. He wrote them solely to express himself, to comfort himself, as it were, in his exile with no hope of seeing them in print. These letters, according to the literary fashion of the time, were addressed to a fictitious "aunt", and the genre, which Mikes acclimatized in Hungarian literature, was a French invention. The most direct influence upon Mikes must have been the correspondence of Mme de Sévigné. Literature in the form of letters released Hungarian writers from the fetters of conventional seventeenth-century genres; much as the *kuruc* poetry broke down the former patterns and limitations of lyric poetry. Mikes wrote of everything and anything, wandering from one topic to another; after all, he was writing letters, wasn't he, communications of a private nature that were nobody else's business, and the reader ought to count himself lucky if he was allowed a glimpse of them. On the other hand, since these letters were after all fiction, a certain framework and a more or less fixed length would inevitably be imposed by the chosen topic. But within these limits a variety and diversity of thoughts and sentiments and emotions are offered, revealing the writer with a frankness and at a length that would be quite unimaginable in stories and fables, in sermons or novels and even in memoirs. The fact, moreover, that the writer was living out his life in exile increased the possibilities inherent in the letter form and created an authentic and tragic tension between the writer and his fictitious "aunt". The aunt, indeed, the "Countess E. P.", is no other than his native land he longs, vainly, to see again. Yet it is no abstraction; it means reunion with parents, family and friends, the sight of one's native town again, the familiar countryside, the hills and flowers and grass and animals of home. "I have come to like it here in Rodosto so much that I cannot ever forget Zágon [Mikes's native place in Transylvania]," he writes in one of the letters; and this sigh runs through all his work.

Significantly, the flow of these fictitious letters stopped after January 1759, when Mikes had obtained permission from the Austrian authorities to correspond with his native country: from that time on he would write genuine letters to the people at home, telling them of his life in Turkish exile. In them he frequently copied passages from his earlier, fictitious letters, and this fact clearly indicates that although letter-writing might in his case have been an activity stemming from the creative urge, the result of a literary ambition, Mikes was not merely indulging himself or following the literary fashion of the time: it was for him a way of fulfilling subjective desires springing from the deeper recesses of the spirit. With the most accomplished craftsmanship he transposed these desires from the world of the subjective to the objectivity of artistic creation. "Practically everyone writes letters," he wrote. "But not everyone can write in a manner that will give pleasure to others. Some will write down whatever they want to say, yet the result is dull, insipid, without flavour. Others have a gift for embellishing the smallest trifle, so as to give it flavour, and make it a joy to read."

Literary digressions in his letters tell us something about his reading. He knew Pierre Bayle's great encyclopaedic dictionary *Dictionnaire historique et critique* (1694), the French translation of the English periodical *The Spectator* (Le Spectateur, 1712–14), Noel Chomel's *Dictionnaire œconomique* (1709) and Montesquieu's *Lettres Persanes* (1712). He translated much of his reading into Hungarian, notably *Journées amusantes* (1722–1731), a sequence of romantic stories by Madame de Gomez. His translations go to show that Mikes's craftsmanship no longer found its roots in the politically-inspired memoir, such as Bethlen's: Mikes was a Rococo writer; his intellectual and emotional world indicated the advent of Classicism.

The Impact of the Memoir Literature

One eighteenth-century diarist, *Kata Bethlen* (1700–1759), a Transylvanian noble-woman, stands out in sharp contrast to the politically-minded statesmen–writers of her time. A part of her diary was printed in 1762, *A Brief Account of Her Own Life* (Életének maga által való rövid leírása). This diary is a striking piece of writing, because in it a woman's mind revealed itself with an openness unprecedented in that age: the diarist was a deeply religious Calvinist married to a Catholic who constantly tormented her, placing great strains on the marriage. Almost totally oblivious to what was going on in the outer world, she turned inwards to reveal a highly personal and almost poetic picture of an introverted woman with great spiritual leanings, completely absorbed in the business of self-observation, probing the depths of her own ever changing yet ultimately unchanged soul.

It is a long way from Mihály Veresmarti to Kata Bethlen, both in terms of time —the gap is more than a hundred years—and in terms of the development, in style and in content, of Hungarian prose. In the history of Hungarian literature, marked for a long period by the almost total absence of fiction in the form of the short story and the novel, the passion for memoir-writing was of particular importance because it served as a substitute for fiction, and consequently helped to create the conditions that later gave rise to the novel. For the memoir, as Kelemen Mikes's work shows, was a bridge to fiction in more ways than one: both in the specific development of prose style and in the writers' practice of encapsulating short stories or brief narratives within the work. The great Hungarian novelists and short-story writers of the nineteenth century were well acquainted with these memoirs, and indeed a distinguished contemporary author, László Németh, has made use of them, rediscovering them at the same time for present-day readers.

16 Popular Baroque Literature

Popular Poetry

The work of militant Jesuits and learned Protestant professors residing in the mansions of the nobility was but one contribution to the literature of the Baroque; another catered for a wider range of less educated readers. Popular Baroque literature was read by soldiers and students, artisans and village teachers and even such farmers and peasants as had acquired a smattering of education. These collections of poems and stories, both secular and religious, originally circulated in manuscript, but from the eighteenth century onwards they appeared in printed form.

This type of literature was particularly rich in poetry. At the beginning popularized versions of Renaissance poetry were common and verse-chronicles emerged around the same time, which, still in the genre of the earlier verse-chronicles, were nevertheless more loosely knit prosodically, and more poetic (e.g., *The Song of István Kádár* — Kádár István éneke, 1658). There were hundreds of dirges, rhymed greetings, soldiers' songs, and laments over the cruel fate of the nation or the destruction of a region or a town.

But most striking of all was the proliferation of love poetry. Manuscript songbooks were full of love lyrics. The influence of Balassi or Gyöngyösi is clear, and even blatant on occasion, but they also showed the influence of Baroque, and even Rococo, writing in their versification as in their exuberant imagery. There is a tendency to heap epithet on epithet: "Gentle rose, little swan, violet, my sweet love, my dearest heart, little Venus!", a line found in the *Mátray Codex* copied some time after 1677. Besides the *Mátray Codex*, many other manuscript songbooks have survived to provide evidence of popular Baroque love poetry. These songbooks, as elsewhere, carry the name of the collector or editor, such as: Teleki's *Book of Songs* (c. 1655), Vásárhelyi's *Book of Songs* (c. 1672), Thoroczkai's *Book of Songs* (end of the seventeenth century).

This love poetry survived into the eighteenth century in the form of student songs. Students of the period revived the old, Goliard poetry of the Middle Ages, kept it alive and passed it on to later generations. They did more than that; in these songs social discontent found a voice something unknown in the manuscript songbooks preserved in the country homes of the nobility. A good many of these students were themselves of peasant stock and they knew the dire poverty of the peasants at first hand:

> *Each sunrise brings the bailiff on a trip*
> *demanding service. Give him any lip*
> *and soon you'll find your poor behind is smarting from his whip!*

(*There is no Man Unhappier than the Serf*
—Nincs boldogtalanabb a parasztembernél;
translated by Tony Connor)

This poem was set to music by both Béla Bartók and Zoltán Kodály: the echoes of this early eighteenth-century poetry reverberated into the twentieth century. Even more important, its impact is evident in the great poets of the late eighteenth century: Csokonai's lyric poetry sprang from this popular college verse-making, raising not only the popular love song but the drinking song as well to the level of conscious art.

Kuruc Poetry

One offshoot of this profusion of popular song-poetry was a branch of poetry with clearly marked themes that throve during a definite period. It is known as *kuruc* poetry. The *kuruc* poems are a by-product of Thököly's and Rákóczi's anti-Habsburg wars. The word *kuruc* (pronounced koorootz) is a corruption of the Latin *crux* (cross), and goes back to the peasant rising of 1514, when peasants originally massed for an anti-Turkish crusade, but eventually turned their arms against their lords, attacking and burning their manors and castles. From that time the term *kuruc* had been applied to insurgents and rebels who rose against the nobles, and later, towards the end of the seventeenth century, was also used for the insurgents who rose against Habsburg rule; hence *kuruc* poetry as a collective term covering outlaws' songs, laments, patriotic songs and invocations, and the warlike songs that sprang up at that time. These poems are recorded in several manuscript songbooks and are mostly by unknown authors, some by nobles, others by common soldiers. A number of *kuruc* poems survived in folklore versions that continued to be sung by peasants.

The earliest *kuruc* poem, of popular inspiration and imbued with revolutionary ardour, *O Hungary and Transylvania, Hear the News!* (Magyarország, Erdély, hallj új hírt!), is associated with the first victories of Rákóczi's *kuruc* fighters. The most widely known *kuruc* air, still sung today, is a victory dance song, *Csínom Palkó,* reflecting the riotous spirit of soldiers making merry by the campfire, flushed with victory on the battlefield.

> *Come on, come on, brothers-in-arms,*
> *Let's drink and be merry,*
> *Let each of us join the ring-dance*
> *With his loving lassie.*

These *kuruc* songs are not only patriotic invocations, campfire dance tunes or drinking songs. Many have a political content conveying the reaction of the people to each new turn in the part of the country under Rákóczi's control. As the campaign wore on growing numbers of magnates and nobles deserted Rákóczi's standard, and tension between the social classes increased. *Conversation of Two Outlaws* (Két szegénylegény beszélgetése, 1706) warns Rákóczi to trust the nobility no longer. Although cast in the form of a poem, the *Conversation* is in fact a political pamphlet. Unusual situtations give rise to unconventional genres, or at the least expand conventional patterns.

The classic lyric form, however, what was known as the poetry of the fugitives, (that is, the *kuruc* partisans on the run following the rout of the insurgent cause) reveals the world of runaway serfs hiding out in reedy marshlands or forests of nobles reduced to penury, servants who rebelled against their lords, army deserters, and scholars fleeing persecution on political or religious grounds. These are the finest pieces of all the popular poetry of the age, the ones that still evoke a quick response today. Endre Ady, the great Hungarian poet of the early twentieth century, quotes them in his *kuruc* poems. *Dew on the Green Forest* (Zöld erdő harmatát...) is still sung today, and *The Song of Jakab Buga* or *The Ex-soldier's Lament* (Buga Jakab éneke), by an unidentified author, is one of the finest and most widely known poems in Hungary. They are full of self-mockery, bitter resignation and sadness over the life of the fugitive and the exile, but at the same time a certain pride and joy in independence seeps through.

> *Old friend, old comrade, why such sore distress?*
> *Surely it's not because you're penniless?*
> *The good Lord gives, the good Lord takes away,*
> *our time will come, we dogs will have our day!*
>
> (Translated by Tony Connor)

The most famous of all *kuruc* poems is the *Rákóczi Song*, although it is now believed to date from the 1730s, long after the War of Independence was over. It was this song that inspired Franz Liszt, and then Hector Berlioz, to compose the justly celebrated "Rákóczi March".

Hungary, fairest land,
now the enemy tears you, my friend!
You are cracked, blotched, stained—
a beautiful vessel ruined,
which was once sound,
admired, enjoyed, esteemed,
O tragic land!

(Translated by Tony Connor)

The Anecdote

Prose written for entertainment was at the same time becoming increasingly secular and middle-class. Books of anecdotes, collections of short stories and fables appeared; the collection by *József Hermányi Dienes* (1699–1763), a Transylvanian Calvinist pastor, though never printed and therefore unknown in his time, is now regarded as the finest example of this type of work. Hermányi Dienes wrote *Weeping Heraclitus and Smiling and Laughing Democritus of Nagyenyed* (Nagyenyedi síró Heráklitus és hol mosolygó s hol kacagó Demokritus) between 1759 and 1762; it is best described as a volume of notes and observations on his contemporaries, written with ruthless irony and a sharp eye for the absurdities of society.

His great strength is his ability to portray character. He calls every character by name, as was the general practice among short-story writers of the age, from the *Cento novelle antiche,* a collection of Italian medieval short stories, to Péter Bornemisza's *Temptations of the Devil.* In a few lines he introduces the chief character, and proceeds to tell a pithy anecdote linked with his name. But he is not merely concerned to amuse; he seeks to give his readers food for thought. But the naming of names, refreshing and realistic as it is, does not mean that the writer drew his subject-matter entirely from life; many of the tales he tells are versions of motifs borrowed from the universal store of story-tellers, from the Talmud to Till Eulenspiegel. Hermányi Dienes's tales come close to literary pastiche and parody, that very modern genre cultivated by his contemporary Diderot and other French writers.

College Drama

As mentioned earlier, college students played an important role in fostering and popularizing Baroque lyric poetry, and the same is true of the drama. Our knowledge of the early development of the Hungarian theatre is sketchy; dramatic performances undoubtedly enjoyed great popularity in the Middle Ages, but there is considerable uncertainty as to which plays were produced and the manner of their production. But as a large number of school plays have survived from the seventeenth and eighteenth centuries, it seems likely that they were actually produced. Since the colleges were denominational establishments, the college plays too can be distinguished on a denominational basis. There were Catholic—chiefly Jesuit-inspired—as well as Calvinist, Lutheran and Unitarian school plays, each marked by their respective beliefs and principles. The most important of them was a play called *Comico-tragoedia* (1693) by György Felvinczi, an alumnus of the Unitarian College of Kolozsvár. This is a Baroque play ridiculing the manners and morals of contemporary Transylvania, obviously influenced by Marcantonio Cesti's opera, *Il pomodoro*. In 1696 Felvinczi obtained permission from the Emperor King Leopold in Vienna to set up a theatrical company. It is not known whether in fact he did so, and if he did, how long it survived.

In the course of the eighteenth century, plays became more and more secular in their subject-matter but they continued to be produced by college students. The influence of Corneille and Molière is quite evident in them. The most prolific adapter of Molière's plays was a Piarist monk named *Kristóf Simai* (1742–1833). He produced a Hungarian version of *Les Fourberies de Scapin* in 1775 and translated *l'Avare* in 1792. *Le Bourgeois gentilhomme* was adapted by *János Illei* (1725–1794), a Jesuit monk, who re-named it *Péter Tornyos* (1789). Illei may be regarded as the leading dramatist of the period; he wrote plays on various national events in Hungarian history such as *Salamon* (1767) dealing with the feuds between King Solomon of Hungary (1064–1074) and Prince Ladislas (later Ladislas I).

The age produced a considerable number of comedies by anonymous authors, the most successful being *The Marriage of Mihály Kocsonya* (Kocsonya Mihály házassága), a bluff, rustic comedy ridiculing the ignorance of the lesser nobles. In this and in several other plays from Protestant colleges the Jesuits' "mythology-mongering" and their taste for the Baroque ornate appears, spiced with a certain amount of comedy. Sámuel Szathmári Paksi's *The History of Phaedra* (Az Phaedrának története 1772–73) and János Szászi's *The History of Dido's Sorrows over Aeneas* (Didónak Eneas miatt lett szomorú története, 1790) rob these tragic myths of any grandeur by the contemporary humour and jokes accompanying them; the behaviour of the characters is eighteenth-century behaviour; they play cards, carry pistols, wear the costume and allude to events of the time.

17 Scholarly Literature

János Apácai Csere (1625-1659)

There was vigorous increase in the spread of education and learning among members of the Protestant middle class around the middle of the seventeenth century. Despite the fact that the economic and political power of the nobility continued to grow, the position of the middle class was greatly improved in comparison with earlier centuries, and its growing wealth led to a rising demand for more democratic procedures, particularly in Transylvania. Blocked in the political arena, these aspirations found an outlet in religion and cultural interests. The Protestant Church intelligentsia—whose members, as in earlier centuries, came from the farming middle class of country towns—was the mainstay and chief source of bourgeois learning and literature.

The most distinguished representative of the Protestant middle-class intelligentsia was *János Apácai Csere*. He completed his university studies in Holland, and returned with a Dutch wife in the early autumn of 1653 to teach at the university of Gyulafehérvár, the seat of the princes of Transylvania. But it was not long before there was an outcry against his teachings; it was claimed that he propagated heresy in the form of English Puritan doctrine and Cartesian principles. Apácai had indeed been studying in Holland at the time the English Civil Wars began, through the execution of Charles I, and up to the time when the news of Cromwell's dictatorship reached neighbouring Holland. It was a time when the Low Countries were under the spell of Descartes. Apácai Csere embraced Cartesian philosophy and maintained it in the face of the outraged opposition of all the theologians of Transylvania; he was first threatened and finally expelled from his position. It is a strange coincidence that in a country far removed from England and Holland, the former court chaplain of Charles I, Isaac Basire, who had gone to live in Transylvania at the invitation of Prince György Rákóczi, had become Apácai's implacable enemy: in his eyes Apácai represented all the forces which had deprived him of his comfortable post. But Apácai stood his ground; with the support of friends he obtained a position as headmaster in Kolozsvár in 1656, and enjoyed it until his death.

Apácai Csere's principal work was the *Hungarian Encyclopaedia* (Magyar encyclopaedia, Utrecht, 1655). From an academic point of view, this encyclopaedia is nothing more than a secondary-school textbook carefully compiled from the works of Descartes, Pierre de La Ramée, Le Roy and others. But it is the first book in the Hungarian language which made the most progressive ideas of the time accessible to Hungarian readers, expounding the essence of the Cartesian theory. It was not merely philosophical ambition that fired Apácai Csere in writing the *Encyclopaedia;* his purpose was practical: he was impelled by an almost obsessive desire to disseminate culture and learning. "Unless we arm ourselves with the light of logic," he said in his inaugural address at Gyulafehérvár, "we shall gape like idiots, like so many stuck pigs, at anything and everything."

Apácai's other works were also inspired by his passionate desire to stop as many compatriots as possible from "gaping like idiots" at the new ideas of the time. *Hungarian Logic* (Magyar Logikácska, 1654) was the first exposition of logic in the Hungarian language; *Counsel* (Tanács) is an essay written in dialogue form exhorting despondent scholars to study, holding out the prospect of enjoying the fruits of their labours, the incomparable sensation of intellectual enjoyment. Nothing could better illustrate the importance of Apácai Csere's work, and the deplorable state of learning in a Hungary groaning under Habsburg oppression, than the fact that in 1803 a new edition of his 1655 Encyclopaedia was censored by the Imperial censor, in an extraordinary display of the official fear felt of all free-thinking philosophy in the age of the French Revolution and the Napoleonic Wars.

Miklós Tótfalusi Kis (1650-1702)

When the *Hungarian Encyclopaedia* appeared, Miklós Tótfalusi Kis was only five years old. But Tótfalusi Kis had the advantage of acquiring his education in schools already benefiting from the work of Apácai and his foremost contemporaries, and on going to Holland in 1680 to pursue his studies, he soon became, as a printer, a European synonym for the dissemination of educational and cultural works. As a highly qualified printer he worked for English, Swedish and Italian clients. With supreme taste and skill he cut and cast every kind of type for his publications. He was responsible, for instance, for the first printed alphabet in Georgian characters. He accumulated considerable wealth in Holland, but returned to his native country after living abroad for ten years, intent on using his skill and knowledge to improve the cultural and educational standards of his country. He established a very fine and successful printing works, and issued a great number of major works in fitting format. It was the intrigue of envious rivals that led him to write his autobiography, in an attempt to explain his publishing policy and cultural views, *An Apology for Himself* (Magamentsége, 1698). He was also notable as a reformer of Hungarian orthography.

The more modern requirements of the eighteenth century gradually broke down the rigid clerical superstructure of the seventeenth century. As then, the authors were mostly ecclesiastics, clergy of one sort or another, but they now dealt with secular and scholarly subjects. It is, however, true that books written by the clergy were limited in their scholarly scope as the umbilical cord binding them to theology could not be cut.

History of Literature—the Beginnings

Gradually the basic conditions were created for the systematic study of the history of literature, history itself, philology and the natural sciences. *Dávid Czvittinger* (*c.* 1680–1743), a burgher from Selmecbánya (now Banská Stiavnica, Czechoslovakia), was astonished to find on a trip to Germany, how misinformed German scholars were about literary activity in Hungary: a German scholar, Jakob Friedrich Reimmann, in his book *Versuch einer Einleitung in die historiam literariam insgemein* (1708), claimed there was nothing to be written about Hungarian literature since it did not exist: "The Hungarians, by their very nature, put more value on a good horse or a shining sword than on an interesting book." Czvittinger promptly settled down to compile information about more than 250 men of letters in Hungary in a lexicon entitled *Specimen Hungariae literatae* (1711).

Encouraged by Czvittinger's pioneering effort, *Péter Bod* (1712–1762), a Transylvanian Calvinist pastor who was for some years Kata Bethlen's chaplain, compiled a more exhaustive work; a lexicon of Hungarian literature entitled *Hungarian Athenas* (Magyar Athenas, 1766), in which he presented over five hundred Hungarian authors with no denominational bias (Czvittinger had ignored "heretical" Unitarian authors). Bod checked his facts carefully, and conscientiously discussed the works of the authors he listed, considering only those he had actually read or seen. Bod's lexicon is a fundamental source book which was, and still is, widely consulted by literary historians of later periods.

Historiography and Topography

Mátyás Bél (1684–1749), a Lutheran pastor of mixed Hungarian-Slovak parentage from northern Hungary, compiled the first historico-geographical account of Hungary, the first reliable survey of the country. His five-volume *Notitia Hungariae novae historico-geographica* (1735–1742) was compiled with the co-operation of a team of tireless associates. Bél had to overcome a good deal of opposition in order to publish his work, and even so not all the material collected was published. He covered each county, each town, country district and village. No detail, however insignificant, escaped his inquisitive eye, and he was interested in every aspect of the subject: archaeological, ethnographical, economic and cultural. Bél made an international name for himself: he became an acknowledged authority, and scientific societies and academies in London, Paris and Jena conferred honorary memberships and fellowships on him.

For their part the Jesuits also made a considerable contribution to Baroque learning. *Gábor Hevenesi* (1656–1715), a provincial of the Jesuit order, in his declining years compiled a collection of sources of Hungarian national and ecclesiastical history running into 140 volumes. His ascetic writings earned him great popularity among his contemporaries, and were translated into German and French.

Sámuel Timon (1675–1736), a Jesuit teacher of theology, wrote a *Synopsis novae chronologiae* (1714–1719) in five volumes, which was a scholarly attempt to fill a gap in Hungarian historiography. "What we are seeking is truth, and not agreement with others," he wrote in the introduction. He sifted masses of records and other documents and was the first to study source materials in the modern, critical sense.

A similarly painstaking and scholarly work can be seen in Sajnovics's enquiry into the origins of the Hungarian language. *János Sajnovics* (1733–1785) was the first to become aware of the linguistic kinship between Hungarian and Finno-Ugrian inasmuch as he demonstrated certain links between the Lapp and the Hungarian languages in his *Demonstratio idioma Ungarorum et Lapporum idem esse,* 1770. The earliest continuous text in the Hungarian language, the *Funeral Oration* of *c.* 1192, was first published in this volume, in the poet Ferenc Faludi's version.

The Hungarian Enlightenment and the Classicist Movement

(c. 1770–c. 1820)

18 The Growth of Literary Life

Historical Background

There was no opportunity in Hungary for any bourgeois state to develop under the royal absolutism that existed. Such Hungarian nationalism as arose in opposition to Habsburg oppression was to be mainly found in the relatively numerous class of medium land-owning and lower gentry, uncultivated and not too well-off, who kept the memory and the tradition of the fight for freedom alive, and most of whom were looked at askance by the Catholic Habsburgs because they were Protestants. As a middle class as such did not then exist in Hungarian society, the lesser nobles, or rather gentry, claimed the role of a "third estate", which, however, they misinterpreted, and indeed proved themselves unfit for the role. Their struggle was ambivalent in that it combined the determination to fight for the interests of the nation on the one hand and to protect the feudal privileges they enjoyed on the other. They were opposed to the enlightened absolutism of Joseph II (1780–1790), which threatened these privileges, but were active in promoting the status and improvement of the Hungarian language as a pre-condition of Hungarian national development, while believing themselves all the while to be offering the same opposition to tyranny as the supporters of the French Revolution in 1789. The vague character of their social and political programme became obvious in the 1790–91 session of the Diet. As however the social implications of the French Revolution became clear, the situation began to clarify itself, and in order to defend the feudal order the terrified lesser nobility and gentry were more than ready to enter into an alliance with the Habsburgs, in the belief that "the nobility cannot survive without the monarch nor the monarch rule without the nobility." It was only a handful of intellectuals who, around 1795, prepared to take active steps towards the development of a nationalist and bourgeois state by way of revolution. The plot, organized by *Ignác Martinovics* (1755–1795), a former university professor, was uncovered at its initial stage, and the mass execution of the chief conspirators followed, with long terms of imprisonments for others, effectively putting an end to political activity in Hungary for almost thirty years.

The Enlightenment and the Cult of the Mother Tongue

It was in the Hungarian literature of this period, however, that a continuing interest in political ideas was displayed. The establishment of a bourgeois, as opposed to a feudal, state became part of its aims, and it reflected a keen interest in the achievements of the French Enlightenment. It was the French Enlightenment which inspired the new educational purposes of literature, and extended the range of its devices and means of expression. In keeping with this spirit, the mass education of the people was regarded as the key to the future development of the nation. And the means to achieve it was seen in the cultivation of the Hungarian mother tongue which, indeed, was the obvious basis of all cultural transmission. The refinement and development of the Hungarian language occupied a central place in the new attitudes on literature which were developing. This was not a specifically Hungarian movement; the same preoccupation with the national language, allied to a sense of nationalist cultural and political development, was to be seen in the other Eastern European countries under foreign domination.

In Hungary, unlike in the Bulgarian, Greek, Serb and Slovak nations, where the national language was in a more primitive state, it was not found necessary to create an entirely new literary language. The revival of the native language and literature of Hungary is more comparable to the same movement among the Czechs. Though there were indeed Hungarian writers of that period who impatiently rejected all previous Hungarian literature, little though they knew of it, the period also marked the beginning of a systematic exploration of the older literature, and a consciousness of Hungarian literary history as a whole, relating old and new. The men who set out to improve the language, found their main difficulty not so much in the limited use of the language as in the inadequacies of its means of expression; and considered the current Hungarian literary language, designed to convey ideas connected with religion and the feudal order of society, unfit and inadequate as the medium of a new, bourgeois type of enlightened national culture. They consequently carried out an expansion of the language, introducing new words and expressions to make it a fit tool for their purpose, which was in fact to use literature as the medium for spreading the improvement of the language.

An added strength to the new literary movement was that the language question was in fact an important political issue. In accordance with his principles of centralization Joseph II introduced the use of the German language into Hungarian official life. The measure evoked strong opposition, with writers raising their voices in defence of the Hungarian language, and from that time on its protection and cultivation became a national issue.

Those, however, who supported the use of their native tongue against the imposition of German were not always inspired by the same motives. The majority

118

of the nobility neither could nor would see the need to create a bourgeois national culture based on the ideas of the Enlightenment, together with the use of the native tongue, and consequently did not regard the improvement of the language as necessary. Moreover, they had no wish at all to extend its use at the expense of the Latin language still in current use in public and cultural life. The result was that by the beginning of the nineteenth century there were two opposing groups, the conservatives who wanted no changes in the language, and the more forward-looking who were in favour of them.

Literary Life

Between 1770 and 1790 a considerable number of new writers made their appearance. The isolation which was a feature of the literature of previous times no longer existed. Writers were eager to establish contact with one another and to organize their literary activities, despite the fact that although national economic and cultural conditions were improving, life was still hard. The elementary requisites of a flourishing literature were lacking; there was no royal court in Hungary to encourage literature, and very few noble patrons. The majority of the lesser nobility made few pretensions to culture. They lived on their country estates, caring for little beyond the boundaries of their counties, and with no intellectual interest. Poets were entertainers who could be hired to make congratulatory verses at weddings, baptisms or name-days, or produce valedictory poems for funerals. The citizens of the few Hungarian towns where the standard of civilization was higher were mostly German; it was the villages where the population was mainly Hungarian.

The soil in which Hungarian literature could begin to grow, and the limited opportunities it was offered, seem almost unbelievable today. Maria Theresa (1740–1780), who was Joseph II's predecessor, invited Hungarian nobles to help form the royal guard, and the sons of the Hungarian nobility were thus given the opportunity to educate themselves in Vienna. They could leave the waste lands of Hungary, and begin in Vienna first to enjoy, then to practise the reading and then the writing of literature, and it was in Vienna that they organized the first society of Hungarian writers. The Imperial city, which at that time was one of the most important centres of European culture, a stronghold of music and the birthplace of German literary movements in the theatre, for long played an important role in the development of Hungarian literature as the French Enlightenment, Italian Rococo, and the various German literary movements that arose in quick succession came to affect it through the medium of Vienna. The collections of paintings, the literature and theatre of Vienna meant European civilization to Hungarian writers as it did to the Serb writers who could get no farther than Vienna. Literary societies, similar to the one founded in Vienna but of less importance, were coming into being in Hungarian towns as well, in Kassa for instance, and Kolozsvár and Komárom. The libraries of Hungarian nobles, Orczy, Ráday, and Ferenc Széchényi above all, who were book collectors and also wrote themselves, became literary centres and workshops of literature together with the monasteries, theological colleges and Protestant schools. In the wave of enthusiasm for the refinement and development of the mother tongue, and the creation of a truly national culture, the religious differences that had previously influenced the cultural life of Hungary, tended to disappear. An important milestone was the foundation of a department of the Hungarian language at the University of Pest in 1791, and the teaching of Hungarian language and literature was introduced in secondary schools all over the country.

The Hungarian capital, lying on both sides of the Danube, at that time consisted of the two separate towns, Buda and Pest, still somewhat underdeveloped as a result of the long Turkish occupation. The two towns together had something less than fifty thousand inhabitants, the majority of German origin who had settled in the country. At that time it was not yet the centre of Hungarian cultural and political life. Even the Diet, in fact, met in the border town of Pozsony. But the main government offices were in the capital, it possessed a university, moved from Nagyszombat to Buda in 1777, and in 1784 to Pest, as well as a German-language and, from 1790, a Hungarian-language theatre, and a growing printing industry, which promised well for its development as the real centre of the nation. Its social life prospered, and it offered every opportunity for the architects of Hungarian literature to establish contact with one another, make the acquaintance of the few Hungarian nobles and well-to-do and cultivated members of the gentry interested in literature. It was in Buda and Pest in 1779 that the first nationwide association of writers, the Society of Hungarian Patriots was organized, which got off to an inauspicious start.

The Masonic movement, which included almost all the educated members of the Hungarian society of the time, played an important role in widening social contacts, and provided a background for a type of bourgeois literary life in both the capital and the major provincial towns.

The rapid increase in the number of books published between 1770 and 1790 also marked the beginning of a new period in the history of Hungarian literature, which was particularly prolific during the ten years of Joseph II's reign. This was partly due to Joseph's liberal policy in the matter of censorship, and partly to the reaction to his royal decree imposing the use of the German language where possible. Twenty-three newspapers and ten periodicals were started during the reign of Joseph II. Among them were the *Magyar Museum* (Hungarian Museum, Kassa, 1788–1792), the *Mindenes Gyűjtemény* (Miscellany, Komárom, 1789–1792), the *Orpheus* (Kassa, 1790–1791), and the *Uránia,* which appeared somewhat later (Pest, 1792–1795). The large number of pamphlets published in connection with the 1790–1791 session of the Diet is evidence of the widespread use of the published word to inform and appeal to the public. The newly opened lending libraries and reading rooms (known as *Lesekabinetts*) made books and other reading matter available to wide circles: readings were even instituted for illiterates. Lipót Sándor, the Palatine of Hungary wrote in 1795 that "the Hungarian papers... are read by the notary to the peasants in most villages." The number of copies of these publications was, however, pitifully small: the *Magyar Museum,* for instance, had 329 subscribers, and only 142 people took the *Uránia.*

From 1795 onwards, following the suppression of the Jacobin conspiracy headed by Martinovics, the literary activities which were then beginning to flourish came to a standstill as writers felt themselves threatened and the censorship tightened. Fewer books were produced and no new periodicals appeared apart from the short-lived *Erdélyi Museum* (Transylvanian Museum), published in Kolozsvár, which ran from 1814 to 1818 and the *Tudományos Gyűjtemény* (Scientific Collection, Pest, 1817–43). The first Hungarian theatrical company in Pest collapsed in 1796, and the only one which continued to give performances was the company founded in 1792 in Kolozsvár. The public activities of writers came to an end; they could no longer organize, and the best of them retired to the country and lived in rural solitude. The movement for the expansion and refinement of the language, however, which intensified around 1810, again aroused considerable public support, and the fact that literary life in Pest began to revive about that time was greatly helped by the energy and enthusiasm of the Hungarian students at Pest University and the revival of the Hungarian theatre.

The growing sense of continuity in literature, linking the past to the present, was increased by a new interest in old manuscripts and documents, and in the field of linguistics and literary history. János Sajnovics, and later *Sámuel Gyarmathy* (1751–1830) evolved the theory of the Finno-Ugrian origin of the Hungarian language. *Miklós Révai* (1750–1807) published the earliest written records of the Hungarian language, and initiated the study of Hungarian grammar on a historical basis before Schlegel and Grimm introduced the science of language development. His debate, mainly on questions of orthography, with Ferenc Verseghy who supported current usage, aroused considerable public interest, and for a time divided writers into factions. Around this time the nobility made their libraries available to the reading public, and this further encouraged the study of literary history. The collection of books donated to the nation in 1803 by Count Ferenc Széchényi (1754–1820) formed the nucleus of a Hungarian national library, which is today the National Széchényi Library. Together with the publication of important texts, a bibliography of Hungarian literature compiled by *István Sándor* (1750–1815) and entitled *The Treasury of Hungarian Books* (Magyar Könyvesház) was of great value, as well as the history of literature written by *Sámuel Pápay* (1770–1827), entitled *Knowledge of Hungarian Literature* (A magyar literatura esmérete, 1808), written in the spirit of the Enlightenment and designed to help improve the language.

Trends in Style

Erudition took first place in the literature of the period, chiefly regarded as a medium for the improvement of the language. This attitude was imported into Eastern Europe at the same time as the ideas of the Enlightenment, and helped to promote the spread of Neo-Classicism. A great many literary works of the period were translations, adaptations or imitations. Writers eagerly experimented with new styles of writing and new literary forms, which, eventually, led to clashes between them. French Neo-Classicism was originally the dominant trend, to be followed at the beginning of the nineteenth century by German Neo-Classicism, which in turn gave way to imitations of the style of Antiquity, reaching back to the Roman poetic tradition via the earlier somewhat Baroque productions of the high schools and colleges. Sentimentality was also one of the more decided offshoots of Neo-Classicism, and it was also the trend that extended beyond the theories of the school which looked on literature mainly as a tool for expanding and enriching the language. Within this framework the demand for originality in content, which dominated the later Romantic school, was realized in practice as part of its programme. Alongside these various versions of Neo-Classicism certain tricks of comprehensible style also emerged in contemporary Hungarian literature, for the most part retaining out of date Baroque and Rococo elements. A version of these, which took on a touch of the popular style, with a little folklore to boot, often coupled with a feudal outlook on life, and antagonism to the ideals of the Enlightenment was sharply criticized by the writers and poets representing the newer trends. In the work, however, of one outstanding poet, Csokonai, the Rococo elements with a touch of folk colouring match with the enlightened and more emotional aspects of his poetry, and are, in fact, democratic in content. The cult of Ossian also foreshadowed the later Romantic movement. Hungarians, frustrated in their patriotic aspirations, felt a kinship with the grief expressed in the melancholy poems of the alleged Celtic bard.

In Hungary the fine arts and music produced nothing of value during this period. The language movement, however, was accompanied by a cult for the national costume, and by light music containing the Hungarian dance and song motifs. This trend was of somewhat ambiguous value, as it tended to an insularity incompatible with an enlightened civilization.

19 The Leading Literary Figures
and their Ideas

With the growing appreciation of the social tasks of literature, and its function as the voice of national interests, the attention of the public was increasingly drawn to the more politically committed writers. This was not an exclusively Hungarian preoccupation. Josef Dobrovský and Josef Jungman in Bohemia, Ignacy Krasicki in Poland, Dositej Obradović in Serbia, and Gheorghe Lazar in Rumania represented the same dawning nationalism in their own countries.

György Bessenyei (1747-1811)

First of these new writers in Hungary came György Bessenyei. He was born into a noble family living east of the river Tisza. He was one of the Hungarians serving in Maria Theresa's corps of guards in Vienna, and it was there he realized the contrast between the advanced culture of the Imperial city and the backwardness of his homeland, dominated by half-educated country squires. He took advantage of his stay in Vienna to become acquainted with the ideas of rationalism that had become fashionable at the time. His favourite authors were Locke, Pope, Montesquieu, Voltaire and Rousseau, and it was they who inspired his cultural schemes, together with the new trends in German literature and the theatre, current in contemporary Vienna. But he was equally influenced by the traditional Hungarian patriotism of his own family and by the rising movement for national independence led by the nobility. Bessenyei came to the fore in 1772, the same year as the leading figure of the Czech literary revival, Josef Dobrovský first appeared. Dobrovský, however, with the Hussite traditions of the Czechs behind him and the sense of fraternity among the Slav nations to support him, could propose a wider and more far-reaching development, even though he wrote in German. Bessenyei, on the other hand, was not certain of his starting point. His early work shows not only his desire to find a personal voice of his own, but also a new voice in Hungarian literature. His Neo-Classicist tragedies (*The Tragedy of László Hunyadi*—Hunyadi László tragédiája, 1772; *The Tragedy of Ágis*—Ágis tragédiája, 1772; *The Tragedy of Buda*—Buda tragédiája, 1773) represented the clash with tyranny in enlightened terms. In his epic poem, *Hunyadi* (1772), written after the manner of Voltaire, he revived one of the most glorious episodes in the history of the Hungarian nation. He delved into philosophical questions in both poetry and prose, such as *The Test of Man* (Az embernek próbája), modelled on Pope's *Essay on Man*, and *Miscellaneous Matters* (A holmi, 1779), introducing secular and even materialistic problems of philosophy, discussed here for the first time in the Hungarian language. He worked unusually speedily, which may partly account for certain signs of immaturity in these works; they are, however, dictated less by the ambitions of an artist than by the anxieties of a Hungarian desirous for promoting the development of his country.

The works of his which exerted the greatest influence were those directly dealing with his own age, and directly addressed to his own people. Such a piece is the comedy entitled *The Philosopher* (A filozófus, 1777). Its plot, dealing with questions of love and marriage, was based on French Neo-Classical models, such as the plays of Marivaux and Destouches. Yet through the skilfully individualized characters that are nonetheless types the author was able to criticize the contemporary state of civilization in Hungary, the affectation of French manners that was the latest fashion as well as the underlying boorishness and conservatism of the majority. Bessenyei's pamphlets, *Hungarian Nation* (Magyarság, 1778), *Hungarian Spectator* (A magyar néző, 1779) and *Modest Intention* (Jámbor szándék, 1781), which suggested a cultural policy for the nation, are rather more important than these earlier books and plays. "The chief hope of a country's happiness lies through knowledge," he wrote in his *Modest Intention*. The more the inhabitants of a country cultivate it the happier they are. Language is the door to knowledge, which to most people who have no opportunity to know other languages means their native tongue. So, perfecting it should be the main task of the nation that wants knowledge to spread among its inhabitants, in order that they should prosper through it. Some of the implications of this motion foreshadow a bourgeois national state, as for instance the statement that the principal characteristic marking off a nation is its mother tongue, or that the word nation includes the serfs as well. It is literature's task to perfect the native tongue, and to synchronize its development with the progress of knowledge. But this meant that he rejected earlier Hungarian literature, describing religious and legal works as books of inferior taste, and demanded that contemporary Hungarian literature should form part of and assimilate to contemporary foreign literature, that it should keep abreast of modern trends through translations, that it should be Hungarian in its language, secular in its contents, and above all, practical in its aims. To realize this programme obviously required unity, which is why Bessenyei tried to organize writers into a society, the Society of Hungarian Patriots, wider in membership than the limited group of fellow enthusiasts in the Guards. The *Modest Intention*, in fact, which proposed the foundation of a Hungarian Academy of Sciences and which was the first to outline the functions of such an institution, was written to promote this society.

Bessenyei left the Guards in 1773, and as he faile to obtain and official post, he returned to Hungary and settled down on his country estate. He thus lost contact with the current of literary life he had been the first to stimulate, and from that time on could find no publisher for his works. The important philosophical poem *The World of Nature* (A természet világa), written about 1800, and *The Hermit of Bihar* (A bihari remete), between 1803 and 1808 and *The Search for Reason* (Az értelemnek keresése), in 1804, the last two designed to provide a summary of his basic views, have survived in manuscript. Had they appeared in print at the time, the passionate reasoning contained in them, and the arguments reflecting an inward struggle would have made them pioneer works in the study of philosophy, a discipline, in fact, missing from Hungarian culture for a long time. His novel, *The Travels of Tarimenes* (Tariménes utazása, 1804) could similarly have justly marked the beginning of the Hungarian novel if it had been published at the time instead of the 126 years after it had been written. In this novel Bessenyei poured the events and experiences of his life and the problems of his age. It no longer simply imitated foreign models, such as *Télémaque* of Fénelon, Montesquieu's *Persian Letters,* and Voltaire's *Candide* and *L'Ingénu,* but used them to provide emotional and intellectual inspiration. No piece of writing containing more intellectual stimulus, more concentrated in its form, and conveying a richer range of experience was produced in the period than this political novel based on the travels of its hero. The barren atmosphere of rural solitude, the luxury of courts, the enlightened views of the Government Minister, the description of the parliamentary debates, the denunciation of the wars of colonization and religious fanaticism, and discussions of love are all represented in this variegated novel. It is however somewhat thin in both plot and characterization. But the variety and poetry of the style which is full of feeling, moving in his moments of nostalgic recollection and bitter and ironical at other times, sufficiently compensate for the failings.

It was in fact Bessenyei's cultural proposals, formulated in his pamphlets, that influenced his contemporaries. They were generally accepted, and for decades they determined the lines along which Hungarian literature developed. Only one character from all his other work has survived as a popular figure: it is Pontyi who in the comedy *The Philosopher* (A filozófus) represents the rather uncouth and uncultivated country gentleman; similar types emerge over and over again in nineteenth-century comedies, novels and short stories. The literary principles enshrined in his novels and other work remained without followers, and consequently, the next generation of writers had to set to work with a limited perspective in front of them.

József Kármán (1769-1795)

It was József Kármán, in the 1790s, who attempted to widen the language movement by insisting on the necessity for originality in literature. He came from an educated Calvinist family; his father was a clergyman, and they lived in Upper Hungary. He studied at the University in Vienna, where he met and mixed with the sons of the Hungarian nobility. There he fell in love with a countess, and the memory of this sentimental attachment is preserved in his letters. On his return to Pest he continued to cultivate the society of the nobility and the intelligentsia, which accepted him, probably because he was a Freemason. He helped to draw up the regulations for the first Hungarian theatrical company, and in 1794 he started a periodical under the title *Uránia*. He propounded his views on literature and education both in the preface to this review and in his essay *The Improvement of the Nation* (A nemzet csinosodása). In it he criticized those who thought too much of the development of literature during the twenty years that had passed since the appearance of Bessenyei on the literary scene. "A certain fuss and bustle has indeed occurred, and there has been some interest, but nothing else has been achieved," he wrote. Although it became fashionable to cultivate literature, he said, no appreciable signs of its influence on wider circles of the public could be seen. In his opinion the majority of the Hungarian gentry were uncultivated, rural life made them narrow-minded, they lacked not only any intellectual interest but refined feelings too. Writers bemused by questions of language, who spent their time translating foreign works into Hungarian, had no value for Kármán who proclaimed the need to produce original works. "Each writer has his own universe with an atmosphere peculiar to it—a universe in which he lives, to which he can turn, from which he draws his material." This appears strikingly modern in a literary world in which the imitation of outstanding models was regarded as the criterion of perfection in art. By stressing the importance of originality Kármán became the precursor of Romanticism. Quite independently of Kármán's literary beliefs but, as it were, reviving them, Kölcsey propagated the same views at the beginning of the nineteenth century.

Kármán wrote for women readers, and what he considered his main task as a writer was to present the life of women in literature. He proposed to influence the attitude of men as well by undertaking to raise the standard of education among women, and to shape their emotions. It was for women, whose task it is to bring up the next generation, that he intended his reviews and his novel of sentiment. *The Posthumous Papers of Fanny* (Fanni hagyományai) is in the form of letters and was written about women and to women. The book may recall Goethe's *Werther* and other sentimental novels, but its main merit is its own. Its heroine is brought to destruction in a world dominated by the hidebound Hungarian gentry of the time, blind to any feelings of a more refined nature, such as those Kármán described in *The Improvement of the Nation*. The beauties of nature, art, friendship and love, that are so dear to the heart of Fanny, are ignored by the world in which she lives. Her sensitive agony, the disease of body and soul fatally consuming her, is psychologically convincing, although the picture of the man Fanny loves is by no means so effective.

The short sentence constructions of Kármán's style are unlike the sentence structure peculiar to earlier Hungarian literature. The play of nature on the mood of human beings, and the individual speech of the various characters are dealt with considerable virtuosity. His articles reveal him as a master of satire and rational argument. Although he coined no new words, the phrases, descriptive terms and similes are unusual and apt, and he can justly be regarded as the best writer of prose of his period.

All his efforts, however, were even less successful than Bessenyei's. He died in his native town, Losonc (now Lučenec, Czechoslovakia) about the same time as Martinovics and his fellow-conspirators were executed. It was claimed he took part in the plot, but the circumstances of his death are obscure. His review was forced to cease publication, and in the course of time he was practically forgotten. He was in effect rediscovered in the 1840s, but it was some time before anyone took up his thesis that literature demanded originality not dependent on models, and that it was important that women readers should be encouraged.

Ferenc Kazinczy (1759–1831)

Greater success attended the plans and projects for Hungarian literature laid down by Kazinczy. Like Bessenyei, he came from a Protestant noble family in eastern Hungary. His father, a highly cultivated man, inculcated a love of literature in the child in his early years. Kazinczy acquired an extensive knowledge of foreign literature, and in particular the new contemporary German-language literature as well as a taste and understanding for painting and sculpture. As a school inspector he enthusiastically supported the enlightened measures of Joseph II. In his translation of the idylls of Gessner (1788) and in an adaptation of Kayser's novel, *Adolfs gesammelte Briefe,* which he published in 1789 under the title *The Collected Letters of Bácsmegyey* (Bácsmegyey öszveszedett levelei), he experimented with the new sentimental style of writing, even before Kármán's appearance on the literary scene. The *Letters of Bácsmegyey,* and his translation of Goethe's *Stella,* are semi-autobiographical, reflecting his own life and love. Kazinczy spent his whole existence among books, and not only gave expression to his life but practically shaped it according to literary examples. Like Kármán in Vienna, Kazinczy found in Kassa, the main town in Upper Hungary, a circle of congenial and sensitive people capable of appreciating the new literature of sentiment. In Kassa he first started the *Magyar Museum*, a review edited with János Batsányi and Dávid Baróti Szabó, and later, separating from them, he founded another, entitled *Orpheus*. The name was, in fact, his Masonic pseudonym, and in this review he propagated the teachings of Helvetius, Holbach, Rousseau, Voltaire and Wieland. The foundation of the first Hungarian theatrical company turned him to the translation of plays for it. Among others he translated Goethe's plays, *Die Mitschuldigen, Die Geschwister, Clavigo* and *Stella;* Shakespeare's *Hamlet* and *Macbeth* (from the German translation of Schröder), Lessing's *Miss Sarah Sampson* and *Emilia Galotti,* and later pieces by Molière and Schiller. His career came to an abrupt stop in 1795 when he was sentenced to death for taking part in the Martinovics conspiracy; the sentence subsequently being commuted into imprisonment for an indefinite term.

He showed remarkable powers of endurance during the six and a half years he spent in prison. Despite the harsh conditions of imprisonment Kazinczy continued to write, at times even drawing blood from his own arm for lack of ink. During this period he clarified his own views on the task of literature, and prepared for the work that lay ahead. He never abandoned his advanced views, but in style came more and more under the influence of Classical and Neo-Classicist models, such as Cicero, Sallustius, Horace, Plutarch, Winckelmann, Goethe, La Rochefoucauld and Barthélemy. He also came to give greater weight to the refinements of taste than the propagation of enlightened ideals. Literature, in which Bessenyei and Kármán included scholarship, for Kazinczy came to mean literature pure, as it is known today. It was he, moreover, who was most insistent on the task of refining and perfecting the language, a task originally projected by Bessenyei. Kazinczy, however, no longer regarded the language merely as a vehicle for general education and culture; he also regarded it as the vehicle of literature and poetry, and as such, an artistic product in itself.

When released from prison Kazinczy could only retire to his small estate, from where, though in financial straits, he nonetheless continued his work of raising the level of public taste, embellishing the language, and successfully reviving literary life in Hungary. By maintaining an extensive correspondence throughout the country, he was able to turn his country residence into a literary centre, and as there were no Hungarian reviews appearing at the time, he published critical essays on Hungarian literature in a German review, *Annalen der Literatur und Kunst in dem Österreichischen Kaisertum* and when, prompted by the Government in Vienna, the "Cotta" Press in Tübingen announced a competition designed to provoke writers to express their true opinion, he seized the opportunity to propagate the argument that the Hungarian language was suitable and desirable for official use and that Hungarian literature was not to be despised. Literature was the absorbing passion of his life, and he continued to publish his works and those of other writers, financing them out of his own pocket. When he died he left a large family in poverty, but literary activities in Hungary had been stimulated to a lively and creative level never reached before.

The Language Reform

In spite of all the difficulties confronting his project for the renovation and refinement of the language, designed to produce a fit vehicle for literature, Kazinczy called into being a movement on a larger scale than that previously created by Bessenyei and Kármán. Kazinczy's importance in this field can only be compared to that of Josef Jungman in Czech literature. With his sharp epigrams, epistles, critical writings, and biographical introductions to the works he edited, he made the development of the language a question of central importance in the literary life of Hungary in the years between 1810 and 1820. The clash between the two opposing parties, the "neologists", inventing and using new words, on one hand, and the "orthologists" or those content with the language as it stood, on the other hand, represented not only the conflict between those anxious to refine and develop the language and the traditionalists but also in different attitudes on literature and art in the wider sense, and even between different social attitudes. Kazinczy emphasized the importance of personal individuality and originality in literature, and of aesthetic considerations. The reformers were also concerned to promote the development of an urban civilization and a bourgeois society when they coined words to fit these concepts, and, when they opposed the linguistic isolation threatened by the use of regional dialects, by their attempt to create a unified literary language. They certainly broke some of the rules of grammatical propriety, and, as their opponents described it, "offended against the spirit of the language," but the overwhelming majority of the words they created later passed into general literary currency, and time has justified them. Their campaigns brought literature to the attention of the general public. Both the pamphlet *Mondolat* (1813), attacking their efforts, and *An Answer to the "Mondolat"* (Felelet a Mondolatra, 1815) mocking conservative taste, are examples of satirical exaggerations of these language theories, presupposing a reading public capable of appreciating such satire, and both familiar with such means of expression and interested in them.

Kazinczy also played an important part in arousing interest in the historical continuity of Hungarian literature. Bessenyei and Kármán had turned their backs on all earlier Hungarian literature; Kazinczy pointed out some of its beauties and achievements. It was due to Kazinczy that Zrínyi's place in the forefront of the older Hungarian literature was recognized and made secure. Nor did the innovation he introduced into the language mean a break with the riches of the earlier language:

many long-forgotten Hungarian words were re-discovered and revived, and by the beginning of the nineteenth century the dispute on grammar between Miklós Révai, supporting historical precedents, and Ferenc Verseghy, defending current usage, was settled by Kazinczy in favour of Révai.

Kazinczy's Literary Principles

In the context of later developments in Hungarian literature, Kazinczy's activities as critic are also of outstanding importance. Although he wrote little criticism, his letters are full of critical observations, encouragement, advice and admonition. His views, however, were often biassed; his classical taste prevented him from appreciating other trends. He taught a generation of writers to insist on strict literary standards, for although he was primarily concerned with language and form, he never neglected the content of literature. It was he who first introduced Dániel Berzsenyi, the greatest Hungarian poet of that time, to the ideas of the Enlightenment.

Yet Kazinczy, unlike Kármán, marked a step backwards on the question of originality in literary content. "We can make progress in our literary craft only if, instead of fine inventions, we are ready to accept the splendid achievements already in existence of nations luckier than we." He appeared to think of literature as a school of painting, was of the opinion that the great masterpieces should be copied in order to acquire technical skill, and consequently considered his translations his chief literary works. He continued to polish and revise them, somewhat to their detriment as they became increasingly artificial with each revision.

The classicist attitude he admired, in Goethe above all, is reflected best in his epigrams, *Thorns and Flowers* (Tövisek és Virágok, 1811). They are intellectually and verbally sharp, witty and concise, and in striking contrast to the prolixity of previous Hungarian poetry. The clarity and intellectual vigour of his epistles casts the Baroque verse-epistle into a disciplined and Neo-Classical framework. His sonnets, the first in Hungarian literature, are more evidence of technical skill than anything else. More interesting, however, are his personal writings, two autobiographical works, an account of a journey, and a collection of his letters in twenty-three monumental volumes, and it is to these, apart from the influence he exercised on his contemporaries, that Kazinczy owes his reputation as an outstanding figure in Hungarian literature. In his autobiographical work *Memories of my Career* (Pályám emlékezete) he draws, not so much a portrait of himself, as of the age in which he lived and his contemporaries—writers, patrons of art and public personalities. He is a master of the character sketch, and his portraits have a note of intimacy and familiarity. His portrait of Joseph II, for instance, whose greatness he appreciates, and of whom he writes with affection, is enlivened by touches about his bad Latin, the slovenliness of his dress, and the patched elbow of his coat. It is also his powers of penetration that strike the reader in the *Journal of my Captivity* (Fogságom naplója). In this he preceded Silvio Pellico, the other famous chronicler of life in Austrian prisons. Pellico is more successful in describing the psychological reactions to such a situation. The subject-matter of a diary of prison life should lend itself to a more passionate treatment than Kazinczy's. But his brief and concise style is pregnant with feeling. Here are lines from the *Journal* on the death of the Jacobin martyrs, Martinovics and his comrades: "On the morning following the day of the execution roses were flowering where it took place. Vases containing them had been dug into the ground."

The achievements of his literary campaigns which survived were the cultivation of the art of literature and the development of the language. Many of his views, however, were out of date even in his own time. Romanticism took the place of the Classicism he propagated. His aesthetic views were tinged with an aristocratic cosmopolitan outlook that was superseded by the new national trends in literature, and his translations, owing to both their subject-matter and their language, which had been designed to set new standards of style, were also soon out of date. But the example he set lived on, and so did the memory of his life and his magnetic personality. "Atlas-like, he maintained the cause of the nation for half a century," wrote Sándor Petőfi. He earned the esteem of his contemporaries who appreciated his devotion to his self-appointed task. Even his opponents were finally reconciled with him, and young writers at the beginning of their literary career, despite their different views, gave him their homage. He was in fact universally regarded as the first indisputably great classic of a reviving Hungarian literature.

20 The Narrative in Prose and Verse

The Beginnings of the Novel

The most remarkable achievement of these men was the production of large-scale works in prose, such as *Travels of Tarimenes, Fanny, Memories of my Career,* and the *Journal of my Captivity.* Scant attention was given to these works, however; the whole tradition of memoir-writing of Baroque times had sunk into oblivion, and the general standard of such works as appeared was very low. But the public showed an increasing interest in a new literary genre, the novel. It was unfortunate, however, that the only novels available were translations or adaptations of novels and tales from Western Europe, for the most part second or third-rate stuff, mangled still further by the translators who, in order to give them a Hungarian colouring, gave them a Hungarian background, with Hungarian names for the characters. In that period the German word *Roman* was still used instead of the word "novel", and it soon acquired a pejorative meaning. Writers with higher aspirations and supporters of the old moral and customary order antagonized by their "erotic" content, nonetheless condemned them in vain; they spread like wild fire. While they certainly helped to broaden the habit of reading and popularized the new bourgeois way of life, they also helped to lower standards of taste. It was typical of the time that Bessenyei's *Tarimenes* was never published, and that Kármán's *Fanny* appeared by instalments in a periodical with only 142 subscribers, while *Kártigám* (1772) by Ignác Mészáros (1721-1800)—a work of little literary value—ran into four editions by the end of the century.

Sándor Báróczy (1735-1809), who was a fellow-writer of György Bessenyei in the Guards in Vienna and who translated La Calprenède and Marmontel, is chiefly remembered for his style. His prose translations, deliberately designed to meet certain aesthetic standards, reveal him a disciple of Kazinczy's. It is clear that he was concerned not only to translate the original piece but also to render the style into elegant Hungarian. "Each time I read the translation," he wrote in the preface of Marmontel, "I found that much of the sparkling spirit which enlivens the French original was missing. . ." He was appreciative of the niceties of Marmontel's style—he called it the *style coupé per incisa*—, deliberately and successfully reproduced his style in Hungarian, thus opening up new prospects for the development of a Hungarian prose style.

132

András Dugonics (1740-1818)

The most popular novelist of the age was András Dugonics, a member of the Piarist order, and a university professor of mathematics. He came from a Hungarianized family of Dalmatian origin which numbered artisans and merchants among their forebears. His interest in old Hungarian folk traditions made him a pioneer in the study of Hungarian folklore. He collected popular sayings and worked on a collection entitled *Hungarian Sermons and Famous Proverbs* (Magyar példabeszédek és jeles közmondások) until his death.

His novel *Etelka* (1788) was the kind of work typified in world literature by John Barclay's *Argenis,* an allegorical political poem written in Latin. *Etelka* is a *roman à clef;* it is laid in the tenth century following the Hungarian Conquest of the country, but this is a covering for the contemporary period of Joseph II: the book is written to advance the views of the nationalist nobility, giving the somewhat superficial and simple advice to the Hungarians to cling to their national customs, language and dress, to try to persuade the monarch, himself a benevolent being, to dismiss his evil advisers, and to convince him of the excellence of the Hungarian nation. The nobility, of course, found this simple political message attractive. It is recorded that a member of the Pest county council, at a meeting in 1790, turned to the writer and said: "You see, Sir, all that we can say here will be taken from your book *Etelka,* we entreat you never to abandon Hungary in your writing, in order to stimulate the Hungarians to be valiant and courageous."

Etelka, however, not only provided a political programme for the Hungarian nobility, but also helped to fill the gap caused by the lack of badly needed historical books and novels. Dugonics was the first to popularize the story of the Hungarian Conquest as described in the chronicle of Anonymus, discovered in 1746. But the historical element was only a prop on which the author built an unrealistic, nationalist attitude. The discovery of the kinship between the Finno-Ugrian and Hungarian peoples inspired the invention of a mythical story on the origins of not only the Hungarians but also the Finno-Ugrians. In his play *Etelka in Karelia* (Etelka Karjelben, 1794), and the novel *Jolánka, Daughter of Etelka* (Jolánka, Etelkának leánya, 1803), sequels to *Etelka,* Hungary and Karelia were portrayed as countries closely related to each other, inhabited by the same people, with a common language. The sentiments of national pride in these tales, which abounded in surprising and thrilling adventures, charmed the readers of Dugonics, whose influence on the reading public was considerable, though hardly beneficial.

József Gvadányi (1725-1801)

Although the novel grew in popularity as a literary genre, by the end of the eighteenth century epic poetry stemming back to an honourable past assumed an importance greater than that of the prose tale, and it was István Gyöngyösi who was revered as the model in this field. "No Hungarian mother had ever given life to a poet greater than he," said József Gvadányi of István Gyöngyösi. His nationalist views and traditional attitude to society make József Gvadányi the counterpart of Dugonics in the field of epic poetry. He was given the title of count when serving in the Habsburg army, and was promoted to general. Stationed in remote villages in north-eastern Hungary, he found his chief relaxation in the writing of poems. They are in general inferior to those of Gyöngyösi whom he greatly admired. Both their style and subject-matter recall the occasional verse and crude anecdotal tales of village clerics, choir-masters and schoolmasters, notaries and rowdy students. The only work of his of any note is *The Visit of the Village Notary to Buda* (Egy falusi nótárius budai utazása, 1790), largely due to its more coherent construction and skilful characterization of its hero.

The chief character in this poem comes to life through the multiplication of details which build him into a convincing figure, and its poetic value is also largely due to the precise presentation of details and accuracy of observation. His other works also contain vivid and living descriptions of some minute circumstance, some characteristic picture or series of pictures that capture the imagination of the reader. It was precisely for this immediate sensuous quality in particular details, and for the vigorous rustic language Gvadányi used, that Petőfi and Arany, the two great classics of the nineteenth century, were attracted to his poetry.

The Visit of the Village Notary to Buda, however, also has conservative overtones which detract from its charm. It is designed to glorify the conservatism of the nobility. The village notary, whose awkwardness involves him in a series of comic adventures, passionately condemns the slavish imitation of foreign manners he finds in Pest. The political message, indeed, is even poorer than that of Dugonics's: don't adopt foreign fashions or clothes, or speak foreign language, don't change the customs of your ancestors, because change is always dangerous. Gvadányi's *Notary* continued to be well known to the public, due to the fact that it went into several new editions, and later on even cheap editions, and a stage adaptation. It certainly introduced the public to "popular realism", but it also exercised an unfortunate influence on taste, and was largely responsible for the public failure to appreciate no more than the superficial aspects of realism, and to extend its political ideas beyond mere nationalism.

Mihály Fazekas (1766-1828)

It was Mihály Fazekas who wrote the finest narrative poem of the period. Entitled *Matyi, the Goose-boy*, it was inspired by Hungarian folk tales. The Hungarian title *Lúdas Matyi* contains a pun on the word "Lúdas", which in Hungarian can mean both "cunning" and "the owner of geese". Fazekas went to school at the famous college of Debrecen, with its rich national and Protestant cultural background. While still little more than a child he joined the army, fighting against the Turks in Moldavia and the French in Belgium, on the Rhine, and in Northern France. His military ardour cooled in the course of these campaigns, and he became increasingly reluctant to act against his conscience. "My hand refuses to shed more blood in service of coats of arms and illustrious names," he wrote in his *Soldiers' Farewell Song* (Katonai búcsúének).

His first poems were inspired by his military experiences and his fleeting love affairs. Instead of the elegant, sentimental and stylized heroines of the fashionable love poems of the time, the heroines of his poems were Rusanda, the Rumanian peasant girl of Moldavia, and Ameli, a French (or German) girl of bourgeois origin. The realism of his poetry, however, does not depend on their rustic or bourgeois origins but also on his convincing presentation of emotions and states of mind, equally true of the later poems which were primarily inspired by a love of nature. But for him nature was not wild and romantic, but his own garden, shaped by human hands. Following Voltaire's advice, as it were, the poet who was also the author of the first Hungarian herbal, cultivated his garden which offered him an isolated refuge in which he could escape the hostility of society in the early years of the nineteenth century. There, however, he could reach beyond his isolation in his poems, like folk songs, manifesting not only his affection and love of people but also his discontent with the feudal system, such poems reflecting the theme of his chief work *Lúdas Matyi*.

The core of this poem, i.e. the threefold revenge of the poor man for the wrong suffered at the hands of the rich man, is in fact a motif found time and time again in international folklore. It first appeared in 704 B.C. in Assyria in the form of the tale of the old man of Nippur and subsequently reached Spain and Sicily through the Arabs, spreading to Western Europe, as far afield as the folk poetry of the Georgian, Russian, Ukranian, Rumanian and Tsango (Hungarian-speaking Moldavian) peoples. Fazekas probably first heard the tale in Moldavia. His plan to expand it into a poem remained with him for fifteen years until it finally came to fruition in 1804. He added incidents and characters which gave it a Hungarian topicality, and turned it into a poem reflecting his age and the conditions of Hungarian society. Matyi, the hero of his poem, is of the stuff of Till Eulenspiegel and Nasraddin Hodja, the famous popular heroes and champions of justice of European and Eastern tales; but his story is more finished, more shaped than theirs, and the character is more individual, clearer-cut. His stubborn defiance of the heartless land-owner who robs him of his geese and has him flogged, at the beginning of the story, is not so much indicative of revolt as of the simplicity and awkwardness of an ignorant lad. It is not however through some twist in the plot, nor because it is necessary for Matyi to become a real hero, that he is able to avenge himself, but because the poet sends him travel in the world, learning trades and acquiring money, all of which enable him to take a triple revenge on the landlord, twice by disguising himself as a carpenter and doctor, and on each occasion succeeding in flogging him soundly. This is how, in Fazekas's poem, the machinery of justice in folk-tales assimilates the principles of bourgeois progress.

Elements of language which at first sight are contradictory form a happy mixture in this narrative poem. The author deliberately makes it simple. He uses both a popular language which almost approximates to prose, and the classic hexameter which had only recently been adopted in Hungarian poetry. The contrast between the homely language and the heroic hexameter provides a bizarre and odd touch which, in turn, enhances the comic effect of the whole piece.

If we turn to its social content, we must recognize *Lúdas Matyi* as probably the most daring poem published at that time in Hungary. Fazekas in fact never thought of publishing it, and when it first appeared it was without his knowledge. He then wrote a preface to it, denying that the poem referred to contemporary times. The discerning reader, however, probably took the statement as ironically emphasizing the actual topicality of the poem.

The daringly democratic character of *Lúdas Matyi* and the realism of its outlook on life found no successors for a long time, despite the fact that its success, with an almost contemporary Rumanian translation of it, the many editions that appeared, its adaptation for the stage showed that it met a public demand more fully than many other works of the time that have since sunk into oblivion. In fact even today literary histories have little to say about Fazekas, perhaps because he played only a minor role in the shaping of its process. But on the other hand, the representatives of the populist trend in twentieth-century Hungarian literature —and especially Zsigmond Móricz and Gyula Illyés—have recognized their literary predecessor in Fazekas.

Of all contemporary genres it was the narrative poem which most clearly revealed the conditions of contemporary Hungarian society, and in this context might have prepared the ground for the Hungarian realistic novel. But the writing of narrative poems lapsed, and was only later revived in the work of János Arany, and the beginnings of the Hungarian novel were quite independent of, and unaffected by, these earlier narrative poems.

21 Lyric Poetry in the Age of the Enlightenment

New Matter and Form

The ideals of the Enlightenment and the movement for a national identity found their most subtle and yet effective expression in lyric poetry, which was also the genre most affected by innovations of form. Many were the poets of that period; few had genuine talent. The Enlightenment gave rise to a philosophical and didactic type of poetry, disposed to abstract generalizations and tending to be arid andstale. Poetry, however, found its stimulus in the campaign for national independence, which revealed a set of common feelings shared by a whole community, in an anxiety to preserve the mother tongue and indigenous customs. The history of the nation received growing attention, on one hand by successful historical researches of the eighteenth century, and on the other by the influence of the poems of Ossian, then popular over the Continent, and was expressed in the first place in lyric poetry, and a few decades later even more powerfully in Romantic poetry. A number of poets of the period experimented with forms and genres, but were rarely successful. The style adapted from the poetry of the French Enlightenment and from German classicist poetry no more lent itself to individual and personal treatment than the poetic imitation deriving from Baroque art. Here and there, it is true, a rather more individual note is struck in poems following the sentimental tradition of the time.

In terms of the history of literature the innovations in form and style were the most important achievements of this poetry. Apart from a few isolated experiments, only the rhythm based on the different stresses of syllables was used in Hungarian poetry up to the middle of the eighteenth century. West European verse patterns, based both on the lengths and stresses of syllables, were interpreted as based on stresses only. The French alexandrine, for instance, was assimilated as a twelve-sylladle Hungarian type of accented line of two beats, each consisting of six syllables.

This ancient type of line, the verse form most frequently employed in old Hungarian poetry, was arranged into traditional four-line stanzas, all the four lines rhyming, and when, following the French example, poets began to use the rhyming couplet instead of the older four-line rhyme, they made what were the first steps towards the reformation of Hungarian verse. But their most significant achievement was not so much this change as the introduction of the metrical principle based on the length of syllables. As the Hungarian language makes a clear distinction between long and short syllables, this metrical principle is perfectly appropriate to it. It developed in two different directions. On one hand, poets adopted the purely metrical unrhyming forms of Greek and Roman poetry. On the other, they introduced the rhyming verse forms of West European poetry, but here they ignored the stresses that emphasize the metres, and treated them as purely metrical. As in the Hungarian language long syllables are not necessarily stressed as well, in the rhyming patterns adopted from the West the metrical stress and the speech stress are independent of each other. As a result, a more flexible and smooth rhythmic pattern arose, parallel with the crisp and sharper rhythm of accentual verse, which provided the basis and technical devices to be exploited with such splendour by the poets of the nineteenth century.

Noble Amateurs of Literature

Among the many poets now appearing were those who had written poems for "the desk", and now came forward to take part in the literary movement called to life by Bessenyei and his fellow-writers. One of them was the greatly esteemed elder poet of the time, Count *Gedeon Ráday* (1713–1792), who after forty years of experimentation with classical metres and West European verse forms, hesitantly published a few of his poems, signed only with his initials. He was not really a good poet, yet the term "Ráday verse", given to the West European metrical patterns he introduced into Hungarian verse has perpetuated his name in the history of Hungarian versification. Kazinczy, in his *Memories of my Career,* gives a pleasant picture of Ráday happily discussing literature, history and theatre in his own library in Pest, or in the foyers of the theatre, and it was he who saw to it that the smiling count, night cap on head, was immortalized in a copper engraving. Both portraits picture him as the wise old grandfather of the Enlightenment in Hungarian literature.

Baron *Lőrinc Orczy* (1718–1789) and *Ábrahám Barcsay* (1742–1806) first made their names together with *The Poetic Effusions of Two High-born Authors* (Két nagyságos elmének költeményes szüleményei, 1789), a joint—and anonymous—production. They had previously corresponded in verse-letters with each other, and their literary background and education were very similar. The French type of education they had been given, the affinity in their attitudes to life, and the literary themes they chose in common largely accounted for their intellectual kinship. In both their poetry and their general views the feudal outlook and feudal traditions clashed with the values of enlightened culture. In Orczy the former was the stronger force, but his naturally cheerful disposition blunted the edge of the conflict between the two. His practical wisdom was based on principles of humanism allied to a stoical philosophy, but he was equally receptive to the idyllic mood of Rococo art. He praised the simplicity of village life as against the busy towns; his pictures of peasant life were affectionate, and he viewed that life from the point of view of the patriarchal land-owner who is at the same time also a philosopher familiar with the ideas of the Enlightenment and aware that peasant labour is the key to the welfare of society. Apart from his cheerful humour, the reader is impressed by the reality of his descriptions, which reveal him as an excellent observer, as, for instance, in the poem entitled *In Praise of the Inn in Bugac* (A bugaci csárdának tiszteletére).

Barcsay, who was in the Guards in Vienna with Bessenyei, was closer to the ideas of the Enlightenment than Orczy, and was at the same time more susceptible of doubt, and reacted to the contradictions of the time more sensitively than his friend. He was the first Hungarian poet to praise scientific inventions, such as the steamship and the lightning conductor, and he was also the first whose reading awakened him to the seamy sides of capitalist development—the pursuit of profits and of the ruthless morality of colonization. He also lauded the simple life as the source of happiness, but the sentiment permeating his poems indicates more the wounded soul escaping to solitude à la Rousseau than the complacent land-owner. His affection for the common people is equal to Orczy's, but he is less patriarchal. The few charming Rococo love poems he wrote stand out in the essentially intellectual and descriptive poetry of the age.

The Pioneers of the Classical Verse Forms

From the sixteenth century onwards a few writers tried to naturalize the classical verse form in Hungarian poetry; and as we have seen with Ráday, they continued to experiment with it in the eighteenth century as well. It is, however, curiously typical of literary conditions in Hungary that the men engaged in these experiments worked without the slightest knowledge of the attempts of one another. Indeed, in the late seventies and in the early eighties three priests, *Dávid Baróti Szabó* (1739–1819), *József Rájnis* (1741–1812) and *Miklós Révai* (1750–1807) all published poems in these verse forms, and fell out over their claims to priority. Although the heated and highly charged dispute began on questions of prosody, they never tried to conceal that their first interest was to settle the question of priority. But, like Ráday, they lacked the true poetic fire. What they were trying to prove was that the Hungarian language was an appropriate vehicle for classical metres, which could be naturalized in it even better than in German. Baróti Szabó was pre-eminent among them. At the beginning of his career he composed occasional verse reminiscent of the

Baroque style but lacking its high-flown quality, poetical epistles addressed to friends, but later his poetry came to acquire a more personal note, and even a political note in propagating the ideals of the nationalist movement as organized by the nobles. Among his poems on this subject, the allegory *To a Walnut Tree that Fell* (Egy ledőlt diófához, 1790) became particularly well known. His contemporaries often criticized him for the mannerism of his language, his unusual phrases, bold epithets, and strange inversions, but these are in fact the main merits of his poetry. He forced the Hungarian language into compliance with new rhythms, and created a poetic style which was both original and effective on account of its very strangeness, so preparing the way for the romantic style to come. *Benedek Virág* (1754–1830), who was a monk of the Pauline order, came to the fore only a few years later than these three pioneers of the classical verse form. His poems crystallized the earlier first attempts of these three men into a mature, developed form. His handling of the formal elements of poetry bore witness to his technical mastery; he adjusted his prosody to the range of Hungarian sounds, the sentences in his verses flow smoothly. Although the three pioneers of classical verse form did in fact translate the classics—and particularly Virgil—into Hungarian, their work was more akin to the Baroque Latin verse of high-school pupils. But Benedek Virág, who translated the complete works of Horace, had assimilated the spirit and attitude of that poet so entirely that they permeated his own poems. The universal ideals implicit in the Horatian odes are to be found in Virág's poems, with certain bourgeois overtones, with the result that they are uninfluenced by the nationalist movement of the nobles, for good or bad. Benedek Virág was a conscious artist. His poetry is clearly distinguishable from the older literary tradition with its Baroque forms; nor does he regard occasional verse as real poetry. Owing to the somewhat rigorous classical principles dictating the forms of his poetry, he lost a great deal of his popularity during the years of Romanticism.

The Poets of Sentimentalism

Pál Ányos (1756–1784) was the first poet of any eminence who introduced a more personal lyric tone into his poetry. He was in contact with all the major Hungarian writers of the time, and his poetry is shot through with a multitudinous variety of ideas and fashions in taste. In the spirit of the Enlightenment, he was in favour of social progress, and opposed the scepticism derived from Rousseau which characterized Barcsay. He was at one with the nobles who organized the movement of national resistance, and was more violently critical of Joseph II than any other contemporary poet as in his poem *The King with a Hat* (A kalapos király). As a spur to the revival of the old patriotic virtues he evoked the earlier history of the nobility, and in so doing started a trend whole-heartedly followed by the Romantic poets of the Reform Era. However, the most profound note in his poetry was struck by the tragedy of his own life: his own inner struggle when he became conscious of the conflict between the thinking and the way of life of the enlightened man of the age and the priest he was; the miseries of banishment, imposed upon him by the clerical authorities, his own illness, solitude and unhappy love. His earlier poems appear to be derivative and affected in style, but the sorrow and grief they express take on a deepening realism with time, as *To a Fading Rose* (Egy elenyésző rózsához); *The Complaint of an Unhappy Soul at the Faint Light of the Moon* (Egy boldogtalannak panaszai a halavány holdnál); and *When I was Heavy with Care on a Sleepless Night* (Egy terhes álomtalan éjjelemkor). It is primarily his images that strike the reader; the verse form he uses is still more or less the traditional two-beat twelve-syllable line, and his language as a whole is, in fact, rather diffuse.

Gábor Dayka (1769–1796), a poet who died young, and who expressed in his poems the sentimental attituoe to life within the conventional classical framework, was a favourite of Kazinczy's. Like Ányos, he too was a priest, and as a priest he too found himself faced with an inner conflict which, in his case, led him to abandon his priestly vocation. In his love poems the Rococo style, the elegant air, the echoes of antiquity, and the anacreontic form were coupled with a sober love of life peculiar to the age of Enlightenment. As with Ányos, it was this inner conflict and the unfortunate conditions of his life—an unhappy marriage and illness—that gave rise to more sentimental poems. Not that these events were directly mentioned in his poems; it was only the grief they caused that appeared. "Some obscure sorrow weighs heavy on my soul" is the beginning of one of his poems, *Secret Sorrow* (Titkos bú). The subject of his grief remained undefined; the poem rather expressed a mood concealed in the innermost recess of the soul than a definite feeling emerging into consciousness, and it is depicted with remarkable subtlety. He was a master of natural description; with a power of presenting the affinity between nature and the inner world of the human being. While Ányos employed the traditional verse form, Dayka also made use of innovations in versification. His poems are written in both West European and classical verse forms. It is probably due to the fact that his highly individual prosody was not found suitable for later poetry, and that his lyric poetry provided no variety in theme or mood, that despite his genuinely poetic qualities, he never became a living influence in Hungarian literature.

The Jacobin Poets

The three Jacobin poets, Szentjóbi Szabó, Verseghy and Batsányi, were connected by a common fate. All three of them were condemned for their part in the movement led by Martinovics. Their eagerness to promote the progress and development of bourgeois society can be seen in their multifarious activities.

László Szentjóbi Szabó (1767–1795), the youngest of these three poets, died in prison. In the course of his short life he worked in several fields: he wrote a play on the renowned king of Hungary, Matthias Corvinus, and he started working on a historical novel with a Hungarian subject. He translated parts of Rousseau's *Emile,* the famous work based on the thesis that "it is the common people who make the nation of mankind". But his chief claim to fame rests on his lyric poetry. It was influenced by the German Rococo songs of burgherdom, and was the kind of gentlemanly Rococo poetry that Ferenc Faludi wrote, only simpler and more straightforward in character. By using certain German formal devices but giving them a Hungarian colour, he produced poems which on occasion were very similar to folk songs. His verse tale *The Simple Peasant* (Az eggyügyű paraszt) enjoyed a deserved popularity. It was a type of poem rarely found at that time, in which the poet painted people, conditions and manners of speech with the kind of realism then found only in the works of Csokonai and Fazekas.

Ferenc Verseghy (1757–1822), whose father was a minor official, and who was orphaned while still a child, became a priest for want of anything better. Through his enlightened sermons, his unconcealed love affair with an ex-nun, his literary activities, and the part he played in the movement of Martinovics he came into conflict with his Church superiors. A variety of styles and literary tendencies meet in his poetry. Like Szentjóbi Szabó, he wrote Rococo songs at the beginning of his career. His musical education helped him to adjust the rhythms of language and music accurately to one another, writing verse for Haydn's and Mozart's music, and he also translated the libretto of Mozart's *Magic Flute.* His poems are principally love poems, full of an unrestrained delight in the joy of life. He also took his share in the political struggles of his time. He warned the nobility at the time of the 1790 session of the Diet to introduce bourgeois reforms, he translated a history of the world by that liberal-minded abbot, Millot, and he was the first to produce a Hungarian version of the *Marseillaise.*

In his narrative verse and prose, such as *Mátyás Rikóti* and *Gergely Kolomposi Szarvas* (1805), he drew pictures of provincial life in Hungary, which revealed an exceptionally keen insight. He was observant, realistic, satirical and comic turn by turn, but though he possessed the power of creating convincing characters, he lacked skill in the construction of his works, which perhaps explains why he failed to produce a really important piece of epic work. The impression of some insufficiency, some shortcoming, is always there. His literary works reveal the influence of Rousseau, Herder and Sterne, while his linguistic studies echo Adelung. As far as his role in the history of Hungarian literature is concerned, he is regarded as one of the forerunners of Romanticism. It appears, however, that Verseghy, who lost courage after he had been released from prison, and found the work of the reformers of the language in full swing, was unable to cope with the situation, and failed to produce works equal to his stature as a personality.

János Batsányi (1763-1845)

His extensive learning and talent should have made János Batsányi a leading figure in the literary life of the time, and it was indeed his ambition. However, the circumstances of his life required that he should leave his country; consequently, for the rest of his life, extending over half a century, he could only watch the development of the literary life in Hungary from a position of exile. He was born into a lower middle-class family of artisans living in Transdanubia. As a tutor in the family of Lőrinc Orczy he had the opportunity to read widely and deeply; he came to feel he had a vocation for literature, and some of his political views also date from this period. As a result of his quarrel with Kazinczy he took over the editorship of the *Magyar Museum,* which he had founded in Kassa with Kazinczy and Dávid Baróti Szabó. Batsányi supported the movement of national resistance, introduced by some of the nobles, but was at the same time an advocate of the ideas of the Enlightenment and of social progress. In the *Magyar Museum* he published a remarkable article on Bessenyei, which marked him as the first among his contemporaries to recognize his importance. He supported the literary programme set out by Bessenyei, but influenced by the nationalist movement, and also by the fervour of the poems of Ossian, which he also translated, dwelt on the national aspect of the campaign far more than Bessenyei. His poems on the miseries of the national past and the grievances and hopes of the present recall the atmosphere of the poems of the sixteenth-century rebels, and indeed anticipated the great patriotic poems of the Reform Era, and Kölcsey's *Hymn* in particular:

> *Lo, the patriot groans in his deprivation,*
> *Orphaned by his hopes he finds no consolation,*
> *And since he be homeless within his own nation,*
> *He utters but plaints and words of protestation.*
>
> (*A Stirring Answer to Benedek Virág* —
> Serkentő válasz Virág Benedeknek)

Batsányi's poems did not only establish a link between the struggles of Rákóczi and the campaigns of the Reform Era; they also unambiguously linked the Hungarian national movement of the 1790s with the contemporary situation in Europe. The French Revolution inspired one of Batsányi's finest poems, *On the Changes in France* (A franciaországi változásokra), as early as the first year of the revolution, that is, in 1789.

> *Ye countries and nations tried by vicissitude,*
> *Groaning in the throes of unseemly servitude;*
> *Unable as yet to break out in defiance*
> *From your ignominious, imprisoning irons;*
> *You whose blood Nature asks, you anointed hangmen,*
> *You, too, butchers of your faithful feudal bondmen,*
> *Come and foresee your fate, which as yet but tarries—*
> *But keep your watchful gaze steadily on Paris!*

The poem is as compressed and concise as an epigram. In its first four lines the poet regards the peoples and countries suffering under oppression, in the next two he addresses the tyrants of mankind, and in the final couplet he directs their eyes to the example of Paris. It is not only remarkable for its significant conclusion, but also for the profound emotional intensity of the author's passionate attack on tyranny. "My mind burns when I compose a poem on such matters," he wrote of another poem in words equally applicable to this, "and on such an occasion I try to express my thoughts and feelings as briefly and effectively as I can, and at the same time with words as powerful as possible. If I could, I would make my poems so compact that each sentence sets the reader's imagination on fire, and melts his sympathetic heart."

Patriotic ardour was the main driving force in his poetry in the period which followed the death of Joseph II, while at the same time he began to diss ociatehimself from the nobility he formerly supported, who were inclined to compromise with the Habsburgs. Torn by doubt and hope, he brooded over the fate of his native land and the revolution, seeing it at the same time in the broader context of Europe as a whole.

> *Will the world awaken from its deadly slumber?*
> *Will it ever break the chains that it encumber?*
> *Or to the century's utter shame eternal,*
> *Will it be toppled down, Freedom's new-raised altar?*

he wrote in a poetic epistle to Ábrahám Barcsay in 1792. But in *The Visionary* (A látó), he was ready to prophesy the victory of the revolution throughout the world. "That glorious nation has risen to be the redeemer of two worlds," wrote

Batsányi of the French. But even while he thus spurred on himself and his fellows, he was well aware that the forces of reaction which were gaining the upper hand in Hungary would stop at nothing to silence him. He was dismissed from his post, and was repeatedly prosecuted for the opinions expressed in his poetry.

Martinovics designed a leading role for Batsányi in his revolutionary move-ment, but the poet refused, as he had no faith in Martinovics. He was nonetheless arrested and, following on his spirited and justifiable defence of himself at his trial, was also condemned to prison. In that prison he wrote his finest lyric poems, the *Elegies Written in Kufstein* (Kufsteini elégiák). For all their revolutionary content, his earlier poems had been in traditional verse forms, which meant that their language and images were traditional too. The Kufstein Elegies introduced a new, softer, more sentimental note. In one of them, *Meditation* (Tünődés), the poet speaks to the moon from his prison window, but the moon is no longer the familiar cliché image, the companion of man, found in sentimental poetry, but in the context of imprisonment is given a new guise. *The Captive and the Bird* (A rab és a madár) is another poem that stands out with its soft lyric tone. As in the free verse of Klopstock or the youthful Goethe, the structure, images, phrases, and even verse form of this poem change as the flow and flux of emotion requires. As in a piece of music, in which the interplay of the individual instruments gradually grows into the leading theme climax and grand finale, so, after a series of irregular lines in the iambic metre, the concluding lines of the poem embody the message of the poet who is at once patriot, revolutionary, and prisoner, in the Alcaic verse form of the heroic odes:

> *To thee, Liberty! To thee he sings.*
> *You have no heart, nor senses strong,*
> *If you are but unmoved stone*
>   *By the sweet sounds of this our song.*

After his release from prison, Batsányi left Hungary and settled in Vienna, and in 1809 he married Gabriella Baumberg, an Austrian woman poet. Following the French occupation of Vienna he moved to Paris, probably because he was involved in the preparation and translation of the text of Napoleon's proclamation to the Hungarians. After the fall of Napoleon the poet was taken by the Austrians, and interned in Linz, where he remained for the last thirty years of his life. He continued to maintain his interest in literary activities in Hungary, but, partly due to his per-sonal antipathy to Kazinczy, he set his face against Kazinczy's innovations in the language, and he was gradually ignored in his homeland. Although his poems never again reached the standard of his earlier work in the nineties, several of them show that his revolutionary ardour remained unshaken. After he left Hungary his prestige increased in the outer world, and he was regarded as a distinguished figure of Euro-pean literature. His ode *Der Kampf* (The Struggle) appeared in Herder's periodical

Adrastea in 1803 without his name, but in 1810 the **Cotta Press** in Tübingen re-published it with a political essay accompanying it. It is a poem which reveals depression and disillusionment, but at the same time affirms the poet's undying love of freedom. It demonstrates, however, that the poet still entertained illusions about Napoleon, and his correspondence with Johannes von Müller, an outstanding Swiss historian and writer, bears witness to the active part he played in the intellectual life of Europe during the period of the Emperor's supremacy.

Sándor Kisfaludy (1772-1844)

The poetry of Sándor Kisfaludy is in many respect different from the poetry of all these poets. He first came before the public some ten years later than they did; he also received a different education, and his experiences and opportunities were also different. His achievements, not only in poetry but also in the formation of the reading tastes of the public, made him an architect of the transition to Romanticism. He came from a propertied noble family living in Transdanubia. In the early 1790s he served in the royal Guard in Vienna, there reading and educating himself as eagerly as Bessenyei had done twenty-five years before. His interest, however, was not directed towards the writers of the French Enlightenment, but to the contemporary German sentimental poets. He learnt Italian from his mistress, Maria Medina, who was a famous dancer at the Vienna Opera, and in 1796 he fought in Northern Italy against Napoleon, was captured and sent to Provence. In his case, however, both these events in his life could be regarded as stages in a profitable tour, at that time becoming acquainted with the poems of Petrarch, and later Rousseau's *Nouvelle Héloïse* through the attentions of his many loves. His diary reveals the portrait of a man with a heart as sensitive as the hero of any novel, fond of reading, playing the violin, meditating and dreaming, a lover of the sea and romantic scenery. The antiquities of the South inspire him to quotations from the Latin poets, mainly Virgil, and then he recalls the cold-hearted Róza Szegedy, the girl he met at vintage on the Balaton, and who refused him when he proposed to her in a moment of fervour. Róza Szegedy herself is described in his diary as an educated young lady and a "delicate soul", and thus eminently suitable to be the heroine of the romantic sequence of love poems he composed in Italy and Provence, in "plains full of melody". The sequence *The Sorrows of Love* (A kesergő szerelem) appeared under the pseudonym "Himfy", and was the first really successful production of its kind in Hungarian literature. The cycle consists of two hundred poems, is interspersed with twenty songs of a narrative character—a story framework for the purely lyric poems in the sequence which would make them more attractive to the reader.

In this sequence the influence of Petrarch is paramount. Its basically sentimental tone embodies all the various trends—Renaissance, Baroque, and Rococo. But at the same time Kisfaludy draws on Hungarian traditions as well. He may be said to have gatherep together in his work all the elements of Hungarian love poetry from the popular romances of the sixteenth century to Amade, Ányos and Dayka. Kisfaludy's sentimentality, however, differs from that of Ányos, Dayka or Kármán; despite its stylization and its bourgeois character it is more compatible with the taste of the nobility than the sentimental strain represented by these three. Kisfaludy, like them, writes of the secrets and the sweet pains of the heart, and clings to the feelings and memories of his own inner life as he contrasts them with reason, fate, and with the uncertainties and rigidity of the exterior world. But this confrontation of the two shows no signs of any desire for a new form of existence. It is the world of the Transdanubian country mansions that he inhabits which he infuses with his emotion in his poems.

Whatever new he produced in his language and verse form was also in complete harmony with tradition. He used the same verse form in all his songs; what is known as the "Himfy stanza" is composed of eight and seven-syllable accented lines, a favourite form in Hungarian poetry. This highly controlled verse form in its way recalls the sonnet, and it strongly influenced the intellectual and linguistic structure of Kisfaludy's poems.

The consistent use of this verse form almost certainly accounts for the somewhat monotonous quality of the contents of his poems, and for their unevenness in terms of art. It was consequently a little unwise of the poet, stimulated by the success of *The Sorrows of Love,* to compose another sequence with the same verse form and the same construction. The new sequence, *The Happiness of Love* (A boldog szerelem, 1807), was written after the poet had won Róza Szegedy as his wife in 1799. But the inspiration provided by happy marital love was less fruitful than the "sorrows" of love. Fortunately, in the new sequence the theme of love is coupled with other subjects; the poet takes delight in sketching the life of the gentry in their country mansions, in descriptions of scenery, which is linked with a patriotic fervour. One of the songs expresses his growing consciousness as a poet: he sings of the poetry of the heart, and spontaneous feeling as contrasted with "scholastic rules". This attitude, in fact, marked both his rejection of imitations of Baroque art, still popular in that period, and of the aesthetic principles of Classicism, and foreshadowed the coming of the Romantic age.

The lyric note of *The Sorrows of Love* and *The Happiness of Love* survives in those of Kisfaludy's romantic narratives also dealing with love, such as *Csobánc, Tátika,* and *Somló.* These poems are of interest more for their historical themes and the patriotic feelings they convey than for the actual love story. In them Kisfaludy makes use of several of the themes of the patriotic lyric poetry of the 1780s and 90s, handing them down, as it were, to the poets of the Reform Era. Such subjects, which the poet employs as a dire warning, include the defeats at the period of the Turkish invasion, the siege of Várna (1444), and the Battle of Mohács (1526)—disastrous events in Hungarian history.

As an "orthologist", Kisfaludy became confronted with Kazinczy and his followers, but when the battle for innovation in the language ended, nothing could prevent his poetry exerting a general influence. Only by then his powers seem to have been exhausted, and the plays he wrote around 1810 and between 1820 and 1830, and his late Romantic narratives, dating between 1820 and 1840, are of no real significance.

The lyric poems of the age of Kisfaludy, in fact, must rather be seen as a preparation for the poetry of the succeeding age than artistic achievements in themselves. Generally speaking, the poets of the period were more important as part of the process of literary history than for their individual work. There were, however, two really great poets in this period: Csokonai and Berzsenyi; and this fact makes Hungarian literature unique among the literatures of Central and Eastern European nations in that writers of similar stature in those countries appeared only in the age of Romanticism.

22 Mihály Csokonai Vitéz (1773-1805)

The career and work of no other writer better reflects the devoted search for new forms of expression, a search characterizing the literature of the whole period, than that of Csokonai. But it represents more than the mere search. He made use of everything he learnt from European literature, transmuting it in his own personal manner, and producing from the synthesis something original and integrally his own. The traditions of Hungary, moreover the elements of folklore in his poetry never date: they enhance its aesthetic value and accentuate its democratic content. He was a miraculously gifted poet, and his wide range of knowledge, acquired while still little more than a child, marked him out as something of a prodigy. When his first critic compared him to Bürger, he, in fact, underestimated him. A comparison with Burns would, indeed, throw more light in his stature as a poet, but it would be misleading, for it would overemphasize the popular elements in his poetry.

His Life

Csokonai's father, who was the son of a Protestant clergyman, was an apothecary and surgeon, and his mother was the daughter of a tailor in Debrecen. They lived in Debrecen, at that time a populous but rather rural town lying east of the river Tisza. Csokonai's parents were well-educated, with a considerable interest in literature. The boy was educated in the Calvinist College of Debrecen, founded at the beginning of the sixteenth century, and it was his teacher in the College, himself a poet and translator of the *Aeneid,* who was the first to discover his talent; another teacher of his, who later took part in the Hungarian Jacobin movement, first opened his mind to the ideas of the Enlightenment. In the late eighties and early nineties, Csokonai and a number of fellow-pupils, stimulated by the intellectual curiosity of the period, founded a society to study the literature of West European countries, the members each undertaking to learn a foreign language; Csokonai chose Italian, but within a short time he had mastered Latin, French, German, Spanish and Greek as well, and he went on to study English, Hebrew, Arabic and Persian. Yet he never left his native country, and at home preferred to wander about the country than travel decently by coach. He was never amditted into elegant society, and never treated as an equal by the upper classes; yet there was no one in contemporary Hungary who could have been more justly regarded as one of that community of geniuses who transcend the boundaries of space and time. He was very well-read in world literature; he knew the classics, the poetry of Ariosto and Tasso, the works of Hafiz and of his contemporaries, Metastasio, Gessner, Bürger, Matthisson and Kleist. He read Voltaire, Rousseau, Helvetius and Diderot, and translated Holbach. János Földi, the poet physician living in the neighbourhood of Debrecen, and Ferenc Kazinczy introduced him to contemporary Hungarian literature. The College of Debrecen was the "alma mater" of the poet in the fullest sense of the word, for his poetry, maturing under the influence of foreign literatures, was firmly rooted in the old poetical traditions of the College. His poems are linked to "college poetry" which embodied the centuries-old literary and popular traditions of poetic song that reached its apex between 1750 and 1800. With the combination of these two traditions, the popular poetic song declined, and a genuine poet was neededto inspire it with new life. The many members of the College indeed formed Csokonai's first reading public. In fact, Csokonai had become celebrated, and his poems spread both by word of mouth and in manuscript form before any of them were published. These poems of Csokonai that circulated in manuscript form are indeed much more representative of his work than the mutilated editions that were published during his lifetime.

1795, when the Martinovics conspiracy was crushed, was a turning point in Csokonai's career as a poet. For reasons that have remained obscure up to the present day, but probably because he was quite open about his advanced views, he was expelled from the College, and left the only community on which he could rely. From that time on he lived a feverish and unsettled life. In Sárospatak, where Bessenyei and Kazinczy had once studied, he studied law, but it held no charms for him. In the autumn of 1796, he attempted to publish his poems in Pozsony where the Diet met, in a series of booklets entitled *Diétai Magyar Múzsa,* but they failed to arouse any interest. Then, in Komárom, he tried to find help from among the nobles mustering their forces for the insurrection of 1797, but again without success. But in Komárom he met Júlia Vajda, whom he calls "Lilla" in his poems. She was the daughter of a well-to-do citizen, and she inspired the finest cycle of love poems in Hungarian literature, written at the same time as the "Himfy" sequence of Kisfaludy's. But he was penniless, and could not hope to win her hand. For a short time, from 1799 to 1800, he was assistant schoolmaster in Csurgó, which was a small town in southern Transdanubia, and then returned to Debrecen. There he was once again frustrated in his attempts to find work and publish his poems. He became more and more of a recluse, only maintaining contact with one or two *littérateurs* in Debrecen until he died of consumption in 1805, at the age of 32.

The Poet of the Enlightenment

The poet's first attempts at verse in the literature classes in the College immediately revealed his talent. They displayed not only a precocious competence in technique, and the essential requirements of style, but also originality and vision, and the "gift of insight". His first major poems were full of broad student humour, spiced with popular overtones, with a strong tendency to mockery and parody. (Such poems are *On the Inconstancy of Women*—Az asszonyi állhatatlanságról; *The Gods' Wrangling*—Az istenek osztozása; *The War of the Frogs and the Mice*—Békaegérharc, modelled on Blumauer's parody of the *Aeneid*.)

The burning politics of the nineties, and the advanced ideas in the air, provided the inspiration for Csokonai's works, for which he is justly regarded as the greatest poet of the Enlightenment in Hungary. Among them *Constantinople* (Konstancinápoly), attacking religious fanaticism, is particularly powerful. In this poem the imaginative description of the glamour and colour of the East, heightened by the erotic fantasy of an adolescent in the image of the Sultan's harem, is transformed almost unnoticed into an attack on religion. The images of the dervish, the mosque, and the paradise reserved for Moslems emphasize the oriental setting, but the poem develops and concludes in what is almost a triumphal hymn hailing the end of the prejudices created by religion. The attack on religion assumes a universal significance; and the victory of the progressive and advanced ideas of the Enlightenment following the abolition of religion is celebrated:

> *The spirit of love overflows the earth,*
> *Man his dear fellow embraces in mirth;*
> *Saint and plaintive voices vanish in the air,*
> *Bells chime, oh, so blissfully, as for a fair.*

It is Voltaire, of all the writers of the Enlightenment, whose rationalist, forward-looking influence can be most clearly perceived in this poem, but his other great poem, *The Evening* (Az estve) shows the influence of Rousseau. The description of nature here is coupled with social criticism, fused together in the lyric beauty of the poem. The poet escapes from the injustices of society to take refuge in nature which offers freedom and equality to all men alike. In the introductory section, the exquisitely drawn images of dusk in the wood are increasingly permeated with feelings of grief and melancholy until the expression of his emotion fills his canvas and provides a transition to the development of the theme criticizing the state of society. Here Rousseau's theories of the primaeval equality of man now lost, and the evils of the class society, take on concrete form in the poet's references to contemporary conditions in Hungary. And finally images of nature and social images appear paired together in contrast. The golden rays of the moon cannot be rented out,

151

life-giving air cannot be divided into sections by engineers, poor shepherds and labourers can listen to the song of the birds of the forest without payment, and the poet can forever be lord of the beauties of nature.

Both the formal design and the language of these philosophical poems, striking the reader with the freshness of their ideas, reveal Csokonai working along the lines laid down by Bessenyei. As in Bessenyei's philosophical poems, the verse form of these poems of Csokonai consists of twelve-syllable lines arranged into rhyming couplets, with all the characteristic features of the classical style. But they are rich in vivid and detailed images taken from life, and the thoughts they convey are charged with emotional intensity so convincing as to be free from the pedantry and aridity so frequently characterizing intellectual poetry.

Tempefői

In his unfinished play, *Tempefői* (1793–95), the picture Csokonai drew of contemporary educational and cultural conditions in Hungary is similar to that in Bessenyei's *Philosopher,* but marked with even more bitterness. The play deals with the efforts of the chief character, the poet, Tempefői, to find someone to help him publish his works, but all in vain: the count, the noble, and the priest all refuse, and the German printer even sends him to the debtor's prison. His picture of the opponents of anything new in literature, the shallow-minded, arrogant upper-class figures, the boorish suitors and poetasters of inferior taste is painted primarily with sarcasm and irony; but in some of Tempefői's outbursts the comedy grows beyond irony to touch on the verge of tragedy. The subject-matter is not only the tribulations of poets and writers; in this play the poet also launches an attack on the basic vices of feudal society. "Legions of army men idle at the court of lords, where they fatten on the toil of serfs; ... while the learned who work for the glory of the nation are starving ..." Tempefői is threatened with prison because in the end he is unable to pay the expenses of printing; but one is aware in one of the speeches of the reference in it to the persecuted writers who took part in the Martinovics conspiracy: "You, orphaned Muses of my country, never let posterity know that was there a time when the prisons of Pest were filled with men imprisoned because they felt for you and loved their country." Characteristically, Tempefői is suspected of spying for the French, but the simple truth is that he admires France for its revolution, proceeding with "giant steps towards perfection". Csokonai originally intended that the end of the play would reveal that Tempefői was himself a count, and that this would have solved his difficulties. He abandoned this plan, probably because he found such a solution inadequate in a play so full of revolutionary material, and the play was left unfinished.

The Rococo Poet

After the reactionary political change in 1795 that followed the crushing of the Jacobin movement, Csokonai's poems began to lose the boldness of tone which characterized his earlier philosophical poems and the other works which criticized society. In exchange, it marked an expansion of his lyric poetry of a personal character, based on the Rococo tradition which emerged in the early nineties. Here the poems of Metastasio, whom he translated, greatly influenced him and helped him find an appropriate and graceful lyric mode of expression which suited his temperament. The Rococo style opened up a world of beauty and happiness for the young poet, and provided him with an escape from the vulgarity of that vast market-town, Debrecen, and the rigid puritanical discipline of its College, and from the poverty, pettiness and boorishness of contemporary social life in Hungary. The young Csokonai, like Ányos, Dayka, Kármán and the youthful Kazinczy, who were all attracted to the sentimental style, was fascinated by the delicacies of the Rococo, alluring him with its vision of a cultivated life befitting a child of European culture. Through the beauties, delicacy and grace of the Rococo, which in Csokonai's poetry is coupled with a faith in the ideals of Enlightenment, the poet was able to rise above a society which he considered both evil and repulsive.

In his Rococo poems, Csokonai was the voice of joyous life and gaiety; it meant that the sentimental style then fashionable in the literature of the time, beneath which lay the sense of *Weltschmerz,* was alien to him. He turned his back on all the melancholy poems of "sepulchres", "gardens shrouded in mist", of the night, the moon and darkling cypresses, the melancholy poetry of the English poets, Harvey and Young.

What he wrote about in his Rococo poems was love: the Laura and Rosalie of his early love poems was the wife of János Földi, his poetry master, and expressed his infatuation and the erotic longings of an adolescent youth. His prose idyll, *Kisses* (Csókok), is similarly focussed on her. Later Lilla, that is, Júlia Vajda, became the heroine of his love poems. The poems are genuine, witty and delicate, in which all the subtle poetic devices employed serve a valid purpose. The idea of the beauties of life sweetened by art fascinated him, and his poems celebrated their prudent enjoyment. The love he exalted in his poetry is realistic even in its gaiety, and earthy in its eroticism. His poems are also very musical. Music was the most popular of the arts in the eighteenth century, and Csokonai as a poet corresponded to Haydn and Mozart as musicians. He was a master of the techniques of versification and could brilliantly and musically marry the old Hungarian stressed beat to West European metres within one and the same line, thus giving it a twofold rhythm. Rhyme was also used to enhance the musical effect. Csokonai uses pure rhymes instead of the feminine rhyme endings and the conventional consonant endings of

153

earlier Hungarian poetry, which, in turn, are unusual, and strike the reader with their newness and, at times, even with their playfulness.

Disappointment in love changed the spirit of his poetry. The Rococo did not, as might have been expected, give way to a sentimental strain, but the gay and playful mood, the poet's whimsical game with the emotions was replaced by a mature and profound lyricism springing from the pains and sorrows of his life.

The poems inspired by his disappointment in love mark the peak of his lyrical output. These poems reflect not only his frustration in love but also his consciousness that his life was a shipwreck, and all hope abandoned him.

The general theme of escaping to find comfort in the solitude of nature expressed in the earlier poem *The Evening* (Az estve), became a fact of life for him. What he described as the misery of society in *The Evening* became his own fate. The merrymaking of the rich, the tyrannical laws of feudalism, the inconstancy of man, the landlord's authority were all sources of pain; only in the escape to nature did he find understanding and sympathy. ("Grave forests, and rugged cliffs and rocks, echo my lament!") Only, he believed, in the bosom of nature, which fosters and stimulates poetic talent, can men live true lives. Like Rousseau, who retired to Ermenonville, he desired to live in the shelter of Tihany, the small peninsula stretching into Lake Balaton:

> *I suppose it's no miscarriage*
> *Nor against some legal code*
> *If I with a virtue, all disparaged*
> *Want to take up my abode*
> *In this coign of lake-locked land,*
> *And like a Rousseau in Ermenonville,*
> *Live a man and citizen.*
>
> > (*To the Echo in Tihany* —
> > A tihanyi Echóhoz)

Only there, released from the bonds of society, can he recover not only his rights as a human being and citizen in nature, but be free to be a real poet.

> *Sole mother o' virtue, Solitude,*
> *Thou hast made all sages good*
> *By spreading to meet infinitude*
> *Their souls and minds of humble state.*
> *In you the poet has his fancy's flight—*
> *Like lightning on a darksome night—*
> *When he creates appearance, essence*
> *And whole worlds out of nothingnesses.*
>
> > (*To Solitude* — A magánossághoz)

154

The poet who thus addressed Solitude, who could create universes out of his imagination, was at that time compelled to live on the charity of his host in Kisasszond, a small village in south Transdanubia. Yet if there were a topography of poetry, the groves of Kisasszond would certainly be placed beside the Lake District in England and Lamartine's beloved Aix-les-Bains!

The inherent musical quality of the Rococo style was present in all Csokonai's poems of this period. In his most popular poem, *To Hope* (A reményhez), the graceful, melodious rhythm of Rococo poetry is used to paint a picture of utter dispair.

The popular poetry of the people that coloured a good many of Csokonai's poems, easily assimilated to their Rococo style. But it was only in the second half of his career that he became seriously interested in folklore. The folk tale included in *Tempefői* was meant to indicate a boorish and out-of-date taste, but later he systematically collected folk songs, and his poems foreshadowed the role that popular story and song was to play in literature for generations to come. In a number of poems he tried to reproduce the very tone of folk song, and figures of the common people appear in his genre poems, such as *Poor Susan* (Szegény Zsuzsi a táborozáskor) and *Love Song to the Leather Flask* (Szerelemdal a csikóbőrös kulacshoz).

Some of the best of his work, the group of *Anacreontic Songs,* Csokonai wrote in the last years of his life. In them the Epicurean note of the school of Anacreon is coupled with an advanced philosophy of life; and the gay note of Rococo is coupled with a strain of mature Classicism, within which complete harmony is achieved between thought and expression.

The best of his last poems are marked with calmness and realism. *On my Pneumonia* (Tüdőgyúladásomról) he expresses, in fever-ridden images, the state of mind of a man tossing between hope and fear in his serious illness:

> *Stifling sirocco's hot assaults*
> *Waste and wither both my lungs,*
> *And icy winds of sepulchres*
> *Bring on fevers and tremors,*
> *An invisible hand has shot*
> *Sharp arrows just below the heart,*
> *And on the bone-vault of my chest,*
> *Two deaths are knocking merciless.*

The Mock Epic

Before the poet took up the post of schoolmaster in Csurgó, he lived in uncertainty, wandering from one country mansion to another in Transdanubia. It was around that time that he collected the material for his comic mock epic *Dorothea* (Dorottya, 1799). The poem is a parody, the trivial subject-matter decked out in epic garb, on the lines of Pope's *Rape of the Lock*. But it is also a satire on the rude and uncultured manners, the lack of national sentiment of the Hungarian nobility; and as such, can be linked to the play *Tempefői*. Csokonai's picture of the Hungarian nobility in this epic is, on the whole, realistic; it is reminiscent of Pushkin's picture of the life of Russian land-owners in his *Eugen Onegin*. In Csokonai's *Dorothea* the plot is deliberately thin, restricted to the carnival feast and the fight of the old maids and widows to secure husbands for themselves, ending in a miracle, which offers the poet little opportunity for a broader picture of society. He exploited, however, all the limited possibilities offered with the greatest skill, and his characters exhibit so many human and social characteristics that it gives the poem an added value. The mood changes from one moment to another; at one minute parody is predominant, at another satire or realism. Sometimes Csokonai's own views appear in the mouths of his characters—such as the nobleman who attacks cosmopolitan luxury; the peasant who condemns the immorality of the upper classes, though they are never, so to speak, "out of character". Nor does the poet himself become a revolutionary as in his *Tempefői,* but remains what he always appeared to the nobility, a wandering poet, happy when allowed to ride in the coach of a lord.

His Work

Csokonai's literary output was immense. He produced a long philosophical poem on *The Immortality of the Soul* (A lélek halhatatlansága), written for the obsequies of a noble, in which the poet, as a materialist himself, rejected such a belief, nevertheless set out to prove that the soul is immortal, even though his materialistic views made their way into the poem in his references to various philosophical and religious doctrines.

There is also the fragment of an epic poem on the Hungarian Conquest. In addition, he wrote a number of plays, and articles and poems on various subjects. His aspirations as an artist were, however, only partly realized, and taken as a whole it is an unfinished torso. But he was the first Hungarian lyric poet since Balassi to succeed in fusing contemporary European trends and the tone of the old Hungarian folk traditions in his poetry, and was consequently able to give an all-round, authentic picture of his own age. Yet, even in his own time, the most authoritative figures in the literary world failed to understand him: Kazinczy thought him less important than Dayka, and those in Debrecen who admired him as a poet did so mainly from a sense of local patriotism. The generation that followed him also failed to appreciate him at his just value, perhaps because his poetry was not a forerunner of Romanticism, but of realism. It was left to the great poets of a later period, Petőfi and Arany, to recognize him as their great predecessor. Ady in the twentieth century wrote about him:

> *Of all Magyars, he most ostricized,*
> *Yet lit me most the Magyar skies.*

23 Dániel Berzsenyi (1776-1836)

If Csokonai's poetry is graceful and vivid, Berzsenyi's is compact, concentrated and noble. For a long time he was called the Hungarian Horace in histories of literature, but to sum him up by describing him as the man who transplanted the wealth of themes and forms of classical lyric poetry and its human poetic attitudes into Hungarian poetry, is not enough. He has in fact no real counterpart among the contemporary poets in Europe. The Classicism of André Chénier, with its overtones of Romanticism, is based on entirely different attitudes. Hölderlin came closer to Greek ideals towards the end of his life, and Matthisson, whom Berzsenyi took as his model in giving his poems at once a classical and a contemporary sentimental tone, was altogether a less important poet.

His Life

Berzsenyi came from a cultivated middle-class family of noble origin, settled in western Transdanubia, at that time an area in which education and the arts flourished. He went to the Lutheran school in Sopron, a town close to Austrian territory, and consequently greatly under the influence of German culture. He never, however, finished his schooling there. Continually in revolt against his father and the school authorities, he neglected his studies in favour of the works of Horace and Gessner which he read with passion, while delighting in wild sports and merrymaking where he could show off his physical strength. He escaped from the bondage of school by joining the army; then left the army, lived in the house of relatives for some time, and again escaped parental authority by marrying the fourteen-year-old daughter of a family connection.

His marriage, however, marked a turning-point in his life. At the age of twenty-three, the wild, indomitable boy slowly changed into a sober, mature man, settled down on his country estate, and managed it with exemplary efficiency, determined to develop the lands he owned, situated in remote villages, and make a success of them.

Yet even so there was still something *outré*, something eccentric in his way of life which distinguished him from other members of the land-owning class. Society had no attraction for him; he liked to call himself the "Diogenes of Somogy" and the "hermit of Nikla". His standard of living was lower than customary with the lesser nobility. With his wife he could only discuss the management of the estate and household affairs; and when later, a well-known poet, he visited Pest, he shocked his fellow-writers there with his rustic appearance, his regional accent, and his preference for gipsy music over the delights of the urban theatre.

It may be that his behaviour was deliberately designed to exaggerate his crude and rustic mode of existence, in order to emphasize the great contrast between his farmer's way of life and his poetry. In fact, his poetry was not the outcome of his way of life, but rather a compensation for what was missing in it. *Fragment of a Letter to a Lady Friend* (Levéltöredék barátnémhoz) is one of the few poems in which the poet unambiguously reveals his own personal feelings:

> *I give you a picture of a vintage evening*
> *When, bidden to bed, my servants all retire,*
> *And I barely hear the merry-makers' dine*
> *Under the old nut-tree, poking up my fire.*
>
> *Drapes wrapt around, I sit leaning on one elbow,*
> *Gazing into the flames of a flick'ring candle,*
> *Fled into Fancy's world, dreams divine and mellow,*
> *And pass sweet, holy hours, not mundane but mental.*

In fact, when the day's work was over Berzsenyi would sit up till the small hours with his poetry. He wrote poems in secret for some six years, and for another six years cherished the hope that Kazinczy, to whom a common friend of theirs had forwarded some of his poems, would recognize him as a poet. But another five years had to pass before a volume of his poems finally appeared in print. The collection, which included the poetic output of more than fifteen years, contained practically all his poems to that time; few of them were dated, no chronological order was observed.

In terms of form, his work falls into two clearly distinguishable groups. The first group are in rhyme, and most of them are no better than the average sentimental lyrics of the age, not particularly outstanding in themselves. Where Berzsenyi truly finds himself as a poet is in the poems written in classical verse forms.

The Image of Prowess

The fact that Berzsenyi's patriotic poems date from the period of the Napoleonic Wars is of special importance. Perhaps no one has called up the great historical event of the era in all its ebb and flow in such monumental flights of the imagination as Berzsenyi:

> *The sea o' th' world runs riot, o Magyar!*
> *Angry Eris' wrath doth now prevail;*
> > *Her dagger, dipped in blood, inciting*
> > > *Multitudes of men to wild forey.*
>
> *Prussia's royal throne has toppled in a day.*
> *Blood paints red Adria's and Baltic littoral*
> > *And Cordilleras and Balkan*
> > > *Are overwhelmed in turmoil.*
>
> *Regions of Persian Baktria call for arms*
> *And rocky Dardanelles reverberate,*
> > *Barriers to nations are crumble,*
> > > *Bridles and tethers burst asunder.*
>
> (*To the Hungarians* — A magyarokhoz)

This poem is reminiscent of the ideas, images and language of the poetry of the 1780s, and 90s, linked to the image of prowess immortalized in the Roman Odes of Horace. This alone, however, could scarcely have been enough. It is the ardour that burns and flows through the poem like fiery lava, that gives its power. The emotional intensity that seems to exist independently of the subject, of time and place that serves, in his best poems, to proclaim the eternal virtues—moral integrity, courage, love of freedom. It is this quality in Berzsenyi's poems that accounts for their popularity in the Reform Era, when politics and ethical values were regarded as indissolubly connected, and it also explains why a poem of his, set to music by Zoltán Kodály, could help to inspire the anti-fascist movement of the 1930s.

Amathus

The more personal poems of Berzsenyi are also filled with the feeling that the time he lives in is out of joint. The poet can only find the idyllic world he is seeking in rejecting society, and attempting to escape from it. The opening lines of the poem in which he likens his life to a stream silently flowing through a grove of laurels, declare that

> *What plots are hatched by Alexander of Gaul,*
> *And the fearful lord of the glacial North,*
>   *What harbours are sealed, what ports threatened*
>   *By England's laureate glory, Nelson*
> *Recks me not.*
>
>   *(Amathus)*

The more personal themes are generally given a universal character, formalized in Horatian language. Some of his poems are similar to those of Sándor Kisfaludy, in painting the self-satisfied contentment of the gentry, but Kisfaludy's poems are full of the actualities of contemporary life, while Berzsenyi's images are comprehensive, general, undating; Kisfaludy enjoys life at his fireside, Berzsenyi takes refuge in an imaginary region which he calls Amathus, Tibur and the valley of Tempe:

> *Amor attends me and mild muse Pierian*
> *Offers me nectar and soft breast ambrosian,*
> *Here life's delightful and passes in mirth*
> *In purple either of Hesperides' girth.*
>
>   *(Amathus)*

His images and phrases are charged with classical allusions; he is fond of Latin words, classical metres, and an elevated style considerably removed from colloquial speech. Together they give his poetry a certain lofty nobility. It was around that time that Novalis wrote that it was the duty of poets to clothe the known with a dignity peculiar to the unknown, and this was precisely what Berzsenyi did.

Steps towards Romanticism

But was there not some affectation behind this mask of antiquity? Did not Berzsenyi pride himself a little ostentatiously on his knowledge, and indulge too blatantly in the role of the *poeta doctus*? The truth is that it was not vainglory that lay behind this cult of antiquity, but something deeper, the desire to escape from his surroundings. In his patriotic odes Hungary appeared as a new Sparta, a new Rome, its rulers as new Pericleses, Tituses and Trajans, and his contemporaries as Hectors and Catos. His own country home was Tibur and the grove of Ilyssus—all reflecting the dream desires of a poet never believing that his visions corresponded to reality. His poems expressed a constantly increasing disillusionment; the sensitive reader can see it in his adaptation of the wisdom of Horace by his continuation of the Horatian passage. "Dum loquimur, fugerit invida aetas, *carpe diem quam minimum credula postero*," wrote Horace, ending his poem on a note of reassurance. But Berzsenyi ends the first phrase differently: "While we speak, time flies swiftly away, *As the arrow or rushing stream.*" Here, the final sentence, with its two images, draws no final conclusion, as Horace does, the arrow and the stream sweep out to infinity.

Such details clearly show Berzsenyi's departure from the classical spirit. "His antique pose conceals the wounded soul and the aching melancholy of modern man. His intensely disciplined art reflects the self-control of the human mind; behind the pagan wisdom of antiquity lingers the resignation of a Christian. In his lyric poetry," wrote the critic János Horváth, "he praises contentment as one who longs for it in vain."

His Language

The peculiar charm of his poetry is largely due to his language. The Hungarian poets who flourished at the end of the eighteenth century did indeed subject their poetry rigorously to the discipline of classical forms and metres, but none of them as rigorously as Berzsenyi. In describing the language he used he compared it to the dramatic sound of a trumpet, and a line taken from his poetry eloquently illustrates how much energy and tempestuous passion it contains. "Like gun-powder and wrath, / It threatens most when stifled." His sentences are final, definitive formulations, gaining strength by repetition. It is not only strength, however, that his language is capable to express, but also gentleness, softness and melancholy, which he achieves through his choice of words and modulations of sound. Every vowel and consonant has its part in producing the desired effect. "The best words in the best order," wrote an English writer defining poetry. "The best sounds in the best order" might be applied to the music of Berzsenyi's words.

Influence of his Poetry

In literary circles Berzsenyi's poetry was generally regarded as the crowning achievement of the new Hungarian lyric; but his contemporaries were unaware of its real value and of the true nature of his poetic genius. Kazinczy introduced him to the ideas of the Enlightenment, which inspired him to some philosophical epistles. As poems they are less important than his earlier odes and elegies, but they reveal a good deal about the development of his attitudes to life.

The youthful Kölcsey's severe strictures on Berzsenyi's work, reproaching him for using dialect, inflated metaphors, and complicated metres, though devoid of malice, were undeserved in view of Berzsenyi's great talent as a poet, lacked understanding, and seriously impeded the progress of Berzsenyi's poetic career.

He began to indulge in philosophical theories to justify his poetic attitude, but became enmeshed in his speculations and lost courage. He aspired to recreate the harmony of Greek poetry to resolve at once the conflict between the Classical and Romantic ideals and his own inner conflict, due to the uncertainties he felt in his attitude to society, and the contradiction between his former and present views and ideals. He has left us few poems of that period, and in them the free flow of emotion has given way to philosophical reflection clothed in an almost impenetrable web of mythological images and classical references, particularly in his last poems.

Berzsenyi explained his attitude to Kazinczy, then dead, in one of his last works: "... I always liked him as a writer, and only opposed those harmful principles of his by which he turned the poetry of the Hungarians, which had already started on its way towards Greek and Roman ideals, in the direction followed by vagabond minstrels lacking all taste." He believed that the principles underlying his own poetry would fail to influence the development of Hungarian poetry later, but in fact the classical verse form, dynamic language, and majestic flow of his poetry exerted a tremendous influence on Vörösmarty, the greatest of the poets of the next generation. Indeed, Széchenyi, the great nineteenth-century statesman who roused the nation to a political consciousness of itself, quoted from his works and was loud in his praise. Berzsenyi, in fact, was both right and wrong in his judgment on the impact of his poetry on the next generation of poets. On one hand, it is true that the main line of Hungarian poetry did not develop along the model he gave it; but, on the other, it was irrevocably influenced by it. His vigorous poetic language in its classical metre, but breaking all classical bounds with its spacious rhythms and great accumulations of words, both appealed to, and inspired, the Hungarian Expressionists of the twentieth century.

The Romantic Literature of the Reform Era
(1820 to 1840)

24 Reform and the Romantic Movement

The Rise of National Consciousness and Romanticism

The spread of Romanticism and its increasing cultivation all over Europe is connected with the Napoleonic Wars, and the shock and ferment they spread through Europe from Spain to Russia. The Hungarians, however, were very largely onlookers. There was fighting indeed, but only in a small section of the country, and only for a short period (1809). The peace inside the country, and the demand for grain in the midst of the turmoil of war outside the country, and consequently the prosperity it brought to Hungarian agriculture, was more than enough to justify the insular complacency of the gentry. In these conditions, Napoleon's proclamation summoning the Hungarians to break away from the Habsburgs, met with no response: nor, unlike in Germany, Spain and Russia, did any national movement arise to fight the French. The hostility existing between the imperial court of Vienna and the Hungarian nobility, still the main driving-force in the political life of Hungary, came to the forefront again after the defeat of Napoleon. The movement of national resistance led by the Hungarian nobles, steadily growing stronger, was stimulated by the growth of similar movements abroad—the revolutions in Spain, Naples and Piedmont, the revolt of the Russian Decembrists, the wars of independence in Greece and Poland, and above all the 1830 July revolution in Paris, all of them attacks on the system maintained by the Holy Alliance. In the course of the sessions of the Hungarian Diet (in 1825–27; 1832–36, and 1839–40) it became clear that the movement initiated by the nobles had expanded into a movement demanding a specific political programme. Among their principal demands were national independence and a change to the conditions of a bourgeois state; although opinions differed on the precise interpretation of these demands and the order and measure of their realization. Yet, the reform movement, confused and contradictory as it was, led to one of the most glorious episodes in the history of the nation, the 1848 Revolution and the War of Independence which followed it.

Inspired by the reform movement, shaped by its different tendencies and agonizingly reflecting its hesitations, the Hungarian Romantic movement in literature emerged and began to flourish.

Hungarian literature has always been intimately connected with public matters,

167

but during what is known as the Reform Era, was even more closely involved with politics. The movement of national resistance led by the nobles inspired a series of historical works in the 1830s designed to strengthen the sense of national identity. Other peoples as well, who felt at this time their national identity equally endangered, and were forced to fight for their independence, also felt the need to justify their national aspirations and provide them with a historical basis. The work of the Czech historian, František Palacký, and the "Dacian-Rumanian" theory of the "Transylvanian School" served the same purpose for their respective peoples. Books with a historical content represent the branch of literature of most importance in terms of national progress. Among them the monumental work of *Ignác Aurél Fessler* (1756–1839), who wrote in German *(Die Geschichte der Ungarn, und ihrer Landsassen)*, proviced a valuable source of material for the Hungarian poets of the age, the Romantic concept of history of *István Horvát* (1784–1846) influenced a number of writers. Eager to glorify the prehistory of the Hungarians, he was frequently carried away by over-simplified or unfounded theories, and, much as writers in the other small nations of Eastern Europe overcome by the desire to exalt their national history, and consequently exaggerated their past glories. The Czech Vaclav Hanka even went as far as forging a heroic epic in order to strengthen the sense of national identity among his fellow-Czechs.

István Széchenyi (1791-1860)

The literature of the 1830s increasingly reflects the need for a bourgeois development. It arose to a large extent under the influence of the July revolution in 1830 and a peasant rising in northern Hungary. But a third influence was *Count István Széchenyi,* the great Hungarian statesman of the Reform Era. Full of ambition, this young Hungarian noble, born into one of the great families of the Hungarian nobility, whose youthful diaries present the picture of a Byronic hero, plunged into the current of contemporary public life around 1825. He was given a very different education from that received by the Hungarian ruling class, generally bred on Latin and law. He was fond of the great authors of European Romantic literature, Byron, Alfieri, and Mme de Staël, as a young man he studied economics, reading Franklin and Jeremy Bentham, and during his many visits abroad he saw the first development of the capitalist system. In his first important work, *Credit* (Hitel), published in 1830, he dealt with purely economic problems; but in the course of his analysis he pointed out that Hungary's position as a nation and her whole future depended on the realization of the transition from feudalism to capitalism. His writing is passionate, romantic, and dramatic, interspersed with shafts of ironic wit. Several of his phrases, concise, epigrammatic and profound, became popular sayings. "Many think," he wrote, "that Hungary once dexiste; as for me, I like to think it will exist."

The European Background

As the transformation of a feudal to a bourgeois state took on greater political importance, eyes were increasingly turned to the contemporary literature of Europe. Hungarian writing between 1820 and 1830, then concentrating on themes of the national past, crawled some way behind the more modern literary development in Western Europe, partly on account of its antiquated sentimental style, inherited from German Romanticism, and partly because the prevailing genre, the epic, was by then out of date. By the 30s, however, it had drawn level. For years Byron was the idol of the literary world in Hungary; in 1829 Walter Scott's *Ivanhoe* was translated into Hungarian; in 1836 the first Hungarian novel imitating Scott appeared; Victor Hugo, and French Romantic drama in general, became the principal literary models; and in 1837 appeared the first translation in Hungary of a novel by Balzac. The press provided information about life in Western bourgeois societies, and this, together with more frequent travel in the West, reinforced the influence of these authors. One of the most popular works of the time was a book by *Sándor Bölöni Farkas* (1795–1842), called *A Voyage to North America* (Utazás Észak-Amerikában, 1834). Both the author and the Hungarians who read his book were fascinated by the picture of American democracy he described, often comparing conditions there with conditions at home. He was enthusiastic, and saw none of the contradictions of bourgeois society. However, he condemned slavery. But there were an increasing number in Hungary whose reading had made them aware of the seamier sides of bourgeois development, and as a result, the Hungarian struggle against feudalism was coupled with a struggle against the contradictions of bourgeois society, and even contained elements of a Utopian socialism. And what complicated the situation even further was that the class leading the campaign for the introduction of a bourgeois system was still the gentry, often to be hopelessly confused in the conflict between the needs of the country and their own interests.

There was no effective bourgeois class at that time, which is why the search for a national ideal and national characteristics in Hungarian Romantic literature focussed on the common people and the peasants, as indeed in the literature of every nation where the bourgeoisie was either weak or lacking. It was Herder who insisted upon the importance of folk poetry; in addition to his collection of folk songs (1778), Percy's collection of Scottish ballads (1765), the fairy tales of Arnim Brentano (1806) and the Grimm Brothers (1812), Vuk Karadžić's volume of Serbian folk poetry (1815), and the Kalevala, edited by Lönnrot (1835), all testify to the new interest in folk poetry. "The driving force of the poetry of the nation," wrote Ferenc Kölcsey, one of the most outstanding poets and critics of the age, "is to be sought in the songs of the common people" (*National Traditions* — Nemzeti hagyományok, 1826).

It was the age of Romanticism which saw the emergence of the great poetic geniuses of the Poles and Russians, Miczkiewicz, Pushkin and Lermontov, and introduced the folk poetry of the Serbs and Finns to the world. There were also attempts to make Hungarian literature better known abroad, but without much success. Together with rather unimportant anthologies containing work by Hungarian writers who wrote in German, the anthology of John Bowring, *Poetry of the Magyars* (London, 1830) attracted attention, but it failed to arouse any permanent interest in Hungarian literature.

The Literary World

From 1820 onwards the centre of literary life was Pest, by that time no longer a small town, but a genuine capital city. After the age of Enlightenment had finally ended religious controversy in literature, regional differences, such as the conflict between the Transdanubian innovators in the language and those coming from the territory of the Tisza, also died away. In literature the early patriarchal feudalism gave way to bourgeois models, and two at least of the major poets of the time, Károly Kisfaludy and Mihály Vörösmarty, were able to make a living from their writings. Kisfaludy's Bohemian nature, however, kept him permanently impoverished, and Vörösmarty also had to compile a dictionary and a Hungarian grammar in exchange for his salary as a member of the Academy. It was around this time, moreover, that writers began to combine their serious work with journalism or the editorship of a paper, and noble patronage and the dependence on authority it entailed was no longer necessary. So when Count Esterházy offered the gift of an additional sum of money to Károly Kisfaludy for his *Aurora,* the most influential of the literary almanacs so popular at the time, he proudly refused it, while József Bajza stressed that literature should be a "republic" where rank and authority should have no place. Personal and informal contacts, of course, there were. In one of his poems Vörösmarty complained that in a country that produced such excellent wines, the poet had to content himself with the inferior sort; he promptly received from readers a consignment of some excellent wine. For it was around then that poets began to be esteemed and recognized as among the chosen of the world. One need only compare the fate of Csokonai to see the remarkable change that had taken place in some twenty or thirty years in the status and conditions of literature. With the growing links between literature and contemporary life—a distinguishing feature of Hungarian Romanticism—readers began to take an interest in the lives and personalities of the authors, with a greater vigour in literary life, as a result, and a closer relation between the writer and his readers.

Between 1820 and 1840 there were fewer truly important writers than between 1780 and 1800. The supporters of Classicism found themselves on the periphery of literary world, and for almost twenty years Hungarian literature was in fact represented by the contributors to an annual entitled *Aurora* (1822–1837), and later the periodical *Athenaeum* (1837–1843). From them sprang the Kisfaludy Society (1836), after the death of Károly Kisfaludy, the first leader of the Hungarian Romantic movement, and they provided the leading personalities of the Hungarian Academy of Sciences founded in 1825. Between 1835 and 1861, its secretary was Ferenc Toldy, and József Bajza was the first director of the Hungarian-language Theatre of Pest, which opened in 1837. The two of them, with Mihály Vörösmarty, the greatest Hungarian poet of the age, formed a "triumvirate", and, after the death of Károly Kisfaludy, they were in undisputed control of Hungarian literary life. Their literary tastes were based on the kind of Romanticism, prevalent between 1830 and 1840, as represented by Victor Hugo. "The new school firmly advocating progress," said József Bajza, "consists not only of the champions of language or literature but also all those who welcome progress of any kind."

The material aids and openings afforded to Hungarian literature were more than they had ever been before. Publishing became a profitable business, and a constant stream of books was assured, with equally assured earnings, however modest, to the authors. In addition, a series of literary almanacs and journals, including critical reviews or year-books, were founded at the time; and in the early thirties the kind of literary magazine long popular in Western European countries found its way to Hungary as well. The distinction between literature as such, enjoying a growing prestige, and scholarship and science became clearer and as a consequence specifically scientific and educational reviews began to appear. There was still, however, no adequate political coverage in the press since the brief, censored new items, without comment that appeared in the papers, could hardly be regarded as such; and when, in 1837, the great leader of a later period, Lajos Kossuth, circulated his own accounts of the sessions of the Diet and county councils meetings in manuscript form in order to avoid censorship, he was arrested and imprisoned. Nonetheless, despite these difficulties, the literary magazines, and especially the *Athenaeum*, provided a limited forum for the expression of political ideas.

Romantic Art

In the Reform Era music and the fine arts kept pace with literature. It was not only that they developed at the same time, but also that a more organic kind of connection was established between them. Although he was not educated in Hungary, the great composer of the Romantic period, Franz Liszt (1811–1886) was admired by his Hungarian contemporaries for the example he set by enthusiastically stressing his Hungarian origin, both in his words and in his works, and in him they saw the great representative of Hungarian art abroad. Indeed, he inspired one of the finest poems of Vörösmarty. It was around the same time that Ferenc Erkel (1810–1893), who took his subjects mainly from contemporary drama, and to whom Hungarian opera owed its success, started on his career. An artist of the period was the sculptor István Ferenczy (1792–1856), well known for his portraits of writers. He still worked in the classical tradition, and the best Hungarian painters of the time, Károly Markó (1791–1860), Miklós Barabás (1810–1898), and József Borsos (1821–1883) similarly represented the period of transition from Classicism to Romanticism. It was some twenty years later, around 1850, that themes from national history, popular in Hungarian poetry, belatedly appeared in the visual arts. But in the meantime, Romantic taste was fostered, on a modest scale, by the inclusion of steel-engravings in the literary almanacs in which the finest productions of the poets found a place.

25 The Emergence of Hungarian Drama

The Theatre in Hungary

"It is obviously and undoubtedly true that the heart of the nation can best be explored through the channels of poetic drama," wrote Kölcsey in 1826, in his essay *National Traditions* (Nemzeti hagyományok); and the writers of the time were fully in accord with him. Books were only printed in small editions, and the theatre could provide a much greater public for literature than the printed page. It was therefore of first importance that Hungarian literary works should be performed on the stage.

Yet, among all the modes of writing of the time, drama was the most under-developed. Although plays had been written in Hungary even before the age of Shakespeare, by Sztárai, Bornemisza and Balassi, and later by Bessenyei and Csokonai, contemporaries of Lessing, Goethe and Schiller, none of them had ever been performed on the stage. It would in fact have been difficult to develop a theatrical culture which would have stimulated the writing of plays: the absence of towns of any size, and consequently of a real urban civilization, delayed the progress of Hungarian culture in general, and in particular did serious damage to the theatre in Hungary.

Between 1800 and 1840 the growth of a theatrical life provided the pre-conditions for a thriving drama later. Although in 1815 the Hungarian-language theatre of the capital temporarily closed down, as it could not compete with the state-subsidized German-language theatre in a city still predominantly under Austrian cultural influence and operating to European standards, nonetheless, in the provincial towns the torch was kept alight. The first permanent Hungarian theatre was established at Kolozsvár in 1790, and plays were also performed at Miskolc, Székes-fehérvár and Kassa. In 1819, 1820, and from 1833 onwards, Hungarian actors put on performances in Pest, and in 1837 the National Theatre was opened under the name of the Hungarian Theatre of Pest.

The repertory of the theatre was somewhat mixed at the beginning. Stimulated by the foundation of the first Hungarian theatre company in 1790, Kazinczy—as has already been pointed out—set out to translate plays by Shakespeare, Molière and Goethe, hoping that these plays would be performed there. But owing to the actors' lack of skill, and the fact that they were geared to satisfy an altogether different sort of public demand, the theatre repertory was made up of mainly inferior plays. Even when masterpieces, like one or two plays by Shakespeare, were in fact produced, they were distorted to the extent that they were almost unrecognizable. The public preferred pieces with a Hungarian setting, so even the plots of these plays were transmuted into themes or characters from Hungarian history, so that King Lear, for instance, came to be identified with the Hungarian chieftain Szabolcs, one of the leaders of the Hungarian Conquest in the ninth century A.D. For a time the repertory of the German theatre in Pest exercised a powerful influence on the repertoire of the Hungarian theatre; if a play was a success in the German theatre, they tried to obtain a translation and produce it themselves as soon as possible. The most popular playwright in the early part of the century was Kotzebue, and the most popular Hungarian author was András Dugonics, whose adaptations were generally taken to be plays of his own.

There were two types of plays popular with both the Hungarian and the German theatres, the sentimental bourgeois play, modelled on Lessing's *Emilia Galotti* and Schiller's *Kabale und Liebe,* and the Romantic *Ritterdrama* springing from the German Sturm und Drang movement, such as Goethe's *Götz von Berlichingen.* As a general rule, practically all the many translations and adaptations of foreign plays, and the few contemporary Hungarian plays that appeared fall into one or other of these categories. József Katona, the greatest writer of tragedy of the time, was nurtured on the Romantic *Ritterdrama,* which, although frequently high-flown and dependent on elaborate sets and trappings, expressed genuine passion in a masterly fashion.

József Katona (1791-1830)

Like Csokonai, József Katona was born into a bourgeois family in Kecskemét, a market-town. While still a law student in Pest he worked with the theatre company there as an amateur actor. His passion for the theatre was increased by his undisclosed love for Róza Széppataky (1793–1872) who as Mme Déry has come down to posterity as a famous actress at the head of a travelling company which took plays all over Hungary. Katona acted, directed, translated and revised plays. Above all, he was passionately fond of history and, his literary apprenticeship over, he turned to historical subjects. But unlike the writers who cultivated Romanticism coloured with nationalism, he had no desire to join in the quest for ancient historical glories. He condemned the boasting about national glory, regarding it as an obstacle to the development of the Hungarian drama. His plays often confronted former great figures of history with posterity, to judge the value of their deeds. He was never an overt moralist, but preferred the play itself to offer conclusions on "what leads to greatness and how to become a genuine hero". In this he was probably influenced by Schiller's views on the drama that were propounded in his work *Die Schaubühne als eine moralische Anstalt betrachtet.*

Apart from an extempore comedy *The Rose* (A rózsa, 1814), Katona wrote four other plays, the first three of them being *Clementina Aubigny* (1813), *Žiška* (1813), and *The Destruction of Jerusalem* (Jeruzsálem pusztulása, 1814), on foreign subjects. Although they are fairly important plays in themselves, they pale into insignificance beside his principal work, *Ban Bánk* (Bánk Bán).

Ban Bánk

In the play entitled *Ban Bánk,* assumed to have been written in 1815, though the final text only appeared in 1819, Katona took as his subject an event in Hungarian history. In 1213, at the time of the Galician campaign of Andrew II, king of Hungary, his queen, Gertrude, who was of German origin and ruled the country in the absence of the king, was killed as a result of a conspiracy of Hungarian barons. Bánk, who was Ban, or Palatine of Hungary, played a part in the movement that opposed the queen, allegedly joining the conspiracy because the queen's brother had seduced his wife. The story is in Bonfini's Hungarian history, a work of 15th-century humanism which made its way into European literature, and was used as a source book by many German, English and French writers, including Hans Sachs, George Lillo and Grillparzer.

The subject could be treated as a historical play or a love tragedy; it is for the dramatist to decide whether to give greater emphasis to the political reasons behind the insurrection against the queen or to Bánk's despair over the seduction of his wife. Katona allowed neither of these two aspects to dominate the play at the expense of the other, but in fact interwove them, which may be the reason why the meaning of the play is still a subject of argument.

Katona's Bánk is not the triumphant national hero bringing about the fall of a vicious foreign queen, and who would therefore appeal to audiences of the past century cherishing anti-Habsburg feelings; nor, as some claim, is he a dependant of the king whose very existence is shattered by his confrontation with the queen on account of the seduction of his wife. Bánk is, in fact, a sober rational politician capable of judging situations and possibilities with discretion, of imposing a discipline on the emotion of others and himself, and one whom the consequences of his act, which he clearly foresees, and his anxiety to maintain the peace of the realm, deter from becoming the leader of the conspiracy. He is also too intelligent to believe that revenge could compensate for the infamous wrong his wife has suffered. Yet he kills the queen; he can do no other in the intolerable situation in which his country finds itself. For him too, as for the Prince of Denmark, "the time is out of joint", indeed a parallel can be drawn between Hamlet and Bánk in several aspects of their characters. "No way but this," says Bánk on the violent deed he is contemplating.

The play, however, does not end with the death of the queen. In the last act, the returning king pronounces judgement. The justice of Bánk's act is, in fact, beyond doubt. "In any case, she had to die, for otherwise our country would have been destroyed by civil war," says Bánk, and the king cannot help repeating these words. "It was just that the queen died, otherwise our country would have perished." Bánk's act as the revenge of a husband is also fully justified, and even though it cannot be satisfactorily proved that Gertrude is also cast in the role of a bawd, and the king can consequently insist on her innocence in this respect, it can also be accepted that it is a revenge directed against a queen instigating her brother under her protection to evil, and humiliating and expelling the woman who fell victim to his lust. Yet Bánk is destroyed. He who always maintained that the consequences of a violent deed were unpredictable, lost his wife in the chaos following the death of the queen. Her former seducer had her murdered by way of revenge. "It was not this—not this I desired," were Bánk's words over the body of his wife. It is not the king condemning him, but the death of his wife, in which he is forced to see the unpredictable but logical consequence of his violent act that finally destroys him.

As a general rule, Katona's plays do not end in tragic deaths but in the reconciliation of opposites, counterbalancing losses with triumphs. In *Ban Bánk* both Bánk and the king lose their wives, but peace is restored with the death of the queen, by the ending of acts of revenge, and the decision not to punish Bánk. But reaching beyond individual tragedies, in the plays of Katona is his unflinching faith in the survival of the nation, and the peaceful progress of the country. It is the faith of the men of the Enlightenment in the future that animates the play and makes it one of the precursors of the Reform Era.

Katona's own plays could not be produced on the stage in his lifetime. The censorship bore more heavily on the theatre than on the published word, and certainly no plays dealing with rebellion against a monarch could be admitted. When, in the 1830s, *Ban Bánk* came to be performed, it was more its democratic tendency, conveyed through the peasant figure of Tiborc, reflecting the national sentiments of the period, that appealed to the audience than Bánk's mental and emotional struggles and his personal tragedy. The first reviews of the play show that it took some time for the critics to come to terms with it. *Ban Bánk* was originally written for a competition for the play which was to open the permanent theatre in Kolozsvár, and was rejected. Not without some reason, though, exaggerating their importance, the critics, who belonged to the generation of the Romantics, criticized the inconsistencies displayed in some of the characters, and found some of the episodes clumsy and lacking in sufficient motivation. János Arany and Pál Gyulai were indeed the first in their critical analyses to consider *Ban Bánk* as a masterpiece, but they were primarily preoccupied with the characters and the tragic element in the drama. It was only in the twentieth century that it came to be seen that the essential virtue of the piece lies in its growing dramatic tension, in its atmosphere of latent passion, in its feverish, yet controlled and expressive dramatic language, and in its organic unity of action and diction. Here Katona outstrips all his Hungarian contemporaries and successors, and can be compared to the greatest representatives of the genre.

Katona wrote no more plays after *Ban Bánk,* and as none of them found their way to the stage, he lost interest in writing, gave it up, and returned to his native town, Kecskemét to practise as a lawyer, ending as Attorney-General. He saw with bitterness that the road to success in the theatre did not run through the higher regions of art. "The play of the dramatist... who aspires to fame," he wrote in a work on the drama in Hungary, "need not be well-composed, only has to be full of vainglory. Nor should it speak of splendid *deeds,* it is enough if it is stuffed with *boastful references* to them; and once a writer acquires such a manner of writing, he will be considered in Hungary as the phoenix of dramatic art." And in saying this, Katona must surely have had Károly Kisfaludy in mind.

Károly Kisfaludy (1788-1830)

Károly Kisfaludy was the brother of the poet Sándor Kisfaludy; yet for him coats of arms, social rank, and landed estates had no importance. Of a rolling disposition, he became a soldier, then a painter, and eventually, an unexpected stage success turned him into a writer. The Székesfehérvár company of actors, who occasionally acted in Pest, put on a whole series of historical plays he had written. Later on even the dramatist was ashamed of these plays, which include *Tartars in Hungary* (A tatárok Magyarországban), *Ilka* and *Mária Szécsi.* Nonetheless, he went from success to success. His best tragedy was *Irene* (1820), a subject for drama which frequently recurred in the European drama. Kelemen Mikes made the first mention of it in recounting the tale in one of his letters. The Sultan Mohammed, who captured Constantinople, is captivated by a beautiful prisoner, Irene, who feigns love for him for the sake of her subjugated countrymen. The viziers and pashas murmur against her growing power over the Sultan, and he, in turns, learns that she still loves her Greek betrothed, and kills her. Both Mohammed, frustrated in his love, and the girl, who sacrifices her love for the sake of her country, are legitimate subjects of tragedy. But both characters are essentially passive, and the decisive episode comes almost accidentally, which prevents the full development of a tragic climax. On the other hand, the psychologically accurate penetration into character and the exquisite texture of speech, make of *Irene* a piece worth attention.

But Kisfaludy's comedies, such as the *Suitors* (A kérők, 1817), *Rebels* (A pártütők, 1819), and *Illusions* (Csalódások, 1828) were more successful than his tragedies. The plots are very often the machine-made situations popular at the time, and the characters stock types; it is not the technical skill of the dramatist that is noteworthy; it is the picture of contemporary upper class that emerges from these plays. Following in the steps of Bessenyei, in his *Philosopher,* and Csokonai, in his *Tempefői,* Kisfaludy attaches great importance to the social and cultural background of his creatures in establishing their character. Here is the foppish aristocrat imitating foreign manners, the lawyer with his Latin affectations, and there is obvious personal knowledge behind the somewhat unsympathetic portrait of the uneducated village noble. He is most sympathetic to those of his characters who advocate the transformation of a still feudal society into a bourgeois one, who are the spokesmen of enlightened ideals, who regard the cultivation and development of the Hungarian language as a patriotic duty. Kisfaludy also wrote a few comedies on historical subjects, all centring on the picture of a noble and patriarchal Matthias Corvinus, which can be regarded as the precursors of the cult that sprang up round the figure of the famous fifteenth-century Hungarian monarch in the Reform Era.

The Successors of Katona and Kisfaludy

The foundation of the National Theatre in 1837 was not in itself enough to stimulate the writing of the drama in Hungary. Quite understandably the great majority of the Hungarian plays put on between 1830 and 1850 have sunk into oblivion. Yet it is worth mentioning two who have been forgotten, Ignác Nagy and László Teleki.

Ignác Nagy (1810–1854) followed Károly Kisfaludy in his type of social comedies. Voicing the attitudes of the more liberal-minded of the public, he used them to attack the conservative nobles spreading their reactionary views abroad. The fact that his tone is sharper, more direct than that of Kisfaludy indicates the growth of democratic sentiment since Kisfaludy's time. His best comedy, *The County Election* (Tisztújítás, 1843) reveals the corruption of public life through the exposure of the abuses of the elections.

László Teleki (1811–1861) was the ambassador sent to Paris by the Hungarian revolutionary government of 1848–49. After the failure of the War of Independence, he was forced to emigrate, and was a leading personality among the Hungarian emigrés until the machinations of the Austrian Government drove him to suicide.

His only play, *The Favourite* (A kegyenc, 1841), was written in the tradition of Katona's *Ban Bánk*. Here again we have a distinguished man of high rank, Petronius Maximus, coming into conflict with a tyrant, the Roman Emperor Valentinian III, and the motif of revenge for the seduction of his wife is also here. Teleki's hero, however, lacks the strong moral foundation of Katona's; nor is the psychological treatment very profound. Yet its dramatic tension and its attack on tyranny qualify it for a certain amount of attention.

In recent times the modern poet and dramatist Gyula Illyés has revised the play, and has also written a tragedy on the life of Teleki, *The Eccentric* (A különc).

26 Romantic Poetry

The Common Voice of Romantic Poetry

Following a period which saw a great variety of authors, styles and subjects, in the age of Romanticism the general voice and style of lyric poetry and narrative verse was more of a pattern. The previous period had seen the cultivation of sentiment encouraging middle-class attitudes, the glorification of Hungarian history, the preference for a noble and often affected "sublimity", which nonetheless went hand in hand with the worship of reason. In the same way a harking back to folklore and folk poetry went with the introduction and use of new principles of versification, while retaining the old Hungarian line, all appearing as separate and even opposing tendencies. The new era of Romanticism assimilated and integrated them all, and they emerged as the constituent elements of a Romantic poetry whole and entire in itself. Its main characteristics were originality of content and a strong predilection for a national colouring and national background, which in turn distinguished it from the poetry of the previous age.

Lyric poetry and narrative verse were more connected in that period than formerly. The Romantic epics of the age are stamped with the desolation and melancholy of the poems of Ossian, and lyrical ballads and romances, as minor epic or narrative forms came to dominate the field of poetry, while more mundane narrative subjects became themes for prose; which is why lyric poetry and narrative or epic verse are considered together in any discussion of Romantic poetry, and why a separate chapter deals with the prose narratives that became increasingly important.

The first poems of *Károly Kisfaludy*, a pioneer of the new poetry, show the influence of his elder brother Sándor. While consistently retaining his patriotic sentiments in later life, yet on the question of language he followed the "neologist" theories of Kazinczy which, as previously explained, meant the enrichment of the language with new words and technical expressions, and even adopted the rhymed metrical verse form which Kazinczy favoured, creating a form of poetry harmonious in language, style and content. In marked difference from the unambiguously lyrical quality of his brother's work, his poems are reflective, cerebral, yet full of grace and delicacy. His finest poem, an elegy, *Mohács* (1824) symbolizes an attitude to the Hungarian past, Romanticism coloured with national pride. It appeared in *Aurora* in 1826, on the three hundredth anniversary of the defeat at Mohács, which led to the hundred and fifty years of occupation by the Turks. The subject links the poem with the historical epics of the previous decades, and in particular with the romances of Sándor Kisfaludy, but it remains essentially a lyric poem. Its conclusion, resolving the melancholy engendered by the memory of Mohács, invoking the present and the future, is remarkable for the fresh, original thought there expressed, anticipating the time when the Reform Era marked by the pioneer work of István Széchenyi will finally come to fruition.

> *Hence ye, morose images, visions of gloom disappear now,*
> *After so many adversities rises a new sun on us;*
> *Hungary lives, Buda stands yet, let the past be a warning:*
> *Ardent in love for the land, let's look forward with trust.*
>
> *(Mohács)*

In the poems of Károly Kisfaludy, such as *The Ages of Man* (Az élet korai), and *The Two Sailors* (A két hajós), the theme of human life is treated in a profoundly philosophical and allegorical manner; they are also pioneer works of their kind. An objective treatment of experience, and a love of philosophical meditation also distinguish his love poems, though on occasion, the individual and personal quality of his experience break through to overwhelm the more intellectual approach, as in the poem *Song at Dusk* (Az alkonyi dal). Yet, somewhat his name is rather enshrined in the history of Hungarian literature than in the minds and hearts of readers. But his influence can be clearly seen in Vörösmarty's, and even Petőfi's, work.

The poems in which he experiments with folk song represent a new mode of writing for him. The German philosophical historian, Herder had made a strong and unhappy impression on Hungarians by declaring that "die Ungarn sind jetzt unter Slawen, Deutschen, Wlachen und anderen Völkern der geringere Theil der Landeseinwohner und nach Jahrhunderten wird man vielleicht ihre Sprache kaum finden," and in the age of Romanticism the reaction of Hungarians was to stress the importance of Hungarian folk song and tradition. Kisfaludy, however, regarded folksong as only suitable for homely and rustic subjects. He must, however, be given credit for the fact that in the course of his folk-poetry experiments, he drew attention to several formal elements in Hungarian folk songs.

There is no clear-cut borderline between his ballads and his romances in environment and setting. They are in part reminiscent of the Romantic narratives of his brother and in part of the wildly Romantic plays of the time, including his own. In faot, the poets who succeeded him, not only outstripped him in the field of the short historical epic, but by producing far finer work on the same themes, relegated his own poems to oblivion. The most remarkable of his epigrams—*Xenias* (Xéniák, 1820)—are on a rich variety of subjects, and include trenchant and witty comments on other writers. These epigrams are markedly influenced by Kazinczy's epigrams, *Thorns and Flowers* (Tövisek és virágok), but the influence of Goethe and Schiller can also be observed.

Ferenc Kölcsey (1790-1838)

Ferenc Kölcsey was the most profound of the thinkers among the Hungarian Romantics. A man of uncompromising morals, he took part in public life, and as "the saintly man", as he was called, embodied the national and bourgeois aspirations of the period. He was born into a Protestant noble family, inhabiting the part of Hungary that lay north of the river Tisza. A thin and sickly child who lost an eye in childhood, he was early left an orphan. Already as a pupil at the Debrecen College he was shy and reserved in character, passionately addicted to reading at a very early age and, like Csokonai twenty years earlier, he laid the foundations of his wide-ranging knowledge at that school, which gave him a grounding in world literature, philosophy and aesthetics. Circumstances forced him to spend most of his life in rural solitude; on one occasion he did not stir out of his country residence for a year. Yet his prolific reading left him better informed on intellectual developments in Europe than many of his widely-travelled contemporaries. Not long after Goethe had produced the concept of *Weltliteratur,* Kölcsey wrote that "nowadays the English go to Rome, the citizens of Rome to Paris, the French to America, the Americans seek out the land of Hungary, and heaven knows where the Hungarians are. The newspaper editor now writes for the world at large, the English and French novelists make hearts throb on five continents, and thus may rightly regard the whole world their own. People today live in a single, huge common country..."

As a poet Kölcsey was originally influenced by Csokonai, but later, under Kazinczy's sway, he developed a preference for the ideals of German Classicism, and was attracted to the sentimental trend in literature. His poems of that period are distinguished by a plaintive note, a desire to escape from the realities of the world, and an indecision of mood and feeling, as in *Feelings Suppressed* (Elfojtódás, 1814). It conveys the same indefinite sensation of sorrow as the poems of Dayka, the sentimental poet of the Enlightenment. In Dayka, however, the melancholy is mitigated by the formal discipline of Classicism, as in *Secret Grief* (Titkos bú), while in Kölcsey both the verse form and the language help to accentuate his distress:

> *Oh, weep ye, weep ye, weep ye*
> *As none have wept before,*
> *Lamenting gladness past now,*
> *As none have wept before,*
> *When pain's embrace's past now,*
> *Can ye weep as none before?*

This example from his first period is typical of the vague *Weltschmerz* permeating them, and his obsession with unapproachable ideals redeemed by the sense of patriotism they also express. Not that Kölcsey ever abandoned the faith of the Enlightenment that informed his youth, or rejected the universal human ideal expressed in Goethe's Classicism. On the contrary, he extended it, reinterpreting it in the light of later ideas. "I hold the view that it is not harmful indifference excluding all patriotic and national feelings that makes one a citizen of the world," wrote Kölcsey in a letter, in 1816. "One should be concerned with the whole mankind, yet at the same time should retain that sweet and almost instinctive feeling binding one to one's native land. The two are compatible, just as human love is compatible with paternal and filial love."

Kölcsey's first outstanding patriotic poem, following *Come, Rákóczi, Come, Bercsényi* (Rákóczi hajh, Bercsényi hajh, 1817), in which he boldly recalls the struggle for independence led by Rákóczi, is the *Hymn* (Hymnus, 1823), which was set to music by Ferenc Erkel in 1844, and has since become the Hungarian national anthem. The framework for the poem is an invocation to God in two stanzas, of eight lines each. Interspersed are six stanzas surveying the history of the country, dogged by disaster and misfortune. The Hungarians suffered under wars with the Mongols, wars with the Turks, and internecine strife. And the present, he declared, was also sad, "... no freedom grows from the blood of the dead." Yet, the dialectic nature of the poem allowed for hope: this nation has already bought absolution for its past and future by its sufferings. The introduction of the theme of sin and punishment, and the religious thinking which lies at the centre of this poem, written by an enlightened and rationalist poet, might appear to us curiously out of date. Yet the presence of this religious strain serves the same purpose as the deliberate use of archaisms in the language; it links the poem to Hungarian patriotic poetry of the sixteenth and seventeenth centuries. The subtitle of the poem is in fact a reference to this deliberate design: "From the Stormy Centuries of the Hungarian Nation." The *Hymn* is not related to any specific historic situation in the past; the message it expounds is universal, of general import.

The ode *To Liberty* (A szabadsághoz, 1825), echoes the call to freedom voiced by the European Romantic movement of the eighteen-twenties, and the allegorical female figure of Liberty visualized recalls the painting by Delacroix, *Liberty Leading the People* (1830).

In his essay entitled *National Traditions* (Nemzeti hagyományok, 1826), Kölcsey did not fail to stress the fact that Hungarian Romanticism took a decided turn towards folk literature, and he saw the preservation of national characteristics in literature as dependent on preservation and adaptation of such traditions. This is reflected in his poems. He began to adopt the tone and spirit of folk songs, as in the fine love poems *Withering* (Hervadsz, hervadsz...), *In the Barge* (Csolnakon), *Evening Song*

183

(Esti dal), *Desire* (Vágy), and *Mournfully it Sounds* (Búsan csörög). At the same time his intellectual poetry was more strictly controlled and its expressiveness increased. The *Wine Song* (Bordal, 1822), or the *Vanitatum Vanitas* (1823) on the vanity of lofty aspirations, must have been inspired by the sense of grievance implicit in folk songs. They reveal that the poet who in a lighter mood, as it were, proclaimed that all great aspirations were vain, suffered intensely in reaching this conclusion.

Patriotism and Progress

His personal development and his close study of philosophy more and more convinced Kölcsey that the supreme value of human life lay in action, and it was in this belief he plunged into public life. Supporting as he did the double cause of patriotism and progress he joined the struggle for national independence and the liberation of the serfs, at first in his native county, Szatmár, and then in the session of the Diet in Pozsony. In his preoccupation with public affairs at that time he could not afford much time for writing. But it was then that constantly confronted with the struggle between ideals and reality which his public activities involved, his patriotic poetry took on a vigour and directness it had never known before. As with other contemporary poets, the development of his views can best be seen in his epigrams. He summed up the fruit of his philosophical and historical speculations in the conclusion that indulgence in mourning the tragic events of the past was incompatible with the spirit of the age, that men should look to the future instead and to opportunities for action affecting the life of whole of society, and this was expressed in his poems *The Castle of Huszt* (Huszt), *On a Memorial Leaf* (Emléklapra), and *Memories of Struggle* (Versenyemlékek). But, as his *Diary* on the proceedings *of the Diet* (Országgyűlési napló) bear witness, the depressing vacillations that on occasion hampered the struggle of the party of reform, seriously troubled him. "It is always his faith in his own strength and in his own army that makes a hero what he is. But when the soldiers will not draw their swords at his signal, but will calmly see their leader surrounded by the enemy, how and with what feelings, I ask you, can he command his army in a new battle?" And many times in his political struggles must Kölcsey have felt himself such a deserted leader. It is basically this experience that gave rise to his last great poems, first among them being *The Song of Zrínyi* (Zrínyi dala, 1830), and *Zrínyi's Second Song* (Zrínyi második éneke, 1838), expressing his despair over the fate of the nation, and conveying a vision of the nation struggling with its threatened death. For his achievement in expressing patriotic sentiment in genuine poetry, Zrínyi, the great poet of the seventeenth century, became the literary model of the Hungarian poets of the Reform Era, and this is the meaning of the reference to him in the title, for the subject-matter of the poems does not deal with Zrínyi or his period, but with Kölcsey's own age. Both these poems are in the form of a dialogue: in the first the poet speaks to a Wanderer, that ever-popular figure in Romantic art; in the second he holds a conversation with Fate. Again, in the first poem, the glorious ancestors of the present generation, willingly sacrificing themselves for their country, are contrasted with their degenerate successors, and in the second the poet forecasts the destruction of the nation, symbolized as an unhappy mother brought to disaster by the baseness of her children. The conclusion of both are terrifying:

> *Wanderer halt! Base in blood the mother,*
> *Gone is the race, replaced by another,*
> *Heartless, weak in mind, degenerate;*
> *And the noble folk that learnt to labour*
> *And in lab'ring won rewards with sabre*
> *Disappeared and but its name's remembered.*
>
> (*The Song of Zrínyi*)

> *The four rivers shall see a home renewed,*
> *A different hymn and men of different mettle;*
> *A more delightful aspect wear the land,*
> *Enchanted he who comes to know this scape.*
>
> (*Zrínyi's Second Song*)

Herder's words that the Hungarian people were doomed to disappear must have sunk deep in the mind of the writer of these verses, and of his readers. It should be remembered that Poland had been dismembered, and its unsuccessful insurrection of 1830–31 had taken place, as it were, before their eyes, in order to appreciate the real sense of possible extinction that possessed the minds of Hungarians, and that consequently, when Kölcsey wrote of the death of a nation, it was no direful poetic image, but a real danger he was envisaging. Not that these two poems are without hope or courage. In his *Diary* on the proceedings *of the Diet*, Kölcsey made it clear that he regarded the main task of the country was to "achieve the liberation of the serfs", that "instead of the seven hundred thousand souls whom idleness and im-poverishment had made degenerate [i.e. the gentry], the country should gain ten million people [i.e. the serfs] who could be raised to a better fortune." Similarly, in these poems the object of the poet's wrath was the leadership of the nobility. He despaired at the sight of the nation being brought to the brink of destruction through the sins of its leaders, though at the same time the destiny of the country could still be changed: "Destroy my tribe and all its horror; Let the curse lie on the ashes of the dead, but spare the country, our bounteous mother, for her to produce better sons who will protect her." The emotional background of the poem is not despair, but rather an incessant attack on the upper class concluding that "they all" or rather "we all" even deserved death. Kölcsey was in fact one of the most outstanding poet-orators of the country, passionately exposing the sins of the nation, one of a line reaching back to the sixteenth century.

He summed up his philosophy of life in *Parainesis* (1837), a piece of prose shot through with poetical writing, in which he propounded his deepest conviction that no one can be happy who lives for himself, and that the harmony of life can be only found in action. The highest virtue therefore lies in serving mankind, and the best way to do it is to serve one's own country.

Kölcsey was also one of the pioneers of the literary ballad in Hungary. He also wrote short stories, and was one of the best orators of the time. His position as a critic will be discussed later in a separate chapter on the literary criticism of the period. His work indeed is more than a purely literary achievement; his writings are also documents that shaped political thought in the Reform Era, and their combative spirit was a stimulus to other public personalities in their social campaigns.

Gergely Czuczor (1800-1866)

It was the dominating personality of the poet Vörösmarty that determined the form of patriotic Romanticism, which reached its climax during the thirties. All the other poets of the age pale into insignificance beside him. One of these minor poets was Gergely Czuczor, a Benedictine monk of serf origin, who excelled in two modes of contemporary poetry, the historical narrative poem and the popular song, in which he followed Károly Kisfaludy. Better known than his monumental epic poems—*The Battle of Augsburg* (Augsburgi ütközet, 1824), *The Meeting in Arad* (Aradi gyűlés, 1828), and *Botond* (1833)—are his ballads, *Szondi, Hunyad, Kont*, etc. These poems, in fact, anticipate in both theme and plot the ballads of János Arany, written in the fifties. His experiments in folk song, on the other hand, were a stimulus to Petőfi. Owing to his serf origins Gergely Czuczor knew the world of the common people better than Károly Kisfaludy; he could introduce typical characters from folk song, descriptions of scenery, and pungent phrases giving the authentic flavour of folk poetry. It is true that, with few exceptions, his songs lack the genuine lyric touch, though the girl in the poem *The Country Girl in Pest* (A falusi kislány Pesten), with her partly real and partly feigned ingenuousness, produces a piquant and lifelike effect.

János Garay (1812-1853)

Like Czuczor, János Garay also wrote historical epics and ballads; though these, in turn, brought him popularity during his life, they have not stood the test of time. He came from a middle-class family living in Transdanubia, became a journalist, and produced poetry conspicuous for its bourgeois character. The achievements of industry, trade, technology and urbanization formed the subject of many of his poems. They were also inspired by the cult of the Biedermeier, roughly corresponding to Early Victorian, in urban life, and were by no means uninfluenced by religious ideas with a petty-bourgeois colouring, both features being quite unusual in Hungarian poetry at that time. His best piece of work, however, *The Old Soldier* (Az obsitos, 1843), had a popular subject. The hero is János Háry, an old ex-soldier who once fought in the Napoleonic Wars, and who gives free rein to his fantasy in inventing enormous lies to embellish the story of his adventures as he recounts them to an astounded village audience. Indeed, the splendid description of the villagers listening to him is as brilliantly comic as the extravagances of his tale, in which humour blends with good-tempered mockery and satire. Comic and ridiculous as they are, the boasting soldier and his rustic audience are always sympathetic. Zoltán Kodály's well-known opera, *Háry János*, is based on this poem.

The Poetry of József Bajza (1804-1858)

József Bajza was primarily a critic, and his critical work is discussed in a later chapter of this book entitled "Criticism and Literary History", but his lyric poetry also deserves a little attention. He gave the German type of sentimental poetry, which so influenced the youthful Kölcsey, some of the characteristics of folk songs, and consequently greater simplicity. He shared Kölcsey's views on the role of folk poetry in the literature of the nation but, unlike others, did not write a species of folk song in the main; at first he specialized in songs of a poetic character, in which bourgeois sentiments and bourgeois taste replaced the patriotic sentiments conspicuous in his contemporaries. From 1830 onwards, however, these patriotic sentiments came to take an increasing place in his poetry. *Apotheosis* (1834) expressed his passionate concern for the Polish nation defeated in their struggle for independence, and it vibrates with the sympathy implicit in the concept of patriotism in those days for all nations fighting for their freedom. The truth of that feeling, founded on the recognition of the common bond uniting these nations, was shown in the tragic defeat of the Hungarians themselves in the 1848-49 War of Independence fifteen years later. Yet this poem, and those written after 1849, end on a note of hope.

It is perhaps no accident that *Prophecy* (A jóslat) is reminiscent in both rhythm and spirit of Schiller's *Ode to Joy*:

> *And former slaves shall be a nation*
> *Free and living under law,*
> *And man shall once more be himself,*
> *As God had made him long ago.*
> *And in freedom's mighty temple*
> *Yes, Truth a throne shall raise,*
> *Which every earthly thing and blade*
> *of grass shall gladly praise.*

27 Mihály Vörösmarty (1800-1855)

Mihály Vörösmarty, the greatest of Hungarian Romantic poets, deserves a place among such poet-giants of Romanticism as Byron, Victor Hugo, Mickiewicz and Pushkin. But he cannot be compared, or be regarded as the Hungarian counterpart of any of them. The importance of his poetry in the history of Hungarian literature is not only that it sums up and epitomizes the work of those who went before, but that something new and original emerged as well: it was not only moulded by the external literary climate of the time but also by the individual dictates of the poet's genius. It was the response of an inspired creative genius to the vital questions of his age.

His Life

Vörösmarty came from a landless Catholic family of noble origin living in Transdanubia. He lost his father, the estate manager of a count, at an early age; and after years of "honest poverty" the large family he left behind were reduced to destitution. Vörösmarty, in fact, had to undertake coaching in order to finish his schooling. While still at school, he fell in love with a girl named Etelka Perczel, the sister of one of his pupils, coming from a wealthy and noble family, and this love, hopeless and undeclared, helped to nurture the romantic sentiments of the poet.

He was still a schoolboy when he wrote his first verses, and between the age of 15 and 23 he composed almost as many poems as during his whole later career. In his youth, of course, every young man of any ambition aspired to literature. But he found in Bonyhád, a Transdanubian village, where he spent the holidays in the company of his pupils, the chaplain with whom he could discuss the plays of Shakespeare, Schiller, and Goethe, and the village parson who introduced him to Homer, Tasso, and Zrínyi. 1823, the year he finished his law studies, coincided with a marked increase in the organized resistance of the nobles to Habsburg absolutism, and Vörösmarty became familiar with the ideals of the reform movement and the social and national aspirations of the time. Love and patriotism, his growing skill in poetic techniques, and his extensive reading in foreign literature, fired him

189

to try his hand at poems and work in a larger dimension, in plays and epics, as well as lyric poetry.

His epic poem, *The Flight of Zalán* (Zalán futása, 1825), laid in the period of the Hungarian Conquest, brought him instant success. He gave up coaching, moved to Pest, and proceeded to devote all his time to literature. At that period, however, no man could earn a living from literature alone, not even a poet with such a successful piece of work as *The Flight of Zalán* to his credit. "... The brain cannot work," he complained, "when the body suffers and the stomach is empty. The mind remains in fetters, preoccupied with cares, and the problems of satisfying daily needs intrude upon it." At the time he considered leaving Pest, giving up literature and becoming a lawyer to relieve himself and his family from poverty. But when his friends secured for him the editorship of the review *Tudományos Gyűjtemény* (Compendium of Learning), he was able to continue his literary work in Pest.

His youthful struggles seem to have ended in the early thirties. He won literary prizes, as a member of the Academy was commissioned to compile a Hungarian dictionary and grammar, and was soon freed from money troubles. He made a name for himself not only in the cultural but also in the political life of the country, and according to a contemporary police directive, was kept under surveillance by the Habsburg security system. He was the centre of a large group of friends, writers, intellectuals and others, meeting in the Snail Inn, with whom he organized the National Club, which played an important part in forming the progressive political views of the capital. Although the physical and financial conditions were eased, his spirit remained restless. In the early forties he fell in love with Laura Csajághy, barely twenty years old, and the experience shattered him emotionally, though he eventually married her. He was deeply involved in the social struggles of his time. His poems, which reveal his emotionally charged response to the events of the period, are on one hand characterized by conflicting trends and attitudes, and by his faith in a national and universal future inspired by the Enlightenment, while, on the other, insisting on a re-assessment of values on a higher philosophical level.

Vörösmarty's output decreased in the years between 1845 and 1850. Petőfi's revolutionary poetry, which appeared around that time, somewhat overshadowed Vörösmarty's popularity, though it did not impair his prestige as a poet. He enthusiastically supported the 1848 Revolution and War of Independence in which he played a political role. He lived another six years after the defeat, suffering from disease, poverty and disillusionment. In the last years of his life he wrote few poems; yet his most magnificent poem, *The Old Gipsy* (A vén cigány), dates from this period. His funeral, which took place in 1855, was the occasion for a solemn demonstration against Habsburg oppression.

The Epics

The poem which first brought Vörösmarty success as a poet was the epic poem *The Flight of Zalán* (1825). This narrative poem on the Hungarian Conquest realized an age-old dream of Hungarian poets of producing a Hungarian national epic which should be a masterpiece. Similar themes had been attempted both before and during Vörösmarty's time. This poem, however, not only outstripped all other experiments in the genre, mostly unfinished, but enlarged and elaborated the subject in casting a Romantic glamour over it, in blending the Classical overtones of Homer and Virgil with the visionary unrealities of Ossian. In this work, the powerless son of an "impotent age" recalls the ancient glories of the past, thus stimulating the nation to make new efforts that in their importance would be comparable to the conquest of the country. Yet, what determines the powerful lyrical tone of the poem is not the pride evoked by the greatness of that age but the mournful, half elegiac spirit which informs it, conjuring up the picture of ancient times, and by inference the contemporary situation. Most striking are the constantly recurring images of darkness, night, and death, symbolizing the transience of earthly existence, as well as a moving description of the fate of Zalán, the defeated Bulgarian prince. This lyric strain, embodying the more "universal" feelings of the poet, exalts a national epic into a work dealing with the universal forces that govern life and human fate. One of the themes exhibiting this universal quality of the poem is the love story interwoven into it. It is completely independent of the main plot of war and fighting; it is about the vain love of the elfin knight of the South for the human maiden Hajna, and its touching beauty probably owes something to the young Vörösmarty's experience of unrequited love. The lyric quality of the poetry is beyond praise, but on occasion tends to blur the logical presentation of what is after all a narrative epic. The poet achieves variety and colour by various devices —the accumulation of adverbial phrases and adjectives with a similar meaning—, he successfully creates a variety of emotional effects, while the rich, monumental images he employs, ranging from heaven to earth, confirm the universal quality of his poetry. The Hungarian hexameter employed is used with the greatest imaginable skill. It is reminiscent of the classics, but is set in conjunction with the colourful, and often luxurious spate of language to create the tension inherent in Romantic art.

Following *The Flight of Zalán* Vörösmarty's epic poetry developed in two different directions. His epics, *Cserhalom* (1825) and *Eger* (1827) and a number of short narrative poems as *Andrew and Béla* (András és Béla), *Kund, the Diver* (A búvár Kund) and *Toldi* recall the historical past, with the same intention in mind as in *Zalán*, and the fantasy embodied in the figure of the "elfin knight of the South" is continued in the poems *The Valley of Fairies* (Tündérvölgy) and the *Southern Island*

(Délsziget, 1826). The epic Hungarian poetry, we repeat, had a long tradition behind it; yet, the fairy element of *The Valley of the Fairies* and the *Southern Island* is something entirely new. Vörösmarty, incidentally, was the first to translate *The Arabian Nights*. "O, mortals, passing so quickly away, ye will know nothing If you forbid the flame of imagination to play upon you" is the beginning of one poem; "Hence with the unbelieving;—far hence..." the beginning of another, and in both the poet gives free vent to his fantasy in the plots, the imagery and the language. In both the subject is the search for happiness, and this, in turn, is also the theme of Vörösmarty's shorter epic poem, *The Ruin* (A rom) which he wrote in 1830. Only the first of these poems, *The Valley of the Fairies,* with its overtones of the folk tale, ends happily. The *Southern Island* remained unfinished, leaving the reader in doubt whether the lovers, whom the "high powers of heaven separated from each other" after their first kiss, ever met again. And *The Ruin* expresses the poet's belief that the fulfilment of human wishes is all in vain, if the final and most important desire, the liberation of an oppressed nation, remains unfulfilled.

In his last major epic poem, *Two Neighbouring Castles* (A két szomszédvár, 1831), Vörösmarty struck a new tone of romantic passion. The historical past here only functions as a background for the poem, a tale of a blood feud between two hostile families. Both the plot and the picture of uncurbed passion which unfolds are full of hyperbole and extravagance; but at the same time, in view of Vörösmarty's own involvement in the emotions described, it is nonetheless more restrained, more classical, than the others.

But at the same time the shorter epic works became more purely lyrical in character. The subjective description of the beauty of the princess in *Hedvig,* the elegiac quality in the account of the banished king's fate in *Solomon,* and the profound sympathy expressed in his description of the grief of the maiden disappointed in love in *Beautiful Helen* (Szép Ilonka), are all examples of the purely lyric quality surfacing in these epics.

Plays

The three romantic trends then prevailing—the preference for national and historical themes, the taste for fantasy and fairy lore, and an appetite for themes of love and unbridled passion—were not confined to Vörösmarty's epic poems; the same predilections can also be traced in his plays. His first plays—*Sigismund* (Zsigmond, 1823), *Solomon* (1827) and the *Exiles* (A bujdosók, 1830)—also deal with themes from the national past. Referring to the national and social problems of the age, Vörösmarty uses them to represent the eternal struggle against tyranny. Shakespeare's influence can also be detected in Vörösmarty's plays, but they are considerably inferior to József Katona's *Ban Bánk* even though based on a similar conflict.

After twenty or thirty years as a dramatic critic, and a number of plays, together with his translation of Shakespeare's *Julius Caesar* and *King Lear,* which was produced later, unsuccessfully put on the stage, he produced a play, called *Czillei and the Hunyadis* (1844), which also met with no real success. Although he was skilful in his dramatic presentation of history, and could write effective scenes and dialogues, they all lack any real dramatic conflict.

Nor are his plays of romantic passion, such as the *Treasure Seekers* (Kincskeresők), *Blood Wedding* (Vérnász), *Ban Marót* (Marót bán), and *Tribulation* (Az áldozat), written between 1833 and 1841, of any outstanding importance either. The plots are artificial, the characters stereotyped or inconsistent, and the tragic potential of the themes is not exploited. On the other hand, the language is at once vivid and majestic, clothing the glowing passion of the protagonists in lines of supreme beauty.

Csongor and Tünde

Csongor and Tünde (Csongor és Tünde, 1831) is by far the best of Vörösmarty's plays. The plot is taken from *Árgirus,* a 16th-century Hungarian romance by Albert Gergei, and the subject links it with the world of medieval fairy-tales; its dramatic structure recalls Shakespeare's *A Midsummer Night's Dream,* and in intellectual content it is akin to Goethe's *Faust.* The play, however, does not appear to be influenced by any of them, nor do they determine its essence. Almost immediately after he has experienced the happiness of love, the witch Mirigy removes Csongor, the hero of the poem, from Tünde. But he sets out in search of his lost happiness, the way leading through a mixture of the real world and the realm of fairies where confusion reigns. In the course of his journey, Csongor meets three merry young imps, and three wanderers in search of riches, fame and knowledge, respectively. And like Sancho Panza, the servant of Don Quixote, the peasant Balga, (meaning "simple") whose hunger can never be assuaged, offers his companionship to Csongor, and the wife of Balga, Ilma, acts as serving-maid to Tünde. Mirigy, who first covets Csongor for her own daughter, and later for Ledér ("wanton"), the frivolous, gaudy peasant girl, does everything in her power to prevent him finding Tünde; indeed, at a given moment it seems that no one will achieve his given goal. The wanderers re-appear; the one who was greedy for riches has been reduced to poverty, the one who desired power had suffered defeat, and the pilgrim avid for knowledge lost his reason.

"Human desires are never fulfilled," concludes Csongor. "The goal is unattainable, elusive and illusory." Yet, unexpectedly, magically, the lovers so desperately seeking each other are granted happiness. The young imps bind the witch Mirigy and carry her away, binding Csongor at the same time in order to bring

193

Tünde to him; she renounces the everlasting happiness which would be hers in the world of fairies for the sake of love and "the fleeting years of joy" on earth. The transitory nature of the happiness of love is stressed in the speech of the Mistress of the Night, preceding the conclusion. It is, in fact, a great Romantic vision of the universe, arising from nothingness, descending into nothingness, in which the life of the individual and the whole history of mankind are no more than fleeting interludes.

Csongor and Tünde is a philosophical work in which the author searches for the meaning of life, and the story and characters are charged with symbolism. The two peasant figures, Balga and Ilma, acting as counterpoint to Csongor and Tünde, illustrate both the difference between the ideal object of human desire and crude reality, and the fact that the two complement each other. The three wanderers represent three dominant human cravings, while the more mysterious and uncontrollable forces of accident and chance are embodied in the malignant figure of Mirigy, rejoicing in evil. The setting of the play is also allegorical: the flowering garden which becomes a wilderness; the crossroads where the choice must be made between the road leading to the Castle of Dawn, the road to the country of Night and the miraculous well reflecting the desires of all who gaze down into it. Equally symbolical are the various episodes, the scene, for instance, in which Balga, failing the presence of a beautiful maiden, embraces a shabby chair, illustrating the repugnant and tawdry nature of mere physical passion, so far removed from ideal love, while the parallel scene where Csongor finds Tünde asleep expresses the insufficiency of spiritual ardour when unaccompanied by physical desire. The curiously magical power of the play lies in the admixture of its moods and attitudes. No other Hungarian poet possesses such variety and subtlety. The confrontation of fable and fact, fairy and imp, the sublime and the simple, philosophy and fun, the fair and the foul, point the many changes of mood and fancy. The language of the play, moreover, is subtly compounded of layer on layer of meaning and image, producing no careless or random effect of colour and sound, but a splendid and complex verbal and visual architectural harmony. Balga's perpetual hunger expresses the torturing pain caused by the insatiable desire as much as Csongor's more spiritual yearnings. Yet the mixture of philosophical and lyric elements makes the play curiously undramatic as a whole, even though certain episodes are in fact excellently constructed dramatic situations. But all in all, apart from the unparalleled beauty of the language, it is the harmonious organization of the component elements that so frequently occur together in romantic literary plays, that makes it a masterpiece. It marks a peak in the history of Hungarian literature, though the literary tradition it represented died with it, and Vörösmarty's Romantic dream-poetry ended with it as well.

Lyric Poems

Although Vörösmarty was undoubtedly a lyric poet, it was only from around 1835 that the lyric as such took precedence over other forms in his work. His lyric genius, of course, gives life to his epic poetry, and equally fills his plays with light and colour. But it was many years before the poet adopted the lyric form as a means of self-expression. At the beginning he made use of the conventional lyric forms of the age preceding his own; later he began to experiment with a more objective type of poem, by composing populist songs describing events or scenes taken from life, as in *The Mourning Cloth* (A gyászkendő), *Hair, Eyes and Mouth* (Haj, száj, szem), *The Complaint of Ilus* (Ilus panasza), *The Complaint of Andrew* (Andor panasza), *The Delight of Laboda* (Laboda kedve), *The Melancholy Lad* (A bús legény), *The Inn in the Puszta* (Puszta csárda). The highly stylized, Neo-Classical epigrams of Vörösmarty's, reflecting the literary fashion of around 1830, are as impersonal as the populist poems; it was only later that, under the stress of strong romantic feelings, the personal, intimate note developed in his lyric poetry.

His most outstanding poems are inspired by profound patriotic sentiments, concern for the fate of mankind, and the passion of love. The poet blends the solemn and sublime with satire, he reproaches contemporary nobles with burning anger, calls on them passionately to cleanse the Augean stables of public life. He is at his best when most transcendent, when fervent enthusiasm alternates with despair, and the volcanic eruption of passion marks the culmination of the poem.

His imagery is cosmic and universal in quality. He is satisfied with nothing less than perfection, and delights in carefully selected detail, a moment of observation; heaven and earth fill his odes with their turbulence and jubilation. Vörösmarty handles the rhetorical devices of Romantic poetry with complete mastery, his questions, his exclamations, repetitions, exaggerations and contrasts of his poetry are never conventional, nor is he ever, like Victor Hugo, diffuse.

The poet's secret love for Etelka Perczel only indirectly found expression in his more objective poems. Although a note of admiration for feminine loveliness, connected with his love for Etelka and intensified by passion, occasionally emerged even when his passion for Etelka had faded, it was his love for Laura Csajághy that gave rise to his really great love poems. They show him torn by dissonant feelings and moods; they are curiously modern; here Vörösmarty completely abandoned the stereotyped forms of love poetry prevalent up to the time. Their basic mood is one of longing and a desire for the person beloved to return his love, expressed in such poems as *Thirst* (A szomju), *To Laura* (Laurához), *You Make me Angry* (Haragszom rád), *Nameday Congratulations* (Névnapi köszöntés), and *Reverie* (Ábránd). The resolution of his passion when Laura accepted him was expressed in a poem *To the Dreamer* (A merengőhöz) written to his betrothed as a wedding gift, echoing the atmosphere of his odes, but permeated with a resigned wisdom of life. It is, in fact, the poem of an elderly poet's dreams and fantasies of a young woman, in which he warns her against the world of dreams and passionate imaginings, and in doing so betrays the deepest springs of his own poetry.

Patriotism

Patriotism was always a main source of inspiration to Vörösmarty. In one of his early poems he introduces Zrínyi asking Fate whether the Hungarians would ever have a "leader-poet" like him again; certainly he aspired to such a role himself.

The *Appeal* (Szózat, 1836), which has become a second national anthem for the Hungarians and is often called the Hungarian *Marseillaise,* stands out among his patriotic odes, and is, as it were, an epitome of all that characterizes them, inviting comparison with Kölcsey's *Hymn.* Both invoke the past to justify the struggles of the present. In Kölcsey's *Hymn* the hopes of a fairer future spring up within a religious framework—a devout belief in the relationship between sin and punishment, and the poet's faith in God; in Vörösmarty's work it is firm and "unshakable" patriotism that justifies all the struggles of the past, and he appeals passionately for the just recognition of their aims and achievements at the bar of the universal commonwealth of nations. That a man's native country is inseparable from mankind as a whole is one of the basic themes in his poetry. Hungary's isolation and loneliness haunts him: "Torn from his tribe, and brotherless, the Hungarian looks west, and then looks back east with gloomy eyes." His imaginative dreams in his earlier poetry reflected a certain universality of vision; his political views in his maturity equally reflect his constant preoccupation with the fate of all mankind. No Hungarian poet has more consciously and confidently proclaimed before the world his faith in his nation: "The sufferings of a thousand years call for life or death," writes the poet. Like Kölcsey, Vörösmarty recalls the sufferings of his countrymen and their vain struggles. He does not, however, see them as punishments for sins but as sacrifices and efforts that will eventually, and inevitably, lead to a better future:

> *So many hearts cannot have shed*
> *Heroic blood in vain;*
> *So many faithful men to die*
> *Of broken hearts, in pain.*

> *It cannot be that might and mind*
> *Should suffer but reverse,*
> *That will so saint should wilt away*
> *Beneath an evil curse.*

196

He sets out the alternatives of life and death not only for the Hungarian nation but for the world as a whole which acts as both witness and judge. And the characteristic image of the death of a nation links with the above motif:

> *The grave in which the nation sinks*
> *All nations will surround,*
> *And tears of mourning glitter in*
> *A million eyes around.*

Yet, death is not presented as an alternative to life; the possibility of death is to stimulate courage for the fight. The two concluding stanzas are imbued with tension produced by the confrontation of life and death. Here Vörösmarty repeats the first two stanzas of the poem in a slightly altered form which at the same time is enriched with the conclusions it brings:

> *Magyar, to this thy native land*
> *Ever devoted be!*
> *It nourished thee, and soon, when dead,*
> *Its earth receiveth thee.*
>
> *No other land than this expands*
> *For thee beneath the sky!*
> *The fates may bring thee bane and bliss!*
> *Here thou must live and die!*
>
> (Translated by W. N. Loew)

Between 1830 and 1840 Vörösmarty's poems were coloured with a certain amount of satire. It was a period when consciousness of the difficult political situation at home, the lack of progress in reform, and the split within the progressive party, was coupled with his growing awareness of the contradictions of bourgeois development in Western Europe, the increasing pauperization of the masses, the evils of colonialism, and the horror of the institution of slavery in democratic America. The news of the peasant rising in Galicia in 1846 shattered him; he saw it as a warning to the Hungarian nobility of what might be expected in the struggle for independence if the question of the serfs remained unsolved.

The Poet of Mankind

The epigrams dealing with the progress of mankind and the future of the nation can be regarded as anticipating his later philosophical poems. One of them, *Lines Written in the Gutenberg Album* (A Guttenberg-albumba, 1840), echoes his most outstanding philosophical poem, *Thoughts in a Library* (Gondolatok a könyvtárban), which was written four years later. In the Gutenberg poem, the poet hailed Gutenberg, the inventor of printing, as the champion of human progress. The poem consists of one masterfully constructed period which fits in with the distichs of this longer epigram harmoniously. It enumerates the manifold possibilities offered by printing, and lists the conditions under which peace and justice, with the spread of culture, can at last rule the world. The question, on the other hand, whether "the world has ever advanced through the medium of books," is also answered in *Thoughts in a Library*: "It has, but the more glorious a nation is the more horrible books make its filth." Vörösmarty knew at first hand the contradictions in the society and culture of his age, and forcefully exposed them in this poem, driving home the fact that there are millions of poverty-stricken creatures all over the world, and that the number of those who can hope for anything amounts to only a few thousand. Recalling that the paper men write on is made of rags, a series of vivid images and contrasts leap from his pen: "Men write of virtue on this sheet which once a scoundrel wore... Laws are inscribed on the whitened pages of books that were once the bloodstained garments of rebels, false judges and tyrants... The vision of madmen can be true; astronomy is but a blind beggar woman who measures the fate of the world on her rags... terrible lies are everywhere." In the poet's view the ideals promoted in books were refuted in innumerable ways by the facts of reality.

Yet he found himself unable to accept this despairing conclusion. "Yet it is not so; Oh no, it is pain that has dictated all this"—"A new spirit finds its way ahead"—the spirit of freedom and equality. But he could no longer believe wholeheartedly in anything. He felt that mankind built Babels over and over again, that progress was inevitably followed by decline. Nonetheless, he was sustained by his patriotic fervour, the desire to perform manly deeds, two mutually complementary sentiments, even though they failed to resolve his doubts: "Our task in the world is to fight for the noblest aims, according to our strength. The fate of a nation is in our hands," he wrote in a strain reminiscent of the conclusion of Imre Madách's great play, *The Tragedy of Man*. In fact, most of Vörösmarty's poems come to the same patriotic conclusions as *The Tragedy of Man*, extolling an almost religious tenacity and persistence, and thus silencing doubts. Yet, almost simultaneously he could write *People* (Emberek, 1846) with the refrain "there is no hope".

Faith and despair fought their battle within him; he was indeed still haunted in the *Appeal* by his forebodings that the nation would have to choose between a better future and a solemn death. But when the Hungarians were defeated in their War of Independence in 1848, and appeared to be facing extinction as a nation, he cried out vehemently against such a fate, protesting that this was not the fate he had foretold or anticipated. Passion had never driven him to such extremities, and his imagery had never been so wild and unrestrained as in the poems he wrote at that time. The first he wrote after the defeat was entitled *Curse* (Átok). And in the poem *Preface* (Előszó) he piles one terrible image on another:

> *Disaster struck. His icy hand of doom*
> *threw human skulls like fireballs into the sky;*
> *His legs waded in human hearts.*
> *Under his breath all life had shrivelled up...*
> *And wher'er he went, along his dreadful tread*
> *The curses of the peoples trodden down*
> *Rose up from hecatombs of broken bones,*
> *And misery layed her helpless head*
> *On the ashes of towns burnt to the ground.*

This was the poem which anticipated *The Old Gipsy* (A vén cigány), written by Vörösmarty in 1854, after years of torturing, almost intolerable poverty, and almost complete silence. It is one of the finest poems in Hungarian literature. It was a few years ago that László Gara, an ardent lover of Hungarian literature, induced fourteen French poets to produce a fitting French translation of this poem which is, in fact, a passionate declamation on the fate of mankind.

The image of the gipsy is a characteristic component of the Hungarian scene. The gipsy, whose music soothes grief and gives comfort, is traditionally associated with the merry-making of the Hungarians. The sentence of command, "Come, play, gipsy!" with which the poem opens and which recurs again and again, is pregnant with the feelings of one lost in despair, feasting half in tears, and to whom only the intoxicating spell of wine and music can offer relief. The gipsy of the poem, however, represents the poet himself, torn by doubt and longing for comfort. In fact, the poet's words are addressed to himself, and for his own encouragement.

In this poem rhapsodic cries, strange visions, hallucinations are all heaped on one another within a context of hope and confidence. There are references to the events of the recent past and the present, to the failure of the Hungarian fight for independence, to the Crimean War, and the armed conflicts in Palestine—"The harvests of mankind are destroyed"; "there is war in the world"; "The grave of God trembles in the Holy Land"—and he speaks of "routed armies" and of the "desperate hopes of mankind". Scattered in between are images of a different kind, reflecting the strains and stresses of a perturbed soul,—"from where has this repressed sigh arisen? What screams and cries in this wild rush? Who beats on the vault of heaven? What is it that shrieks like the mills of hell?" Now recalling the fratricide of Cain, now the sufferings of Prometheus, he reflects how the sins and miseries of mankind are never-ending. Yet the concluding image of the poem, in which the home of mankind, "that miserable earth" is represented as a "blind star" revolving in its own "bitter exhalation", changes the underlying mood of the poem in opening up a cosmic perspective of confidence, a resurgence of hope, the beacon of the future flaming in the far distance. Earth is purified in the "bitter exudation" of suffering, and the appearance of the Ark of Noah marks the beginning of a new world. "Despite all, the world will feast in the end!" cries the poet; the old gipsy, who speaks for Vörösmarty himself, becomes the serene prophet of the new world; the feverish tone of the poem dies down into the solemnity of an ode; and the last stanza breathes the absolute serenity and happiness of the choral conclusion to Beethoven's Ninth Symphony.

Vörösmarty's poetic works represent a peak in Hungarian poetry; yet, he has not achieved the place in international literature he deserves, which not only diminishes the fame of Hungarian literature in the world but deprives the stock of international Romantic poetry of something as rich and rare as the poetry of Vörösmarty.

28 The Rise of the Novel

Prose Narrative

With the coming of the nineteenth century the more astute publishers in Hungary poured out a succession of novels, since increasing interest was being shown in the new genre, and not even the censorship on novels could stop their popularity for a long time. Prose, however, of a type inspired by Kármán's *Fanny* and by Bessenyei's *Travels of Tarimenes* had not as yet made any general appearance. Nor were the majority of translations and adaptations of the time of particular importance. Rather bad translations of one or two of the works of Voltaire, Goethe, Richardson, Sterne, and Goldsmith appeared at intervals, occasionally so distorted that it was impossible to recognize the original in them. Hungarian Romantic writers, in fact, despised Hungarian novels; they were both "cheap and lamentable", wrote András Fáy who, for one, tried to improve on such novels by stressing the elements of originality and realism in his own works.

Károly Kisfaludy pioneered the way in the field of prose narrative. The same relationship exists between his historical tales and those that took their subjects from contemporary life, as between his tragedies and comedies. His historical novels, such as the *Chalice and Blood* (A vérpohár, 1822); and *Tihamér* (1824), make use of all the conventional features of novels of chivalry, which, though highly improbable, somehow manage to convince; while his modern tales, as, for example, *The Adventures of Jónás Tollagi* (Tollagi Jónás viszontagságai, 1822–27), and *Simon Sulyosdi* (1823), are remarkable for vivid and satirical pictures of the various types of contemporary Hungarian nobles: Sulyosdi, the noble, incapable of action, and wasting his days in idleness, recalls Goncharov's *Oblomov*, though a more superficial character.

András Fáy (1786-1864)

András Fáy's writings are only one aspect of his many activities. He organized the first Hungarian Savings Bank, was a theatrical director, a Member of Parliament, and president of the Kisfaludy Society. A fellow-writer neatly called him the national man of all work.

His most important work, *The House of the Béltekys* (A Bélteky-ház, 1832), is a social novel, and as such is the first of its kind in Hungarian literature. In this novel the conservative and progressive sections of the nobility confront one another in the spirit of Széchenyi's reform programme. The protagonists are two members of the same family, father and son. That the author regarded their differing social and political attitudes as a generation conflict, seen through the life of a single family, might have aided in economy of construction. The novel, however, is rambling and diffuse. Fáy loses himself in the elaborate manipulation of the plot, and the lack of construction bedevils the situation of the many figures in it. The novel has other shortcomings as well. The character of the progressive-minded young Bélteky is sketchily drawn; so much happened before the novel began that the plot is confusing, and the long reflections and soliloquies interspersed throughout the book constantly hold up the action. The novel is couched in the new forms and words introduced by the language reform, many of which sank into oblivion within a relatively short time. The public forgot it all the more easily as some time later Mór Jókai produced much better novels on similar subjects.

Yet, even though the book is not successful as a novel, it contains a wealth of ideas. Its characters discuss economics, education, literature and art; and it also contains an account of a study-tour abroad. Fáy modelled himself on a second-rate German writer, August Lafontaine, but some of the details resemble Goethe's *Wilhelm Meister* both in intellectual content and in mood.

Miklós Jósika (1794-1865)

Baron Miklós Jósika, the father of the Hungarian historical novel, was considerably more talented and successful as a writer than András Fáy. His career as a young soldier was, like Sándor Kisfaludy's, interspersed with romantic love affairs. He fought in the wars against Napoleon, travelled through half Europe, and like Széchenyi, was in Vienna during the Vienna Congress, where he lived the pleasant life of a well-born army officer. He left the army to settle in the country, contracting an unhappy marriage that ended in divorce.

Jósika was forty-two when his first novel appeared. He was still a novice, but his reading had been extensive. He was familiar with German, French, Italian, English, and Spanish literature in their original tongues, and practically the whole range of contemporary novels.

Walter Scott was his literary model. His native land, Transylvania, meant to him what Scotland meant to Walter Scott. It is the same kind of romantic country, mountainous and wild, and had been independent, at least nominally, from the middle of the sixteenth century. Nominally, for it remained in truth in the hands of the great powers, first the Turks, then the Austrians, as well as subject to the oppressive conduct of its own ruling class. It is perhaps the result of the vicissitudes through which it passed that the Transylvanian sense of history was particularly strong, and the memoirs written in Transylvania in the seventeenth and eighteenth centuries are outstanding in the prose of that time. It was these surroundings and this history that stimulated Jósika to produce his historical novels.

The first, *Abafi* (1836), laid in Transylvania towards the end of the sixteenth century, is also his best. The meticulous and accurate description of the historical period forms the background to a thorough and convincing portrait of the principal character, coupled with a fast-moving, eventful plot and a generally progressive attitude. The young hero, sunk in debauchery, redeems himself through force of will, and eventually finds a meaning to his life in a noble love and work for the public good. The unusually enthusiastic reception of the novel did more than arouse the author to a sense of his own abilities, it led him, perhaps, to overrate them. Be that as it may, none of the novels he produced in quick succession came to the level of *Abafi*.

The novels with a certain social content show the influence of French Romanticism, and of Eugene Sue in particular. In most of his historical novels, and indeed in *Abafi* as well, it seems clear he was endeavouring to provide what the public wanted in the form of an exciting plot and plenty of adventures. But as Jókai's novels increased in popularity, his own fell out of favour, though one reason for that was that with the failure of the 1848 War of Independence, he was obliged to leave the country to escape the death sentence passed upon him by the despotic Habsburg regime. Several of his novels appeared in German translation; he also attempted to write some of them in the German language, but neither these nor his memoirs of the War of Independence (*Zur Geschichte des ungarischen Freiheitskampfes*, 1861) aroused any interest.

His main quality as a novelist is also his main defect: pandering to public taste. It is true that by doing so he increased the size of the reading public, and thus indirectly performed a valuable service for Hungarian literature. But he progressed no further; indeed, by catering to the public taste he lost the opportunity of improving his work.

Minor Prose Writers

Fáy and Jósika were not in fact the only prose writers of the period. Between 1830 and 1840, there were other writers of novels and short stories. A somewhat strange figure in the history of Hungarian Romanticism was *Péter Vajda* (1808–1846). He was of serf origin, and is unique in Hungarian literature in representing the German

Romantic pantheism of the period, while at the same time retaining the intellectual and artistic heritage of the Enlightenment. Pantheism and his passionate love of nature find expression in his somewhat ornate and high-flown prose poems, often with esoteric meanings, as in *The Realm of Songs* (Dalhon, 1839–43). On the other hand, his tales on historical and exotic subjects contain a good deal of enlightened social criticism. Anachronistic elements are deliberately introduced into his historical narratives, *The Most Beautiful Maid* (A legszebb leány, 1834), and *Bende Tárcsai* (1837), in order to smuggle the philosophy of the Enlightenment and social satire into them; and in his exotic and Oriental tales and short stories, such as the *Vaj-koontala* and *Manahor the Slave* (Manahor, a rabszolga) he makes use of the same device to expose the contradictions of society. His collected articles, *Letters from Pest,* are, in fact, the first satirical sketches in Hungarian literature. All in all, these works and his public activities made him a champion of bourgeois progress.

It was between 1835 and 1840 that literary sketches appeared in Hungarian literature for the first time. One might call them genre pictures or episodes from life. The speedy proliferation of magazines and reviews created a demand for this sort of writing, and as metropolitan life became livelier it provided plenty of themes for these sketches. Urban life entered Hungarian literature by this means; very often the purpose of these frequently satirical articles was to eliminate obstacles to bourgeois development. As with Dickens, the sketches led the way to the novels in the case of *Ignác Nagy* already mentioned as a dramatist. He saw literature as a craft, and the purpose was to entertain. His chief merit as a writer was his satire, and his best work was the novel *Hungarian Secrets* (Magyar titkok, 1844–45). On this novel which developed out of his satirical sketches, in which he drew a picture of the life of the capital, he imposed a romantic plot modelled on Sue's *Les Mystères de Paris*. But the tale lacks unity. Although the background of life in the small Hungarian capital is convincing, the elaborate criminal machinations at the centre of the plot are less than plausible.

Another novel based on Sue, but more remarkable than Ignác Nagy's, was one by *Lajos Kuthy* (1813–1864). As a distinguished and recognized author, and the personal secretary of a count, he moved in upper-class circles and received little sympathy from the progressive writers of the time. The antipathy, indeed, turned to downright hostility when he entered the service of the despotic Habsburg regime after the Hungarian defeat in the 1848 War of Independence. This fact has affected judgments on his work in later histories of literature; it has been consistently underestimated. His novel *The Secrets of the Native Country* (Hazai rejtelmek, 1846–47), possesses considerable merit: it is coherently planned, not strung together in episodes as the novel by Ignác Nagy, and gives a wide-ranging and comprehensive picture not only of life in Pest but also of the many aspects of contemporary Hungarian society. Kuthy is a gifted observer. He is strongest in his descriptive passages. The romantic and extravagant plot is given plausibility through the authenticity of the details and the background, and even the careful description of objects and clothes painted with a realism reminiscent of Balzac. Although his style is somewhat artificial, there is evidently a kind of creativity to be found in it.

The Romantic narrative prose of the Reform Era produced no conspicuous talent. The Hungarian novelists, Eötvös, Kemény and Jókai, who left a name behind them, belong to the period following it. But the prose writers of the Reform Era carried out a pioneering task in introducing new subjects, creating new genres, and turning far wider sections of society into a permanent reading public.

29 The Rise of Literary Criticism and the Study of Literary History

The relatively regular appearance of literary criticism and reviewing around this time made a further contribution to the development of Hungarian literature. In earlier days when literature was, as it were, running wild, developing in unco-ordinated directions, and serving largely as a vehicle for the expansion and evolution of the Hungarian language, each piece of writing was regarded as a patriotic act, particularly as the writers in those days earned no money from their work. The few reviews or critical observations interwoven into works of a different character had little effect; or rather, the only effect was an impatient rejection of such criticism by both the writers and the reading public in general.

Kölcsey's Critical Work

Kölcsey published his critical studies of Csokonai and Berzsenyi, the two greatest Hungarian poets in the beginning of the nineteenth century, in 1817, and they were equally rejected by writers and public alike. It is, of course, true that despite his honest and careful exploration and evaluation of the personality and essential art of these two poets, and his many valuable comments, his final assessment of these poets was wrong. His work is rather an account of his own development as a poet, and his abandoning of his previous models, than inspired criticism accurately evaluating the value of these poets. Between 1820 and 1830, Kölcsey, together with a fellow-writer, founded a critical review, *Élet és Literatura* (Life and Literature), in which he also published his *Nemzeti hagyományok* (National Traditions, 1826), the most significant of all theoretical works on Hungarian Romanticism. Basing himself on Herder's philosophical approach to history Kölcsey discussed in it the possibilities of an organic development of Hungarian literature. Following a review of world literature, in which he reached the conclusion that only the Greeks had an organically developing national literature, he criticized the Hungarians for imitating foreign writing, especially since the beginning of the age of Enlightenment. National tradition, through which the Hungarians could establish a literature of their own, was to be sought in the "songs of the common people," he declared. The identification of the national element with the popular was immensely important not only in the development of literature but also in the creation of a sense of national identity in the people. This placed Kölcsey squarely on the side of those who stood for national unity based on democracy, as opposed to the far more limited objectives of the more liberal-minded nobles.

József Bajza (1804-1858)

Although Károly Kisfaludy had also planned to start a critical review, it was in fact József Bajza who became the father of Hungarian literary criticism. He came from a noble land-owning family, and began his career as a lawyer. Pretty soon, however, he relieved himself of the management of his estate by letting it, at the same time abandoning his legal practice in order to dedicate himself completely to literature, the only passion of his life. He wrote poetry in his early days, later various studies on different types of poetry, such as *A Theoretical Study of the Epigram* (Az epigramma teóriája, 1828); and *The Novel* (A románköltésről, 1833). It soon became clear that his real forte was literary criticism. Not that he ever wrote long, analytical studies on theory and general literature, but rather that he considered his main task was to give literary criticism a free and firmly established status, while, incidentally, he encouraged the bourgeois values in literature. "Only merit, reason, and intellectual qualities should matter, and not the privileges of birth and rank," he wrote in a debate with Count Dessewffy. "Only these can I recognize as authorities, and I will never bow to others or to noble titles." He wished to make literature a public matter. When he took part in discussions and debates, and let his critical views be known, it was for the sake of the readers whom he wished to save from cheap and tawdry writing. He found, for instance, the encyclopaedia *Conversations Lexicon* unsatisfactory and misleading, and promptly sued the editor for deceiving the public. Sure of himself, he pursued with passion debates and discussions on this or that issue. "It is not the goddess of discord but the goddess of honesty who stimulates me to speak when I find the use of words both necessary and my duty."

Bajza was a severe critic. The criticism is couched in the argumentative style of a litigant lawyer, and his harsh and militant temperament Hungarianizes, as it were, his background of German aesthetics. His dramatic criticisms are particularly interesting. As the first director of the Hungarian Theatre of Pest from 1837 to 1838 and in his role as guide and mentor correcting the views and instructing the dramatic critics of the time through his polemical writings, he did a great deal for the Hungarian theatre. Together with Vörösmarty, he favoured the French Romantic drama of the time, as set against the sentimental drama of the Germans; he found it closer to life, more authentic, and also more humanitarian in its moral attitudes.

He had a great esteem for Shakespeare; yet, in the dispute which raged between 1840 and 1850 between those who wanted more realism in literature like Shakespeare and the advocates of French Romanticism, Bajza supported the latter. The presentation of crude reality in a piece of literature was abhorrent to him, and he believed that even the performance of actors should contain some element of the sublime and the ideal. It was, in fact, his taste for Romanticism, his knowledge and his extensive reading, particularly of Lessing, Tieck and Schlegel, influenced by Neo-Classical principles, that prevented him from appreciating the best Hungarian plays, such as *Ban Bánk,* which had already been produced on the stage at that time.

As critic, his sense of Hungarian nationalism took first place. He maintained that "everything should be subordinate to it, and therefore the arts as well should serve national interests above all else." He too regarded literature as a political battlefield; by 1845 his interest had shifted from literature to politics pure. He was the editor of the most outstanding political publication of the age, the almanac or year-book *Ellenőr* (Controller, 1847), which he published abroad to avoid its censorship in Hungary; and later, during the period of the 1848 War of Independence, he was made editor of Kossuth's *Pesti Hirlap* (News Magazine). Like Vörösmarty and Garay, after the defeat of the Hungarians he lived in poverty and destitution.

Ferenc Toldy (1805-1875)

It was Ferenc Toldy, the best friend of the youthful Bajza, who first applied the principles of German Romantic aesthetics to Hungarian literary works in his critical articles. Later on, however, he found in history the vocation of his life. He came from a German family of bourgeois origin, living in the capital, and his original name was Schedel. He studied medicine and became professor of medicine at the University of Pest. He was later appointed director of the University Library, and became a teacher of Hungarian literature. While still a young man, his enthusiasm over the progress of Hungarian literature during the twenties led him to write himself. In a series of articles written between 1826 and 1827 on the early epic poems of Vörösmarty, he pointed out with great perception several inherent features of Vörösmarty's Romantic art. Yet, neither in the articles, nor in his later criticism did he pay much attention to the question of a Hungarian national consciousness that dominated Hungarian Romanticism; and as a result his estrangement from the experiments in literature increased. By 1840 he no longer shared the views of Bajza and Vörösmarty; nor did French Romanticism appeal to him. He repudiated both the democratic principles of Victor Hugo as well as the democratic sentiments of Eötvös and Petőfi, and was by no means in accord with the democratic spirit of the forties.

His first work dealing with literature was a two-volume anthology, *Handbuch der ungarischen Poesie* (1827–28), which appeared around the same time as the critical articles already mentioned, which contained an introduction outlining the history of Hungarian literature, continuing the work of the early literary historians who made it their business to show the world that the Hungarians had a literature worth knowing. He gave a central place in the history of old Hungarian literature to Zrínyi; emphasized that with the appearance of Bessenyei a new literary period had started; and stated his conviction that Kazinczy, Károly Kisfaludy and Vörösmarty formed the backbone of new Hungarian literature, while giving less importance to Csokonai, Kölcsey and Berzsenyi than they deserved, and making no mention of Katona at all—but for this not Toldy is to blame but the literary tendencies of the time.

An incredible diligence and energy marked Toldy's labours as a literary historian. He not only devoted himself to the development of the literatures of Western European countries, like the majority of his contemporaries, but also took an interest in the literatures of the Slav nations.

He was the first in Hungary to write about Pushkin and Mickiewicz. But in the main he concentrated on the history of Hungarian literature, particularly after 1848; but the task he set himself proved greater than he anticipated, and his monumentally comprehensive work remained unfinished: *A Literary History of the Hungarian Nation* (A magyar nemzeti irodalomtörténet, 1851) stopped at 1526; and in his *History of Hungarian Poetry* (A magyar költészet története, 1854) the last poet he dealt with was Sándor Kisfaludy. Only his *Handbook of Hungarian Literature* (1864–65), for school use, contained a complete review of Hungarian literature.

Toldy is commonly regarded as the father of the history of literature in Hungary; a title he deserves in view of the pioneer works full of information he produced, and the many literary texts and biographies of writers, and studies he edited and wrote, even though his views on literature were behind the times.

The critical work and the study of the history of literature, it must be admitted, of that period are less original than the literature of the time, nor as good. The critics of the time, generally speaking, were unable to free themselves from the influence of Herder, Lessing, Schlegel, Jean Paul and Tieck, and they frequently fitted the literary work they criticized to these theories. As far as the study of literature was concerned, the search for foreign models proved more an obstacle to development than a stimulus for the simultaneous growth of literary consciousness and literature.

Populist Literature
(c. 1840–c. 1870)

30 The Populist Movement and Romanticism

The Populist Era

The literatures of the Eastern Central European nations were equally influenced and became part of the great wave of Romanticism sweeping across Europe in the early nineteenth century. In these nations, however, the natures and role of Romanticism was often somewhat different. As a general rule Romanticism in its first phase meant the birth or revival of a national consciousness and a sense of national identity; in the second an increasingly democratic process for the national culture. In this second phase, in particular, the change in the nature of Romantic literature in certain countries even led to a number of essentially Romantic writers considering themselves adversaries of the Romantic movement and refusing to be regarded as Romantics at all. Even Petőfi, for instance, who did indeed want to be the leader of the "Hungarian school of Romanticism," was substantially affected by the changing trends which, still within the framework of Romanticism, attempted to portray contemporary society more realistically, an attempt which included a certain amount of social criticism and a desire to change that society. This was a trend generally prevailing in the Western novel and poetry of the time: the literature of *Vormärz* and the radical French movement in literature prior to the revolutions of 1848, a combination of all the Romantic and realistic elements of the poetry of those days.

This second phase also developed in Hungary, and was dominant in the decade preceding the 1848 Revolution. It was known as "the era of the people and the nation", after the style and main choice of its subject-matter, and the movement was finally known as *népies* or populist. In some later days the expressions "national Classicism" and "*népies* Classicism" are also to be found. It was a fusion of Romantic and realistic elements, with a steady—though sometimes cautious—stress on the latter. From 1840 onwards realism became the dominant trend, especially in the works of the newer, younger authors.

For Western Europe in general it was a transitional movement marking the change from Romanticism to realism. But due to particular circumstances this transition developed into a full-blooded and independent movement of its own among the Central European nations. It was not in addition of one trend to another,

213

but an alloy; a new quality. The nuances of this movement were innumerable, from near realism such as the "middle" period of Eötvös to the quasi-Romanticism of Madách. And they were moreover often combined within a single writer such as Petőfi. There are many Petőfis of a sort in Eastern European literature, Nekrasov, Słowacki, Stur Alecsandri, and even in the West we have Heine, Béranger and Keller; but due to the special conditions of Hungary none were quite like him.

The Continuity of Romanticism

The essence of these "special conditions" was the momentum which clearly distinguished the Hungarian Revolution of 1848 and the national movement of resistance which followed its defeat from similar events in European history. During the first decades of the century Hungary was concerned with the threat posed to its existence as a nation in particular by the Habsburg empire. Of all the ideas implicit in Romanticism the dominant element in Hungary was the notion of the nation. It was the question of the nation which became the subject of the new philosophical awakening in Hungary in the works of Berzsenyi, Kölcsey and Széchenyi. The lesser nobles and the gentry, who with the intellectuals who joined them were the leaders of this movement, believed it was the main task to arouse a national consciousness which would be their best defence against this threat.

Once this had been successfully achieved they turned with ingenuous optimism to the next task: the transformation of Hungary into a bourgeois state, a pressing need since the 1830s. Since political activity was denied them by the Habsburg regime literature served as the main vehicle in this task. But the literature which had fulfilled a national task in earlier times by glorifying the past had always centred on the Hungarian noble and was unsuitable to present needs. Influenced by Herder, the German pioneer of the Romantic movement, they turned to the folk world and the folk poetry of Hungary for an answer to the fundamental problem of bourgeois development which in Hungary was the question of the serfs. All the more because by that time, a significant plebeian peasant power had emerged. The immediate aim was to study the poetry of the people: to depict their lives, to give voice to their spirit. The *indirect* aim, the much-desired *final* aim still remained the modern expression and interpretation of the "national character". The difference between the two periods was the change in the notion of national character that occurred during the *népies* era. By then "what a nation should become in its essence" had become the idea of a *free community of free citizens* whose kinship was based upon their common past, their common manner of thought and feeling, and their common values and aims.

The basic problem which nineteenth-century philosophy faced from capitalism was alienation. It was first recognized by Rousseau and Herder; it was later scientifically treated by Hegel and Marx. Romanticism was caught in the grip of alienation: the dilemma of Romanticism took the form of a doubt whether a nation could be regarded as the sum of its individual members. The promise implicit in the aim of liberal Romanticism of the development of the True Man, the one who is true to himself, was interpreted in Hungary as a promise about the True Hungarian—the Hungarian who is true to himself. A philosophical question was thus transformed into a national question. Petőfi, the outstanding figure of the first half of the nineteenth century summed up his pessimist judgement on the Hungarian people in 1846: "The Hungarian forgets or is ashamed to be Hungarian. And such a degenerate nation has no claim on life." He regained his faith in them in the revolutionary summer of 1848: "The Hungarian is again Hungarian," he proclaimed. Arany, the leading poet in the second half of the nineteenth century, was inspired by another ideal which he took from Herder. Hungarian poetry had grown away from the Hungarian people, the true embodiment of the nation and its essential character, it had to be guided back to true nationalism through the "populist" movement. "I love our national poetry," he wrote, "in its present *népies* disguise, and I shall love it in its unmasked purity." In the Romantic era, the Herderian idea of an autonomous national community based upon the traditional order prevailed, in the populist period, more democratic principles, characteristic of the age of Enlightenment, came into play—and the idea of a free national community in particular. The abolition of serfdom had become the overriding principle of national existence, and it is to this that all these changes were due. All this required, and finally produced, means of criticizing and condemning society, and were more characteristic of radical Romanticism and realism.

But the conditions of the time and place imposed their limitations on these aspirations. There was no middle class of importance in Hungary; the role it played in other countries was here undertaken by the lesser nobility and the gentry. The choice of subject-matter was consequently restricted, and reduced to descriptions of provincial life among the gentry and the peasants. And what was even more important, the lack of a middle class held back the development of social criticism, since the landed gentry leading the movement had to achieve bourgeois progress at the same time as national independence, and this called for the careful preservation of national unity. After 1849, indeed the absence of a bourgeois class produced even sharper problems. For a better understanding of this, a brief account is required of certain aspects of the political history of the country.

The Consequences of 1848–1849

On the 15th March 1848 a successful revolution against Austrian domination broke out in the capital. The court in Vienna was compelled to accept its demands: it ratified its Constitution and appointed a responsible Hungarian government, but subsequently recanted and tried to revoke the concessions it had made. As, alone, it failed to break the heroic resistance of the well-organized troops of the lawful Hungarian government, it called upon the army of the Czar of Russia to crush the country in its hour of freedom. The revolution was broken; bloodthirsty reprisals and some fifteen years of despotism and repression followed. The Habsburgs, defeated in their wars with Prussia, their position in the world declining, and faced with a Hungarian movement of passive resistance, were in no position to resist the demands of the Hungarians for some form of autonomy, and the Compromise (Ausgleich) of 1867 was signed.

But the failure of the 1848 Revolution had brought changes in its train. The aims of the ruling social strata changed, as did the roles which they assumed. Changes also occurred in the inter-relationship of the various strata and the liberal ideas then prevailing came to be seen in a new light. All this had its effect on the cultural life of the country. The writers of the time, however, imbued with the spirit of passive resistance, were blind to these changes. They felt compelled in both their literary and social activities to abide by the reformist, not yet revolutionary, principles of the pre-1848 *népies*, populist period. They only came to realize the changes that were taking place and their significance between 1859 and 1861. Until that time the trends and style of Hungarian literature had remained virtually the same as in the pre-1848 period, even though signs of change began to be apparent. Between 1859 and 1861 writers themselves began to explain that the aims of the populist movement before and after the revolution could not be the same. The same essential aesthetic ideas and the populist aims were bound to play different roles in the arts and in society in the different social and political situations of pre- and post-1848 Hungary. And indeed even those ideas and aims remained the same only in words. Some of them fell into disuse, and the meaning of others became unclear; the messages of those still remaining were consequently modified.

National resistance to the Habsburgs was led by the Hungarian nobility. They had not been counter-revolutionary, but they were in fear of revolution. In addition to the class interests of the nobility, this was also due to an important factor in the War of Independence which followed the March Revolution, and needless to say, however indirectly, this factor affected their interests too. The Habsburg court had originally tried to crush the Hungarians by making use of the non-Hungarian nationalities of the country, Slovaks, Rumanians, Serbs and Germans who made up over half the population. As these nationalities developed socially and economically, they too were influenced and animated by the same ideas of national liberalism that had inspired the Hungarians. They equated the True Man with the True Slovak, the True Rumanian, or the True Serb, and they too, like the Hungarians, developed demands for greater democracy such as equal rights, free and equal economic opportunities and a call for the destruction of the existing social hierarchy. The belief that the Hungarian state, once it would be bourgeois and independent, would either inspire voluntary assimilation on the part of the other nationalities or, at least, an acceptance of the existing framework, proved utterly naive and unfounded. More than four-fifths of the nobility were Hungarians who, although vis-à-vis the Habsburgs were an oppressed nation, in the eyes of these nationalities were themselves oppressors. The Habsburgs managed to exploit this conflict of ideas to the full. Despite the experience of 1848–49, the general attitude in Hungary, clinging to the ideas of liberalism and the interests of the ruling class, continued to identify the integrity of the nation itself with the territorial integrity of the country.

The majority of those playing an active role in politics and literature were on the whole broadly united in their ideas before the Revolution, but, after its failure, emerged with varying contradictory attitudes. The internal contradictions of national liberalism began to make themselves felt, as did the fact that they conflicted with the interests of the ruling class—the landed gentry. Liberalism had promised organic development but developed into radicalism; it had promised to strengthen the social and national unity of the country but had led to the separatist movement of the nationalities, it proclaimed brotherhood but ruthlessly enforced individual and class interests. This led to widespread misgivings, and even disenchantment with their vision of the historical future and the meaning of progress. At the same time it was evident that, in order to preserve the nation and stimulate effective resistance to the Habsburgs, some sort of political concept was necessary as a foundation; and that it would have been inadmissible to resign oneself to a passive disillusionment. Criticism of the liberal attitude, an understanding of the situation, and the discovery of a solution had all to be combined to emphasize unity and avoid discouragement. The journey from the liberal to the radical-democratic attitude, from emphasis on the national to emphasis on the social aspect from Romanticism to realism was consequently retarded by these considerations, to the extent that there was even a sort of Romantic revival. Most of the writers of the time failed to make full use of this intermediary stage, and considered that extremes of both realism and Romanticism would be of no benefit to the nation. They rejected what was purely emotional or personal as they had rejected crude reality. They shunned the lyric, preferring epic poetry, which, they considered, was more disciplined and objective. Following Herder, they believed that the final purpose and value of history was for a people to realize themselves fully as a nation. Individual values could only be realized as national values. The nation was an organic unit and its individuality was collective, preserved in its purest form in folk poetry and in national tradition and as such was to be cherished and developed. This was the essential central mission of literature, only so could the enrichment of mankind as a whole be achieved. For this reason national tradition once again took an importance. Before 1849 attention had been focussed on the radical, revolutionary aspect of folk tradition; and this was particularly true of Petőfi; it was now the aspect stressing national order, organic continuity and hierarchical values that took first place. The *népies* movement which had already before 1849 made the break with Romanticism now fostered its re-introduction. Historical subjects became popular again, and the professed purpose of literature, the demonstration of examplary national ideals and actions, rather than disrupting criticism, was more easily realized in this manner. This retreat into nationalism, of course, ended in insularity, which can be clearly seen in the post-1848 *népies* period. Of those untainted by insularity, Petőfi made his mark and remained the literary focus of the national consciousness, while Eötvös, for instance, was relegated to the background in the eyes of the majority, not only of readers, but of future writers. It was Jókai who represented that period.

Despite these influences, the second half of this period was a remarkable time in Hungarian literature. Although outwardly they seemed to regress, in fact the main branches of literature were advancing towards realism, and this was reflected in the allied fields of psychological, ethical and philosophical thought. Hungary had always possessed writers, such as Balassi, Csokonai, Berzsenyi and Vörösmarty, equal to any of their Western contemporaries, but this period was the first to produce writers, such as Petőfi, Jókai and Madách, who were known and admired in the West. It is, on the other hand, true that a number of writers of equal standing, in particular Arany, were ignored.

Kossuth and the Political World

New talent sprang up everywhere, and not only in literature. First to appear was Széchenyi, and in his wake came other important public figures. *Miklós Wesselényi* (1796–1850) who came from Transylvania, a man who combined rare perceptiveness with romantic passion; at once the proud oligarch and the faithful democratic friend of the people; a man who realized and proclaimed the need for tolerance in dealing with the problem of the national minorities. There was Count *Aurél Dessewffy* (1808–1842), the intellectual leader of the Conservatives, whose dry, humourless and precise style and disdainful detachment inflicted more wounds on his rivals than the most biting irony ever could. There was *Ferenc Deák* (1803–1876), the maker of the 1867 Compromise between Hungary and Austria; a man whose modesty and sober demeanour masked his remarkable legal knowledge and logical powers. And, most important of all, there was *Lajos Kossuth* (1802–1894), the leader and symbol of revolution in politics as Petőfi was the symbol of revolution in poetry. He was a remarkable orator, turn by turn ironic, down to earth, majestic, tragic, infinitely moving; he was very well-read in literature and science and had made an exhaustive study of European politics and the political ideas of the period. Whatever the subject, his arguments were always coloured by his personal convictions and whole-hearted commitment, his dramatic choice of language and delivery making an intense emotional appeal to his hearers. Kossuth was a man with a fine figure and a deep resonant voice; he was imperious, with a trick of appearing obliging and there were few who could resist his appeal. His rivals, and indeed critical historians as well, reproached him both for his vanity and for pandering to the expectations of the public instead of considering the demands of history, for being slow to recognize opportunities; it took him ten years to appreciate the opportunity he had lost in failing to support a confederation of the peoples of the Danube basin. There was, however, no greater or more consistent representative of liberal democratic policy than he. He was at all times willing to reconsider his ideas and revise his views, even throughout his forty-four years of exile (1850–1894).

Yet even more important than any individual figure was the creation of the first political school of thinking on the lines of those in Western Europe. It was the Centralist school of thought, made up of Antal Csengery, László Szalay, József Eötvös and Ágost Trefort among others. These men had been nourished on Western, and particularly English, liberalism; their interests and their activities embraced economics, literature, criticism, folklore, history and the arts. They were the true Hungarian counterparts of the early Victorian essayist–politicians; Hungarian Macaulays, Gladstones, and Disraelis. They looked to economics, political science, and modern administrative and economic practice to provide answers: they abhorred sentimentality, rhetoric and guesswork. Their influence was strongest before the 1848 Revolution, when they withdrew from active life, and afterwards, during the fifteen years of Austrian repression, it was they who propagated the moral arguments in favour of self-discipline and self-restraint based on the philosophical arguments drawn from history and the social sciences.

The revolution gave scope to the activities of a handful of politicians of the lower classes. The most notable was *Mihály Táncsics* (1799–1884), a teacher who had been born a serf. His life was in itself symbolic; a tale of horror, comparable only to the lives of the most reviled Russian writers. He led a life of poverty, a permanent outcast, with ten years of underground hiding, imprisonment which robbed him of his eyesight, and facing continual warrants for his arrest for the publication of his essays abroad. Well-known political figures had dabbled in semi-socialist ideas before him, they, however, warned their readers against these ideas rather than propagated them. Táncsics, like Petőfi, was devoted heart and soul to these principles, in particular those of Cabet, and his novels and his essays were deliberate vehicles for the propagation of such ideas.

Cultural Life

It was in this period also that Hungarian art began to become a part of cultural life. Permanent exhibitions were opened, and portrait and landscape painting which, in early days, had followed the Austrian Biedermeier in its leanings towards Romanticism and Neo-Classicism, gradually turned for subject-matter to Hungarian history and later to the Hungarian landscape and characteristically Hungarian type of men and women. Following the Neo-Classical sculptor *István Ferenczy,* who was a pupil of Canova, *Miklós Izsó* became the representative of the period with his excellent, idealized peasants. National and folk music similarly claimed the attention of composers such as *Franz Liszt* and *Ferenc Erkel,* and similarly, *Róbert Volkmann* and *Mihály Mosonyi* composed Romantic symphonies based on folk and historical themes. Concerts and opera became a regular part of the cultural life of Budapest.

In fact, the most important development of this period was the growth of Hungarian cultural life. At last there was a demand and a public prepared to provide the incentive and money for books, newspapers and scientific and art publications. Books were no longer bought by patrons of literature, but out of a real desire to read, and literature became a profitable business for an ever-increasing number of publishers. Authors even managed to make a living from their royalties, and the translation of the best works of foreign writers was no longer a matter of private generosity but a business supplying a demand. By the end of this period, translations of Shakespeare, Goethe, Cervantes and Molière as well as foreign contemporary writers—Hugo, Dickens, Heine, Byron, Pushkin and Turgeniev—had appeared.

The creation of this new public was largely due on the one hand to the spread of education and on the other to the press which had managed to rid itself of its former provincial character. The Romantic period had seen the dominance of newspapers dealing with general subjects of interest; in this period there was far more specialization. News of the outside world had previously been taken from foreign papers, principally from the Augsburg *Allgemeine Zeitung;* there was now lively competition between several Hungarian newspapers and reviews. Before 1848 Kossuth's *Pesti Hirlap* was the most important; in the years of Austrian despotism that followed, the *Pesti Napló* took its place. It was in the columns of these newspapers and in the growing number of specialized reviews that philosophical discussions and inquiries first appeared. *János Erdélyi* (1814–1868), a professor of peasant origin who compiled an excellent collection of folk poetry, first exposed his attempts to incorporate the folk-based aesthetics of Herder within the Hegelian system. The teachings of Western liberal historians, economists, scientists, social theorists and ethnographers, the names of Macaulay, de Tocqueville, Bentham, Mill, Liebig, Fechner, the Grimm brothers, Herbart and others, and discussion on their work, together with the studies of Hungarian historians such as *László Szalay* and *Mihály Horváth* also became familiar to Hungarian readers through these publications. Nor did scientific progress lag behind. *Ignác Semmelweis* discovered the cause of puerperal fever; *Ányos Jedlik,* a professor in Pest, constructed a dynamo earlier than and independent of Siemens.

In short, what was happening was the provision of the right conditions, a public and all the resources needed for the emergence of modern literature. This period saw the gradual growth of an ill-defined capitalist economy and an urban way of life. The failure of the revolution retarded it, but could not stop it.

Literary Genres

It was the novel which made most progress in this period. The growth of a large reading public, benefiting from a middle-class, Western education, made publishing a profitable business. And the ruling genre in Western Europe, with which both writers and reading public had the strongest ties, was the novel. Above all, novels and plays best expressed the whole range of problems presenting themselves as the raw material of art. The capitalist transformation of society, the slow death of outmoded ways of life and thought produced conflicts eminently suited to these two genres, though the lag in the development of urban life gave the novel a headstart over the drama.

Lyric poetry retained its popularity, although during this time it was shared with the epic poem, the novel and the short story. Lyric and epic poetry were closely connected in this period, especially as poets wrote in both genres. The populist movement, then the main trend, made the greatest impact on these two genres. The poets were not only the principal representatives of the populist movement; they equally represented the *zeitgeist* of the period. In the first half of the period a variety of basic dicta were enunciated about the meeting and symbiosis of the poetic ego and the world, of man and society. The second half was more introverted, and its best work was deeply concerned with the ethical problems of human potentialities. The first period was characterized by a popular and democratic directness of approach and style, the second by a style which, though based on populism, was more consciously sophisticated. Petőfi and Arany respectively were the leading figures in these two phases of writing, and they were both among the great poets of Europe.

31 Sándor Petőfi (1823-1849)

His Life and Personality

Petőfi is still the Hungarian poet best known abroad. He was the beloved of the gods, lavishly endowed with everything a great poet needs: talent, the right historical situation, a manifest destiny. He lived twenty-six years in all, and left behind a body of work which in both quality and volume cannot be ignored in any assessment of world literature. At the same time it constituted the turning-point of an era in the literature of his nation. And he was given what was only given to Byron: a death which made of him a symbol and a myth. This poet of love, liberty and faith in life died on the battlefield as a volunteer in the cause of freedom. In Hungary, his name is synonymous with the very word "poet". It is not that he had no forerunners: Csokonai and Kölcsey, as well as such Romantics as Vörösmarty, contributed a great deal towards the foundations of the populist movement. But all the hopes and endeavours of the *népies* period, still regarded as one of the peaks of Hungarian literature, found their consummation in Petőfi.

He arrived at the right moment. As the poet of revolution and populism he came as fate demanded. His family no longer belonged to the peasant class, but had not yet achieved bourgeois status. His father, whose name was Petrovics, was of Slovak origin; his mother, Maria Hruz, who was a maid before her marriage, could not speak Hungarian well. His parents soon adopted the Hungarian way of life; at that time the short cut to the bourgeoisie was to become Hungarian. The father was a hard man who tried his hand at a number of things; inn-keeping, leasehold-farming and later as butcher in various villages and market-towns on the Great Plain. He went bankrupt more than once, but invariably managed to make a fresh start. It was his earnest desire that his elder son should be educated, become an intellectual, and move up in the social hierarchy; he retained his younger son at home to work in his trade. The young Petőfi (who made up and took this Hungarian sounding name when he first achieved success as a poet) early left the village for school and was given an early opportunity to gain a varied experience of the world.

As is usually the case with socially insecure people, he became defiantly sensitive to insult. It would have been difficult for him to make a place for himself in the social hierarchy, so he ignored it. Equality was what he required; it was a basic assumption of his in his social dealings and went hand in hand with his cult of the individual character. His father continually changed his school; out of necessity when times were hard, out of fastidious ambition when things improved. His school results were quite inconsistent. After one term, when his results were particularly bad, his father, who at that time happened to be bankrupt, disowned him; so, at age of seventeen he set off, deciding to become an actor.

The next three or four years represented one colourful episode after another in his life. At one time he was employed as an extra at the National Theatre in Pest. He then joined the army as a volunteer, but his fragile health was unable to stand its rigours, and on the recommendation of a friendly medical officer he was discharged. With the help of relatives and patrons he continued his studies; then went back to the stage; worked as a copyist for a paper in Pozsony and as a translator of novels in Pest, and then again returned to the stage, but this time in the eastern part of the country, where he spent a sick and miserable winter in Debrecen. Finally, after wandering all over the northern part of the country on foot, he arrived in Pest. In 1844 he became an assistant editor of a review, and from that time he lived by his writing. From the beginning of 1842, his poems appeared at regular intervals, and in the course of these two years he made his name as one of the leading poets of the country. He settled in Pest, but continued to travel extensively throughout the country. It was on one of these trips that he met Júlia Szendrey, the daughter of a noble family; against the wishes of her father, a man proud of his birth, they eventually married each other. During the 1848 War of Independence he joined the army as a volunteer and became aide-de-camp, interpreter and friend of the legendary General Bem. He died—no one knows where or when—in the battle of Segesvár, (now Şighişoara, Rumania), when the troops of the Czar overran Transylvania. His grave has never been found.

He was an "autobiographical" poet. His poems are almost a diary in the account they give of all the events and changing circumstances of his life, his intellectual and emotional development. It was swift, powerful and assured, and was accompanied by changing attitudes and choice of genres, subject-matter and the poetic means employed. As a result his poetry, produced in no more than seven or eight years in all, can be clearly divided into periods, which in turn provide a series of frameworks for the study of his work as a whole.

The Poet of the People

His early poems were imitations of folksongs, genre scenes and autobiographical outpourings. He rejected the high-flown stateliness, rhetoric and ornamentation of Romanticism for the natural ease and directness of folk song and its structural simplicity. He preferred the Hungarian metre based on stress to one based on the length of syllable. He wrote on the joys and sorrows of love, the sadness engendered by the lack of love: *I Turned into the Kitchen* (Befordúltam a konyhára), *All Along the Village Street* (A faluban utcahosszat), *To Blazes!* ... (Lánggal égő), *Love, Love* (A szerelem, a szerelem), *There are Thousands* (Ezrivel terem), etc. He was particularly attracted to village scenes and characters which were also popular with the Romantics. But Petőfi's genre scenes are not the "interesting" figures depicted by the Romantic poets but the ordinary people he met on his wanderings—the shepherd, the innkeeper, the strolling player, the schoolboy, the field-guard. His humour does not derive, as it so often did with the Romantics, from the exposure of an inferior character to a superior point of view. He identifies himself with his characters in understanding and sympathy; he is not laughing at their expense, they are both comic and likeable as in *Csokonai, The Inkpot* (A tintásüveg), *Master Pinty* (Pinty úrfi), and the *Meditation of a Thirsty Man* (Szomjas ember tűnődése). His characters are dramatic characters; they speak in the first person, he enjoys throwing himself into the personality of the tippler, the happy-go-lucky fellow with no heed for the morrow. But some honest, revealing personal poems are already beginning to appear. The poems in which he reveals his inner self, as well as his village pictures and songs, clearly show how an element of Romanticism broadens and develops into a new quality in his poetry. The Romantics also sought out what was natural and genuine, and they also expressed it in terms of characters and people. But their characters and people were idealized and stylized and their concern for them was more a matter of nostalgia for an ideal past and lack of faith in the present; it was an expression of their hopes rather than their knowledge and assurance. For Petőfi the natural and the right of his subjects to be seen as they were, unclothed by romantic fancy, was a matter of everyday fact. In his poetry things are what they are, he did not feel as the Romantics did any inability to understand the world around him.

The Development of a Populist Programme

Quite characteristically, he expressed his conscious revolt against the Romantic attitude with an excellent parody of the heroic poem. This marks the beginning of his second period, when he consciously adopted populism. The two epic poems which are the most typical examples of this period are his parody *The Hammer of the Village* (A helység kalapácsa, 1844) and a narrative poem, *John the Hero* (János vitéz, 1844). The first is laid in the village pub where two village gallants "Big-handed Fejenagy", the blacksmith and the "tender-hearted local cantor" vie for the favour with the "chaste Erzsók". The whole village appears in this poem, and the rivals, of course, end up with a fight. This is not just a straightforward parody of the Romantic epic as a genre. The real parody lies in the down-to-earth story and the down-to-earth characters dealt with in a high-flown Romantic style. *John the Hero* is just the opposite. The tale, the trappings are stock Romantic; the treatment, the picture projected, is anything but Romantic. The hero, John, is a foundling, brought up by his cruel shepherd stepfather. He falls in love with the orphan Iluska who is equally badly treated by the stepmother. One day, while dallying with Iluska, John's flock strays and the sheep are lost; he is driven out of the house and sets out to seek his fortune. Iluska dies of grief. After a number of adventures, typical of folk-tales, János arrives in Fairyland where he becomes the prince of the country and is reunited with Iluska. This poem not only symbolizes the victory of the poor and defenceless; it is not only an example of the new "epic", written in the language of common speech and the form of versification used by the common people, it also reveals the changes which had taken place in the relationship and outlook of man to the world and to life in general. In Romanticism, realistic themes generally took on a mysterious irrational meaning; with Petőfi, even the irrealistic subjects were treated rationally and realistically. The poems breathe out a faith in man as he is, an emotional and "intellectual" faith typical of populism in general and Petőfi in particular. Romanticism was impregnated with uncertainty and mistrust towards man and the world; Petőfi was assured and confident that the world could be understood and ordered aright.

Personal and Poetic Crisis

Petőfi never lost the faith and certainty so characteristic of revolutionaries in revolutionary ages; but there were times in his life when they weakened and on occasion seemed to fail completely. The worst of these periods followed the completion of *John the Hero* and is known as the "Clouds" period. The progressive political movements, to which Petőfi had by now given his whole-hearted support, ran into difficulties, he lost some of his friends and felt painfully lonely. In his cycle of poems *Clouds* (Felhők, 1846), his rejection of the world, his profound pessimism and his anarchic rebellion can be seen in the fragmented, aphoristic style and in the hyperbolic images and phrases. To find an appropriate form for such feelings he turned to the novel: *The Hangman's Rope* (A hóhér kötele, 1846), and to drama: *Tiger and Hyena* (Tigris és hiéna, 1845). In action, situation and characters both these works conform to the pattern of French Romanticism, but they are pervaded by the same sense of suffering as the poems of the *Clouds* cycle, and it is this lyric element that gives them certain value. They are important more for the stages in his development they reveal than for their intrinsic merit. The need to face the contradictions of the society in which he lived, helped the poet to work out an intellectual and political foundation for his hitherto spontaneous faith in life, which brought him into line with contemporary revolutionary thinking. His style, which up to that time had been developed to express personal feelings and emotions, broadened to take on a more philosophical and reflective colour.

By dealing successfully with this crisis in his life, his work, and the popular style he had adopted, benefited in three different ways: he integrated poetry and politics; his love poetry became more subtle, structured on several levels, and his narrative poetry acquired a philosophical character.

His Political Poetry

Although he had written political poems all along from the beginning of his career, they had been written spontaneously and, as it were, by the way. From this period onwards, his political poetry was consciously, directly conceived, influencing his images and descriptions. The sinking sun was compared to the bloody despot expelled from his country:

> Like a king banished to the border of his land,
> the sun looks back over the rim of the world,
> he gives one last glance
> from his angry face,
> and as soon as his eye reaches the further horizon
> the kingly head loses its bloody crown.
>
> (The Puszta, in Winter — A puszta, télen;
> translated by Edwin Morgan)

the clink of wine glasses to the clanking handcuffs of captive nations (*My Songs*—Dalaim). By this time he was known and appreciated by the radical public, and had won a devoted friend of equal poetic stature, János Arany. He made several attempts to form literary circles in support of his political ideas (The Society of the Ten and the circle connected with the journal *Életképek*). He had won a number of friends (amongst them the novelist Jókai) and he regarded Arany's epic poem *Toldi* as another token of the persuasive success of their literary and political work. The letters the two poets exchanged preserve the memories of a warm friendship and trace the formation of the policy and programme of the new movement: "When the people rule in poetry, they will be near to ruling in politics as well, and this is the task of this century," was how Petőfi expressed it.

He was one of the greatest poets of world literature with a deliberate political mission. Even Goethe would not have applied his derogatory *garstiges Lied*—squalid song—to Petőfi, so personal, so deeply subjective, so truly lyrical was Petőfi's political poetry. This was true from the beginning of his career and it was not at the battle of Segesvár, where he died, that his famous lines gained credit:

> *Love and Liberty*
> *Are all the world for me!*
> *For love I'd sacrifice*
> *My life on every day,*
> *For freedom I would give*
> *My very love away!*
>
> (Translated by J. Grosz
> and A. Boggs)

In politics he moved from the centre left of national liberalism to the extreme left of the revolutionary movement.

He was politically widely read and very well-informed, familiar not only with the figures and events of the Great French Revolution but also with the complete spectrum of its ideas. His revolutionary and democratic beliefs led him to give the general ideas of progressive Romanticism a definite and specific significance. The Romantics, for instance, believed that one of the criteria of the True Man was the love of one's native land. Petőfi shared the feelings expressed in the Romantic question of Sir Walter Scott: "Breathes there a man, with soul so dead, / Who never to himself hath said, / 'This is my own, my native land!' " But he believed that one's native land could only be loved if it gave freedom, life and equality to its sons. Romanticism continued to glorify the "People" and demanded a place for them at the centre of national culture. It was Petőfi's belief that the "People" should also have a place at the centre of the nation's political life. Nor was it for his own nation alone that he desired freedom. He answered the great vexed question of Hungarian politics, the "national minorities" question, by demanding freedom for all nations and nationalities. In a great poem, *One Thought Keeps Tormenting Me...* (Egy gondolat bánt engemet, 1846), comparable in its power to the greatest Romantic-Symbolist visions, he dies exaltantly in the final battle for world freedom.

> *Let it be there they take up my scattered bones*
> *when the great day of mass burial comes,*
> *and with measured, solemn music of the dead*
> *and black-draped banners lifted up ahead*
> *the heroes are given to their common grave.*
> *Sacred world-freedom, it is you who must grieve!*
>
> (Translated by Edwin Morgan)

He admired Béranger, in common with many others in Europe at that time, but in reality he was closer to Shelley and Schiller's white-hot love of freedom than to Béranger's mediocre versification.

It was also politics which led him to abandon the Romantics' idealization of the past. Unlike Vörösmarty and his disciples, he saw little beauty in the past, the time when the people, he believed, lived in permanent degradation. Like Michelet, he despised the history of kings, priests and nobles. He advised Arany never to write about even the best of kings, yet nonetheless a king. He regarded revolutionaries as alone worthy subjects for celebration in verse. He looked towards the future with whole-hearted ardour, and even welcomed technological progress as the inseparable counterpart of capitalist development. The redeeming and reformist attitude of Romanticism acquired a concrete meaning in his work, and merging with his patriotic feelings, intensified into a Messianic fervour. The national consciousness of the Romantics was nourished on the great deeds of the past; Petőfi was inspired by the belief that he stood in the front line in the battle for national freedom.

The Romantics had chosen Hamlet as a symbol of their doubts and indecisions; Petőfi saw the solution of human problems in the useful social deed and not in brooding meditation: "Whether it will be useful or not? / That is the question of questions. / Not 'to be or not to be'." (*Light!*—Világosságot!) This utilitarian and hardly poetic principle, so much like Goethe's *"wahr ist, was fördernd ist"*, brought him, of all his contemporaries, closest to Heine and the Russian revolutionary democrats. The main dilemma of Romanticism centred on the relationship between social man and the independent individual; Petőfi found the answer to the contradiction in social action.

His Love Poetry

After the early cycles (*Cypress-leaves*—Cipruslombok, 1845 and *The Pearls of Love* —Szerelem gyöngyei, 1845) his most beautiful love poems were those written to his wife, Júlia Szendrey. These poems have been the subject of criticism in later times. His critics have reproached him for continuing to write love poems to his wife, and to her alone. These poems are, they claim, chastely conventional productions, "average", "normal". There is some truth in this, especially if considered from a psychoanalytical point of view. But it is a matter of approach. In one of his best-known love poems (*September's End*—Szeptember végén), in autumn melancholy the young husband asks the wife bending over him:

> Tell me, if I die first, will you shed tears
> and cover up my body with a shroud?
> Or could another man bear out my fears
> and second love then blot my name quite out?
>
> (Translated by Edwin Morgan)

His critics remonstrated that in his poetry the "game of love and death" was set in a framework of ordinary life, treated melodramatically, almost bordering on banality. His love poetry is none the less very powerful poetry, for he accepted and lived the "game of love and death" as an unadorned everyday fact of normal life.

It is in fact this very aspect of his love poetry which was new. This is what love is like in the lives of the common people: it is one of the facets, parts of a whole life. Love was worthy of consideration as such, and the "man in love" remained his own essential self. One seeks in vain the myth or mystery of love in Petőfi's poetry. It is untainted by the decadent morbidity of contemporary poetry, the demoniac elements of Romanticism and, as a general rule, by eroticism erected into a myth. Yet his love poems were not written purely for their own sake: explicitly or implicitly, there was always the desire to communicate. It was inspired by the love of family and common human existence and the desire for a constructive life. Not only being in love, but also appreciating the woman as a partner in life. For Petőfi, a well-balanced person, love was not a refuge from life, but at once a concentration and a dispersion of all his life-force. His most famous love poems are: *What Shall I Call You* (Minek nevezzelek), *The Sad Wind of Autumn Speaks to the Trees...* (Beszél a fákkal...), *The Bush Trembles* (Reszket a bokor...), *Answer to the Letter from My Beloved* (Válasz kedvesem levelére), *I Love You, My Sweet* (Szeretlek, kedvesem), etc.

Descriptive Poetry

Petőfi's descriptive poetry appeared in epic and lyric form, in genre poetry, and in his own disguised self-revelations, and runs through reminiscences, meditations, anecdote and many other poetic forms. Yet the main characteristic of his descriptive poetry is that the subject-matter is always taken from ordinary landscapes or figures and events of common life. His is the world of the common people, a world ordinary but never vulgar or uninteresting. He succeeded in giving intensity and substance to moments and objects of daily existence. The Romantics were tormented by the emptiness of life. For Petőfi everything was infused with an emotional fullness, a mood of intimacy: a winter evening at his parents', sunset over the snow-covered Puszta, the noises of animals in the half-dark of the warm stable, the distant soughing of the wind mill in a hay-scented field, the trouble-racked life of his father and his comic old man's grumbles, the revels of the village lads, the delicious midday meal of the shepherds, a bonfire at night on the bank of a flooding river, his mother's faithful old dog and her only hen, the deserted inn, a funeral procession in a village, a village wedding, the market, and countless similar scenes, as in *The Plains* (Az Alföld), *The Ruined Inn* (A csárda romjai), *The Puszta, in Winter* (A puszta, télen),

229

Kutyakaparó, Old Sári (Sári néni), *Panni Panyó, The Tisza.* The Romantics, it is true, were also attracted to such objects and settings. But the Romantics, such as Stifter and Wordsworth, Lamartine and Brentano, Coleridge and Eichendorff, used them as means of escaping from their own lives. Here, again, Petőfi began as one of the Romantics, only to develop and transcend them. It was a natural consequence of his political and intellectual evolution that he should exalt ordinary landscapes and the speech of the common people. Neither his sketches nor his intimate genre poetry ever lapsed into escapist idylls, nor his style into mannerist simplicity. Just as his political attitudes were founded on a realistic appraisal of the common people, his development as an artist was based on a realistic understanding of their ways; he recognized that their virtue lay in their essential being and not in their outward peculiarities, and that what would provide opportunities for renewal and further development was not the forms in which it was couched at present, but the possibilities offered them.

Whatever he touched was impregnated with his youthful confidence. The landscape of his poetry, the salt Plains between the river Danube and the river Tisza, which had up to that time been considered the least poetic of Hungarian landscapes, under the magic of his pen became the conventionally "beautiful Hungarian landscape" for a century to come. The Romantics sought a characteristic national landscape. Petőfi created it. But it was not, as his imitators believed, the "characteristic", "exotic", "eastern" Hungarian quality which shines through his poems, but the faith and confidence which brightened the landscape. There too is the implication that life can be made beautiful and meaningful, thus fulfilling the aspirations of the Romantics: he treated landscape as existing in its own right for man to make of it what he will: the "home of life". Lenau, who was the only important precursor of Petőfi in his description of landscape, was wont to describe this world as the fairyland of a much-desired simplicity and naturalness. It was this part of his poetry which most clearly revealed his keen sense of humour. Humour is a rare gift in a young revolutionary poet, especially one in the main stream of Romanticism. The Romantics displayed cruel satire and bitter irony, but little humour. Petőfi indeed could also write searing satire, but it is his humour which his readers remember. He writes, indeed, of the injuries inflicted by the reactionary noble, and some of his poems at least were composed in an outburst of rage. But his nobleman, Pál Pató, a listless bachelor leading a shabby existence, whose answer to every suggestion—a new roof for his house, a better crop in his field, a young wife in his home, is "Oh, we've plenty of time for that" in time became a proverbial figure. So did another "Hungarian noble" boasting that he cannot read or write, and expecting his privileged position to get him into Heaven. Petőfi transmuted into literature the sometimes coarse, sometimes tender humour of the world of his youth, the peasants, strolling players, craftsmen and students, very much as Burns did in Scotland.

His Poetic Language

By the time he had written *John the Hero* Petőfi had developed a use of language and an individual style peculiarly his own. After 1846 it slowly grew into a language and style capable of embracing the whole variety of life, and we can therefore justifiably call it a "democratism of style". It was not the "language of the people" nor the "language of folklore", not even the language of folk poetry. He used the common speech of everyday—purified, refined and enriched. Everyone understood it, everyone felt that were he to write he would write in the same way. And his language gave his readers a sense that their lives too were the subject of poetry. He established a democracy of words, sentence construction, poetic imagery and objects, in which every thought and feeling was expressed by a word, image or gesture which subconsciously called up immediate and spontaneous associations in the great mass of the people. The Romantics sought a direct and natural approach; Petőfi found it. The Romantics suffered from the gap between life and poetry, between the poet and common man, Petőfi filled it. Yet, the perfection of his form was as extraordinary as his knowledge of literature, and his cultural equipment. He was well-read in German, French and English; he translated Shakespeare. One dazzling piece of bravura followed another; he moved effortlessly from one type of poetry to another, adopting new metres and styles as he wished, and solved the most difficult problems of technique with grace and ease. Were he not so ardently a man of the people, so impatient a revolutionary, so motivated by such strong political beliefs, he might be called Mozartian. For over a century his successors and imitators were enchanted and misled by this very ease. Believing it was enough to sing "as it comes", they claimed that Petőfi sang "as a bird sings".

The Revolutionary

At the time of the 1848 Revolution, Petőfi embraced the extremes of radical Jacobinism and advocated republican views of total equality in society. Apart from shorter poems, such as *Judgement* (Az ítélet), *A Sea Has Wakened Up* (Föltámadott a tenger), *Life or Death* (Élet vagy halál), *National Song* (Nemzeti dal), *I Dream of Bloody Days* (Véres napokról álmodom), *Italy* (Olaszország), etc., the main evidence of his growing radicalism is to be found in the Romantic epic, *The Apostle* (Az apostol, 1848). Its hero is a foundling by the name of Sylvester. Brought up by a beggarwoman and an old thief, he struggled to obtain an education and became inspired by great ideas. He worked as a tutor in a rich family, and later as a village clerk, always ready to defend and teach the peasants. Driven out by the lord and the local priest, he lived in misery in the city with his wife and child, and was imprisoned as a propagator of dangerous ideas. But he retained his faith that his ideals would finally triumph, even if he himself died in the struggle. Petőfi was successful in portraying social and political contradictions hitherto beyond the grasp of even the radical politicians of Hungary. The ideological significance of this work lies in the extent to which his conclusions reached out beyond those of all his contemporaries, while at the same time, some of Sylvester's monologues attain philosophical heights unprecedented—except for a few poems by Kölcsey—in Hungarian poetry.

That the common people may still be misled, should not dishearten those who fight on their behalf, nor will it lessen the historical value of revolutionary ideas, was the way Petőfi summed up his failure as a candidate in the parliamentary elections, where he lost to his rival, a local landlord. In the lull in the revolution he wrote a few beautiful poems, full of quiet memories and longings for his family, and also a small number of reflective poems (*The Skylark Sings*—Pacsirtaszót hallok megint; *At the End of the Year*—Az év végén; *On the Death of My Parents*—Szüleim halálára), but most of his work at this time was written as a call to battle (*Battle-song*—Csatadal; *Onward to the Holy War*—Föl a szentháborúra; *Respublica; Europe is Silent* — Európa csendes, újra csendes). In the summer of 1849, Petőfi hurried to join Bem in Transylvania; and the poet of the people died in battle and was probably buried in an unknown grave of the fallen. The political ideas he personified sank underground for a long time, but the new literature he brought into being remained the dominant trend of the whole period.

32 János Arany (1817–1882)

His Life

The other great poet of the period was János Arany. He was born into a small, closed world and a strictly disciplined and strongly traditional environment. His father was a peasant owning a house and a small plot of land in Nagyszalonta (now Salonta, Rumania), a sizable village on the Hungarian and Transylvanian border. The family, however, which could trace back its ancestry for a century and a half, regarded itself as being of so-called "noble" origin, which often meant simply freeman and not serf status, and worked hard to prove it by means of various documents. Petőfi owed the first stirring of his genius to the schools he attended, which were not uninfluenced by the liberal cult of freedom and individualism of the time. Arany learned to read and write from his father who draw the letters of the alphabet in a pile of ash; his first introduction to literature was provided by the Bible and a kind of simplified pre-Romantic, Baroque literature in the chapbooks on sale in the market-place.

His career started off in the way the careers of poets seemed, by tradition, to start. At the age of ten he was already acting as assistant of the local schoolmaster. This skinny, talented peasant boy, unsuited for work in the fields, was sent to Debrecen, the centre of conservative Calvinist culture, in the hope that he would eventually return to be the pastor, teacher or notary of his community. Old-fashioned though the school was, it awakened his talent and aroused his consciousness of the existence of art. At the beginning he wanted to become a sculptor or a painter. Then, after eighteen months at school he joined a band of strolling players. This venture was a catastrophic failure. After a few months spent wandering, frightened by the uncertainties of such a life he returned to apologize humbly for his conduct to the community of his native place—which needed considerable courage, given the traditional conservative tendencies of such a community. He then proceeded to adopt the career originally marked out for him, becoming the intellectual leader and administrator of the peasant community, an assistant teacher in a nearby village and, later, the notary of his own village. So he remained throughout the first period of his career, up to the age of thirty. During the revolution, under the influence of his friendship with Petőfi and his own early successes in literature, he became the editor of a popular newspaper; and he, too, joined the army, for a brief period, in the War

233

of Independence. After the defeat in 1849 he was offered a teaching post in Nagy-kőrös, a small town of the Great Plain. In 1860 he was appointed director of the Kisfaludy Society in Pest. Finally, in 1865, he became the General Secretary of the Hungarian Academy of Sciences. He retired in 1877 and spent five more prolific years in retirement. In 1882 he died of pneumonia, originating in a common cold. In Pest, he had edited the *Szépirodalmi Figyelő* (Literary Observer), the first Hungarian review of literary criticism, and then the literary magazine *Koszorú* (Wreath). He had two children. His son, László, became a writer and a banker; his daughter, Juliska, married a pastor and died young.

His Early Career

When, after his venture with the strolling players, Arany resolved to take a job in public administration, the most permanent element in his life began to show itself a certain ambivalent attitude compounded by uncertainty. He became an exemplary office worker; he dispatched the affairs of his community with considerable expertise and goodwill. But, although he had made up his mind to be "just like anybody else, an ordinary man", although he settled down in the manner of any village clerk and threw himself into his notarial duties, his nights were devoted to reading. He read political papers and a great deal of literature, but only the classics, ending with Goethe and Schiller, obtaining them from one of his former headmasters. He learned English by reading Shakespeare, French by reading Molière; he read Virgil in Latin and Homer in Greek. He not only read, he wrote poems and made translations. All this was done spontaneously for himself, for an "ordinary man" would be given no literary commissions. At the time he was still unfamiliar with the contemporary authors in his own country and abroad. The only exception was Byron. This proud, rebellious and homeless noble, this archetype of the Romantic spirit, made a lifelong impression on the conscienscious, exemplary clerk who had retreated to the traditional world and was by now the ideal head of a family. But the ordered life and the personality of a poet, the role provided and the role desired, no longer coincided. His final decision was exactly the opposite of what he had originally intended, as he was later to write in *Looking Back* (Visszatekintés).

> *Much as I crave independence,*
> *Still my chains I gladly wear*
> *Lest at last my bold resistance*
> *Make my lot the worse to bear:*

Like the wild beast of the saying,
Which the ropes though never tore,
Yet in struggling and in swaying
Got itself entangled more.

While his lower-class liberal political views, fostered by his newspaper reading, won him a number of sympathizers in his village, his ideas and dreams as an artist, stemming from his reading of the classics, and his "writer's personality" tended to set him apart. Later, in maturity, he regarded the happenings in the world, the titled office-bearers in public life, from his own private viewpoint. He felt himself above them; he saw through them; and while he stood in fear of them he also despised them. His first work, *Lost Constitution* (Elveszett alkotmány, 1845), was born out of such sentiments. He had not originally intended to write a literary work. He had planned to amuse himself with an ironic picture in a series of grotesquely Baroque scenes of the same lies told in their demagogic election campaigns by the liberals and the conservatives. As the rhetoric of both parties was very similar to the bombastic Romantic epics of the time written in hexameters he parodied that genre deliberately or otherwise. The work has no plot as such: it is more a series of election episodes centred on the leaders of the two parties. The long poem, headed by a didactic allegory on mutual understanding and the great role to be played by the "small and simple people" who work for the community, was entered in the competition for a satirical work organized by Kisfaludy Society. He won the competition, and the leading body in literature consequently recognized in him a writer of importance. Although he was then thirty, he had still developed no individual style. Familiarity with the Romantics had taught him what to reject but not what he wanted.

Toldi

It was Petőfi's poetry that liberated Arany and gave him a sense of direction. It proved to him that he could indeed give open expression to the vision of that true and simple world which he had created for himself. Within six months he had written his narrative poem *Toldi* (1847) and hardly any other work of Hungarian literature has enjoyed a greater success. Briefly, the story runs as follows: Miklós Toldi, the younger son of a noble family but brought up to work almost as a peasant on the family estate, lived in a village with his widowed mother. His brother György, an effete courtier at the court of King Louis the Great returning home on a visit, taunted Miklós and even allowed his soldiers to insult him. In a moment of anger Miklós accidentally killed one of the soldiers and was forced to flee. He finally managed to enter the royal court in disguise and unrecognized, and there he defeated

the hitherto unbeaten foreign knight, thus redeeming the reputation of his country
The king pardoned him and took him into his service.

Toldi contains all the elements which Romanticism had introduced into Central
Eastern Europe. The subject was historical, recalling the days of national glory.
The hero was a historical character from the Middle Ages, whose memory had
been preserved and enshrined in folk legend. He had lived, it is true, on the periphery of great historical events, but had been in touch with some of the central
figures in these events. His character and his deeds had caught the popular imagination. He lifted millstones, fought with wolves, he broke bulls with his bare hands.
He fell in with robbers, and untrained, defeated the professional foreign fighter.
He is the strong man of folk imagination, the hero who avenges the outraged
feelings of the people. And whatever the folk legends and the desires of liberal-
democratic Romantics failed to supply was supplied by the poet. Toldi is not
only a strong man. He is the natural, simple soul, untainted by the vices of civilized
society, by the false world of his superiors. He is unselfish but self-respecting and
is conscious of himself as a man. He wishes to fulfil his natural destiny as dictated
by the demands of his own nature, but is hindered by the depravity of the world
and the unjust disposition of society. The poem tells the story of a brave, simple,
true man of the people who overcomes all obstacles and gains his due becoming
the ideal hero and the man who is master of himself in the process.

The work also answers the special needs of Hungarian Romanticism. Toldi
is the embodiment of national solidarity. He is of noble origin, yet lives among
the people. The nation is presented as it once was, according to the Romantics,
and as it should be again: a family community, governed by the rules of justice
and nature. Toldi is essentially a lyric work, as Arany himself later pointed out.
It presents no Utopia, it illustrates no thesis, it is an inner reality, a vision.

> *As on autumn nights a shepherd's glowing fire*
> *Shines across the puszta's vast empire,*
> *So Toldy's face looms large in imagination,*
> *Wellnigh from a depth of nine-ten generations.*

—begins the poem. It is a dream, the dream of a man feeling himself in the grip of
a world alienated from all that is human, who in his loneliness envisioned a world
of his own: a true world, a democracy of his own. It is the vision of one who was
both a man of the people and an intellectual; who rising, left the peasant world,
but still preserved the feeling, the desires and the imagination of that world. It is
a Herderian, a "patriarchal" vision. His belief in its reality infuses Toldi with an
idyllic sense of joy, running bright through the poem. Although he was no adherent
of Petőfi's "style-democratism", this sense of joy gave Arany's complex style a
flavour of populist directness and natural simplicity. Petőfi became attracted to

him, aroused by his faith in a democratic future which made them friends and allies, although their views were never identical.

The success of *Toldi* placed Arany among the leading writers of the time. He now had the opportunity to gain insight into public and literary life, and this led to *Toldi's Eve* (Toldi estéje, 1847–48). This new work describes how little Toldi's desires were satisfied at the court of the king, and how little this world understood him. Here the poet shows no great sympathy for Toldi. He even treats him with a certain ironic humour. He is well aware that the road which the world takes leads to the court and its ways. But he is fearful that this will not end the alienation by mankind. The road which history had taken had led to capitalist development, and not to a patriarchal democracy based on family trust; such a society promised little for the world he aspired to see. The sheer poetry of the second work is even more evident than the first work. Although Toldi is treated with a loving humour, this humour is outweighed by the elegiac tone of the whole. *Toldi's Eve* is an elegy in the form of an epic, one of the most beautiful elegies in Hungarian literature.

Towards the end of his life Arany wrote the middle part of the trilogy, *Toldi's Love* (Toldi szerelme, 1879). It dealt with the adventures of the hero in his full manhood, the deeds that led to maturity, and his disappointment in love. The self-irony is unmistakable; the treatment suggests that compared to *Toldi* the poem is not much more than the trifling of an elderly man.

The Lyric Poet

Arany whole-heartedly espoused the cause of the revolution and the struggle for freedom; he even took up arms. But his confidence and certainty had ebbed away. The collapse of the revolution confirmed that something had been lost forever.

After 1849, Arany turned to lyrical poetry, something which he had no desire to do believing his gift lay in epic poetry. In the period immediately following the revolution, he tried to write a national epic poem. His lyric poetry was a kind of by-product in achieving this. But, in the final attempt of this kind, his epic poem *The Death of Buda* (Buda halála), the "means" were more modern in tone; the lyrical aspects of his work had become more modern than the epic.

These lyrics were born out of the conflict between the ideal and the reality in the years following the revolution, heightened by the subjugation of the nation.

By that time Arany was the man of the widest knowledge in literature and philosophy in the country. His lyrics reflect the various currents of European thought around the middle of the century. The disintegration of the "whole", doubts concerning "cognition", the relativity of truth, the lack of "universal" historical objects, scepticism concerning the equation of "development" and progress, the conflict between "moral" responsibility and material determinism, the immorality of "power" and the defencelessness of labour, the fragmentation of the "traditional" community, the disaccord between the individual and the community, between individual man and social man, and his increasing loneliness and alienation—all these were the subjects of Arany's poems.

> *Indifferent the world, the living,*
> *A ballroom crowded to extreme:*
> *It brings abundant tears to eyes*
> *If friend a friend should recognize.*
>
> *The people seen as through a curtain,*
> *I do not know a face for certain...*
> *Oh, what a crowd! And I alone,*
> *Although their ways are all my own.*
>
> (*In the Garden*—Kertben)

and again, in *Thoughts* (Gondolatok):

> *Gain and effort fall miles apart,*
> *And cheating, made a perfect art,*
> *Sits high, enthroned in every heart.*

or again, in *In the Garden*:

> *... Man, a selfish,*
> *Gluttonous lump of flesh and hide,*
> *Like a hungry caterpillar;*
> *Gains his advantage and takes a bite.*

For ten years of his life, he lived in this state of doubt and aimlessness, overwhelmed by a sense of futility. And he suffered the usual outcome of such feelings: the wish for death, the longing for an existence unencumbered by consciousness, the attraction of the refuge offered by an irrational freedom.

> *My soul, sailor of the ocean,*
> *Fears to pull in newer harbours...*
> *Let's away then, off with cautions,*
> *Rock, my ship, on currents streaming,*
> *Rushing I shall have no notions*
> *What is death, and what's out dreaming.*
>
> (*My Hope*—Reményem)

He wrote at the beginning of that decade. At the end of it he wrote:

> *Every moment but frightens me,*
> *And what comes next a burden be;*
> *My steps tread on the serpent's head,*
> *Today I hate, tomorrow dread.*
>
> (*The Eternal Jew*—Az örök zsidó)

He referred to himself as Hamlet, choosing the hero of doubt, the Prince of Denmark, as the symbol of a disillusioned generation. It is perhaps for this reason that he was able to make one of the best European translations of *Hamlet* (1865).

Yet all this is not Romantic lyricism. Nor can it be compared to the disillusioned, self-analytic lyric poetry of the Positivist period. It lies somewhere between the two, perhaps a little closer to the latter. Arany was not indifferent to the need to resolve these contradictions and achieve a single, integral, moral and assured image of the world. Nor did he lose touch with reality or delude himself with illusions; while not succumbing to complete and final disillusionment. His lyric poetry is of confrontation, the poems have two poles. One is constant: a desire for the ideal. The other fluctuates: he takes an episode from daily, contemporary life in which to clothe his thoughts: he quietly grafts the trees in his garden; he looks out from his room at the misty tedium of the autumn; he says goodnight to his small son, and ponders on the child's future. His poetry is highly subjective; his work is empirically analytical, soberly reflective and intellectual in character.

The language and the whole style of his lyric poems were something he deliberately created. Not for him was the style derived from folk or populist poetry—straightforward, unambiguous, natural. His aim was preciseness, the preciseness of the Classics. He deliberately went to the literary language of ancient writers and primitive folk poetry and saying, chose the words and phrases most loaded with possible meanings and associations. The language, the fruit of his intensive reading and research, makes him consequently, one of the most "difficult" of Hungarian poets. He makes use of every possible stratagem and device offered by language, cunningly devised to enhance one another; words, sounds, phrase-structure, embodying a thousand carefully controlled nuances, allusions and combinations; at once concrete and tangible, and yet universal. True to the tradition of Herderian Romanticism, he believed that such a use of language is the most effective in folk poetry and the "primitive" epic. It is for this reason that he considered the ideal to be folk poetry.

There is a musical principle in his constructions. The work unfolds through gradual progression in time, achieving complexity through variation. The poet forces a fragmentary and contradictory world into the unity of a harmonious work.

And it is all done with a touch of irony, a breath of melancholy, suggesting that he neither denied the need for unity, nor its possibility.

As a result the beauty of his poems is seldom revealed at first reading. They do not sweep the reader away or overwhelm him with a flow of words and dramatic appeal, offering instant experience. He is far from the great spontaneous spates of declamation and rhetoric of Hugo and his followers. The poems of Arany are rarely suitable for declamation. They were conceived in meditation and are for meditation.

Hardly any trace is to be found in Arany of the hard complete disillusionment of Baudelaire and his like who represented the new and "sensational" element in Western poetry of that time. His work is much more akin to the gentler disillusionment seen in the lyric poetry born *"zwischen Himmel und Erde"* in the grip of the real and the ideal, the *"poetischer Realismus"*, halfway between a harmony created by free will and stark unharmonious reality. His nostalgic, stocky humour and his cult of remembrance recalls Keller, his kinship with nature and immediacy of his descriptions Storm; his detached discipline of form and his retreat behind a wall of objectivity, Meyer. And also Tennyson, but the Tennyson who, on occasion, dared to be unharmonious.

Often, however, he managed to achieve a balance between the ideal and the real by references to and associations with styles alien to the experience and to the logic of the work itself such as Romanticism, Biedermeier, the cult of sentiment, didacticism, and in consequence he only managed to produce some twenty faultless poems during this period in an original style completely his own. *Years, You Years to Come* — Évek, ti még jövendő évek; *I Put down the Lute* — Letészem a lantot; *Autumn* — Ősszel; *In the Garden* — Kertben; *Looking Back* — Visszatekintés; *Dante; A Drop of Balm* — Balzsamcsepp; *On the Slope* — A lejtőn; *A Beautiful Autumn* — Kies Ősz; *Oh, do not Look at Me* — Oh! ne nézz rám; *To my Son* — Fiamnak; *Morning and Evening* — Reg és Est; *The Eternal Jew* — Az örök zsidó, etc.)

The Epic

The importance of Arany's lyrics of this period was made clear in the second half of the twentieth century, in the light of the lyric poetry written by Babits and Attila József, at a time when attention was focussed on the position of the individual. But it was accepted in Arany's time that the lyric poem took second place to the epic. Such was the strength of this view that Arany himself, after his earlier lyrics which he simply regarded as the outcome of the compelling circumstances of the moment, considered the epic his chosen field. He prepared himself for his role and mission as an epic poet by the study of critical and analytical works on the theory of poetry and of modern and ancient authors, and by unceasing meditation. He believed that the task of the poet was to create and revive in a contemporary context the common and single-minded national consciousness, feeling and character that had been lost. And the most effective way of doing this was to treat some historical subject in an epic manner. The present had no ideal heroes to appeal to the nation as a whole and would raise questions, especially that of "pauperism", to which the poet could not give an answer or offer a solution. On the other hand, to ignore such questions would only widen the gap and increase the uncertainty. Such thinking came perilously close to that somewhat reactionary aspect of Romanticism which combined the national–popular element in the doctrine of Herder with the philosophy of history enunciated by Savigny, leading to pseudo-historical ideas and the idealization of the peasant as an idyllic figure.

The extent to which his work suffered from this attitude can be seen in the fragments he wrote on contemporary subjects, especially in *The Village Fool* (A falu bolondja, 1851), in which the talented son of a peasant drifts away and, in assuming a series of undignified, laughable roles, becomes the village fool.

Fortunately, Arany also incorporated into the work a typically "un-Romantic" element. He held the view that although the national character is best preserved in the common people, it may become primitive because of their intellectual isolation, therefore, it should be impregnated with values originating in the superior culture of the day. He saw his age as Virgilian: it was not destined to create anything new in culture or art; its main task, therefore, was precisely that work of impregnation. This is a typical "educational" postulate of the age of Comte and Herbart.

The Death of Buda

This twofold theory is the basis of the epic poem *The Death of Buda* (Buda halála, 1863). It is the first part of a trilogy, but can in fact stand on its own as an independent work. It deals with the struggle for the throne between the great Hun king, Attila, and his brother Buda. Arany forced the material of a magnificent psychological novel into a form which was archaic and obsolete, bringing his power of artistic discipline and his vast fund of knowledge to bear on its composition. This work is imbued with all the delicate perception found in the analytic novel to the development of a tragic situation which from its first conception develops inexorably, through the minutest reactions of mind and heart, moving inevitably to its tragic climax.

In this work he warns that catastrophe cannot be avoided unless we submit to the dictates of common sense and the laws of nature through mental discipline and self-knowledge.

The Death of Buda is a tragedy of role and personality. King Buda, in a moment of impetuous generosity, divides his power between himself and his younger brother,

241

Attila. They both accept roles which are inconsistent with their personal characters, the one of them is too weak, the other too strong to share power. It leads to their deaths. Buda dies first at the hand of Attila, and as the other parts of the trilogy were intended to illustrate, Attila then meets his death as a result of his crime. Apart from the warning implicit in the work, this wonderfully concentrated work contains another motif or rather another overtone. It may have been deliberately intended by Arany, or it may have emerged from the devices of style employed—the tragic note, balladistic tone, the short, melancholy summing up. It is the rolling of history, of destiny. Not the mysterious, mythical history, the "destiny" of Romanticism but the horrible cogwheel system of the Positivist era, coldly exposed with critical detachment. The question of the system is clear; the process by which the cogwheels shred all who fall between them is equally explicit, but its object remains concealed. This aspect of the work is no more than an undertone, yet it reveals how few illusions Arany had retained concerning the historical development of his time.

The Ballads

The Death of Buda was the climax of Arany's ten years' search for an epic role; it was his intention that the work should take the same place in public estimation as *Toldi*. But in vain. Apart from *Toldi,* Arany, desiring fame as an epic poet, is still best known for his famous ballads. These ballads were in fact earlier than the search for an epic role. He began to write them in 1853, five years after the failure of the War of Independence, a time when the Hungarians opposed a passive resistance to Habsburg domination. Arany was attracted to the group headed by Kemény and Csengery, the leaders of the movement for passive resistance; he made friends with them and accepted some of their views. In particular, he was concerned to preserve national unity and promote the moral strength of the nation, and it was with this aim in view that he composed his ballads. Their subject-matter is generally taken from sad and difficult periods in national history, especially from the fourteenth and fifteenth centuries, the periods of Anjou and Hunyadi, and from the period of Turkish occupation.

László V (1853) deals with the unhappy son of Albert Habsburg, his conflict with the nation, his breach of faith and his atonement. *Mátyás's Mother* (Mátyás anyja, 1854) is about the imprisonment in Prague of the young Matthias Corvinus and his mother's struggle to secure his release; *Klára Zách* (1855) about the criminal participation of the wife of Charles Anjou in the rape of a noble's daughter, and *The Two Pages of Szondi* (Szondi két apródja, 1856) about the loyalty of a castellan's pages. Arany's subjects included tales from common life. In *Mistress Ágnes* (Ágnes asszony, 1853), for instance, he deals with a peasant woman who, with her lover, killed her husband, and went mad as the consequence of her crime.

When Arany wrote, the ballad was an outmoded genre, only to be found in the village and market-place. Arany raised it again to the rank of literature, and in this type of poem one might rank him next to Goethe. They were excellent means of arousing the national consciousness and a national determination to survive. But they were at the same time objective projections of his ambivalent attitude, his suffocating mood and his moral strength. This is clearly shown by the *Bards of Wales* (A walesi bárdok). The Emperor Franz Joseph only visited Hungary for the first time five years after the 1848 Revolution had been crushed. The authorities requested writers to produce poems of welcome. Arany replied with the ballad of the Welsh bards who went to the scaffold for refusing to pay homage to the conquering English king, Edward I, a story based on legend.

Arany's ballads were greeted with unbelievable enthusiasm. The nation celebrated in them its greatness and its moral superiority to its oppressors, and its right to the tragic assumption of a better future founded upon this "superiority" and "greatness". It neither could nor would listen to the poet struggling painfully with uncertainty and doubt, which echoes through the ballads as it vibrated in the lyrics. It clung to the illusion that national sentiment and will were omnipotent, an attitude by no means rare during the more tragic periods in the history of small nations. Arany's ballads were read as the counterparts of Jókai's romantic novels: the readers were firmly reassured about the national character, the national feeling, the national will; all that mattered was to end foreign oppression.

The range of Arany's art was extremely wide, but especially reveals the psychological associations of the Hungarian sentence, which it would never be possible to reproduce in translation. A single line often contains implicit references to different experiences, judgements, approaches, feelings and distances. Many writers of ballads followed in his footsteps. The ballad is at once the easiest and the most difficult of genres. His imitators chose the easier aspects, and Arany himself, either because of the appearance of a host of imitators or perhaps because the ballad could not replace the great epic of his aspirations, gave up writing them.

His ballads were welcomed with passionate enthusiasm while *The Death of Buda* with obligatory enthusiasm and total incomprehension. The public expected and believed that it had been given in these ballads an overall image of the world, a faith in life justified by simple sentiments of nationalism and a knowledge of the national will. In *The Death of Buda* they were in fact given a poem which embodied Arany's inner struggle with the strict teachings of self-knowledge and self-control, self-discipline, and the ethical discipline of feelings and will, in a form which was too difficult for, and too alien from, the period. The result was that *The Death of Buda* did not bring the poet close to the nation, nor did it enable him to fulfil what he believed to be his mandate, or resolve his doubts and uncertainties.

The Final Period

After the reception accorded to *The Death of Buda* and his four long years of failure as the editor of a literary review, he could not but become aware of his loneliness and his alienation from the people. "You don't want me as a *praeceptor*—very well, you don't want me," was the way he summed up his situation in a mood of bitterness. His alienation from the world became unmistakably clear to him in 1867, when a certain amount of independence was restored to Hungary, and the part liberal, part capitalist and part feudal world of the Dual Monarchy was established, with its mob of lesser nobles and junkers which, while maintaining the privileges of the landed class, introduced into Hungary the selfish, corrupt, jostling society and class characteristics of the bourgeois establishment. Arany did not even begin to work on the other parts of his trilogy. He turned to silence. He buried himself in his work as the General Secretary of the Hungarian Academy of Sciences and threw himself into the translation of the complete works of Aristophanes. *"Seul le silence est grand,"* he too could have written on the next ten years of his life.

But it was with a painful, wise resignation, rather than in bitterness, that he ended; he left with an elegy. A few years before his death, after retirement, he spoke again. It was not that he now had more leisure, but that he was no longer a public official.

The lyric poetry of his later years wonderfully reflects the autumn light of an old man's life. The style is far more even, more contained and consistent than that of his first lyrical period. He was, however, too old and too tired for the great disillusionment peculiar to the second half of the century, as exemplified first by Baudelaire and then by Nietzsche. In some of his poems, however, we hear the note which accompanied him throughout his career—the tragic sense of misgiving, of a mistaken life, an existence missed. But his work did not lead to any final confrontation. It remained mostly on the level of objective recollection, a summing-up, a farewell. Most often he recalled his childhood not directly, but in the form of wonderful "peasant" ballads akin to the doomed and concentrated mystery of Storm's *Schimmelreiter* and to Hardy's descriptions of village life (*Corn-husking* — Tengerihántás, 1877; *Red Rébék* — Vörös Rébék, 1877; *Ordeal of the Bier* — Tetemrehívás, 1877). He bade farewell to his unfulfilled dreams in poems characterized by nostalgia and melancholy, lightened by humour, but elegiac in the deeper sense. He came a step nearer to *"poetischer Realismus"* but a gentler, more "poetic" version. These melodious poems are more concerned with emotion, with gentle memories, than with argument and the inner drama of conflict. There is even a touch of Impressionism in his enjoyment of colour, his love of word-play and soft music. What is most authentic of the man is the dignity with which he registers objectively, undramatically, with a proud, sour reserve, without a smile or tear, that he did what he was able to do, and must accept what is still left for him. His poetry is infused with the most profound of his qualities, his firm, humane, moral sense. Most beautiful of these poems are *In the Market* (Vásárban); *Under the Oaks* (A tölgyek alatt); *Naturam furca expellas; I Have No Need of the Hoar-frost* (Nem kell dér); *This Life* (Ez az élet); *Until the Very End* (Mindvégig); *Dreary Hour* (Meddő órán); *Once More This Time* (Még ez egyszer), etc.

It was undoubtedly his role to sum up and to crown all that had gone before. Not only populism, even though he himself claimed throughout his life to be a "populist" or "popular–national" poet. But, while Petőfi—the true populist poet—had a strong aversion, like the other members of young Europe, towards Goethe, Arany regarded him as the king and final word on his kind of populism. Arany absorbed, summed up and then developed further whatever Hungarian literature had until then created or adopted. His work, consequently, was also closely related to Classicism which it continued and transmitted.

33 The Populist Poets

Mihály Tompa (1817–1868)

In contemporary eyes Mihály Tompa was regarded, after Petőfi and Arany, as one of the chief populist poets. In later times he was acknowledged to be one of them, but rated considerably lower than the others. His place in the history and development of literary taste was undoubtedly important; he transmitted the sentimental, the "Biedermeier", the didactic elements of pre-populist Romanticism to the populist movement, and even beyond into the post-populist period.

He was the son of a drunken provincial bootmaker, and managed to finish school by acting as a servant to his wealthier schoolmates. His whole adult life was passed as a pastor of the Calvinist Church, working in the villages of northern Hungary. His constitutional melancholy was aggravated by the traumas of his childhood, by social injustices, and by an illness contracted in his youth, (believed to be V.D.), which afflicted him throughout his life, sometimes reducing him to a state of lethargic apathy. Physically strong—he could snap a horseshoe with his bare hand—, mentally he was unstable. He was extremely ambitious, yet tormented by doubts of his own talent; he was longing for company, frustrated in his yearning for the idyllic warmth of family life, for his children died one after the other, suspicious, quick to imagine neglect or insult, and consequently very testy in company. He hated critics with all his heart and soul. Only Arany, endowed with unlimited tact, could endure him, and indeed gave him invaluable support in the years of his growing confusion, when he was at times driven to the brink of suicide, and their correspondence makes fascinating reading.

His work divides into three periods, all equally worthy of consideration. The first was devoted to legend and saga (*Folk Legends, Folk Sagas*—Népregék, népmondák, 1846). Following the English and German Romantics, perhaps even inspired by them, he either invented legend or had recourse to existing legend and then proceeded to associate them with some specific object in nature or in history; a waterfall, a rock, ruins, a flower, an animal, a social custom. The tale would be sentimental in tone, full of moral dicta, cast in the form of romance. He can be included among the populist poets only insofar as he makes use of folklore and genre scenes, and his language is rich in folk and country expressions and words. His poems were essentially didactic, while at the same time designed to introduce "popular" principles and values to other strata of society, and his work often contains democratic as well as moral implications.

Tompa's second period, the period of allegory, began after the battle of Világos in 1849 when the Hungarians were finally crushed, and Austrian despotism made it impossible to speak openly about the anguish and future hopes of the nation. He changed easily from the sentimental to the allegorical and elegiac, from moral didacticism to heroic grandiloquence and rhetoric. His grandiloquence is full of pain; his rhetoric is dignified, and the poems expressing the general suffering of the Hungarians still move the reader (*To the Stork* — A gólyához; *The Bird to his Breed* — A madár, fiaihoz; *On the Puszta* — Pusztán, etc.).

Although the subject-matter of the third period had already begun to make its appearance earlier, it only really dominated his work from the mid-fifties onwards. His poems breathe the moods of a doubting soul, tormented by scepticism and shifting and changing values, by the transience of life, by the perplexity of the mind. His sentimental treatment of nature is elevated into a form of pantheism, the allegory of his romances is transformed into symbolism; his didacticism to a noble stoicism; his deeper emotions find expression in the gentle music of sad and nostalgic verse (*Autumn*—Ősszel; *To an Autumn Landscape*—Őszi tájnak; *Do not Call*—Ne hívj; *Summer Evening*—Nyári estén). Tompa is not an intellectual poet; his work is a mingling of mood and emotion. His poetic career began with Biedermeier and sentimental Romanticism and passed through populism to pre-Symbolism and pre-Impressionism. Although he is indeed for the most part close to Petőfi and Arany, in his last period he comes nearer to Vajda and is a forerunner of Reviczky. There was a time when Tompa was the most widely read Hungarian poet of all, particularly in the provinces and among the half-educated, and his role here in the formation of literary taste, as a preparation, a link, was very important. These readers found their way to Petőfi and Arany through their pleasure in Tompa's legends and sagas; and to Reviczky through the melancholic outpouring of his verse.

Gyula Sárosi (1816–1861)

Gyula Sárosi was more receptive than Tompa to the humorous genre scenes of folk life, the lyrical ballad, the love poetry based on folk song and folk language in general, but in style he advanced very little further than Petőfi's first period. He expressed in his work the views and the way of life of the lesser nobility. His parody of an epic, *The Golden Trumpet* (Aranytrombita, 1848–49), written in the form of a reportage, and directed against the Imperial court and the supreme command, shows signs of the influence of Petőfi's satirical poetry; after the Hungarian defeat of 1849 he was imprisoned for it. The disgrace of it broke him. Never a strong character, unaided by any of the resources provided by education, he sought refuge in low amusements. During this period, however, he produced a number of pleasing poems harking back to the Romantics. Such a poem is *At the Rebirth of Ingeborg* (Ingeborg újjászületésekor) in which he expressed the hope that both he and his nation would finally emerge from their present distress.

The Poetry of Pál Gyulai

The poetry of the well-known critic, Pál Gyulai (1826–1909), were greatly influenced by those three dominant poets, Petőfi, Arany and Tompa. In the construction of his poems and his simple and direct language he comes close to Petőfi. Another who greatly influenced him was Heine. His poems resemble songs, limpid in form with uncomplicated rhythms, dealing with slightly sentimental and romantic situations, and composed in the first person. Another aspect of his work is seen in the poems dedicated to simple and single themes, nostalgia for an old love, youth, the moods of the seasons, the pleasures and the idiosyncrasies of company (*Lieutenant*—Hadnagy uram; *I would Like to See you Again* — Szeretnélek még egyszer látni; *On the Rosehill of Buda* — A budai rózsahegyen; *Before the Ball*—Estély előtt). As a critic he was permanently at odds with his contemporaries, but he had made up his mind to continue on his way unabashed. He loved Arany, but the pain and suffering found in Arany's verse was something alien to his muse. He comes closest to him in a few brooding poems comtemplating the defeated country, and meditating on the loss of faith, and was also akin to him in the careful attention he devoted to every word and line of his work (*While Reading Horace*—Horatius olvasásakor). Nevertheless his type of melancholy was more akin to Tompa's than Arany's, his poetry, in fact, falls between Petőfi and Arany.

The Imitators of Petőfi

Apart from the individual poets, there were two groups of poets around that time which call for attention. The first group such as *Kálmán Lisznyai, László Szelestey,* and *József Székely,* are usually known as the "imitators of Petőfi". In general, they copied the style and themes of Petőfi's first period. They imitated the more obvious outward features of his work, reproducing and exaggerating them to a degree that made them absurd. Petőfi's addiction to role-playing, his gaiety, his natural and spontaneous style, his use of the tongue degenerated in their hands into buffoonery, the vulgar joke, the tawdry spree, combined with lack of skill, provincial boorishness and triviality. The majority of those who imitated Petőfi were members of the ill-educated lesser nobility who had come to Pest from the country, and could not adapt to city life. Their poems reveal their taste or, rather, their lack of taste. Only one of their number rose above this level: *Kálmán Tóth* (1831–1881). He possessed some of Petőfi's feeling for melody and some of his oratorical brilliance. But Petőfi's deliberately revolutionary and democratic principles degenerated in Tóth's hand to crude nationalist slogans, Petőfi's charm became *naturbursch*. When Gyulai, Arany and Erdélyi destroyed this trend by their ruthless criticism, Tóth took their words to heart; his writing became more subtle; his self-knowledge deeper, his style more disciplined. A few of his gentle songs and lovely patriotic poems have indeed stood the test of time (e.g. *A Cloud Covers the Forest* — Felleg borult az erdőre; *Forward* — Előre; *Who Were the Freedom-fighters* — Kik voltak a honvédek).

The Imitators of Arany

The other group of poets is known as the "imitators of Arany", its most outstanding members were in fact contemporaries of his. Their virtue lies in their literary skill and their use of the common tongue, but polished and elevated to a classic level, and in their scrupulous concern over versification. Like Arany, they preferred themes taken either from national history or from the peasant world suitable as subjects for epic or for descriptive treatment. These men had no perception of the struggle to balance the ideal and the real faced by Arany. Liberal nationalism they regarded as an absolute virtue, and it dictated the form of the idealized heroes of their epic poems as well as the emotions expressed in their poetry. Their poems were flat, empty of inner conflict, turgid and middle of the way. They won no small number of official awards; after 1867 they filled important and well-paid posts; were endlessly active, and led long and blameless lives. In their moral complacency they were the provincial cousins of Longfellow, indeed, they translated much of his work. They were, as a matter of fact, closer to Tompa than to Arany, though lacked Tompa's profound melancholy and scepticism.

Perhaps the best of these poets was *József Lévay* (1825–1918), who was a friend of Arany and Tompa. He wrote a few simple, carefully shaped poems about the sorrows of the nation, nature, and the joys and sadness of country life. (*Mikes; Our Grapeharvest* — Szüretünk; *I Remained in the Valley* — A völgyben maradtam; *Jupiter Pluvius; Harvest* — Aratás.) He demands a certain amount of respect for his knowledge of his own limitations: he never aspired to more than his emotional and intellectual powers permitted.

The Arany school of poets enjoyed the support of the authorities—the Academy, the educational world, the Churches,—until the end of the century, becoming increasingly sterile in the process. These men are to a great extent responsible for the conservative image given to Arany, and the fact that the progressive elements in the country viewed him with disfavour. These men, after all, enjoyed official support, and all literary patronage and rewards passed through their hands, with the result that young or unknown poets received very little in the way of assistance from them.

34 Mór Jókai (1825-1904)

The Novel

It was Romanticism that produced the Hungarian historical novel. It also went some way towards establishing the "social" novel, the novel concerned with social problems, but it attracted no public worth speaking of. The novel only became an accepted genre in the 1840s. The historical novel lost popularity in the years prior to the 1848 Revolution, and it was only in the following years that it came to the fore again. And then it was no longer in the form of Jósika's rather simple descriptive accounts of history; it was then involved in the political, moral, philosophical and psychological aspects of history and the historical content was designed to point a moral for the living present. It is true that even before 1848 the historical novel had to some extent been concerned with social problems. But, interestingly enough, after the 1848 Revolution exactly the opposite occurred, and the social novel acquired some of the features of the historical novel. The transition of the novel from Romanticism to realism was more obvious before the revolution than after. Before 1848 there was a growing tendency to a general criticism of the social system, but afterwards introverted psychological analysis took over.

The populist movement did not have the same direct and effective impact upon the novel as it did on lyric and epic poetry. This is because the novel primarily dealt with the world of the still semi-feudal nobility, and its main aim was a spirited criticism of such a society. It was sympathetic to the plight of the peasants, though not written from the angle of the peasants themselves. The three leading novelists, Jókai, Eötvös and Kemény, and in addition Gyulai, who only wrote a single novel, projected the mentality and feelings of the nobility, although each writer was concerned with a different group of the nobility, with its own distinctive form of behaviour. But then, European literature can boast of few novels written specifically from the peasant's point of view. Peasant life, so central to lyric and epic poetry, is merely episodic in the novel. Romantic lyric and epic poetry, even the theatre, drew much of their inspiration from songs and folk tales; the novel with its complex structures, found no such examples in folklore; only the short story made use of it to some degree.

His Life

Mór Jókai was Hungary's greatest Romantic writer of prose. His works enjoyed a wide reading public who still prefer him to any other novelist. Jókai was born in Komárom, and enjoyed an eventful and happy childhood. His father was a respected and wealthy lawyer of noble origin, but the spirit of his home was rather that of a city intellectual than that of a provincial land-owner. Neighbouring land-owners, however, were also frequent visitors to the house, being relatives, clients or friends of his father.

His native town, famous for beautiful and well-kept gardens, was a busy port on the Danube and was one of the commercial centres of the country. His family lived in an atmosphere of hopeful liberalism, confident of the security and superiority of the Protestant Enlightenment. The schools which Jókai attended had already been powerfully affected by French Romanticism and the radical-liberal spirit of Young Europe, eager with expectation, Byronic in their yearnings and despairs. These influences can be seen in his first works, written at the age of twenty, a tragedy (*The Jewish Boy* — A zsidó fiú, 1843), a novel (*Weekdays* — Hétköznapok, 1846), and a number of short stories.

Immediate success attended him and, together with Petőfi, he became a leading figure among the young writers of Pest, and editor of *Életképek,* a review to which he had contributed. This slim, blue-eyed young man with his gentle manners and humour was popular everywhere. He was a man easily swayed by other, more dynamic, more decisive people, and this was equally true of his marriage. During his first years in Pest, he married an actress, much older than himself, who was a favourite of the aristocracy. According to Jókai's contemporaries, this woman, capricious and vain, loving the material goods of this world, was partly responsible for Jókai's later opportunism. On the other hand, it was largely due to her determination that mundane troubles never crossed the threshold of Jókai's study.

During the 1848 Revolution, Jókai worked as a journalist and editor, wavering between the two sides. On occasion he seemed to support the republican cause; and then again to be in favour of a compromise with the ruling dynasty. And always from conviction. He took his convictions from the political company he kept, who were then and later the leaders of the wealthy nobility. After the failure of the 1848 Revolution he was forced to go into hiding for some time, and wrote under a pseudonym, but during the ten years of repression that followed under the restored regime of the Habsburgs, he became the most popular Hungarian author of his time. He was the first Hungarian author to make a prosperous living by his pen. Between 1867 and 1896 he was a Member of Parliament. He also edited a number of magazines and newspapers, including a very popular comic newspaper.

He was a born journalist. Not a man of logic, factual argument or intellectual conviction, his politics were largely emotional, buttressed by brilliant and dramatic rhetoric. As journalist and politician his tactics were to encourage his supporters and discredit his opponents, largely by the use of ridicule, biting irony, telling anecdotes, insinuation and sharp parody. In the later years of his life, his work as editor and his position as a Member of Parliament were no more than nominal, his rule was confined to making propaganda for his party. At this time he wrote practically no political articles. But memoirs, sketches, anecdotes, short stories, and prose poems, especially descriptions of landscape, poured profusely from his pen. He took his subjects from human and historical curiosities from the four corners of the earth, but later Hungarian history and descriptions of Hungarian landscape still predominated. Although he played practically no active part in politics in later life, he still enjoyed considerable political influence. He had a child-like faith in the ability of national liberalism to put the world to rights, in the bright future of the Dual Monarchy. He did indeed enjoy personal relationships with some of the royal family. His publicity work for the regime and his novels were equally responsible for the acceptance of this belief by the middle classes: he, more than any one else, created the national illusionism. His popularity declined after the turn of the century, but his death was still a national event.

The Short Stories

His literary work only really developed after 1848. He began with short stories (*Battle Scenes* — Csataképek; *Diary in Hiding* — Egy bujdosó naplója, 1850–51). At twenty-five Jókai appeared to be a perfectly mature writer, a master of the Romantic short story. Blended in his work are the rhetoric and vision of Hugo and the sentimentality and love of nature of Rousseau. His treatment gradually eased from the grandiloquent to the poetic, from the striking to the intimate. In long idyllic lyrics, he dealt with nature—the forest, the marsh, celebrating the simple life far from civilization which acted as a refuge and cure for the persecuted, the disappointed, the aimless. In his dramatic manner, he elevated the recent past to visionary heights, always doing full justice to the vanquished and setting them above the victor. His short stories won him great popularity. Already, at this stage, one of the main reasons for his success was clear: his ability to identify with the prevailing mood and sentiments. Others, such as Arany and Kemény, struggled to comprehend the causes and consequences of the 1848 tragedy, tormenting themselves and the nation in the process. Jókai quite spontaneously expressed and exalted both the national sentiments of genuine patriotism and the illusory conviction of superiority.

The Novel of Incident or Anecdote

Jókai consolidated his popularity with the novels which followed his short stories, and thenceforward his principal preoccupation was the novel. His novels can be divided into four types. One of the earliest and most important—*A Hungarian Nabob* (Egy magyar nábob, 1853)—falls into the first category of these types. It is the novel based on a series of genre-scenes and anecdotes. The genre-scene, dealing not much with a subject or plot, but with everyday life and surroundings, unidealized, whether rustic or middle or upper class, was also popular with the populist Romantics changing from the idyllic, the purely imaginary to the realistic. In prose this change occurred in *A Hungarian Nabob*: a general picture of a class of society, of a national way of life, emerges from the fragments of the novel. The other component—the incident, the anecdote—was a classic element of the market-place chapbooks of peasant stories and tales about the life of the nobility. Jókai made use of both types, restoring the ancient function of the anecdote in use in the European Renaissance: gives the essence of social situations and human types in the flashlight of the point of the story. The subject of the work, as in most novels of this kind, is the nobility in the Age of Reform. János Kárpáthy, a wealthy aristocrat and bachelor, is surrounded by an odd circle of the provincial lesser nobility. Fellow-toppers, shooting-companions, administrators, entertaining fellows, excelling in the invention and retailing of one anecdote after another. His nephew, following the fashion of the ultra-reactionary aristocrats of Paris, who has squandered everything abroad, now impatiently awaits his uncle's death in order to lay hands on his fortune. But Sir John tricks him; he marries a middle-class girl who bears him a son.

Eötvös painted the more repellent aspects of the nobility, Jókai the more attractive. Although he makes no attempt to conceal the general illiteracy, public ineptitude and egoism of his chief characters, he always manages to find one good point in them—their willingness to enlist in a good cause, generally stemming from their patriotism and liberal sentiments. Eötvös bent all his energies to stirring the nation, and the nobility in particular, to radical reform; Jókai to keeping a national consciousness and a liberal attitude alive. The crisis of liberalism, which shook so many of his contemporaries, hardly touched him. His simple faith in the liberal doctrine of continued progress is not likely to worry the reader in this novel, as it primarily appears indirectly in his pictures of different types of human beings. He is mainly concerned to justify men, not movements or ideologies: his simplicity is that of the fairy tale. He lends colour to and describes with immense affection all the awkwardness and faults of his heroes. They are the subject-matter of his best humorous writing. Generally speaking he fails whenever his irony or satire is based on any kind of ideology. The villains of the piece promptly become unreal and lifeless when he attempts anything of the kind. He came closest to the optimistic "realism" of Dickens's

Pickwick Papers in this type of novel, especially in *The New Land-owner* (Az új földes-úr, 1862), another excellent example of the same genre, where he describes how a convinced anti-Hungarian official of the oppressive Habsburg regime is transformed in a few years into an enthusiastic Hungarian patriot. This novel is structurally better composed and possesses a more clearly defined "ideological" aim. And precisely on this account, is somewhat ambiguous. His failure to confront the crisis of national liberalism has serious consequences here. He may have meant to prove the moral superiority of the oppressed, but all he manages to assert was the moral superiority and irresistible appeal of his nation, or, indeed, simply of his class. He nursed the myth of his class and his nation sustained of themselves, which later proved so injurious, and helped to shield them from their need for self-knowledge.

The Novel of Heroism

Although the novel of incident is still to be found among Jókai's later works, it ceased to take first place after 1867. In the following years he concentrated on the heroic novel—or something called novel-epics. The subject is usually an episode from one of the Hungarian struggles for national independence. Some believe they were inspired by Jókai's opposition to the Compromise of 1867 and these dramatically coloured tableaux were designed to create an ideal for present and future struggles. The most famous of them is the long novel *Sons of the Stony-hearted Man* (A kőszívű ember fiai, 1859). The plot of this novel, like the others of the same type, is involved and monumental, with a tendency towards idealization combined with a propaganda purpose, and the method is one of sharp contrasts in black and white, as Romantic as Hugo himself. The setting is pre-1848. The stony-hearted man, Kázmér Baradlay, a noble loyal to the Habsburg dynasty, was anxious that everything should go on according to the order of feudal hierarchy. In his will, he marks out three posts in the service of this hierarchy for his three sons. But it is the eve of the revolution; his sons and his wife refuse this order of his, and set out to serve and defend the cause of freedom. In describing their adventures, the author gives a vivid picture of the 1848 War of Independence.

This novel, together with his other novels in a similar vein, enjoyed an exaggerated popularity in Hungary on account of its political attitude and aims. It would be no more than an adventure story for boys today. The more original, more personal aspects of his writing, and making use of more realistic material, were relegated to the background, and the description of the manners and way of life of men and women, brought to life with inimitable vivacity and humour in the genre-scenes and various incidents of the tale, which gave such power to the *Nabob,* are hardly given a chance in this novel. Nor, lacking any compensating touch of reality does the other aspect of his talent, the one akin to the spirit of the French Romanticism have the best opportunity. The motivation of the novel is poor; the construction of each incident artificial and theatrical; his exposition of his ideas naive and bombastic; the characters are juxtaposed in a simple angel-devil confrontation; the dialogue rhetoric odd; the tension that of the adventure story. The criticism, the self-scrutiny, so badly needed by the public at this juncture, is practically non-existent. In the scenes taken from common life, his hopes for the future found expression in his pictures of human character, and, thus, in the manner of the "folk-tale", his "liberal", his "national", ideas were conveyed, transformed in human situations and this was one of the main sources of his magic. In this particular novel, such a transformation was wanting, and his unquestioning political optimism became over-simplified and indeed, counter-productive.

The Novel of Personal Confession

His most charming novel belongs to the third type which one may describe as the novel of personal confession. *The Man with the Golden Touch* (Az aranyember, 1872) reached quite as high a standard as *A Hungarian Nabob*. This is a novel of inner crisis, like most of his writings of this kind (for instance, *By the Time We Grow Old* — Mire megvénülünk, 1863). By the 1870's, he must have become aware that liberalism was unable to fulfil his hopes in the economic, social or moral-intellectual sphere, and he could no longer ignore or avoid the crisis presented. Personal experience, including a love affair late in life, only added to his disorientation. In *The Man with the Golden Touch* all the elements of his first great period of crisis, the period of his earliest short stories, *Battle Scenes* and *Diary in Hiding,* are present. But the subject is now all handled with the faultless mastery of an experienced writer, and is enriched by the vivid, realistic atmosphere of the scenes from common life. The melancholy inherent in the contrast between the ideal and the real and the transience of life had, up to this moment, been only spasmodic in his novels; it was now the central element in his work. In those short stories of 1850–51, he painted the conditions of hopelessness and disillusionment which were experienced; here he described the process of their emergence. None of his novels revealed greater realistic psychological depth than this highly Romantic work. He did not analyse in the manner of contemporary realism but by evocation, by the use of internal monologues, by lyrical descriptions of landscape. Symbolism and Impressionism make themselves felt in this novel, and in none of the novels is Rousseau's feeling for nature so present. Indeed, the conflict of the novel is resolved in a Rousseauesque spirit.

In this novel, laid in the beginning of the nineteenth century, a brave intelligent Danube sailor, Mihály Timár, acquires by dubious means the treasure of a wealthy

Greek merchant in flight from the Turks. He educates, then marries the young daughter of this merchant who knows nothing about the treasure. His aim is to repair the wrong to her and satisfy his conscience. Their marriage is unhappy. In vain he heaps all that the heart can desire on his wife, out of his ever-increasing wealth. They are bound by no more than ties of gratitude and a mutual affection. He becomes disillusioned with the world he knows, founded on money and acquisition, and finally finds happiness on a "no man's island" in the Lower Danube with another woman and her mother, also repudiating the world of money and wealth. But that Jókai described was neither a naive utopia nor commercial-minded Romanticism. This "no man's island" is described with painful melancholy as something deeply desired but doomed as impossible from the outset.

The Novel of Adventure

Nonetheless Jókai has to be described as an inveterate optimist. As soon as both national and personal troubles began to abate, he promptly returned to his optimist attitude, with no great searching for a reasonable foundation. It became, however, increasingly dated. His output was no less, but his books were emptier and more and more out of touch with the world as it was, at the same time his way and means of representation becoming more and more obsolete. His fourth type of novel, the novel of adventure, dominated his last years. The subjects and settings were extremely varied, and anyone unacquainted with Jókai, judging these novels on their content, would see him as a counterpart of Dumas père. Jókai did in fact borrow from him, especially in story-turns and matters of technique and dénouement, as well as from others, such as Sue, Jules Verne, and even Zola. But certain features emerge in these novels that are his alone, and he succeeded in raising this type of novel above the level of the average adventure story. One reason was his wonderful gift of story-telling. Cartoonists often depicted him with an encyclopaedia in one hand, twisting its dry facts into colourful stories with the other. Whatever he read or heard immediately became plot for him; an anecdote, a tale of common life or adventure. He once confessed that he in these novels relived his rich colourful childhood. He wrote easily and with pleasure; it was practically a mode of existence for him. Yet, all in all, his adventure novels are the least important of his books. None of his novels, of course, can be said to belong purely to this or that type, nor can the periods be taken strictly either. *Eppur si muove* (1872), for instance, is essentially a heroic novel about the Reform Era, but its first pages contain one of Jókai's most beautiful scenes taken from common life, and the prologue is a mixture which includes adventure and personal confession as well. The sequel to the *Nabob, Zoltán Kárpáthy* (1854), the story of the Nabob's son, is also a mixture of these styles of novels.

Black Diamonds (Fekete gyémántok, 1870), being essentially a work of social criticism, and extremely anti-clerical, is at the same time also an adventure novel. Throughout his life he attached great importance to the historical novel. On the surface, he would appear to be a pupil of Scott and Hugo. But the signs of their influence are generally only external. The attraction of his historical novels lies in the intimate, though anachronistic, description of the setting and the episodic genre-scenes. A famous critic of Jókai, Jenő Péterfy, wrote that the action and characters of his historical novels belonged to the operatic stage. But there is an exception here, too. *Prisoner Ráby* (Rab Ráby, 1879), is based on the memoirs of a supporter and confidant of Joseph II. He gave an honest picture of this strange man of the period of the Enlightenment, so cruelly reviled by the feudal world. But he transformed the sad end of this man into an episode ending in felicity.

The predominance of incident and anecdote and genre-scene in Jókai's work and its result—a lack of individual characterization—influenced later writers. It hindered the action and especially the development of central figures in a novel. Mikszáth and Móricz are examples. On the other hand, his influence was helpful to all his successors in the use of settings and interior descriptions, in dialogue and the creation of atmosphere. Particularly indebted to him in this respect are those, like Krúdy, who specialized in the tale of an incident, the single anecdote, which was Jókai's first phase of writing. These qualities were of real value in the development of the short story. It would be hardly possible to imagine the Hungarian short story at the end of the last century without Jókai's mastery of detail. His great contemporary, János Arany, pointed out in a critical work that these were the elements by which Jókai adapted the literary prose of Romanticism to the populist period. And it is in these qualities of Jókai that the transitional character of the period between Romanticism and realism is best revealed. He himself, indeed came closest to realism by virtue of these qualities.

35 The Novel—from Romanticism to Realism

József Eötvös (1813-1871)

The other two important novelists of the period are Eötvös, very nearly a realist writer in his views on history and society, and Kemény, who trod the same type of path in psychology. Although Eötvös had, prior to 1849, already shown a tendency to introduce a more radical element in populism, both he and Kemény were further away from populism than Jókai.

Baron József Eötvös was born into a loyal family of office-holding nobles. He spent his childhood on the estate of his maternal grandfather, an old liberal soldier of German origin who, despite a certain unworldliness, was a pioneer of capitalist development. His father employed a member of the Martinovics conspiracy, who had spent some time in prison, as a tutor for the boy, to provide an example which would deter him from radical thought. The plan miscarried: young Eötvös absorbed the liberal ideas of his tutor, and when his father, threatened with bankruptcy, planned to resort to certain unethical business practices, the young man broke off relations with him. From then on, his career and opportunities were rather those of an official of the upper classes than of an aristocrat. His marriage brought him some landed property again, but he lost most of it through inexperience. He entered politics at an early age. He soon overcame the distrust of progressive circles towards his family—his father had supported the Austrian court in 1848,—by his conscientious pursuit of liberal and democratic aims. He became one of the leaders of the Centralist Party, and held the office of Minister of Religion and Public Education in the Government of 1848 in the early days of the revolution. He was opposed to the break with the dynasty, and the proclamation of a republic that followed, and during the fighting he resigned and went abroad. He returned in the early fifties; immediately after the Compromise, he took office again and remained Minister of Religion and Public Education in the Hungarian Government until his death.

The writing career of Eötvös began in the circle of Kölcsey and Kazinczy. The first inspiration derived from German Classicism; he was later influenced by French Romanticism, as well as his readings in liberal theories of politics, law and state. Most of his poems were written during this period. They combined German Classicism and French Romanticism with the sentimental Romanticism of Kölcsey, characterized by a warm philanthropic feeling for the oppressed and the suffering, an elevated moral sense, and the correct patriotic sentiments of the time. His poetry consistently reflects the predominant literary modes of his period; sentimental pathos, philosophic melancholy, meditative reflection, musical language, the introduction of new words into the vocabulary and a good deal of high rhetorical flourish, dominated by an overall romance-like tone. His most important poems are: *The Frozen Child* (Megfagyott gyermek); *Oh if I were...* (Oh lenné...); *I would Desire* (Én is szeretném...); *Farewell* (Búcsú); *Will* (Végrendelet); *The Flag-bearer* (A zászlótartó). Despite his strong lyrical streak, he was not really a lyrical poet. Nor was he a dramatist, although he wrote a number of plays, his best being the comedy *Long Live Equality* (Éljen az egyenlőség, 1841). This is a satire on the middle ranks of the nobility, anxious for equality with their superiors, but utterly averse to any suggestion of equality with their inferiors. The action of the play is sluggish, with no clear-cut dénouement, the whole too speculative and complicated, while the dialogue and the whole approach are both clearly those of a novelist.

He was a radical reformer, who strongly believed not only that needed reforms would prevent revolution, but that failure to institute them would inevitably provoke it, and his whole life and work were devoted to this belief, applying the same criteria both to situations and events abroad, as in his studies *Poverty in Ireland* (Szegénység Irlandban, 1840) for instance, as at home in *Prison Reform* (Fogházjaví-tás, 1842).

His Novels

His first novel, *The Carthusian* (A karthausi, 1839) was not written explicitly directed to these aims. Yet in this work he overcame the Byronic-Romantic melancholy of his generation and class, the Romantic anarchy and pessimism of his circumstances, and also clarified his objectives. The novel is set in France. Gustave, the son of a noble French family, became disappointed in love, friendship, in the integrity of the middle classes and the aristocracy. The corrupt atmosphere of the kingdom of Louis-Philippe I poisoned relationships, with everyone pursuing his own selfish interests. Disillusioned, he joins the Carthusians only to realize that he was himself pursuing his own selfish interests in doing so, even though his means were somewhat purer. "It is only the selfish for whom life contains no consolation" is the final conclusion of the novel.

Before Eötvös, no Hungarian novel combined social criticism with psychological analysis. His work was therefore greatly influenced by French Romanticism and, to a lesser extent, German Classicism and the novel of Sentiment. But he managed to fuse into one the pioneering efforts of Fáy and Kármán and, as a result, this novel, which is set in France, became the first genuine and important Hungarian social novel. The work does, however, have serious faults: it is too full of meditative reflections and poetic flights, and the character-drawing is often merely descriptive with elaborate dialogue and language.

Eötvös's literary qualities and his primary purpose in writing are fully revealed in this novel. Liberal–democratic reforms pursued needed, he thought, criticism and further impetus, and Eötvös was prepared—like the Junges Deutschland or Hugo's circle—for his work to be branded as propaganda poetry. In a passionate essay, *Reform* (1844 and 1846) he attacked all the sins and stupidity of feudal Hungary, and in a passionately satirical novel, *The Village Notary* (A falu jegyzője, 1845), he brought all the faults and fatuity of this feudal Hungary to life. He built the overwhelming and exhaustive arraignment around a crime: the act of the reactionary noble party in arranging for the theft of the letters-patent of the liberal village notary, Tengelyi, to prevent him from running for office again. For the first time in Hungarian prose, the peasants are given heroic and important parts to play in the tale and are given real and individual characters instead of the former, invariable presentation of them as subsidiary comic characters. It was his deliberate intention in this novel to demonstrate the pressing need for reform and, in his next novel (*Hungary in 1514* — Magyarország 1514-ben, 1847), the consequences of neglecting such reform. In the second novel he describes the Hungarian counterpart of the German peasant wars at the close of the Middle Ages. The peasant armies, together with the craftsmen and priests who joined them, originally called together to go on crusade that never took place, are led by Dózsa, and begin by seeking reasonable reforms from their lords. The latter resist these demands, stubbornly and brutally, and the peasant movement turns to revolution and civil war, with Dózsa's cruel death and an inhuman retaliation which set back the progress of the whole country. Eötvös's novels show a certain similarity to Scott, and also to English novelists of the eighteenth century, in his objective treatment and pedestrian manner; the clearly defined plot and construction of his books, on the other hand, are akin to the *Wahlverwandtschaften*. Both these novels are more masterly in construction and proportion than the earlier *Carthusian*. But one feature is less in evidence: the psychological study of the individual, which began to take shape in the first novel, developed no further, and was actually suppressed. He clarified and accepted his objectives, he put his trust in reason and in the superiority of ethical man and in liberal progress. He was a political thinker, untouched by the specific problems of philosophy. The philosophical basis of his liberal ideas and activities, the nature of the opportunities and limits of reason and ethics seldom troubled him. When, in his old age, he read Kant, he called *The Critique of Pure Reason* strange and incomprehensible. His own self-confidence enabled him to become the first Hungarian to practise a realism which was critical of society, but it perhaps prevented his realism from acquiring a psychological foundation. It is for this reason that

The Village Notary is superior to *Hungary in 1514;* individual characterization is not as essential a requirement in satire as in the novel.

Eötvös also wrote a most illuminating study of Petőfi. He considered his poetry in the light of its ideas and social significance, and appreciated the poet's popular style at its just value, though his own work was far from such a style, replete as it was with cycles of long sentences, logical structures, and rhetorical dialogues. The incidental or anecdotal type of novel, the genre-scene, the brief maxims so characteristic of Jókai's prose were alien to him. It was partly on this account, and partly on account of the critical attitude he adopted, that his influence on the development of Hungarian prose in the second half of the nineteenth century was comparatively small, and far less than he merited.

Some years after the collapse of the revolution in 1849 he wrote another and last novel (*Sisters* — A nővérek, 1857), a rather weak "educational" novel. First in exile, and later on his return to Hungary, he continued his campaign in the cause of Hungarian unity, liberal democracy, the welfare of the people and general education, with pamphlets and essays in Hungarian and German, including the first Hungarian account of liberal theory of state: *The Leading Ideas of the Nineteenth Century and their Influence on the State* (A XIX. század uralkodó eszméinek befolyása az álladalomra, 1851–53). When, in 1867, he once more became Minister of Religion and Public Education, and found his more democratic educational plans thwarted by the Church and a growing body of reactionary land-owners, in anger he reached for his pen again. Death, however, prevented him from writing his projected novel, *The Barons of the Nineteenth Century* (A XIX. század bárói), which might have given a new direction to the Hungarian novel. A strong, realistic work, on the lines of *The Village Notary,* might have opened up new paths at a time when the dominance of Jókai's romantic illusions and anecdotal style was proving a restrictive influence.

Zsigmond Kemény (1817-1874)

The third novelist of that period, Baron Zsigmond Kemény possessed those very qualities which Jókai and Eötvös lacked: a philosophical bent, a passion for psychological analysis, the ability to create individual characters. But he was wanting in several qualities which the other two possessed—the ability to construct a tale, and the gift of story-telling. He was born into a distinguished but impoverished Transylvanian family. His father married twice and acted with brutality towards his family, and Kemény's childhood was spent in scenes of family discord. A scholarship to one of the famous schools of Transylvania, where he studied under an outstanding liberal thinker, came to him as a blessing. As a protegé of Miklós Wesselényi, the famous liberal politician, he entered politics early, and soon became the leading advocate of the liberal opposition in Transylvania. He studied English and French liberal politics and economics, the history and development of both of these countries, as well as German Romantic philosophy and the literatures of all three countries. He read medicine at the University of Vienna, and he was well aware of the problems connected with the beginnings of Positivism, and was even acquainted with the ideas of Western socialism. He later moved to Pest and aligned himself with the Centralist Party. He withdrew during the revolution, and later supported a party in favour of peace with the Habsburg dynasty. Nonetheless, after the collapse of the revolution, he was imprisoned for some time. He then became one of the most prominent leaders of passive resistance to the Austrian regime and edited Deák's organ, *Pesti Napló* (Pest Journal), a paper of the patriotic land-owning class. In 1859–61, when political life in Hungary revived, he was one of its most important intellectual leaders. But he was not given any important post after the Compromise of 1867. His unbalanced way of life (at times he lived a bachelor life in hotels and even in brothels, at other times in ascetic isolation) and his illness finally undermined his nervous system. His mind gradually gave way; he spent the last years of his life in complete darkness of mind in his native place in Transylvania.

This man who was so obsessed with psychological analysis could himself have proved a fitting subject for such a study. His personality was an unbalanced union of opposing qualities: the comic and the tragic; the deeply ethical and the immoral; the idyllic desire for happiness and the inability to be happy. He and his characters have often been compared with Dostoievsky's. And not without reason. Jenő Péterfy, an authority on the European novel, declared that nobody more nearly rivalled the great European masters, and Zsigmond Móricz considered him to be the best Hungarian novelist of all. Eötvös's books had been published in German, French, English and Italian; even Jókai gained a certain following abroad. But Kemény's works never crossed the frontiers of his country, possibly on account of his previously mentioned shortcomings, which, apart from his artistic make-up, could also have been the consequences of his views.

From the outset, he adopted a sceptical attitude towards the liberal philosophy of history. His opposition and scepticism centred on two points. One was the possibility of changing the course of history; the other concerned the relationship of the individual and history. He did not reject the liberal concept of progress, but doubted whether liberal programmes would succeed in influencing the march of history. Any artificial intervention was bound to upset the balance of society, nation and state, and their organic development; it would cause tragic harm. His views combined the fatalism of Romanticism and the determinism of positivism. It was his belief that any disruption of the European situation and the structure of the Habsburg monarchy could only lead to chaos and tragedy, and prove a check to progress. He consequently advocated the slow, organic development of the bourgeoisie and capitalism.

He believed that the workings of history, which would bring about collective improvement, would ultimately destroy the happiness of the individual and render the maintenance of his individual personality impossible. He held that to reject this fact was nothing more than plain madness; the only possible way out was stoic self-knowledge and disciplined adaption to circumstances. In his pamphlets (*After the Revolution* — Forradalom után, 1850; *One More Word after the Revolution* — Még egy szó a forradalom után, 1851) he urged such stoic adaptation to the situation and tried to prove by the Romantics' belief in national characteristics that Hungarians are by nature unrevolutionary, and therefore Vienna's reprisals for revolutionary activity were senseless, for it was not the nation but a mere handful of individuals under the leadership of Kossuth who were responsible. There is an element of shrewdness in this, but the need to comply with the workings of history is undoubtedly one of the fundamental tenets of his thought. Kemény's novels are also concerned with such ideas.

His Novels

Kemény's first novel of any importance was written prior to 1848 (*Pál Gyulai*, 1847). It is set in sixteenth-century Transylvania, at the court of the Báthoris who then ruled Transylvania, the focal point for all court machinations, for conflict and intrigue between Turk and German, Catholic and Protestant, burgher and noble, prince and subject. *Pál Gyulai* is the chief adviser of the unpredictable ruling prince Zsigmond. In order to preserve his personal integrity and loyalty to his task, for various reasons he is forced to accept the appearance of disloyalty and betrayal. His noble intentions thus lead to the most tragic of results. His loyalty to his Prince and his sense of honour and personal integrity drive Gyulai to tragedy, and in the end destroy that honour and integrity.

After 1849 Kemény wrote short stories and a novel on social problems, such as *The Whirlpools of the Heart* (A szív örvényei, 1851); *Hazy Scenes on the Horizon of the Spirit* (Ködképek a kedély láthatárán, 1853); *Husband and Wife* (Férj és nő, 1852). But is was not until around 1855 that he found himself as a writer. In his subsequent historical novels, he pointed out ways the tragedy might have been avoided. The novel, *The Widow and Her Daughter* (Az özvegy és leánya, 1855), which is set in the period of the Reformation, demonstrates how religious fanaticism, family selfishness, a lack of discipline and an unwillingness to adapt to circumstance destroy human life and happiness. Mrs. Tarnóczy, a Calvinist, forbids her daughter to marry her lover who is a Catholic, but forces her to marry a wealthy old Protestant and thereby causes her death. The subject of another novel, *Fanatics* (A rajongók, 1859), is religious fanaticism; the work is set in the same period and is a study of the unbridled passions of religious enthusiasm and intolerance. Elemér, the nephew of the Calvinist chancellor, Kassai, is in love with the daughter of his political and religious opponent, the Sabbatarian Pécsi. The conditions of the time tear them apart; hatred brings about the death of both Pécsi and Elemér, and brings misery to the country. In this novel, as well as in his last great novel, *Stormy Times* (Zord idő, 1862), his aim is to show that the pre-condition for the controlled restraint of passion is self-knowledge, which must be based on a knowledge of the workings of history. The subject and the background of this novel is the Turkish occupation of Buda in 1541. The story deals with the unhappy Barnabás, an honest and estimable young student whom circumstances transform into a monster: the humiliation he has suffered and his lust for revenge lead him to become a traitor, a Turk; but when it suits his new masters, they hand him back.

Kemény's last works were really historical novels. With a historian's insight he shows the causes and roots of individual and public tragedies, with a writer's skill he brings the atmosphere of the time and the personality of his heroes to life. His strength lay in the description, exalted yet detailed and precise, of the movements of men's souls, but he was weak on construction, with little narrative sense, and the incidents and dialogues are awkward and clumsy. The psychology, in fact, was brilliant, the narrative poor, made up of Romantic clichés. Here, too, the contradictions in his literary attitudes can be detected. His powers of analysis of different situations is comparable to those of the great realist writers; his vision of fate and history is Romantic. In fact, while opposing Romanticism, he sustained it. He was both an impediment in the development of realism, and at the same time its precursor. His novels were not read by the general public in his own day, nor have they read them since. On the other hand, he is forever being rediscovered by writers and men of letters for his wonderful psychological insight. He is a writers' writer.

The Novel of Pál Gyulai

To the work of these three novelists must also be added the single novel of Pál Gyulai (*The Old Mansion's Last Owner* — Egy régi udvarház utolsó gazdája, 1857). This work is most akin to the European realistic novels of the period, especially to Turgeniev. It also rejected the Romantic plot, adopting one which could not be simpler. An old noblemen spends the two years of the 1848–49 Revolution in hospital. He returns home, after the defeat, with his old ideas, habits and methods of farming intact, to find himself a Rip Van Winkle in a changed world. His family abandons him and disperses; his servants treat him as a joke; his estate goes to rack and ruin: he becomes a man unneeded and unwanted, and dies. This is the first example in Hungary of the realistic novel of disillusionment; the psychology is brilliant and the autumnal atmosphere, the society of the time, are faultlessly reproduced. Gyulai views his hero with melancholy and irony; he sees him as the bearer of a great human and national inheritance which has fulfilled its function and must now disappear. What would come next is a question neither he nor disillusioned realism attempted to answer. But this was certainly the liveliest novel of that period, and it is to be regretted that the path he opened was not followed before the seventies or, indeed, before the end of the century.

Minor Novelists

The minor novelists of the time followed in the footsteps of Scott, Jósika, Jókai or the French Romanticism. *Gereben Vas* (1823–1868) was the author of novels about the recent past, full of stirring incidents and plots, somewhat rambling, couched in elaborate folk language (*Great Times, Great Men* — Nagy idők, nagy emberek, 1856; *The Workers of the Nation* — A nemzet napszámosai, 1857; *Kinsfolk at Law* — A pörös atyafiak, 1860). His populism is of an earlier type than Petőfi's and connected with the post-1849 peasant plays. The lesser nobility, whose level of education was low, found that he expressed their views of life and people. *Lajos Abonyi* (1833–1898), master of the idyllic, painted scenes of village life on the lines of the Austrian *Dorfgeschichte*, and produced in particular the type of work which dilutes the love romance and folklore into a story. *Alajos Degré* (1820–1896) wrote in the "French" style; the subjects of his novels were drawn from the bourgeoisie. His memoirs of the 1848–49 War of Independence (1884) are more important than his novels (*Two Years in the Life of a Lawyer* — Két év egy ügyvéd életéből, 1853; *Adventuress* — Kalandornő, 1854, and others), which combine liberal-radical rhetoric with unwieldy action. *Albert Pálffy* (1820–1897) followed Jósika in his writing, with rather more psychology and a better sense of construction, but with less of the spirit and colour of Jósika's world of adventure (*The God-daughter of the Prince* — A fejedelem keresztlánya, 1857). Another was *Károly Bérczy* (1821–1867), the translator of *Onegin,* who wrote carefully motivated short stories and a novella, *The Healed Wound* (A gyógyult seb, 1864). *László Beöthy* (1826–1857) took as his model the satirical novels of the English writers of the eighteenth century and Jean Paul. His subjects were taken mostly from the world of commerce (*Golbach and Co.,* 1858).

To sum up, the period saW the blossoming of the novel. Out of all of them, the works of Jókai must be accorded first place; in manner and style they were close to the main genres of populism, the lyric and the epic poetry. The short story on the whole made little progress during this period, but Jókai, whose novels in fact were frequently a series of short stories, laid the foundation for the triumph of the short story at the hands of Mikszáth and other writers at the end of the century.

36 Theatre in the Populist Period

Drama and the Populist Movement

It was a propitious period to the drama. The size of the theatre-going public in the cities rapidly increased. The emergence of a political life concerned with the well-being of society led to the birth of new types of plays. The debate between the Conservatives and the Liberals, the conflict between village and city life, between the nobility and the middle class, provided scope and subject for serious, satirical and comic plays, with especial emphasis on comedy and what are described in Hungarian literary history as "plays of the middle kind", those being neither comedies nor tragedies. The Liberal confidence in the future and the fact that even the political extremists on both sides were not for national unity pushed the irresolvable social conflict, and the satire and tragedy which fed on it, into the background. The butt of the comedy would be a harmless, even likeable figure often converted to better ways at the end, and the conflict was never bitter, and usually resolved by a final grand reconciliation.

The writers of comedy, *József Eötvös* (*Long Live Equality* — Éljen az egyenlőség, 1841); *József Gaál* (*Lead Sticks* — Ólombotok, 1842); *Imre Vahot* (*Restoration* — Restauráció, 1845), adopted Ignác Nagy's style with hardly a deviation including historical comedies. In this type of play the transformation of Romanticism can already be seen; by then liberal-democratic thought had accepted the idea of the non-hero and even the comic or farcical representation of national heroes. It was even more significant that, although at this time folk figures were rarely historical heroes, historical heroes were often given folk characteristics and identities. Matthias Corvinus, for instance, is not only painted as a friend of the people, but is also given qualities explicitly associated with the common people; a certain cunningness and shrewdness, love of sententious maxims or pithy folk-sayings, a ready tongue, and a spontaneously robust love of life, *Vahot* (*Poet and King* — Költő és király, 1846); *Gaál* (*The King at Ludas* — A király Ludason, 1837); *Szigligeti* (*Kinizsi*, 1842).

None of the fashionable genres of drama were really suited to the *népies* spirit. It was considered necessary to show both the moral nobility of the people, the injustice they suffered, their intellectual maturity, and the need for national unity and leadership by the thinking section of the nobility. The people were full of good will and hope, following the leadership of those urging reform, but their patience was coming to an end and their situation was intolerable. Plays "of the middle kind" proved the most effective vehicle for exposing these questions. Few things were so characteristic of the transitional nature of the *népies* movement in relation to Romanticism and realism as the way in which it transformed this kind of drama and created a quite specific genre—the "play about peasant life" *(népszínmű)*. This lies somewhere between comedy and serious play, more dramatic before 1849, more comic afterwards. The "play about peasant life" dealt in strongly defined types, and was weak in individual characterization; there was more idealization and less analysis, the motivation was more general, the descriptions of milieu more stylized; greater play was made with local colour and the comic element. The emotional range was also more limited, it dealt in basic emotional situations, especially those connected with family life; the conflict usually revolved around complications in love and marriage. Folk customs, folk traditions were present in every aspect, particularly in descriptions of the background environment. The "play about peasant life" was designed to aid the common people, but it still regarded their world from a position of superiority. While the Romantics desired bourgeois development, they possessed at the same time a nostalgia and illusory yearning for an ancient, pure, simple and patriarchal "folk world".

Ede Szigligeti (1814–1878)

The first writer of "plays about peasant life" of any note was Ede Szigligeti. He was born into a family of the lesser nobility, and first studied law, then joined a group of strolling players, had little success as an actor, and so decided to turn his hand to the writing of plays. He moved to Pest and, after success came to him, made a career of the theatre life: he was a director of the National Theatre, a professor at the Drama School, the author of theoretical works, translator of plays, a stage director and a critic. His output was prodigious, but little of value remains. Yet he made a very considerable contribution to the cultural education of the people in general, particularly in the theatre; for over forty years he supplied the Hungarian theatre with actable plays which often approached the modern. It was only in his first period that he produced "plays about peasant life". *The Runaway Soldier* (Szökött katona, 1843) was not only his own first important piece, it was also the first important work of this kind. It was an attack on the forced conscription of peasants, and revolved round the love and marriage of a peasant lad. His other notable play of this kind was in fact his best play, *The Horse-herd* (Csikós, 1847). The love and marriage of a shepherd boy is obstructed by a young noble who, in order to save himself, diverts suspicion for a murder to the boy. The play is given a happy ending, as in *The Runaway Sol-*

dier, although the clash between the classes is more pronounced. As a result, many believe that Szigligeti was on the path from "plays about peasant life" to serious folk drama. But the collapse of the 1848 Revolution gave both his work and this particular genre a different direction.

His true bent was "the play of the middle kind"; he took his material from city life, which included strikes and socialist movements. He made several attempts in this genre, making use not only of social conflict but also of the psychological thought of his day (*The Waif*— A lelenc, 1863; *The Strike* — A strike, 1870). But the general situation was not propitious to, nor the public mature enough for, such subjects, and he consequently often turned to the romantic-national recipe of the historical play. In these plays he tried to emulate the psychological approach of Dumas fils and others, but with scant success. The sentiments are rapid, the rhetoric empty, the moral messages without taste.

His successors, such as the actor-writer *József Szigeti* (1822–1902), also attempted to produce a genuine, serious folk drama, but after 1867 this type of play became a vehicle for comedy and even farce. Combined with the dances of vaudeville and smart flippancy of the music-hall song, the spectacular, sentimental and mock-naive characteristics of the Viennese *Volkstück,* the "play about peasant life" as opposed to genuine and serious folk drama came close to operetta.

Stagnation in the Theatre

No form of art suffered so great a setback from the collapse of the 1848 Revolution as the theatre. The ebullience of the forties vanished. It produced neither a great writer nor a great work; those ten years were too brief and too eventful for any writer to develop the necessary expertise and polish. But it was rich in experiment, especially in subject-matter, and genre, many of them in the sphere of tragedy, as in the tragedies of *Károly Obernyik* (1814–1855). The son of a pastor, and himself a tutor, he was for some time one of the circle surrounding Kölcsey, he made friends with Petőfi, and was full of the liberal, even radical, ideas of the period. It was under their influence that he wrote his play, *Lord and Villein* (Főúr és pór, 1844). The title indicates the conflict, the author siding whole-heartedly with the villein. In subject-matter he aligned himself with pre-revolutionary populism; in style he remained influenced by the French Romantics, and in his comedies and comedies of manners, it was closely related to the popular genre-scene (*The Unmarried Husband* — A nőtlen férj, 1846). After 1849 he, too, sank into silence, returning to the historical play after 1850 *(György Brankovics).*

Szigligeti and Obernyik are typical of the whole period. Between the collapse of the 1848 Revolution and the beginning of realism in the seventies, no important work was written, no interesting experiment undertaken. The censors of the Habsburg régime, in restricting the possibility of genuine drama emerging, joined forces with a theory of national self-restraint in anything that might endanger national unity in the face of Habsburg absolutism. It is true, though, that the censors would, for political reasons, pass a certain number of plays on social subjects. The position on problems of a moral or psychological nature was very much the same: to dwell on them, it was claimed, could have endangered the stability of traditional morality and traditional thinking. The storm over one of Jókai's plays was typical of this attitude: he had presented Dózsa, the leader of the rebellious peasants, with a certain sympathy (*Dózsa*, 1857); Eötvös, in his novel *Hungary in 1514*, written before 1849, could write in the same vein with impunity. The leading critics of the period, moreover, such as Gyulai and Salamon, based their judgements on principles of world order and poetic justice. All conflict had to contain an element of sin, stemming from some infringement of the natural order of the world. The traditional order, morals and way of life of the nation are the most important manifestations of this order of the world. In a good play, therefore, the figure attacking this order had to be punished so that the sense of natural justice should not be outraged. With such restrictions imposed on it, the drama returned to the well-beaten track of the Romantic historical play or, in the case of the *népies* plays, avoided all real conflict and verged on operetta. The return to Romanticism was apparent in the serious play as well, but here the pseudo-Romantic took the place of genuine Romanticism. The towns and cities were, however, growing and developing, so the increasing demand for plays was satisfied by foreign classics, and above all the importation of French boulevard pieces. In the second half of the *népies* period there was scarcely any advance in dramatic writing, which remained the weakest point in Hungarian literature. It is customary to point to Madách's great work, *The Tragedy of Man,* but this is really a dramatic poem and belongs to the field of lyric poetry, one of the great European Romantic poems of the period.

37 Imre Madách (1823-1864)

Of all the Hungarian writers of the nineteenth century, it is Imre Madách, in addition to Petőfi, whose name is more than an entry in an encyclopaedia for the educated European. It ranks beside great European names like Goethe, Byron, Ibsen, Hugo and Mickiewicz; his great work can be compared with great European works like *Faust, Manfred, Peer Gynt, Légende des siècles* and *Dziady*. His name stands or falls by this one work—*The Tragedy of Man* (Az ember tragédiája). All his other writings are not much more than a gloss on it.

No other Hungarian work has stirred up more argument and debate than *The Tragedy of Man*. The great Hungarian writers entered the lists for and against him. The first to defend him was János Arany, the foremost poet of the age; the first to attack him was János Erdélyi, the most important literary critic of the period. Writers with generally conflicting views often came surprisingly close to one another in their appraisal of him, sworn allies parted ways over him. Both Bishop Prohászka, the leading exponent of the anti-Marxism of Hungarian Catholics in the twentieth century, and György Lukács, the outstanding writer on twentieth-century Marxist aesthetics, rejected him for his "pessimism". He had no faith that human reason could guide history in the direction of progress, said Lukács; had no faith that divine providence can direct history into the harbour of salvation, said Prohászka.

The genre is unique in that transitional period between Romanticism and disillusioned realism, liberal philosophy of history and Positivism. It is the most comprehensive epitome of ideas and ventures in the period of crisis following the 1848 Revolution. Madách was a man of ideas. He was at home in the ideological sphere of reality. He also regarded the events of daily life from this point of view.

His Life

Madách was born into an old and distinguished family of declining fortunes, some-where between the greater barons and the middle nobility. He, like his father, an introspective man who died early, was delicate and of poor physique. But his mother, a strict and ascetic woman of title, proved a tower of strength when left to cope on her own. Her deeply personal and ethical Catholicism was combined with a re-spect for other people and a love of culture. This powerful woman instilled into her family and friends a faith in ideas and a consciousness of their importance. The administration of the estate remained in the hands of this indomitable mother who survived her son.

Madách read law at the University of Pest, and then obtained an important post in the country administration, where he took part in the political struggle on the side of the radical liberals. Although he was ill during the revolution, he was afterwards arrested and imprisoned for having hidden Kossuth's secretary. While he was serving his sentence, his wife was having affairs with the officers of the oc-cupying forces. After his release they were divorced. He returned to public life during the 1859–60 movements, which inspired him to write his great work. He sent it to Arany whom he had never met. After its enormous success, he fell ill again and died in 1864.

Madách the Writer

Limited as he was in practical activities by his dominant mother, Madách discovered himself through solitary meditation and reflection when quite young in life. Under the influences of an age feverish with reform, it was his desire, with an ardour verging on fanaticism, to devote the best part of his talent to the propagation of liberal ideas. In his eyes, they were directed towards the restoration and modernization of the former happy state which man enjoyed before he proved unfaithful to his nature. The sins which stemmed from this betrayal stood in the way of the restoration and recreation of that state. But there are also intrinsic contradictions in man which multiply the stultifying consequences of his sins. Young Madách desired to expose these sins and their consequences in the terrifying and purifying light of tragedy and to call attention to these opposing tendencies in man. His plays: *Commodus,* which is set in Rome; *Andrew of Naples* (Nápolyi Endre) set in Naples under the An-gevins; *Man and Woman* (Férfi és nő), the subject of which is taken from Greek mythology; *Csák's Last Days* (Csák végnapjai) is set in the feudal anarchy of the fourteenth century.

His heroes echo the great Romantic Titans, and illustrate the Romantic idea of life generated by liberal ideas. Madách was a young enthusiast who cast a tragic eye on the world from behind the protective and insulated circle of his ideas. But the world was in no hurry either to understand or implement these ideas. His views are tragic, not pessimistic. He has no doubt as to the value or the final victory of his ideas. In his early plays, he warns—urgently; they are calls inspired by his deepest reflections. What is most valuable in them is their poetry and a certain defiant emotionalism reminiscent of French Romanticism. Not only do the ideas expressed in his principal work already appear but many of the elements of his later style are also present. But there are as yet no signs of real conflict: that inner conflict which gives rise to the real dramatic work. His absolute faith in the years preceding the revolution concealed the recurrent internal contradictions of his thinking.

The Hungarian defeat in 1849 brought these ideas to the fore. Madách's personal circumstances were such that the national catastrophe made a far more dramatic impact upon him than upon most people, largely due to personal troubles, the most serious being his wife's infidelity. What made this the more tragic was that his marriage had been founded on his Romantic-Liberal ideas. He had believed the girl in question freer and closer to his ideas than girls of his own class, had married her against the wishes of his mother and friends, and anticipated that ideally happy relationship which he hoped his ideas would provide for mankind.

After his divorce, he withdrew to his books, for the most part books on contemporary science, which was then interesting him, and he also turned to lyric poetry. Desolation, annihilation and a sense of the futility of all endeavour dominated his poems. His themes were the indifference of nature, crippled and incomplete man, and the emptiness of ideas. Yet the basic tone of his work was not pessimistic. It was rather the expression of a fear that such pessimism might prove to be true, and of the desire to continue to search for the better, or, at least, the hope that his search was not useless or impossible (*Poetry of Death* — A halál költészete; *Cemetery in Nyír* — Egy nyíri temető; *Hollow Song* — Síri dal; *Midnight Thoughts* — Éjféli gondolatok).

About 1860, when the reviving hope of national independence drew him out of his isolation and solitary meditation, he wrote a caustic one-act comedy after the manner of Aristophanes about the "civilizing" activities of the authorities, the argument the Imperial government invoked to justify its despotism in the eyes of Europe (*The Civilizer* — A civilizátor, 1859). He then returned to the ideas from which he at one time hoped would flow an understanding and regulation of the world and the construction of a national life; vacillating between scepticism and hope, he still maintained them. The outcome was *The Tragedy of Man*.

The Tragedy of Man

This work is a dramatic poem in fifteen acts. The first three acts and the last act form framing acts to the others. They are situated in Heaven, and God himself appears in them. The eleven acts between them call up visions of the great periods of history: the building of the pyramids in Egypt, the public meetings in Athens, the orgies of Imperial Rome, the debates about dogma of the Western Crusaders in Byzantium, the court of the Emperor Rudolf in Prague with Kepler, the French Revolution at the time of Danton's fall, the streets of bourgeois London, a Fourier socialist phalanstery, and finally, a world in a state of entropy. The three main characters are Adam, Eve and Lucifer. The historical scenes occur within a dream of Adam and Eve, which Lucifer sends them on their expulsion from Eden to show them the future of mankind. They are the three main characters of each act. Adam is in turn the Pharaoh with absolute power; Miltiades the hero of liberty; Kepler the scientist; Danton the revolutionary, and so on. Eve is the wife, the mistress, the beloved of Adam, as circumstances direct. Lucifer accompanies them throughout to comment on the events.

The external, historical structure encloses an internal structure of an historical-philosophical nature. The "philosophy of history" was for the period of Romantic liberalism what "reason" was for the Enlightenment. It justified faith in the process of history, in the intelligibility of life and the possibility of a principle of order. Of the various philosophies of history, Madách chose the highest and most universal: the Hegelian. Adam-Pharaoh finds his absolute power, founded on the defencelessness of others unbearable: it bars him from experiencing the essence of human nature. In the Athenian scene that follows the contrary occurs: he has became Miltiades, champion of democracy. Here again his hopes fail him; his enemies take advantage of the opportunities for abuse provided by democracy and obtain the people's assent to the proposal that he should be condemned to death for treason. Next, in Rome, he is still seeking a possible way of life and a method of enjoying it that should be consonant with his character. So Adam turns to hedonism, but it is followed by disgust, which leads him, encouraged by the words of the Apostle Peter to a new hope of fulfilment through equality born of love under the influence of Christian ideas. But Christian ideas in turn give rise to an inhuman fanaticism and, in Byzantium, people are slaughtered for the iota in the homousion-homoiusion dispute. As Kepler, Adam turns from religious faith to science, again he is deceived; the age demands, not science, but horoscopes and pseudo-science. Desperately he dreams of a noble era in which all social barriers are demolished and reason is triumphant. But here again the hope turns to dust. Robespierre sends Danton-Adam to his death in the name of fraternity. Adam then places all his hope in the free competition of powers and talent, but the capitalist society of London becomes a hotbed of humiliation, force and chaos. Next comes hope in the planned society, the socialist phalanstery, but here Adam sees that Michelangelo is used to carve chair-legs and Plato to herd cattle in this order of things, that it destroys art, the spirit, love, in short everything that speaks of the individual.

As with Hegel, in Madách's play each stage of history creates its own excess and contradiction and the struggle of these opposites gives rise to the next historical stage. But, unlike Hegel, the second stage is not necessarily superior to the first. In the last "historical" scene, the cooling earth is seen as imagined by the age of Positivism on the basis of the theory of entropy. Man has sunk to a level hardly higher than that of the animals. Awakening from this vision of history, Adam wants to kill himself, in order to prevent such things happening. But it is too late, Eve is pregnant and Adam must accept the struggle before mankind, though aware of what the historical process will hold. The voice of the Lord is heard: "Man, struggle and have faith." The poem ends on these enigmatic words.

Before the revolution, Madách's reading had centred on the Romantic-liberal teleological theory of history. After the Hungarian defeat in 1849 his main reading was the positivist-materialist scientific literature of the age. Nothing was more despised at that juncture than the philosophy of history; no name more abominated than Hegel's; no viewpoint more laughable than the teleological; no method more ridiculous than the deductive. As a result, "two souls dwelt" in Madách's breast. Adam's faith and enthusiasm was based on the liberal reading of history; Lucifer's confutation was based on positivism. Each fresh start by Adam demonstrates his desire to prove the truth of his reading of history; and each failure strengthens the Positivist confutation.

Both the atheists and the devout who are antagonistic to the tragedy reject the enigmatic final words of God. And, as these words occupy a key position in the structure of the work, they reject the work itself. This ending is an "arbitrary conclusion" and outside the logic of the piece; the atheists, Hegelians in particular, hold that Madách sinks from a pessimistic final conclusion of history, based on false views of a declining class, into the irrationality of religion. The conclusion is correct, claim the devout, but the previous historical scenes neither load up to it nor justify it.

But *The Tragedy of Man* is not a treatise of philosophy nor is it a play. It is a dramatic poem. Poem is the genus, dramatic poem the species. Its hero is poetical, and the lyrical Ego is the poet himself. Adam and Lucifer represent the duality of his soul: he believed in the rationality of existence and in the existence of the real. The former took the form of action based on free will, the harmonization of the individual and history; the latter meant the determinism of action and the denial of free will and the individual. Unable to find a scientific or philosophical solution to these opposing beliefs Madách tried to resolve the contradiction through lyric poetry and in the sphere of ethics. He rejected the practical contents of the liberal philosophy of history and its teleological bent, but retained its moral commitment to the search.

275

He rejected the mechanistic determinism and world-concept of Positivism, but retained the moral commitment to reality. Adam and Lucifer are symbols. Symbols of the two halves of the spiritual Ego of the poet. But Eve is also a symbol. Before pronouncing his enigmatic words, the Lord refers to her as a symbol, a symbol of the resolution into unity. Adam and Lucifer are opposed to each other, but together they oppose Eve. With Eve, and with his poem as a whole, Madách wished to symbolize his belief that the interpretation of one age would necessarily cancel the other; that life would always devise the new interpretations necessary for its survival. There are some who suspect that he foresaw the rebellion against Positivism at the end of the century and anticipated it by introducing the "life" concept of vitalism at the close of Romanticism.

Arany, who was always unbiassed as a critic, even with his friends, defended the *Tragedy* against his opponents as well as against his own allies. There was no one closer to Madách than Arany and the aged Vörösmarty. Not only on account of the ideas they held in common. Madách's opponents attacked the *Tragedy* on the grounds of its style and old-fashioned language. And it is true that compared with the poetic narrative style of the *népies* poets, with the smooth flow of their song and descriptions, his language was heavy and crabbed. His Romantic images, symbols, and allusions are archaic, and characteristic of the 1830s. But even on this count Arany came to his defence. He realized that Madách's language achieved power and tension. His grammar and syntax may be strained, his language dramatic, highly concentrated and grandiloquent, but it is all controlled by a disciplined objectivity, and subordinated to the description of the development of the experience of thought. The verbal rhetoric of Romanticism, and the Romantic rhetoric which enjoyed the sound of its own voice, were as repugnant to Madách as to Arany. He can be placed somewhere between Vörösmarty in his old age and the lyric poet Arany. As for style, Madách believed, like Arany (in a Herderian way) that the poetic treasures of a people, which have become universal, such as the Bible, the great Greek and oriental myths, the folk epics, are the real models of poetic form and its eternal inspiration.

The *Tragedy* was often performed on the stage. In most cases it was not much more than an excuse for a grandiose spectacle. But it is not really a play for the theatre, nor even play for the study; it is a dramatic poem. It is a confrontation with the crisis of Romantic liberalism, within the framework of what is, *par excellence,* a Romantic genre.

After *The Tragedy of Man,* Madách began to write a Biblical play. The new work revolved round Moses, brought up at the court of the Pharaoh but becoming conscious of his national identity and how he and the Jews came together, as the leader of the people and the people who followed him (*Moses,* 1861). Those who defend *The Tragedy of Man* are justified in their claim that in his rejection of liberal teleology Madách did not discard the will to progress. But nor is this work of his, strictly speaking, a play; it is rather a dramatized Romantic epic.

38 Literary Criticism

Around this time the essay arrived to join the hitherto existing forms of non-fiction, which also underwent a change. But the essay on aesthetics developed in the direction marked out by Kölcsey. Before 1849, the aesthetic principles laid down by János Erdélyi dominated the scene; after 1849 came Pál Gyulai, János Arany and Zsigmond Kemény.

János Erdélyi (1814–1868)

Erdélyi, the son of a serf, who fought his way up to the position of director of the Calvinist College in Sárospatak, began his literary career under the influence of Herderian ideas and the aesthetics of French Romanticism. He considered the social function of the writer to be indispensable. It was the writer's duty, he believed, to voice the aspirations of the national community, especially the common people, to paint the picture of their world, to react to it, to help develop its self-awareness, historical knowledge and ethical principles. He rejected both the extreme individualization of Romanticism and the extreme idealization of Classicism. He was consequently a supporter of the populist attitude while already engaged in preparing the transformation to realism. In literary principles and attitudes he was the precursor of Petőfi. His own poems helped to develop the *népies* movement, but he was better known for his collection of folklore based on the folk-principles of Romanticism (1846). His opinions changed later under the influence of Hegel; by adopting the Hegelian teaching he lent a historical perspective to Herderian ideas and gave a theoretical basis to Herder's views on genres. Before 1849, when the *népies* movement was threatened by its fixation on scenes of common life and conventionalized descriptions of types, he stressed a more individual treatment of character. After 1849, he preferred to stress the need for idealization to further the struggle against relativism, and consequently, against his own wishes, he involuntarily contributed to the process of re-Romanticization, although he fought very hard against its cheaper manifestations, especially against the imitators of Petőfi. His main works

277

are: *On Folk Poetry* (Népköltészetről, 1842); *The Individual and the Ideal* (Egyéni és eszményi, 1847); *A Quarter of a Century of Hungarian Literature* (Egy századnegyed a magyar szépirodalomból, 1855).

Pál Gyulai (1826-1909)

Pál Gyulai was an outstanding critic in the fifties, and later an equally outstanding biographical essayist. His critical writings are empirical, normative and much concerned with history. He was a writer himself, and his views were distilled from his own works as well as from the great works of others—such as Shakespeare, Molière, Schiller, Arany, Petőfi, and Kemény. His aesthetic theories were based on the work of third-rate authors like Planche and Julian Schmied, the best source he drew from being the dramatic studies of A. W. Schlegel. Herderian theories also greatly influenced him, but he acquired them at second-hand through Kölcsey, Arany and Kemény. His concern with history was not with a philosophical foundation for the study of history, but was rather literary empiricism, the sympathetic study and comparison of earlier literary works. Nobody did more than he to secure recognition for the *népies* movement of Petőfi and Arany, but by setting up the *népies* principles as a criterion for future Hungarian poetry, he was largely responsible for impeding the total disentanglement from Romanticism. This was mainly due to his lack of appreciation of the very elements in the poetry of Petőfi and Arany which were furthest from the ideas and aesthetics of liberal Romanticism: the late poetry of Petőfi, which is mainly reflective, and the lyric poetry of Arany written in his years of crisis. He called for realism in describing the objects of idealization and demanded that the moral order should be respected. Here he was referring to the moral principles of national liberalism, which combined elements of the Enlightenment and religious sentiments. He also insisted that the emotions expressed in a poem should be controlled and balanced; that the action of a novel should be built upon well-motivated characters; that drama (about which more is said in the chapter on drama) should contain a conflict justifying the "world order". He was implacable in his condemnation of Jókai, believing that the morality of Jókai's novels was frivolous and irresponsible and his psychology naive and crude.

Gyulai created the language and style of modern criticism in Hungarian. Criticism became a creative work in his hands. Fervent in dispute, passionate in defence of his own opinion, explicit in his judgement disregarding all secondary considerations, he combined these characteristics with disciplined and logical argument, lucid construction, and a fine rhetorical style. He was a master of the precise, unambiguous word. Every criticism he wrote became a further justification of his own views. In his biographical essays, he asserts rather than argues; he is objective and his argument almost matter-of-fact, in the manner of the Positivists, while the construction of the work possesses the simplicity of Classicism. The style he adopted in his essays came very near to the style in the period of realism. His most important critical studies were: *Sándor Petőfi and our Recent Lyrical Poetry* (Petőfi Sándor és újabb lírai költészetünk), in which he demolished the imitators of Petőfi; *Our Female Writers* (Nőíróinkról), a work directed against the revival of works of sentimental and cheap Romanticism; and *Mór Jókai's Latest Novels* (Jókai Mór legújabb regényei). His most beautiful biographical essays are on Vörösmarty, Arany and Kemény.

Arany the Critic

Arany is a quite different kind of critic. He wrote only a few studies of a general aesthetic nature (*Our Literary Principles* — Irodalmi hitvallásunk; *Trends* — Irányok, 1862). Each of his critical works discusses the aesthetic questions of the period from newer and fresher angles. He learnt a great deal from Erdélyi, but was not always of the same opinion. They were in agreement on the Herderian-Hegelian concept of history, but Arany gave greater importance to Herder. And, in dealing with Hungarian nationalism, Arany included the social angle. What is even more important is that he was of the opinion that Hegel paid insufficient attention to the part played by the individual in the creation of literary trends and tastes. He feared that this would lead to the criticism of a work being limited to the criterion of the principles governing the philosophy of history, and the individual merits of the book would not come under discussion.

It was on this point that he came into conflict with Gyulai as well. His criticisms are situated on two planes. One of them foreshadows the achievement of twentieth-century structuralism. He examines the work from the point of view of the author's intention, as an individual and independent whole which gives meaning to its component parts. On the other, he estimates the work according to his own aesthetic principles. The intention and the matter of a work in themselves are justified no further than the actual artistic performance allows. If he considers that to be good, he will praise work which in other respects is alien to him, and consequently his range of appreciation is greater than Gyulai's. Gyulai is always in the judge's seat; he pontificates on principles and pronounces judgement. But Arany at his desk meditates and considers. His critical writings are usually "difficult"; they demand not only a receptive mood in the reader, but considerable thought as well. In his biographical essays, and in the essay on *Gvadányi* especially, he offered a very modern model of literary criticism, subtle on many levels, not only excelled in his own time but even in the twentieth century. To what had already been achieved by the Romantic version of the history of literature, he adds, as if in anticipation, the contribution of positivism; all this is done inductively, spontaneously, with the directness of an essay and the objectivity of a thesis, and a great feeling of identification with the writer under discussion (*Gyöngyösi, Gvadányi, Baróti Szabó, Orczy,* 1863–64). He was one of the first masters in the comparative study of literature in Europe as well as in Hungary. The essayists of the twentieth century still return to Arany's essay on *Zrínyi and Tasso* for material on these two great Baroque poets.

The Essays of Kemény

Kemény wrote a few critical works, but his aesthetic studies are of great importance (*Thoughts on the Novel and the Drama* — Eszmék a regény és a dráma körül; *Life and Literature* — Élet és irodalom) from different points of view: the relationship between society and literature, the development of genres and social change, and the traditional and contemporary taste. He considered that the direct influence of social and political life upon literature is stronger than that of literature upon social and political life; that writers do not act upon society directly, in the manner of prophets, as the Romantics believed, but indirectly, by creating new ideas, new standards of taste and life, new values. For this task, in a bourgeois age, the most suitable vehicle is the novel. Its chief strength lies in its power of psychological analysis, enabling it to expose the origins of ideas and values, and usually "debunking" them in the process. In short, it disillusions. In these works, Kemény came close to the disillusionment of realism. But he also contributed to the maintenance of liberal national Romanticism, in for instance placing epic poetry before the novel, and the historical before the social novel. He held that the principal aim of literature was to paint the ideal picture of the national character, and also help to secure its continuity. For such purpose epic poetry and the historical novel are most suitable. For Arany, the national past was that of the "people". For Kemény, it was that of the "historic nation" and the "historical classes". He was considerably influenced by the essays of Macaulay. While he was less capable than Macaulay of treating social themes effectively, he was better in the handling of psychological detail, and was in fact at his most masterly in the biographical essay. As in his novels, the figures in his essays are raised to the position of symbols. He concentrates on their personalities; and on the relationship of history and the individual; his suppressed passion and his restrained outbursts are proof that his essays are primarily a form of self-expression and self-confession, as for instance *The Two Wesselényis* (A két Wesselényi); *Széchenyi,* etc.

The Essay, and the History of Literature

Apart from these writers, *Ferenc Salamon* (1825–1892) is worth mentioning as one who excelled in dramatic criticism and gave even more stress than Gyulai to the need for idealization and the protection of the moral order. There was also *Ágost Greguss* (1825–1882), who began his career with critical works reminiscent of radical French Romanticism and then turned to general aesthetic studies of a conservative nature, along lines similar to the academical aesthetic thinking in Germany and France.

The period produced no important literary historian. *Ferenc Toldy* continued to assemble his material and write comprehensive volumes with incredible diligence, treating national development along the lines of Gervinus. The evolutionary ideas of Kemény, Gyulai and Arany in particular had, however, a decisive effect upon the subsequent writing of literary history.

It was most in the essay above all that the literary leaders of the age insisted on the ideas of national–liberal Romanticism as their means of self-defence. Whatever they accepted in the way of Positivist ideas or methods, they used to propagate national-liberal ideas. To compare the aims of these essays and Arany's lyric poetry, Madách's dramatic poems and Kemény's novels is to realize the discrepancy between the objectives and the real situation after the revolution, and this discrepancy explains at the same time why the progress of Romanticism towards Realism was delayed and the return of a certain degree of Romanticism.

The Emergence of Realism
(c. 1870–c. 1905)

39 The Period of the Compromise and Realism

The 1867 Compromise

In 1867, an agreement, known to history as the Compromise *(Ausgleich)*, was finally reached between Hungary and the Habsburg dynasty. The Empire was transformed into the Dual Monarchy, with Hungary, which formed one half, achieving independence in internal matters. As a result Hungary regained much of her independence as a state. Nevertheless, between the more industrially developed Austria and agrarian Hungary a certain dependence and subordination confirmed by law still existed. Developments in Hungary over the following fifty years must be understood in the light of this dual relationship. In Austria, power rested in the hands of the Court aristocracy and the upper middle class; in Hungary it was the large and medium-sized land-owners who controlled the country. In Austria the power of the upper middle class increased with time and became predominant; in Hungary, the power of the middle class as a whole was negligible at the outset and its growth was slow, though inevitable. It is for these reasons that the Compromise is often regarded, as far as economic and class relationships are concerned, as the pact between the Austrian capitalists and Hungarian land-owners.

It took the new Hungarian authorities ten years to establish themselves. The medium-sized land-owners considered their share of power and economic opportunity insufficient, and they formed an opposition demanding complete separation from Austria, only personal union under the crown to be retained. In the meantime, however, the competitive nature of prospering capitalism and their own outmoded farming methods and lack of capital had finally deprived this class of medium-sized land-owners of their money and power. Crisis followed crisis. Finally, in 1875, an agreement was achieved between the party responsible for the Compromise and the party of the medium-sized land-owners and they merged under the name Liberal Party. The general administration fell into the hands of the medium-sized land-owners. Filling administrative posts up and down the land they were able to supplement their incomes with the salaries attached to them. It was from this class of society, especially from those who lived from their lands as well as from their official posts, that the typical Hungarian gentry emerged. For half a century they were to determine Hungarian taste and the Hungarian way of life (especially in the provinces), which, in turn, determined for long the image of the Hungarian "national character" held by foreigners.

Within the Dual Monarchy, that is to say, within the new Europe that was born after the Franco-German war of 1870, there followed some thirty years of quiet, fairly substantial development. But, beneath the surface the predictable contradictions of capitalist development were brewing among the various groups of the social structure. By the turn of the century, the crisis had become acute. From this time onwards, until the collapse of the Dual Monarchy after the First World War, after a number of unsuccessful and temporary attempts at minor reform, the system could only be maintained by force. Within the Hungarian state, the contradictions were partly social: from the nineties onwards, the middle classes were demanding first a greater share of power and then control, and from 1900 the workers' movements steadily grew in strength. The other immediate problem was what was known as the nationality question: the numbers of Rumanians, Croats and Slovaks, who formed substantial non-Hungarian minorities in the country, were demanding, first, autonomy within the Hungarian state, then separation from it.

The Towns and the Middle Classes

Over this forty years the face of the country changed considerably, and the towns changed in particular. Budapest grew from a provincial town to a European industrial city: its population tripled, reaching almost three quarters of a million. Joining the Austrian and Hungarian banks, already in the city, which possessed large capital resources, came the great banking houses of Europe hastening to establish branches in Hungary. With Budapest as its centre, a dense network of railways spread over the country. In short, Hungary ceased to be a totally agricultural country; a third of it was industrialized. The middle classes moved from their position on the periphery of society to occupy a central role. This rapid progress created a sizable proletariat, not only in the towns but also in the villages.

Parliamentary life had, since 1875, been nothing more than a sterile debate between the ruling Liberal Party and the Opposition, the small Party of '48, which called for complete independence. Groups with different social aims began to appear in the nineties; the Conservative Party with their agrarian, religious, and nationalist policies, in defence of the interests of the land-owning class; the New Liberals and the Radicals, who roughly represented the interests of the middle classes; and the Social Democrats.

But, while struggling for power, these various groups fought for the enforcement of their particular tastes, culture, and way of life. The cultural needs and resources of the middle classes were far greater than indicated by their share in economic and political life. Budapest was not simply the capital of an agricultural country but, as far as politics and culture were concerned, the second largest city in the highly industrialized, capital-orientated Habsburg Empire. The larger cities were Hungarian as well as part of the Empire. Around 1900 a number of new papers, publishing houses, colleges, theatres, music-halls, galleries, artists' workshops, scientific associations and conservatoires were functioning in the country, and, generally speaking, their standard was reasonably high. The Opera House was built and maintained at huge expense, and for years engaged international talents, as for instance Mahler as conductor. And, although the more conservative sector of the public continued to admire Mihály Munkácsy, who painted in the Classic–Realist style, the *plein-air* Impressionists and Secessionists influenced artists and found militant supporters such as Pál Szinyei-Merse, Károly Ferenczy and Simon Hollósy around the same time as in Berlin or Vienna. Not without good reason was Budapest called the sister-city of Vienna.

Disillusionment and Realism

The events of the time exerted considerable influence on literature, but not directly, nor immediately. Within the period, three different stages can be distinguished: the three phases in the evolution of realism in Hungarian literature. The first was characterized by an overpowering sense of disillusionment, based on the difficulties that followed the 1867 Compromise. The lesser nobility and the gentry found themselves increasingly impoverished and the younger generation, which grew up during the period of passive resistance between the 1848 Revolution and the Compromise, and who flocked hopefully to the cities, was the most affected by this disillusionment. The new Hungarian state could not give them what they hoped for as the reward of their passive resistance; Hungary had obtained its internal independence, but these young men found themselves unprepared for the tasks of a capitalist state. They were left helpless, with neither professions nor incomes, even more helpless indeed by the influx of new trends in European thinking after 1848, especially the determinism of Positivism and the pessimism of Schopenhauer, which until then had been hidden from them by the emotional fervour and promised prospects of the resistance movement. They felt incapable of action, unneeded and unnecessary. The writers of this generation were concerned to expose the reasons for this feeling of paralysis and the remedy. Most of them belonged to the emergent middle class. They were acquainted with the Positivist-utilitarian ideas of Comte, Mill and Spencer, and applied them to the Hungarian situation and to a national liberalism which was leading to the formation of a Hungarian bourgeoisie. The belief of the Romantic liberal writers, that it was their duty to intervene directly through their writing in the development of a national society, was combined with the cult of the factual and the empirical and the analytic attitude of positivism. Within this framework, they analysed the relationships which resulted in this disillusionment and criticized the nobility for preferring to sink into the position of impoverished gentry, rather than gird up their loins and become an active part of capitalist society, taking to industry and commerce. Such criticism demanded a type of *Bildungsroman* enabling them to follow the development of their hero's character. The first phase, therefore, in the development of Hungarian realism was marked by a mood of disillusionment, an attitude of criticism and suggestion, social and psychological analysis, and the *Bildungsroman*.

In the second phase, this particular economic crisis had been resolved, and was followed by a wave of prosperity, enabling the different groups to find places for themselves. The gentry all too happily took power and the middle classes took advantage of the opportunity to thrive. The country, and the Habsburg Empire as a whole, was dominated by pseudo-romanticism trading under the name of security. Jókai, Johann Strauss, and their joint work, the *Gipsy Baron,* are the names which typify this phase. There were no longer any unneeded or useless classes generally speaking, only individuals here and there who could not fit themselves into the framework of society. These people felt, like Ibsen, that there was a lie somewhere, that Establishment values were not based upon anything real, and the disillusionment continued. But the Establishment continued to function effectively, so their disenchantment was not related directly to national—and rarely to social problems. The Ibsenite problem rarely found an Ibsenite form of social criticism. And indeed what affected them was rather the second wave of Positivism, the sceptical views of Renan and Taine regarding all things as relative and atomized. This was further strengthened by the philosophy of Schopenhauer, which by then was widely known. Their disillusionment was both "narrower" and "broader" than that of the previous generation. It had narrowed to the concept of the individual ruled by biological factors; it had broadened to take in the question of universal existence. Such a trend favoured the production of writing designed on a lesser scale, work suitable for expressing subjective emotions. Lyric poetry took the lead, firstly Impressionist and then Symbolist in style (Vajda, Reviczky, Komjáthy, Endrődi), and the short story also took second place, lyrical, melancholy, Impressionist and Symbolist in turn, or written with a wry resignation in the form of anecdotes (Mikszáth, Petelei, Gozsdu). Realism continued to evolve, but certain forms of it, especially those characteristic of the realistic novel, met with difficulties; there was little demand for objective, impersonal reporting and rational and constructive social criticism. Prose took first place in this phase of the literature of realism, but in the form of the short story and not the novel.

Towards the end of the eighties, in the third phase, when the contradictions underlying the illusion of social unity and the security of prosperity began to be felt, the short story became even more dominant. Writers and readers believed the main cause of tension lay in the conflict between the middle classes and the landowners, heightened by the dissatisfaction of the lower classes and by the social, intellectual and artistic unrest in Europe. This phase was impregnated with the repercussions growing from active social involvement and with social criticism.

At the same time, there was little attempt made to produce a synthesis or theory which would have embraced the general experience, and would have given the novel a greater scope. Positivism was no longer, and vitalism and Marxism was not yet, a dynamic and obvious influence capable of co-ordinating various attitudes. Yet all made themselves felt. The most frequently quoted names were those of Spencer and Taine. Empiricism, the principles of causality, environmental and biological determinism, induction and analysis, utilitarianism and a faith in competition, tolerance and hedonism, all principles strengthening the position of the middle classes, dominated the scene. It was a late revival of liberalism without the attempt at synthesis characteristic of classic liberalism. It was held to be sufficient to record the many versions of the facts and disorders of society for common sense to recognize them as fundamental contradictions. The most popular genre was consequently the short story, objective in attitude and concerned with social conditions. It was this type of writing that was most successful as the first period of Hungarian realism, realized in the work of Bródy, Tömörkény, Ambrus and Papp.

The Secession (Art Nouveau)

It was in the heyday of the short story that the first signs of what was known in Central Europe and Germany as the *Secession* and in Western Europe as *art nouveau,* appeared. They had their effect on the short story, but in the period in question it was in the field of literary journalism that they assumed the function of character determination and style organization. In Hungary, the literary form of the Secession movement represented the attempt of the wealthy and liberal middle class to assure recognition of their taste, their aesthetic and ethical values alongside traditional Christian national values. Their principal tool to this end was a belief in relative as opposed to absolute values. Tastes and values were considered subjective, and therefore equally valid. They widened this belief in the relative nature of judgements to subsume all literary elements. The most important literary consequence of this attitude was the introduction of free association to ease the structure of a work, transforming it completely; though this was more apparent in the literature of the next period. During the period in question the Secession remained as a trend which influenced the other literary tendencies of the time; without it the new realism of Móricz and Babits in the next period could not have come about.

289

40 The Novel of Realism

Bildungsroman

In Hungary, as in the rest of Europe, prose took first place, first as the novel and then as the short story. The generation under discussion found a need for *Bildungsroman*. A number of highly poetic versions, this type of novel came into existence: the novel in verse, the novel of confession, the *Ich-Roman*, the novel illustrating a moral thesis. This marked the last surviving elements of the *népies* movement and Romantic Liberalism though combined with the wry longings of Romanticism. The "historical necessity" of these versions is shown by the fact that even the older generation experimented with them: Gyulai wrote *Romhányi*, a novel in verse (1871); Arany just managed to finish his *Istók the Fool* (Bolond Istók, 1873), no more than the size of a short story in verse form, and at the same time Jókai wrote his poetic novel, *The Man with the Golden Touch* (Aranyember, 1872). János Vajda also wrote these modern narrative poems which might be discribed as novels in verse, *Meetings* (Találkozások, 1873), *Alfred's Novel* (Alfréd regénye, 1875).

László Arany (1844-1898)

The most outstanding representative of this generation was Arany's banker son, László Arany. He was a highly-cultivated man and while still a student at the university, compiled the best collection of Hungarian folk tales up to that time (1862). After completing his law studies, he joined the group of politically-minded intellectuals who helped to bring about the 1867 Compromise and also made a successful career as a banker.

Besides a number of excellent studies on folk poetry, prosody and language, literature and politics, in which the Liberal idea of the national progress to capitalism were combined with the thinking of Stuart Mill and Spencer, he wrote a single novel in verse, *The Hero of Daydreams* (A délibábok hőse, 1872). The chief character, Balázs Hübele, is typical of the generation which grew up in the fifties. He is an honest man, full of noble aspirations, but the series of grandiose undertakings on which he ventures are beyond him. He plans to write a tragedy that would spark off a revolution; he then joins Garibaldi's army in order to return as a liberator. But even his more useful, realistic enterprises, such as the attempt to establish in his native land an industrial and capitalist economy on the lines of the English system, end in disappointing failure, for he is unaware of the laws of society and has no knowledge of himself and the age in which he lives. Finally, after even humiliating the love of his youth, he sinks back into the hopeless existence of the provincial land-owner in an access of a pitiful self-deception.

László Arany was fond of Byron, and even more so of Pushkin and Lermontov. Inspired by these writers and by his father's work, he was fortunate in his choice of genre. In his work, there is the confrontation of two mentalities. One is Balázs, who might have been the young author himself: the intuitive, the passionate, the "Romantic". The other is the character chosen and created by the author as his opposite, secure in his understanding of reality, acting in accordance with the dictates of his intellectual and ethical principles. From this second frame of mind, he looked with "Russian" irony at the first. And, with a sense of profound melancholy and nostalgia he deliberately chooses the new, intellectual form of behaviour, though it lacked the glamour of Romanticism and the emotions of his youth. And again, he looked upon the nostalgia he experiences with ironical resignation. "We are born without teeth, hair and illusions. We die without teeth, hair and illusions," he says. The lyric poem was indeed far more suited to the deeply personal nature of his work than prose. The enduring value of his work is perhaps due to the fact that he managed to relate the problems of his age to the eternally human, moral moment of choice and decision.

He had no wish to abandon the style of the *népies* period, but he transformed it fundamentally. The naive, directly personal, narrative manner, the folk images of the populist tales were replaced in his work by the analysis of motives, the creation of distance through irony, an urban language and images drawn from contemporary culture.

The Novels of Disillusionment

János Asbóth (1845–1911) was the son of a field engineer and general in the 1848 Revolution, he was trained as an engineer himself but his real bent was towards journalism and politics. Darvady, the hero of his novel *Dreamer of Dreams* (Álmok álmodója, 1876), written in the first person, his only major work, passes through various political, philosophical and emotional disillusionments to reach the conclusion that the only worthwhile form of human conduct is the stoical fulfilment of duty. This novel echoes the theories of Stirner and Ruskin in denouncing mechanization and mass production. Asbóth rejected the world of the provincial gentry as well as that of the middle classes of Western Europe, and advocated a "conservatism" akin to the Romanticism of the pre-capitalist period, in order to renew and preserve human relationship and the dignity of work. In addition to its musical qualities and its symbolism, a certain amount of social and psychological analysis can be found in Asbóth's novel.

István Toldy (1844–1879), son of the great literary historian, Ferenc Toldy, was himself a journalist, novelist and playwright, who was also concerned to make a break with the populist movement. He, too, was one of the first writers of realistic prose in a way which combined pre- and post-realistic trends, the Romantic novel and the naturalist thesis-novel. The preface to his novel, *Anatole* (1878) is sometimes compared to Hugo's preface to *Cromwell* or with the pronunciamentos of Zola. The novel tells of the love and political frustrations of a promising young Frenchman who finally ends by killing himself. Toldy also wanted to investigate and clarify the intellectual evolution of his contemporaries. Man's behaviour, he considered, was determined by his environment and his biological inheritance. The reason for his hero's failure was that he ignored these vital factors. According to Toldy, it was the duty of the novelist to present a scientific exposition of ordinary human lives, and not to write about ideal heroes, and Toldy's book is a burning indictment of the aesthetics of idealism. But his use of the principles of Positivist psychology was excessively dogmatic, and he was inclined to regard the human spirit as a multiplication table of these principles.

Typical of this generation were the two novels, *Márton Bíró* (1872) and *Béla Kálozdy* (1875) by *Zsolt Beöthy* (1848–1922), who was later to become a conservative literary historian of great influence. Both novels dealt with the frustration and sense of futility felt by the young gentry of that time. The central characters of both novels are weak-willed early-orphaned young men. The author excels in his pictures of the background and the environment of his characters, and in his ability to create a poetic atmosphere especially in the first of the novels, which, like Asbóth's novel, is narrated in the first person.

Lajos Tolnai (1837-1902)

Lajos Tolnai was the most prolific writer of his time. His long career was marked by a series of aggressive works, indicting, satirizing, even including personal attacks in the form of pamphlets. But his attacks were not directed against old or outworn thinking. He attacked on conventional moral grounds, on behalf of the traditional, sober, rational morality of the little man, against the sins and sinners that caused the difficulties of the period. He belonged to the lower class of provincial intellectuals; his father was a notary. He became a Calvinist pastor, but without a sense of calling. He was a passionate, angry man, who made enemies easily. In Maros-vásárhely (now Tîrgu Mureș, Rumania), where he worked as minister, he used to attack his enemies with a stick; later, being afraid of insult, he carried a gun to the services. During the last decades of his life, he abandoned his ministry and became the headmaster of a school in the capital. He wrote first ballads, then prose. The only part of the general European culture of the day that interested him was literature (especially Thackeray and his predecessors), but even this affected him on an intuitive rather than a conscious level. He sensed the growing crisis in the country as it was reflected in individual lives; he never meditated on it as a problem of the philosophy of history or a political question.

His first important novel, *The Masters* (Az urak, 1872), dealt with the disinte-gration of a well-to-do peasant family; it advocated the transformation of the traditional way of life and morality in the direction propounded by middle-class utilitarian liberalism. The satiric and the idyllic are equally well balanced in this as in his subsequent novels. After the Hungarian gentry took power, he lost his any sense of measure and self-restraint. His novels became *romans à clef* in which he let loose his satirical and even pamphleteering inclinations. While his early, better novels, such as *Baroness Mistress* (A báróné ténsasszony, 1882), *The New Lord Lieutenant* (Az új főispán, 1885), gave promise of a writer who would follow up Eötvös's *Village Notary* or for a Hungarian Thackeray or Shchedrin, in fact most of his novels lack psychological development and social context. He returned to the literary resources of horror-Romanticism. His passionate autobiography, *Dark World* (Sötét világ, 1894), stands out among his latter works.

The Novel of the End of the Century

With the period of disillusionment over, the eighties saw the novel, and in par-ticular the *Bildungsroman,* in a state of decline, although there were more novels written and translated, numerically speaking, than ever before. The period of light reading had begun, but there were very few serious attempts to develop the realistic novel. One attempt was made by *Ödön Iványi* (1854–1893), a writer who matured slowly and died young, leaving behind him short stories and one important novel, *The Bishop's Kinfolk* (A püspök atyafisága, 1888). He was concerned to paint the involvement of the gentry with capitalism and finance, viewed from a middle-class standpoint in the manner of Balzac. Task and subject were complex; there was no precedent for this type of novel, and in fact he failed to reach the literary level of the short stories of the period.

Zsigmond Justh (1863–1894), another writer who died young, also produced a number of novels. He was an aristocrat, moving in the best society of Paris, where he acquired an interest in literature, being influenced by Taine and Zola. His theory was that the biological and intellectual decadence of the Hungarian aristocracy could be reversed by interbreeding with the peasantry. This simple naturalistic and romantic but absurd idea was not alien to the French, nor to the ageing Renan, and accorded with the ideas of the Hungarian agrarians. He tried to describe this decadence and rejuvenation in several of his novels, such as *Fuimus* (1895) and *Julcsa Gányó* (1895). In planning his novels he followed Zola's example, but the only really effective parts are his pictures, ironic, resigned, nostalgic, of the way of life and feelings of his own class. His *Diary* (Napló), published several decades after his death, is more interesting than his novels, especially the section dealing with his life in Paris. Although spurred on by loneliness and ambition, he made the acquaintance of most of the writers of the period he remained fundamentally an odd, isolated figure.

But by this time the short story had replaced the novel as the leading prose genre. Kálmán Mikszáth, the most important prose writer of the period, produced original and important short stories, and when he turned to the novel he adopted a loose, anecdotal structure.

41 Kálmán Mikszáth (1847-1910)

Kálmán Mikszáth, one of the masters of Hungarian prose, was with Jókai the most widely read of nineteenth-century writers. And also one of the most controversial. The argument over Madách was from the outset the struggle of two opposing attitudes. But, in so far as Mikszáth is concerned, almost every essayist offered a completely different interpretation. He was treated as the "last of the liberals" and the witness to the failure of liberalism; the guardian of the traditions of 1848, and the critic of its mistakes; the last great Romantic, and one of the first "critical realists"; the writer of the gentry and the protector of the people; disillusioned cynic and depositary of revolutionary ideas; the master of the provincial anecdote, and the Hungarian master of *fin-de-siècle* European irony; a frivolous entertainer and a perceptive historical thinker.

His Life

He came from a peasant background, from a family in Upper Hungary, still conscious of noble antecedents. After completing his studies in a provincial secondary school, he began to read law, but never finished the course. He became an official and secretly married the daughter of his superior who was one of the gentry. He then moved to Pest to realize his plans as a writer. There he met with misery and humiliation, and compelled his wife to divorce him, sending her back to her parents to spare her the bitter experience of his life. He himself left Pest for Szeged, one of the largest cities in the provinces, where he worked as a journalist. It was here that he wrote the volumes of short stories, *The Good Palots* (A jó palócok) and *The Slovak Yokels* (Tót atyafiak, 1882), which brought him fame overnight. He returned to the capital, where he remained until his death. He then remarried his former wife, and worked for the major newspapers. Although he had worked in Szeged, and in Pest too, at least at the beginning, for an opposition newspaper, he accepted a post offered by the ruling party, and became one of the inner circle around the Prime Minister, as a confidential friend and congenial companion at cards. His popularity grew steadily and official awards of every descriptions were heaped on him. He died unexpectedly, still at the height of his creative powers.

For a considerable time he remained under the spell of Jókai, fortunately the Jókai of the *Nábob,* the master of the genre-scene, the anecdote, the painter of types and a hundred varying ways of life. But his years in Pest freed him from the illusions which beset Jókai. The result was that the very values he questioned were those which the age admired and wished to embody. Mikszáth realized that the leading figures in society, those who were successful and belonged to the upper classes, did not in fact believe or subscribe to such values at all. He consequently looked for a world where genuine values could be found, and especially a world where this paradox, this lie, was absent. It was the influence of Dickens, Bret Harte, Daudet and the regional literature long cultivated around Szeged that led him to turn his attention to the peasant world of his childhood.

The Populist Short Story

The short stories in both *The Good Palots* and *The Slovak Yokels* are brief. This was his first period, and these are his never-fading, most-readable works. But the critics were confused over them from the outset. At one time they said they were pieces of social criticism; at another, romantic idealization. The subjects are mostly drawn from folk poetry. Not the folk tale or narrative, but from the poems, songs, ballads, romances and dirges of the country people. They throw light on the essence of a life, a character or a situation seen in a concentrated dramatic moment. The character and the means employed also belong to folk poetry. Profound psychological observation alternates with descriptions of naive, superstitious illusions, and crudely realistic manifestations of rebellious and revealing social motives with mythic, animist-fatalist explanations. Like Jókai's art of the episode, the structure of these short stories is anecdotal and the description is in the manner of the genre-scene. But they are not folk songs transposed into prose or anecdote, nor Jókai with an added touch of poetry, nor Bret Harte or Dickens. From first to last, Mikszáth's art is unmistakably personal and individual, in the sentence structure, in the sound and the modulation of the language. There is a touch of nostalgia, a breath of sadness in most of his work, yet it is wry, ironic and humorous at the same time. The world of the "people" is beautiful because it is a real world; there, word and intention, feeling and action are identical. There is no lie. It is this that the story suggests. Nonetheless it is a world full of suffering and irrationality; and, in any case, one might ask, does this world actually exist or is no more than a memory? And if it does exist, will it or can it survive? There is undoubtedly an escapist attitude in the short stories. But the author's respect for fact and reason, and his firm belief in the necessity of progress, prevent him from taking refuge in the idyllic. It is for this reason that these works are claimed to be Romantic, realistic, escapist or revealing in turn, according to the impact made on the reader by the story and its atmosphere.

Irony and the Novella

He wrote a number of *népies* short stories in a poetic-nostalgic vein in his later periods, but these were no longer characteristic of him; his later writing was purely ironical. They deal with the lives of the provincial gentry and small-town inhabitants, and are cast in the form of the novella. They are still based on the incident or anecdote and the technique is still based upon the genre-scene with echoes of Cervantes's Don Quixote, in the picture of the outmoded, obsolescent life, ways of thought and fading power of the noble, on the one hand, and of Gogol's *Inspector* in the exposure of the corrupted compliance of the middle class on the other. Mikszáth was a Member of Parliament supporting the ruling party and a friend of the Prime Minister's, but he was in fact outside the real circle of power. His exposures seldom took the form of a direct attack; he denied, but his denials were hints: "It's not quite like that;" "That's different;" "It may appear otherwise through the eyes of another." He cast doubts, raised questions on the attitudes of the Establishment; he drew attention to its false and wavering values. But the opposition also had its share of the good things provided for the Establishment. So the hint, the doubt "It's not quite like that" applied to their values and aims as well. The result was a superlative use of irony, striking out in many directions, even on occasion at himself.

This attitude determined his choice of characters, the structure of his stories and treatment during this period. He had a taste for the peculiar, the grotesque, at times exaggerating these qualities and carrying them to the limit of the absurd. Frequently, and more particularly in his best work, this penchant of his produced odd characters and incredible situations. His novel *The Siege of Beszterce* (Beszterce ostroma, 1894), for instance, concerns Count Pongrácz, the lord of a castle, who resolves to enforce his inherited feudal rights in the middle of the nineteenth century. He forms an army from his peasants and wages war against the neighbouring estates, castles and towns, collecting dues, taking hostages and even abducting a girl. The authorities are compelled to enter into the spirit of the game in order to stop him. The book could easily have been a straightforward satire, an exaggerated attack on obsolete feudal mentality. But Pongrácz cannot be simply dismissed as a madman. He is better than his contemporaries, the sons of a mercenary, opportunist age, for whom strength of personality, positive action and the need to create genuine values is neither desirable nor possible. He is a tragicomic figure; his failure does not lack melancholy. The same situation is even more pronounced in *New Zrínyiad* (Új Zrínyiász, 1897). He

297

used the old trick of the writer in placing the main character, the sixteenth-century heroes of Zrínyi's epic, in a nineteenth-century setting, described with all the accuracy and fidelity of a reporter.

When describing ironically, with great realism, the manners and distorted mentality of a whole class, he is irresistible. In these cases the Romantic is subordinated to the realistic, and the realistic to the ironic. The anecdote here is not the sign of an as yet unachieved realism, but the means to a certain form of realism. He shows certain similarities to Anatole France and Gottfried Keller. He caricatures not only characters and events, but the novel and the cult of realism as well, and it gives his writing a beautiful and subtle grace. His lines are permeated with experience of life, a profound knowledge of human nature and an almost contemplative atmosphere. This is very apparent in the novel most admired abroad, *St. Peter's Umbrella* (Szent Péter esernyője, 1895). An old, dishevelled, lunatic Jew fixes an ancient red umbrella on to a basket in front of the door of the priest's house, where the priest's young sister is sleeping, while outside the rain pours down. The poor priest is wracking his brains how to educate the little girl. The umbrella, however, brings fortune to the girl; the peasants, who had never seen an umbrella before, spread the rumour that St. Peter had personally delivered it himself, and the priest is unable to scotch it. But the rich miser had concealed his securities in the handle of the umbrella before his death, and the umbrella, sold and lost, was being sought by his son. The handle is destroyed, but the young sister of the priest and the miser's son eventually find each other. This operetta story, treated with unrestrained humour, is a rich storehouse of wise irony, with everyone getting his share. In that flawless novella of his, *The Gallants* (Gavallérok, 1897), he describes a wedding he attended. The wedding guests ride in fine coaches from the manor houses of the county to the mansion of the couple. With regal grandeur, they present the new couple with their gifts. But on their return home, we discover that the coaches were borrowed, that the gifts cannot be taken seriously, and that the characters will now resume their lives as small clerks. They had been aping the customs of their forefathers, intent on presenting an appearance and acting as if they were really rich. Hardly ever has the anachronism of gentry life been so deftly, so economically, so delicately exposed.

The same can be clearly seen in his historical novels. He liked to show the great heroes of history as children, or in comic situations; the king or the high priest climbing a tree, the national hero chasing chickens in the courtyard. The sardonic "it is not quite like that" and "it can be interpreted differently" was designed to deflate the idealization of Hungarian history so strongly favoured by the Establishment after the Compromise (*The Magic Caftan* — A beszélő köntös, 1889; *The Two Poor Students* — A két koldusdiák, 1885; *The Women of Szelistye* — A szelistyei asszonyok, 1901, etc.).

Occasionally he abandons this indirect approach to follow the example of contemporary Russian and Western realist writers, directly attacking abuses, as in his novella *Sipsirica* (1902), which deals with the organized and brutal destruction of a clerk, solely because, out of a sense of humanity and a love of the truth, he dared to confront the members of the ruling order.

The Novels

The critical dangers beginning to gather around the turn of the century called for more than the short story and the novella could give. The last ten years of his life were devoted to a search for a new answer and a new vehicle for it. Three lengthy novels indicate the directions his mind was taking. The first, *Strange Marriage* (Különös házasság, 1900), deals with marriage entered into under duress and continued by force, showing how even in the most intimate and personal matters, the individual is at the mercy of inhuman, impersonal and reactionary forces, in this case the feudal Church and feudal orders, intent on safeguarding their power. In a second novel, *The Noszty Boy's Affair with Mari Tóth* (A Noszty fiú esete Tóth Marival, 1908), all the nobility of the county join forces to gain possession of the wealth of a middle-class girl, in order to maintain their outmoded way of life. In the third novel, *Black City* (A fekete város, 1911), a burgher town revolts against the institutions of the nobility and its representative, the county sheriff. In these novels, he attacks the Hungarian land-owning class more vehemently than ever before. He is concerned with questions of how things that were once of value become valueless, and even harmful, and whether new values will replace the old.

In *Noszty,* the answer is a definite "yes": the father of the middle-class girl who revolts against the conspiracy of the nobles is an honest man, although less vigorously drawn than the portraits of the nobles themselves. And the county sheriff in *Black City* is undoubtedly a more attractive character than the middle-class heroes of the novel. Nonetheless, Mikszáth puts his faith to the class which is superseding the gentry, even though he can only vaguely perceive its features. But he is really uncertain about liberalism. For Mikszáth, the whole problem of values in society was concentrated on two points: whether a satisfactory power would supersede the land-owning class, and whether liberalism would be replaced by a satisfactory set of principles. And when, finally, he was forced to face the issue, he considered liberalism, with all its faults, to be the most acceptable system, which demonstrates the class-bound quality of his choice.

Opinion varies widely on these three novels. Some regard them as his most ambitious works. Others, while not disputing his intentions, judge that the means he selected were inadequate. The Romantic devices and other technical tricks which he had employed, used with irony and even parody in his novels were here used in deadly seriousness. These critics usually refer to Mikszáth's own statement made in his last years, to the effect that were it possible for him to begin again, he would follow the path of Dostoievsky, as evidence of his dissatisfaction with these novels. Although there is some truth in this, Mikszáth began to write in the new manner while he still retained his old attitudes and beliefs. The psychological truth of his characters, and his social views, are conveyed obliquely in the turn and twist of his style, and so insinuate themselves into acceptance. He deliberately maintained the air and atmosphere of operetta to heighten the irony. It is, admittedly, difficult, if not impossible, to produce a successful tragic novel in this way, but it is possible to achieve an effect which is ironic or melancholy, and in this sense he is both kin and forerunner of the great ironic novelists who flourished from 1900 onwards.

Mikszáth had an enormous influence on the development of Hungarian litera-ture. Due to him the outdated Romanticism inherited from Jókai, of whom he wrote an excellent biography (1907), was finally consigned to oblivion. He made Jókai's genre-scene and Jókai's episode or anecdote the focus or pivot of his tales, and his wry, melancholy tone was in step with contemporary writing in the Western world. He freed the Hungarian short story from idealization, rhetoric and excessive, dramatic, emotional appeal. But any form of deep psychological analysis, the charac-teristic of bourgeois realism, was alien to him. Irony supplied its place. He was a master of the short story, and even in his novels this quality provided the artistic, the modern, the realistic element. It is largely due to Mikszáth that the Hungarian short story around the turn of the century achieved such heights.

42 The Heyday of the Short Story

The Hungarian short story around the turn of the century, in the work of Mikszáth, depended on the intimate tone and the immediate personality of the writer. He did not conceal himself behind an impersonal style, factual accounts, objective analysis and the detailed description of character. He himself is always present, the tone and nuances of his own voice are always heard, and it was through this personal flourish, this personal approach that the reader could be brought to perceive the trickery and falsity behind the varnish of the ruling authorities, even if they could not grasp it objectively as a whole. These writers hinted, suggested, lifted a veil here and there, and it was the authenticity of their own intimate voice speaking, with irony, with melancholy, with resignation, with nostalgia, that gave validity to their critical attitude of rejection. They were akin to Anatole France, Turgeniev and Keller rather than to Maupassant, Tolstoy and Zola. It was Impressionism and psychologism which most influenced their works, or the last heritage of Romanticism, or Symbolism, with a touch of naturalism.

István Petelei (1825-1910)

Besides Mikszáth, the other important short-story writer of the time was István Petelei, the son of a wealthy Armenian merchant family living in Transylvania. He first studied theology, then turned to science and archaeology, and ended up as a journalist, working as an editor in Kolozsvár and Marosvásárhely. But he soon became disillusioned in this career as well, and gave up journalism. He subsequently led the hidden, at times ascetic life of a hermit, and scarcely tolerated anyone but children. Later his nervous disorders took complete possession of him, and he died in total solitude.

Although he was also a master of the *Stimmungsnovelle* he was a very different type of writer from the author of *The Good Palots*. He wrote of the suffering and dispossessed of the earth, and of the invisible and inevitable approach of tragedy. He found his subject-matter in three different milieux: the old small towns, the peasant villages surrounding them, and the declining village gentry. The themes were ordinary: death, estrangement, the loneliness of old people, the disintegration of a family, the failure of a way of life, and the like. The moment which concerned him was when a man abandoned his way of life, his moral attitudes, his will to live, that is himself, drifted out of the mainstream of society and became an outsider, an alien to normal life *(Orphan Lotti* — Árva Lotti; *Mayer, The Jewish Cobbler* — A zsidó suszter; *The Horse of Csifó Frajter* — Csifó frajter lova). He was well acquainted with the theory of positivism and biological determinism. But, as opposed to the naturalist school, he seldom depicts man as so determined purely by biological inheritance; he attached more importance to his social environment and intellectual background. He wrote an excellent sociographical essay: *The Way of the Mezőség* (Mezőségi út, 1884). In his determinism there is always a moral element: passivity. His heroes are passive: they do not shape their own fate, it happens to them. Petelei, with the sensitivity of the dispossessed, throws light on the ever-increasing number of tragic moments behind the illusion of a thriving but essentially false system.

His style is deliberately monotonous: a recitative, a musically composed monotony. He used few technical devices, but was painstaking with them. Three of them are of especial importance: the ballad-like style, the inner monologue, and his symbolic descriptions of nature. The main virtue of his short stories lies in their atmosphere, their poetic tone. He often used what the cinema calls flash-backs: he would begin with the final outcome, before dealing with the path that led to it. Some form of analysis is nearly always present, but rarely in the objective descriptions, when it is, its presence is unfortunate. His lyricism does not bear open analysis. There is something provincial in his exaggerated use of lyrical monologues as well as in his moral attitudes and limited choice of subject-matter.

Elek Gozsdu (1849-1919)

Elek Gozsdu is usually regarded as being rather like Petelei, although Petelei's limited themes and provincialism are not characteristics of his work. He lived in many different kinds of places, from remote small towns to the capital. His middle-class family was a mixture of Macedonian, Rumanian, Armenian and north and south Transdanubian Hungarian blood. He studied law, retiring to Temesvár, already a large city, where he worked as district attorney. He was more closely connected with his fellow-writers than Petelei, and enjoyed discussing literary and philosophical questions with them.

But his position was also that of the outsider, and his main artistic virtue was the tone of his writings. He was familiar with the philosophical and sociological implications of Positivism; and also with the emerging anti-Positivism. Most of his short stories were concerned with one of the principal ideas of the age; he pondered on the question of whether they could be justified as art because they presented vital human and Hungarian material or because they help in a deeper understanding of human nature and the Hungarian situation. He was interested in the problem of inheritance, the relationship of genius and madness, biology and decadence, race and character, power and morals, eroticism and culture, nihilism and vitality, and similar themes. Unlike Petelei, he did not avoid socialist ideas. Although in his own lifetime he was considered a more "modern", more "philosophical" writer than Petelei, today the reverse is true. His stories illustrate a particular argument and are often ephemeral, strained, and of only passing interest. Later, when he realized he was considered an outsider, he became interested in Dostoievsky and Turgeniev; human suffering, expressed in a symbolical and lyrical way, became the main preoccupation of his pen.

The Progress of Social Criticism

The further development of the realistic short story was appreciably conditioned by the fundamental contradiction of Hungarian society, the conflict between the land-owning and the middle classes, which became acute and obvious to all concerned by the 1890s. In 1897, all the tinsel and glamour of an apparently prosperous era was used to gild the celebrations of the millennium of the Hungarian Conquest of the land a thousand years before, even though the country was already full of unrest. All the important writers were essentially middle-class in their views, employed the method of a socially critical realism. Each of them responded to European influences, but differently, according to their individual background and social attitudes, though none of them, however, was strong enough to oust realism. The strongest influences were naturalism and the Secession, followed by Symbolism and Impressionism.

At the beginning of this century a number of important experiments were undertaken in the novel, apart from those initiated by Mikszáth; but the short story still took precedence; and indeed even strengthened its position. Some of the features of the earlier type of short story persisted, especially its poetic qualities, but they were subordinated to a more objective, critically oriented approach. The Hungarian short story never attained so high a general standard as around this time.

Sándor Bródy (1863-1924)

The first of these writers to appear on the scene was Sándor Bródy, who was also, historically speaking, the most important. He played a part in, or introduced most of, the literary trends of the time, although he was most closely associated with naturalism and the Secession.

He came from a poor provincial Jewish family, and was employed as a clerk for a firm of lawyers. After reading Zola's *Nana* while still a very young man, he published a volume of short stories entitled *Misery* (Nyomor, 1884), "on the principles of naturalism". It met with both wide approval and fervent opposition. He became famous, moved to Pest and worked as a journalist there, taking his first steps on the path to the greatest writing career of the period. He was a passionate, wilful, handsome man, with vast expectations from life and great ambitions. His path was paved with success and failures, both amorous and literary. Except at the end when he was subjected to the humiliating racial persecution initiated by the 1920 counter-revolution, he always managed to right himself again. But that time he was forced to leave the country, and went to Vienna and Italy. It was in these years that he wrote his best short stories, but it was in these years he went to pieces, and he died soon after his return to Hungary.

He was a multi-faceted, prolific writer, working in a variety of styles and genres. In addition to many volumes of short stories, he wrote a number of novels and plays and a great deal of journalism. He took his subjects and background anywhere he found them, but two types of characters constantly re-appear—the little man who leaves the traditional country way of life and drifts into the still amorphous world of the changing city, and the bourgeois longing for a career, for the "big life". He started out under the influence of Zola, but Jókai and Mikszáth affected him to at least the same extent. He tried to combine the romantically poetic, the radically critical and the naturalistic life-like. He was attracted by extreme individuality and strong passions, but had a strong sense of social solidarity and was prepared to write and argue forcefully on its behalf. His views, however, were multicoloured. He echoed almost all the fashionable ideas of the age, from the role given to biology by Positivism and the aestheticism of the Secession, to the individuality and life-cult of vitalism.

It is in his short stories that his best work is to be found. The limited scope of the short story and its strict rules gave him a feeling for proportion and enhanced the poetic value of his language. His language, indeed, is one of his chief assets. It is at once grandiloquent and rhythmic, grotesque and rhetorical. A peasant simplicity and the ease of folk song combines with slang to produce an exciting lyrical, tender style. Nowhere else has naturalism and movements such as Symbolism, Impressionism and the Secession, which are anti-naturalist, combined into an organic style as successfully as in his short stories.

Two of his types of short story are outstanding. The first are his "maidservant stories" (*Nanny Elizabeth and Other Maids* — Erzsébet dajka és más cselédek, 1902). They are made up of a mixture of romance and tragedy, a yearning for the good and true life, and the desolate cruelty of reality. His maidservant heroines begin full of confidence, with a naive trust in the goodwill of their masters. They would be content with very little, but meet with nothing but the uninhibited selfishness that considers them as mere objects. The other are the *Rembrandt* stories written before his death. In his humiliation he relived the life of the old outcast Rembrandt. Personal confession is mixed with objective description, tragic personal reticence and suppression with memories, together with a strict attention to historical accuracy, combine to make them a short-story cycle of striking quality.

His wild mixture of attitudes and views and his lack of artistic discipline had a bad effect on his novels (*Silver Goat* — Ezüstkecske, 1898; *The Knight of the Sun* — A nap lovagja, 1902, etc.). The action of these novels often follows the patterns of Romanticism, and their characters are conventional and typed. His style which, in his short stories, radiates a personal charm of its own, becomes artificial and mannered in the longer context. We shall return to his plays in the chapter on the drama of the age. His journalism has already been mentioned, as this won him a name in Hungarian political journalism. It was journalistic writings that introduced the growing influence of the Secession into journalism, even influencing better writers than himself, as Ady, for instance. He was in fact considerably more important for his innovations, and the seminal influence he exercised, than for accomplishment as a writer proper. Until the appearance of the *Nyugat,* he was the symbol, patron and promoter of all that was new.

Géza Gárdonyi (1863-1922)

The other author of the period who exercised considerable influence was Géza Gárdonyi. But while Bródy's influence was paramount among writers, Gárdonyi's was effective on the reader of a later period. With Jókai and Mikszáth he made up the trio most popular with the public. He was the son of a German blacksmith, who had become a Hungarian revolutionary in 1848, and a peasant girl who was a devout Catholic. He became a teacher and worked in various Catholic schools in the provinces in miserable circumstances, exposed to all sorts of clerical humiliations. Throughout his career, he fought against the Church, but in his own mystical inner world he remained bound to it. His marriage was unsuccessful and his progress as a writer was slow. He abandoned teaching and worked in Szeged as a journalist, supplementing his salary by writing anonymously anything that came to hand, pornography and adventure stories and short tales guying the peasants. His first successful book was *My Village* (Az én falum, 1898), a volume of short stories. From that time he lived in the capital from his earnings as a writer. He later retired to the home of his school days, Eger, where he lived in seclusion among his books, with a deteriorating nervous disorder, and great crises of conscience, in intellectual agony.

A self-taught man, he was an introverted, slow, passive character. He was only attracted to those ideas of the age to which his sufferings made him sensitive, and he constructed his philosophy of life around them with touching determination and simplicity. His main experience was also the decline of all the old values. But while Bródy sought a possible basis of new values in new phenomena, Gárdonyi turned to the passing reality, wishing to preserve its values and thus became the interpreter *par excellence* of the provincial town and village.

Like Bródy, Gárdonyi also wrote novels, plays and poetry, and the short stories which contained his best work. His tales mostly concern themselves with a quite ordinary episode or event which brings out the common human virtues in all their emotional and ethical fullness: an old roof-tiler falls, and lies on his death-bed awaiting the arrival of his only son; at the moment of death, the father–son relationship is irradiated with restrained beauty and simplicity (*Wish Pesta would Come* — Csak már a Pesta jönne). He is generally appreciated for his attitude in considering the soul of the peasant as valuable as that of the other classes of society but was, on the other hand, criticized for idealizing the village and perpetuating the romantic view of the people. Both criticisms are justified but are immaterial in the light of his wish to demonstrate the honest and enduring value of the joys and sufferings of the poor, as opposed to the false values prevailing at the time. He is aware of suffering, even of its social causes, but it is elevated into a sphere of eternal necessity, and both enduring it and alleviating it are virtues. This concept of suffering gave his work a sad, elegiac atmosphere. He was not a striking writer or an advocate of action. Faith in moral, psychological and social value is always present, strengthening self-respect, but it is often too sentimental.

Gárdonyi's finest books are his historical novels, but he lacks the power to delve into complex relationships and development of character. These novels are short stories, extended by meticulous descriptions of background and surroundings, and by the vivid accounts of incidents and events. *Stars of Eger* (Egri csillagok, 1901) is about a couple of children who grow up, fall in love and marry. The story is set in Turkish times in the sixteenth century, and includes an account of the famous defence of Eger against the Turks. This novel achieved supreme success with young readers. Another book, *The Invisible Man* (A láthatatlan ember, 1902), revived the times of Attila, the Scourge of God through the story of two hopeless lovers. *God's Prisoners* (Isten rabjai, 1908) was yet another novel written with the utmost attention to detail, set in thirteenth-century Hungary, after the devastations of the Mongol Invasion, seen through the eye of the fresh and realistic simple lay-brother serving in a convent where the King's daughter is a nun. The attraction of his historical novels stems from the very virtues displayed in his short stories: the admirable moral attitudes of ordinary people and their wise, sad, stoical acceptance of life. His social novels are rather weak, apart from *The Old Gentleman* (Az öreg tekintetes, 1905), which deals with an old man who drifts into the city, his tragedy and his suicide, using him not to protest against the city in favour of the village but to express the horror of the impersonal business world of the city.

István Tömörkény (1866-1917)

As a realist writer, István Tömörkény is most akin to Gárdonyi. He was, by choice, a regional writer. His short stories concentrate on the peasants and the small men of the Tisza region. His work is quite as uneven as that of Gárdonyi or Bródy. His subject-matter and technique are limited. After reading twenty of his short stories, one can guess the pattern of the other five hundred. But he wrote nevertheless enough good short stories to fill a volume that would rank with the best of Hungarian short stories.

Tömörkény was born into a middle-class family of German settler origin, which by then was completely Hungarian, had settled in Szeged, and had acquired land there. His father was the owner of a railway restaurant; he himself became a pharmacist. It was while he was doing his national service in the desolate mountains of Bosnia that he became aware of his talent as a writer and of the subject-matter which interested him most. On his return home he worked as a journalist. He also took a keen interest in folklore and archaeology, and as a result, became the director of a museum in Szeged. He hardly ever moved outside the region; the whole of his uneventful life, entirely devoted to his work, was spent there. Although he tried his hand at novels and plays, he remained essentially a short-story writer.

Unlike Gárdonyi, Tömörkény himself stands aside; he refuses to identify himself with his characters or become involved with their situation. He describes; he reports from within the thoughts, language and attitudes of his heroes, as if a third person, part of their world but uninvolved in the situation, reports on his neighbours, tells the story, records the event. The logic, motivation and conclusions of such an assumed attitude is, of course, indefensible, grotesque and absurd from the point of view of the author's own attitudes and cultural standpoint. Ordinary events provoke a sour humour; tragic events, a painful sense of shame. A lonely, abandoned peasant is burnt to death in a fire in the loft where he sleeps. Next day, his charred remains are inspected by the others. They comment; they discuss the dead man with the best of intentions, but from a peasant's point of view, and what emerges from their conversations is not only the unforgettable tragicomedy of life, but a whole attitude to the world. Tömörkény seldom openly espouses social or political ideas, yet his best work provides a more shattering social indictment than the more deliberately planned attacks of his contemporaries. The reader is forced to ask himself whether life is really as petty as this, and is it endurable that it should remain on this level in the face of its highest possibilities. Tömörkény never idealizes the attitudes of his characters; although not uninfluenced by naturalism, he never reduces them to the merely animal either. Within the bounds of their own mentality, they mean well; they are reasonable and honest. It is, in fact, this aspect that completes the tragic nature of his stories: their conclusion reveals the contradiction between the attitude and action.

In the majority of his stories, his method of writing becomes a mannerism, he often uses folk phrases without any appropriate function in the context: the reasoning is distorted and illogical. The result is a petty-bourgeois form of humour, relating incidents or anecdotes in the manner of the "plays about peasant life", often accompanied by a philanthropic sentimentality. We know hardly anything of his intellectual or aesthetic development; apart from the positivist respect for fact which became a fundamental principle of his work, there is little else to note as characteristic, but it is a quality which suits the short-story writer. It also tends to restrict him somewhat, but nonetheless he was an excellent writer of the realistic short story, and the objective trend found in a later generation, derive in part from his work.

Zoltán Thury (1870-1906)

The best work of Bródy, Gárdonyi and Tömörkény was concerned with the world of the lower classes, ordinary people treated with sympathy and encouragement. The social and political views of these writers were, however, vague and undefined. Their younger contemporary, Zoltán Thury, went further: to the threshold of socialism. The working class and the overt social struggle were the usual subjects of his work. His method and style are more dramatic and more passionate, but at the same time more objective and reflective, more "ideal" than the three elder writers. But it was only in the last years of his life that his work rivalled that of his contemporaries, for he matured slowly and died young. His main virtue lies rather in what he initiated than in what he accomplished.

He was the son of an army family from Transylvania. He worked as a journalist in various towns, and his foreign travels, combined with wide reading, turned his mind to socialism. The theatre held a strong attraction for him, but his plays never reached the level of his later stories, which bear a certain resemblance to Chekhov's stories though there is more action in them and the outlines are firmer. He makes considerable use of reporting techniques, both where his scenes of action and his language are concerned. *Death of a Man* (Emberhalál), for instance, reads like a legal report. Ady and the whole radical wing of his generation regarded Thury as their immediate predecessor.

Portraitists of the Middle Classes

Bródy, Gárdonyi, Tömörkény and Thury were as much involved with the middle as with the lower classes. And a number of writers might justly be called portraitists of the middle classes. Tamás Kóbor, Dániel Papp, Károly Lovik, Zoltán Ambrus and Ferenc Herczeg all represented different layers of a heterogeneous class. They were closer than these four writers to the *Nyugat* movement and social and educational problems were combined in their work.

The newly assimilated Jewish middle classes, especially the poorer middle class, formed the subject-matter of much of *Tamás Kóbor's* work (1867–1942), who saw and described their world from within. He wrote novels which generally take the form of chronicles and better short stories, in fact he was more of a journalist than a writer pure. He is not of great importance but his love of truth and his passionate plea for mutual toleration touch a sympathetic chord.

The provincial middle class found its spokesman in *Dániel Papp* (1865–1900). He came from the prosperous southern part of the country, from Bácska, where there was a colourful mixture of religions, national minorities and cultures. He himself was half-Hungarian, half-Serb, the son of a titled family whose income was provided by posts in the administration. For some time he was a theological student in a Unitarian seminary. He then worked as a journalist, first in the provinces and then in Pest. Throughout his life he worked very hard, he had a large family and died young of tuberculosis. The whole body of his short stories was written in some ten years or so filling only a few volumes. But they showed promise of future mastery. His knowledge of life was rich and complex; he was well acquainted not only with the provincial intellectual world but also with the world of the Church, the Serb peasantry and the Hungarian gentry. His cultural background gave him a feeling for proportion and matured his judgement, saving him from the narrow outlook of the self-taught. Original ideas and a strong sense of atmosphere permeate his short stories. The atmosphere is provided by the evocation of background and surroundings which he learnt from Mikszáth, and the intellectual angle by the explanation and interpretation he placed on them. He does not lecture, nor does he describe; he prefers to reveal character through dialogue and the inner monologue. He is interested in the extent to which men are bound by the rigid customs of their social class, and consequently prevented from developing their personality and achieving mutual understanding. He considers, for instance, how a priest comes to realize that what makes up his life is not, in fact, original to him; how a peasant acts according to irrational norms. His voice is sympathetic when he talks of the lower class, ironic when the upper classes are his subject. His power of creating atmosphere is greatly heightened by the symbolic element often present in his work. He combined the qualities of the masters of the previous generation, Mikszáth and Petelei, but took them even further.

On the borderline between the middle class and the gentry stood *Károly Lovik* (1874–1915), the son of a middle-class family connected with the gentry, the youngest of his generation. He was a sports reporter who loved the races and was an expert horse-breeder. This occupation kept him in touch with the gentry as well as with the wealthier members of the middle class. He was at home where these two worlds overlapped. Other writers regarded him as something of an amateur, and he himself looked upon writing as a pastime. As a result his work was often sketchy, but this, in fact, occasionally added to the quality of his writing. He was the observer of one of the company who, for his own amusement, watches the others, "a thief among them taking notes", usually in the form of portraits, sometimes as an account of some incident or other. He was more given to pungent observations and an epigrammatic summing up of the situation than to analysis or interpretation. He watched wrily, from his vantage ground, the decline of the gentry, and the middle class imitating the gentry as they acquired wealth. There is often a nostalgic, as well as ironic, overtone to his work, which is on occasion transmuted into a Romantic and Impressionist dream-world. In later life his criticism of society and moral demands increased, and his late short stories, like those of most of the other writers of the period, proved his best (*The Golden Citizen* — Az arany polgár, 1908; *Migrant Bird* — Vándormadár, 1909). He ceased to be a detached painter and became a committed critic.

Zoltán Ambrus (1861-1932)

The most outstanding member of this group was Zoltán Ambrus, a follower of the analytic French school, who is often compared by Hungarian literary historians to Anatole France. Despite his strong nationality and his "doctus" attitude, he was far more emotional and romantic. He came from a provincial family earning their living in clerical jobs, which had already been influenced by the urban way of life; he became a lawyer and subsequently worked as a bank official. He made a number of visits to Paris, where he came under the influence of Positivism. He later devoted himself entirely to literature and journalism, and was for some time the director of the National Theatre in Budapest. He eventually retired, but remained a much-respected figure. He also wrote novels, but his best works were his short stories.

His work was usually set in the world of the middle and upper-middle classes, but he was also drawn to the world of artists, especially in his novels. His approach is generally psychological in nature with strong social overtones, and he is frequently concerned with the conflict between the different cultural strata, between various types and ways of life; the conflict between real and false culture, the educated man and the snob. In place of the discredited values of the old world he offers justice, toleration, understanding, and a love of culture. He is close to Renan in his educational ideas and also in his scepticism. In method and style he is related to Taine, analysing with the calm objectivity and mastery of the university lecturer. The irony he uses is always equal to the subject whether it be the matter of the tale, himself, his art or his public. But it changes to satire when confronting the mental intolerance of the outdated class of the gentry or the false culture of the nouveau riche, as in his famous cycle of short stories, *Baron Berzsenyi and His Family* (Berzsenyi báró és családja). He was a mediocre sober-paced writer, never sinking to the worst levels of Gárdonyi, Tömörkény or Bródy, and seldom reaching their highest flights. He could write about anything, yet rarely offered his reader a genuine literary experience. It is human behaviour as glimpsed in his tales, rather than the tales as such, that strikes the reader.

The *fin de siècle* face that emerges from his novels is marked with nostalgia rather than irony. He suffered from a lack of certainty and conviction, and the difference between life and art, the typical symptoms of the middle-class dilemma at the end of the century; but there was, however, a certain complacency in the suffering. His novels (*Solus eris*, 1901; *King Midas* — Midás király, 1906) are for the most part "novels of the art world", following each new fashion of the era, especially the Secessionist style. He often gives the disturbing impression that he forces a method and a dimension alien to him. While his intellectual qualities are attractive in his short stories, the dogmatically partisan approach of his novels repels.

Ferenc Herczeg (1863-1954)

The writer of that generation who enjoyed the longest career, Ferenc Herczeg developed in exactly the opposite direction as Lovik did: he changed from being a critic of the gentry to become their champion. He came from the southern part of Hungary, born into a well-to-do, provincial middle-class family of German settler origin, and he learnt Hungarian at school. He became a lawyer, and began to write in the eighties, first novels and short stories, and then plays. (*Mutamur*, short stories, 1892; *Occidental Tales* — Napnyugati mesék, short stories, 1894; *The Gyurkovics Girls* — A Gyurkovics lányok, novel, 1893; *The Daughter of the Nabob of Dolova* — A dolovai nábob leánya, play, 1903.) In his early days he regarded the gentry from a liberal, middle-class moral standpoint and criticized, in particular their frivolity and idleness. He wrote with ease, with a feeling for proportion, and an economy of language, and showed, above all, a sensitivity to the nuances of style. He admired the playful irony of Mikszáth. From the very outset he was nonetheless attracted to the elegant superiority and self-assurance—and irresponsibility—of "upper-class life" viewed from without, and it showed through his didactic criticism. For some time he excused this attraction, saying that he needed a close knowledge of the milieu in order to describe it, and this could only be obtained from within it. This close knowledge was eventually so successful that in the course of a few years he became the darling of the middle classes. He found himself unable to resist the lure of the popularity and the role it demanded he play. He was first the entertainer of the middle class; then he aspired to become its conscience and proceeded to adopt the central principle of the gentry, i.e., that the national character is concentrated in this class. He assumed the hopelessly outmoded, liberal–Romantic role of "the writer of the nation", in place of short stories and comedies, wrote historical plays and novels on the turning-points in national history (*Pagans* — Pogányok, 1902; *Byzantium* — Bizánc, 1904). In later life he returned several times to the genres and themes which had brought him success in his younger years—psychological love stories in play and novel form. These brought him success abroad, made his books bestsellers, and his plays stage successes. (*Blue Fox* — A kék róka, play, 1918; *The Golden Violin* — Az aranyhegedű, novel, 1916.)

He was undoubtedly a clever writer, managing to clothe superannuated views with some appearance of modernity, and he was very readable. His popularity was enhanced by the weekly he ran, *Új Idők* (New Times), which spanned the years 1895 to 1945, enjoying a vast circulation and catering for the conservative tastes of the middle classes. He lived alone, working on his memoirs. All in all, he produced an immense body of work, but, due to his narrow provincial and conservative views, and despite his talent, no more than a couple of volumes of his short stories are of lasting literary value.

43 The Drama of Realism—Its Beginnings

Dramatic Trends

This period also failed to produce any outstanding dramatic works. The growth of towns favoured the growth of theatres but good drama could not be produced on the popular illusions of the time.

The new school around the beginning of the period was what was called the Neo-Romantic school, akin to the work of Nestroy and the Viennese *Volkstück*. It was primarily designed to provide the new middle-class audience with light entertainment. But it was at the same time a protest, however cautious, against the tyrannical rule of traditional moral standards in favour of themes taken from national and peasant life. Love was the dominant theme, and, under cover of legend and myth, a certain erotism was even introduced. They also on occasion voiced a protect against the prevailing social hierarchy. The plays were set in remote and romantic places and times, history turned fairy-tale: Spain and India, the Middle Ages, the Hellenic Age. The dramatists were mostly lower middle class in origin, more particularly from the newly assimilated German and Jewish groups.

During the seventies, social problems treated realistically were also more openly discussed in the theatre. *István Toldy*, already mentioned as a novelist, wrote such plays. They were realistic; they might even be called propaganda. It was his comedies that were most successful. He revitalized the manner of Károly Kisfaludy, using a skill in dialogue and a wealth of detail and settings learned from Jókai, to please the new middle class and serve the ideas of utilitarian liberalism. In *The Good Patriots* (A jó hazafiak, 1872), he caricatures the life of the provincial nobility and their bombastic patriotism. In *The New People* (Az új emberek, 1872), he praised the resourcefulness and adaptability of the middle classes. In his tragedies (*Kornélia*, 1874; *Lívia*, 1874), he criticised the ambivalent morality of the rapidly developing urban way of life. He was strongly anti-clerical, lashing the religious pretensions of Church and laymen with sweeping criticism of traditional morality. In this he took Dumas fils as his model, but while displayed greater moral force and sincerity, his theatrical sense and his technique as a playwright was inferior to that of his model. Had he not died so young, he might have equalled Ibsen in his achievement.

The genre of the *népszínmű*, or "play about peasant life", also produced new results in this period. *Ede Tóth* (1844–1876), a dramatist who began his career as a strolling player, wrote plays about the social conflicts of peasants and poor towns-folk, but it was only in certain parts of his plays, that he managed to avoid the idyllic and didactic elements. (*Scamp of the Village* — A falu rossza, 1875; *The Vagrant* — A tolonc, 1876; *The Family of Organ-grinders* — A kintornás család, 1876.) Further development was ended by his early death. As prosperity and pleasure in romantic illusion displaced interest in social questions, no other playwrights followed his lead. The idyllic, pseudo-Romantic, half-operetta plays, making use of singing and dancing, took over the genre of "peasant life" plays, and were exceedingly popular. These peasant half-operetta plays became almost a symbol of the common social illusions of the different classes: special theatre was founded for their performances (1875). (Principal authors: Jenő Rákosi, Ferenc Csepreghy, Tihamér Balogh, etc.)

Gergely Csiky (1842–1891)

The theatre prospered with the prosperity of the eighties. First-class companies performed the classics, mostly Shakespeare and Molière, but with particular emphasis on the French "social plays" of Sardou, Augier, Dumas fils and others. But there were Hungarian playwrights who also wrote such "social plays". One of them, Gergely Csiky, was a writer of considerable talent. His theatrical sense rivalled Sardou's; his capacity for work Jókai's and Szigligeti's. He came from a clerical family, became a Catholic priest and was put in charge of marital affairs in his diocese, where his experience of human conflict was extensive—and very useful. Nonetheless, his first plays were written in the Neo-Romantic manner. A lengthy stay in Paris gave him other ideas, and from then on he turned to the life of the gentry and the middle classes. His successful play, *The Proletarians* (A proletárok, 1880), brought him into conflict with the Church. He then became converted to Lutheranism and married. His incredible capacity for work finally failed him. His health was undermined and he died some ten years later.

He, too, was mainly concerned with the contradiction between reality and appearance, with false values and hypocrisy. *The Proletarians* dealt with the treacherous manipulation of national feelings and the falsity of the concept of gentlemanly honour. The central issue of *Mukányi* (1880) was the social climbing of the middle classes and the opportunist nature of contemporary bourgeois scholarship and science. *Tinsel Misery* (Cifra nyomorúság, 1881) exposed the stupidity and corruption of the impassionate defence of their position and status, *Bubbles* (Buborékok, 1887) attacks the humbug of old family ties and current morality through the financial collapse of a gentry family. His pictures of such backgrounds and surroundings are usually realistic and critical. In the first acts of his plays, these milieux emerge in a stronger

314

critical light than Mikszáth ever produced. But, as his excellent critic, Péterfy, said, the real conflict is left downstairs in the hall, and after the first act everything falls into the cliché-ridden pattern of fashionable French drama. And in the third act, the artificial reclamation of one of the characters eliminates the conflict entirely: instead of failure, a solution miraculously appears. For instance, in *Bubbles,* the noble family which was originally ready to sell the girl to lay hands on the bridegroom's money, redeem themselves from moral failure since the bridegroom's father suddenly becomes aware of his "paternal feelings" and gives his consent to the marriage and thus, looking back, the whole immoral speculation becomes no more than a mild comic intrigue.

Csiky was obsessed with the idea of success. What he worked for was faultless theatrical effects. In the end, he gave the public what it wanted: a superficial consideration of their problems, easily solved in a glow of illusion and goodwill. He was the Sardou of the Hungarian stage: he taught Hungarian playwrights the value of striking, colloquial dialogue which was capable of carrying the action of the play and of the well-constructed plot.

The Plays of the Short-story Writers

Around 1900, when the social contradictions of the system began to make themselves felt, conditions favoured not only the development of theatre, but of drama as well. The willingness to compromise displayed by the middle classes and the lack of a firm standpoint which would give coherence to a work, on the other hand, impeded the development of a worthwhile drama. "Plays of the middle kind" in which the conflict was promptly and easily resolved held the stage. Nor did there any writer emerge who was essentially a playwright. Playwrights were in fact, for the most part, short-story writers, and most of their plays were adaptations of their short stories. And even after achieving success in the theatre, they remained pre-eminently writers as of the short story. The best of them, in theatrical talent and the part he played in the development of the drama, was Bródy. His plays possessed the same virtues as his short stories. They were built around the social contradictions of the time. The two best-known are *The Nanny* (A dada, 1902), and *The Schoolmistress* (A tanító-nő, 1908). The first deals with a peasant girl in service as a nanny; it describes her mental and physical defencelessness and humiliation at the hands of her masters in the city. The second play is about the struggle of a poor teacher for her profession and love against the official and ecclesiastical authorities who control the distribution of the various posts. Although Bródy's technique reveals the influence of French drawing-room comedy, as well as the Hungarian *népszínmű* or "play about peasant life", his work also bears a certain resemblance to that of Hauptmann and the poetic atmosphere so magically conjured up by Chekhov. And although Bródy could never have known it, *The Nanny* is in some ways similar to Gorky's *Lower Depths*. But here again, his character and way of life militated against his art. He loved success and admiration; his extravagant way of life called for a great deal of money. So he wrote two endings for *The Schoolmistress:* one was tragic, in accordance with the logic of the play; the other was a happy ending designed to please the public. And this was the more fortunate case, too. More often he combined both solutions, usually at the expense of the dramatic conflict inherent in the play.

The plays of Thury and Herczeg are also worth mentioning. Thury possessed a sense of social conflict, Herczeg a skilled theatrical technique and a feeling for psychological development. The subjects of Thury's earlier plays were taken from the officers' mess. His most famous play, *Soldiers* (Katonák, 1898), which was banned, revealed the conflict between the limited opportunities available to officers on little pay and the life of luxury led by the high-ranking officers. He later attempted to write about the proletariat, but the lack of any traditional guidance and his early death prevented him from developing this opening any further.

Herczeg adapted his short stories for the theatre, but also wrote a number of successful original plays. His social plays followed the model of French "social" drama and the patterns set by Csiky. His early works contained a certain amount of social criticism; later, he gave way to a tendency to moralize and exhort, and especially to the skilful use of the fashionable theories of psychology prevalent at the time (*The Gyurkovics Girls*— A Gyurkovics lányok, 1893; *The Gyurkovics Boys* — A Gyurkovics fiúk, 1895; *The Daughter of the Nabob of Dolova* — A dolovai nábob leánya, 1903). He experimented with historical subjects several times in *The Seven Swabians* (A hét sváb, 1916), for instance, and even ventured into the field of historical tragedy (*Byzantium* — Bizánc, 1904).

Gárdonyi also tried his hand at writing for the stage, and his only play, *The Wine* (A bor, 1901), was a great success. He tried to raise the level of the *népszínmű* or "play about peasant life" to the level of modern folk-drama and to show that peasant life is as suitable for the presentation of psychological conflicts as any other.

The plays of all these writers were nothing like as good as their short stories. Nonetheless, as a body, and Bródy and Thury in particular, they contributed to the development of drama by the social criticism and psychological realism in their works. Although their technique was more old-fashioned than that of Chekhov or Hauptmann, they introduced a number of elements which were the outcome of naturalism, Symbolism and the Secession, and so they successfully transformed the traditional style of play left by Csiky and the *népszínmű*. The successful playwrights of the twentieth century, like Ferenc Molnár, built on the dramatic style of these writers.

44 Lyric Poetry in the Period of Realism

Lyric poetry was becoming less important than it had been before. The beginning of this period witnessed the paradox that while the novel took on lyrical qualities, the lyric lost some of its lyricism. Around 1880 it began to flourish again in the work of solitary writers outside the Establishment and its fictional values. The late lyric poems of János Arany fall into this period and must be seen in the light of this development. But the more typical figures of the period were those who broke away from the populist styles or completely transformed them: Vajda, Reviczky, Komjáthy and József Kiss.

János Vajda (1827-1897)

The eldest—and most important of them—was János Vajda, whose life spanned most of the nineteenth century, and whose name had become the symbol of opposition to populism. His talent matured slowly. Although he had begun to write before the 1848 Revolution, his lyric poetry only developed into a coherent body of work in the second half of the seventies. His father was a gamekeeper. He went to school in Pest and at quite an early age joined the political and literary circles of the radicals. After 1849 he was conscripted as a private and sent to Italy as a punishment for his activities; after he was demobilized, he worked in an office and also as a journalist. He remained in essence a solitary man; he failed to be accepted by either the leading literary or political groups, and wrestled alone with the problems of his age. Two pamphlets (*Self-criticism* — Önbírálat; *Development of Bourgeois Civilization* — Polgárosodás, 1862) contain his political thinking. He stressed the primary importance of bourgeois development as against national independence; for he believed that bourgeois development would eventually lead to national independence. He was profoundly sceptical about the leadership of the nobility: he described their moral attitudes and their culture with caustic irony. He demanded that literature should give the "human" the same value as the national: he claimed that in literature "man as such is overshadowed by the Hungarian". His pamphlets, coupled with rumours that he was prepared to edit a government paper, put the seal on his solitude and his exclusion, which not even the Compromise of 1867 could resolve, because he denounced it at the time as not offering adequate opportunity for bourgeois development. He was often in money difficulties, and it was only in his last years, when a whole younger generation hailed him as their master, that he received a modest amount of government help.

He himself was his own worst enemy in this respect. Vajda was a "Romantic". Most of his ideas and political views dated back to the period before 1848. He was fired by visions of greatness and glory; Napoleon's picture adorned the wall of his room. He was only concerned with what adverse circumstances prevented him from attaining, and in fact, nothing was given to him easily. Nor was he more successful in his private life or in his love-affairs. He fell in love with the beautiful daughter of a barber, who did not return his love, becoming the mistress of an aristocrat instead. His solitude and his failure began to prey on his mind. His hatred and disgust, his desires and devotions increased to an abnormal degree.

He meditated constantly on problems of politics, love and death. At first it was only in politics he was able to find a suitable form to express himself. He followed Petőfi's populism, into which he integrated the passion-driven rhetoric and visions of Vörösmarty and the atmospheric, symbolic style of Tompa (*The Vigil-keepers* — A virrasztók; *Lusitanian Song* — Luzitán dal). He later became more disillusioned, and his poetry more intellectual filled with the philosophical grandiloquence of his confrontation with existence, and his style took on a Symbolist character. It was at this point that his love poetry became infused with a modern spirit. Love was elevated from a thing of the fleeting moment to an opportunity for a universal experience, a value which gave life shape and coherence. Unfulfilled love, on the other hand, meant exclusion from the experience of human life; it symbolized the waste of life. In terms of their subject-matter, these poems were untraditional love poems. Vajda made no use of situation or incidents or the description of sentiments. He linked up ancient elemental symbols—stars, mountains, sea, flames, the sun, summer—with fundamental words imbued with emotional and intellectual implications—the universe, the world, creation, birth, death—in intensive combination ("at the meridian of creation, a shame-stigma burns in the sun, there is no decency in the stars, existence is impoverished to the level of a beggar," etc.) in order to give expression to his passionate love, his ecstatic joy or despair. The philosophic quality of the love poems of his later years can be seen in the treatment of time. Time is the barrier to fulfilment; fulfilled love gives dead, neutral time a value, makes it immortal.

> *Only unappeased desires,*
> *Unfulfilled dreams, unburnt-out fires,*
> *The missed out, lost, infertile hour,*

318

> *These can't be made good, they turn all sour;*
> *These only dead and doomed for ever,*
> *These brought back by no endeavour.*
>
> (*Ghosts* — Kísértetek)

The idea of death was usually present in his philosophical poems. Often it was death which gives peace through the consistency of non-existence, a mythical, aesthetic death. But for the most part it was a death which clamoured for an answer as to what life really is. Existence should not be missed, because no answer is given; time must not be felt unfulfilled on this account. Here Vajda came close to Arany and Madách. But his questions were more direct, firmer, more open. He searched for all the answers contemporary thought could offer, the Christian religion (*Autumn Landscape* — Őszi tájék); the irrationalism of "life is a dream" (*On a Reedy Lake* — Nádas tavon); the materialism of Ludwig Büchner (*Under the Trees in Bikol* — A bikoli fák alatt); the principle of the eternal, immortal yet changing recurrence of matter (*Infinity* — Végtelenség). But in all the poems he questioned, never asserted. His philosophical knowledge was neither deep nor extensive. The popular conclusions of various philosophical systems epitomized in phrases are often encountered in his poems. But it is not the philosophy but the questioning which attracts us in his poetry, confronting as he does a tremendous emotional desire to believe with the intellectual rigour of an insistence upon reality.

The same is true of the rest of his themes. In his nature poetry, for instance, there is little real description, although from early childhood he had known and loved the forest. In his poetry, the objects of nature differ not through their qualities and attributes but as different expressions of his consciousness of life. And the same sense of consciousness is to be found not only in the different subjects he chooses but also in the various genres which he chose to express himself, for he also wrote short stories and novels in verse. The importance of the narrative poems or novels in verse essentially lies in their poetry (*Meetings* — Találkozások, 1873; *Alfred's Novel* — Alfréd regénye, 1875). Objective, narrative treatment was unsuited to his talent, his character and his experience. Even his short stories are, in fact, outdated examples of the patterns of French Romanticism.

Vajda made hardly any changes in populist, Romantic forms of rhythm, rhyme, stanza and verse structure. What was new in his work was his images and metaphors. His images usually embody a vital moment in some natural process. Nature that is calm and at rest was alien to him. His poetry is pantheistic, it is an inverted pantheism; man is not part of Nature, Nature is part of man; his life is enlarged to cosmic dimensions. He made considerable use of symbols, but taken as a whole no individual poem is Symbolist. In his use of symbols he was nearer to Baudelaire than to Verlaine or Mallarmé. He employed objects as a means of interpreting individual existence, and to achieve this, he heightened one of their original qualities to an abnormal dimension. In the same way, his images are ecstatic; the superlative is essential. And all this, already present in the work of the Romantics, results emotional rhetoric. Vajda is distinguished from Baudelaire by this power of dramatic emotion and by a lack of cool objectivity and irony. His lyric poetry may be more Romantic than that of Baudelaire, but it is no longer truly Romantic. His ecstatic images and superlatives mostly reflect poetic situations through realistic psychology.

His poetry was uneven. He wrote more good lines than good poems. Nonetheless he is an important writer. He experienced and introduced to literature a new form of solitude, urban solitude. He was the first to search with passion for a meaning to life, for full existence, for new values in a new, bourgeois situation. And he preserved and renewed the attitude of a revolutionary poet in an age which was essentially anti-revolutionary. His example encouraged every new attempt during the long period of Neo-Classic imitation of the *népies* movement. He was the first ripple of the wave which culminated in the lyric poetry of Ady.

Gyula Reviczky (1855-1889)

Gyula Reviczky was born in northern Hungary. His life would have made good material for a novel, a sad and moving *fin-de-siècle* novel. He was the illegitimate son of an officer of the Guards, of good family; his mother was a poor Slovak maid. But his father's wife cared for him as if he had been her own child. After her death, his father squandered all his money, including the boy's inheritance, and neglected to legitimize him. The boy was suddenly forced to face the fact that he was penniless and that not even his distinguished name belonged to him. He was passed from one relative to another, eventually going to Pest to make his living from journalism and poetry. But his poverty drove him back to the provinces where he became a tutor. After being disappointed in love, his ambitions again drew him to the capital. Further misery and disappointment ensued until, finally, at the age of 32, he obtained a full-time post on a big newspaper and began to be appreciated as a writer. But it was too late; his health had been undermined and he died at the age of 34, full of ambition to live and work at an age when he was in complete control of his poetic resources.

He was an intellectual proletarian: his situation marked him out for rebellion. But his rebellious attitudes only concerned his intellect and emotions, his life and artistic ideas, and took the form of rejection rather than attack. Alone, he tried to come to his own conclusions about the world, turning to Schopenhauer and the philosophy of positivism. But he also borrowed from Christianity and was influenced to some extent by Tolstoy, especially in regard to Tolstoy's insistence on sympathy and love. Certain ideas dominated his thinking; that the poet was the man who really understood existence, the interpreter of life, ranking above the philosopher; that our knowledge and experience are relative and subjective, determined by our biological inheritance, that lucid observation without the will to act is a liberating force and that the most profound form of behaviour is a stoical acceptance, an understanding, a superior smile in the face of suffering, and that Christ, Buddha, Goethe and Arany were from that point of view humanists. He wrote a number of studies in aesthetics on the question of humour: *Humour and Materialism* (Humor és materializmus), *The Psychology of Humour* (A humor pszichológiája), *Humour in Art* (Humor a művészetben). With this essential Quietist philosophy he combined a principle of active love and sympathy: the sufferer, the fallen one, the sad one has to be consoled and protected, and the truth about him has to be told. Looking within, at himself, his key-word was humour; looking outside, at others, they were love and sympathy.

His poetry is melancholic and reflective. It has the air of recollections in a dream, in his work even the present seems no more than a memory. He wrote of a love of his youth, an encounter with a prostitute, an outcast of the city, a humiliating relationship, a sad meeting, a childhood landscape, the desires of a lonely man in the age of reason, and of his dreams and reflections. The title of his first volume was *My Youth* (Ifjúságom, 1883); his second work was *Loneliness* (Magány, 1889). He could be called a semi-autobiographical poet: all the most close and most remote moments of his life reappear in his poems. But culture, religion and public life also have a place in his work, in the form of personal memories interwoven with reflections: the Sermon on the Mount as well as the shame he felt on seeing Turgeniev's grave covered with weeds. On such occasions he slides from the elegiac to the dramatic, from the humorous to the satirical, from a rejection representing indirect rebellion to direct and aggressive social criticism. This is especially the case with his prose. He wrote a small number of short stories marked with a strange atmospheric power, but it was his semi-autobiographical novel, *Paternal Inheritance* (Apai örökség, 1884), which was his really important work. It is a continuation of the form introduced by László Arany, a novel of human development equipped with brilliant, cruel, self-biting psychological insight and a perfect re-creation of the milieu. The explanation of the development of the hero, Tibor Fejértájy, the mirror-image of the author, into a hesitant, superfluous human being is somewhat theoretical, based on assumptions of biological inheritance. But nonetheless, Fejértájy appears as at once the embodiment and the victim of a class and age. Many regard this book of his as far more important than his lyric poetry.

But he was a lyric poet. It is debatable whether his poetry was Impressionist or Symbolist. Images seldom evolve into a system in his work. What was new in

321

his work lay not in his images but in the rhythm, his sentences and the music of his verse. The two-beat line, in particular the iambic, became a popular feature in Hungarian lyric poetry through his gentle, murmuring verses. And even more important than his metre was the music of his lines. Past and present appeared to merge into a resigned memory, the transient moment merged into the universal, allowing the emotional and atmospheric tone of his composition to dominate. His famous poem, *On Myself* (Magamról), could be considered as the first Hungarian proclamation of Impressionism. It was also proof that, as in the rest of Europe, it was positivism which provided the intellectual foundations for Impressionism in Hungary. The closing lines of the poem read:

> *Now the world—don't overlook it—*
> *Stands it neither straight nor crooked;*
> *Home of neither grief nor pleasure*
> *But an image of your measure.*
> *Some would mope, prefer, some revel would:*
> *All the world's a passing mood.*

He can be compared to Tompa among his predecessors, the poet who transmitted Biedermeier sentimentality; Gyula Juhász, the young Kosztolányi and Árpád Tóth among his successors.

Jenő Komjáthy (1858-1895)

The other new lyric poet of the period between 1870 and 1900, Jenő Komjáthy, was a forerunner of Symbolism. On the one hand he allied himself with the visionary Romanticism of Vörösmarty; on the other he foreshadowed the Symbolism of Ady. At times he shows a certain similarity with Baudelaire, but, more often, it is Nietzsche, the lyric poet, whom he resembles. Reviczky was, as we have already seen, pushed to the fringes of society; Komjáthy was outside society altogether. Reviczky questioned the dominant mentality of his age; Komjáthy attacked it. But even then his rebellion remained indirect.

From the outset he was born into a distinguished family of noble origins which had resigned itself to its straitened circumstances and clerical jobs. He became a teacher, working first in a small town near the capital and afterwards in a remote Slovak village. He lived there in depressing misery until the end of his days, surrounded by his large family, as if in exile, in a community speaking a foreign language.

From the outset he was concerned with philosophical questions. Philosophy—and poetry—became his refuge in exile. The philosophical notes which he left behind amounted to several volumes. But he completed no more than one article on criticism. Although he too was influenced by Schopenhauer, he needed something more in his solitude, was drawn to Spinoza's pantheism and to the mystic principles widely studied in those years. It is doubtful whether he had read Nietzsche, but he resembled him in his attitude; only in one aspect, true, but a crucial aspect: the almost hysterical and euphoric belief in the necessity, the possibility and the aggressive thrust of the *Umwertung aller Werte,* that man will be great and free like God, that he will be God. His idea of freedom is irrational, almost mystical, and implies a rejection of the determination of matter, of causality and of the limits of time and space. But, contrary to Nietzsche, his idea of freedom embraces complete social freedom. The tragic loneliness which Nietzsche's free man accepted with pride was unacceptable to him. He preached that freedom and liberation from false values would usher in the era of a great and happy brotherhood of spirits. He held that freedom and love were complementary. His lines ring with the mysterious prophesies of happiness to come and the Dionysian joy of an obscure metaphysical–social Utopia. At no time was he merely the anointed prophet of this belief; he saw himself as the forerunner of its fulfilment: he reached the final stage of hallucinatory nervous tension, the threshold of a nervous breakdown. Mednyánszky, one of the best painters of the period, also an outcast from society, painted a portrait of him. Frighteningly dilated eyes, staring into the distance: the face of a highly intellectual madman with a countenance like Christ.

The social significance of his attitude is clear: the destruction of everything that justifies the existing order; the teachings of the Church as well as those of utilitarian Positivism. His poems are "hymns" of a philosophical or metaphysical revelation. His basic sentence exclaims; it rather announces than orders, announcing the changes occurring during the revelations through the use of symbols. His tone and manner bear a considerable resemblance to Nietzsche's *Zarathustra.* But seldom do these symbols represent a complete system of symbols; they form a sequence rather than a system. They mostly derive from Christian symbolism and the religions of the Orient.

> *I who am the light, lived in darkness,*
> *hid myself from the world;*
> *in the vast unknown distance,*
> *I blazed in solitude.*

These are the opening lines of one of his famous poems, *From the Darkness* (A homályból), the title-poem of his book. The last lines read:

> *I carry in my heart a flame,*
> *I carry in my heart the sun.*
> *Oh, kindle then a kindred flame!*
> *I see! See you a kindred sun!*

323

No one had left the Neo-Classical *népies* spirit further behind and come nearer to the great lyrical trend of the century than Komjáthy. Poets of this trend discovered a poet who, in his own lifetime, was only recognized by a small circle of friends and hardly understood even by them.

József Kiss (1843-1921)

The poet who most changed contemporary taste, and was best known and understood, was József Kiss. Yet his role as a forerunner is not as clear as these others. Nonetheless the part he played in the creation of a new poetry was extremely important. He was the son of a poor Jew, a village grocer, barely emerged from the former isolation of the small Jewish community in Hungary. His family intended him to be a rabbi, but he acquired a passion for poetry under the influence of an educated Calvinist minister. Success came to him late in life; his own individual style and inner confidence came even later. He began with lyrical and narrative poems, written in the *népies* manner, in imitation of Arany, for the most part ballads about sad, seduced girls.

The social conditions of his life were very different from those of the other Hungarian poets. He was no social outcast. He worked as a clerk for the Jewish community in Temesvár; he later tried to set up on his own account, first in the provinces and then in the capital. The Jews, who around 1867 had been more or less completely outside Hungarian society, were by now in the course of rapid assimilation. In this respect society was civilized; those, assimilated to the Hungarian norm were accepted as full Hungarians. In keeping with the pattern of capitalist development in Central Europe, Jews joined the merchant-craftsman class. By the nineties, they were also pressing for social reform. The poet's social criticism and re-assessment of social needs never departed from those accepted by his class; if petty, so was he; if it was radical, so was he. The *Story of a Sewing Machine* (Mese a varrógépről), for instance, is a sentimental, romantic story about a seamstress; *Kniaz Potemkin* is a dithyrambic echo of the Russian revolution of 1905. It explains his success as an editor; his weekly, *A Hét* (The Week), founded in 1890, which depended entirely upon the support of a middle-class readership, made a major contribution to the transformation of public taste.

He was able successfully to tell stories from his childhood illuminating the world of ancient Jewish customs, beliefs and rituals, and at the same time to handle urban subjects as well. In his highly emotional poems, reminiscent of folklore and romance, he came close to the new musical Symbolic-Impressionist style of Reviczky.

The mature Kiss was an extrovert, an "optimistic" poet. There is a feeling of pleasure, of enjoyment, in his work. When he became a famous poet and a prosperous editor, he filled his flat with objects of art, silks, brocades, marble and bronze. His sorrows—it might be the late arrival of a love, it might be the late arrival of success—as well as his joys—the pride he felt in his career or his pleasure in becoming one with Nature—were all subjects of delight. He was not a striking poet, even in his best poems his charm, his sorrowful moods, the grace of his joy, are always engaging. He took great care over his poems, and the art he exercised with great delicacy can be seen in his rhythms, his verse construction and the musical combination of different kinds of rhythm and line. He was excited by rhythmical variation and musical tone-play, and the charm, grace and atmosphere of his poems stem largely from these qualities. His work is to some degree akin to Symbolism, but, chiefly on account of his musical techniques, it is a mixture of Impressionism and Symbolism, nearer the former than the latter, which means he was closer to the fin-de-siècle poets than to the generation of Reviczky. As a result from that, around the turn of the century, for some fifteen years he was Hungary's most popular poet. Vajda, Reviczky and Komjáthy never won such recognition. But they are constantly being rediscovered, which is hardly likely to happen in the case of Kiss. His achievements were important foundation-stones on which later lyric poetry was built, and his better poems are standard pieces in anthologies; but only rarely do they bear witness to any depth of poetic revelation, thought or attitude.

Minor Lyric Poets

Alongside the four great poets of the period, there were a number of minor poets who enjoyed popular acclaim. In the first place there were Vajda's followers and imitators, such as *Sándor Endrődi* (1850–1920), a poet with a pantheistic approach to nature. The excellent versifier, *Emil Ábrányi* (1851–1920), followed Byron, Heine and especially Hugo in creating a social–political, rhetorical poetry of opposition. But neither he nor the others went further than an abstract verbal radicalism, combined with a benevolent moral stance, which served as a refuge from the crisis of the times.

Of the next generation, *Lajos Palágyi* (1866–1933) was a bitter, passionate poet of lower middle-class origins, one of the first writers of poetry with specific socialist tendencies; and *Gyula Rudnyánszky* (1858–1913) contributed to the creation of a Symbolist style with poems confusedly combining socialist and Catholic ideas.

The end of this period, from 1870 to 1905, when realist fiction and the short story were in the ascendant, did not produce any lyric poets of importance. There was *Jenő Heltai* (1871–1957) who mostly wrote plays and fiction prose, but he really falls into the next period of Hungarian literature. At the time in question he was known as a lyric poet producing various combinations of the French *chanson*, the kind of song found in Heine, *népszínmű* and the cabaret. His originality, flavoured by the free association of the Secession, consisted in taking the lyrical situations of romances, imbued with the neo-sentimentality of the period, and turning them into ironic, grotesque poems, bringing the idealized sentiments of the old-fashioned literature form to earth. . . . There was *Emil Makai* (1870–1901), less important than Heltai, adept in combining different moods, moving from religious Jewish poetry to a sentimental and frivolous love poetry without a pause. There was *Géza Szilágyi* (1875–1958), with his erotic poetry influenced more by Baudelaire than Heine. He wrote sombre, even tragic verse, and a recurrent theme of his was the attraction and the repulsion of women.

45 The Positivist Influence on the History of Literature and Criticism

The History of Literature

The literary essay was influenced by Positivism, which shaped the framework and methods of contemporary criticism and literary history. *Budapesti Szemle* (The Budapest Review), in which essays were published, was complemented by scholarly journals such as the *Egyetemes Philologiai Közlöny* (Universal Philological Gazette) dating from 1872; and the *Irodalomtörténeti Közlemények* (Gazette of the History of Literature) dating from 1891. Literary criticism and the history of literature became separate subjects; at the beginning of the period Ferenc Toldi with his Romantic ideas and methods embodied the principles of literary history, by the turn of the century the study of literature had at its command a number of specialists and a series of serious publications.

One of the best-known literary historians of the period was *Zsolt Beöthy* (1848–1922). Originally a writer and critic, he became professor of aesthetics at the University of Budapest. He modelled his theories on Spencer's organicism and Taine's racial theories in his attempt to maintain the principles of populism. He believed that literature was invariably national in character, and only work which gave expression to the national character and "spirit" could be part of the national literature, defining the Hungarian character by the qualities of the gentry. His fundamental views were expressed in his book *The Tragic Quality* (A tragikum, 1885), in which he declared that all conflicts arose from the violation of either the moral order of the world or the organic nature of historic evolution. From the nineties onwards, he was one of the chief opponents of all progressive movements. *Frigyes Riedl* (1856–1921) held the chair of Hungarian Literary History at the University of Budapest. He was a follower of Taine, and especially of Taine's methods. But he combined various methods and views in almost every book that he wrote (for instance, Taine's method with J. Burckhardt's methods of reconstruction). His approach was Impressionist; his main interest was the portrayal of period and character. His principal work was his monograph on Arany (1887) in which he modernized the views of Gyulai in the light of positivist theories. *Gusztáv Heinrich* (1845–1922), a follower and friend of W. Scherer, was the professor of German studies at the University of Budapest; he researched into source-material and the use and borrowing of motifs and was an exponent of an extreme, factual Positivism. He is still considered important; he educated generations in the methods of exact research and established the organized framework of research. *Zsigmond Bodnár* (1839–1907) was a lecturer at the University of Kolozsvár; he was one of the first to rebel against positivism. He believed history was a series of alternating periods of the ideal and the real, of revolution and anti-revolution, driven by idea-power (*History of Hungarian Literature* — A magyar irodalom története, 1891). *Lajos Katona* (1862–1910), who was originally an ethnographer, was also a professor at the University of Budapest. He was intent on demolishing both National Romanticism and Taine's Positivism by using the results of Positivist methodology and the comparative study of literature and culture. His main subject was the Middle Ages.

Jenő Péterfy (1850–1899)

One of the most important figures in Hungarian literary criticism, Jenő Péterfy, whose life came to a tragic end, first came to the fore in the eighties. He studied the violin, but was obliged to become a teacher. With his exceptional knowledge of philosophy, literature, art and music, he taught in various secondary schools until he found the apparent meaninglessness of his life too much for him, and put a bullet through his head.

His views were founded upon the philosophy of Hegel, though he was not a Hegelian. His attitude towards the literary trends of his day was inspired by the need to confront one philosophy or theory by another. He considered Taine from a Hegelian standpoint, and Hegel through the eyes of Positivism; Zola from the viewpoint of the Wilhelm Meister type of Classicism; and Classicism from the angle of experimental realistic psychology. The duty of the critic, he believed, was to conduct this permanent process of confrontation and comparison, and correct his opinions accordingly, a duty hardly ever fulfilled by the busy man or artist of the period. He believed that man's knowledge was constantly growing; that every period and every trend contributed to such growth, although to varying degrees. In his eyes, the final character and value of new or developing periods and trends was decided by the attitude to man by the degree to which the contributions made in the different periods deepened a knowledge of man, and strengthened his consciousness and independence.

This approach is expressed in his three famous essays on Kemény, Jókai and Eötvös (1881–82). He thought Kemény's failure to produce a great novel was due to his Romantic attitude of fatalism to history and life; and similar failures by Eötvös and Jókai to the credulous, liberal rational–utilitarian historical outlook of the one, and the self-deceiving, Romantic–liberal rose-coloured view of the Hungarian nation of the other, a view which was the fashion of the time and the principal obstacle in the path of realism. As opposed to Beöthy, who saw the birth of the tragic element in the violation of "world order", he regarded the conflicts of opposing historical powers as the origin of the tragic. He believed that a man of any period could only affirm his own personality if it were founded on the knowledge and acceptance of reality, however tragic or bleak, and that all art was finally designed to serve this end. This task could only be fulfilled by such works as satisfy the requirements of both social–historical dependence and a firm conviction in the validity of a man's own art. It was the opinion that Art had the particular and irreplaceable duty of creating the right values for mankind.

He was an advocate of realism in art. But when realism took over predominance, he withdrew exhausted into Greek philosophy and tragedy. Personal reasons alone did not account for this. This realism was based on one-sided social objectives and motivation, and Péterfy, the outsider in the literary word, aspired after a more philosophical and psychological form of realism. He is appreciated today for his ideas, but also for his style. His writing is a combination of superior irony, hidden poetry, and a lurking melancholy. He managed to marry conceptual rigour and objectivity to imaginative richness in a style of effortless grace and restrained discipline.

Ignotus (1869–1949)

New critics of any importance in the nineties mostly worked for *A Hét* (The Week). The best known of their number was Ignotus (Hugo Veigelsberg), who was of German-Jewish origin. Upon completing his law studies, he became a journalist and joined *A Hét* Later, in 1905, he was one of the founders and the chief editor of the review *Nyugat* (The West). He represented the liberalism of the prosperous middle class. He wanted no radical transformation of the social system, only equal share of power for the middle classes, and these ideas were most cleary expressed in his cultural and literary criticism. The main criteria, in his mind, were taste, personality, talent and effect. Taste was determined by character, so it could only be individual and subjective, and for this reason any system of aesthetic values had to be relative. Any trend, any genre, any style was justified if the writer had the talent to achieve the intended effect. The duty of the critic was to grasp a work intuitively and to employ his skill as a writer to convey his experience to the reader. These were the maxims of Impressionist criticism, and Ignotus added nothing to them of any theoretical significance. His great virtue lay in the way he implemented his principles, and his purpose. He became the leading figure of the Hungarian Secession, and campaigned against the dominant and conservative ideas on the nation and the national character, and especially the *népies* trend.

His writing was based on his determination to assert relative as opposed to absolute values, values which maintained the judgement. The most different categories and sets of values were combined and reconciled in his work, which caused him to be frequently accused of frivolity. Papal infallibility and abortion, the primitive magnificence of Giotto and the misery of the peasants along the Danube, the stupidity of army officers and the love-affairs of the Royal Family jostled one another in the same article, paragraph or even the same sentence. Some of his articles can be regarded as regular short stories, while other writings combine the essay, the editorial, the short story, personal confessions, or diary. High-flown writing, bombast intermingled with city slang; French, English and German quotations with pithy folk-sayings. And all was marked by a pleasure in the very act of creation, by the hedonistic happiness of a person thoroughly enjoying himself.

His impact was tremendous: the middle-class public devoured the literary criticism produced by Ignotus and his colleagues. It gave the *coup de grace* to conservative populist taste. The writers working at *A Hét* cleared the way for the rapid disappearance of Secessionist influence, to usher the great period which followed, and left the way clear for the untrammelled development of the new prose realism of Móricz, Babits and Kosztolányi and the poetry of Ady, Babits and Kosztolányi.

Conclusions

This half-century, during which realism finally came into its own, could hardly be called a golden age. The truly outstanding writers of the first half of the period, Arany and Jókai, belonged to the previous era of *népies* Romanticism. The second half of the century produced only one writer of comparable quality: Mikszáth, and even his importance and status is still a matter of argument. But as a stage of development the period is significant. During these years the time-lag between Hungarian and European cultural developments disappeared. Not in every field of literature, true, but in the sphere of prose Hungary managed to keep pace with the rest of Europe. Nor is it without importance that it was during this period that Hungarian culture absorbed the classic works of old Hungarian and foreign literature, and made them an organic part of its intellectual landscape. Literature, which had formerly been the concern of a small literate stratum of society, became a social necessity. And it was from this background that, around 1905, emerged the next great literary period, the second golden age of Hungarian literature. The period under review was not simply transitional; it was rather preparatory. It produced many of the resources and means needed for the next great literary period; all that was left for the emergence of a new, great literary era were the social and cultural conditions which would breed new talents and open up new opportunities.

Years of the Nyugat (1908–1941)

46 A Country of Contradictions

Around the turn of the nineteenth century Hungary developed more and more into an organic part of contemporary Europe. A comparatively advanced industry was rapidly evolving; the country was crisscrossed by a dense network of railways, and there was a marked increase in the numbers of office workers. And at the same time the contradictions characteristic of a modern world power became increasingly apparent. Rather like the busy centres of colonial power, benefiting from technological advances on the one hand and the exploitation of their enormous colonies on the other, Hungary was made up of the capital city on the one hand—its population tripled over the past forty years to almost a million, and had taken the European character of Vienna as its model—and, on the other, the backwardness of the greater part of the country. The enormous eclectic buildings of the 1890s gave a distinctive character to the inner districts of the capital. The Parliament building compared in size and structure with those of the European powers, and the first underground on the Continent ran under Andrássy Avenue with its imposing Renaissance-style mansions. Mascagni and Puccini themselves conducted the first performances of their works in Hungary, Mihály Munkácsy won general acclaim for his paintings in Paris. And yet, down in the villages quacks were still selling their cures and the stewards of the great ecclesiastical estates were exercising their legal right to beat their servants. There were forged trials of Jews for the ritual murder of children, and the paintings of Tivadar Csontváry Kosztka, undoubtedly the greatest Hungarian painter of the time, were being sold off as late as 1920 as sacking material. While the chauvinist Jenő Rákosi (already mentioned as a dramatist), the chief propagandist of gentry interests, was dreaming of a Hungary with a population of thirty million, almost a million and a half landless peasants in those twenty years emigrated to America, and the phenomenon of the only child emerged: the process of the self-destruction of the peasants began. Modern machinery, it is true, was used in agriculture, but there were still places where the peasants harvested with sickles. While Leó Frankel, a member of the 1871 Paris Commune, was on a visit to his homeland organizing the workers' party, Prince Pallavicini was permitted to pull down the houses of peasants unable to pay their debts, with the aid of gendarmes. Great battles were fought in Parliament for more independence for Hungary within the Dual Monarchy, but at the same time that same Parliament put up a stubborn resistance to the demands of the many national minorities in the country. Despite the fact that in many places there were stirrings of socialism in the countryside, upper classes, together with the newly developed middle class, regarded socialist ideas as alien infiltrations. They continued to cling to their fanciful picture of the peasant, a picture born of a fusion of romantic and early nineteenth-century German ideas. The musical taste of the country gentry, now in a state of decline, was satisfied by tunes layed by Gipsies which bore little relation to either to Gipsy or Hungarian folk music. In the towns Viennese operettas coloured with Hungarian motifs, more modern and of a somewhat higher standard but artistically of no importance, were popular. The Social Democratic Party had already gained a strong hold among the workers in large urban enterprises, and the seemingly cloudless and cheerful world of pre-war days was disturbed by strikes demanding universal suffrage and the secret ballot as well as wage increases. In 1912 there were even outbreaks of fighting in the streets.

Social conditions in Hungary around this time indeed fostered the new forces which were to bring the second proletarian state in world history into existence. The establishment, however, continued its attempts to preserve a social system long since outmoded by disguising its essentially conservative character under a mask of modernism.

A Cultural Renewal

It was against this background of contrasts and contradictions that what might be described as the greatest generation of men in the cultural life of Hungary up to this date first emerged. Béla Bartók and Zoltán Kodály were among those who began their careers at this time. There were also the historian Gyula Szekfű, the linguist Zoltán Gombocz and the literary historian János Horváth (1878–1961). György Lukács devoted himself to the study of aesthetics, a subject long neglected in Hungary, and working in cognate disciplines were Lajos Fülep, the art historian, and Béla Balázs, an early pioneer in film aesthetics. Film producers such as Sándor Korda (Sir Alexander Korda) and Mihály Kertész (Michael Curtis) were to find world fame abroad, as were many scientists born about this time, such as the mathematician Lipót Fejér, the physicist Leó Szilárd, the psychologists Géza Róheim, Sándor Ferenczi and Géza Révész. There were whole groups of distinguished writers and artists. The group known as the "Seekers" was formed in 1909. This group of avant-garde painters looked for something beyond both the accepted conservative tradition and Impressionism. It included Róbert Berény, Béla Czóbel, Dezső Czigány, Károly Kernstok, Ödön Márffy, Dezső Orbán, Bertalan Pór and Lajos Tihanyi. From 1911 on these painters organized their exhibitions under the name of "The Eight". These men, however, were not condemned to the role of lonely and neglected geniuses, as the remarkable scientists, the two Bolyais, father and son, embittered in their Transylvanian isolation, for they found favour in the eyes of a bourgeoisie which, although still relatively undeveloped, already exercised a substantial influence. The cultural needs of organized labour as it began to develop also provided a field for their activities, for which the previous generation had partly prepared the way.

These years also saw the appearance of a number of journals and reviews in Budapest, as in other large Western European cities, and some of them provided fairly extensive opportunities for the writers of the time to make their work known. But the establishment of a literary review which was to represent and express their beliefs and aspirations was left to the writers themselves. In 1908, after several unsuccessful attempts, they succeeded in setting up *Nyugat* (The West), a fortnightly review designed to meet the needs of an educated and intellectual readership, and providing a forum for works of a high and demanding standard, as opposed to the "family" weeklies with large circulations. In 1908 and 1909, with the financial help of Lajos Hatvany, the literary son of an industrial magnate and a historian, a a two-volume anthology *Holnap* (Tomorrow) was published in Nagyvárad (now Oradea, Rumania), the provincial city where the new bourgeois influence was probably strongest, which provided a second forum for the new literary revival.

The majority of the intellectuals most receptive to new ideas lived in Budapest. Yet in addition to the capital some of the towns in the provinces enjoyed an active cultural life. For the rest, only odd teachers and doctors living scattered in the country gave weak but increasingly felt support for these new impulses.

In the dozen or so theatres of the country, apart from the "plays about peasant life" and operettas, third-rate romantic and society plays filled the stage. Nonetheless, in the first few years of the twentieth century it was an expression of the cultural revival taking place that the works of Strindberg, Hauptmann, Ibsen, Gorki and Chekhov were already being played at the Vígszínház in Budapest as well as by some of the smaller companies. These companies included the short-lived Thalia Company, which had established contacts with workers, and the reactionary press promptly responded to these performances by attacking them. The first Hungarian performance of Gorki's *Lower Depths* was one of the earliest in the world, as was the publication of *The Mother*, an indication of the interest shown in Russian literature, reinforced by a certain similarity in conditions in the two countries at the time. Generally speaking it was around this period that the substantial publication of foreign works began.

Several groups had already attempted to win to themselves the radical intelligentsia which had emerged in the first twenty years of the century. The need to abolish the relative time lag between Hungary and the more developed European countries and catch up with them was strongly felt, accounted for by the fact that the dissemination of the views of Darwin and Einstein, Bergson and Spencer, came only very shortly before the acceptance of the teaching of Marx and Engels, and the ideas of Nietzsche and Freud.

One result of the interest in modern foreign literature, and especially poetry, was that the majority of the finest Hungarian poets turned their hand to translation. The body of work translated from foreign tongues into Hungarian, already substantial, now proliferated, maintaining an extremely high standard; indeed, ever since that time many of the best poets have made translation into Hungarian part of their work.

Directions in Art and Literature

Young artists discontented with the cultural establishment of the time sought guidance from various periods and movements. Artists revolting against the painters who followed the Munich historical school and who had produced prettily popular pictures of still life turned to Constructivism (József Nemes Lampérth) or *art nouveau* (József Rippl-Rónai), the latter leaving its mark on the taste of the whole period under review. Other trends, *plein air,* Impressionism and early Expressionism, also appeared very shortly afterwards. There were also realist painters with a strong psychological tendency (László Mednyánszky) and others more objectively inclined (János Nagy Balogh). Tivadar Csontváry Kosztka produced an original style of his own in fusing and remaking the characteristics of various trends. The group who called themselves "The Eight" went beyond Impressionism. They took Hungarian painting a further step forward under the inspiration of Cézanne on the one hand, and the contemporary avant-garde, the Fauvism, Expressionism, Cubism and Futurism.

The same thing was happening in literature. Symbolism, Impressionism, Naturalism, *art nouveau,* Expressionism, even if they did not all make their appearance simultaneously, were all regarded as new and exciting at much the same time. Even the publication of the principle of *l'art pour l'art* was considered an act of bravery at a time when nationalist and religious–ethical literary values were dominant, and when writers in sympathy with the working class were voicing their commitment to the social responsibility of art. It was mainly the daily paper of the Social Democratic Party, *Népszava* (The Voice of the People), which provided a platform for such views, and it was paradoxical that both these attitudes on the social commitment of art could have seemed to be the new direction for a young beginner in their common opposition to official, dogmatic views on the function of art and literature.The major offices in the Academy, the literary organizations and the educational world were filled by men who subscribed to the official view.

Nyugat embodied the many different aspirations of new movements not free of

336

contradictions of their own. The editors adopted a broad, liberal line in their direction of the review. The staff of *Nyugat* included Ernő Osvát, blessed with a great deal of literary sensitivity and a passionate love of the arts, the experienced critic and journalist Ignotus, as well as the literary patron and writer Miksa Fenyő. Lajos Hatvany, another enlightened patron and prominent figure in cultural life, who had an influence on the review, shared the views of its editors. The most important writers associated with *Nyugat,* however, Endre Ady and later Zsigmond Móricz, were concerned to make it a mouthpiece for the expression of radical social views.

The Revolutions

The First World War destroyed the superficial tranquillity of Hungarian life, bringing the hidden trends inherent in the entire imperialist system to the surface. But at the time it was the progressives who were defeated. This was partly due to the fact that at the beginning the Social Democratic Party, in their opposition to the Czar and imperialist Czarism, had supported the war. By the third or fourth year of the war, however, it was not only the best of the workers and intellectuals who opposed the war. The enormous sacrifices of lives, the increasing privation, the enormous gains of the war profiteers had a revolutionary effect in much wider circles. The revolution broke out in 1918.

The "aster" revolution, named after the asters worn by the revolutionary crowds in their caps, produced what was largely a bourgeois transformation. The desire for peace and opposition to the war were the main causes of the outbreak. But the process of radicalization which was affecting a substantial number of intellectuals also played a part, and the revolutionary leadership also opted for national independence. The Government vacillated, incapable of meeting the peasants' clamour for land and the demands of the workers fired by the example of the Russian revolution. Nor was it capable of defending the national frontiers or the revolution itself, when the Entente powers answered its peaceful approach with further territorial demands. As a result the Government resigned in March 1919 in favour of a Socialist Democrat and Communist coalition, the parties of the organized proletariat, and the Republic of Councils came into existence, only to be defeated after four months, outnumbered by foreign troops, Rumanian, Czech and French, who were aided by the counter-revolutionary movement then in the process of formation.

It was during this revolutionary period that the progressive Vörösmarty Academy was set up and began to function. Among its members were the best writers of the time. Mihály Babits, Lajos Fülep and Géza Révész were nominated to university chairs. György Lukács became a People's Commissar, and Béla Bartók, Zoltán Kodály and Zsigmond Móricz played an important part in the organization of cultural life. Only a few really understood the full implication of the revolutionary class struggle of the modern working class, but the events which had wrought such a profound change in the life of the people left a deep impression on the thought and perceptions of many, even after the success and stabilization of the counter-revolution, even though this awareness was not without its own contradictions.

The Nyugat and Its Significance

In the period following the victory of the counter-revolution in 1919, the contents and character of *Nyugat* underwent certain modifications, but did not change in essentials. The double tendency in its editorial policy it had earlier manifested continued under the joint editorship of Mihály Babits and Zsigmond Móricz. Ignotus was forced into a long exile from Hungary; Osvát died in 1929; the poet Oszkár Gellért continued rather longer with the editorial board. As the times changed, gifted writers with different ambitions were given opportunities to express themselves in the review, but it still remained primarily the platform of the "great" generation of intellectuals who had begun their careers together. During the first period the review played an important role in publishing work untrammeled by the reactionary political attitudes then current, and even the work of writers espousing radical views of society. After the twenties, however, it failed to maintain the position of leadership it had so unhesitatingly enjoyed in the past *vis-à-vis* other reviews of a high standard which provided greater freedom for the expression and the artistic and political aspirations of the time. In the end it was only known to a tiny section of the population; its subscribers numbered around a thousand. It ceased to appear in 1941, during the Second World War, when Babits died, when the reactionary government of the day refused to renew its licence to print.

During its life the review not only provided a platform for new writers but for new critics as well. These were for the most part the writers and editors themselves. They all had one characteristic in common, a general, humanistic view of the world in opposition to the reactionary and parochial views held by the great mass of the conservative critics of the day. They respected the personal and subjective attitudes of the artist, adopting indeed such a stance themselves, and above all they demanded a high literary standard. But in the same period, especially between the two wars, other and completely different critical trends of no less weight emerged.

All in all, the *Nyugat* was more than just one important review among many. Its name is inseparably linked with those of the writers of the first, "great" generation, and consequently with a broadly-based literary movement. It was this movement, this generation which brought Hungarian literature into the European mainstream to make its own valuable contribution.

47 Endre Ady (1877-1919)

One of the most influential, and perhaps one of the most complex characters in Hungarian poetry was born into this period of tension and internal contradictions at the turn of the century. He was Endre Ady.

His Life

Ady was born in a village in the border zone between Hungary and Transylvania. His family was Protestant, of the lesser nobility or gentry, reduced to poverty, in which opposition to Habsburg rule was traditional, as was a certain somewhat Calvinist mode of liberal thinking. Against the wishes of his father he became a journalist, first in Debrecen and later in Nagyvárad. His articles expressed a patriotism increasingly tempered by a passionate rejection of the excesses of nationalism, and an unqualified support for freedom of thought.

He very soon realized the importance of the strong mass movements of the world, and drew adequate conclusions. His first volumes of poetry show the traits of neither a novel nor an original poet, and do not display a radical outlook or an understanding for timely problems, so typical of his articles. The decisive change in his art, germs of which only can be found in his early poems, came about in the wake of a private experience. In 1903, he made the acquaintance, in Nagyvárad, of a cultured lady of the bourgeoisie, Adél Diósi who, till 1912, meant "the great love" for Ady. The woman, sung of in Ady's poems as Léda (anagram of Adél), and the great experience of Paris are inseparably bound up for Ady who sojourned in the French capital as a correspondent of the newspaper *Budapesti Napló* (Budapest Diary), and who came to see Paris as Life and Light, the breeding ground of modern art, of radical ideas and of revolutionary tradition. He became deeply rooted in Paris as in a second homeland; nevertheless, he often returned to his mother and to the village. The way there led him, from time to time, through Hungary's bleak fallow, through morass and desolation. The two experiences—Paris, where Ady observed not only throbbing, pulsating life but also the disease germs of modern capitalistic

339

society, and the Hungarian plains with its long-standing customs and weird super-stition and so full of social contradictions—became the two poles of Ady's new poetry; and the tension between these two poles stimulated him more than any-thing else.

The first genuine Ady volume appeared in 1906, under the title *New Poems* (Új versek). From that moment, part of his readers received Ady's poetry with boundless enthusiasm as a revelation, another part—the much greater one—with blind hatred and repulsion. The most prominent reactionary politician, Prime Min-ister Count István Tisza, attacked him personally. Ady came up also against the vehement aversion of Jenő Rákosi, leading political writer of reaction, and became the target of comic papers and an easy subject for cabaret farce writers. His poetry was qualified as incomprehensible, immoral, unpatriotic and pathological. The best representatives of the new literature, however, unanimously considered Ady as their leader, and those who demanded a radical, or outright revolutionary, change of society took the same stand. In spite of this, *Népszava*, the daily paper of the Social Democratic Party, also challenged Ady's poesy so different from the cus-tomary, popular and conventional party poetry. Nevertheless, Ady's partisans proved to be the stronger lot.

His hectic and unbalanced way of life, his excesses in love and drink attacked Ady's health; also, he suffered from the consequences of syphilis he fell victim to in his younger years and from which he could never be completely cured.

From the very outset, Ady violently protested against the world war—a fact making him the target of the cross-firing of his nationalistically enthused adversaries. In the war years, he married Berta Boncza, a young girl from a family of noblemen. At the outbreak, in October 1918, of the Hungarian revolution, Ady received the greatest official distinction by having been elected chairman of the Vörösmarty Academy founded in those days. Physically, Ady was already a broken man. Though he welcomed the revolution, his shock suffered over Hungary's collapse was greater than his enthusiasm. He died in January 1919, and was buried with full honours by the revolutionary Hungarian Republic of Councils.

The New in Ady's Poetry

The volume *New Poems* was the first to contain most of the traits of Ady's poetry of later days. The strong impression evoked by this volume can be attributed to the fact that Hungarian readers fairly well-informed about the contemporary prose literature of other countries knew precious little about the European poetry of this era and the preceding one. The Symbolists, and even Walt Whitman, were known only to the cultured few. And Apollinaire, Stefan George and Rilke, who found their form of expression at the time, were even less known. The best representatives of French Symbolism, interpreted to Hungarians by none too adequate translations, if taken cognizance of at all, were registered rather as curiosities. Ady's modern Hungarian poetry, a broad, mighty and relatively uniform current, represented the stirring and, from many a point of view, shocking novelty in literature. However, Ady's lifework has not only the merit of having approached Hungarian poetry to contemporary European one and, thus, to have re-established contacts; his poetry possesses higher and unique values.

The different Hungarian strands that influenced Ady's poetry have been traced back in part to Jenő Komjáthy, in part to Gyula Reviczky and János Vajda and the works of a few minor poets. But there is a new voice heard in *New Poems*. One of the most obviously individual features of his poetry, which can be traced throughout his entire work, is the desire for a world which is one whole. In contrast to his Hungarian predecessors he puts this in the first place. What, moreover, he has to say about suffering and the secret intimations of the soul has little of the typical overtones of *fin de siècle* writing, or the enervating decadence of *art nouveau*. He prefers to stress the will to struggle, the fighting spirit in man, as revealed in the poem beginning "I am the son of Gog and Magog...". In this opening poem of one of his volumes of poetry he speaks as the descendant of mythological giants, as one who vainly "knocks at gates and walls" in order to gain the right "to cry out", to express the tragicomic nature of life.

In the Hungarian literature of the period the vigorous expression of pain and annihilation paradoxically enough meant action. Ady's complex and symbolic poetic world, in which everything is simultaneously immediate to the senses and yet beyond reach is the whole-hearted expression of this general attitude to life.

Ady also introduced a number of new elements into Hungarian love poetry. The unresolved conflicts in relation between man and woman were given open expression which could reach tragic heights. Ady transposes his inner struggles into a vision of a ruthless battle between two hawks, high in the air, tearing each other before they drop (*Hawks' Embrace on the Dead Leaves* — Héja-nász az avaron).

The Need for the Whole and Full Life and Romanticism

Ady's poetic attitude has much in common with the Romantic poets, but generally speaking he did not use the means adopted by nineteenth-century Romanticism. He did indeed very definitely repudiated the world view embraced by nineteenth-century Romanticism. For Ady it was not the prosaic nature of bourgeois life which conflicted with the world of visions, of the beauties of the past. It was rather the backwardness and ignorance of the time which came to be seen as the deadly "Waste-

341

land", the "Hungarian Cemetery", killing all true poetry and thought, every "fine resonance of the soul". For Ady the Hortobágy with its galloping stallions was no longer the setting and symbol of a fine free life, nor did it hold exotic attraction it had held for the romantic Petőfi or for Lenau. For him it rather meant "wild, uncouth, dull-minded shepherds"; it was the symbol of backwardness, the "sunless East" (*The Bard of Hortobágy* — A Hortobágy poétája).

But it is the consequence of the need to live a full life that brings consequences that are more important. Ady's thinking—this is most apparent in his articles and essays—was primarily influenced by the rationalist spirit of French radicalism. But he was also influenced by the "heroic pessimism" of Nietzsche. This "heroic", or in a more general sense "romantic", attitude is of necessity accompanied not only by a passionate denial but also by the acceptance of an often apparently hopeless situation. Life is welcomed by Ady, chaotic, even squalid as it may be, and yet for all that a magnificent whole. His books of poems are built throughout cycles opposing one another in argument and persuasion which nonetheless complement each other. He wrote one Léda poem after the other, fired by sexual passion, which reveal tragic loneliness and which yet accept the fate of the "two holy sailors" thrown upon the same path. But at the same time he wrote poems full of a fresh, lively sensuousness as well. In *The Owl of the Horror Tales* (A rém-mesék uhuja), the hallucination of a bird blundering blindly into a darkened room and beating at the window in vain, together with the sanity which dispels it, brings the sense of alienation to vivid life. Yet at other times Ady was ready to accept the very transcendence of loneliness: "I am, as every man is, majesty, / North Pole, secrecy, estrangement, / distant light that deludes" (*Nor Successor...* — Sem utódja). He equally awakens the reader to the hidden beauties of the old primitive world in the wilds of the Hungarian Wasteland in the same paradoxical manner. "The smell of flowers long gone intoxicates as though in love" (*On the Hungarian Waste* — A magyar Ugaron). At one and the same time Ady felt himself the inheritor of the pagan, barbaric world of the "ancient Orient" and the son of the sophisticated culture of the West. He looked about him on the banks of the Tisza with a startled sense of alienation, yet he still spoke of it as "for me, my home".

On Being Hungarian

The patriotic feeling which played an extremely important part in the poetry of Ady can again only be understood by keeping in mind his desire for completeness. The poem *The Old Scoffer* (Az ős Kaján), in which Ady expressed both the tragic and the comic aspects of a breakdown into conflict and oblivion, in which he reviewed his entire life, at the same time voiced the question of national loyalty. This voice is an organic part of the whole work: "My Lord, my soil is Hungarian soil, barren, exploited. / Why encourage us to unmindful rapture? / What is worth of pledges in wine and blood? / What may the worth of a Hungarian be?" This last, much quoted question is far from the conventions of Romantic nationalism. Ady's poems on what being a Hungarian means, formulate basic human questions and express basic experiences.

Ady lived emotionally through all the tragedies and losses of Hungarian history: the wars which time and again threatened the existence of the nation, the struggles for national independence failed or thwarted, the tragic failures of heroic experiments in the struggle for a better existence. To all of them he opposed the panacea of universal renewal through revolution. He felt that a failure to rebel threatened the existence of the Hungarian nation. "If we do not tread under those who bar our way / Everything here is lost for eternity"—he wrote. For Ady the existence of the Hungarians was not merely a question of national independence. National existence meant above all the preservation and nurture of what were, for him, the most valuable folk or national characteristics. Some of them reached back to the mists of time, some of them originated in the last few centuries. In these "Hungarian" poems we find equally passionate denial and passionate affirmation turn by turn, faith and doubt: the poetry embraces it all: "Young man who has broken away from the muddy brook, escape, escape"—cries as the only possibility for those who desire to live truly human lives. He accepts as final the fate of the stone tossed in the air, flying up and up, but each time falling "back into the dust from which it came" (*The Stone Tossed and Tossed Again* — A föl-földobott kő). For Ady being Hungarian involves the acceptance or rejection of conflict and struggle.

Loneliness to Ady is part of the experience of living through the Hungarian destiny, for at times the whole Hungarian nation appeared to him as a solitary people condemned to a particularly tragic fate. At other times his poems dealt with the experience of alienation *within* the Hungarian nation. Here with the "growth beyond the race" is the tragedy of those who vainly attempt to take action for the good of their country. Isolated, they can do nothing. These poems create a true "myth of Hungarianness", the myth of a lost people doomed at once by the pressure of a historical fate and by their own errors, their own fearful passivity (*The Lost Horseman* — Az eltévedt lovas).

Ady's Symbolic Myths

The myth of being Hungarian is just one among many. Money is something that also takes on the form of a frightening fetish in Ady's poetry: Desire, the kiss appear as superhuman powers in his symbolic world. Nor is Léda herself merely an individual woman but the hidden female force embodying those guiding passions which make for the fullness of life. In his poems Ady is a Symbolist in the narrower sense of the word. Feelings, thoughts, intimations are objectified in pictures which often lack definition but are enormously effective in atmosphere and suggestion. The poet recognizes himself in the "phantom-ridden ancient castle" with its deserted halls, or in a noble stallion tethered and vainly longing for freedom. A strange ship bears him swiftly to the newer and newer waters of his imagination, while the magic dawn bird of joy flutters between his hands.

Ady is supreme in the use of poetic techniques to create a strange and mysterious world. He frequently uses words evocative of colour and shades of colour; the influence of the Impressionist painters can be felt in his verse. The reader is transported into a world imbued with shifting hues and a pulsating vibrancy by the unusual, unexpectedly abrupt rhythm of his poems. This rhythm is a fresh and original fusion of the iambic metre and the stress-based (often called Hungarian) rhythmic form which Ady adapted and transformed.

The collections of poems which followed hard upon one another, *Blood and Gold* (Vér és arany, 1907), *In Elijah's Chariot* (Az Illés szekerén, 1908), *I Would Love to be Loved* (Szeretném, ha szeretnének, 1909), *The Verses of All Mysteries* (A Minden-titkok versei, 1909), *Escaping Life* (A menekülő Élet, 1912) continue the trends and colours of *New Poems* still further. The tone is characteristically bourgeois (perhaps most close to Baudelaire) and decadent. In some of the most outstanding poems the poet wrestles with the problems of loneliness, death and the peculiar difficulties which confront the artist (*Before the Good Prince of Silence* — Jó Csönd-herceg előtt; *The Black Piano* — A fekete zongora; *The Dance of Widowed Young Men* — Özvegy legények tánca).

The peculiar settings and beings in these poems remind one of some of the poems of Edgar Allan Poe. The poems are intensely evocative, cunningly wrought, and highly complex. The sounds, the visual associations, the expressive force of the words, and the fantastic quality of dreams with their own dissonances and fluidity, are welded in the end into a finely constructed poetic whole.

The Revolutionary

On the one hand Ady had a profound love for the Hungarian people, but on the other he detested the conditions of life in his home country, and the two together merged into a passionate espousal of revolutionary principles. The revolution was to be broad in scope and democratic, a bourgeois revolution which was nevertheless to secure important rights and responsibilities for the workers and peasants. In one poem the poet wrote of the peasants on the farm of a noble count mourning the lost harvest after a devastating fire although it was not theirs by right (*On the Count's Threshing Floor* — A grófi szérűn). In another the peasant is a harvester beaten down by worldly misfortunes and the powers of nature, still continues to carry out his tasks, because "life and hope have for so long been harvested in Hungary in the midst of decay" (*A Hungarian Harvest* — Arat a magyar).

Nonetheless he noted the seeds of revolt, the example set by struggle in the ranks of the workers (*On Máté Csák's Land* — Csák Máté földjén). He admired them as "the white hope of the future". They will wage the war for which he felt himself too much a creature of the past to wage himself. "Hunger for bread, hunger for the word, hunger for Beauty drives you on," he wrote. The oppressed with their longing for a full life on the one hand, those greedily appropriating the goods of this world, and who yet do not know in reality how to live, stand opposed to each other. And therefore the socialist masses struggling for a complete reformation of the world and the isolated man set on fire by new ideas and his love of beauty have much in common. In some of Ady's poetry they fuse and become one, even though he was well aware of the deep gulf separating the poet imbued with the experience of his bourgeois environment from the organized masses. "Our bond was decreed by fate. Not merit, not guilt, not virtue, not need, nor indeed guile: oppressed people, oppressed poet—we met, you and I" (*I am Sending the Ark of the Covenant* — Küldöm a frigyládát). In another poem he takes the two converging parties, those who walk solitary in their high vocation, and the revolutionaries, and symbolizes them in a vision of storm-rent mountains with their lonely peaks and great, spreading masses (*The Alps and the Riviera* — Havasok és Riviéra).

When the revolutionary wave of 1917 was about to break Ady felt beneath his feet the earth-shaking movement of long-suppressed energy. He gave a sense of the frightening tension of silence before the storm in *We Race toward Revolution* (Rohanunk a forradalomba). He sees the coming revolution sweeping aside all that is past in a single stroke, heralding universal change and bringing new life to all the oppressed peoples of the Carpathian Basin (*To the March Sun* — A márciusi Naphoz).

Ady is not only sensitive to the tragic in life; he is also wide open to rebirth and to the blossoming of life—landscapes bathed in summer showers, women's bodies glowing with health, the fine, virile bodies of men (*After a May Shower* — Májusi zápor után; *On the Banks of the Kalota* — A Kalota partján). "Life seeks to live for reasons which are holy"—this poetic affirmation of a deep conviction is at the core of Ady's work.

Poems on God

In his poems Ady's abstract concepts are clothed in sensuous, bodily form. The figure of God plays an important part in them as the bodily representation of the forces distilling the essence of human, social, and national life. This is not only because the figure of God is one of the most universal of symbols, but also because centuries-old tradition and myth had already invested his image with a wealth of association and colour. Ady spent much time reading the Bible, for he saw it as one of the most perfect examples of the old Hungarian language before the language reform of the nineteenth century. It was more primitive, elementary, nearer the natural sources. As an artist, Ady's view of the world was greatly influenced by Calvinist determinism, and he found inspiration in the Bible, and particularly the Old Testament. The God of the Old Testament has not been transformed into spirit; he leads battles, decides the fate of nations, argues with man. In various poetic cycles Ady invoked the aid of this God both in his own personal struggle and his country's. He also saw in this God the greater forces driving men, forces against which they contend and on which they depend. But there are also poems more closely linked to Verlaine, where the poet, tired, lonely, racked by pain, turned in submission to the Christian God of suffering.

Human Dignity

There is a cruel honesty in the poem he wrote at the ending of what was the great love of his life. It is to "Léda", the woman who now wants him back: "Break again spell, broken a hundred thousand times, a hundred times / Thus I let you go—once again—finally. / If you thought that I held you still / And you thought that yet another letting go was called for" (*Farewell* — Elbocsátó, szép üzenet). Here the poet dispatches the woman who was his inspiration, stripping her of all that he had woven around her in his poems. An imperial pride speaks within him—but no longer in tones of romantic and emotional magnificence. His sentences press slowly forward, given weight by echoes and repetitions, with all the clarity of disciplined logic. The lines are informed with a sense of human dignity. We hear the voice of a man who has come to know the great unforgiving laws of life and who has made them his own: "Stricken a hundred times, thus I throw you, to you the rich, noble mantle of my forgetting / Put it on, for it will be colder still / Put it on for I pity us. / I pity us for the great shame of an uneven battle / For your humiliation, for I know not what. / So now it is you, you only, whom I pity... I wanted to see your graceful fall / From my proud breast, which is great and insatiable." Here we have an unapproachable dignity—and it is not the patrician calm of Stefan George. On these heights it is even possible for a human warmth to infuse the irrevocable judgement he passes. Ady demanded of the woman who, as he wrote, "was fulfilled only with my coming" that she should understand the need for the tragic ending of their love. He demands this of the person who was transformed from a bourgeoise to the timeless symbol of the desired woman in his poetry. He demands of her that she should realize that she had played her part in the context of greater matters—and should play it thus to the end.

Ady, who insisted on human dignity, lived in an age in which human dignity was a scarce commodity. In his mature period he was deeply conscious of the profoundly antisocial tendencies of his time.

The Defence of Human Integrity

Carriage Way into the Night (Kocsi-út az éjszakában) is one of the poems expressing the feeling that characterized the Romantics, that a fulfilled human life was unattainable in his age: "Every Whole is broken / Every Flame burns only in part / Every love is in pieces / Every Whole is broken." This poem is an exposition of the problem of fragmentation. Ady dealt with it even more intensely when the contradictions of the imperialist world order came to the surface in their most extreme manifestation during the war, reducing the established order of things to chaos. "Every Separate has congealed / And yet everything has fallen apart," is Ady's cry. "The entire weft of the world has unravelled," he wrote.

The yearning for a full, rich life and the destructive powers of society were sharply contrasted during the First World War, and this contrast was reflected in Ady's poetry. In describing the imaginary summer night that saw the outbreak of the war, the most fearful moment comes with the phrase that "Thought, the proud youth of Man... was crippled, became no one" (*Remembering a Summer Night* — Emlékezés egy nyár-éjszakára). "Again and again the face of Man falls into the mud", he cries (*On the Margin of the Book of Isaiah* — Ésaiás könyvének margójára). "Humanity and virtue only words / and the shifting / The frightened world is nowhere / And it hurts that I am / And it hurts that I cannot be proud / That I am a man" (*There is Nothing, Nothing* — Nincsen, semmi sincs). Here he is at once fearful for mankind and denouncing it, as he was formerly fearful for the Hungarian people while attacking them. Even so, he does not abandon "man's faith woven in beauty"; he guards his beliefs, derided as they are, as seeds under the snow. For even in war Ady saw the greatness in struggling mankind. He saw it in the soldiers going into battle, gone to their death for interests which were not their own. "Life seeks to live for reasons which are holy", and the thought expressed in a variety of ways occurs again and again in his poems. Another constantly recurring theme was the conviction that the struggle, apparently vain, but which nevertheless gives a meaning to life, should never be abandoned. Even at the end of his life, Ady defended the growing revolutionary spirit; he spoke for all men concerned to end the meaningless slaughter, if necessary by the use of armed force (*The Complaint of a Discontented Young Man* — Elégedetlen ifjú panasza).

347

The Search for a Modern Form of Expression

Even at this period some of Ady's poetry still maintained its mythological and personified forms. In his earlier verse it had been the powers which had inhibited effective action which had been personified, so now it is the unleashed powers of death and destruction. But there is now a certain simplification. *Farewell* does not rely on the atmosphere generated by the choice of words, on the subtleties of feelings and emotion, nor on richness of colour. A new style is introduced in the slow movement of the sentences, unimpeded and unembellished by rhyme, as well as by the powerfully logical construction of the poem and its clear-cut conclusions. This process of simplification can be seen, for instance, in those of Ady's poems akin to dramatic and more psychological monologues (*With Brows Beaten Bloody* — Véresre zúzott homlokkal). Rather more removed, but still belonging to this simplified category, are the poems addressed to Csinszka, his last love, in which a lyrical inner voice makes itself quietly heard.

The style and structure of Ady's verse shows other changes as well. From 1910 onwards a general loosening of structure can be observed. Not only words, but entire images and lines are juxtaposed in a logically freer manner. "The Autumn, his sun-dial stopped / Watches the timid approach of our lips / Sometimes the mist brings the smell of snow / Many-coloured dead leaves make up our bed / And from the autumnal forest comes the song / Of the deathly faith of our love's fear" (*The Fear of Autumnal Forests* — Őszülő erdők rettegése). Here Ady no longer describes himself and the world in one sensuous image or in a structure concentrated around some future act. Here the images springing from his sensitive reactions to the chaos in the world around him are allowed to flow more freely, with an objective, less embellished sense of his own actual condition. These poems are often quieter in tone, less emotional, but more nervous, more confused. They have points of resemblance with the poetry of Apollinaire and with the developing Surrealism of the early twenties.

These, however, are not Ady's most characteristic poems, and his readers gave them less attention. They were accustomed to his earlier poems, and preferred their flamboyance or their morbid *art nouveau* elements. Viewing it as a whole, there was some decline in the standard of his work from 1912 onwards for a certain time. But it was at the end of what might be described as a search for new directions that the most important of Ady's war poems were written. The best poems of this last phase are to be found in the volumes *Who Saw Me?* (Ki látott engem?, 1914) and *In the Vanguard of the Dead* (A halottak élén, 1918).

Ady is the first and greatest pioneer of modern Hungarian poetry. Most of what he has to say is of universal value. He wrote poetry where the "I" is central and where everything is subjective in the manner of the middle-class poets of the second half of the nineteenth century. This "I", however, with its own particular humanism, lives through the events of the entire world, as it were, as an intensely personal experience. This "self" is more closely related to the collective ego of the Expressionist than to the subjectivity of Baudelaire and Verlaine. Endre Ady is one of the representatives of the second wave of Symbolism, of which Rilke, Verhaeren, Blok and Arghezi formed part. Ady's road, however, led to an expansion of the poetic world, beyond the boundaries of Symbolism.

His Lifework

The poems written during the war expressed the tragic view he took of the national fate calling at the same time for revolution and fearful lest it be denied. His work came to an end when he died in January 1919, in the midst of the 1918–19 Revolution.

The rich and complex nature of Ady's language makes it particularly difficult to make his poetry known to foreign readers. His archaic usage make the translator's work harder than usual; his system of images and symbols is strongly rooted in the Hungarian past.

Ady's short stories deserve a mention here. But his work as a journalist, extending over many years, is more important. He wrote small daily columns, editorials, theatre criticism, political commentaries and social essays. His outlook on the world is reflected in his evaluation of both events in Hungary and in the world at large (the Russian revolution of 1905, for instance, the reorganization of the Social Democratic Party, the Social Democrats' role in Asia, etc.). His articles are often the forerunners of poems dealing with social topics, and the same strength of passion informs them both.

48 Zsigmond Móricz (1879–1942)

Their contemporaries more than once drew a parallel between Ady and Móricz. And indeed the role the one played in revitalizing poetry was similar to that played by the other in revitalizing prose. Just as in the earlier period of renewal Petőfi greeted Arany in verse, so too did Endre Ady greet Zsigmond Móricz (1879–1942). Móricz was a fellow-spirit, moved by the same basic motivation, though at the same time a more tranquil and better balanced man.

His Life

He was born in a small village on the Great Plain in 1879, the first son of the marriage between an enterprising, fiery-spirited peasant, who owned about seven acres of land, and the daughter of an impoverished Protestant minister. During his childhood he experienced turn and turn about the deprivations of the poor peasant family and their financial recovery, but he also absorbed a compelling urge for education and a higher kind of life. He later went to one of the distinguished Calvinist schools, and studied intermittently before becoming a journalist in Budapest. With others he wandered in the country collecting folk poetry, and on these trips not only found many valuable examples of an inimitable folk culture but once more came into contact with the social world of his early days.

Móricz first came to notice in 1908 with a short story entitled *Seven Pennies* (Hét krajcár) published in *Nyugat*. From that time on he was intimately associated with *Nyugat*, and in fact became one of its most influential collaborators.

During the war he was a war correspondent. His earlier accounts paid tribute to the courage of the common soldiers, his later ones described their suffering and the general desire for peace. When the revolution broke out in the autumn of 1918 and the Hungarian Republic of Councils came into being he greeted both with enthusiasm, as did most of the progressive intellectuals of the time. But the consequence he most desired was the division of the land among the peasants. His articles are full of hope for the formation of agricultural co-operatives. He had, however, no firm set of social principles. At times he seemed to find in the revolution the realization of Christian ideals, but in the end he was somewhat alienated from the politics of the Hungarian Republic of Councils. Nevertheless, at the time of the White counter-revolution he was execrated and even spent some time in prison.

His social position, however, gradually improved. His novels appeared one after the other; some of them were re-written for the stage, and he became a co-editor of *Nyugat*. His development as a writer took place under the crossfire of criticism, but he did not wait long for recognition, even though poverty sometimes led him to produce hasty and somewhat superficial work. In his attempts to bring culture to the masses he re-worked some of the remains of ancient Hungarian litera-ture which had been neglected and which were hardly, if at all, known by the wider reading public, as for instance, Péter Bornemisza's *Electra* and the prose of Lajos Tolnai. In this type of work Móricz was most drawn to realistic, characteristically Hungarian material.

In those days he also made regular trips to the countryside, finding remote and hidden villages as he had done in the days when collecting folk songs. He greedily noted and absorbed everything that he saw and heard. Disillusioned by political struggle, he saw the only possible road to national progress and survival in work, in strengthening the impoverished masses on both the material and moral plane. In the later part of the thirties he worked partly parallel to, and partly together with, the village research movement of the "folk" *(népi)* writers known as the populists. In 1939 he took over the editorship of the literary review *Kelet Népe* (People of the East), which gave space to contributions from writers with a peasant background and dealt mainly with peasant problems.

The Beginnings of His Career

Móricz became the greatest figure of Hungarian realist prose, but he did not begin to write in the still-existing tradition of the nineteenth-century Hungarian realists. In his youth he was influenced by Jókai, and later by the anecdotal, slightly idealizing prose written in the spirit of conservative "folk-national poetry".

The famous short story, *Seven Pennies* (Hét krajcár), which appeared in *Nyugat*, can be traced to these influences. He gave a picture of the happy side of the life of the poor, in a short-story style, but he was already clear-minded about the fate of the poor. He looked into a world where one accepts coins from a beggar, and where the laughter which seeks to overcome misery turns to coughed-up blood.

There is thus a certain two-sided approach already visible in *Seven Pennies*, and although Móricz's work was to undergo many changes this dualism can be found in almost everything he wrote. He is concerned to show quite frankly the depths of human misery, but at the same time he is also concerned with positive values in life, in human features undistorted by misery. Sometimes the balance is perfect, sometimes one outweighs the other.

As his career progressed Móricz brought fewer and fewer illusions to his picture of society. In *Tragedy* (Tragédia, 1909) for instance, he deals with a starving agricultural labourer who, invited to a rich peasant's feast, in blind hunger and greed, partially fuelled by hatred, stuffed himself to death. His meaningless death goes as unnoticed as his life. The tone is apparently objective. But this short story, written with digressions, with a strict economy of means directed to precise goals, is charged with the emotional tensions of a writer who has looked into the depths of human existence, and reveals the frightening aridity in a section of society hitherto unobserved.

His Naturalism

Naturalism is a strong feature of the work just discussed, as it is of Móricz's later writings, especially of the novel *Pure Gold* (Sárarany, 1910). This work deals with the disintegration of the life of a peasant of strong capabilities and passions, urged on by an active temperament. His failures in love and personal ambition are tellingly revealed, and he who could have become the leader of the villagers in their struggle for land against the noble land-owner, becomes in the end the land-owner's murderer, for the sake of a woman, in order to satisfy his male vanity. Naturalism here takes the form of the strain imposed by crude physical passions, exhibited in the unfettered language of the characters, in the realistic background, in the uncompromising display of avarice, the sensuous immediacy of material objects. Móricz is not trying to write a "scientific experimental novel" like Zola, nor does he lay inordinate emphasis on material detail. Parts of the work display different aspects of the misery of village life, balanced however by encomiums on the magnificence of nature and the energy and spirit lying dormant in man. The characters are forcefully drawn, vividly alive, despite the difficulties of creating a chief character imbued with unusual powers. In this work of Móricz it is already clear that the author is addicted to tense and dramatic scenes where both strong human passions and representative characters from the different social worlds are shown in conflict. *Pure Gold* is a picture of a typical Hungarian village slowly experiencing the influence of capitalism. *Poor Folk* (Szegény emberek), a short story written in 1916, during the First World War, is one of Móricz's finest essays in realism, and at the same time an excellent example of the two aspects of his work. The truth which Ady voices in the language of ancient jeremiads in *Poor Men Kill, Merely Kill* is repeated by Móricz in an objective prose which conceals a deep dismay within it. It uncovers the inhumanity of war with the sharpness of steel. It deals with a soldier home on leave, who tries to help his debt-ridden family by stealing. But in the end, as a consequence of the theft and the need to kill bred in him at the front, he commits a double murder. Móricz paints the main figures in minute psychological detail—based not so much on a cold analysis as on the description of their inner selves: the soldier who gradually becomes aware that he has not changed his fate by his action, that he has only sunk deeper in the mire, the wife who will cling to her husband absolutely, despite his growing confusion and his crime. The reader feels the remains of humanity in his hero even through the final dehumanizing process. The short story is written in purely realistic terms, with no forced contrasts or extremes. The man, who becomes increasingly revolted by his deed, comes to final recognition of the real situation sitting on the banks of a ditch, thinking of the trenches on his way home with the things he has stolen: It is not the man of a different nationality who stands on the other side in war, who is opposed to the poor. As things are, he realizes that on one side are those "who have a stinking hovel, whose boots are in tatters, who have no bread to eat, but who have only lots and lots of children". On the other side stand those who get officer's treatment, who are "good men who don't hurt a soul because they give a penny to beggars".

Symbolism and Lyricism

The novel *The Torch* (A fáklya, 1917) was partly influenced by the war. Here Móricz is no longer satisfied to register the relentless laws of the world, what he now expresses is the desire for change. The fervent nature of the novel provides an outlet for his more "lyrical", more romantic tendencies. This uneven work is close to *Pure Gold* in subject, but it is even closer to Ady's poems on the subject of Hungarian Wasteland and Hungarian "Messiahs" incapable of action. In the frightening, debilitating world of the Hungarian countryside even those who started out as torch-bearers of good causes fall by the way or do harm. Here it is a gifted Protestant minister fired by a vocation akin to that of the preachers of old, at odds with the crippling strains of life. He fails, and in the end he is forced to question his original sense of vocation, and, with the whole world against him, he curses it. It is as if his curse were answered in the fire which breaks out as a result of a stupid accident, and which brings mass death and destruction during the village festivities. This is the first appearance of destruction by fire which appears later at the conclusion of several of Móricz's works. The minister's last words are said in a feverish semi-consciousness: "It has come to pass, but nothing has become clearer." And the frightening scene of death and destruction provides a symbolically charged background to these words.

A similar scene closes *Gentlemen Make Merry* (Úri muri, 1928), written some ten years later, after the war and the 1918–19 Revolution and counter-revolution. The action, which takes place at the end of the nineteenth century, is concerned with a single feast, lasting several days. Móricz not only condemns a declining section of society, the gentry, but as in Ady's verse, crowds past centuries into the present. The work moves gradually from a narrative to a dramatic form. The strong sense of atmosphere permeating this work has an almost poetic quality. Every small detail, indeed, is realistic: the weary conversation born of boredom, the fly droppings on the tablecloth, the dust of the stifling summer in the street. Yet all this is the symbol of a world more extended in time and space. Each movement seems to retain the memory of ancient ceremonies, the scene of action is bounded by a cupola-shaped sky. By their merry-making the main characters try to deny their economic and moral collapse, or at least to regard it as merely temporary. The increasingly frantic dance of death of the feast takes on a frightening dimension for just this reason. Here are small-town people confined in a rigidly conventional framework, and the village men fired by ancient passions: the ex-land-owner, now reduced to selling books, who foretells and explains the ruin of the country, the eccentric landlord who regards the exploited peasants as a joke, but who lives and dies for his animals. Such men surround, humiliate and finally destroy the man trying to change things, to escape. In the hurlyburly of the festivity, the minister sets fire to the roof above them, and shoots himself in the heart.

All the old strength and ancient obduracy of the East, all its old virtues and vices are concentrated in this novel. Móricz is also concerned with the duality which Ady writes of in *On the Hungarian Waste* (A magyar Ugaron): the historical past, the hypnotic effect of tradition, the stubborn pride of centuries and the lack of responsibility that inevitably lead to destruction. The central characters in Móricz's novels are also driven by a longing for a whole and fulfilled life: their failure means the end of the splendid possibilities of life. The narrative writer, however, needs to give a realistic representation of the failure of his characters and of the causes of that failure, a task that Móricz fulfils admirably: he gives a clearly comprehensible picture of the inner inevitability of failure for the man without any opportunity of active participation in society, and so losing his moral base.

An earlier work by Móricz, *Until Break of Dawn* (Kivilágos kivirradtig, 1926), is akin to *Gentlemen Make Merry* both in plot and theme. Here all the signs of financial and moral collapse behind apparent tranquillity come to the surface in a single night of increasingly hectic merry-making.

Critical Realism

A strong sympathy and an even stronger—illusionary—faith originally connected Móricz with the better elements among the gentry. But to a certain extent already in *The Torch*, and certainly in two works under discussion, he realized that this whole class was doomed. A final judgement without any trace of illusion is expressed in *Relatives* (Rokonok, 1930), a novel which follows the more traditional forms of realism, closely related to Móricz's earlier work, *Behind God's Back* (Az Isten háta mögött, 1911), which in turn is a deliberately grotesque version of Flaubert's *Madame Bovary*. In the life of the small town, stifling, boring, petty, even Madame Bovary-type attempts to escape become dull and ordinary. The suicidal jump of the unfaithful wife ends with her landing on her backside; the deceived husband cannot even understand why the magistrate who commits suicide should call him Mr. Bovary. Life continues at the end of the novel exactly where it began.

This terrifying vision of extinction is not death but more a bitterly precise account of life which has lost its meaning.

The same theme runs through *Relatives* as in *The Torch* and *Gentlemen Make Merry*. Móricz sets his scene in contemporary life, around the nineteen-thirties, among the bourgeois intellectuals and gentry burdened by the remains of a feudal past. A city councillor, responsible for cultural activities, is elected to the post of chief attorney. His efforts to purify and reform the system are frustrated by opposition from the mayor, who dominates the town and whose cynical ruthlessness is masked by an easy and familiar manner. The failure is pitiful rather than tragic. The chief attorney is brought by a kind of necessity to a point where his plans must fail through a variety of reasons: through the manipulative skills of the real rulers of the town, better adapted to the tempo of modern life, through his own ambition to succeed, and through the relatives looking for security by means of his influence. The novel is centred on the main character. The unexpected exception comes in the final chapter where, in sharp contrast to the ending of *Gentlemen Make Merry*, we are only given the bare news of the suicidal shot. We do not even know whether or not he dies. Here there is no sense of the greatness of the struggle with death. The concentration is on the attorney's inner life, its ups and downs, contradictions, and the process of its disintegration are charted with a sober clarity. One of the characteristic intellectual flaws of the century, self-deception, is displayed in this novel. Kopjáss, the careful tactician, deludes himself that he is representing the interests of the poor even when their cause is a mere tool for his own advancement, since he has long since only been interested in the furtherence of his own career. Even at the end he feels that his failure is the failure of a man battling for a genuine cause, whereas by that time it is only his unwillingness to take risks and his lack of foresight which distinguishes him from the powerful group riding roughshod over him.

355

Historical Novels

Móricz was also interested in larger and more universal questions than those of small-town life or the fate of self-deluded officials. In 1921 he embarked on an enormous historical trilogy, *Transylvania (Erdély)*, which was only finished in 1935. He took as his subject Gábor Bethlen, the seventeenth-century Protestant ruler of Transylvania, who united this small country, later to play an important role in Europe, portraying him as the exemplar of the strong monarch who was dependent on his people; who promoted the development of a middle class and who brought unity and peace to warring national groups. The figure of Bethlen is reminiscent in various ways of Heinrich Mann's Henry IV. A good deal of detailed and serious historical research went into this work. The turbulent, colourful life of the period, the two worlds of the rich and the poor, are recreated in slightly archaic but powerful language; the action is lively, the character convincing.

Particularly successful are the portraits of Bethlen and Gábor Báthori. Báthori is the ruler who is the antithesis of Bethlen; his visions are bold and far-reaching, his abilities great but marred by an ungovernable temper. (Did Móricz model his two central characters on himself and Ady?) The human picture of Bethlen is intensified by his conflicting emotions for two women: the intelligent, disciplined wife with her inner purity, cherishing her husband, and the mistress offering free and uncontrolled passion but lacking moral strength. This attraction of opposites is present in a number of the other novels as well (*Pure Gold, Gentlemen Make Merry, Relatives,* etc.). Móricz built a veritable mythology out of these contrasting types, the "mythology" of the two basic categories of woman.

The chief character of his other historical cycle of novels, written at the end of his life, is a folk hero—Sándor Rózsa, the famous lowland outlaw of the mid-nineteenth century. (The concept of the outlaw had long attracted him; the central figure of The *Outlaw (Betyár, 1937)* became the champion of the oppressed against the oppressor.) The work was planned for three volumes. The first is a masterpiece of his maturity. But in the second, written in considerable haste, Móricz tried to integrate both the 1848 struggle for Hungarian freedom and the figure of the outlaw who took part in it, which somewhat upsets the balance of the structure. The end of the work deals with the loss of hope, "everything has an end, only poverty stays forever". The first novel, *Sándor Rózsa Jumps his Horse* (Rózsa Sándor a lovát ugratja, 1941), carefully organized, vigorous in language, is rich in a magnificent panorama of men set against their natural background, as it pictures both the lonely hero and the busy, multifarious life of the people. And the second novel, *Sándor Rózsa Puckers his Brow* (Rózsa Sándor összevonja a szemöldökét, 1942), despite its loose structure, is no less remarkable. The completed trilogy would have crowned his achievement—but he was not allowed time to finish it. The third volume remained no more than a plan.

Human Fate and Autobiography

During his writing career Móricz often recurred to the problems of childhood. No doubt this was connected with the bitterness of his own childhood years, but it may also have had something to do with the fact that even after grappling with all the adult questions of the individual and society, he retained something of a child's amiability. It was after the successful counter-revolution of 1919 that he wrote *Be Faithful Unto Death* (Légy jó mindhalálig, 1921), which is a sensitive psychological portrait of the helpless struggles of a hurt and exploited schoolboy, set against an admirable picture of the sterile life of a students' hostel and the small-town characters of a Hungarian province. *Little Orphan* (Árvácska, 1941), moreover, written in Móricz's last period deals with an even greater degree of exploitation. The novel is about the subhuman life of an orphan, passed from one peasant family to another. It also ends with a devastating fire as the only "solution". The final image is that of a blanket of snow covering everything: "There was nothing to show that a house had stood there and that people had lived in it, and that those people had perished here under the snow."

The Peasant

The fate of the peasant is also a recurrent theme in Móricz's work, particularly in the novel *A Happy Man* (A boldog ember, 1932). It is written in an easy voice, in the first person. It slowly unfolds the character of a peasant, looking back from his present penury, who sees the years before the war as happy ones, even though that life was also nothing but sheer poverty and work, with no hope of escape. Even so it is not merely because of the even greater poverty of the post-war period that his earlier life seems happier in retrospect. It is because within its narrow limits that life had more contentment, and yet the peasant survives despite the harsh conditions of his existence. He lived, he passed on life to his children; he worked and loved, and neither joy nor the appreciation of beauty had died in him.

This work is perhaps the nearest in tone to *The Story of My Life* (Életem regénye, 1938), the autobiography which gives such an authentic and perceptive account of the writer's childhood, revealing at the same time the spirit and customs of the age. If Thomas Mann in the *Joseph Trilogy* explains myth and brings it close to man, Móricz elevates the story of his family to the status of myth. We see the intermingling of the lives of the independent peasant boy with his great vitality and mental strength and the gentle parson's daughter. All the warmth and immediacy of the events are vividly conveyed to us, while at the same time the careful analysis and examination to which they are subjected give us an understanding of the peasant in Hungary at the turn of the century.

The Short Stories

It is no accident that Móricz first came to the attention of the public with his short stories. In his prolific output of this genre are a number of short-story masterpieces. These dense, often dramatically structured tales are various in tone, sometimes stark, sometimes light, sometimes bitterly ironic. They deal with the fundamental problems confronting man in his dealing with nature and society, and expose them in a contemporary context.

One of the most outstanding is *The Barbarians* (Barbárok, 1932), which is as far from *Seven Pennies* as it is from *Tragedy*. The action takes place in that "semi-past" which left its effect on Móricz's own time, that is, the second half of the nineteenth century. The story is simple: a shepherd and his child are beaten to death by two other shepherds, and his flock is driven away. His wife searches for many months until she comes upon the dead bodies. One of the murderers, now in prison, and in any case due to be hanged for other offences to which he has confessed, nonetheless stubbornly refuses to confess to this particular crime. Or at least until he unexpectedly sees the dead shepherd's belt, which had already played an important part in the story. The judge is taken by surprise, but sends the shepherd to receive the additional punishment of twenty-five strokes of the birch, adding one word to the sentence— "barbarians". And indeed, the story takes us into a world of men living like Asian barbarians "red in tooth and claw". And indeed, dominating the whole tale is the sense of the chasm of incomprehension and indifference separating the world "above" from the world "below". Yet in the latter there are certain beauties: the woman who searches for the man she rarely sees, travels through half the country in the manner of mythical heroines embodying a primitive loyalty to a bond assumed for life. The different sections of the story merge to form a unity: at times its economy is reminiscent of Hemingway, at times of the poetry of the folk-tale or the ballad.

The atmosphere of the old ballads, the close relationship to the essence of the art of the common folk, is somewhat akin to the work done in contemporary music by Bartók and Kodály. It is also related to the work of the younger generation of populist writers. But Móricz's work is not local: it belongs to the wider currents of world literature. It is a more poetic version of his early naturalistic–realistic *Tragedy*, namely, *To Eat One's Fill* (Egyszer jóllakni). This story is not set in the narrow world of a single village; it is set in the endless wastelands, and the peasants who live in it battle against the age-old hunger of the poor. The chief character in the novel is not simply a peasant dulled to stupidity by the conditions of his life. He cries out that a peasant cannot stomach everything, and the cry has a wider meaning. At the climax of the merry-making arranged by the squire, he plunges his knife in the breast of the policeman, who represents the power of the landlord, with a passion reminiscent of the Gypsies of García Lorca.

His Lifework

Others of his later stories worth a mention here are those about the life of the urban proletariat, about the struggle between man and woman and about the upheavals of adolescence. But his finest works, in addition to *Gentlemen Make Merry* and *Transylvania,* are those dealing with peasant life. His greatest achievement lies in his stark but often poetic picture of more than half a century of Hungarian peasant life, in the tales of strong and active figures living in close communion with their surroundings. They bear a certain relationship to those of Reymont, but they are by no means slavish copies. His best works take their place alongside the work of twentieth-century writers like Solokhov, Steinbeck, Laxness and Nexö, in the realistic tradition of Tolstoy and Balzac in their sense of strong social responsibility.

49 Mihály Babits (1883-1941)

After Endre Ady, or perhaps beside him, the most important figure in the Hungarian poetic revival of the early twentieth century was Mihály Babits. In the period between the wars only Móricz equals him in reputation. But while both Ady and Móricz were concerned with radical social aspirations, Babits represented a rather more exclusive, "purer" literary–cultural attitude.

His Life

He was born at Szekszárd, a small town on the vine-covered hills of what was once Pannonia. His father was a pastor with a taste for classics, and Babits himself began his career as a teacher. His poems had aroused interest when he was at Budapest University, and it was there that he met two men who were both to become outstanding poets and who later contributed to *Nyugat,* Gyula Juhász and Dezső Kosztolányi. Babits taught in various country towns, when his name appeared in the pages of the anthology *Tomorrow* (Holnap). By that time his poems were being published by *Nyugat.*

During the war proceedings were taken against him on account of the anti-war attitude of his poetry. During the 1919 Hungarian Republic of Councils he was given a university professorship, but was deprived of it when the counter-revolution succeeded. He never supported the rule of the workers, indeed he openly opposed it during the counter-revolution, but nonetheless he always opposed, even if non-militantly, the Horthy regime. After his temporary retirement he came to play a larger and larger part in literary life. In 1927 he became curator of the literary award which was founded by the German art connoisseur of Hungarian descent, Ferenc Baumgarten, and which for twenty years was the most important literary prize in the country. In 1929 he became editor of *Nyugat.* This gave him an influential position, and swelled the numbers of those who sought his favour, but it also made him enemies. In the end he was a lonely man, with few intimates. In 1937 he contracted cancer of the throat. His illness required a number of serious operations, caused him much suffering, and finally deprived him of his voice. He died in 1941.

The death of Babits brought the era of *Nyugat* to an end. By this time few of its great contributors were still alive. Móricz, who was then writing for *Kelet Népe* (People of the East), lived only a further year. The review itself survived until 1944 and the German occupation of Hungary. After the war it was revived under the title of *Magyar Csillag* (Hungarian Star), edited by Gyula Illyés.

Decadence and Neo-Classicism

It is in the early part of Babits's career especially that we note the powerful element of *poeta doctus*, where the influence of his education is most strongly felt. At this point Babits was interested in exercising all his poetic facilities. The decadent influences of the aestheticism and eclecticism prevalent at the turn of the century as well as the influence of foreign poets, (Poe, Baudelaire, Swinburne) can be seen in Babits's poetry of this period. There is Classicism in his poems too, and not only because he often follows the example of particular classical poets. In the opening poem of his first volume *In Horatium* he speaks of the need for new ways, but not with very great enthusiasm: he cites the wisdom of ancient authors and in classically disciplined verse forms affirms the never-ending necessity of an ordered world.

Many of his early poems, like Browning's, are spoken through the voices of different characters and in different times; here is a Gypsy song, there the airs of medieval German *minnesingers*, or again the ribald songs of the soldiers in the inn at Golgotha after Christ's death.

A central insight voiced by Babits is one that characterizes the Symbolists, that the meaning of phenomena is concealed, is only to be surmised. "Light is the painter of surfaces" whereas in reality "black is the inner frame of things", "the soul of matter" (*Black Country* — Fekete ország). Behind the wooden façade of a country hotel "the corpse silently decays". The monotonous walls of the eternal passage are lit from mysterious sources (*The Eternal Passage* — Az örök folyosó): even the visible and prosaic light from city tenements have secret destinies latent in them. The most mundane objects of life "cry out though they have no words" (*Sunt lacrimae rerum*).

For Babits, unlike Ady, objects do not only carry the tragedy of things, of inanimate matter, within them. In one poem a young dustman carries his load with movements suggesting an antique ceremony, and the dust rising in the strong morning sunlight glistens like gold dust. (*The Lad with the Bells* — A csengetyűsfiú). To the poet this commonplace movement is imbued with an essential beauty which he transmits to us. *Let your Fame Be Woven among Eternal Things* (Örök dolgok közé legyen híred beszőtt) is the title of one of his poems. For it is not the least of his duties as a poet to raise the mundane and ephemeral to the rank of "eternal things".

As a result the things of this world conserve their bodily, tangible properties. Babits does not simply intimate, he is concerned that the reader should really *see* deep into the disciplined order of poetic creation. His early poems, it is true, are occasionally mannered and slightly precious, as he plays with verse forms, parading his facility with rhyme, rhythm and alliteration. Yet it is largely due to him that in the poetic mode of the time, dominated by emotional and romantic enthusiasm and the simple folk-song forms so much in vogue, the sense of poetry as a craft came once more to be recognized. For Babits there was a certain moral or ethical quality in this attitude. Talking about his sonnets, he deliberately expressed the view that writing poetry was "goldsmith's work", that each of his poems was "a miniature altar" (*These Are Cold Sonnets* — Ezek hideg szonettek). In this thought we find both the cult of beauty as defined by Baudelaire and the naive, deeply felt respect of the medieval artisan, as guardians of their craft.

Babits also wrote of the ferment and terror of life in large towns, of the plots of horror films, of the decay of dwellings on the edge of the city. Yet it is the aesthetic rigour of the anonymous medieval icon painter which gripped him in this poem: "We are kin, brother of long ago: / Like you hidden in your cell, / I make my drawings for myself, / and continue what you have begun. / What are you now? Dust in the ground: / But he whom you drew lives for ever. / Thus I now, before I fall / leave the memory of him whom I have seen, / So that others may see him and love him / I close my eyes in peace, / And remain forever unknown, / Pictor Ignotus" (*Pictor Ignotus*).

Babits's work has many aspects: he surprises with the image of a church attempting to fly; he evokes the Danaids in a strange, lulling rhythm (*The Danaids* — A Danaidák); he paints for us the glistening figure of feminine beauty (*Light-beam* — Sugár); he juxtaposes all the variety of an imaginary landscape with the calm green of the familiar Transdanubian plain. He writes a satanic ode to evil which is reminiscent of Baudelaire, and plays with the gentle sounds of his mother's name. Babits himself realized that this concentration on craft and form led to a certain lack in his work. The immediate experience was narrowly based, and in his concentration on the purity of the poetic art he remained rigidly centred on the personal "I". He admitted in the concluding poem (*The Poet's Epilogue* — A lírikus epilógja) of his first volume *Leaves from Iris's Wreath* (Levelek Írisz koszorújából, 1908): "Only I can be the hero of my verse, the first and last in every song: I seek to encompass everything in verse, but I have reached no further than myself."

Babits's intellectual approach and his tendency to abstraction were also directed toward an escape from the "prison" of this "magical circle" of himself. The long philosophical poem *Campaign in the Void* (Hadjárat a semmibe) is a case in point. Here Babits explores the secret laws of the infinite, freed from all limitations to a comprehensive whole.

Social Responsibility

It was the ferment and turmoil in the world around him which first shook Babits out of this purely formal attitude to poetry. As early as 1912 the workers' demonstration of "Bloody Thursday" produced an unwonted note in his work. This was when he wrote the poem *May 23rd at Rákospalota* (Május huszonhárom Rákospalotán): "Let mortal justice fall on corrupted life, / Let approaching death stand watch in the streets: / nothing matters more! let the depths of the ocean erupt! / bring the pus to the surface! let revolution come! / Let barbarism come! Let us at the least have the truth, / after so much dishonesty and dissembling!"—he cries, describing his thoughts as he stands in the disordered and deserted streets. Yet this poem, dealing with the struggles of the masses, yet cast in an ancient poetic form, expresses no more than cautious intellectual solidarity. Two years later, however, by the beginning of the First World War, emotion, intellect, and Christian humanism all find themselves at one in his cry of passionate dissent: "And if my lips are torn to tatters, even then... I do not celebrate the victor... but he, whoever he may be, who will first say... enough!" he cries in *Before Easter* (Húsvét előtt), writing of the peace that is to come and of the forgiveness that is to follow. In *Fortissimo* he expressed emotions which come very close to Ady's as he accused a God who is indifferent to the prayers of the suffering.

Babits's opposition to the war gave his verse at one and the same time a more personal and more socially central angle. War employed the machinery of the modern age to destroy human and cultural values. And for this reason he no longer sought out the new but rather saw himself entrusted with the task of safeguarding the more humane moral order of earlier times.

"Barbarism comes, like a snowbound spring, / with a lash in its hand; song, / has already / sought dumb shelter under the eaves; and this the Good / which no longer understands and has abandoned our age." In this poem *The Best Depart* (A jobbak elmaradnak), written at the beginning of the nineteen-twenties, prefigures the coming horror of fascism. In *Dangerous World View* (Veszedelmes világnézet), written during the First World War, he denounced the dangerous latitude allowed to the unreason and the barbarism of modern philosophies. The announcement of his plan for a new classicism was designed to counter these trends.

In the poetry of Babits there is a conflict between the individual life and the more general forces of society. His new design was summed up in the title of one of his poems, *The Smallholder Builds a Fence* (A gazda bekeríti házát). But at the same time a passionate grief runs through another in which he pictures the "poor, mad woman" who is the symbol of his country. The woman staggers on her way in the night, scattering her jewels in the mud as she goes. While official Hungary celebrated the centenary of the revolutionary poet Petőfi, whose character they falsified, Babits encouraged the youth of his nation to action in the spirit of the real Petőfi (*The Woman Scattering Diamonds* — A gyémántszóró asszony; *Petőfi's Wreaths* — Petőfi koszorúi).

Although after the war Babits made no move towards introducing further innovations in his poetic methods, and his somewhat conservative world view was complemented by a reverence for the discipline of artistic form, his poetry nevertheless showed a certain affinity with Expressionism, which can be seen in the choice of themes, form of expression and poetic construction of some of his poems. But more important is the effect of Expressionist "man with a capital" which in Babits merges with the Christian–humanist idea of man. This is particularly important with respect to Babits's affirmation of life, connected as it is with the fear for mankind which had sprung up in him in the course of the war. His passions, fired by the sufferings of the masses, could not be contained within the discipline of strict poetic form.

In the main, however, Babits's poetry at this period can be characterized most aptly by the allegory of the fence built round the house. The attitude he adopted was that of the artist who cultivated his garden à la Voltaire, carrying on his worldly affairs in a humane fashion, from a strongly ethical standpoint, but within the relative protection of his own small world.

But his work is nonetheless closer to actual experience than that would imply without damage to artistic form. In *Verse Diary* (Verses napló), he brings to life the "music of grave, sweet bells", he recognizes the peace inherent in the ordered life, in the morning-to-evening of quiet summer days. Eternally recurrent renewal is expressed in his descriptions of blossoming springtime. In the arrival of autumn he sees "the rhythm of years, the rhythm of God's poem". There are no more obvious archaisms in his poetry of this period; he no longer steps from his own world into a strongly stylized other world. Nor any sign of his earlier desire to master a great variety of verse forms. This new poetry is closer to actual experience, but in some respects the horizon is narrower than the earlier verse.

The cancer of the throat from which he suffered in the last years of his life seems to have given his final poems a more personal quality, more inspired by reality, more imbued with emotion. In a sense this was a continuation of the process which began in the poems opposing the war. In *Balázsolás**, a poem looking with great courage into his inner self, Babits remembers a childhood experience, and prays to a saint of long ago whose throat was cut by pagans, first with a childlike zeal and then with a manly emotion as he contemplates the operation on his larynx and the imminent approach of death.

---

* Balázsolás: a procession of school-boys on St. Blase's day accompanied by singing.

The Book of Jonah

This experience of suffering breaking through the discipline of classical restraint animates the most important of Babits' later work, the lyrical-discursive poem *The Book of Jonah* (Jónáskönyve, 1939). An even greater influence in the creation of this poem was the dangerous barbarism unleashed by the war. The sense of poetic responsibility displayed in this poem was only equalled by the poems written during the First World War. Babits here recreates the story of the Biblical Jonah—the man who refuses the burden of carrying God's message and is only concerned to escape from the guilt and corruption of life into isolation. Babits both identifies with Jonah and views the figure with a certain irony. The man who escapes the hell of the whale's belly and the tempests of the sea, he who "abhors the office of prophet" finally awakens to the fact that there is no escape to privacy from the vocation to which he is called. This is so not merely because "the Lord" can reach him everywhere, but also because "he who remains silent amongst sinners conspires with them".

It is with manifest delight that Babits paints the epic sections of his poem in Old Testament colours. His methods of injecting irony into the stark style of the poem are masterly. The theme of the poem is the recognition of responsibility for others. Despite the anger and force of Jonah's prophetic utterances, they are tinged with irony, because each of them is contradicted by events. It is only Jonah's final recognition of his destiny that the irony disappears in whole-hearted emotion. In Jonah's prayer there is nothing but the whole-hearted acceptance of his vocation. Here we recognize the sick poet, Babits himself who, in the voice of Jonah prays for aid in the wording of what he has to say before he "disappears in the mouth of an even blinder and eternal whale", who prays that "...my words may stand in faultless ranks / as He intimates, bravely / let me speak as my weak voice will allow / and let me not tire before evening / or until the powers of heaven and Nineveh / let me speak and let me not die".

Prose

The novel *The Stork Caliph* (A gólyakalifa, 1931), in common with much of Babits's early poetry, deals with the unsettling dichotomy between the world of surface appearances and the reality they mask. Babits's early output of short stories is also dominated by themes drawn from the period of *art nouveau*. His novel *The House of Cards* (Kártyavár, 1920) unmasks the corruption of small-town capitalist society. His short story *Virgil Timár's Son* (Timár Virgil fia, 1922) is concerned with a set of moral and psychological problems, involving the struggle of a teacher priest for the intellectual guardianship of a boy left in his charge, and his failure in his opposition to the boy's father. The novel *Elza, the Pilot, or the Perfect Society* (Elza pilóta vagy a tökéletes társadalom), 1933, belongs to the genre of fantasy novels fashionable at the time. It carries the reader into the world of an imaginary Second World War and imaginary totalitarian states. *The Sons of Death* (Halálfiai, 1927) comes closest to the most carefully constructed and mature of Babits's poems. This realistic novel of family fortunes, of the transition between different generations and different ages, is peopled by excellently characterized Hungarian types. It also carries on the themes of *The Stork Caliph* and of *Virgil Timár's Son*. Babits's prose, however, is a little stilted, as though the poet, used to the discipline of verse, had failed to discover the rather more recondite discipline of realistic prose. That which seems natural in poetic language is likely to seem mannered in prose. Indeed, Babits's far-reaching knowledge and vast culture is seen to best advantage in his essays. In addition to his essays and criticism dealing with contemporary Hungarian literature and with some of the great historical figures of Hungarian literature, an extremely important work is *The History of European Literature* (Az európai irodalom története, 1936). This is proclaimedly no systematic literary history, but rather a history of ideas in the form of a chronologically arranged set of essays worked into an organic whole.

The Translations

Babits played an important part in raising the standard of Hungarian literary translation to its particularly high level. At first he tended to produce work *based* on the original, but he later concentrated increasingly on giving a faithful rendering of both the form and the content of the original, in order to reproduce the total experience created by the poem. One of the towering achievements of his prolific career as a translator of both the ancient and modern classics (Sophocles, Shakespeare, etc.) is the translation of Dante's *Divine Comedy*, for which he received the San Remo Prize.

Babits's work and the part he played as a leader in the world of literature exercised its main influence on the bourgeois tendencies of Hungarian poetry. However, the generation which followed him and which tended to Classicism was also influenced by his verse. Babits's place is among those twentieth-century poets desiring to create order in the face of chaos and dissolution. His work is a link between the earlier exponents of this trend and its more modern representatives. In recent times people have increasingly come to recognize his kinship to T. S. Eliot, more on the grounds of a common view of the world and their perceptions of human action than on the basis of formal similarities.

50 Dezső Kosztolányi (1885-1936)

The other important figure, in addition to Babits, among the "bourgeois" group of *Nyugat* contributors, those furthest from the revolutionary–popular leanings of Ady and Móricz, was Dezső Kosztolányi. Although his writing does not possess the depths of Babits's best work, the rich variety of literary forms in which he achieved excellence assures his place amongst the greatest figures of his generation. He first came to the attention of the public as a poet, but his interestingly contradictory work played just as important a part in the development of prose.

His Life

His father was a secondary school teacher, and he himself took an arts course at the University of Budapest, where he met Babits and Gyula Juhász. Leaving his studies uncompleted he began a career as a journalist, which offered him both an easier life-style and greater chances of success. He settled in the capital and wrote for both left and right-wing papers. *Nyugat* published his poems from the start and also published his short stories regularly. In contrast with Babits's *homo moralis*, Kosztolányi took *homo aestheticus* as his model. He attacked the great poet of his age, Ady, after his death, but at a later point in time came out in support of the socialist poet Attila József. He was the first chairman of Hungarian PEN and he maintained a relationship with many foreign writers (as for instance, Thomas Mann and Gorki, whom he visited). He also translated the work of a great many foreign poets into Hungarian, aided by his knowledge of languages and his wide cultural attainments. He was a prolific author, and succeeded not only as a poet and imaginative writer but also as a strongly impressionistic critic and essayist, a man interested in the development of the Hungarian language and an all-round journalist.

His Poetry

As a poet Kosztolányi began, as did Babits, with the spectacular attempts to impress. In his first volume he set out to express the philosophy of Nietzsche in verse; to express the emotionalism popular at the turn of the century; to proclaim clamorously the right to suicide; to encapsulate Hungarian heroes in the space of a sonnet; to prefigure revolution in the symbol of black factory chimneys. He did all this with marvellous ease, but the slight theatricality of a large number of the poems indicates a still half-adolescent attitude. In his early volumes, *Autumn Concert* (Őszi koncert, 1911), *Mágia,* 1912, etc. a strongly decadent influence can be felt.

In this period his most genuine and authentic poetry appears in the verse-cycle *The Poor Child's Complaints* (A szegény kisgyermek panaszai, 1910). The child which was to live in Kosztolányi to the end found its voice naturally in the recollection of years gone by. The wonder at the world springing from childhood experience and the attitude which finds a secret hidden behind all things, here connect themselves spontaneously with Impressionism and Symbolism.

The rather more sober, unadorned titles of Kosztolányi's later work indicate the process of change in his life and work, as in, for instance, *Bread and Wine* (Kenyér és bor, 1920), *Naked* (Meztelenül, 1929), *Accounting* (Számadás, 1935). The First World War also played a part in stripping Kosztolányi's work of its poses and giving it greater depth. *How Close* (Milyen közeli), dealing with the spectacle of a young, strong deserter shot in the street, is saved from superficial morbidity by the consciousness of the mass killing going on. The words of mourning for the dead youth are also filled with that compassion for the common man which is an essential element in Kosztolányi's work.

The events of the time involved Kosztolányi more closely with the actualities of his world. Particularly important in this respect is the volume *Naked,* which bears signs of the influence of the *neue Sachlichkeit* (and to a lesser extent Expressionism). Kosztolányi, however, does not deal with the lives of men in the mass, but concentrates on the small human tragedies which break in on everyday life. He illuminates these, without drama, in simple, restrained language. In *Anna* he concentrates the lost dreams of an office-girl into five lines. In *Execution* (Kivégzés) he notes concisely, accurately the signs of old age indicating the imminence of death. Or again, he presents the figure of a conductor sitting down in the half-empty tram, who, strangely, is now seen to be "human, like a passenger" (*The Conductor* — A kalauz). In this period of his life Kosztolányi often wrote in free verse, but the inner structure of the verse is under rigid control.

At other times he juggles with rhyme and rhythm with marvellous dexterity, on occasion in sheer delight, on occasion with ironic overtones. The music of poetry annuls with "playful ease" through the "gymnastics of the mind". This music "hums as it soothes... and quenches sorrow with a pleasing rhyme". There are times when he makes a song out of trifles, out of nothing at all. In *Flag* (Zászló) he celebrates the fact that flags transcend the wood and linen of their composition. In *The Song of Kornél Esti* (Esti Kornél éneke) he praises "saintly, empty foolishness" in a playful, whimsical manner. But in *Marcus Aurelius* he declares unrhymed that he only respects the man who "is in contact with the earth, who experiences with courage the stony terror of Medusa-reality, and affirms that 'there is this' and 'there is not this', 'this is truth', 'this is reality'." In Kosztolányi's novel *Nero* different viewpoints are expressed in the different poems which round off the sections of the novel. For Kosztolányi truth is terrible: it is the complete fragmentation of the world (*Despair* — Kétségbeesés) or even death (*Funeral Oration* — Halotti beszéd).

In *February Ode* (Februári óda), however, he is no longer content to record everyday manifestations, imminent death, or wifely devotion, in a "workmanlike, objective" fashion. He is concerned to create the eternal image of human action in an ordered verse form which always ends emphatically with a Sapphic line. This poem is no longer akin to the bourgeois decadence prevalent at the turn of the century, it is much closer to the characteristic voice of the twentieth-century socialist poets speaking for humanity, the voices of Eluard, Hikmet and Aragon.

The modern immediacy of the poems does not prevent them from achieving the heights of more traditionally conceived poetry. "I would tell you this—I hope it won't bore you," begins one poem, "Last night..." the poet opens another of his notable achievements (*Daybreak Drunkenness* — Hajnali részegség). The prosaic present, the childhood enhanced in remembrance, the objective vision free from illusion, the unfettered imagination, all merge in one great poem which is in essence a passionate affirmation of life.

Just as some of the themes of Kosztolányi's poetry recur again and again in the course of his poetic career with always deepening significance, so we find the full flower of his maturity in some of his late poems.

The Short Stories

There is a strong *art nouveau* influence in his early short stories, as in the work of many of the writers around 1900. There is also an atmosphere of unreality in them, a sense that, indeed, the visible world is illusory. In Kosztolányi's tales the influence of E. T. A. Hoffmann's Romanticism as well as overtones of Hofmannsthal, Maeterlinck and others can be felt. The stories are based on the bourgeois life of Kosztolányi's own time, and deal with the ruined and oppressed of that world. These early stories suggest the effervescence of the poetry of Babits and Kosztolányi when young, in both decorative quality and their stylized language. There is a deeper meaning in most of the events and actions portrayed than appears on the surface. It is the atmosphere of the stories which is most appealing.

But, like the development of his poetry, there is a growing tendency toward greater realism in Kosztolányi's prose. What remains of the fantastic helps to show up the realism of the rest of his work by contrast. A mourning bridegroom, for instance, is visited by his dead bride, resurrected for an hour, and the "great reunion" finally ends in yawning boredom. In his last tales, the fantastic element is reduced to almost nothing. Traces of it in the author's otherwise astringent style are only noticeable at dramatic or exciting moments, in the use of an "exaggerated" sentence or phrase. He possesses the power of capturing a whole hidden life in a gesture, or through actions that would appear to the casual observer to be insignificant in themselves—an agonizing toothache intruding upon the marriage night, or the restless activities of a judge who is accidentally shut into his room for an hour. Kosztolányi's short stories often deal with the lives of men as they turn to ashes, losing all importance and meaning. His sense of compassion and his disillusioned irony merge in his restrained and disciplined style. An old man comes to look for his old file in an editorial office, and has finally to be bluntly told that he never wrote the short story around which he had woven the paltry legend of his past (*An Old File* — Egy régi-régi tárca). A clerk is raised for a moment from insignificance by an appendectomy, and subsequently comes to cling more and more desperately to the memory of this event *(Appendicitis)*. His characterization of men and women is reminiscent of Chekhov and Pirandello in its precision, intellectual flexibility, and seemingly dispassionate ease of style. Sometimes it is not a situation, but an object, such as a Chinese jug, a clay angel, or a lost walking-stick, around which he builds his tale with effortless economy.

Kosztolányi is a ruthlessly accurate observer of men's spirit, of their thoughts and passions, of their timid impulses and their suppressed hatreds. His whole conception of the psyche was influenced by Freudian theory. But his psychological analysis often develops into an analysis of society, and the author often turns his beam on the inhuman relationship existing between the oppressors and the oppressed, and on the hypocrisy of human relationships in general.

The Novels

A certain number of Kosztolányi's late short stories are set in distant times and places, such as ancient Rome, and centre on abstract philosophical or moral issues, such as questions of power and morality, wisdom and justice. His first novel, *Nero, the Blood-stained Poet* (Nero, a véres költő, 1922) is of this type. The chief character is the poet-emperor who compensates for his lack of talent by striking poses of genius and terrorizing the society around him. First among those who oppose him is Seneca who represents the dignity of intellect. Here we have the open debate, and more often, the intellectual tension that exists between two mutually incompatible views of the world which provides the life of the novel. The fundamental issues are poetry and politics, and morality and action. In an indirect manner the novel directs itself towards the danger of the irrationalism of the age and the release of the powers associated with that irrationalism. "Every truth is two-faceted and I saw both at once..., I held all truth in my possession, they could not have endured it... I protected the only life I had, the life which would never return, in an age in which it was not natural to be alive;" says the dying Seneca. The short novel *The Lark* (Pacsirta, 1924) is a more constricted but faultlessly written work. The central character is a girl who has never married and who has gradually become the tyrant of herparents through her incessant care and supervision. In the account of her parents who escape her overpowering solicitude for a few days, Kosztolányi succeeds in displaying the trivia of everyday life with compassionate irony. *Anna Édes* (Édes Anna) concentrates on the part played in life by unconscious passion and on the inhumanity latent in the social order. In this novel with its coldly ironic "scene-set", a peasant girl, after the victory of the counter-revolution, ends up in a gentleman's household. Obedient and all-enduring, she becomes the proud possession of the lady of the house as a "perfect servant". This state of affairs continues until one night, apparently without explanation, her long suppressed resentment erupts and she kills both master and mistress, an act subtly presented by Kosztolányi as inevitable.

Kosztolányi's particular qualities in his stories can be seen in his larger works as well. His realism is, in fact, of a highly stylized kind. His compact construction and style are suffused by a kind of restless energy.

Perhaps the novel with the widest range and compass is *The Golden Dragon* (Aranysárkány, 1925). Here the author catches the atmosphere of a small Hungarian city at the beginning of the century in a subtle piece of writing, free from all illusion. It deals with the tragedy of a high-school teacher, buried in his scholarly pursuits. The epilogue in particular lays bare the sterility of this small-time world. The daughter of the teacher who had been nearly driven to suicide by the agony of young love has now, only a few years later, recovered, to live the life of the petty bourgeoise, just like all the others.

There is a more direct treatment of the hopelessness of life in the sequence *Kornél Esti* (Esti Kornél, 1933). This fantastic–satiric, now symbolic, now amusing work declares in effect that actions which seek to change "the course of things" make no sense. The city where the truth is invariably told is even more intolerable than the world of customary hypocrisies. The man who has been saved from drowning gradually becomes the tyrant of his saviour who in the end is forced to toss him back. The hero finds the whole inner life of a Bulgarian conductor opening out before him through a touchingly bizarre conversation, in which he can only contribute two words of Bulgarian. Their relationship is nevertheless no better and no worse than those of others who have the language at their fingertips. In creating Kornél Esti the author created his alter ego; the anarchic, cynical, Bohemian version of himself.

The books Kosztolányi wrote in his maturity influenced later writers. The modern, more clearly intellectual literary products of the twentieth century were largely due to their influence.

51 The Nyugat Poets

The Two Opposites

One can more or less distinguish the whole of the poetry of the review *Nyugat* as lying between Ady and Babits. The works of the one are by and large marked by a vigorous and open commitment to the masses, the other to a bourgeois humanism, passive until forced in final desperation into action. In the one a contemporary spirit of emotional self-expression plays the larger part, in the other a concentration on formal considerations and the demands of art. In Ady, a desire to change predominates; in Babits, it is the permanent qualities of life persisting within change which prevail. Yet it is hardly possible to divide the poets of *Nyugat* into different groups on the basis of these attitudes. Neither in their lives nor in their activities did they polarize into different groups, styles or trends. Gyula Juhász and Árpád Tóth are closest to Ady. This is especially true in their more emotional verse taken up with conditions in Hungary. This poetry, in identifying with the oppressed and exploited poor, occasionally even reaches revolutionary fervour.

Gyula Juhász (1883-1937)

While at the university, both Babits and Kosztolányi revered Gyula Juhász whose poetry was already greatly admired. In later years they occasionally gave material aid to the poet out of esteem and friendship, but also with a certain condescension, when the poet remained buried in the countryside. The change of attitude was due both to Gyula Juhász himself and to external circumstances. He was born in Szeged, in 1883, into a petty bourgeois family. He first enrolled in a seminary to train as a priest, but later turned to teaching. After a year spent teaching in the more lively atmosphere of Nagyvárad, he was transferred to smaller towns, then back to Szeged. By this time he was writing as a journalist, devoured with love for an insignificant actress who did not love him. The *Nyugat* often published his poems, and the local press various other pieces. He took part in the 1918–19 Revolution, for which he was fiercely attacked afterwards, was forbidden to teach, and forced into obscurity for the rest of his life. He was very neurotic, a state of affairs which had begun in his

373

youth and grew steadily worse, and as time went on wrote less and less. He attempted to commit suicide several times and, in 1937, on his final attempt, medical help arrived too late.

Some of his early poetry is strongly akin to the older tradition of nationalist, rather rhetorical socialist humanism. He protested against the oppression of Hungary, celebrated labour and the working man, and wrote a hymn to humanity. Yet his sonnets also bore witness to his love of beauty and art, expressed in sad and melancholy terms.

Juhász was more intent on giving vent to his innermost feelings than following fashion; some of his poetry is frankly autobiographical. His work is also affected by the misery and poverty of the peasants in the Hungarian countryside (*Hungarian Scene, with Hungarian Brush* — Magyar táj, magyar ecsettel). In these poems, the often delicate yet varied colours of Impressionism, the enervation of *fin de siècle art nouveau* and certain realistic elements and tendencies flow into one another. In his early work the influence of both the Parnassians and the theories of Nietzsche and Tolstoy exerted a strong effect. Later on, he was more concerned with the exterior world. His poems charm the reader with the rich variety of their adjectives which induce a mood of melodious sweetness, like Verlaine, with lines built up of mellow consonants. They paint quiet scenes on the Tisza, mild sunsets, and the emotional life of people who can only escape from their village isolation through dreams. He writes with almost the same compassion of ill-fated servant girls as of the Christ hanging on a wayside cross, a symbol of the landless poor whose only hope resides in Him (*The Christ of Tápé* — A tápéi Krisztus).

He frequently calls up the past, especially in some of his love poetry, as in one of the masterpieces of the "Anna" poems, written to the woman he loved (*How Was It* — Milyen volt. . .). There are delicate parallels and contrasts built up in the three verses written to the same pattern, and the poem containing them is a synthesis of both free and classical writing. The lines simultaneously voice a painful renunciation of the unattainable and a gentle defiance of the fate which excludes him from the world. They show an appreciation of the beauty of the universe, a resignation felt over the passage of time and faith in eternal regeneration. The sequence of spring–summer–autumn expresses all this with a hint of alienation from it all.

On occasion his inner need to oppose fate and his consistent sympathy with the oppressed and suffering coincide, and then the profound humanism of Juhász's poetry deepens into revolutionary feeling. Here Ady's influence is demonstrable. Juhász identified with the exploited poor of both ancient and contemporary times and voiced their passionate bitterness. He brought to life the sleeping spirit of the murdered peasant leader, György Dózsa, by evoking echoes of old songs (*The Head of Dózsa* — Dózsa feje), gave voice to the burning passions engendered in the sunburnt countryside (*Hungarian Summer, 1918*— Magyar nyár, 1918), and proclaimed his hatred of those who live without working. He was waiting for the age "when all you see are workers", and during the anti-revolutionary White terror of 1919 he declared his faith in the revolution. Other poems are warm with a generous love for humanity; allied with a rephrasing of the attacks against the Germans of the ancient, heathen Hungarians, is the love of other, and especially Slav peoples.

He repeatedly revived the memory of Hungarian artists destined to a tragic fate and identified with them. The best of these poems are those dedicated to Lajos Gulácsy, his emotionally unstable painter friend, one of the greatest in the Hungarian *art nouveau* movement. Against his memories of the lives of young artists and the prosaic reality of the bourgeoisie stands the vivid picture of his artist friend. He "remained beyond space and time" where "eternal nothing proceeds under the blind sun". The frightened soul of the poet has returned, probably for the last time from the world "where the soul ticks like a clock, but does not show the time".

The most outstanding of his later poems is the *Wedding of Tápa* (Tápai lagzi), imbued with terrifying and tragic atmosphere generated by Ady and recalling folk ballads. In this unusually powerful poem, the misery of peasant life flashes out in the events of the night of a village wedding. The work finishes with the huge supernatural image of Death gathering his harvest over the horizon. He uses the medium of the festivity, slowly twisting and turning into a Dance of Death, to reveal the harshness of peasant life.

Towards the end of his career he wrote his tiny, delicate poems in a "Japanese style", but his decreasing poetic output shows little sympathy for modern aspirations, and he reacted only indirectly to the new problems of the time. His socialistically inclined poems derived from his peasant background entitle him to be regarded as the precursor of the next generation of popular poets. His close love of the countryside, his sympathy with human life and the realism of his poetry all had a definite influence on Attila József who was then beginning his career and whom he personally helped.

Árpád Tóth (1886-1928)

Babits and Kosztolányi sought to refine, to reduce to order, to introduce a sense of realism; Árpád Tóth sought the same qualities noted in Babits and Kosztolányi. His work probably changed least from beginning to end, and is the most consistent among those of the "great generation". He spent his childhood in Debrecen, a conservative, tradition-bound agricultural town. The son of an unsuccessful sculptor, he suffered all his life from a weak constitution with an inclination to tuberculosis. He studied for an arts degree at the University of Budapest but failed to complete his course for lack of money. He worked as a journalist and most of his poetry was published in *Nyugat*. Normally a quiet, modest personality inclined to self-irony,

375

he greeted the formation of the Hungarian Republic of Councils in 1919 with enthusiastic verses. He was later attacked for them, but even during the anti-revolutionary White terror he continued to publish translations of poems through which he could express his opposition to them: Wilde's *Ballad of Reading Gaol,* Lenau's *Epilogue for the Albigensians.* After repeated stays in sanatoria, he finally died of tuberculosis.

His poetry, more than that of any other Hungarian poet, resembles the bourgeois poetry of the Western world, the poetry of Poe, Wilde, Verlaine and Samain. His translations of Rilke, Shelley, Keats and the vitally important Baudelaire translations owed their artistic perfection to the fact that he made the originals completely his own; he recognized himself in them. They helped him to find his own distinctive voice without plagiarizing. His is the voice *par excellence* of tired, disembodied melancholy and the desire to break out of the claustrophobia and disunity of the bourgeois world of the 1890's, and through it the trivia of the real world come to life. He contrasts the dirty grey of a city dawn and the beginning of bleak drudgery with the moment when the rays of the sun bring back the magic of colour (*Dawn on the Boulevard* — Körúti hajnal). He also brings back to solid earth the ecstasy of love taking him into increasingly spiritual regions (*Evening Halo* — Esti sugárkoszorú).

His poems, especially in his young days, were exceptionally rich in similes and metaphors, although he rarely used symbolism. His favourite words are those which evoke fatigue and grey monotony. His poems achieve unity through the use of allusions through which he expresses his love of life and art at the same time.

They are indeed permeated all through with a human warmth, and in this respect they fall between those of Babits and Gyula Juhász. While Babits talks of his yearning to break out of an enchanted circle, Tóth believes it is vain to hope to reach other souls in this eternal loneliness. His skill and artistry are nearly equal to Babits, but his verses are more intensely related to the spontaneous ones of Gyula Juhász. On the other hand, the sympathy that Juhász feels for the masses rarely appears in his poems, which do no more than recall affectionately the memory of "shaggy, serf ancestors". Or, at most, while pondering over the inexorable passage of time, he is concerned for the fate of the country as a whole (*The Tavern of Aquincum* — Aquincumi korcsmában). He respected Ady as a model, but always felt himself to be distant from the masses.

Nonetheless, he felt bound to protest with warm humanity during the years of the First World War (*Elegy in Memory of a Fallen Youth* — Elégia egy elesett ifjú emlékére; *Elegy to a Furze Bush* — Elégia egy rekettyebokorhoz). His elegiac sorrow is tinged with a faint remoteness, though without the old-fashioned rigidity of ancient odes and elegies. In the majestic poem he wrote to greet the birth of the Hungarian Republic of Councils (*The New God* — Az új Isten), he drew with all the rich colours of Impressionism the picture of the Red God marching on his immense feet "from the red East to the pale West". Shivering "rivers of tears" as well as the evocative twilight found in the shadow of churches haunt his lines, and he is equally sensitive to the myriad tiny moments of life: the discarded matchsticks which vainly try to burst into flame (*Flame* — Láng), or clumsy human movements. And there is a hint of irony in his moving description of his emotions when preparing for death (*Good Night!* — Jó éjszakát!). Occasionally the youthful tones of happiness and good humour are heard too. In his translations he tried to be more faithful to the originals than the other poet-translators of the *Nyugat* generation. His version of Shelley's *Ode to the West Wind* is remarkable; Babits called it "the most beautiful Hungarian poem".

Milán Füst (1888-1967)

If we paint a picture of the poetry of the period, it would be the poems of Milán Füst which would provide the brightest patch of colour.

He was born in 1888 into a middle-class family. During his lifetime a whole series of legends circulated around his person, because he led a very retired life, devoted to his art, and only allowing access to a most select circle of admirers. When he taught aesthetics at the University of Budapest at the end of the forties and the beginning of the fifties, though seriously ill, he was punctilious in delivering his lectures. They were published in book form under the title *Vision and Passion in Art* (Látomás és indulat a művészetben). He died in 1967.

He spent many years polishing his relatively few poems, and fused elements of antiquity and modernity in their creation. Where most of his fellow-poets attempted to express the mysteries of life to produce in a formal style elements of reality from their own lives, he strangely called up the figure of a solitary horseman on the banks of the Arany creek, wrote odes to an imaginary artist, spoke with ancient monarchs, echoed the sound of ancient psalms or choirs, or described the slow movements of a pastor wearing an old cloak, or a vineyard worker. All this had little to do with a simple romantic return to the past; it was more that the restlessness and flux of *art nouveau* merged with a classical monumentalism and a desire to achieve tranquillity. The unusual subjects, often derived from art sources, were not an excuse for playful experiments in literature, as was sometimes the case with the young Babits. Just as Ady's wild, magical countryside was an expression of his profound consciousness of being Hungarian, so in all sobriety Füst created his own world to express his struggles with the problems of life or artistic destiny. "Oh vision, halt! Let me know why I existed!" he cried in the *Song of the Dead* (Halottak éneke). It was not a personal question, nor is the whole poem a personal one. He meditated on youth and old age, activity and mortality, the law and the need to change it, crime and justice, life and death. This can be seen in his description of the 1912 Budapest workers' rebellion and especially in the figure of Lenin in *By Candlelight* (Gyertyafénynél), *Apparition* (Jelenés). He mingles philosophical abstraction with flexibility, shrill colours melt into softer shades, his bizarre visions resemble those of Bosch and Chagall; in some poems melancholy speaks with Shakespearian coarseness, in contrast to other mellower tones of delight.

His public was limited, but his literary influence can clearly be seen in the poets immediately following him. It was the structure of his poems which set a trend capable of development. Through powerful articulation with classical discipline, but without following the rules of regular versifying he shows a close relationship to free verse.

Other Poets of the Nyugat

Many talented poets belonged to the *Nyugat* circle, but a detailed description of them would not add much. To the right were poets trying to reproduce their inner experiences in different ways, mainly through poems in the first person, which also occasionally expressed a desire for social change. This was true of *Zoltán Somlyó* (1882–1937) whose deepest passions were mirrored in his writings and who was also one of the last practitioners of the art of the long narrative poem which had had an important part to play in the history of Hungarian literature. *Zoltán Nagy* (1884–1945) was more restrained, gentle and musical; in the main he resembled Árpád Tóth. There was also the decadent poet *Simon Kemény* (1883–1945), and *Ernő Szép* (1884–1953) whose poems retained some of the naiveté of childhood.

Many excellent writers, whom we mainly regard as prose writers, also contributed to the poetry pages of *Nyugat*. *Frigyes Karinthy* was one of them. His poems resemble those of Milán Füst in their form and are on occasion characterized by a certain didacticism. He makes no attempt to deal with contemporary matters, and his poems show some intellectual sterility. Nor does he cultivate self-expression, but is more concerned with general truths. He is happier in gay and sparkling experimentation than in the expression of profundities.

Margit Kaffka was another writer of prose who won recognition with sincere but conventional family poems and free verse, some of which was remarkable for its torrential outpouring as well as for its revolutionary fervour (*Rhythms of Dawn —* Hajnali ritmusok).

There were a number of women poets at that time, and *Anna Lesznai* (1885–1968), who was later forced to emigrate, was one of those writing excellent verse. She was among the first to give voice to liberated women, and her work expressed serene dignity and passionate eroticism, in form combining Secessionist, Symbolist and Classical influences.

Other Trends

Important poetical experiments also appeared outside the circle of *Nyugat. Béla Balázs* (1884–1949) was an individualist of some importance among these writers, with an influence in other fields of literature as well. It was German rather than French culture which moved him. At first he was in theory a follower of the Symbolists, and strongly affected by the *art nouveau*; and it was partly due to this that he later turned to folk poetry. His poems became increasingly ideological, and during the years of his forced emigration, after the 1918–19 Revolution, he gradually progressed from poems exposing his loneliness to collectivism and socialist humanism.

Andor Gábor (1884–1953) progressed from writing biting, sometimes crude cabaret songs during the time of the Hungarian Republic of Councils and later to propagating the ideas of the socialist revolution, with heated denunciation of oppression. In style he continued the tradition of Heine, but he also re-created the revolutionary tones of Petőfi. The poems of *Andor Peterdi, Zseni Várnai, Sándor Csizmadia, Emil Gyagyovszky,* and *Antal Farkas* were published in *Népszava* (Voice of the People), the Social Democrat daily with an important literary supplement. Their style echoed the rhetoric of the new nationalism or the Neo-Romantics, rather than the style of *Nyugat.* Their strongly socialist leanings and their occasional bursts of antimilitarism broke new ground, and so deserve to be mentioned in the same breath as *Nyugat.*

Gábor Oláh (1881–1942) was among the first in Hungary to write free verse. His expression was similar to that of Ady, though he was hostile to him through personal jealousy. He could not, however, overcome an old-fashioned Romanticism and was unable to keep abreast of the intellectual thought of his time, and so remained a curiosity to be ranked among unsuccessful contemporary poets. *Géza Gyóni* (1884–1917) came to public notice with his powerfully pacifist verse and the fact that he had experienced the horrors of war at first hand. His *Only for One Night* (Csak egy éjszakára) is a work which also attracted attention abroad.

The poems of *Lajos Áprily* (1887–1967) also belong to this period. They were written somewhat late in life, in the interwar years. He spent most of his life in the Carpathian mountains and his poems are embued with Symbolism and Classicism, strongly influenced by his feeling for nature.

Conclusion

When we sum up the qualities of the poems of the *Nyugat* period, we note that they were strongly influenced by Impressionism, *art nouveau* and Symbolism, but none of them, especially those written before the First World War, can be classified into this style or that. Their place in world literature is not clearly determined yet. The historians of comparative literature have not yet established, for instance, how the poetry of young Kosztolányi compares with that of Hofmannsthal and Rilke, or how the candour and sincerity of Gyula Juhász's poems, coloured by his religious–mystical East European symbolism, compare with the Russians or with the Rumanian Arghezi who had a similar sympathy for the masses. The relationship, nevertheless, is noticeable. It is also clear that the more important poets all progressed well beyond any imitation of their models. It is their later, more objective, less vivid, less formal, yet more sincere and humane period which was aesthetically superior. By then they had largely overcome the sense of decadence so apparent in earlier days. The writers of *Nyugat* played a most important part in the literary period before the 1918–19 Revolution, because at that time their work was still unconventional and new, more European than provincial, and more demanding than unassuming.

52 The Prose Writers of the Nyugat Period

Margit Kaffka (1880-1918)

It is no accident that it was this writer who wrote a novel which is identifiably about *Nyugat* itself, for it was her life which was perhaps most intimately bound with that review.

Margit Kaffka was born in a country town with a conservative background. Her family were impoverished gentry who had played an important part in the life of their country. Her father died while she was still a child, and she was educated by nuns, then trained as a teacher. She taught first at Miskolc and then on the outskirts of Budapest. She began her creative career as a poet and was a member of the inner circle of *Nyugat* from its earliest beginnings. As a consequence of the emancipated attitude in her work she was loudly disowned by the gentry of her birthplace. She was, however, much admired by her fellow-artists, among them Endre Ady. Her stormy life, complicated by emotional and other problems, came to a sudden end when she fell victim to the influenza epidemic of 1918.

She was already writing short stories at the beginning of the century. The women's movement, which began to take shape around that time, formed a theme in her writing. The figures of women and girls trying to free themselves, to live their own lives, recur repeatedly in her novels, together with the impulse to rebellion, often nipped in the bud, and the subsequent resignation and disillusionment.

In her early work, Margit Kaffka was interested in highly psychic conditions and in mysticism in general. But she was at the same time fascinated by the facts and laws of everyday existence, and this tendency increasingly asserted itself with the passing of time. She wrote of ethical problems, of the social options open to women, and the contrast between illusion and reality as they are mirrored in the human psyche. Margit Kaffka contemplated her central characters from the point of view of a human being seeking to lead a rich and fulfilling life. She wrote with both a sense of poetic identification with the inner lives of her characters, and a cool and sober objective detachment. In her best work she both judged and understood. Her talent for producing atmosphere is evident even in her earliest writings, but precision of characterization is equally so.

Of all her novels, *Colours and Years* (Színek és évek, 1912) is the best. It deals with the upbringing, marriage and gradual destruction of a gentlewoman. She is both the cause and the victim of her undoing; at once an oppressed creature and a parasite. She had no opportunities open to her apart from those conventionally provided. And she is unable to face her destiny and the conditions of her life with anything but romantic dreams. Her petit-bourgeois first husband, with his own modest needs, is driven to suicide because he succumbs to pressures to try and achieve a life style beyond his means. Her second marriage to a cosmopolitan violinist which promises more than the first, ends with even less fulfilment; the "life of the artist" becomes no more than stupidly modish pattern of bohemian dissipation. The county gentry continue to live as in the past, in the illusion of permanence, while inner decay undermines the whole society. In the family it is only the grandmother who is the genuine guardian of the values of the past. The brothers of the central character, Magda Pórtelky, embody the decay of traditional virtues. The brother who was designed by the family to become a bishop cannot take the emotional strain of religious devotion. The brother who begins a career as an army officer ends up as an alcoholic vagrant.

Margit Kaffka takes the typical theme of the decline of the old European families and weaves it into a picture of a society incapable of providing individuals with valid lives and aims. She precedes Móricz's best novels about the life of the gentry in her sketch of the hopelessness of human aspirations in the provincial culture of Hungary. But unlike Móricz, she writes soberly and eschews dramatic scenes. It is not the suicide who is the central figure—the event is marked only by a brief announcement—but rather the character forced to face the hopelessness of her life from one or two insincere gestures, from hints, implications and misplaced phrases.

This novel passes an unmistakable judgement on society. Its basic realism is heightened by an Impressionistic touch in the rhythms of the novel by turn sharp and nervous, then steady, written in the form of memories recalled. As the years pass the colours change; among the memories of long afternoons, of sunlight filtered gently through the trees, harsher images appear; images of yellowed faces, of dulled eyes.

Maria's Years (Mária évei, 1912), Kaffka's next considerable work, is a half-successful experiment which attempted to find a new form for the psychological novel. The central character is a woman who is only able to conceive her future as a choice between extremes, between the soul-destroying ties of bourgeois life and absolute freedom. The novel chronicles her quest for fulfilment, which ends in senseless tragedy.

Her longest novel, *Stations* (Állomások, 1917) is like many of its contemporaries, a novel *à clef*. It deals with the unsettled life of the writers and artists associated with *Nyugat,* focussing on a woman attempting to find fulfilment in a free, artistic life. Many of the characters are taken from figures well known in the Budapest of the day. There is a sensitive treatment of political and social questions, but from a purely formal point of view the novel cannot be regarded as truly mature.

Anthill (Hangyaboly, 1917), can also be ranked among Kaffka's more important novels. This somewhat symbolic work deals with life in a convent school and its peculiarly sterile alienation from life. This short novel, however, is written with a stricter objectivity than the earlier works.

Margit Kaffka's early death frustrated her further development as a writer, as well as the completion of her more ambitious literary plans. Even so, she is the most important woman in Hungarian literary history, and her best work, *Colours and Years,* is among the best of Hungarian realistic fiction.

Gyula Krúdy (1878-1933)

Kaffka was concerned to find a way out of the social disintegration she described. Gyula Krúdy, on the other hand, whose career began earlier and who was only partially connected with *Nyugat,* was entirely absorbed in pinning down the process of decay. His attitude to the world was even more strongly influenced by the past, although tendencies more modern than Margit Kaffka's can be recognized in his style.

On his father's side he inherited the traditions of the middle gentry who had taken part in the revolution of 1848, together with a peculiar kind of restlessness. His mother, on the other hand, had originally been a mortar carrier whom his father had married only after the birth of their eighth child. In opposition to his father's wishes Krúdy chose the career of a writer rather than taking a job in the county administration. After working as a journalist in various country towns he settled in Budapest. His unconventional manner of life almost immediately gave rise to legends about him. At first he lived in poverty, then he became a successful and prosperous writer, and lapsed into poverty again; he fought duels and tossed money around, he lectured rowdy officers of the hussars in coffee houses, but always wrote diligently, following a daily plan. He wondered around old sections of the city, he was contemptuous of official recognition, and yet between two nights of adventure he would spend a day studying historical documents in libraries. He enjoyed a close relationship with Endre Ady. In social life, however, he sought the greatest possible freedom from ties, and never joined any identifiable group.

Expressionist and Surrealist writers in Western and Middle Europe deliberately echoed the works of the romantic school, and especially the German Romantics, in whom they recognized to some extent the forerunners of their own work. In Hungary, however, mainly due to the delay in the development of the bourgeoisie, there was an immediate and spontaneous contact between the Romanticism of certain still living authors and the beginnings of modernist literature. Thus there was a direct relation between Ady and Vajda, who, in turn, was directly linked to Vörös-marty, the greatest Hungarian Romantic poet of all. And in much the same way there was a relationship between Krúdy and Mikszáth who can be seen as the heir to Jókai's Romanticism.

Krúdy certainly owed a literary debt to Jókai who still had faith in the heroic Romanticism of the world he pictured. Mikszáth, who was soberer and more clear-sighted, was nonetheless incapable of breaking away from the spell of romantic beauty. Krúdy, who made his appearance as a writer earlier than his contemporaries in *Nyugat,* took his point of departure from Mikszáth, and in some respects continued to work in the same vein until he came to see one class, and through it the whole of life, from an utterly disillusioned point of view. The whole body of his work was nonetheless suffused by the nostalgia he experienced for the nobler traditions and patrician values of a lost poetic world. In place of the courageous, adventurous lives of Jókai's heroes we increasingly find in Krúdy portraits of static and pointless lives. Human failures, dead ends take the place of heroic victories and defeats, but none-theless Krúdy's writing is touched with a peculiar lyric quality. He employs a strange, magical style to describe ordinary and mundane matters, grotesque peculiarities, and hackneyed gestures and words, dissolving them all in a dreamlike mist. Some of his characters live in the clouds, ignoring the practical aspects of life in favour of romantic love, refined and elegant gestures, gallant flattery and protestations of high-minded nobility. Yet it is their creator who perhaps sees their lack of reality most clearly. Sometimes they live on the memory of their own or their ancestors' past, but are themselves come down in the world. It is not difficult to find among these characters those whose lives border on, or no longer even border on, empty preten-sions and moral dissipation. The imaginary and the real, the present and the memory of the past blend into each other in the mellifluous tones of the narrative, while at the same time we are made to feel the anachronism, absurdities and lack of reality in his characters and situations.

Through this nebulous style, a condition of timelessness is achieved at moments. Figures which are the remnants of the past and twentieth-century characters appear together in situations existing in the Hungary of the 1890s, or, indeed, in the time-lessness of inertia. We find in Krúdy indeed the preoccupation with time, which plays such a large part in the twentieth-century literature of Western Europe. It is closest to Proust, but tinged with elements of an old-fashioned Romanticism.

Krúdy's favourite character indeed is Sindbad who appears in a series of tales; Sindbad of the tired smile, who belongs both to the 1890s and the Arabian Nights. He is the sailor who wanders in measureless time and space yet at the same time within the confines of defined years and decades. A central place in these tales comes to be occupied by an old-fashioned and strange "crimson coach", for ever setting out on newer and newer journeys, but for the most part staying within a single country.

The journey-motif of German Romanticism is transposed in Krúdy's work to the Hungarian scene. Strangely-named figures giving final proof of the death-throes of a manner of life appear in strange confusion—aristocrats, strangers to all forms of work, who play cards, drink, and gamble on the horses; reporters, country dancing masters, unsuccessful poets, ladies of pleasure and old, faded gentlemen. Amongst them there is the occasional sensitive soul drawn with poetic tenderness, side by side with earthy characters from the countryside. In addition, there is the occasional sketch of the sober bourgeois defending the moral values of an earlier time. Although Krúdy supported the revolution when it came, there are no social classes or forces who consciously seek something new and worthwhile in the world of his creation; who represent any kind of renewal. For him, as a writer, it is only decay and decline which are important, and it is these he paints, hopelessly, yet with clear-sighted sobriety. His tales are vivid in the evocation of colours, voices, tastes and smells; he uses the methods of Impressionism, Romanticism, *art nouveau* and realism turn and turn about, but it is the last of these that gradually takes over.

Action plays a small part in Krúdy's work. The main secret of his work is in his style. His sentences are musical, music which springs from a relaxed ease, which suggests spontaneity, almost to the point of negligence. Irony and emotional involvement, delicacy of description, and straightforward fact are all to be found in sentences built up out of chains of loose associations.

The most important works in his erratic, but essentially not very varied output, which was huge, and included a number of historical novels, are the following: The *Sindbad* novels (1911–12), *The Crimson Coach* (A vörös postakocsi, 1914), *The Seven Owls* (Hét bagoly, 1922), and *In the Happy Days of my Youth* (Boldogult úrfikoromban, 1930).

Frigyes Karinthy (1887–1938)

The work of Frigyes Karinthy is essentially more rational in outlook than the work of Krúdy, and is far removed from his evocation atmosphere and "magic". Karinthy was born in Budapest and was the son of a businessman. His work began to be published as soon as he had finished school, and appeared in various Budapest reviews. He belonged to the circle centred on *Nyugat*, and was close friends with Dezső Kosztolányi until his death. He was an extremely prolific writer; his lighter works won him much popularity, and he is the best of Hungarian humorous writers.

Karinthy was first noticed for his brilliant parodies of the styles of others. He made ruthless fun of the conservative writers, but no less apt were his imitations of the styles and affectations of the new, liberal and left-wing writers. His arrogant, intellectual wit found its best outlet in parody. These parodies were collected in a volume entitled *The Way You Write* (Így írtok ti, 1912), which went through numerous editions.

Karinthy's short stories mainly deal with the moral and psychological problems of the isolated bourgeois and intellectual. In style they are closest to Kosztolányi. His fantastic, Utopian works *Journey to Faremido* (Utazás Faremidóba, 1916) and *Capillaria* (1921) belong in part to the tradition of Swift, and in part to the book of Wells. In the intellectual world of this writer a respect for the enlightenment and for intellectual capacity is mixed with a rather more modern scepticism and relativism, which, however, inspired an abundant play of thoughts and ideas more than any systematic philosophy. Paradoxes proliferate in his work. He was intensely interested in the relations between men and women, but less in the relations of man and society, between instinct and intellectual judgement, or even man's relations with his own inner self. He wrote highly original plays, sometimes bitterly satirical, though the satire quite often degenerated into merely surface wit.

One of Karinthy's most original works is *Please, Sir* (Tanár úr kérem, 1916). Here he brought the world of the schoolboy to life by concentrating on the events in the innermost recesses of his being rather than on external action. This work, with its exceptional psychological insight, is not merely a story about adolescence, but also, either directly or indirectly, illuminates the paradoxical and singular nature of adulthood and life in general. But above all, it radiates gaiety. *A Journey around my Skull* (Utazás a koponyám körül, 1937) is an account, in the form of an autobiographical novel, of his illness and the rescuing operation performed on his brain. Respect for the inquiring, analytical intellect retaining control even when contemplating illness and the danger of death, dominates this precisely realistic novel written in the form of a diary.

Jenő J. Tersánszky (1888-1969)

Jenő J. Tersánszky trod a highly individual path. He cared little for any of the conventions, and in his free life-style he differed from his contemporaries. He experimented with painting. He fought through the First World War. He worked for many other reviews besides *Nyugat,* and later he even played for a while with a group of wind-players in various places of entertainment.

His major work is *Marci Kakuk* (Kakuk Marci, 1942). This was formed into a whole cycle made up from a number of independent pieces of his. The vagabond who never does a day's work, who is bound by no moral conventions and who is secure in his own independence, is a stock figure in German Romantic writing. But Tersánszky's hero bears very little resemblance to the idealized, highly coloured fantasy figures of the Romantics. This very earthy figure of Tersánszky's is more akin to Steinbeck's hoboes and Till Eulenspiegel.

Throughout his work Tersánszky attempts to give the impression that he is entirely unfettered by the limitations of any particular style, clearly avoiding naturalism with his adventurer hero. The light picaresque cycle gains interest by the variety of events in the life of the gay and confident vagabond who tells the stories himself, and is further enriched by many subtly drawn figures taken from all social classes. This lively style of story-telling, which had long been traditional in Hungarian literature, though broad and natural, still differs substantially from an anecdotal style in attitude and theme, which gives it one of its chief claims to originality. But its popularity rested on the fact that it opposed a hero akin to the victorious, cunning heroes of the folk-tales to the creatures of a world in decay.

Tersánszky's short novel *Goodbye, My Dear* (Viszontlátásra, drága), written during the war, is also outstanding among his many works. It is a careful, psychological portrayal of a girl who lives in the path of troop movements in wartime, and is written in the form of letters. The central figure, who is helpless when faced with the breakdown of accustomed order, sinks by degrees into complete moral chaos. After the first conventional affair she has a series of shallower and shallower relationships, and in retrospect the first affair appears in a romantically coloured light to the disturbed woman.

A similar theme inspires the novel *The Song of Daisies* (A margarétás dal, 1929) which concerns itself with the same problems. Tersánszky also wrote other books dealing with sexual questions and women such as *The Harlot and the Virgin* (A céda és a szűz, 1924). The writer's highly personal style, embracing a subjective and soberly objective view of the world at one and the same time, retains the effect of effortless, natural ease.

Milán Füst

The most consciously "artistic" prose of the period is that of Milán Füst. His aesthetic works are evidence of his mastery of the writer's craft, and his knowledge of what goes to the making of a work of art. His prose is a joint product of his serious and deeply humane vision of the world and his assured technique as a writer. The result is a cultivated body of work which is highly stylized and shows all the signs of precise craftsmanship. These writings are only tangentially related to the objects which surround human beings and to any form of social reality, and the influence of the *art nouveau* period is clearly visible. They take us into a world where the stress laid on certain details produces a strong emotional effect—as opposed, for instance, to Krúdy's remote and magic world—but which is nonetheless also somewhat unreal and intangible. And the same is true of the relationships in time he describes. Franz Kafka or Musil are the most likely parallels, but their world, and especially Kafka's, is more frightening and more irrational than Füst's.

His short novel, *Advent* (1920), deals with an ancient English emergency tribunal. The work was written at the time of the counter-revolutionary terror of 1919, which no doubt influenced it. His chief work is *The Story of My Wife* (A feleségem története, 1942). Here a Dutch ship's captain tells the story of his relationship with his wife and of her unfaithfulness. It is only on the surface that the narrative seems loosely constructed; its development is linked to the logic of a subtle psychological analysis culminating in a confession expressing both a resigned bitterness and perplexity and bewilderment at the course of life.

Minor Prose Writers

Gyula Török (1888–1918) made one of the *Nyugat* group. He gave promise of becoming a talented realist writer, but died very young. His works reveal many contemporary influences. His best novels (*In the Dust* — A porban, 1917; *The Ring with the Green Stone* — A zöldköves gyűrű, 1918) are written with lightly poetic realism. These novels, particularly *The Ring with the Green Stone,* are late examples of a tradition that has unfortunately died out, which began in Hungary with Pál Gyulai's *The Old Mansion's Last Owner* and was related to the work of Russian writers such as Turgeniev and Chekhov. They are set in the period after 1848, and exhibit the beginnings of the decline of the gentry.

Géza Csáth (1887–1919) was Kosztolányi's cousin and his equal in the cultivation of a strict economy of style and a soberly objective psychological realism. His tragic psychological decline and early death prevented the full fruition of his talent.

Less realistic, more stylized prose with romantic and *art nouveau* characteristics, was written not only by Milán Füst, Gyula Krúdy, the young Kosztolányi as well as Babits at the beginning of his career, but also by *Gyula Szini* (1876–1932) in his lyrical short stories. Both Symbolism and Romanticism influenced this writer whose early work was marked by a freshness of outlook. His later books, however, were disappointing; they tended to repeat themselves in a routine manner. He was preceded on the literary stage by *Viktor Cholnoky* (1868–1912) whose work was even more characteristic of late Romantic tendencies in its search for the exotic and the fantastic. But it also had its more modern side: at times he was capable of sensing, with a frightening directness, the futility of bourgeois existence. His younger brother *László Cholnoky* (1879–1929) frequently wrote similar short stories with highly poetic overtones, and novels characterized by an atmosphere in which realism and flights of visionary fancy were combined, and which dealt with the lost creatures of urban life, often alcoholics, with a private inner life of their own. *Dezső Szomory* (1869–1944), also a dramatist, displayed *art nouveau* and Symbolist tendencies in a slightly languid style designed to achieve visual and musical effects, though a later book, *The Paris Novel* (A párizsi regény, 1929), revealed a growing realistic tendency.

These men were not all connected with the circle of *Nyugat,* but they were all part of the literary tendency represented by that review. *Kálmán Harsányi* (1876–1929) indeed, was hostile to the group associated with *Nyugat,* yet he can be regarded as a parallel phenomenon. This not only because he also opposed the official literary establishment, but especially because he was influenced by the new trends in art which were appearing. In his chief work *Crystal-gazers* (Kristálynézők, 1914), the tendency to documentary prose was as noticeable as the influence of Symbolism and *art nouveau. Crystal-gazers* gives a picture of the ferment surrounding new ideologies and new trends in art around 1900.

Ferenc Móra (1879-1934)

Of all the writers who began their careers around 1900, it was perhaps Ferenc Móra who was least influenced by *Nyugat.* All his life he lived in the country at Szeged. There he worked as teacher, journalist, and as Tömörkény's successor as the director of the local museum. As a writer of short stories he was also a disciple of Tömörkény's, following him in the choice of themes and in the manner of his writing; he also is principally concerned with the peasant and the little man. But he writes with more personal force than his master; his radical social ideas are present in a more personal and direct way. He does not, however, match his teacher in objective, tangible dramatic force. But his novels are, on the other hand, better balanced between the personal and the objective, between poetic and narrative qualities. An example of this balance is *Song of the Wheatfields* (Ének a búzamezőkről, 1927), about the prisoners of war; ordinary men everywhere hate war and recognize each other instinctively as fellow-humans. Here his insight into the character of man and the nature of the countryside are coloured by elements of religion-mysticism. Móra's novel *The Golden Coffin* (Aranykoporsó, 1932), takes us back to the time of Diocletian. He works with Gárdonyi's historical tools, but is the more faithful to historical facts. Perhaps the works of his most likely to last are those written for the young. In these works there is the happiest mixture of reminiscence and story, teaching and moral conclusions as in, for instance, *The Treasure-hunting Smock-frock* (Kincskereső kis ködmön, 1918). Between the wars, as a serious journalist, he did indeed raise his voice against fascism, but as a narrative writer he remained in the 1900s.

The Prose of the Nyugat

The complete picture of *Nyugat*, therefore, includes a fair variety of prose as well as poetry. In terms of its aims nothing radically new was introduced in this field. Trends were further developed that had already been present at the end of the last century in the work of Gozsdu, Petelei, Lovik, Bródy and Thury, if on a higher level and in newer and more individual forms. A common factor in these trends was the rejection of certain old and tired conventions. The more important writers of that generation were in the main closer to the facts of contemporary society. They were impatient of idealization, "poetic justice", romantic embellishment of the real world, and easy literary solutions. They were not afraid of the problems confronting them. They rejected the anecdote, the type of narrative intent on transmitting immediate experience, with its tendency to switch suddenly from the main narrative to the interpolation of little tales and stories, which had become the traditional manner of the classics of nineteenth-century Hungarian literature and even later. They put in its place a more conscious concentration on artistic form; the emphasis on construction is noticeable in nearly all of them. Within these more general tendencies the work of Móricz, Kaffka, Kosztolányi, Tersánszky and in particular Babits's *The Sons of Death* (Halálfiai) represent that stream of twentieth-century realism which developed and renewed the traditions of the nineteenth century.

This was the period in which much greater attention to style began to be paid in Hungarian prose, and a variety of short story and novel forms developed.

53 Drama

Drama and Theatre

Of all the literary genres drama was the least remarkable in the *Nyugat* period. This was partly because Hungarian dramatic writing had little tradition behind it, and had been unable to pose any serious challenge to the great flood of shallow popular entertainment. A good play becomes a completed work of art only on the stage, and to achieve that end an audience is required cultivated enough to support theatres for the purpose. The audience needs to be willing to back works of artistic and social significance instead of "Establishment" works and easy entertainment. The Hungarian progressive movements of the time, however, were neither strong nor broadly based enough to provide the support required for a progressive theatre.

Yet in spite of all the difficulties, the standards of Hungarian theatre rose appreciably in the early years of the twentieth century. It was greatly stimulated by the work of the outstanding producer and director *Sándor Hevesi* (1873–1939). He supported naturalism on the stage, demanded a very high standard, and produced a whole sequence of fine contemporary plays from all over the world.

It was typical of contemporary Hungarian dramatic writing that many of its best plays were adaptations of novels, and those most closely connected with the life of Hungarian society. Such a work, for instance, is Móricz's *Gentlemen Make Merry* (Úri muri, 1928, 1942) which shows the inevitable decline of a class of Hungarian society. This novel was "improved" for the stage; the tragic ending was replaced by a happier one.

Of all the major trends in the international drama of the time it was naturalism which took pride of place on the Hungarian stage. And the better Hungarian plays became a more or less modest branch of this movement.

But the development which began at the turn of the century with the work of Bródy and Thury soon gave way to a flourishing commercial theatre.

Ferenc Molnár (1878-1952)

Ferenc Molnár was the most popular playwright of the period. He had great talents as a dramatist, but he lacked the appreciation of the noble human values necessary for true greatness. He originally studied law, and then turned to journalism. His name first became known between 1900 and 1910, and gradually he achieved a worldwide fame. At the time of the First World War he worked as a war correspondent sending some deeply moving reports from the Russian front. In 1918–19 he supported the Hungarian Revolution of 1918–19. He wrote novels, numerous essays and short articles. His book *The Pál Street Boys* (A Pál utcai fiúk, 1907), a touching adventure story for the young, was, and still is, particularly successful. *Music* (Muzsika, 1908), is a collection of obliquely poetic short stories written with slightly bitter humour. One of them, *Coal Thieves* (Széntolvajok) show a social interest uncharacteristic of the rest of Molnár's work.

From the beginning of his career he spent a great deal of time abroad, especially in Italy, Switzerland, Austria, and France. As a refugee from fascism he finally settled in the United States in 1940. It was there, in 1952, that he died.

His plays are mainly marked by an abundance of inventive ideas and a masterly theatrical technique. Here the main influence was Scribe. But his attitude to the world was closer to Wilde's. Other influences included the French writers of the "problem play", such as Bernstein, Bataille and Sardou as well as Hauptmann and Pirandello. He touched on a number of contemporary social and psychological issues, but mostly in a completely superficial way. His plays are a combination of Impressionism, naturalism and drawing-room comedy. They are given freshness by the ease of their construction and their sparkling dialogue, but on occasion border on the sentimental. They are neither the culmination of earlier trends nor an advance to something new. But they won popularity on the Budapest stage from the typical urban audiences of that time, and as far as audiences abroad were concerned, the usual stage situations and settings were embellished with a few Hungarian touches.

Ferenc Molnár took the theatre itself as his starting-point. The laws of the theatre directed his work—successfully. He gives his audience a spectacle, makes them laugh, and at the same time moralizes a little, makes fun, or is a little sentimental. Nor is he any stranger to a form of light cynicism. His work has connections both with enlightened rationalism and a kind of mysticism. As Molnár's informed and educated self finds expression in his plays, so too does his political naiveté and nostalgia. On the whole he is dominated by the need for a bourgeois existence, but one more honest than the one in existence, as can be seen when he uncovers the hypocrisies of bourgeois life. But the adoption of a more active social attitude is as alien to him as is any profundity of thought.

The central idea of *The Devil* (Az ördög, 1907), is taken from Faust, but beyond this there are few similarities. It is the question of female sexuality that occupies the foreground (suggesting perhaps a Freudian influence), and the play passes judgement on the cowardly bourgeois mentality which denies desire. *Liliom* (1909), which Puccini thought of setting to music, is still often played as a musical under the title of *Carousel*. The central character is a fair-ground operator who irresponsibly exploits a young servant girl from the city. The man, whose better self wants to redeem his earlier brutal behaviour, lapses back into his customary behaviour despite himself: the movement of the hand intended to be a caress turns into a slap. The play dealing with the lives of ordinary men with a certain sentimentality, combines aspects of naturalism and Symbolism.

The central character of *The Guardsman* (A testőr, 1910), is an actor, who is determined to test his wife's fidelity by seducing her in the guise of an officer of the guards. At the last minute, however, he reveals himself. The comic ending, where it is the wife who acts out the pretence that she was only playing a part, is a brilliant dénouement. The more serious aspect of the play—the question of rôle-playing in human affairs–is not really explored at all. Both *The Swan* (A hattyú, 1920), and *Olympia* (1928) satirize the life of a feudal aristocracy which has outlived its time. *Harmony* (Harmónia, 1923) makes fun of the dreams and idylls of the philistine bourgeoisie. The all-pervasive power of money is the theme of *One, Two, Three* (Egy, kettő, három, 1929), with its complicated plot, and the subject of *The Play's the Thing* (Játék a kastélyban, 1926), is play-acting itself; the birth of a play for the theatre. Here, as in *The Guardsman* or in one of the sections—*Marshall*—of the three-part *Theatre* (Színház), Molnár touches on the relationship of play-acting and reality.

Menyhért Lengyel (1880-1974)

The career of Menyhért Lengyel is somewhat similar to Molnár's. He worked as a journalist in the country before settling in the capital, joining the circle around *Nyugat*. At one time he directed a theatre. After numerous stays abroad he left the country in 1937 in the face of advancing fascism. He worked for many years in Hollywood and in Italy.

His most interesting work is *The Great Ruler* (A nagy fejedelem, 1907), which shows the strong influence of Ibsen, and deals with the conflict between power and justice. A statue is erected to a former ruler in a small town. It is only later in the play, just before the statue is to be unveiled, that a historian finds a new and decisive bundle of documents revealing that the ruler he had earlier celebrated as a noble character was in fact a bloodthirsty tyrant. All the various sections of society in the town turn against the scholar. In the end, it is the historian who is forced into failure before the statue which remains as a symbol of the endurance of power and hypocrisy.

Lengyel achieved international recognition with *Typhoon* (Taifun, 1909), even though it is a less interesting work. Much of its success is due to the subject-matter, the "yellow peril". Here the brilliant theatrical construction helps to produce suspense in the development of the plot. It makes the play theatrically effective, but fails to evoke a genuine dramatic conflict between two types of behaviour.

Lengyel's later plays follow the same path. However, the plot for the ballet *The Miraculous Mandarin* (A csodálatos mandarin) is particularly well-known because it was set to music by Béla Bartók. This work, written in an *art-nouveau* spirit, deals with ancient, primal passions (and the wild and tragic greatness of romantic love) in the style of Eastern myth.

The Plays of Milán Füst

Although he had no particular talents as a dramatist, the poet and novelist Milán Füst experimented with drama. He wrote his first play *The Unhappy Ones* (Boldogtalanok, 1915), in a naturalist style. This play probes with deeper and deeper insights into the moral and material misery of a semi-proletarian family living on the outskirts of the city. His characters develop into almost comical creatures, but Füst is able to bring to life the inner drama played out underneath surface appearances. This intellectual and psychological orientation is even more pronounced in *King Henry IV* (IV. Henrik király, 1931), which is a more characteristic work of his. He makes a universal human drama of the story of the ruler travelling to Canossa. The play deals with the struggles of the large-spirited human being capable of standing his ground against anyone, even when abandoned by others, and who in the many changes in his life lives through all the possible ranges of experience. This work is similar in its concern with those of the early years of the century which centre on the need for "individuality" and "human greatness". But the themes prevalent in the transitional period of the early twentieth century are perhaps to be found more distinctly in some of the works of Dezső Szomory and Béla Balázs.

Dezső Szomory

Dezső Szomory, who also produced a good many short stories, wrote historical plays tempered with subtle psychological studies of the characters (*The Grand Lady* — A nagyasszony, 1910; *Marie Antoinette* — Mária Antónia, 1913; *The Emperor Joseph II* — II. József császár, 1918). He also wrote social dramas with echoes of *art nouveau*. *Little Georgina, Dear Child* (Györgyike drága gyermek, 1912), is the most important of these. This play attacks the ultra-refinements of pseudo-morality, making an interesting and ironical use of irrational and grotesque elements. After a promising beginning Szomory succumbed to the temptations of the commercial theatre in his later work.

Béla Balázs (1884-1949)

Béla Balázs began as a poet, but later experimented with various media. He fought in the First World War, and then took an active part in the struggles of the Hungarian Republic of Councils. He was later forced to emigrate to Vienna to escape the White Terror of the counter-revolution, then to Berlin and finally to Moscow and there worked actively with other left-wing exiled writers on behalf of communism. He returned to Hungary in 1945 and died a few years later in Budapest.

His plays are strongly intellectual in character. He examines the development of the individual, the life of the artist, the relations between men and women in the light of moral and philosophical considerations. Some of his work is strongly influenced by Ibsen; on the other hand, his more arcane plays, shot through with a strong poetic element, show the influence of Maeterlinck. *Bluebeard's Castle* (A kékszakállú herceg vára) in particular achieved world fame because it was used by Béla Bartók as the libretto for his opera of that name. It was also one of his works which formed the basis of another of Bartók's compositions, the ballet *The Wooden Prince* (A fából faragott királyfi).

Béla Balázs wrote other libretti later on as well as short didactic pieces for Piscator's theatre. For him film represented the synthesis of music, visual art and expressive thought conceived according to the aesthetic principles of Wagner in his later years. The potential of film as a means of mass education also intrigued him, as his artistic interests began to move in a communist direction, and his theories exerted an influence on the Soviet films of the thirties. He worked on scripts for films both in Berlin and Moscow, and on his return to Hungary he took part in the development of Hungarian films. His script provided the groundwork for *Somewhere in Europe* (Valahol Európában, 1948). This was one of the first important productions of early post-war Hungarian films. His most important work in film aesthetics was *Der sichtbare Mensch* 1924.

Socialist Ideas and the Development of Modern Trends

(The Period between the Two World Wars)

54 Literature in the Interwar Years

The influence of *Nyugat* lasted until the 1918 Revolution. The chief *Nyugat* writers in the period following the revolution, important in themselves, can be regarded as already inseparable from the new directions literature was taking.

The New Aspirations

The most outstanding characteristic of the writers and artists of this period—which began fifteen years after the revolutions—was not that they were no longer predominantly concerned with national life and the role of the men and artists within it. It was twentieth-century life that interested them: it was not only the idyllic Biedermeier world which turned out to be false, or rather, unbearable, but also, for most of them, the artificial illusions of the inner man. They were aware of modern technology, promising new life and new possibilities, as well as the terror of modern mass destruction; they were aware of the socialist revolution born in the spirit of conscious, organized resistance, of the resultant fascist counter-revolution, as well as developments of modern science, constantly illuminating previously unsuspected areas. The arts were developing and expanding, and in part expressed the sharpening and occasionally exploding contradictions of both the modern metropolis, capitalism and imperialism. Partly as a contrast, the artists of the age reached back to older forms, free from mannerisms of *art nouveau*—a trend which meant a movement towards closer relationship with the common people, and the appearance of peasant styles. They were, therefore, working on the creation of a more vigorous and social literature as opposed to the exclusive concentration on self of the decadent period. The ideal of beauty was increasingly replaced by that of life, and the place of the writer, possibly socialist in his principles, but concerned with the writer as artist, was replaced by the writer actively involved in social matters. Literature reflects the futility of the twentieth-century world and protested against it. These writers wanted to create order out of chaos, but an order purged of artistic affectation. They wanted to make their readers see, with a minimum of personal reflection, the changing world

399

of society and nature. They exploded traditional forms in favour of new modes of writing or in opposition to the over-refined mannerisms of the past.

But there was no development of a single, unified style in this period, in fact the differences became even more pronounced. With hindsight, the most obvious tendencies were Expressionist–Activist and a Romantic–Surrealist in style, with peasant overtones, a vigorous and constructive form of creativity with classical and objective, though naive-realistic characteristics. A more intellectual approach encouraged the writing of essay. Regarded from another point of view and from an even greater distance in time, one can see attempts to relate to external objective and social conditions. These different styles and aims shift and change even in the work of a single writer and even intermingle within the same work.

Although these various trends are also grounded in the life of their own period, their social importance is less dominant than their writers' political stand. Yet writers' and artists' groupings and organizations were decided by their political attitudes, which frequently found admirable literary expression in their better works. The public and political trends in Hungarian literature were particularly pronounced, if not overwhelming, during this period. Those who were quick to grasp the manifestations of the external world had to adopt some sort of position on the social questions of the time.

Revolution and Counter-revolution

The ruin and devastation of the First World War made clear the brutal laws of war. The economic damage done to the country was one of the important factors in the discontent brewing among the masses, unallayed by the 1918 bourgeois revolution. The Communist Party, which was formed in 1918 and came to power in 1919, in coalition with the Social Democrats, was born of the international revolutionary movement of the twentieth century which went well beyond any spontaneous domestic development. With the socialist revolution, society headed bravely for the future. Banks and factories were nationalized, socialist measures multiplied, artistic treasures were also nationalized, and men, such as György Lukács and Zoltán Kodály, were placed in positions of leadership. But the counter-revolutionary forces, exploiting the weaknesses of the young regime, such as the nationalization instead of the expected re-distribution of land, came to power with the help of various foreign armies, and they restored the past as completely as they could. (The only difference was national independence from Austria and a condemned "liberalism".) They were nonetheless forced to resort to various socialist measures, yet the oppressions of the regime were better organized and more vicious than before. From the very beginning of the counter-revolutionary regime, a certain fascist tendency was noticeable. Not only during the White Terror of 1919 did they torture and murder in the most bestial manner those who took part in the revolution—killing a multitude of sympathizers as well—but in the 1920s, following the "consolidation", they also tortured and executed numerous imprisoned members of the illegal Communist Party. And it was not only the communists who went through the prisons of the Horthy regime; many radical and progressive thinkers suffered the same fate.

The semi-feudalist social system which had outlived its usefulness now forcibly restored, had almost paralysed the economy, already greatly damaged as a result of the war and the subsequent upheavals. The position of the oppressed masses consequently became a question of national survival, especially in the 1930s, in the shadow of spreading German imperialism. In bad years a large proportion of the agricultural workers literally starved, but the often unemployed workers in the cities fared little better. The country became the nation of "three million beggars". This was particularly true in the Depression of the 1930s which brought the workers to the verge of revolution once again.

The regime attempted to blame the economic ills of the country on the Peace Treaty of 1919, which had greatly reduced the territory of Hungary, and attempted to channel the passions building up against neighbouring peoples. The ambition to regain the lost territories was encouraged by German fascism, and as a result the country became an ally of German imperialism, prepared to help Hungary to achieve these aims, and as a result Hungary became embroiled in the war against Yugoslavia and the Soviet Union. The inner sympathies of the reactionary regime also were naturally oriented towards the fascist regimes, and they introduced racial discrimination against the Jews—especially in the *numerus clausus* limiting the entry to universities—as soon as it had gained control; the excuse was that Jewish intellectuals had played a considerable role during the 1919 revolution. Although the years of widespread terror were broken by the more liberal period when István Bethlen was Prime Minister, and tried to establish good relations with Western democracies during the '30s, as soon as Gyula Gömbös, an admirer of Hitler, acceded to the Premiership, many anti-Semitic laws were passed and relations with Germany strengthened.

After the tide turned against Germany, and after the destruction of the 200,000-strong Hungarian army, the regime started to put out feelers for the possibility of a withdrawal from the war. In reprisal, Germany occupied Hungary in the spring of 1944, and in the autumn of that year they installed their most contemptible collaborators, the hordes of the Arrow-cross Party, under Szálasy in command, thus setting up a total fascist dictatorship. Left-wing forces in Hungary attempted to demonstrate their opposition to the war and to fascism in different ways, by legal and illegal publications, occasional mass demonstrations, some armed action, and the organization of an opposition in the army. Many died in this resistance, but they could not achieve any significant results; the machine which had been built up over the years and which had the support of the occupying German forces, was too powerful.

The conditions of publishing were to a certain extent inimical (and had been all through the interwar years) to the propagation of the truth. Until the German occupation the anti-revolutionary regime had given an appearance of democracy, one of the manifestations of which was the apparent freedom of the press. There was no lack of subjects, but a lack of money, or rather the fear of a lack of customers, often restrained writers and publishers. There was also the distinct possibility of lawsuits, and it could also happen that the local policemen beat up the local peasant-writer using the capital as a forum for his works on fine arts, sociology or politics. But those writers who were socially determined enough, could still make themselves partially heard, and those works which could not be published inside Hungary were either published through one of the emigré outlets or in the publishing houses of the Hungarian minorities in neighbouring countries.

Revolutionary Socialist Groupings

The earliest avant-garde periodical for literature and the fine arts, with a vigorous pacifist programme, first appeared in 1915, during the First World War. It was called *A Tett* (The Deed). After it was first banned, it appeared from 1916 to 1919 in a more moderate guise under the title *MA* (Today). Authors who, due to their political radicalism, were dissatisfied with the attitude of current periodicals formed this circle, and during the time of the Hungarian Republic of Councils played a predominant role in the press, becoming the nucleus of the later groups of communist writers.

Those writers who played any sort of part during the Revolution of 1918–19 were imprisoned and generally harassed during the counter-revolution. Those particularly compromised were mostly forced to emigrate. At first they published rather short-lived periodicals and then books in Vienna, later they mostly operated in Berlin, and worked in theatre and films. After Hitler came to power, the majority of the communist emigré writers took refuge in the Soviet Union, where they pursued both their political and literary activities. The non-communist emigrés for the most part returned home in the 1920s, during what was called the "consolidation". On the whole the counter-revolution scattered the ranks of the communists, but they made valiant efforts to organize their forces. By the time, however, they were able to work under more stable conditions in the Soviet Union, the personality cult was developing, and this influenced their work and activities. Their most important periodical there later became the *Új Hang* (New Voice, 1938–1941) which followed the politics of the Popular Front. Those in Hungary, mainly younger writers, first grouped themselves around the review *100%* (1927–1930), and after it was banned, they flocked to *Gondolat* (Thought, 1936–1937), which also supported the radical, anti-fascist front. An important forum for their views was the Rumanian *Korunk* (Our Age, 1926–1940) as well as the Czech *Az Út* (The Road, 1931–1936). The fact that they were either scattered in exile or oppressed at home was partly responsible for the divisions that arose among them; nonetheless their work influenced a wide range of progressive intellectuals.

The Populist Writers

The group of populist (népi) writers was formed during the 1920s, and they became the most influential writers' groups of twentieth-century Hungarian literary and one of ideological life. The core of their beliefs was that after the massive 1919 defeat of the proletariat, and consequently the revolution, it would be the peasants who, after a radical land reform, would provide the mass strength for national renewal and the base for the emergence of a new middle-class, intellectual leadership. This movement was widespread, but also full of internal contradictions. Some of its members came from the ranks of poor peasants, the rest were intellectuals in sympathy with them and naturally the workers as well. Not only were they hostile to the growth of the bourgeoisie, but they also disliked the type of socialism which was coming into being in the Soviet Union. One of their main theoreticians, László Németh, wanted to create "quality socialism" in Hungary, to be based on economic and intellectual communities created by peasant unions and which would build a bridge between East and West. At the same time some of their members held that the only way ahead lay in a certain kind of middle-class development. The left wing of the populist writers kept in contact with the workers' movements (József Darvas, Ferenc Erdei). But there were also members of the movement, who were closer to fascist ideology and occasionally even to the fascist movement itself.

Yet in spite of their differences, there were many similarities in their ideas; they all agreed on the need to change the lives of the peasants who made up the great majority of the population. Their literary, ideological and sociological forum was the periodical *Válasz* (Answer, 1934–1938), then later *Kelet Népe* (People of the East, 1935–1942).

Middle-class Trends

Some of the progressive bourgeois intellectuals published their work in the review *A Toll* (The Pen, 1914–1938) as well as *Nyugat;* later *Szép Szó* (Fine Words, 1936–1939) attracted some of them. The development of opposing camps of "urban" and *népi* writers became a very unfortunate fact of literary life. The "urban" writers reacted more sensitively to the expression of fascist tendencies, they were more concerned with world literature, and they were unsympathetic towards peasant demands and promising peasant talents. The anti-capitalism of the *népi* writers often showed itself in a lack of understanding of bourgeois culture and a certain provincialism, indeed some of them were even anti-Semitic.

The changing vagaries of political life naturally influenced changes and development in literary "fronts"; sometimes the inner contradictions were heightened, sometimes lessened. During the forties the fascist danger from the Third Reich led to the formation of anti-fascist intellectual fronts among the intellectuals. The illegal Communist Party did its best to help these activities (it was to this end that Gyula Illyés edited the *Magyar Csillag* (Hungarian Star, successor to *Nyugat*) from 1941 till 1944, but they remained insufficiently organized and relatively powerless.

Although they played no major part in the new literary currents, conservative writers had great powers in the official literary life of that period. The Academy and the other leading literary associations were under their control. Their leader, Ferenc Herczeg, was the only remaining "elder" writer, and was heaped with official honours. The petty-bourgeois weekly *Új Idők* (New Times), which he edited, and *Napkelet* (Sunrise, 1923–1940) became their main mouthpieces and the conservative rivals of *Nyugat*. The *Protestáns Szemle* (Protestant Review, 1899–1944) and the Catholic *Vigilia* (from 1935) were also vehicles for conservatives, but also provided a forum for their more modern writers.

There were many, moreover, who followed a middle way from thinking men open to new influences to popular writers intent on satisfying the market and winning official goodwill with their entertainments. But none of the talented young writers came from their ranks.

The younger men started a few reviews with no decided social views nor any particular literary attitude, but they rarely lasted. Among the independent publications which appeared over the years, the *Pesti Napló* (Pest Diary), a daily with a left-wing bourgeois bias, played an important role in opening the pages of its Sunday literary supplement for talented writers.

The new literature had already reached many more classes of readers, and was welcomed by them, than had been possible earlier through *Nyugat,* even though this popularity could scarcely compete with the flood of "official" or different kinds of light literature.

The Position of the Arts

The unparalleled burgeoning of the arts in the first twenty years of the century could not fail to lose its momentum under the depressing conditions of the counter-revolutionary regime. Many fine artists left the country either for openly political reasons or because of lack of opportunity. The sculptor József Csáky and László Mészáros, the painters Béla Uitz, László Moholy-Nagy and Victor Vasarely, the conductor Eugene Ormandy, the violinists Joseph Szigeti and Endre Gertler, the architect Marcel Breuer and the film directors Alexander Korda and Michael Curtis all settled abroad. The growth of fascism at the beginning of the Second World War also forced Béla Bartók to emigrate. The fact that after the First World War Hungary had become a minor power with limited outlets, after having been an important part of the great Austro-Hungarian Empire, was also a reason for the emigration of all these gifted people.

On the other hand, many fine artists continued to work within the country. There were in particular many outstanding painters: Gyula Derkovits, József Egry, István Nagy, Aurél Bernáth, Róbert Berény, Vilmos Aba Novák, Lajos Vajda, Jenő Barcsay and others. It was during this time that the sculptors Ferenc Medgyessy, Béni Ferenczy and others produced their best work, and in addition to the two great masters of music, Bartók and Kodály, Ernő Dohnányi, Leo Weiner and Sándor Veress composed notable works. Modern architecture also established itself in the thirties and forties, although it was official policy, especially in the earlier years, to encourage older styles, such as the Baroque. The film industry, which had made a very promising beginning in the first twenty years of the century, was the art most influenced by financial considerations, and operated on a very low, mostly commercial level, and only produced one or two good films (those of Pál Fejes and István Szőts).

The theatre managed to maintain the standards reached in previous years, due to the many excellent producers and actors available, but the writing of plays made little progress as a whole. It is true, however, that the period did produce certain plays of an introspective cast, of such a high standard that they could be validly performed abroad, and which were nonetheless solidly based on Hungarian literary traditions as well as the facts of Hungarian life. The successful plays of Ferenc Molnár were written during this period. Plays which were written to satisfy the needs of the commercial theatres by the writers of this period did not really rank as dramatic literature. The plays which were actually staged were lighter and more colourful than those which were published in book form. For those who wrote for the stage Ferenc Molnár was the model, but even the better writers could not approach his professional standards.

The Liberation

In 1944–45, the Soviet army liberated the country from the German occupation and from fascism—at the price of hard battles in which they were modestly assisted by the actions of the Hungarian partisans and the tardily formed democratic army. This was followed by changes in society and the lives of artists. Not only was the damage caused by the war particularly heavy—a large section of the capital was in ruins—but the fascist terror had taken the lives of hundreds of thousands: more than a hundred novelists, literary historians and journalists, for instance, were killed, among them many outstanding talents.

After the damage was repaired, the nation applied itself to the building of a new society. It increasingly adopted socialist measures and a socialist policy, following inter-party struggles. In the early stages, even under the conditions, it was writers of the past twenty years who were most vocal. The activities of a large proportion of them were identified with the developments, and the emigrés who returned contributed towards the new literary life of their country. On the other hand, in the course of the revolution and its aftermath a few of the older writers left the country and continued to publish their works in new Western emigré outlets. Many of the earlier writers either completely withdrew or were forbidden to publish for years, especially between 1949 and 1954. They have now, however, all returned to the literary scene. With liberation and the building of socialism, Hungarian literature began a new period and a new stage of development.

55 The Avant-garde: Progress and Indecision

The Hungarian Avant-garde

Lajos Kassák was the editor and leading personality of the new review *A Tett* (The Deed), and Dezső Szabó wrote the leading article in its first number which appeared in 1915. It opened with a stentorian proclamation of principle and a name which indicated intentions of immediate activity. There was ten years' difference in age between Kassák and Ady, but Kassák was only one year older than another of the "great men" of *Nyugat*—Árpád Tóth, and Dezső Szabó was the same age as the older men in that group, indeed he had earlier been connected with it. Their rejection of it, consequently, could not be explained in terms of a generation gap, but rather as a result of their inner need and their literary development. The two writers came from different backgrounds and they soon parted, but their short meeting was more than just chance. They both hoped to build something new, comparable to *Nyugat*, but they were also linked by the fact that they held the works of Endre Ady in the highest esteem, and felt most drawn to him. Their future was also similar. They both originated important developments in literature, though later the groups they led were considerably smaller. Those who took their first steps on roads pioneered by these two, and under the influence of their theories, moved further and further out of the orbit of their former masters—though the original influences were always perceptible in their work.

At the crest of the wave both Lajos Kassák and Dezső Szabó insisted that certain burning social issues could not be avoided. They both had an important, and Kassák a vital, role in the development of a new, life-affirming form of art, a new literary style which in expression and structure suited the needs of the time. It was Kassák who first drew attention to the urban proletariat and to the socialist workers' literature then beginning to appear. Dezső Szabó, who a few years later became the intellectual and aesthetic leader of the counter-revolution, strengthened and modified the Móricz-derived peasant cult with his own pseudo-peasant fables. He paved the way for the activities of the "populist writers" coterie, with their contradictory attitudes. Kassák's work, after the failure of the 1918–19 Revolution, produced nothing substantially new, especially when compared to the "aestheticist" group at *Nyugat*. These characteristics later showed affinities with the "urban" bourgeois writers' apolitical humanism.

Of the two, Kassák, who appeared later on the literary scene, was the first to play an important part. His influence lasted longer, and there was an impetus in his work which could have been the beginnings of a sound literary movement.

Lajos Kassák (1887-1967)

Although his poorly-paid father wanted to help him to an education, he became a locksmith and then an ironworker. He took part in the organization of the strikes of 1905, and later roamed as a locksmith through Western Europe, and became familiar not only with a worker's and wanderer's life but also life in the metropolis, educating himself at the same time in modern movements in art. He wrote poems during his journey and sent them home for publication. Although he had been writing earlier, it was the world of art revealed to him during this period which awoke his intense love for the arts. After his return home he worked in factories in the capital for a while, and then turned to a life of literature and art. He soon became the leading figure in a group of left-wing young writers feverishly intent on new ideas and new ways.

Epic in a Wagnerian Mould (Éposz Wagner maszkjában), his first volume of poetry, appeared in 1915. Although *Nyugat* recognized his talent, they always remained aloof, and Babits distanced himself from Kassák's group with a satirical article; but even more revolutionary authors emerged from Kassák's circle at the end of the war. During the period of the Hungarian Republic of Councils he was active in the organization of cultural life, but he found himself in opposition to the leading revolutionary, Béla Kun, over the direction of literature by the Party. During the counter-revolution he was imprisoned; after his release he took refuge in Vienna, where he took part in emigré activities. He returned home in 1926, but no longer played a part in the workers' movement. During the twenties and thirties he edited several long or short-lived art reviews with a strong social content (*Kortárs* — Contemporary; *Dokumentum* — Document; *Munka* — Work). He was highly respected by his young avant-garde followers. From the beginning of the 1920s he also worked in the visual arts, creating Constructivist architectural designs and collages.

His poems showed Expressionist, Futurist and decadent tendencies. His extravagant and turbulent hopes for the future which he expressed were soon balanced by the firm and disciplined structure of his verse, though the stream of words was governed by neither rhyme nor stress, nor regular rhythm. It showed the influence of both Whitman and Apollinaire. Nor were the poems divided into verses. A significant proportion of them are very definitely structured. His words, with their concrete, conceptual meanings, emotional associations fit solidly into the construction of the poem, or rather, they are the construction, and in some lines, and in the poem as a whole, they follow one another in vigorous curves. The adjectives in his poems, as opposed to the loosely used decorative adjectives of Impressionism and *art nouveau*, cannot be interchanged to quite the same extent; the word order is tauter, a tautness necessary for the formation of the structure, aided by the fact that Kassák was clearly aiming for simplicity on the one hand, and yet on the other has produced a majestic, almost Biblical effect: every word is weighed like the speech of the ancients. They seem to carry universal meanings; "mountain", "gate", "town", "fruit", "worker", "creek", "house" carry this biblical echo through their use in the poem.

The Construction of a New World of Art

In his early stages Kassák identified himself with the revolutionary workers' movement, but from the 1920s onwards he moved further and further away as he consciously aimed at a fundamental renewal of poetry and painting and the re-creation of a clearly constructed world of art. He went beyond the expression of the personal self found in bourgeois poetry; and if he seems to speak personally in many of his poems, this "I" is not his real persona, it is a universal man or worker who observes the world and who responds to everything, these two melt into one another. The earlier bold, "tight" and later freer associations often weave inner and external perceptions into one another.

During the revolutionary period a strong sense of social dissatisfaction was to be found in his poems. These poems are dynamic; modern technologies and inventions play a large part in his mode of seeing and expressing. Driving-belts, soaring bridges, reverberating sheets of steel, high-tension cables all testify in his world to Man's "self-realization". The prime mover, the combatant for this is the working class, endowed with fabulous powers. A working class which is still cruelly oppressed by modern society:

> *Someone has preached in stupidity: We are the force!*
> *Creation! Life! In a moment the flames of joy burnt out the centuries*
> *of pogroms from the head of Jews,*
> *Street-walkers wiped the masks of shame from their bodies,*
> *Every day emaciated mothers supported their sons with rickets*
> *and even the oldest workers shook off the terrors of*
> *factories, churches and pubs.*

Everyone threw themselves into the joys of fulfilment...
Then suddenly the vision was obscured,
in a moment no one could feel their partners beside them,
and the resounding guns mercilessly injected them with death.

(*Public Meeting* — Népgyűlés)

Kassák lamented the crushed revolution with the *Song of the Bonfires* (Máglyák éne-kelnek, 1920)—a poem in a lyrical style somewhat similar to that of Mayakovski, but more loosely structured. But from then on his work no longer reflected a rev-olutionary tone. In *The Horse Dies, the Birds Fly Out* (A ló meghal, a madarak kire-pülnek), faith in the ripening of the new age and complete despair alternate with each other. The work he produced in the twenties shows affinities with Surrealism. Later on they became sadder in tone, and in them he retreated to a self-constrained world. Instead of the vigour of battle, he turned to the ethos of building a new world (*The Greeting of Masters*—Mesterek köszöntése), or from major events to the moments of everyday life: his work reflected the attitude of an observer rather than that of an activist. This change was partly caused by the altered conditions of society around him. He writes, for instance, in a later poem called *Saturday* (Szombat):

My clasped hands rest in my lap.
It is evening.
The city is clothed in dark velvet.
The depth of the silence is impenetrable.
This is my best hour.
I have done my chores,
before me a glass of wine
I shall be more humble and tender if I empty it
without
anxious thoughts
weak fears.

He did not gain importance through any individual poem but rather through the value of his pioneering work in poetry taken as a whole. The poem which appears most often in anthologies is his *Craftsmen* (Mesteremberek), written in 1915, with its socialist outlook, uniting the great powers of expression and firm construction of his earlier poems.

His prose works are more traditional in style, though less so in theme. They link naturalism with proletarian realism, the most important being *The Life of a Man* (Egy ember élete, 1928–1939). This book is an autobiography dealing with the events of his life up to the moment when he was forced to emigrate. In it he describes how as a child he chose the path his life was to take, how he took this road and followed it until he rose from a locksmith's apprentice to become an acknowledged artist. This was the end of a period in his life in more than one respect. In the course of it, he left his small community and roamed Europe. He came to know the great cities, the world of revolutionary movements beginning to shake Europe, and took part in them. Soberly, without romantic protestations of guilt, he describes his slow growth into maturity in a series of vivid descriptions. This work is distantly related to the *Bildungsroman* of Goethe and Keller, and more closely, to the autobiographical novels of Gorki and Nexö, even though it does not quite equal the deep humanity of Gorki's or his gift for the living detail.

Another important work, *Angyalföld* (1929) is a novel which immortalizes the outer suburb of Budapest called Angyalföld (Land of the Angels). The novel centres on the difficult development of a young working-class lad and his growing consciousness of his own identity.

Dezső Szabó (1879-1945)

Kassák expressed in his poems both dynamism and irrationality, and paints in his poems and visual art the needs of the new world coming to birth. In his prose, he aimed at the objective grasp of social realities as yet unexposed by others. Dezső Szabó turned prose into something "lyrical"; he expressed discontent and pantheistic joy in the passionate rhetoric of his own desires and hopes.

Dezső Szabó was born in Kolozsvár in Transylvania, became a teacher of French and Hungarian, and taught in small towns. At first he was interested in language and literature, but his absorption with the philosophy of Nietzsche later overpowered his interest in French culture. He published his first articles in *Nyugat*. He went to Budapest during the revolution, but later found himself in opposition to the Hungarian Republic of Councils. Then in the summer of 1919 he published his novel *The Village that was Swept Away* (Az elsodort falu, 1919). It appeared in several volumes, an ideologically confused racist work, which passed unnoticed until the counter-revolution and then several editions were published. Engrossed with his vocation, capable of theatrical poses and with a striking personality, he attracted many of the young intellectuals. When he realized that the counter-revolution was not after all his "real" Hungarian revolution, he turned passionately against it. Although his racial theories and his irrational philosophy often coincided with its tenets, he was a determined opponent of fascism and all its Hungarian supporters. More and more out of touch with the times, increasingly bitter, he quarrelled with nearly everyone, seeing himself as a tragic genius, mainly publishing his work in his own publications. He died during the siege of Budapest.

His most important work, *The Village that was Swept Away*, was an attempt to

411

give a picture of the years before the war, and of society during the revolution and the war which ended with the collapse of the country, and was designed to point the way to a possible future. In it he described with telling effect the stifling, neurotic lives of provincial intellectuals, the breakdown of old values, and the decadence of the rootless life of artists in the city. But in his tale, it was a descendent of the old nobility who found the answer; he returned to the village and married a peasant girl. He embodies the idea of strength and activity in the face of nervous unease, and unconquerable life in the face of destruction. Tolstoy's revolt from civilization in favour of peasant life, Nietzsche's mythology, and the naive romanticism of Mór Jókai all meet in this novel. The style is a synthesis of Romanticism, naturalism and Expressionism. Dezső Szabó's heroes live at a very intense level. They embrace, they laugh, they weep, they harvest and eat, they are either overcome by tremendous wrath or great goodness. Their opponents are usually sick, life-denying characters. These extremes are not really appropriate for an epic canvas of the twentieth century. On the other hand, Dezső Szabó with his verbal mastery possesses a capacity to create great dramatic scenes. His dynamic phrases contain individually coined words, his unexpectedly tightly structured, sweeping sentences bring vividly to life the intoxication of the crowd with war, the terror of refugees forced from their land, the soldiers' increasing desire for life, men, sated with killing, who discover one another while celebrating peace.

The story of a musical genius hounded to death is the theme of *Help!* (Segítség!, 1925). It is too romantic, but Szabó is merciless in his ridicule of the "notables" and the characteristic types of the counter-revolutionary regime. Here, his characters are outstanding; their ludicrous nature is set against the tragedy they cause. In a satirical short story called *The Resurrection at Makucska* (Feltámadás Makucskán, 1932), an old village disturbs the Easter holiday by producing a genuine resurrection. The affair becomes a national scandal and ends up in Parliament where the bickering ministers are finally united behind the statement of the Prime Minister's; that the resurrection in a Hungarian village would have to be suppressed with bayonets if necessary, because "Hungarian history recognizes the living and recognizes the dead, but does not recognize the resurrections or the resurrected". His other novels are not so good, and some are complete failures, and his output of short stories was modest. His bold dynamic style, with the coinage of words and subtle word associations, is very appealing at first reading, but his mannerisms are apt to prove wearisome on second reading. The populist writers took over his passionate commitment to the national interest and his orientation towards the peasants as well as some of his ideas, but the only writer to be influenced by his descriptive style was Áron Tamási.

56 Attila József (1905-1937)

In the Hungarian literature of this century only Attila József's lyrical poetry can rank in greatness with Ady's, although the character of their work is very different, and their lives developed along very different lines. Their position in history, and the different nature of their goals mark this contrast. Ady's task was to innovate, start a literary revolution, József's to unite and fulfil. Ady's fresh new voice exploded suddenly on to the Hungarian literary scene; József slowly developed and matured over a period of ten years in forming his own totally new creative world. His role, and the value of his work, were consequently slow to gain recognition.

His Life

Attila József was born in one of the working-class districts of the capital, the third child of a part-Hungarian, part-Rumanian soapmaker and his washer-woman wife. When he was three years old, his father, in an attempt to improve their miserable lot, left in order to emigrate to America, hoping to be better able to support the family from there. This did not happen, but he never returned to his wife and children. Attila was fostered out in the country for some time, but later returned to endure all the privations and miseries of a slum child in the capital. In 1919 his mother died, and the sense of loss and loneliness which possessed him was given no relief by the treatment meted out to him as a poor relative by his older sister's husband, a lawyer, who provided only for his most basic needs, and had him educated in the provinces. He published his first booklet of verse at seventeen, with the help of Gyula Juhász. In Szeged he studied arts; in 1925 he went to Vienna and in 1926-7 to Paris, where he continued to study in poor and miserable conditions. During this period he became familiar with Marxism and the workers' movement as well as the attitudes and aspirations of contemporary artists. His books appeared one after another, but no one recognized their importance. His opposition to the existing social order deepened, and after an earlier casual association he joined the illegal Communist Party in 1930.

In the early thirties he took an active part in the work of the Party, and indeed, his volume of revolutionary verse, published in 1930, was seized by the authorities, and he himself was often prosecuted. His work in the movement brought him friendship and appreciation among the workers. He lived with Judit Szántó who linked him even more closely to the Party. His intellectual activities, which will be discussed in the chapter on literary achievements, also began around this time.

In the early 1930s, for various reasons—partly theoretical, partly personal—he came into conflict with the Communist Party and was expelled. He was unable to find work, being without any qualifications—he never finished university. Often entirely destitute, he only just managed to survive on his meagre earnings from his writing. The volume entitled *Night in the Slums* (Külvárosi éj), which appeared in 1932, revealed his full maturity as poet, yet the critics still failed to comprehend him. More isolated than ever, he had a breakdown, and the psychoanalytic treatment he underwent did him no good.

In 1934 a collection of his work appeared entitled *The Bear's Dance* (Medvetánc), and in 1936 a final volume, *It Hurts a Lot* (Nagyon fáj). A few critics were by this time giving him the attention he deserved, and he became one of the editors of the review *Szép Szó* (Fine Word), begun in 1936. But the wider recognition came too late; his private life had become extremely unhappy, he was separated from his life companion and his love for another woman was not returned. He was also embittered by the fact that he was not chosen as the Hungarian representative to the Soviet Writers' Congress. He broke down again, and was forced to return to the sanatorium at the expense of sympathizers. This was an intense humiliation for him, a man who had been tortured by the sense of being reduced to dependance on strangers since childhood. He had, moreover, lost effective control of the review *Szép Szó*. When, in the late autumn of 1937, in a small village by Lake Balaton, where his sisters had brought him to recuperate, he finally believed he was uncurable, he threw himself under a train.

Appreciation of his literary importance only began to grow after his death, but official recognition could and did only come with the arrival of a democratic Hungary.

His Work

At the outset of his career, there was no dearth of educated and talented poets. The first generation of the poets of *Nyugat* were at the peak of their careers, and the new wave of poets had already made their *début*. Verses inspired by Expressionism, Futurism or Surrealism were by this time as hackneyed as the old folk songs rejuvenated and employed in the modern idiom. In his first volumes Attila József showed himself to be a gifted poet, and his work was already marked with the imprint of his own personality; yet the whole of his creative being had not fully emerged. From Kosztolányi he took a certain powerful realism, devoid of all illusion, and the ability to respond to the immediacy of the moment; from Gyula Juhász an intimacy with his country and his fellow man, the lyrical expression of his deeply compassionate feeling for the poor; from Babits his pursuit of Classicism. Later he acquired from Kassák a more daring and expressive form of construction, broke away from conventional verse patterns, and, again like Kassák, made use of modern scientific and technical words and phrases. Contemporary writers awoke his interest in the simple rhythms of the folk song, and the dissonant forms of its first beginnings. But after his year in Paris, his verse showed the influence not only of Surrealism but also of the revolutionary zeal of Ady and Mayakovski, the raw sincerity and turbulence of Villon's verse and the descriptive lyricism of Verhaeren. Yet despite these marked influences on his work it was always original and unique, and its originality and importance stands out even more clearly when we look at it as a whole. One of his earliest masterpieces is a sonnet, *Study of a Head* (Tanulmányfej), which displays the influence of Gyula Juhász and Dezső Kosztolányi. The dense splendour of the epithets in places recalls these earlier poets, but the face he is looking at—that of a vagabond or labourer seated in shadow—is from the depths of a social class neither of them ever penetrated. The precision in the construction of the poem also surpasses the work of the two who influenced it. From the infinity of early morning the picture narrows to the enclosed room, to the man settling there, the face, and finally the eye. As the sense of space narrows down, so the mood deepens: from observing the sleepy atmosphere of the morning outside to the consciousness of a ruin of a life within. There are other, later masterpieces related to this sonnet, *Hunger* (Éhség) focussing on the lunch-break of a handful of farm labourers, or the intimate tone of *A Tired Man* (Megfáradt ember).

He also learned his craft from other sources. The simple melodies of the folk song are honed to perfection in each line and verse, as in *Now Reeds Sway* (Holott náddal ringat), and *Coral Beads* (Klárisok). He defines and reveals the social bitterness implicit in other folk poems, as in his "Poor Man" poems, the *Ballad of the Poor Man* (Szegényember balladája), *The Poor Man's Lover* (Szegényember szeretője). He finds his rhythms occasionally in the free association of Surrealist verse, in a style which is at once formal and grotesque, as in the cycle of *Medallions* (Medáliák), introducing us by turns into a world of terror and primitive panic and one of simple and happy wonder. In his poems echoes of Villon and Brecht seem to resound in the turbulence and bitterness of the abandoned workers in their struggle, as in the *Ballad of Capital Profit* (A tőkehaszon balladája). Mayakovski's dramatically revolutionary cry becomes warmer, more cordial in József's *Socialists* (Szocialisták) and *The Crowd* (Tömeg), melting into prose in the lines that tell of demonstrations and the struggle for the revolution. There are poems about the urge to be one with the world, or affirmations of that unity, sometimes expressing an enthusiastic pantheism, sometimes with an open-hearted simplicity: *Bless you with Sorrow, with Joy* (Áldalak búval, vigalommal), *See?...* (Látod?...). The passionate desire to improve, to change, is intermingled, entwined in his poetry with the torments of Expressionism (*A Fine Summer Evening*—Szép nyári este van); yet side by side with it can be found the exquisitely precise description of the smaller things in life, as in *The Ant* (Hangya).

The lyrical qualities of his poetry gradually intensified, but did not reach their full flowering until 1931. The works he wrote at that time, of great poetic depth and dimension, contain many of the influences already mentioned, but they have been fused and changed in this new, epoch-making poetry.

Description and Reflection

His greatest poems are his poems of description and reflection. This, however, is not to imply a rigid categorization, or even a firm definition, since both romantic sentiment and political beliefs are equally present in each of these "categories"; yet concept and objective description are very closely connected in Attila József's mature poetry.

Descriptive poetry has a long tradition behind it in Hungarian literature. Sándor Petőfi's verses describing the Hungarian Great Plain and the people living there gave a realistic picture of them and mirrored a calm self-confidence; a similar attitude permeates part of the narrative works of János Arany. Nature provided a wealth of inspiration for both of them. This tradition was transmitted to Attila József through the *Nyugat* poet Gyula Juhász. József's objective portrayal of reality, however, was intermingled with the subjective trends of the time: the material world in its existing forms of time and space varied and dissolved according to the writer's state of mind.

Representation of Reality

József was interested in representing the material external world, and in stressing that the order within it was determined by material and objective laws... "I am sitting here on a glittering wall of rocks"; "I am standing at the corner of the ironworks..." he wrote. He placed his all-observing self on a spot immovable in space and determined in time: by the trunk of a weather-worn, "rust-leaved" tree leaning out of the twilight; or on the top of a hill overlooking all below it. He saw and expressed the material facts of the external world which the subjective inner self cannot change: material things, social conditions, universal laws. In *Tiszazug*, the fleecy softness of twilight gives way to the icy hardness of the night sky, and the apparently peaceful village is revealed as lifeless and numb. Or, in *My Country*

(Hazám), his eyes fall on sleeping figures in the street, jolting him out of the daze of the "airy, mild, warm" spring night. The man escaping into the magic of youthful memories is reminded by the cell-bars of the coldly sparkling stars above him and the dull sound of a clock breaking the silence that the world is locked into the indissoluble bonds of time and space (*Consciousness—Eszmélet*). Not only does the external world recover its own objective character in his poetry, but we are made aware of its tangible, palpable character in every line.

BY THE DANUBE

1

On the bottom step that from the wharf descends
I sat, and watched a melon-rind float by.
I hardly heard, wrapped in my destined ends,
To surface chat the silent depth reply.
As if it flowed from my own heart in spate,
Wise was the Danube, turbulent and great.

Like a man's muscles bending at his toil,
Hammering, pitching, leaning on the spade,
So bulged and then contracted in recoil
Each wave that rippling in the current played.
It rocked me like my mother, told me a wealth
Of tales, and washed out all the city's filth.

And drops of rain began to fall, but then,
As though their fall had no effect, they stopped.
Yet still, like one who stayed at the long rain
Out of a cave, my gaze I never dropped
Below the horizon. Endlessly to waste,
Drably like rain fell all bright things, the past.

The Danube just flowed on. And playfully
The ripples laughed at me as I reclined,
A child on his prolific mother's knee
Resting, while other thoughts engaged her mind.
They trembled in time's flow and in its wake
As tottering tombstones in a graveyard shake.

2

I am he who has gazed a hundred thousand years
On that which he now sees for the first time.
One moment, and fulfilled all time appears
In a hundred thousand forbears' eyes and mine.

I see what they could not because they must
Drag hoes, kill and embrace, for this enrolled,
And they, who have descended into dust
See what I do not, if the truth be told.

We know each other as sorrow and delight.
I, in the past, they in the present live.
They hold the pencil in the poem I write.
I feel them and evoke what they now give.

3

My mother was Cumanian, and half Szekler
My father half Rumanian or entire.
The nurture from my mother's mouth was nectar
And from my father's lips the truth was pure.
When I stir, they embrace. Then, soon or late,
This makes me sad. This is mortality.
Of this I am made. Such words as these: Just wait
Until we are no more—they speak to me.

They speak to me, for now I am they, robust
Despite whatever weakness made me frail,
And I think back that I am more than most:
Each ancestor am I, to the first cell.
I am the Forbear split and multiplied
To make my father and my mother whole;
My father and mother then in turn divide,
and so I am made one, a single soul.

I am the world; all that is past exists;
Where nations hurl themselves against each other,
With me in death the conqueror's victory lasts,
In me the anguish gnaws of those they smother.
Árpád, Zalán, Werbőczy, Dózsa, Turks,
Tartars, Rumanians, Slovaks, storm this heart.
If in great depths a quiet future lurks,
It owes the past, to-day's Hungarians, part.

418

I want to work. Enough of conflict goes
Into that need which must confess the past.
The Danube's tender ripples which compose
Past, present, future, hold each other fast.
The battle which our ancestors once fought
Through recollection is resolved in peace,
And settling at long last the price of thought,
This is our task, and none too short its lease.

(Translated by Vernon Watkins)

Constructive Poetic Structure

This tangible quality does not only emphasize the material reality of things. It makes us aware of their dissociation from men, their general irrelation. The external world conjured up in these poems is furthermore vaster and more complex than that found in the works of the poets of a century ago. *Winter Night* (Téli éjszaka) or *Freight Trains* (Tehervonatok tolatnak) set the scene against a sense of cosmic distances, in an infinity in which the whole visible world is a tiny atom, a group of sparks revolving in smoke, a mere microcosm. *By the Danube* (A Dunánál) and *Consciousness* (Eszmélet), however, deal with the fate of man and his momentary environment in the "whole of time". A sense of a whole is at its best in *Winter Night*, and *Elegy* (Elégia) combines lively, human aspects, and a sense of alienation at the same time.

ELEGY

Like a dense downdrift of smoke
between land and leaden sky,
my spirit hangs low,
close to the ground.
It sways, it cannot fly.

O my hard spirit, supple imagination!
Follow reality's heavy tracks,
take a look at yourself here,
where you came from.
Here, under a sky at other times so dilute,
near a solitary, gaunt, bare wall,
poverty's sullen silence
menacing, pleading,

419

washes away the grief
hardened on a brooding heart
and stirs it
into those of millions.

Man's whole world is made here,
where everything is in ruins.
In an abandoned factory yard
a hardy dandelion opens its umbrella.
The days go down
the faded steps of broken little windows
into dampness, into shadows.
Answer now:
are you from here?
Are you from here, so that you are never left alone
by the grim desire to be
like those other sufferers
into whom this great age wedged itself
to distort and deform their every feature?

Here you can rest, where the crippled
picket fence, with its harsh cries,
upholds and protects
a greedy moral order.
Can you recognize yourself? Here,
waiting for a well-constructed, fine
and concrete future,
are souls with the emptiness of vacant lots
lying around idle, mournful,
dreaming of tall buildings that weave
the noise of life. The tortured grass
is watched by glazed, fixed eyes:
bits of broken glass in the mud.

From time to time a thimbleful of sand
rolls from a mound. And at times
a blue or green or black fly
buzzes by,
drawn here from richer regions
by human waste and rags.
In its own way

the tormented soil
lays the table even here:
yellow grass blooms in a rusty pot.

Can you tell
what consciousness, what barren joy
attracts and drags you
relentlessly to this place?
What rich suffering throws you here?
This is how the child
who was shoved and beaten by strangers
returns to his mother,
Only here can you really smile or cry.
Soul, only here can you bear yourself.
This is your home.

(Translated by John Bátki)

The city scenes of Verhaeren are in some far-off sense predecessors of this type of poetry. In József's poetry scenes and the elements which compose them are built into a vision of the world regarded from a modern scientific viewpoint. Contrary to the majority of today's objective poets, his works give a picture of a whole, constructed according to the laws of actual reality. They conjure up a systematic world, permeated with contradictions, every particle with its own secrets, yet penetrable to the disciplined human intellect. This world was built up of an endless line of microcosms and macrocosms, and in it man, abandoned to himself, must stand his ground. Both the dialectic of materialism and the attitude of the twentieth-century proletarian fighter, betrayed to foreign powers, yet totally committed to the struggle for a human existence, pervade these poems, expressing the emotions of an extraordinarily sensitive but strictly logical artist.

Between 1925 and 1930 József, having outgrown the influence of the avant-garde, returned to the use of rhyme. This was, however, only a partial return to an earlier form. His precise construction is different from the artistic discipline of his earlier work, which was manifest in his perfect handling of verse forms, e.g. the sonnet. The near-linear inner structure of *Study of a Head* (Tanulmányfej) was replaced by a construction built out of the dissonant tensions of strongly contrasting sections, and the symmetrical external form also gave way to an apparently asymmetrical pattern. Long and short lines, variable rhyme apparently somewhat like prose, the existence or non-existence of rhyme, or rather its position and nature, play in almost every case an individually determined function in the poem's construction. This structure takes as much from the original individual style of Kassák as from the "traditional" school of poetry.

421

The Basic Questions of Human Existence

József was, to the end, both an intensely isolated man and yet vividly aware of the artist's need completely, joyously to integrate with the world outside him. This duality is displayed equally in his works as a whole, and in individual poems, e.g., *Ode*. Through the completely concealed, and yet regular construction of this poem passes a procession of pairs of patterns—almost archetypal in depth and changing form from time to time—above all that of change and permanence.

ODE

1

I am sitting
here on a glittering wall of rocks.
The mellow wind of the young summer
like the warmth of a good supper
flies around.

I let my heart grow fond of silence.
It is not so difficult,
—the past swarms around—
the head bends down
and down hangs the hand.

I gaze at the mountains' mane
every leaf reflects the glow
of your brow.
The road is empty, empty,
yet I can see
how the wind makes your skirt flutter
under the fragile branches of the tree.

I see a lock of your hair tip forward
your soft breasts quiver
—as the stream down below is running away—
behold, I see again,
how the ripples on round white pebbles
the fairy laughter spouts out on your teeth.

2

O *how I love you*
who made to speak
both the wily solitude which weaved its plots
in the deepest caverns of the heart
and the universe.

Who part from me, in silence, and run away
like the waterfall from its own rumble
while I, between the peaks of my life,
near to the far,
cry out and reverberate
rebounding against sky and earth
that I love you, you sweet step-mother.

3

I love you like the child loves his mother,
like silent pits love their depth
I love you like halls love the light
like the soul loves the flame,
like the body loves repose.
I love you like all mortals love living
until they die.

Every single smile, movement, word of yours
I keep like the earth keeps all fallen matter.
Like acids into metal
so my instincts have burnt
your dear and beautiful form into my mind,
and there your being fills up everything.

Moments pass by, rattling
but you are sitting mutely in my ears.
Stars blaze and fall
but you stand still in my eyes.

Like silence in a cave,
your flavour, now cool,
Still lingers in my mouth
and your hand upon the waterglass
and the delicate veins upon your hand
glimmer up before me again and again.

423

4
O what kind of matter am I
that your glance cuts and shapes me?
What kind of soul and what kind of light
and what kind of amazing phenomenon am I
that in the mist of emptiness
I can walk around
the gentle slopes of your fertile body?
And like the word
entering into an enlightened mind
I can enter into its mysteries...

Your veins like rosebushes
tremble ceaselessly.
They carry the eternal current
that love may blossom in your cheeks
and thy womb may bear a blessed fruit.

Many a small root embroiders through and through
the sensitive soil of your stomach
weaving knots, unwinding the tangle
that the cells of your juices may align
into clusters of swarming lines
and that the good thickets of your bushy lungs
may whisper their own glory.

The eternal matter happily proceeds in you
along the tunnels of your bowels
and the waste gains a rich life
in the hot wells of your ardent kidneys.

Undulating hills rise
star constellations oscillate
lakes move, factories operate
millions of living creatures
insects
seaweed
cruelty and goodness stir
the sun shines, a misty arctic light looms—
unconscious eternity roams about
in your metabolism.

5
Like clots of blood
these words fall
before you.
Existence stutters
only the law speaks clearly.
But my industrious organs that renew me
day by day
are now preparing for silence.

But until then all cry out.
You,
whom they have selected out of the multitude
of two thousand million people,
you only one,
you soft cradle,
strong grave, living bed
receive me into you...

(How tall is the sky at dawn!
Armies are dazzling in its ore.
This great radiance hurts my eyes.
I am lost, I believe...
I hear my heart beating
flapping above me.)

6
(By-Song)

(The train is taking me, I am going
perhaps I may even find you today.
My burning face may then cool down,
and perhaps you will softly say:

The water is running, take a bath.
Here is a towel for you to dry.
The meat is cooking, appease your hunger,
this is your bed, where I lie.)

(Translated by Thomas Kabdebo)

It is from this position of "here and now" that József most frequently raises, and answers, the fundamental questions of human existence. He does this in *Consciousness* (Eszmélet) and *Incidental Poem for Ignotus on the State of Socialism* (Alkalmi vers a szocializmus állásáról Ignotusnak). In *Consciousness* he calls human existence a tragedy, owing to the non-fulfilment of the great potentialities of humanity, and the failure to achieve a grand world order:

> *I looked up in the night*
> *and saw the cogwheel of the stars.*
> *The loom of the past was weaving laws*
> *from glittering threads of chance.*
> *Then, from my steaming dreams*
> *I looked up at the sky again*
> *and saw that the fabric of the law*
> *would somehow always have its flaw.*
>
> (Translated by John Bátki)

In the other, however, he recognizes the irrepressible, beautiful pulse of life as stronger than the contradictions of the material world about him, and the capacity of men to be part of it: "Should the pillars framing the mine collapse, the tunnels will guard the treasure, and it blazes... And as long as their hearts beat, the miners will always reopen the shaft..." With this recognition he releases the human ego into the outside world: he sees it "not in the grass, not in the trees, but in everything..."—as fraternizing with everything—as the dusk silently smooths out the outlines of a cloud.

Revolution and Solitude

This expression of the disintegration of law in his verse reflects the rise of fascism in Germany. Around 1930 he wrote passionate revolutionary poems imbued with a consciousness of the near approach of class war: *The Crowd* (Tömeg), *Socialists* (Szocialisták), *The Woodcutter* (Favágó), *Workers* (Munkások), and *On the Outskirts of the City* (A város peremén), which so perfectly embody the teachings of historical materialism. Later, when he no longer felt the creation of a socialist society imminent, he once more invoked the question of a life worthy of man: *Welcome to Thomas Mann* (Thomas Mann üdvözlése), *A Breath of Air!* (Levegőt!).

WELCOME TO THOMAS MANN

> *Just as the child by sleep already possessed,*
> *Drops in his quiet bed eager to rest,*
> *But begs you: ,,Don't go yet: tell me a story,"*
> *For night this way will come less suddenly,*

And his heart throbs with little anxious beats
Nor wholly understands what he entreats,
The story's sake or that yourself be near,
So we ask you: Sit down with us: make clear
What you are used to saying; the known relate,
That you are here among us, and our state
Is yours, and that we all are here with you,
All whose concerns are worthy of man's due.
You know this well: the poet never lies.
The real is not enough; through its disguise
Tell us the truth which fills the mind with light
Because, without each other, all is night.
Through Madame Chauchat's body Hans Castorp sees:
So train us to be our own witnesses.
Gentle your voice, no discord in that tongue;
Then tell us what is noble, what is wrong,
Lifting our hearts from mourning to desire.
We have buried Kosztolányi: cureless, dire,
The cancer on his mouth grew bitterly,
But growths more monstrous gnaw humanity.
Appalled we ask; More than that went before,
What horror has the future yet in store
What ravening thoughts will seize us for their prey?
What poison, brewing now, eat us away
And, if your lecture can put of that doom,
How long may you still count upon a room?
Ah, do but speak, and we can take heart then.
Being men by birthright, we must remain men,
And women, women, cherished for that reason,
All of us human, though such numbers lessen.
Sit down, please. Let your stirring tale be said.
We are listening to you, glad, like one in bed,
To see to-day, vefore that sudden night,
A European mid people barbarous, white.

(Translated by Vernon Watkins)

His verse is inspired by a world where "freedom is the norm" and which will also include a light-hearted, playful love of life. Clear enlightened intellect and the instinct to find a companion everywhere, in all things, make up the innermost essence of man, he feels: "My ocean is the soft warm shade of embracing arms, my sky the light of humanity understood…" (*Long, Long Ago… — Már régesrég…*). And this is why he believes the struggle for a society worthy of humanity is one of the chief duties of the artist and of man:

Other poets—what concern of mine?
Wallowing in fake imagery
belly-high and fired with bogus wine
let them ape out their ecstasy.

I step past the revels of today
to understanding and beyond.
With a free mind I shall never play
the vile role of the servile fool.

Be free to eat, drink, make love and sleep!
Weigh yourself with the universe!
I shan't hiss my inward curse to creep
and serve the base bone-crushing powers.

The bargain's off—let me be happy!
Or else all men will insult me;
Growing spots of red will mark me out
fever will suck my fluids dry.

(From *Ars Poetica;*
translated by Michael Beevor)

In the last years of his life, loneliness dominated his thoughts: he felt part of "the world staggering in empty space." "My heart is perched on nothing's branch," he wrote in *Without Hope* (Reménytelenül). "The things I have listen to my person like empty desks to a mad teacher," "it doesn't touch me, what I touch", he lamented elsewhere. He spoke of disintegration, of falling apart, even of captivity, during the time of his own decline: "My eyes are jumping from my head. If I go crazy, please don't hurt me. Just hold me down with your strong hands" (*My Eyes are Jumping* — Ki-be ugrál). Yet even the horrors of his disintegrating mind materialized in pictures of perfect clarity and classical precision. There is a detached, psychological realism in his final work, alongside an agony culminating in an almost apocalyptic whirlwind of pain, in *It Hurts a Lot* (Nagyon fáj); but at other times he described his state of mind in an entirely detached manner. One critic wrote that "the reader could not support his message were it not for the sweet music that breaks through in his every line." The earlier light lyricism remained as an important ingredient in the later poetry of his maturity.

428

A Personal Poet

Attila József's poetry varied greatly in his choice of versification and poetic forms. There are simple ditties, poems written in metric form, unrhymed free verse, sonnets and sonnet cycles. Sound and melody are also varied: sometimes they are subordinated to the conceptual or pictorial development, while at other times they play a comparatively independent role.

Another feature of his work is its strongly personal aspect. It is full of vivid sketches and echoes drawn from the multiple experiences of his own life as well as from the situation of his class, his nation, and humanity at large. In the last he follows an enduring tradition in Hungarian poetry, but at the same time turns it into something new. He solved the universal artistic dilemma of the time: experiencing to the full and giving expression to the shattered twentieth century, a world permeated by contradictions, he yet retained a deep sense of order, and created a solid system in the world he conjured up. He felt and described man's solitude, flung out into the world, and he gave valid answers to the basic question: man's task is to take the intellectual measure of the world, discover his place in it, and to struggle for a revolutionary change in social conditions to attain it.

57 Poetry

Interwar Developments

Attila József brought about a synthesis between the rather narrow realism of the *Nyugat* poets, certain kinds of Impressionism, and various avant-garde trends—especially Expressionism, Surrealism and a poetic structure which owed a great deal to Kassák. These various tendencies are an indication of the more complex nature of this period, and at this time other tendencies appeared as well. Of these three can be immediately isolated: the first is a trend to Classicism, which, in the verse of Miklós Radnóti, is to be found together with avant-garde elements and the immediate influence of Attila József. The second is a strongly objective, humanist, socially-oriented poetry, represented by Gyula Illyés. The third is the kind of verse which turns away from the social and objective world to concentrate on the world of the mind; here Sándor Weöres is pre-eminent.

One of the main concerns of the poetry of the interwar years is communal and social life. It is no accident that, for instance, Babits's poetry, which had earlier been a poetry of isolation, later became, more or less deliberately, considerably more vigorous in its social concern during the period under discussion. In this poetry a major role was played by the emotional life of the working man and the poor peasant, but at the same time it expressed the passion of the powerless intellectuals, robbed of opportunities to fulfil their hopes and ambitions. These themes are to be found again and again in the writing of the first twenty years of the century and in the early thirties. Before the Revolution of 1918 the tone was more confident, after its failure the overtones were darker. Poetry which concentrated on the problems of the artist and the inner life of the individual took a more prominent place in the thirties. The growth of fascism, however, evoked a corresponding growth in the expression of humanist opposition, combined with a sense of hopelessness.

In so far as form is concerned, although the powerful effect of the avant-garde in art which preoccupied writers between 1900 and 1920 can be felt in nearly all important later writing, at the same time various "traditional" verse-forms came back into favour. The adoption of these forms is due partly to the folklorists, József Erdélyi for instance, and partly writers, such as Miklós Radnóti, turning to classical forms. But the resurgence of traditional forms must also be put down to the fact that the Hungarian language provides exceptional opportunities for both rhyme and the exploitation of strict rhythmical forms.

As the appearance of Kassák indicates, the avant-garde was the first of the major poetic tendencies of the period to appear. Of all the poets who began their career in Kassák's circle, or rather, in the reviews associated with him, Sándor Barta and Aladár Komját were the two who carried on the avant-garde movement he initiated. But they soon parted from their master on ideological grounds, and became the pioneers of socialist poetry, preceding the mature period of Attila József's poetry.

Sándor Barta (1897-1938)

was connected with the workers' movement and one of the groups of left-wing intellectuals as a young man. At the time of the Hungarian Republic of Councils he worked as a journalist, and then, as an emigré in Vienna, edited a number of short-lived reviews. For a while he found himself attracted by anarchist tendencies, but finally joined the Communist Party and in 1925 emigrated to the Soviet Union, where he took part in literary life until, in 1938, he fell victim to the purges.

For some time his work showed anarchist tendencies, and he was also influenced by Dadaism. He made use of associations that were generally daring and exciting, though sometimes overstrained.

His poems are relatively little guided by logic, but his structuring of images is firm. His poetry is less organized than Kassák's, but in some way it is more absorbing, more revolutionary. Some of his work, conceived on the grand scale, deals with the horrors of life and all its frightening possibilities. *Primitive Holy Trinity* (Primitív Szentháromság), for instance, describes dramatically the relentless march of the oppressed from the depths. Later he writes of achievement:

> *. . .there it stood before us on the*
> *face of the sleepy Asian steppes, steeped*
> *in soot and fire, with the glowing pupils*
> *of its fiery ovens, the sun's bronze clip*
> *in its tangled, untidy smoke-hair, Magnitogorsk.*

His later work, however, failed to come up to the standard of his earlier poetry.

Aladár Komját (1891-1937)

who was older than Barta, worked in an industrial firm after he had finished his law studies. During the First World War he helped to organize an antimilitarist movement. In 1917, together with a number of his companions, he left Kassák and his friends because he did not find them sufficiently radical. He was one of the founders of the Hungarian Communist Party. During the brief period of power of the Hungarian Republic of Councils in 1919, he edited a pro-revolutionary review. He was afterwards imprisoned and then became an emigré in Italy, Vienna, Berlin, Switzerland, and finally in Paris. He helped to edit a number of periodicals, including *Imprecor,* the seven-language journal of the Communist International, in the period between 1925 and 1933, and worked as a party official until his death in 1937.

His poetry gained considerable strength from the bold impetus of Expressionism, and to a lesser extent, from Futurism. The strident and dramatic voice of revolution cries out in his work. His poems express, in highly evocative terms, the stormy yet disciplined desire for something new and better, as well as for the fulfilment of the demands of the spirit. He exclaims, he cries out, he demands, but nonetheless the force of logical argument animate his poetry. The words and images hammer home their meaning by repetition, and special weight is given to certain lines through the use of rhyme in a rhymeless context. He is the first consciously communist poet of Hungarian literature. The abstractions of his youth were later replaced by more object-centred, more descriptive poems, occasionally in the form of ballads, and rhymed verse became more frequent. All his work expresses a passionate affirmation of life, as in *To the Engineers of the Soul* (A lélek mérnökeihez):

> *Dip yourself into the flowing river,*
> *take in through your mouth, ears, nose,*
> *eyes, heart, brain,*
> *this entire,*
> *suffering, happy*
> *cowardly and heroic,*
> *filthy and gleaming,*
> *dying and rejoicing,*
> *but victorious life.*

Other works by Komját include *The New International* (Új Internacionálé), *The Revolution is Dead—Long Live the Revolution* (A forradalom meghalt!—Éljen a forradalom!), *Hamburg's October* (Hamburg októbere), *The "Yellow Rabble" has Arisen!* (A "sárga csőcselék" fölállt!), *The Hungarian Proletariat is on the March* (Proletár-Magyarország marsol), *The Anthem of the International Brigade* (A nemzetközi brigád indulója), and *Joy* (Öröm).

432

Other Socialist Poets

The poetry written by other close followers of Kassák only played any important part at the time of the 1919 Revolution. For ideological reasons later socialist poets abandoned the path marked out by Kassák. Their common view of the world formed a strong bond between the socialist poets, but there were wide differences of style. Apart from the original genius of Attila József, and the actively political Sándor Barta and Aladár Komját, there was *Antal Hidas* (1899–1980) whose prose books were more important, but who wrote propaganda poems using more traditional verse-forms. His literary work developed in the Soviet Union, but a couple of his poems became popular workers' songs in Hungary. Among the more modern socialist poets, whose work was closer to that of Attila József, and who adopted a rather more subtle style, were *Ernő Salamon* (1912–1943), *László Lukács* (1906–1944) and *Antal Forgács* (1910–1944), whose life and work were so tragically cut short.

Socialist poets such as *László Benjámin,* who began to write in the interwar years and who were members of a group of "worker writers", were to a large extent influenced by topical and literary developments after the liberation in 1945 and since their work matured in that period of Hungarian literary history, they will be discussed when we come to it.

Lőrinc Szabó (1900–1957)

The work of one of Attila József's most important contemporaries, Lőrinc Szabó, though it shows signs of the more bourgeois aspects of the avant-garde, cannot really be placed in any specific category.

He was the son of an engine driver, and after high school went to Budapest at the time of the bourgeois 1918 Revolution. His brief career as an arts student spanned the confused period of the White Terror. It was during this time, soon after the death of Ady, that he began to write. Babits's interest was immediately awakened by the young, impoverished writer who sent his articles to *Nyugat*. He later worked on the daily *Pesti Napló* (Pest Diary). In 1927 he experimented with the founding of a new review, and later made contact with the "populist writers".

For a period he adopted right-wing nationalist views, occasionally expressing them in his poetry, but later he corrected these errors. In the last ten years of his life, like many other poets, such as Gyula Illyés and László Németh, as well as the painter József Egry and the sculptor Miklós Borsos, he lived by Lake Balaton.

A variety of influences went to make up Szabó's poetry. For a time it was mainly Expressionism, seen most clearly in *Earth, Forest, God* (Föld, erdő, isten, 1922), but also, in a somewhat changed form, in later poems (*Give me Poison, Give me a Revolver* — Mérget! revolvert!, *Wild-West Europe* — Wild-West Európa, *Grand Hotel, Miramonte*). To a lesser extent he fell under the spell of the *Neue Sachlichkeit* in the poem, for instance, *The Bell Rings in the Basilica* (A Bazilikában zúg a harang). Out of them, however, he forged his own individual style. And he was obliquely influenced by his first master, Babits. It was Babits's work that he found the strongest example of poetry which was objective in its stance and was concerned with general philosophical and moral problems.

His picture of the world around him is less stylized than Babits's; first and foremost of the world of the bourgeois intelligentsia. This was partly due to the indirect influence of Expressionism which through its own particular means brought about a new perception of reality. For Szabó, this was matched with a more personal, emotional and intellectual form of self-expression.

In Lőrinc Szabó's poetry there is no affectation. The poem always "says" what is said by the conjunction of all the sentences contained in it. The words, too, signify themselves. The shape of the images is clear, they have an almost tangible sharpness, and so does the logic of the thoughts expressed and the overall structure of the poems. At the worst the sentences are sometimes overlong and are broken in the attempt to express a highly condensed thought or an inner turbulence and emotional disturbance. This poetry does not work by suggestion or by invocation or magic, it catches the attention by the immediacy of its communication.

It is perhaps this poetry which is most characteristic of bourgeois verse in all Hungarian literature.

The loss of illusion is a theme frequently found in his poetry. In *Morning* (Reggel) and *Lovers in the Forest* (Erdei szeretők) a man wakes up from a world painted by a young, vividly pantheistic imagination to the turmoil of the modern metropolis and comes to realize the inhuman anxiety and anguish of life in a capitalist society. In other poems, the man sets out in life with a fervent faith in change and improvement, and finally relinquishes all hope of it. And while the young Ady looks on money as a fearful fetish, Lőrinc Szabó writes grimly that "there is no money, and we must eat". It is the world of contemporary everyday life which appears in his free verse, though indeed, some of his later poems were in rhymed forms.

One of Szabó's constant themes is the ruthless nature of the laws of life in general, and the pointlessness of human struggle (*Separate Peace* — Különbéke). But he still valiantly affirms a belief in life. *All for Nothing* (Semmiért egészen), for instance, deals with the conflict of men and women confronting each other in relationships of love. He voices the demands of the ego in love in words of raw honesty, based on logical psychological analysis: "I want you to become a working part of my fate". In the austerely unadorned sentences, however, there is the turmoil of strong emotion, even at times reminiscent of Shakespeare. It is these emotions which build up the tension of the poem to the full circle of the close.

Let the law save those who are
good as their fellow-men;
beyond the law, like an animal,
be like that, I'll love you then.
Like a lamp that's turned off, you
mustn't be if I don't need you to;
don't complain, don't even see
a prison that's invisible;
and I in my mind will guarantee
that you forgive my ruthless rule.

(Translated by Edwin Morgan)

A substantial portion of his work is made up of his philosophical poetry. He has one basic thing to say, that man's helplessness is due to his subordination to higher laws outside himself. But his work cannot be compared with that of Attila József or Gyula Illyés in profundity of thought. He wrote a poem about the all powerful nature of matter (*Materialism* — Materializmus), and it was in part written in the spirit of nineteenth-century materialism. At the same time, *The Dream of Dsuang Dsi* (Dsuang Dszi álma) he adopted a solipsistic position, and he frequently voiced ancient Eastern, Indian, Chinese thinking in his slightly didactic poems.

In addition to such influences he was also influenced by Goethe. This influence can be felt elsewhere in Szabó's poetry as well, especially in the irrational pantheism of his view of nature in his later work. The experience he translated into these poems, in which, unlike the poems of his youth, the objective observer was also given a substantial role, was that of connection with a universe infinite in space and time. This characteristic ambivalence between the objective and the subjective was also a feature of, for instance, *On the Jetty at Földvár* (A földvári mólón) in which he pro-duced delicate and precise reflections of the rhythm of the waves, even to their half or quarter-beat intervals. He gave as close an account of the tiny movements in the picture as is possible and perceived the stability of the rhythms within it. At the same time, he used repetition and close enjambment to give the effect of breathlessly rapid speech, to express the transport and ecstasy of the spirit.

His objectivity, his logical qualities and the realism implicit in his methods of work inclined him towards narrative poetry. Thought and feeling are often con-nected with descriptions of the external world. *Cricket Music* (Tücsökzene, 1947) is made up of a loosely connected chain of poems, in fact, three hundred and seventy poems of eighteen lines each. They are descriptions of episodes picked from the whole course of his life in a mode reminiscent of Proust. The style is on occasion so stark that the value of some of the poems is entirely dependent on the intensity of the experience or thought expressed. In Szabó's late writings, however, the position is

435

changed. The rhymes he used were not only a means of expressing an ordered reg-
ularity and composition of the whole, but also it could be of a kind of inner turbulence. They are sometimes given a value of their own: the whole effect of the
poems on the ear is to make them more musical, more vivid to the senses. This
development is due to the fact that the poems are no longer concerned with the
disillusioned acceptance of the ruthless nature of life but rather with experiencing
its joys.

Szabó's final book of poems was inspired by Shakespeare. It contains 120 sonnets. This is *The Twenty-sixth Year* (A huszonhatodik év, 1957), dedicated to the memory of a love lasting twenty-five years. It adopted a more introspective and at the
same time a more human stance than most of his earlier love poetry. The broken
phrases of the poems breathe the feelings of a spirit transported by love. But here
too he accepts without illusion the fact of death, of unbridgeable distance. The
contrasts brought about by this ambivalence, emphasizing now one, now the other,
in complex verse structures, help to make the sequence of an intensely moving experience.

Another of his more striking poems is the relatively early ballad, or rather
oratorio, *Mourners of Brethren* (Testvérsiratók) which brings alive the memory of the
Waldensians, transported to the galleys. The whole work is instinct with Szabó's
pantheistic adoration of nature, the raw strength of his emotions and his sense of
both realism and humanism.

In some of the features of his writing, the long sentences, stark rhymes, the
objectivity of his style, his intense and yet controlled expression of emotion, he is
close to, and in part a follower of, Gyula Illyés. His philosophy is nearer to that of a
poet who began to write later, Sándor Weöres.

Sándor Weöres (b. 1913)

Sándor Weöres was already writing poetry of an accomplished kind at the age of
fourteen, and within the space of a few years he developed from a prodigy into a
mature poet. He paid frequent visits to the Far East. For some years he worked
as a librarian, but from the beginning of his career he held himself aloof from
any kind of involvement in communal or social affairs, living only for his work
as a poet.

Weöres's poetry is unbelievably varied. It extends from poems of a single word
to long narrative poems, from rhymes for children to tragic philosophical works,
from poems expressing Christian fervour to bizarre gestures in verse, making use
of an enormous assortment of methods and modes of writing through his magnificent verbal facility and virtuoso technique. His skill appears to be almost instinctive,

and yet he continues to seek new avenues, learn to handle new techniques, take himself to school again and again. And in terms of sound his works range through all the transitions between the allurement of verbal music and the dignity of prose.

In the enormous variety of his output he comes closest to Attila József. But whereas for József "man is the measure of all things", relying on himself and seeking to find himself in the activities of the world, for Weöres, at least from the intellectual point of view, the human, traditional centre of poetry and of art in general fades into insignificance. He is more sympathetic to those things "which bear their submission to natural laws than to men who regard mortality as tragic and who revolt against those laws". "This world is not my world", "Another world has sent me"—he repeats again and again, especially in the period between 1930 and 1950. (*Another World . . .* — Egy másik világ..., *De Profundis*.) As he sees "reality come alive" in the rhythmic, harmonic movements of the dancer (*Dancers* — Táncosnők), so equally he declares that "this" life is only a version of the other, forced into material form. The "other" is more spiritual in nature, and is to be found in the beauty of form, in the play of lines approaching one another, in the tuneless rhythms of colours and movement (*Attic Window* — Padlásablak). Real wisdom, according to him, is recognition of the fact that the mind directed toward worldly ends is "only the paltry shadow of the mind: it only touches the surfaces of things". As for the immediate world, which adulterates and distorts the laws of the "other" world, it has been irrevocably despoiled "because the horrible has spread to the heart of being, because fear has broken into the heart of non-being: there is no more peace in death"—he repeats in different forms in *The Book of Lost Hope* (A reménytelenség könyve) written in 1944. "At night, if the tread of horses sounds, it is the hooves of nowhere to nowhere." He indicates his complete loss of direction in lines which are now strongly tinged with atmosphere, now dryly logical. The material world appears in the form of piles of sterile objects, and according to Weöres "eternal darkness" falls on "the inner surface" of things.

It is experience of Kafkaesque alienation and nightmare which sweeps through these poems:

> *It is not built upward, but downwards*
> *the temple. The hell.*
> *Its slates falling in constant dissolution.*
> *His great book bound in green*
> *lies about on a chaotic bench.*
> *If you ask for the great book bound in green:*
> *you get a copy of the plan for dissolution instead.*
> *Great, rustling rolls of paper.*
>
> (*The Book of Lost Hope* — A reménytelenség könyve)

437

This, in a very schematic form, is one aspect of Weöres's poetic world. The other is the translation into actuality of the beauties of the "real world" as they are seen or surmised, and the expression of wonder they engender. The verses for children also lie on the borders of this realm of experience. The desire for oblivion in playfulness and the naiveté and tenderness of childhood is expressed in other poems as well.

One of his more famous poems, *The Lost Parasol* (Az elveszített napernyő), describes the return to nature of a parasol—a man-made object from nature's materials—discarded by a pair of lovers, and its slow, progressive but complete disintegration and absorption into the animal, vegetable and mineral world; as background he paints the dazzling, changing colours and tiniest movements of its surroundings, and the great churning spool of the thunder until:

> *a smile dawns eternity on man,*
> *its arches bend and march on their way*
> *between watery shores,*
> *Theatrum Gloriae Dei.*
>
> (Translated by Edwin Morgan)

Aspects of this world appear in many of his less important works, and the duality of the "two worlds" is itself a subject of inspiration. In the abundance of his works, he portrays the world as a conglomerate of pairs of opposites, confronting man and woman, "up" and "down", a harsh, clear radiance of light and the intimate dimness of valleys, silent blocks of rocks and organic life in its multitude of forms—elements which form a whole. In a number of poems mythical figures are given new, individual interpretations, elsewhere the sphere of everyday life is transsubstantiated (*Medeia; Orpheus; The Legend of the Brook* — Patakmonda; *The Song of Grades* — Grádicsok éneke). The expression of a sense of alienation from real existence finds expression in his poems alongside the joy of melting into existence with abandon. He runs through all the different agonies of life, and plays with words (*Hungarian Etudes* — Magyar etűdök; *From the Rag-Carpet Series* — A rongyszőnyeg-sorozatból). He gives expression to emotional unrest and to light-hearted eroticism in *Fairy Spring;* depicts other artists, penetrating into the very essence of their style, as in *Three Œuvres* (Három emlékmű) and *Tolstoy* and takes us into distant phantasy worlds, as in *The Ruin of Mahruh* (Mahruh veszése).

In an important group of poems he gives pre-eminence to the way words sound. He treats certain sounds, groups of sounds, words and word-constructions much the same way as the composer handles notes or the artist-craftsman the marbled stones or a piece of strangely wined wood—now with light-hearted playfulness, now with bold associations, at the same time, however, subordinating them to strict structural laws in order to obtain from them some linguistic form. Such poems depict neither a clearly outlined plot, nor do they furnish us with some unambiguous message, yet they are rich in artistic meaning (*Fugue* — Fúga; *Fughetta; Four Chorals* — Négy korál; *Drum and Dance* — Dob és tánc).

His poetic drama, *Theomachia,* is a new interpretation of the deeds of the Greek. He shows how non-existence is turned into the ancient rigid state of *being* which develops into organic *life,* varied and colourful. He also shows how *human* life becomes separated from all the other phenomena of the world in the sense that it faces its own existence as a problem. His poem *The Rape of the Earth* (A föld meg-gyalázása) is a self-contained myth, a re-interpretation of the Orpheus myth. Medeia rises from her barbarous, selfish love through tremendous suffering to the moral heights of unselfishness and sacrifice. He looks upon the relationship between man and woman as a mythical connection. Man is related to the Sun, the life-giving energy, while woman is of the substance of water. Their confluence is the completion of the universal laws of existence (*Sixth Symphony* — Hatodik szimfónia; *Uniting* — Az egyesülés). Real connection with the universal can be achieved in the heat of love, in the unconsciousness of dream, in playing, and artistic activity. One of the main subjects and aims of Weöres's poetry is the possibility of freeing oneself from the barriers of the self (*Window to the Night* — Ablak az éjbe; *The Unchanging in the Changing* — Állandó a változóban).

He happily dons the most extraordinary disguises — a Hungarian woman poet of the previous century (in his *Psyche* cycle), a barbarian warrior, a Ukrainian minstrel, a South-Slav monk, each of them clothed in turn in appropriate rhythms and language—ancient metric versification or the introduction of new "barbaric" rhythms, picking up the poetic styles of the most diverse eras and regions. This is also true in another connection: the classics of traditional European verse, Hungarian folk poetry, and the creations of various oriental cultures were not without influence on his attitude and style—nor the various "isms", primarily Surrealism, with their distinctive word order, imagery and form.

His poems are sometimes characterized by tight syntactic construction, at other times they are loosely woven, giving place to free association. The result is often a poem resembling a musical work.

Though part of his work is profoundly intellectual in content, he is not interested in finding solutions to problems; his answers are sometimes unacceptable not only to socialists, but to all rational, thinking people of the twentieth century. He is more concerned with the difficult mental struggle involving the whole of one's being in an attempt to see and understand the problem (*Song in Three Parts* — Háromrészes ének). His intellectual approach is in itself an aesthetic quality through the remark-able imagery he employs. The foundations of his ideas have remained unchanged for a long time—and here we can expect no change, even the social upheaval around him produces little reaction—but he continues to write, and his recent volumes provide still newer problems for those wishing to evaluate his work.

439

His plays and oratorios are less significant. The most important among them is *Octopus,* a handling of the Saint George legend centred on the questions of the transfer of power.

His extraordinary knowledge of verse and language makes him one of the greatest living translators. His translations of Oriental poetry are especially important.

József Erdélyi (1896-1978)

The influence of folk poetry on such different poets as Sándor Weöres and Attila József has been marked, and is to be seen again in the work of Gyula Illyés. With these poets, however, the folk influence was just one feature—of greater or lesser intensity—in the development of their work. With József Erdélyi his interest in folk poetry played a dominant role. Of peasant origin, he grew up in poverty to become a well-known poet. His early work was full of rebellious, revolutionary passion, and in the early 1930s he was one of the "populist writers" movement. Later, however, he drifted to the extreme right, and supported the fascist demagogues in his verse. After the liberation he fled the country, but later returned and presented himself before the authorities. In 1947 a People's Court sentenced him to three years' imprisonment, and it was only ten years later that he was able to publish again.

During a period when various heavily stylized tendencies made themselves felt in a self-centred, strongly personal form of poetry, his main contribution in 1920 was to produce poems of a natural simplicity, with the spontaneity of the folk song, with a sense of kinship with the earth and air, with trees, with the voice of the poor, combined with a call to action. This populism, though different in kind, vaguely recalls that of Petőfi. Erdélyi sings of the poor peasant bled white by landlords and tenant farmers, and voices their experiences and their feelings in lines that are on occasion raw and vigorous, on occasion sinuous and melodious. His imagery, the lively rhythm of his verse and its light, firm vigour suggests, either directly or indirectly, the feeling that the entire world which surrounds man can be made something more human. His most important works are: *Polo on Blood Meadow* (Lovaspóló a Vérmezőn), *Pile-drivers* (Cölöpverők).

Poets of Folk Myth

To some extent József Erdélyi was the forerunner of the slightly classical, soberly realist Illyés school which specialized in clear, precise images and lucid sequences of thought and feeling.

The more dissonant, turbulent elements in folk poetry were brought to the surface by *István Sinka* (1897–1969). His verse, influenced by ballads, shares something with those Spanish poets of the twentieth century inspired by democratic feelings—notably García Lorca. His forbears were herdsmen, and like Erdélyi and many others of peasant origin, self-taught in their art, his work is full of gloomy images, bold associations, mostly in free verse. He wrote some fine narrative poems, such as *Herdsman's Song* (Pásztorének), and some superb poems, such as *My Mother Dances a Ballad* (Anyám balladát táncol). The trend which drew its inspiration from folk poetry—akin to Bartók's *Allegro Barbaro* or *Cantata Profana*—made its influence felt less vividly in Attila József's work. Of the populist writers, the best of them in this vein was the learned but unevenly talented *Pál Gulyás* (1899–1944) who sought his inspiration in ancient myths, but failed to create a synthesis of ancient and modern as József had done in some of his masterpieces.

These trends re-appeared after the liberation, transmuted to a higher level, with the new generation of important poets like Ferenc Juhász and László Nagy.

Urban, Humanistic Trends

Apart from the groups of poets under discussion, an army of fine poets were writing at this time, from socialist idealists to devoted adherents of the Catholic faith. A certain urban attitude, an intellectual hunger, and a humanist tendency—despite their differences—unites all of them. The poetry of *József Fodor* (1898–1973), who began his career simultaneously with Attila József, and was a well-known poet in his early years, is grave, solemn, and highly intellectual, influenced by Shakespeare, Shelley and Ady, and permeated in early years by bourgeois radicalism, and later by socialism. A wry, half-melancholy erudition is represented by *Zoltán Jékely* (1913–1982), the son of the poet Lajos Áprily; *György Rónay* (1913–1978) created a modern poetry based on Christian humanist views and rational sobriety. *István Vas,* who is of the same generation as Radnóti, Jékely and Rónay, will be discussed later, as his work falls more into the post-liberation period.

The work of the Rumanian–Hungarian poet *Jenő Dsida* (1907–1938) also belongs to this period. Although influenced by Expressionism, he was also to a certain extent a follower of Kosztolányi in the bravura, buoyancy and flexibility of his verse, and in his ability to freeze in a single phrase the fleeting moment in the lives of ordinary people, and to cast a magic light on simple objects.

György Sárközi (1899–1945), who was murdered by the fascists, was a populist poet of the classical school, and wrote poems of a Romantic–Expressionist tendency of some value, expressing his inner strains and stresses, and lyrics influenced by folklore.

Béla Pásztor (1906–1943), a victim of the fascists in the labour camps towards the end of the war, whose poetry was touched by Surrealism and folk influence, and on occasion ardently socialist in tone, demonstrates the range and variety of the Hungarian poetry of the period; another was Radnóti's beloved teacher, the priest *Sándor Sík* (1889–1963) whose conservative Catholic humanism permeated his work. Another poet priest of the era, *László Mécs* (1895–1978) earned a name for himself in the 1930s for his religious poetry in which he gave voice to social dissatisfaction and expressed sympathy for the average man.

The poetry of the period, rich in nuance and colour, reaches a summit and can be summed up in two fine poets: Miklós Radnóti and Gyula Illyés.

58 Miklós Radnóti (1909–1944)

His Place

Order, the affirmation of harmony, respect for reason, the vigorous structure of the poem and the task of building it into disciplined form, which was also an important consideration for Attila József, were all characteristic of Miklós Radnóti, combined with a strong leaning towards the classical.

A certain degree of Classicism, resulting in stylization of a fairly abstract kind, began in twentieth-century Hungarian poetry with Babits, in which torment was contrasted with peace, fragmentation with fulfilment, permanence with change. Both Attila József and, as we have seen, his contemporary Lőrinc Szabó were affected by this trend and, although in a different form from Babits, it could also be seen at one time in the work of Gyula Illyés, but it was never a dominant factor with any of them. With the young Radnóti, however, it became a definite feature of his modern style. What had been a surface addition to their poetry was rejuvenated and transmuted into something deeply relevant to the events of that terrible period.

His Life

Radnóti came from an educated and intellectual family in Budapest. He obtained a degree in Hungarian and French at the University of Szeged, but due to his Jewish origins and his progressive beliefs, he was unable to obtain a teaching post. At the university he formed part of a left-wing group, through which he came into contact with the workers' movement and the illegal Communist Party. For his second volume of verse, he was prosecuted on grounds of indecency. For a time he worked as a clerk, but in the main he made his living by writing. During the war he was called up for forced labour service as a Jew, which meant hard labour in the camps or on the front. Some of his poetry was sent home from here. In the autumn of 1944 his group was marched from the labour camp near Bor in Yugoslavia, through Hungary towards Austria, and the retreating Nazis shot those unable to keep up with the group. Near the Hungarian village of Abda, Radnóti was also murdered. His last poems were found in his coat pocket, after his exhumation from a mass grave.

Pastoral and Expressionist Influences

From the beginning he was attracted by pastoral poetry, as the titles of his first volumes demonstrate: *Pagan Salute* (Pogány köszöntő, 1936), *Song of Modern Shepherds* (Újmódi pásztorok éneke, 1931), and verses such as *Sun-bodied Virgins, Shepherds and Flocks* (Naptestű szüzek, pásztorok és nyájak), *Landscape, with Lovers* (Táj, szeretőkkel). The squalor of the Hungarian village was, however, too far removed from the Virgilian eclogue; therefore, a poetic world based on such endeavours became, by necessity, strongly stylized. It had few points of contact with the age, or rather it had insofar as it offered a counterpoint to reality. Radnóti's favourite subject at this time was the joy of life and a wholesome eroticism.

Such a biblical, classical "pastoral poetry" was not unrelated to the solemn, peaceful quality of Kassák's lyrics in his time. His influence can be felt in Radnóti's construction, in which he juxtaposes words and "stretches" them more boldly than is acceptable in purely classical writing. The whole poem will often conceal some secret tension, slowly mounting to the surface. Expressionism had a disturbing, tormenting effect on his verse. He had after all made contact with the workers' and village movements, he was inevitably affected by the atmosphere of an age in which social tension was ready to explode.

He writes of the murder of a black writer, relates grimly the death through tuberculosis of a Hungarian worker (*John Love, my Brother* — John Love, testvérem; *Sunday* — Vasárnap), visions of dead Far Eastern workers appal him and he sees the shadow of the local police falling over the landscape (*Peace Dissolves with a Whistle* — Füttyel oszlik a béke; *Landscape with Change* — Táj változással). He senses the enormous power in the tiniest things: "there's a breeze on the green, a foaming forest over there! But here, a gale bends the militant pine!"

In verse written in the mid-thirties the reader is aware—and at times it is openly revealed—that the poet was in contact with the revolutionary workers' movements. A socialist attitude to the world permeates his work through and through.

His language was affected not only by Expressionism but by his work in translating Apollinaire into Hungarian, the first time this was done. It stimulated and broadened his imagination and his word associations. But it was under the shadow of fascism that he reached out beyond his contemporaries to attain an outstanding level of work. He was keenly aware of, and expressed magnificently, the superficial calm that hid the terrible power on the verge of explosion. At this time, however, what he anticipated was the coming of barbarism and terror, instead of revolution. The silence of death threatens everything, everywhere—not a heroic defeat, but a senseless fate, like that of Kafka's hero in *The Trial*. The title of his volume which appeared in 1936 makes this clear: *Walk on, Condemned!* (Járkálj csak, halálraítélt!).

The Role of Classicism

It was around this time that the classical elements in his work came to full perfection, combined with strands of poetic realism. The restrained majesty of Virgil and the classical poets was united to an intellectual approach deriving from socialist humanism, and Surrealist images and Expressionist constructions took their place amid the strict hexameters.

His verse is in part intimately personal, but elsewhere he speaks in the quality of the Poet. The Poet, the artist, raised to an impersonal, universal level but springing from the present: a time of unleashed barbarism destroying the spiritual and cultural values of thousands of years, a time when "trees grow crooked and gnarled, and the mouths of salt mines cave in; bricks in a wall must scream..." The eloquent expression of present terrors is set against the objectivity of art in the desire for eternal beauty. His work is thus firmly set in the exterior world of his day, which gives aesthetic contrast to the classic idyll. Tension and struggle in his poems suggest a more important message:

> *Pastoral Muse, offer help! in this age it is poets who die like...*
> *heaven will topple on us, no grave mound marks our dust here,*
> *nor will a nobly conceived Greek amphora hold it; if one, two*
> *poems of ours remain...*

> (*Third Eclogue* — Harmadik ecloga;
> translated by Emery George)

His Poet sees his chief task as the defence of classical values, and as constant creation, and thereby the protection of human existence. In reporting everything precisely, apparently with cold objectivity, as in *Sky with Clouds* (Tajtékos ég), in raising the "tiny flutters of the world" from momentary to eternal time, he masters terror. The attitude of the classical artists falls into its place in the twentieth century. "Reality, like a cracked flowerpot, no longer holds form, and just waits to fling to the winds its useless shards"—he writes in O *Peace of Ancient Prisons* (Ó, régi börtönök); "Write on the sky when all below lies wrecked!" answers a Voice in the *Fourth Eclogue* (Negyedik ecloga), unfolding higher truths and universal commands to the Poet. But occasionally even the Voice from lofty eternity gives way to a more characteristically twentieth-century "unpassionate passion" and the bitter, ironic tones of resignation. But this resignation is in itself of value, bearing witness to human endurance: "...Poets write; cats can say meow; a dog must howl; that little fish will lay coyly her roe..."—replies the Poet to the proud Pilot's blithe encouragement. "Will you write about me?" the anxious Pilot asks at last, worn out by the hell of war. "If I live. And there's anyone around to read it," the Poet answers in the last line of the *Second Eclogue* (Második ecloga). The classicism which penetrates

445

the metre and imagery of his poems is not over-elaborate for the by no means very classical beauties of the twentieth century. The common events ennobled by his verse do not seem to be real events, but memories or dreams. "Evenings, gentle and old, you return as memory's nobles!", he wrote in a late poem of his, *À la recherche*... inspired by the great novel of Proust's. While the hell of barbarism and war rage, tiny details crystallize in memory to symbolize peace and a fruitful existence. An intimate morning in a garden, the figure of a woman waiting for her husband by the hedge, glasses clinking, discussion over a line of verse. The slightly surrealist details, as if set out and framed, become the details of a kind of modern, loose psychological realism: the poem directly expresses the poet's state of mind, and clearly affirms that only what the mind experiences was real to that tired, dreaming mind:

> *Gleaming table, crowned as by laurels with poets and young wives,*
> *where are you sliding on marshes of irretrievable hours?*
> *Where are the nights when exuberant friends were cheerfully drinking*
> *auvergnat gris out of bright-eyed, thin-stemmed, delicate glasses?*
>
> *Lines of verse swam high round the light of the lamps, with bright green*
> *epithets bobbing up-down foaming crests of the meter;*
> *those now dead were alive and the prisoners, still at home; those*
> *vanished, dear friends, long since fallen, were writing their poems;*
> *on their hearts the Ukraine, the soil of Spain or of Flanders...*
> ....
> *Where, where indeed is the night? that night which shall never return now,*
> *for, to whatever is past, death itself lends another perspective.*

(Translated by Emery George)

Respect of the Intellect

Respect for the workings of a cool clear mind is a dominant feature of Radnóti's later poetry. As in Chagall's revelation, the far-flyers come dazedly to life in his poem, the *Seventh Eclogue* (Hetedik ecloga):

> *Ragged, with shaven heads, these prisoners, snoring aloud, fly,*
> *leaving Serbia's blind peak, back to their fugitive homesteads.*

Nor is a cinematic "other" reality missing from this vision: "Only the mind, it alone is alive to the tautness of wire" *(Seventh Eclogue)*. Dreams, memories, desire and the immediate present are all clearly separated one from another by a disciplined mind, and by the clear articulation of the poem, and are paired with the solemn

446

hexametric form. He contrasts the heat of desire with the "sobriety of two times two", and we see his self-analysis in the milder tone of *Letter to my Wife* (Levél a hitveshez):

> *When may I see you? I hardly know any longer,*
> *you, who were solid, were weighty as the psalter,*
> *beautiful as a shadow and beautiful as light,*
> *to whom I would find my way, whether deafmute or blind;*
> *now hiding in the landscape, from within,*
> *on my eyes, you flash—the mind projects its film.*
>
> *You were what is real, returned to dream in essence,*
> *and I, fallen back into the well of adolescence,*
>
> *jealously question you: whether you love me,*
> *whether, on my youth's summit, you will yet be*
> *my wife—I am now hoping once again,*
> *and, back on life's alert road, where I have fallen,*
> *I know you are all this. My wife, my friend and peer—*
> *only far! Beyond three wild frontiers.*

(Translated by Emery George)

Dreams, the wild surge of desire, and the sober objectivity of intellect; the union of an emotional flood of personal confession and perfectly crafted classical poetry characterize his poems, most of which were conceived in different labour camps. In the age-old qualities of a humane culture, in the delight of the senses, and in clarity of intellect he saw values worth saving for "a better world than this": that was his basic faith. It was for this he raised his voice, called on the will to battle on, summoned up the gnarled figures of wrathful prophets (*Eighth Eclogue* — Nyolcadik ecloga). The agony of his situation, however, provided little inspiration. He was impelled to speak of horrors, of the exhaustion of men falling during a forced march. Among the "filthy, stinking crowd" of his fellows, intent on avoiding being shot, he can yet rise to the heights of the "Poet" as he writes with the stub of a pencil, "in half-dark, blindly, in earthworm-rhythm ... inching along on the paper", in his tiny notebook—writing perfect poetry. Even as Attila József, on the verge of insanity, wrote of his consciousness, of the decomposition of his being.

This poetry is one of the peaks of antifascist verse. He was not a prolific writer, but what he wrote remains a part of the glory of Hungarian literature.

59 Fiction 1920–1940

Prose written during the twenties and thirties mirrors the diversity of literature as a whole at that time. Ideological divisions can be seen in the themes writers chose. The subject-matter of the largest group of novels and short stories was the harshness of workers' lives, the challenges it presented, and the contradictions, distortions, and changes in peasant life. The books taking the intellectual and moral problems of the bourgeoisie as their central theme form a second group. The socialist or peasant-oriented writers are clearly distinguishable from the "refined" writers who chose to remain within the bourgeois ambience. These categories do not necessarily apply to every writer. The socialist character of Béla Illés's or Tibor Déry's books, for instance, consists not merely of dealing with the life of the working class but also analysing it. And it would be oversimplification to place Áron Tamási, Andor Endre Gelléri or Károly Pap in one group or another.

Prose styles can be distinguished by their degree of realism, by whether influenced by the different aesthetic theories of the day, and by whether they are action-oriented or simple essays. But the different trends rarely appeared in their pure form.

Hungarian prose of that period is more realistic and traditional than European writing of the time. This was partly due to social causes, and also partly because realism in nineteenth-century prose arrived late, and so the tradition of Hungarian realism had not yet been exhausted. Is is fair to say that prose, especially in the form of the novel, failed to achieve the standard of the poetry of that period. It is worth noting indeed that autobiographical writing made up an unexpectedly large part of these novels. The fact that this led towards the essay form is also relevant. Apart from Móricz and Kassák, who wrote autobiographies in this period, Lajos Nagy, Péter Veres, János Kodolányi, Andor Endre Gelléri, Károly Pap, Gyula Illyés and Sándor Márai as well as the painter Aurél Bernáth also wrote similar works (*The Way we Lived in Pannonia* — Így éltünk Pannóniában), and the excellent autobiographical work of the architect Pál Granasztói *Confession and Farewell* (Vallomás és búcsú) also belongs in this category. Some of the authors of this period also wrote plays, but apart from those of László Németh these were considerably fewer and less important than their novels and short stories.

Lajos Nagy (1883-1954)

He was the same age as the younger *Nyugat* generation, and the two masters of prose of the interwar years, Kassák and Dezső Szabó. He emerged as a writer much later than his contemporaries, and this was very important both in his career and in his adherence to different artistic groups. He was the illegitimate child of a housemaid in a lowlands community of the Plain. He lived in poverty in both the countryside and the capital, but his mother managed to give him an education. For years he worked in different offices, then came a period as a tutor, and he finally succeeded sufficiently to live from his writing. For a while he was in touch with the social democratic and communist movements, and in 1934 he took part in the Soviet Writers' Congress with Gyula Illyés.

He was first and foremost a short-story writer; the smaller events of life attracted his attention; complicated plots held no attraction for him. While the realism of Móricz was inspired by great human tragedies and conflicts, which is why his works are so strongly rooted in the past, the tales of Lajos Nagy are set in the present and are shot through with disillusion and bitterness. The peasant hero of Móricz *Just To Eat One's Fill* (Egyszer jóllakni) buries his knife to the hilt in the breast of the gendarme sitting beside him; but in Nagy's *Farm Story* (Tanyai történet) the peasants humbly submit to the blows of the gendarme. He also paints realistically the desire in the wife of the beaten man for the stronger man, who leads an obviously better life, mixed with feelings of solidarity towards her husband.

Beautiful human faces only appear very indirectly in his pieces. His sentences are spare and severely objective, and, like the poems written by Lőrinc Szabó in his revolutionary period, deal with facts which leave no room for illusions of any sort. The aesthetic skill of his best short stories lies in the harmonious combination of spare construction and the concentrated brevity of the subject-matter. Much of his writing is concerned with man's inhumanity to man. Especially horrifying are his descriptions of the early manifestations of anti-Semitism in the years of the White Terror. The austere, apparently dispassionate style contains within itself the controlled passion of protest. Bitter sarcasm and ruthless caricature appear in much of his writings. Nor is he above a certain amount of didacticism: he frequently deals in abstractions, his characters are often stereotyped. The confrontation of the Rich Man and the everlasting underdog, the Poor Man appears in several forms, as for example in *The Road Accident* (Utcai baleset). All this gives his work a similarity with that of Brecht, but the simultaneous technique which he occasionally uses also recalls Dos Passos to the reader.

Kiskunhalom (1934) was a work in his new style, in which he assembled a day in the life of a large village out of several parallel short stories. Ordinarily dull, in-human or tragic events and figures pass before our eyes, without comment, and finally the work becomes a completed whole. This novel was a forerunner of what came to be known as village research or "sociographical" literature. *Budapest Café* (Budapest Nagykávéház, 1936) is a similar outstanding work about middle-class life. Some of his other short stories which could be classed as masterpieces, *The Lesson* (A lecke), *January* (Január), and *May 1919* (1919 Május), all cruelly satirize human self-abasement. He adapted the last into a one-act play called *The New Guest has Arrived* (Új vendég érkezett), in 1954. Of his few novels, two of autobiographical interest are *The Rebellious Man* (A lázadó ember, 1949) and *The Fleeing Man* (A menekülő ember, 1954). His articles and sketches, moreover, had a keenly critical eye for people and conditions in the anti-revolutionary period, and were written with a passion barely concealed in a dry, factual style.

To some extent Lajos Nagy occupied a central position among socialist writers until the mid-thirties. Because of his leftist attitude, the emigré communist writers regarded him as a comrade, and many of his works helped to form the "sociographical" style. While the objective, dispassionate writing of Lajos Nagy is firmly connected with avant-garde trends, the majority of revolutionary socialist writers and the populist writers continued on the road of traditional narrative.

Béla Illés (1895–1974)

was the most important of the communist emigré writers. He continued the tradition of the anecdote as earlier exemplified by Mikszáth in his novels, renewed with fresh topical and ideological content and social realism. He was born in Kassa, fought on different fronts in the First World War from 1916 on, and also in the battles of the Hungarian Republic of Councils of 1919. Later he was chief secretary of the World Union of Proletarian Writers. During the Second World War he enlisted as a militiaman in the Soviet Army, and in 1945 he returned to his homeland with the rank of major. Since then he has been a respected member of the Hungarian literary world and his works have been published in numerous editions.

His first important novel was *The Tisza is Burning* (Ég a Tisza, 1929) which perpetuated the memory of the struggles of the Hungarian Republic of Councils. This critical picture of the 1918–19 Revolution was influenced by Expressionism and contains a number of character sketches. *The Carpathian Rhapsody* (Kárpáti rapszódia, 1939), a trilogy which is held to be his masterpiece, is on a higher level altogether. It has heroes; strong lumbermen who long for a better life, timber workers who are becoming aware of themselves and organize, the Jewish village doctor who expounds the theories of humanity and social responsibility until he is shot during the war. The story begins at the turn of the century and most of it takes place over the next twenty years embracing the defeat of the Hungarian Republic of Councils and subsequent events. It is a comprehensive description of society, from a communist viewpoint, but never degenerates into propaganda. The novel is full of action and the characters are sympathetic. It is a world defending old traditions, but fighting new problems.

This novel of Béla Illés's is among the first and most successful examples of socialist realism. In those of his novels dealing with Hungary's part in the First World War, and also parts of *The Carpathian Rhapsody,* the episode and traditional narrative tend to take too prominent a place to the detriment of the work as a whole. But they are of value for their documentary qualities (*Conquest* — Honfoglalás, 1954).

Communist Emigré Writers

In addition to Béla Illés, a large number of writers who emigrated to the Soviet Union made a contribution to socialist literature. *Máté Zalka* (1896–1937), who died a hero's death at Huesca in the Spanish Civil War, was planning a long cycle of novels. It would have dealt with the years leading up to the Revolution and then the period of the Russian Civil War. Only the first volume of this work was completed, titled *Doberdo* (1936). It was a work of realism describing the lives of the masses, the soldiers of the world wars, and the processes which gave them revolutionary consciousness. *Frigyes Karikás* (1895–1938), who fell a victim to the purges, wrote short anecdotal stories which were sympathetic and joyous, though often ending in tragedy. They usually portrayed battles of 1919 or episodes from the history of the workers' movement. *Sándor Barta* (1897–1938) was a noted poet, but he wrote a novel *Gold Diggers* (Aranyásók, 1935), which shows the influence of Dos Passos and Upton Sinclair. It deals with the contradictions of life in Budapest at the turn of the century. *Antal Hidas* (1899–1980) was more important as a novelist, though he wrote poems as well. His novels *Mr. Ficzek* (Ficzek úr, 1936), *Other Music is Needed* (Más muzsika kell, 1959), and *Martin and his Friends* (Márton és barátai, 1963), compose a cycle dealing, with a humour and satire reminiscent of Hašek and Ilf-Petrov, with typical figures of the first twenty years of the twentieth century. *Sándor Gergely* (1896–1966) changed from his earlier Expressionism to a style reminiscent of the early Móricz. His best books are *György Dózsa* (1936–1945), a trilogy which brings the 1514 peasant rebellion to life, and parts of his autobiographical cycle, *Thorny Path* (Rögös út, 1955), *Forbidden Roads* (Tiltott utak, 1961), and *Promoted to the Upper Grade* (Felsőbb osztályba léphet, 1964). *Knights and Heroes* (Vitézek és hősök, 1938), a play which is set in the time of the Horthy regime, sets communist principles against the compromising half-hearted behaviour of the bourgeoisie. *József Lengyel* was also a communist writer forced into emigration, but he wrote most of his works after the liberation and therefore will be discussed in another chapter.

Ervin Sinkó (1898–1967), who spent most of his life in Yugoslavia, had also been an emigré. His prose writings were strongly committed to socialism, highly cerebral and very didactic. In *The Optimists* (Optimisták), he dealt with the period of the 1918–19 Revolution, and his diary, *The Story of a Novel* (Egy regény regénye), discussed the publishing history of his *Optimists,* and the effect on it of the period of the purges in the Soviet Union.

Several Hungarian authors living in Rumania must also be counted as socialist writers. *András Szilágyi* (b. 1904) wrote *The New Pastor* (Új pásztor), and both *István Nagy* (1904–1977) and *István Asztalos* (1909–1960) depicted the struggles of the peoples of the multi-national territory of Hungary and their interdependency clearly and decidedly, and sometimes humorously. *The Grandchildren of the Oltyáns* (Oltyánok unokái, 1943), by Nagy and *The Wind Does not Blow* (Szél fuvatlan nem indul, 1949), by Asztalos were their most important works. Their style is very much the style of Zsigmond Móricz and is linked to the work of the populist writers.

Péter Veres (1897–1970)

The fact that a strictly objective description of reality became very important to a group of writers known as the populist (*népi*) writers, was connected with the emergence of village research or "sociographical" literature, and the writing of rural sociology. There were some among them, Ferenc Erdei, Imre Kovács, and Zoltán Szabó, whose activities were not really literary at all in the strict sense of the word. Others were simply narrators—Pál Szabó and Áron Tamási. But the works of Péter Veres, for instance, show a very close connection between sociology and fiction, and so do the youthful works of József Darvas.

Péter Veres was born into a poor peasant family east of the river Tisza. He educated himself while working as an agricultural labourer and ended as a widely cultured man. He was victimized for his revolutionary feelings and was arrested several times. In addition to his sociological and literary works, his interests extended to a wide variety of social questions, and his critical works on literature are also of great interest. He was a Cabinet Minister for a while after 1945, until the dissolution of the Peasant Party, and then he was President of the Hungarian Writers' Association for many years.

Accounting (Számadás, 1937), an autobiography, *The End of the Village* (Gyepsor, 1940) and *The Test* (Próbatétel, 1951), volumes of short stories, and *Plate-layers* (Pályamunkások, 1951), which was a loosely organized novel, were all written in a carefully restrained style and were designed to describe facts in the same way as the "sociographical" survey which measured counties or villages. He observed the lives of poor peasants from the inside, and wrote about them in a realist style, describing their subhuman lives in a succint and unpretentious manner. These writings lack the bitterness which runs through the work of Lajos Nagy. He never ignored, and often made a point of noting, the continuous development of the human being through work, poverty and struggle, sensitive at the same time to the beauty which can be found in the lives of the poor.

Three Generations (Három nemzedék, 1951–1961), which later appeared under the title *The Story of the Balogh Family* (A Balogh család története), is a powerful trilogy of this type written after the liberation. In its way, this work is unique. It gives a comprehensive and faithful view of the lives of poor peasants in the first half of the twentieth century. A few outstanding types are presented, and in one powerful section he gives a sensitive picture of men and women facing the difficult trials of normal everyday life. The novel is not as great as the theme would imply, partly because there is too much dry sociographical material in it; in some places it is simply a series of disconnected episodes and at other times the action degenerates into mere anecdote. The world which was going through increasingly complex changes could no longer be successfully described with the tools of naive realism.

Pál Szabó (1893-1970)

Szabó's books are more "romantic" and poetic than Péter Veres's strict fidelity to reality. He was born in a village of the eastern plains and worked as a peasant and village bricklayer. He later joined in the production of different publications of the populist writers and after the liberation he went into politics and he was a member of the Presidential Council.

His best work is found in his short stories—*The Trumpeter* (A trombitás), *Anna Szegi's Kiss* (Szegi Anna csókja), *The Legend of the Hired Woman* (A béresasszony legendája), etc. Poor peasants who aspire to lead decent human lives, but are tragically frustrated by social conditions, are the centre of his stories. The action meanders, a multitude of episodes follow each other in a loosely organized chain, and the lively descriptions of peasant life are almost ethnographic in their detailed observation. He is keenly aware of the connection between man and nature, and despite the moments of tragedy, his writing is informed with a dynamic sense of life (*The Wedding, Christening, Cradle* — Lakodalom, Keresztelő, Bölcső; *The Mills of God* — Isten malmai). Some of his critics classify him with Giono; but this is a mistake, since Pál Szabó's outlook on life is basically different from Giono's deliberate neo-primitivism and hostility to civilization. Szabó catches and transfixes the ancient unchanging misery of the peasants, and nevertheless sees the poetry in their lives. *The Wedding, Christening, Cradle* (1942–1943) is a trilogy which was used as the basis for a very fine film after the liberation, called *The Soil Under Your Feet* (Talpalatnyi föld).

453

János Kodolányi (1899-1968)

In his best works he was intent on expressing the realities of the world. He was born into a middle-class family, but broke off all connections with them as his political sentiments became increasingly radical. For a while he was close to the workers' movement and the illegal Communist Party, but he later joined the populist writers movement and his attitude became increasingly nationalist and anti-revolutionary, and he was unable to publish and lived in obscurity between 1945 and 1954.

He also used naturalist and realist methods of writing to depict the hard and often cruel life of the villages of the Great Plain, the life of peasants who live in spiritual darkness and a self-destructive environment, a life in which beauty or the memory of a brave, great act appears as a rare contrast (*Darkness* — Sötétség, *Unarmed* — Fegyvertelenül). His most successful dramatic works also deal with this theme, *Earthquake* (Földindulás, 1939). At other times he writes of the members of the decaying middle class. His analysis of character and the construction of his short stories are excellent (*Sweltering Summer Day* — Rekkenő nyári nap). He was one of the most talented of the populist writers as far as the description of character, nature and the organization of his novels were concerned. His style is related more closely to that of Móricz than anyone else, but for many years his interest was concentrated on the period after the defeat of the revolution and on the problems of peasants in the interwar years. Later, in his monumental novels *Brother Julianus* (Julianus barát), *The Sons of Iron* (A vas fiai), *Blessed Margit* (Boldog Margit, 1936–1938) and others, he wrote of social developments of the thirteenth century, and the time of the Mongol Invasion, using them to exemplify contemporary problems. Later, he turned to the world of myths: *The Flood* (Vízözön), *New Sky, New Earth* (Új ég, új föld), and to autobiography in *Happy Times of Peace* (Boldog békeidők, 1956) and *The Watershed* (Vízválasztó, 1960).

Áron Tamási (1897-1966)

Among the peasant writers were some who united a strict adherence to factual truth with a Romantic style. Áron Tamási was one of the most original talents among these authors, a talent as far removed from the strictly objective style of Péter Veres as possible.

He was born in the mountains of Transylvania in a peasant family with many children. He lived in the United States from 1923 to 1926 and then settled in Kolozsvár. In the nineteen-forties he moved to Budapest. He soon gained popularity and recognition with his novels and short stories, but the reading public showed much less interest in him in the last twenty years of his life.

Although his work is romantically inclined, it does not mean that the picture he gave of the inhabitants of the Transylvanian mountains was false. The subject of the peasants and lumbermen living in poverty and hardship attracted him through the poetry that welled up through their bitter lives. The natural background is painted in fresh colours, and the plot and events are treated in both whimsical and dramatic fashion. But above all, it is the beauty of his characters' faces on which he dwells with the greatest intensity. The tragic atmosphere of old ballads can be felt in some of his works, and an apparently innocent simplicity in others. The poetry of folk-tales and ballads is revived and renewed in his novels and in some of his short stories. Among the former, the most outstanding is his *Abel* trilogy, especially its first part, *Abel Alone* (Ábel a rengetegben, 1932). The hero, who as a child was forced into becoming a forest guard, withstands the trials and tribulations with which both nature and the forces of society confront him. At times he escapes from his difficulties with mischievous cunning, at times he suffers a setback, but he never cracks completely, he is always finally saved by his unique sense of humour.

A Romantic–pantheistic view of nature permeates all his work which at first sight bears a resemblance to Giono's books. His great awe and respect for nature is not, however, as contrived, and does not serve as a decorative cover for retrograde social views. At least, not in his best works. But occasional mythical, irrational tendencies do appear in his works. The more "prosaic" forms of realism obviously did not appeal to him and the novels in which he describes and criticizes society never rise above a mediocre level. The world of the snowy mountains disappeared in the twentieth century, and this prevented him from continuing to produce works of an equally fine calibre as his best which in the form of novella are among the best works of fiction in Hungarian literature, e.g. *Tamás Szász the Heathen* (Szász Tamás, a pogány), *Breathe in, Little Mihály* (Mihályka, szippants), *Take Some Fire* (Tüzet vegyenek), *Beautiful Anna Domonkos* (Szép Domonkos Anna), *Dawn Bird* (Hajnali madár), *Flowering Goat Horns* (Kivirágzott kecskeszarvak).

His experiments in writing plays are also interesting; plays which employ the methods of character analysis, deal with real people and real problems, and have charming elements of mysticism and fable. His best plays, e.g. *The Songbird* (Énekes madár, 1933), are very attractive in their whimsical light-heartedness and their poetic qualities.

Andor Endre Gelléri (1907-1945)

Gelléri was, next to Tamási, the best "Romantic" novelist of the period. He was born in an outer suburb of Budapest, and worked as a manual labourer for many years. Being of Jewish descent, he spent the war years as a forced labourer. His health, naturally good, was ruined through privation and cruelty. He was deported after the German occupation of Hungary, and in May 1945 he died of typhoid fever.

Apart from his voluminous autobiography, *The Story of a Self-regard* (Egy önérzet története, 1957), and *Laundry Works* (Nagymosoda, 1930), a loosely constructed novel, he only wrote short stories, mainly about transport workers, house painters, unemployed people ruined to vagabondage, and the little people of the cities. Dezső Kosztolányi aptly named his style "fairy realism". In his works the familiar life of everyday is a dream, a world of fantasy and drawn with a magical touch. The styles of Andor Endre Gelléri and Áron Tamási have much in common, with the difference that Gelléri drew his themes from the outskirts of the city rather than from the mountains of Transylvania. Apprentices hungry for women (*Thirsty Apprentices* — Szomjas inasok), "honeymooners" heading for the hills of Buda, who overcome their poverty with their fun and delight (*The Honeymooners of Hűvösvölgy* — Hűvösvölgyi nászutasok) all come to joyous life in his works. At other times he is touched by the desire for beauty in people who may live through an instant of wonder in dreams, or find it in the rare and fleeting miracle of a moment in time.

The themes of his tales can scarcely be called magical, but a magical quality runs through them. He encircles his characters with sparkling colours—as if to emphasize the real tragedies that lie behind the grey, seemingly unimportant events of every day (*Old Panna's Mirror* — A vén Panna tükre; *Carnival* — Farsang). His taste runs to the outcasts of society, or those who live on the periphery; and they give his stories a genuine reality. The tramp in *The House on the Vacant Lot* (Ház a telepen) is repeating the primitive development of civilization when he knocks together a little shed on a vacant lot, finds an old stove to shelter his fire, and finally takes a woman to it—and experiences true tragedy when the land-owner knocks his shanty down.

Many other short stories by Gelléri deal with the joys and tragedies of ordinary people. Occasionally a raw, robust, and even cruel realism appears in some of them (*Port* — Kikötő; *At the Carriers* — A szállítóknál). His later tales are sparer, greyer, more disillusioned (*Georgi, the Barber* — Georgi, a borbély; *Fifty* — Ötven).

Károly Pap (1897-1944)

who was murdered by the fascists, had certain affinities with Gelléri, but he cannot really be identified with any particular literary category. His powerful short stories often express crude and sombre passions. He took a pitiless view of reality in treating a variety of themes; he was interested in social problems, and the effects of both Jewish mysticism and modern Symbolism can also be felt. He wrote about the members of his own circle as readily as he worked over stories from the Bible. Social dissatisfaction appears in his short stories discussing moral problems, deliberations on the relationship between the body and soul. A cycle called *You Freed me from Death* (Megszabadítottál a haláltól, 1932) is the best of his narratives. His novel *Azarel* (1937) is based on events in his own life. He is masterly in his descriptions of anguished and passionate childhood and of the community of unassimilated Jews very conscious of their Jewish heritage whom he knew in his own childhood.

Middle-class Writers

Literary worth and general popularity have rarely parted company to the extent that they did between the two world wars. The authors discussed so far only became popular with the changed tastes of the reading public after liberation. Before that time the emigré communist writers had no means of reaching the Hungarian public. By contrast, an extensive proliferation of middle-class bestseller literature developed, which satisfied the reading and leisure needs of the middle classes. Writers who often made promising beginnings frequently lowered their standards to meet the tastes of the middle-class public for the sake of success, to the detriment of their art writing as a whole. *Lajos Zilahy* (1891–1974) was one who achieved great success with his novels and plays in middle-class circles. His novels were professionally skilful, but false in their social comment. His superficial novels dealing with the passions of love were: *The Two Prisoners* (A két fogoly, 1927), *The Water Carries Something* (Valamit visz a víz, 1928), *The Fugitive* (A szökevény, 1931), dealing with middle-class life, and *Ararat* (1941), a novel criticizing the upper middle classes. He went to live abroad in 1947. *Irén Gulácsy* (1894–1945) made her name with rather shallow historical novels, and *Miklós Surányi* (1882–1936) and *Zsolt Harsányi* (1887–1943) with their undemanding and entertaining social and biographical novels. *József Nyírő* (1889–1953) was also a typical Transylvanian, and resembled Áron Tamási in his style, although not quite so fine a talent. He mainly wrote short stories, *Bence Uz* (Uz Bence, 1933), and novels, e.g. *Under the Yoke of God* (Isten igájában, 1930). *Sándor Hunyady* (1890–1942) was a writer of short stories on a higher level. They were polished and cultured, written from only entirely middle-class viewpoint, and he also wrote plays which made concessions to the audience with their trivial, easy solutions.

Sándor Márai (b. 1900)

He was the most important of the bourgeois writers before 1945. He came from a respectable middle-class family of German descent. During his student days he supported the 1918 Revolution and later left for Germany, where he lived for a considerable length of time. After his return his works appeared in left-wing publications for a while, but he then became more conservative, and very popular with the bourgeoisie. He left the country in 1948, and since then his works have appeared abroad, i.e. the United States.

His most important work is a semi-autobiographical novel, *The Confessions of a Citizen* (Egy polgár vallomásai, 1930). The subject is a bourgeois family shackled to tradition and yet managing to survive quite comfortably. He paints it very vividly, and coolly analyses it at the same time. It was written to suit the life-style of the Hungarian middle class never fully developed, which viewed the world with a slight feeling of intellectual superiority, but never showed any serious interest in the genuinely urgent problems of contemporary Hungarian society. *The Sulky Ones* (Sértődöttek, 1948) is a novel, the title of which is indicative of his feelings, in which he reacts, with his refined worldly sensitivity, to the barbarism of fascism.

One of the characteristics of his style is his economy of language. He was influenced by both Impressionism and Expressionism. His sentences are all delicately and subtly constructed, but occasionally overmannered. Here he continued and modified the tradition of Kosztolányi and Krúdy. Some of his work was strongly influenced by Western writers such as Mann, Cocteau and Duhamel. Much of it, in conformity with one of the trends of the times, was more intellectual in its approach than the fashion of previous writers. Some of his other important books are: *Baby or the First Love* (Bébi vagy az első szerelem, 1928), *The Rioters* (A zendülők, 1930), *Csutora* (1930) and *Guest Performance in Bolzano* (Vendégjáték Bolzanóban, 1940).

Endre Illés (b. 1902)

is a master of prose style. He has an eye sensitive to the significance of small incidents, and is adept in reproducing the minutest shades of life, employing a fine irony in describing characteristics and changes in emotional states. He writes in a very realistic style, but with Impressionist overtones. His characters are mainly modelled on intellectual contemporaries, which gave him an indirect chance to discuss political and moral themes and principles, frequently passing judgement on people's behaviour, e.g. in *The Judgement* (Ítélet), *Double Circle* (Kettős kör). *The Ambitious* (Törtetők, 1941) is a play satirizing the careerists of his age. *Anger* (Méreg) is a study of emotion, and was an important milestone in Hungarian interwar dramatic literature. His vigorous intellect and excellent style has made him one of the best twentieth-century essay writers in Hungary (*Chalk-sketches* — Krétarajzok, 1958). As publisher and editor he has played an important role in Hungarian literary life.

The Emergence of Essayistic Prose

One of the characteristics of Hungarian prose from the thirties on was the emergence of intellectual content. This tendency, which in extreme cases led to an essayistic style, to a certain extent represented a renewal of the line of Kemény and Eötvös and others in the sadly neglected tradition of Hungarian narrative prose.

Somewhat further removed from these younger writers was *Aladár Kuncz* (1886–1931), who belonged to an elder generation and whose work *The Black Convent* (A fekete kolostor, 1931) dealt with his internment in France during the First World War. It is a coolly objective and carefully analysed study of the psychology of different characters forced into close proximity, the "other world" of the camp, its stratification into classes and conflicts.

The intellectual content of the works of the essayist and literary historian *Antal Szerb* (1901–1945) is important, but he also wrote novels, such as the fantasy *The Pendragon Legend* (Pendragon-legenda, 1934), which is situated in an English castle and is a parody of a detective-cum-ghost story. His bourgeois conformist *Traveller in the Moonlight* (Utas és holdvilág, 1937) revolves around self-discovery and the plot is linked to a trip in Italy. He was directly influenced by the new Romantic current from the West, and his work is dominated by a skilfully presented light-heartedness which made one to feel that the author did not take the story seriously. He is distinguished from the old-style Romantic writer by a mild irony and his essayistic style. His last novel, *The Queen's Necklace* (A királyné nyaklánca) is a neo-Romantic, sad, ironical story of disillusionment set in the 1789 *ancien régime* of pre-revolutionary France. He was murdered by the fascists a few months before the liberation of Hungary.

The writing of essayistic intellectual prose was mainly confined to the so-called "urbanists". *Emil Kolozsvári Grandpierre* (b. 1907) wrote a highly critical psychological and social analysis of bourgeois life and morals in his carefully organized autobiographical novel *Yesterday* (Tegnap, 1942). *Zsigmond Remenyik* (1900–1962) also wrote a largely autobiographical novel, *Guilty Conscience* (Bűntudat, 1937) exposing and condemning the life of the gentry. He described bourgeois ideology and behaviour with bitter sarcasm in *Flea Circus* (Bolhacirkusz, 1932) and *The Living and the Dead* (Élők és holtak, 1948). His plays which are filled with bitterness over social conditions, include *The Blőses Owe Everybody* (Blőse úrék mindenkinek tartoznak, 1934), *Hotel Old Europe* (Hotel Vén-Európa, 1941). The literary scholar

István Sőtér (b. 1913) made use of Surrealistic elements in some of his work, but his short stories and novels are closer to neo-realism (*Quixotry* — Fellegjárás, 1939, and *Fall into Sin* — Bűnbeesés). *Miklós Szentkuthy* (b. 1908), an erudite and cultured scholar, rejected all traditional elements in his novels, as in *Prae* (1934). *András Hevesi* (1902–1940), who died serving in the French army, produced an analytical novel *Rain in Paris* (Párizsi eső, 1936).

The essay style and the preference for intellectual content was not exclusive to any special group of writers. Perhaps the taste for semi-autobiographical writing is partly responsible for it, as here form, plot and action are largely relegated to the background, and analysis and judgement given more importance. This trend is also present in different forms in the communist writer Tibor Déry and the populist writers Gyula Illyés and László Németh.

60 László Németh (1901-1975)

His Life

He was born in 1901, and in the period between the wars he was a member of the populist writers' group: he was indeed one of the leading theorists of this movement, yet his varied literary output can in no wise be described as populist.

His father came from a peasant family, but became a secondary school teacher. He himself first followed an arts course at the University, but then switched to medicine. His first published work, a short story, appeared in *Nyugat,* but he later severed all contacts with that review. Dezső Szabó exerted a great influence on him, but being cooler and more scholarly by nature, he came to reject the latter's rather pompous affectations. His novels and plays soon won him public acclaim. He became a leading inspiration to young men of the thirties and forties. From 1932 to 1936 he published a review called *Tanu* (Witness), written exclusively by himself. He was greatly influenced by the books of Spengler, Dilthey, Ortega y Gasset, Henrik de Man, and Fried. László Németh's opposition to capitalism was a romantic anti-capitalism, but he found himself unable to identify with Marxism, and sought a third possibility between socialism and capitalism; he had a vision—an illusion— like the bourgeois reformer and his Utopia, of little communities, "islands", which would reorganize society. Another aspect of this "third way" was that the leading force in renewing society was to be the intelligentsia. Although in his novels and plays he describes the failure of an "exodus" and the island theory, he did not rid himself entirely of his erroneous views until the late fifties. It was only then that he was able to return to literary life: during the early fifties he was only allowed to publish translations.

Novels

Németh's prose renewed the traditional forms of the novel of realism. It is interesting to note that when there was such a vogue for short stories he wrote practically nothing but novels. He is undoubtedly one of the most important Hungarian novelists of the century. His books are usually in the form of a straightforward narrative, about the events in the life of one man, and the whole of the work is concentrated on develop-

461

ing that line. Each individual movement, thought, word, mental or instinctive process of the different characters are precisely connected with one another.

The highly intellectual gifts of the author are demonstrated in the handling of complex and intricate problems facing his heroes, and in their profound, frequently clinical, precise exposition, treated with the greatest artistic refinement. This in no way impairs the fabric of the novel, though it may slow the action a little.

There are two chief characters in one outstanding, and somewhat different novel, *Guilt* (Bűn, 1936), which highlights a very real social problem. The hero is a man of intellect who wants to identify with the people and support them, and improve society not unlike László Németh himself, but is finally broken by internal conflict and commits suicide, for he cannot genuinely tear himself from the way of life he is trying to reject, nor equally can he resign himself to a half-and-half existence.

His best novels are those which portray the fascination a certain kind of woman holds for him, and her reactions to certain situations. First among these is *Mourning* (Gyász, 1936). We are shown the figure of a woman who lost her husband early, and cannot reconcile herself to the role dictated by village custom. By degrees she retires within herself, and confronts the world around her with arrogant defiance.

Another in this genre is *Revulsion* (Iszony, 1947), concerning an energetic but lonely woman. Her father's unexpected death virtually paralyses her, she marries a man in every respect her exact opposite. A few years of marriage inevitably lead to her killing her husband, neither intentionally, nor accidentally. The tale is told in the first person, and Németh views the world through the coldly appraising eyes of his heroine, seeing nothing but human frailty and falsehood. The woman is endowed with the universal, unchanging qualities of humankind, yet the individual, particular traits of her own personality are perceptively and convincingly presented. From her strict analysis, determined in time and space, he unfolds his thoughts: this type of person must go into the service of higher, more universal concerns, if it wishes to find its way.

It is this course that *Eszter Égető* adopts, in the novel of that name (publ. 1956). The book gives a broad, graphic picture of the Hungarian middle class from the turn of the century to the nineteen-fifties. The central character is a woman who, despite disappointment and discouragement, persists in her attempts to create a community; she brings families together, encourages peasant talent, and takes up the cause of the persecuted.

In *Mercy* (Irgalom, 1965), the heroine, a medical student, begins by passing strict moral judgements on her fellow beings. Experience slowly teaches her to modify her attitudes and understanding and a healing compassion takes its place. In the end she gives herself to a lame boy whose zeal for the defeated proletarian revolution leads her to see that her calling is "to give faith to lame mankind, so that it can run,

and to care for its foot that it should not trip over its own lameness". The novel
shows that the author has accepted the socialist view of the world, coupling the
warmth of humane compassion with revolutionary determination.

Plays

Németh occupies a unique position in the relatively inferior field of Hungarian drama.
Like his novels, his plays are constructed on the old, traditional pattern; he is untouched by the innovative tendencies of the avant-garde. He can best be described
as a follower of Ibsen; his plays are realist, he concentrates on the development of
character, the revelation of hidden realities, on the disintegration and collapse of
the inner being. As in his novels, much of his characters are patterned on himself
—the chief protagonist is invariably an idealist trying to arouse a sense of service to the
community in men's consciousness, and in the process struggling with himself—or
rather with the world around him—family, society, country—which exploits his
weaknesses. Although he wins moral victories, his plans never come to fruition, and
his propensity to abstract moral principles leads to the distortion of his human qualities, eventually turning him into a monster. In *Galilei* (1954) Németh has managed
to create a person devoted to the highest universal aspirations for progress and wisdom, whose acts are indeed in accordance with his nature, but which appear as
spontaneous, almost irresistible self-interest. At the end of the play, this spontaneity
grows into a sense of moral responsibility, as the hero revokes the oath made under
coercion. "There was no special law made for me on Mt. Sinaï." The psychological
insight and profoundly intellectual approach produce complete conviction, it is
probably the best example of László Németh's devotion to his vocation.

His best plays are *Lightning* (Villámfénynél, 1936), *Cherry Garden* (Cseresnyés,
1939), the chief character an idealist who loses all in organizing a Utopian community;
Gregory VII (VII. Gergely, 1939), who is finally left to stand alone; and *The Two
Bolyais* (A két Bolyai, 1961), the struggle of those two entirely different great men
of science who were father and son.

Essays

László Németh did not specialize in any particular branch of learning, but his wide
knowledge of medicine and mathematics, philosophy, politics, education and the
arts provided an exceptional background for the writing of essays. These essays are
logical, sensitive, and thought-provoking, though the influence of Dezső Szabó and
the school of *Geistesgeschichte* at times led him to the enunciation of irrational theories.

His later works are free from such influences. His review *Tanu* contained many of his essays and articles. The subjects are various, the philosophy behind them always consistent. Three plays of García Lorca, the problems of literary translation, the poetry of Ady and the folklore of the South Slavs, the possibilities of combining the ancient and modern in art, or the mathematical and philosophical works of János Bolyai all engage his attention. Whatever his subject, he always has something new to say, something substantial and often worthy of discussion. His opinions are based on a great store of knowledge, whether on the subject of ancient Greek culture, Hungarian verse forms or modern Hungarian and foreign writers. These essays and articles were published in a collection of volumes called *The Quality Revolution* (A minőség forradalma) in 1948, and a more recent book of essays *Nights in Sajkód* (Sajkódi esték) in 1961.

61 Gyula Illyés (1902–1983)

Another great member of the "populist" writers' group was born a year after László Németh. His work, however, like Németh's, soon broke the narrow bonds of that particular movement, and even before the Second World War he was recognized as a leading writer of the era. His work as a whole, moreover like that of Tibor Déry's, belongs rather to the following period, when a new literature appeared.

His Life

He was the son of a mechanic, born on a large estate in Western Hungary. He grew up among the children of the servants on the estate until a concerted effort by his large family sent him to secondary school. At sixteen he became involved in revolutionary politics, and during the 1918–19 Revolution fought against its enemies on the Rumanian front. After its defeat he remained in Hungary for a while as part of the underground movement, but was soon forced to emigrate. His journeyings took him through Germany and Belgium, and finally to France, where he lived until 1925, working as a labourer and yet managing to attend lectures at the Sorbonne. At the same time he was active in the workers' movement, and found time to meet and get to know the exponents of French Surrealism.

On Illyés's return to Hungary Mihály Babits almost immediately perceived his exceptional gifts: by the end of the 1920s he was recognized as an outstanding poet. During the 1930s he became a leading figure in the emerging populist writers' group. In 1934 he and Lajos Nagy represented Hungary at the Soviet Writers' Congress. He became an editor of *Nyugat* and, when Babits died in 1941, he continued to run it, almost unaltered, under the name of *Magyar Csillag* (Hungarian Star), supporting the policy of the Popular Front. When the Germans occupied Hungary in 1944 he was forced into hiding. After the liberation he edited the populist *Válasz* (Response) for a time. In 1965 he was awarded the Grand Prix of Poetry at the Knokke Biennale, in 1978 that of the French Poets' Society. He wrote many fine prose works and plays, but his fame rests chiefly on his poems.

In the course of a career spanning several decades the work of Gyula Illyés underwent a number of changes, yet it nonetheless retained clearly identifiable features present in all his works from his first maturity as a poet. First and foremost are his objectivity, his concentration on an almost tangible clarity, and a simple, straightforward sense of order. For over ten years, from roughly 1930 to 1940, he wrote of the people among whom he was brought up, the labourers and employees of the great estates. The subject matter, the concern and, as a consequence, the expression of social dissatisfaction, as well as the simplicity of his style and his inclination to narrative, link him to his predecessor, József Erdélyi. Illyés's poetry was from the beginning consciously and carefully designed. His early surrealism is not to be found in his later work, but the influence of both older and more modern poets is always in evidence.

His sophisticated, sensitive and intellectual approach only appears indirectly at first: where necessary he diluted naiveté with mild irony, slipping from the subjective to the objective point of view, merging lyric and narrative in just and delicate proportion. It is this sense of proportion which his descriptive poems display, such as *Youth* (Ifjúság), *Three Old Men* (Három öreg) and *I Speak of Heroes* (Hősökről beszélek), poems written in the early thirties.

Idyll and Revolution

In *Youth* he painted a realistic and classically clear picture of the twentieth-century idyll of young love. The poem deals with the love of a sixteen-year-old country boy and his girl, and their plans for a happy and beautiful life. There is a slightly classic touch to the poem, with subtly ironic overtones. The simple, timeless beauty of the story is violently offset by the circumstances surrounding it; the boy fought for the revolution and is now in hiding.

I Speak of Heroes has a similar theme, although in a wider perspective; it concerns the events of a single night, and reaches a no less dramatic climax. The night is the night of "recovery", when, following an ancient custom of the poor, the people steal something from the produce which was the perquisite of the lords of the manor. The deed takes on a symbolical significance, representing an act of natural justice, the natural justice which will be triumph when the revolution abolishes the corruption of the existing social order. It is a feeling, completely convincing picture of the people and the countryside, in which a gentle humour and a revolutionary passion intermingle to create a masterpiece.

He uses concrete details to illustrate the appalling life of the poor peasants with the same ease. In the style of the *Neue Sachlichkeit,* he brings his peasant figures to life, their gestures and words conveying a sense of utter despair, as in *Elegy* (Elégia) and *The Sad Farm-hand* (Szomorú béres). He conjures up the image of Wonder Castle, taken from an old Hungarian folk-tale, seeing himself rambling up a hillside dotted with the villas of the wealthy, and remembering the Plain and its people. He envisages a treadmill with workers and peasants trudging round and round and revolving the "wondrous round thing" within which a delicate mechanism provides all the good things its inhabitants desire.

> *Outside the garden—where daily*
> *a crunched bridge and hospital*
> *melt on the tongues of this charmingly*
> *cavorting throng, not to mention thirty thousand*
> *stillborn infants—*
> *a parade was on: the milling casual*
> *lookers-on applauded, laughed.*
>
> (*The Wonder Castle* — A kacsalábon forgó vár;
> translated by Kenneth McRobbie)

Illyés is equally passionate, and equally sober, building the poem up with tiny observed details in *Carrion Eaters* (Hullaevők), written during the Second World War, where he contrasts the man eating chicken in an elegant restaurant with the peasant conscript losing his arms, legs, and life in that man's defence. His description of György Dózsa the peasants' leader in *György Dózsa's Address in the Market in Cegléd* (Dózsa György beszéde a ceglédi piacon) departing to do battle with the nobility is similarly realistic. He has the power of personifying and embodying the most abstract characteristics in concrete form. Many years later, after the liberation, the remains of a sculptured group of figures inspired him to a poem which incarnated the past, the present and long-desired future of the country *In the Garden of Statistics*) (A Statisztika-kertben). The gnarled and scarred hands of his grandfather inspired a poem on the universal labour of humanity, entitled *Two Hands* (Két kéz).

The Intellectual Approach

From the mid-fifties the poetry of Gyula Illyés took on a more deliberately intellectual approach. He ceased to see the ultimate answer lying in the hands of the peasant; or in those of the nation as a whole. Once again, in *On Seeing the Reformation Monument, Geneva* (A reformáció genfi emlékműve előtt) a piece of sculpture conjures up a myriad associations, and invites speculation on the eternal verities. In *Horsehair, Catgut* (Lószőr, macskabél...) he marvels that over thousands of years horsehair, catgut, resin and wood have slowly solidified and been transmuted into violin and music, and discovers in this process an incentive and a lesson for himself and for the twentieth-century poet.

To the questions on the philosophy of art asked by his generation, he replies in *Bartók*.

> *Picasso's two-nosed women,*
> *six-legged stallions*
> *alone could have keened abroad*
> *galloping, neighed out*
> *what we have borne, we men...*
>
> (Translated by Claire Lashley)

But he adds that "by speaking out the horror "dissolved". His earlier method of taking a small scene or event and magnifying it, his concentration on clarity and order are maintained in his later work. His work is nonetheless more irregular, more "rustic" than Attila József's. In the more intricately structured works he uses disharmony to make harmony.

Recent Lyric Poetry

The poems of Gyula Illyés of the late fifties and early sixties show a change. The former revolutionary speaks with greater resignation, his poetry is gentler, lighter, as in *Snowfall* (Hóesésben), or *Paris, Love* (Párizs, szerelem). The earlier style, deliberately pitched in a cruder voice, alternates with one more musical in tone, or an unrhymed structure, sublimated into poetry by its intellectual clarity and sinuous delicacy. The subject-matter also changed. The objective-narrative poetry of his earlier days became more inward looking, and at the same time, as in *Charons' Boat* (Kháron ladikján), more recognizably lyrical. In many of his later verses he was preparing for the "good death" which in its very senselessness makes sense at the end of life to which it puts a worthy full stop *(Mors bona, nihil aliud)*. In this too, we see his characteristic desire for order. A critic once said of him: "If Illyés has only a glass of wine by him, at once there are two of them, he and the glass," and his recent work showed him on occasions making "two of them" with death, dissolving its terrors, preparing himself, tuning himself to receive death, while, void of illusion, he looked annihilation in the face: "for there is no perdition, or other world, or God."

But while the writer prepared for death, his work continued to move on in new directions. His poems written in the '60s, especially his prose-poems, hark back to his earliest, Surrealist period. These later poems are more original, greater, more finely constructed than the earlier ones. They are visionary in places, yet spring from a vigorously materialist point of view. They deal with extreme opposites, life and annihilation, non-existence and the desire to rule the world, or just the rapture of the will to live. They are reticent in tone, yet from time to time passionately lyrical, often composed of very different units into an organized whole, which produce entirely new values, not only in his own work, but in the development of Hungarian poetry, examples being *At Dusk* (Alkonyatban), *Successful Effort* (Sikeres erőfeszítés), *The Maker* (Teremteni), *The Elders Drink the New Wine* (Aggastyánok isszák az újbort).

His most recent poems were written in the same vein. He dealt with the fate of mankind and the human condition which he saw in a context of mythical proportions, amid recurring tragedies, around which, as it were, only the scenery changed capriciously. Yet they express, with a pathos more restrained than earlier, the imperative of the attempts at making life meaningful *(Breach of Promise* — Az ígéret megszegése; *The Swallow and the Leaf* — A fecske és a falevél; *The Defeat of Time* — Az idő lebírása; *First Night* — Bemutató; *Wreath* — Koszorú).

Prose

This development is also apparent in Illyés's essays. For although in his poetry his flexible, sensitive style, the methods of composition, dictated by the experiences of his older years, only developed in middle age, these qualities were present in his prose from the beginning. While the young poet could be compared to József Erdélyi, the young prose writer was inspired by the best of Dezső Kosztolányi. Shortly after writing *I Speak of Heroes,* which predicted the revolution, he wrote one of the most outstanding non-fiction works of Hungarian literature. In it he takes a subject previously ignored by earlier writers, and paints a distressing picture of the heavy lot of the employees on large estates, at the mercy of the lord and landowner. *People of the Puszta* (Puszták népe) is at once an objective sociological document and a semi-autobiography. Detachment alternates with anger, irony with humour. The powers of a poet, imbued with a strong feeling for the community which he sprang, are joined with that of a Paris-bred essayist writing with cool reasoning and sophisticated grace.

One of the most important of prose works is his life of *Petőfi* (1936) which remains the best biography of that poet. In contrast to the many mistaken interpretations of Petőfi, Illyés first makes clear, and then analyses in depth, the political views, acts and poetry of the man, and their cumulative effect in making him a revolutionary. His own great sympathy for Petőfi matched with a slightly ironic detachment combine to bring the poet more convincingly to life than all the earlier biographies. He manages to extract the essence of the man, to give a vivid and scholarly account of the aesthetics, psychology, sociological and historical environment of a young poet, introverted, a little naive, driven by an inner fire and poetic ambition, who became the revolutionary hero of his country. The essay is both accurate in terms of literary history and enchanting to read.

His own individual style shines out most brilliantly in *Lunch at the Mansion* (Ebéd a kastélyban), published in 1962, containing shorter pieces from various periods. Intellectual and peasant experiences are here synthesized. He also wrote travel books, volumes of essays, and an autobiographical novel, *The Huns in Paris* (Hunok Párizsban, 1946), recalling the years he spent in that city, a poetic and gently ironic book. His most traditional creation in prose, *Early Spring* (Koratavasz, 1941), re-creating the events of the revolution, is somewhat inferior to his major works. Of greater significance, both as a work of art and social document, is *Beatrice's Page Boys* (Beatrice apródjai, 1979), in which he depicts the years of 1918–20 with the help of memoirs, contemporary documents and analysis.

The Playwright

Illyés began to write plays later in life. His first play, *The Eye of the Needle* (A tű foka, 1944), was written at the peak of a personal emotional crisis. More recently, he produced one historical piece after another, chronicling tragic or heroic events of various periods, as well as folk comedies or satires ridiculing some aspect of the present time. Prominent among the former are *Torchlight* (Fáklyaláng, 1952), and *The Favourite* (Kegyenc, 1963). In the first of these, portraying the struggle of the two chief protagonists in the 1848–49 War of Independence, historical events are interwoven, and in the process questions of importance to humanity in general are probed. The play does not only concern itself with the tragedy of the two men, both leaders, but of the nation as a whole. During the last and decisive battle of the 1848–49 Revolution, two men face each other: Lajos Kossuth, the leader of the movement, and the Chief Commander of the Hungarian revolutionary army, Artur Görgey. In three, increasingly violent clashes they argue and dispute whether and for how long it is necessary to carry on fighting. Kossuth, vacillating between the nobility and the people, discovers in the hour of tragic defeat that the cause of the revolution can only be brought to fruition by relying on the people. The play's epilogue stresses the same theme, with an ironic airiness which sets off the vigour and drama of the preceding scenes. *The Favourite* has its action in the distant past and is based on a play by the ill-fated Hungarian politician of the 1860s, László Teleki. It is set in ancient Rome, removing the action to a stylized background in which the heroes can rise at tragic heights, as against characters in plays of private life. The hero Maximus, always consistent, even to extremes, is ready to sacrifice all—himself, his wife, his honour, for the Absolute State, and commits a tragic deed. He is the confident of the Emperor Valentinianus, and is convinced that the position of Emperor is no more than an office, a function, and whom he must therefore serve and influence in the interests of the nation. He is gradually forced to realize that this absolute power resides in a man who is merely mortal, who can abuse his position to become a repellent tyrant, seeking unlimited power and the right to probe into the innermost recesses of men's souls. Finally, after events which destroy both him and his family, Maximus's wife, who would rather believe in him than in the numerous gods of the age, leads him to discover the truth: "By mocking man, we serve no god."

This work illustrates the development of Illyés as a playwright from the slightly romantic, factual and descriptive to the intellectual and rational. To the end of his life, Illyés remained the spokesman for the same sense of community values as the younger Illyés long ago: in essence he was the vigorous mouthpiece of the humanity of the common man which he voiced so ardently in his early years. In *The Pure* (Tiszták, 1969), probably the most significant piece of his latest plays, he depicts the tragic fate of the Albigenses who were ready to die in a hopeless fight in order not to turn traitor to their ideas.

62 Tibor Déry (1896-1977)

His Life

Tibor Déry is generally regarded as the finest writer of socialist prose. He was born in Budapest into a well-to-do family. In 1919 he supported the Hungarian Republic of Councils, and then became an emigré in various Western countries. Years later he returned, but continued to spend longer or shorter periods abroad. Some of his works appeared in *Nyugat,* but he was never a regular contributor to that review. He had connections in the Communist Party. The Horthy regime banned his plays as well as one of his major works, but after 1945 his various works came out in large editions and often led to considerable discussion.

His political activities immediately before and after the counter-revolution of 1956 created much friction, but any problems surrounding his person have long since been resolved and Tibor Déry, up to his death in 1977, was one of the most important literary figures in Hungary.

Early Work

His early work was Expressionist or even Surrealist in character; his later work showed the influence of Kafka and Thomas Mann in the sharply pointed yet whimsically sarcastic style he employed. From time to time the irony of Anatole France made its effect felt, as well as the influence of Proust. From these influences Tibor Déry created his own unique and highly individual style, and his subject-matter is very different from theirs. He often discussed events in connection with the communist movement, and sought to find in it an answer to universal issues. But even when he dealt with other subjects, his thinking was decisively based on the socialist ethic, and his point of view governed by a vigorously socialist humanism. A dominant feature of his work is his absorbing interest in moral problems.

His major work before the liberation in 1945 was *The Unfinished Sentence* (A befejezetlen mondat), which was written between 1934 and 1938, but was only published in 1947. Its immediate predecessor, *Eye to Eye* (Szemtől szembe, 1934), which took as its subject German communism destroying itself in its tragic battle

472

with the ever-growing threat of fascism. *The Unfinished Sentence* is about the revolutionary crises of the thirties, and the struggles of the illegal Communist Party and its inner workings, set in the framework of contemporary society. There is the working woman who knows no compromise, who masters her personal feelings with iron determination, who ranks the class war above all else; there is the morally bankrupt city inhabitant; there are the intellectuals, caught in their own dilemma, seeking a purpose in life, partly finding it, partly destroying themselves. A complex and animated plot is accompanied by a wealth of actual and detailed material. The time structure of the novel is highly individual. The traditional method of telling a consecutive story is interrupted in many places; the consciousness which analyses the inner logic of the events and personalities summons up fictional or real pictures of the future, thereby deepening and modifying the "present" of the story. *The Unfinished Sentence* is made up of the artistic need for totality of concept, a loose time structure, and from the constructional point of view, a strictly disciplined documentation of fact. The story is related from several viewpoints, the characters, with the aid of linguistic peculiarities, portray a senseless world in the grip of merciless powers, which is compelled to create the instrument of its own destruction.

This is one of the best novels in the modern Hungarian literature of socialist realism. It is true that in the rigid world portrayed here the essential humanity of the revolutionary heroes we have come to know through the works of Gorki or Solokhov is missing. The works in which such rich and real characters are to be found only appeared after the liberation.

The *Answer* (Felelet) series: two of these novels were written between 1950 and 1952. They recount the story of the struggles of a working-class boy, representing the depressed, and a university lecturer, representing the élite. The author successfully realized his aims, but owing to certain weaknesses in construction, and to the largely undeserved criticism and impatience of the sectarian literary politics dominant at the time, it was not well received. Déry no longer felt close to its hero, who achieved his ambitions after the liberation and developed his full personality, and consequently he left the series unfinished. Nor did he ever again attempt to write a realist novel of a comprehensive nature.

Some of his short stories are in the same vein as *The Unfinished Sentence*, with a large element of the bizarre and grotesque in them. The pattern and design of the detail lends a certain lightness to his later work, some of the short stories being almost a musical counterpoint in their arrangement. They deal for the most part with questions of responsibility and conscience, but above all with the acceptance of a sense of humanity. If his earlier novels and stories were concerned with men perishing from the non-fulfilment of their inner needs, his later work dealt with men living in a society still burdened with the residuum of its past, but seeking renewal, and more especially with those racked by the injustices of the personality cult, who were

473

still able to retain their essential humanity. With strict objectivity, and an almost pedantic exactness, and yet with a poetry of its own, *Niki* (1956) relates the story of a dog, through which the life of a married couple in the years between 1948 and 1956 is revealed. They are years of tragedy for them, and the novel displays the conditions of the time with clear and convincing mastery. The destinies of dog and man are skilfully paralleled and contrasted in this little masterpiece, in which didacticism and gaiety, irony and a grave solemnity are intermingled.

Mr. G. A. in X (G. A. úr X-ben), a novel of fantasy written at the end of the fifties and published in 1964, takes us into a completely alien, frighteningly strange world, a novel which satirizes both capitalism and the era of the personality cult. Its oppressive atmosphere is lightened by passages of lyrical beauty from which emerges a passionate love of life. The book is in essence about the nature of freedom, but though designed on an extensive scale, fails to achieve the integrated, whole effect we are entitled to expect. In *The Excommunicator* (A kiközösítő, 1966), which is set in the early years of Christianity, he refers to the present, but also takes pleasure in evoking the past. The chief character in this novel is Ambrose, Bishop of Milan, whose faith and fervour brings about, among other achievements, the conversion of Saint Augustine. The events of his life, its vicissitudes and triumphs, are presented with biting humour and a bold insouciance. Ambrose serves his faith with wisdom and endurance, he is persistent and firm, sparing neither himself nor others, but he finally falls foul of the Emperor himself. In the end we find him facing death, and asking himself the profound questions which we also have to ask ourselves: "Did we lead a righteous life?... What kind of world do we leave behind us?"—The answer, achieved in pain and tribulation—"With long and laborious toil much of it could still be helped..."—is clearly the answer of the writer as well, and in its way a distant echo of the conclusion reached in László Németh's last novel.

Recent Work

There is no Judgement (Ítélet nincs, 1969) is Tibor Déry's autobiography, in which a procession of his dead contemporaries moves before him. Material precision and imaginative understanding alternate in turn, and the grave tones of the wisdom life brought him are lightened by the writer's quiet humour. This mosaic of an autobiography, intermingled with sections devoted to analysis and meditation, results in an essayistic style. The work, whole and complete, is without doubt one of his major creations, and is indeed among the best of twentieth-century autobiographies.

The novel *Imaginary Report on an American Pop Festival* (Képzelt riport egy amerikai popfesztiválról), published in 1971, embodies the fantasy of *Mr. G. A. in X,* the loose, airy attitudes of *The Excommunicator,* in a "musical" form. Released through loneliness, lack of self-respect, and inhuman violence from all moral restraints, these almost animal conditions, permeate the work, and give it a disturbing vigour; it is imbued with a concern for the welfare of mankind, for good, sound life in the future. This short novel equally demonstrates the constant self-analysis of the author, as well as the consistency of his moral standards. Among his latest works, *Dear Beau-père* (Kedves bóper, 1973) displays his love of life and the presence of serenity, though not without his usual irony. Déry's finest work undoubtedly lies in the realm of narrative prose, but his poetry and plays are also far-reaching in their scope and splendid in style. The poetry written in his earlier years bears the stamp of Surrealism; in later years he gave up writing verse. An important later poem, however, *To Face it* (Szembenézni), struggles, like Gyula Illyés's equally large-scale work, with the problems of man in the twentieth century. An outstanding play, *The Giant Baby* (Az óriáscsecsemő), written in the twenties but not published until much later, a Dadaist piece of the absurd, is also concerned with universal questions, and forces despair into a grotesque and grimacing mask. The production of this play might have been a most important first step for a Hungarian avant-garde theatre.

63 Literary Criticism

Directions of Literature

From the beginnings of the review *Nyugat*, with the arrival of Ady, all innovation and new directions in literature were bitterly opposed by the traditional literary scholars of the time. From the University, and the academic world in general, came one misconceived and reactionary attack after another directed against all progressive writers. The Positivist trend which dominated scholarly circles at the time led to ever drier, duller and trivial literary experiments, which agreed well enough with the platitudes of conservative social and national politics. The Hungarian Literary History Society, formed in 1911, with a fresh outlook and more modern forms as its original aim, soon became a bastion of conservative Positivism. The final downfall of the declining Positivist school is exemplified in the eight-volume *History of Hungarian Literature* compiled by Jenő Pintér during the 1930s. Already outdated when it was published, its only value lay in its biographical data and the bibliography of the writers listed within it. The appraisal and explanation of their works is elementary, its understanding of modern writing totally inept.

The lines along which the study of modern literature developed in the interwar years endeavouring to assess modern forms by scholarly levels, witness the Russian Formalists, the Czech Structuralists, and later Practical Criticism and the New Criticism, found no echo in Hungary. The school of *Geistesgeschichte*, however, which originated in Germany, made its influence felt from roughly 1920 to the 1940s. Marxist study of literature increased and progressed producing more and more important works. Many literary historians employed the techniques devised by a number of different literary movements, occasionally somewhat eclectically, at other times evenly balancing them, and used them together in their works. Despite the regrettable isolation from certain trends, the interest of scholars in literature increased considerably in the twentieth century. In the twenties, widely read scholars, contemporaries of the first *Nyugat* generation, were writing with great maturity. Alongside them grew up a newer generation tending towards the more flexible form of the essay.

János Horváth (1878-1961)

If we define the writing of literary history more narrowly, the works of János Horváth stand out as pre-eminent. Pál Gyulai and Jenő Péterfy were his teachers in Budapest, and Brunetière, Lanson and Bédier helped to form his exploratory style. He taught at Budapest University, and his teaching methods exerted considerable influence on the teaching of literature, and on scholars of the succeeding generation.

He never joined in the worship of Positivism, so prevalent at the time, and from the beginning it was clear that he meant to break through the barriers it posed. He began work on a synthesis of Hungarian literary history, his *Study of Hungarian Literature* (Magyar irodalomismeret, 1922), designed to clear up some of the theoretical problems in this field. Scholars consider the content of the written words as an integral part of the process of development, and within this process they see the evolution of taste as playing an important role; they do not separate the author and his work from that which calls it into existence and embraces it—society. One of the categories central to his theory is "the basic literary relationship"; this is "the spiritual relationship of writer and reader, through the medium of the written work." The author sees the conceptual powers of the *Geistesgeschichte* combining with sociological analysis to result in a more realistic view.

This great scholar, however, who could draw on a vast knowledge of his material, and who had remarkable analytical abilities and theoretical learning, was never able to understand the literature of his age and of his own generation. In outlook and taste he remained bound by Gyulai's conclusions; he only enlarged upon and echoed Gyulai's ideas on literary history. According to him, János Arany's works, and those of Petőfi's which he considered to equal them, form the climax, the peak of Hungarian literature. Horváth's conservative ethical principles objected as much to signs of decadence in literature as to the lack of reality in Romanticism and other similar movements. His ideal was the era of sober realism and "national classicism". As a result, he looked for strands in early history leading to this era, and condemned all later departures from it. He supported the view of the historian Gyula Szekfű, who at that time considered revolution and any progressive movement—that is, the rejection of a cautious reform of conservative–moral–national concepts—as being responsible for "the collapse of the nation".

Although conservatism could not affect literature to any great extent, for literature is of necessity more closely in touch with real life, it wielded considerable power within the enclosed limits of the academic world. János Horváth nonetheless wrote a number of works which are still classics of their kind, even though the best among them are those which deal with the past: *The Beginnings of Hungarian Literature* (A magyar irodalmi műveltség kezdetei, 1931), *The Repartition of Literary Cultivation* (Az irodalmi műveltség megoszlása, 1935), *In the Name of the Reformation*

(A reformáció jegyében, 1953). Although his lack of any understanding of Petőfi in his revolutionary aspect is lamentably evident in his biography of the poet, *Sándor Petőfi* (1921), the analysis of his verse and the widely-based material information it provided is much valued by modern scholars. Horváth's main contribution was his pioneer work in the analysis of rhythm in Hungarian poetry in *Hungarian Poetry* (A magyar vers, 1948), *Concise Hungarian Prosody* (Rendszeres magyar verstan, 1951). In 1956 he published a collection of some of his early and later work, entitled *Studies* (Tanulmányok).

Critics and Scholars

The most consistent advocate of the movement of *Geistesgeschichte* was the authority on German literature, *Tivadar Thienemann* (b. 1890). Together with János Horváth, he founded the Minerva Society in 1921, and wrote in the review of the same name as a spokesman for that movement. His most important book, *Basic Concepts of Literary History* (Irodalomtörténeti alapfogalmak, 1927–1930), is a study of theory and methodology. He was above all a great source of inspiration to the supporters of comparative studies.

The chief protagonist of the comparative school was *József Túróczi-Trostler* (1888–1962), a man conversant with every period of literature, whose life-long study of the subject found expression in *Hungarian Literature—World Literature* (Magyar irodalom—világirodalom), published in two volumes in 1961. *János Hankiss* (1893–1959) specialized in the study of the theory of literature. *Sándor Eckhardt* (1890–1969) pioneered work in Central European comparative studies, and also engaged in philological researches of great value.

György Király (1887–1922) was another outstanding philologist, and was esteemed as an understanding critic of the progressive writers of the twentieth century. *Aladár Schöpflin* (1872–1950) wrote some interesting accounts of the contributors to *Nyugat*, and especially of Endre Ady; *Béla Zolnai* (1890–1969) developed stylistics, until then neglected in Hungary. An admirable attempt to organize a compilation of aesthetic theories was made by the learned priest-poet and literary historian *Sándor Sík*, in his *Aesthetics* (Esztétika, 1943). Many literary historians had already published a number of brilliant studies even before the war, and after it were considerably influenced by Marxism—*József Waldapfel* (1904–1968) was one, *János Barta* (b. 1901), *László Bóka* (1910–1964), also noteworthy as a writer, and *István Sőtér* (b. 1913) were among many others.

Antal Szerb (1901-1945)

Szerb's scholarly work belongs to the school of *Geistesgeschichte*. He was initially attracted to the novelty of Expressionism, but later, influenced by the work of Gundolf, Dilthey and Strich, turned to Romanticism. He was affected by Spenglerian cultural morphology and by Freudian psychology. He did not force his conclusions into the theories of *Geistesgeschichte* and Freudian psychology, but retained from all these influences a strongly intuitive approach and the desire to see everything in perspective. His witty, slightly frivolous works are not always based on sufficiently solid facts, yet in every case they contain something of value, which later, more firmly based research could not ignore. With all the elegance of a writer of belles-lettres he nevertheless maintained a foundation of solid sense in his novels, while as a historian he was gifted with the power of bringing subjects to life, and making the communication of facts enjoyable.

His major work was *Hungarian Literary History* (Magyar irodalomtörténet, 1934), in which he made the division between religious, aristocratic and bourgeois literature from the first written work to his own time, noting the development of style along the way. His views on the novel were expressed in *Weekdays and Wonders* (Hétköznapok és csodák, 1935), in which he wrote of the possibility and the need for a renewal of Romanticism. Although mainly interested in English literature, his *History of World Literature* (A világirodalom története, 1941) is an interesting and well-organized piece of work.

The Essayists

Antal Szerb had translated the heavier "specific gravity" of literary history into the lighter essay form, and in this attempt he was not alone, for Mihály Babits was moving in the same direction. Between the two world wars Hungarian essay writing took on new life. Some of the best essays were written by established authors, such as László Németh (q.v.), as well as Albert Gyergyai, Gyula Illyés, Endre Illés, Aladár Komlós, István Sőtér, and László Cs. Szabó, who also made their contribution to the literature of the time with their essays and critical reviews.

It was perhaps the work of *Gábor Halász* (1901-1945) which took first place in the interwar period. He only published one book, entitled *The Search for Reason* (Az értelem keresése, 1938). Reflecting on the literary failings of his own time, he began to concentrate on the discipline afforded by Classicism and the respect paid to Reason by the Enlightenment, rejecting the subjective attitudes of the Romantics, Symbolists and Impressionists. He discounted the inspiration of the Muses, and came down in favour of craftsmanship serving a well-balanced and disciplined world view. His somewhat aristocratic opinions did not prevent him from noting much that was good around him, and recognizing the value of the objective approach in the short story, or, for instance, the novels of Hemingway and Steinbeck. His choice of methods seemed to give promise of greater mastery; first came single individual portraits, then the development of connections between them. He did not live to fulfil that promise: together with Antal Szerb he was murdered by the fascists in a labour camp towards the end of the war.

The Beginnings of Marxist Criticism

The great movement of the future, a Marxist critical literature, was pioneered in Hungary by a few writers in the interwar period. Among them was *György Bálint* (1906–1943), the first man to recognize the poetic genius of Attila József. He made his name as a literary journalist. His best works are a combination of thought and experience, fancy and fact, the subjective and the objective. He wrote on political events or art, travel, literature, but permeating it all was his insistence on the need to preserve a humanist outlook, to improve the quality of life. Rising above petty prejudices, he was always concerned to reach the heart of the matter. He consistently and continuously raised his voice against fascism and all it stood for, employing every device of irony, wit and ridicule to achieve this purpose. He succeeded in maintaining a delicate balance between his response to innovation and his firm Marxist beliefs. His broad learning and expert connoisseurship formed the basis for many critical articles on Hungarian and foreign works which have stood the test of time. He too was broken by the war; he died in a punishment battalion and his body was never found.

Bálint and *Zoltán Fábry* (1897–1970) shared similar attitudes. Fábry later became a leading figure among the Hungarians in Czechoslovakia. Generous-minded, steadfast and incorruptible, he became something of a legendary figure, almost a symbol, even though he lived in a remote village far from the centre of things. He was a dedicated opponent of fascism, passionately exposing its brutality, inhumanity, demagogy and cultural nihilism. As a literary critic he wrote critical articles on J. R. Becher, Thomas Mann, Stefan Zweig and Isaac Babel, among others, analysing their work from the standpoint of socialist humanism. He was also among the first to recognize Attila József, but living as he did out of touch with the realities of Hungarian life, he was unable to appreciate the developments in literature after Ady's death.

Attila József himself deserves a mention in any discussion on the development of Marxist literature, although it is not so much his critical but his aesthetic contribution that demands our attention. Unfortunately he only left a mere sketch of his aesthetic philosophy. He believed that all true works of art are divisible into a certain "artistic constant" and an "artistic variable". The former is the structure of the work, whose "every point is Archimedean", that is, dependent upon all the others; and the latter is the message the work conveys, which is determined by the current attitudes of society, and the social classes within it. József developed the framework for a flexible, dialectic Marxist theory of aesthetics out of what had previously been a rigidly dogmatic Marxist exercise.

György Lukács (1885-1971)

His name is associated with the profoundly philosophical Marxist essay, and with works discussing the fundamental questions of Marxist aesthetics. He studied law and philosophy in Budapest and Berlin, and in 1918 joined the then infant Communist Party. He took an active part in the 1919 Hungarian Republic of Councils and was appointed a Commissar, but after its collapse was forced to emigrate first to Vienna, and finally to Moscow, spending many years in Berlin in between. After 1945 he became a professor at the University of Budapest, and until 1956 was active in national affairs. After 1957 he devoted himself entirely to scholarly activities.

His early friendship with Max Weber and Simmell directed his interests towards the *Geistesgeschichte,* which produced *The Soul and the Forms* (A lélek és a formák, 1910), and *Die Theorie des Romans,* published as a book in 1920. His absorption in German classical philosophy stimulated him to study Hegel and later Marx. His interest in literature was in fact from the outset intertwined with his philosophical investigations, and all his various writings reflect this connection. Taking his stand firmly on the side of materialist realism, influenced by Marx and Engels as well as by the ideas of Hegel, he worked out his own theory of realism, which was to have a great effect on Hungarian Marxist literary scholars. To some extent these views were already present in the works he wrote before he actually formulated them in his aesthetics, the corner-stone or perhaps starting-point of which was the analysis of literary works, including prose works and plays.

His main field of study was the classical (or what has ripened into classical in the twentieth century) writers of Germany, for example, Goethe and Thomas Mann, but his dissertations on French and Russian literature are also interesting and important. A relatively modest but immensely valuable section of his varied and prolific output was devoted to Hungarian writers such as Arany, Ady, and Déry as well as a number of others.

Lukács did not ignore the question of continuity in literature or problems of development, yet his interest was not primarily in the history of literature. He was seeking the most important constant factor in all its variants when he discussed the works of various writers, paying little attention to autobiographical detail, the

481

psychology of personality and creativity or the discovery of other elements in the work. He examined with care the relationship between the period and the work: what conditions favoured the creation of masterpieces, certain types and genres of literature, what compelled a writer intent on preserving essentials to look for newer directions, or what carried him easily along the road to decline. From the beginning he considered the castigation of all forms of decadence as of the greatest importance. For him decadence included more than there is generally accepted by literary historians: any work which, voluntarily or otherwise, abandoned the defence of integrity, was decadent. *The Problems of Realism* (A realizmus problémái, 1948), is a collection of essays on the possibilities open to literature in the twentieth century for a vigorous depiction of reality, and on the pitfalls of doing without it. In *Balzac, Stendhal, Zola* (1945) he directed attention to the aesthetic values which elevated realism above naturalism. *The Historical Novel* (A történelmi regény, 1947) discussed literary genres. Even though his main preoccupation with philosophy took up most of his time and strength, he remained actively in touch with the literature of his age to the end.

His interests, his whole system of values were naturally enough guided by aesthetic considerations, and their most complete expression is to be found in *Die Eigenart des Ästhetischen* (Az esztétikum sajátossága, 1963), which is the first part of a planned three-part study of aesthetics. Certainly controversial, it is undeniably the most significant, most thoroughly accomplished piece of writing in the Marxist literature of aesthetics. Lukács's system is based on two specific corner-stones. One is the concept that all literary work mirrors reality, the same reality shown by science, but in a manner determined by society. He considers this mirror-image to belong to the sphere of the "specific", in which there is movement to the concrete, the particular, and back again, and to the abstract, the general, and back. As the extensiveness and intensiveness of the images of reality which result determine the value of the work, true art is realist art. The other corner-stone of his system is the concept that the work in its construction strengthens man in his humanity, through its power of evocation. Art therefore is humanistic in essence, and serves to defend man's integrity. Mirroring reality as it does, serving to enrich mankind, it must of necessity play a part in the decisive battles of humankind.

József Révai (1898–1959)

The Marxist attitude to literature as exposed by Lukács exerted a great influence on Révai, although the two men repeatedly found themselves holding confronting viewpoints. He began his career by writing poetry, and contributed to Kassák's avant-garde reviews. His pursuit of revolutionary aims soon took him beyond

Kassák's more moderate political views: he became one of the founder members of the Communist Party. After the fall of the 1919 Republic of Councils, he worked sometimes as an emigré, and sometimes as an illegal Party member at home. In 1945 he returned home from the Soviet Union, and until 1956 played a leading part in the state administration, especially in cultural fields.

Révai consistently upheld and enforced all the Marxist–Leninist imperatives of committed art, and in analysing the means needed to attain this mirror-image of reality, he attached greater importance to the didactic, agitational aspects of literature, directly addressed to the community. In this, his work was more closely allied with the old tradition of Hungarian literature, strongly imbued with the sense of a national mission. In all his writings on literary history Lukács remained essentially a philosopher, while Révai was the proponent of cultural policy; this can be seen in the style of their respective works.

Révai has analysed the works of Ferenc Kölcsey (1938) with considerable sensitivity and perception to the human drama of men who pledge themselves to the service of fundamental questions, and he has a deep comprehension of their problems. In his book on Ady (1940–41) both his intellectual approach and his love of poetry are evident. His writings are not afraid to deal with revolutionary ideas usually left undiscussed, nor does he gloss over the contradictions in the works he studies. He placed the controversies between the "populist" and the "urban" writers in their correct light, and thus directed attention to the need to reach an accommodation between them. His literary and historical studies only became known in Hungary after his return at the end of the Second World War. After 1945 his work was mainly devoted to questions of literary policy, but his studies of Attila József's and Madách's poetry are nonetheless of great importance.

Contemporary Literature—an Outline

As with earlier literature, the frontiers of contemporary literature cannot be clearly demarcated. The works of Illyés, Németh or Déry are as much a part of the literature of today as Móricz's later works are inextricably part of the interwar generation years; some of them are as modern as the latest trends of today, not only on account of their subject and the message they convey, but also because of their construction. Nonetheless the generation which followed the liberation, during the growth of socialism, is linked by a certain common bond which separates them from all who went before. What is presented here is not a comprehensive survey but a brief outline to be filled in and amplified by the literary historians of the future.

The Socialist Transformation

The great changes in the literature of this time were brought about by the revolutionary changes which took place in the country. The liberation of Hungary from the German occupation and Fascist terror, the end of the ravages of war and the collapse of the semi-Fascist, counter-revolutionary regime that was in power between the two wars opened up new horizons and opportunities for the rebirth of the nation. The land reforms of 1945 and the progressive nationalization that followed broke the power of the propertied classes. The Communist Party, legalized after the liberation, gained increasing support among the population. It consolidated the revolutionary spirit of other parties around itself, and soon became the leading political power. Following a few years of transition, Hungary embarked on the road to socialism between 1948 and 1949.

This great step naturally created entirely new conditions for writers. In later years a need was felt for the chronicling of the social struggle—the successes and occasional failures—of the country as a whole. The new literature could not ignore the fact that after the ruin and desolation that followed the war, the poverty that had been so widespread in earlier days had slowly disappeared, the enormous gulf that separated village and town diminished, and the ruling class had been overthrown.

The position of the different classes changed, partly in relation to one another, and partly in their proportions: the working class increased, but the numbers in the educated class also rose to a significant degree as opportunities to learn opened up before the eager children of the formerly oppressed classes. As a result the internal structure of the intelligentsia also changed. As Hungary became part of the socialist system, the adherents of a "separate Hungarian solution" fell away by degrees, and the effect of their beliefs was reduced. Marxism, previously outlawed and suppressed, gradually became the dominant ideology, and the country began to take its place as an active component in the general development of Europe.

Literary Life

Fundamental changes were also taking place during this period, in the literary life of Hungary as well. Left-wing writers forced into exile returned, and those at home were able to publish works in their own country which had previously been impossible to print there. Soviet literature, equally inaccessible to Hungarian readers up to that time, was now being translated and published in large quantities.

Between 1945 and 1948 many new literary reviews appeared: *Fórum* and *Csillag* (Star), published in the name of the people's front movement by the communists, and *Magyarok* (Hungarians) and *Válasz* (Answer), the paper of the populist writers also reappeared. Slightly more advanced was the *Valóság* (Reality) edited by students of the people's colleges (politically active working-class and peasant students in free universities). *Újhold* (New Moon) was the organ which preached art for art's sake among young writers. These, and the short-lived *Kortárs* (Contemporary), expounding Kassák's avant-garde theories and beliefs, as well as a number of other reviews of art and literature provided new outlets for writers.

Later, between 1948 and 1950, following the nationalization of industry, publishing houses and theatres also came under state ownership, and thenceforth cultural life as a whole enjoyed Government support. At the same time the directives of the state and the Party leadership became an important factor in literary life. The proportion of good as opposed to *kitsch* literature published increased significantly, and found acceptance in ever-growing circles, while at the same time there was a recrudescence of interest in the film industry.

In 1949 the Hungarian Writers' Association was founded, made up of the majority of important authors from the start, and later joined by every notable Hungarian writer. In addition to their original periodical, *Csillag* now recast, *Új Hang* (New Voice) and *Irodalmi Újság* (Literary Journal), became the forums for writers; and various regional papers also sprang up. They all provided a platform, not only for discussion on literary matters, but on topical, communal and political issues as well.

After 1953, in addition to the justified denunciation of dogmatism, revisionist tendencies appeared, which identified socialism as such with the personality cult, and the sectarian leadership of the Party was unable to distinguish between legitimate criticism and attacks on the very essence of socialism.

The serious upheaval of 1956—in the course of which some writers sided with the counter-revolution—was followed by a reorganization of literary life, which provided a sounder atmosphere for literary work. New reviews replaced the old ones: *Kortárs* and later *Új Írás* (New Writing) became the two most important periodicals, but a large number of city and regional publications, including *Élet és Irodalom* (Life and Literature) also gave scope to writers and their critics.

The books and periodicals of the Hungarian-speaking minorities in the neighbouring countries also played an active part in the nurture and development of Hungarian literature. Among them were *Irodalmi Szemle* (Literary Review) in Czechoslovakia, *Igaz Szó* (True Word) in Rumania, and the Yugoslav *Híd* (Bridge).

Since 1956 the products of world literature have been made familiar to the reader by *Nagyvilág* (Wide World), and from that time on modern world literature and drama have been more readily available to reader and theatre-goer alike than in the immediately previous years.

Socialist Realism

Between 1949 and 1953, in the course of the formulation of literary policy, a very important role in its direction was played by József Révai, a man of considerable talent. Unfortunately, he followed the dogmatic and rigid line current in Soviet literary politics at that time, and though he was concerned in the development of socialist realism, the concept was interpreted in a narrow and conservative spirit, partly as inheriting the mantle of nineteenth-century realism and partly as implementing so-called revolutionary romanticism. This literary policy was subserved by the politics of the day—which were too often wrong. As a result, alongside, but sometimes in place of, genuine talent, various pseudo-geniuses gained recognition and attained important positions, such as the award of the Stalin Prize to the mediocre works of Tamás Aczél, who later moved to the West, and the approval given to many writers who were later to sink into oblivion.

Literary policy continued to regard socialist realist literature as its primary concern in later years, and does so today. Yet the change is remarkable. This is in part due to the fact that the programme does not, since 1956, exclude the publication of works based on other principles, and in part to the fact that open discussion among critics, literary historians, students of aesthetics, and writers has broadened and modernized the meaning of socialist realism, not limiting it to a predetermined style.

A considerably more colourful literature has resulted from this broader interpretation of socialist realism, one that is impregnated by socialist thought and is vitally contemporary in its outlook.

In the 35 years since the liberation, a new era has opened for Hungarian literature. Writers who began their careers before the war and those who came to the fore in the postwar years have developed into a new generation producing rich, varied, and original works. Although the social aims, views and behaviour of this group is more homogeneous than the previous generation, the complexity and rivalry of various groups, literary trends and styles are highly characteristic of the period. As this is a process which is still continuing, their final value, role and position in history is difficult to assess at this stage. In the following chapters therefore, only a brief introduction to each writer will be given, not in any chronological order. Most of these writers began their career after the liberation, but many who, although they were writing much earlier, produced their most important works after it, e.g. Benjámin, Lengyel, Darvas, will also be discussed.

László Benjámin (b. 1915)

Benjámin, together with Ernő Salamon, began as one of the so-called working-class writers. With his strongly socialist and community-minded poetry he had become a propagator of the Communist Party, identifying himself not only with the theory and goal of communism but also with the tactical steps of the party. Even if in the early 1950s it was in part due to the pressure of the current cultural policy, it was essentially a conviction held with great sincerity on his part. He disseminated the principles of this universal idea, this world-wide movement, its humanity and responsibility, for example in the poem *Account* (Számadás) in words that were at once sensitive and firm.

Benjámin's clear and logical train of thought was accompanied by intense feeling, and his poems became especially rich and varied when he finally realized that in previous years there had not been, as he had claimed "each day a victory", but that he had supported trumped-up charges on which many men—some of them his friends—had been condemned. A deep moral sense of responsibility and guilt, and his fundamental loyalty to his ideals struggled within him during the mid-fifties. The clearest, most concisely composed answers to the questions of the age are provided by his intellectually disciplined verse, inspired by Attila József's example. He does not merely regret the disintegration of his dreams. "Denying what is a crime, I carry the burden of the whole", he admits, and his lines dissipate the bitterness in brusque rhythms, while expressing his tenacious acceptance of life in *No shame, no swagger* (Ne szégyenkezz, ne legénykedj). "The Idea must be found, if we have to dig out of the mud with our fingers / for we have given it our lives / and held it up, clean for the world to see," he declares in *The Way we Are...* (Így vagyunk), expressing both the passion and the ceaseless tortures of anxiety which beset him. One of his best poems is *Two Decades* (Két évtized), in which he expands a description of the tiny events of daily life into the provision of answers to universal questions, while guiltily weighing up all that his self-sacrificing wife has given him.

Man stands firmly at the centre of his beliefs: social man, who begins again after each *débâcle,* seeing the struggle for a better life "through the surface of all things" and never abandoning it, making sense of the realities of life by his knowledge and inspired activity (*What's on the Other Side of the Moon?* — Mi van a Hold túlsó felén?, *Under Blood-stained Flags* — Vérző zászlók alatt, and *Brushwood Fire* — Rőzse-láng). He speaks of this type of man and of his world, passionately and without affectation triumphing over bitterness and disillusionment. And then he turns to paint satirical but resigned pictures of himself and his immediate surroundings *From the Vadaskerti Road to Calvin Square* (A Vadaskerti úttól a Kálvin térig).

In his more recent poems, influenced by Aragon, Benjámin very largely abandons regular verse-forms. The bolder, more visionary nature of these poems is held in shape by their more concentrated and meaningful content. The very clear-cut forms are developed from the arrangement of the words, and patterned, like the later work of Illyés, into tense and vigorous pieces of writings: *In the Captivity of the Oceans* (Tengerek fogságában), *The Stopped Clock* (A megállt óra), *The General's Demotion* (A tábornok lefokozása), *North Wind* (Az északi szél).

István Vas (b. 1910)

also began to write well before 1945, and although his work was not concerned with the events and the characteristics of the age directly or graphically, it could not fail to be influenced by the same historical contexts and factors, though in a more subtle and transposed manner. István Vas's poetry, forceful as it is, is less politically oriented; his urban upbringing and his more intellectually based education incline him to a meditative, moral–intellectual attitude, though in general in accord with the developments leading to the transformation of society. Middle-class values and socialist humanism can barely be distinguished from each other in much of his work. It is not on the whole a sharp individuality that emerges from his poetry: it is rather its complexity. His views, his technique are drawn from many sources, but they are by no means mere replicas. He has learnt from the philosophic, contemplative János Arany, from the spirit and dash of Kosztolányi, the rigorous discipline of Mihály Babits, from the strict simplicity of Lőrinc Szabó, and even from avant-garde Lajos Kassák. His poems express anguish and delight, tragedy and quietude, the passing

491

moment and eternity; they reflect sensual and intellectual experiences, and private and public happenings, in often disturbing, but in the final analysis harmonious, combinations. His poetic output is remarkable for its consistent unity, and cannot be characterized by singling out a few outstanding pieces.

An important work is *Difficult Love* (Nehéz szerelem), a semi-autobiography in which he dissects himself and others with the same unsparing exactitude. The second part is published under the title *Why Does the Vulture Scream?* (Miért vijjog a saskeselyű?). He is also considered one of the greatest translators of foreign poetry into Hungarian. He has written several plays in collaboration with Miklós Hubay and Endre Illés.

Ferenc Juhász (b. 1928)

is a writer of poems which are more torrential in associations, richer than those of Benjámin, more fundamental and vigorous than those of István Vas. Juhász only began to write after the liberation. He was following an arts course at Budapest University in 1948 when he met there and became friends with two other poets, László Nagy and István Simon. Two years later, by 1950, when his second and third volumes of poems were published, he was already well known.

In the beginning he wrote narrative poems, but later turned to the lyric form. He renewed the tradition inaugurated by Petőfi and Arany and Illyés in his first major works (*The Sántha Family* — A Sántha család; *My Father* — Apám, 1950; and *The Cock-patterned Frost Flower* — A jégvirág kakasa). In his hands not only even the coarsest features of the world take on an enchantment, but his poems also seek to probe the innermost recesses of the human soul. In his choice of subject-matter he frequently returns to the changes that took place in his own early peasant life, tells of the peasants at last obtaining possession of the land and later working it communally.

His early lyric poetry reveals a man rejoicing in the harmony of the world, though this naive bliss was shaken a few years later by growing disillusionment. Around this time his taste was turning from the narrative to the lyric which produced a body of fine, diversified poetry. The heroes of his poems of symbolic meaning survive through terrible agonies to be betrayed, to see apocalyptic horrors taking place before their eyes, as in *The Prince who Wished to be Immortal* (A halhatatlanságra vágyó királyfi, 1953). In *The Spendthrift Country* (A tékozló ország, 1954), the peasant uprising, painted on a monumental scale, goes down to defeat, and all that remains is the tortured lament of the narrator, weeping over the terrible *débâcle,* the unresolved philosophical questions that beset him, and the scenes of destruction all around. His verse is impregnated on the one hand by a desire for the creation of a better life, to be enjoyed to the full, and on the other, by the bitterness of tragic experiences. The first is rooted in socialist principles, and is supported and strengthened by its great ideals, the other is born of terrible fear of nuclear war, and of the errors committed in the course of building socialism. Woven through with opposites, what began as fresh and vibrant verse evoking a myriad images and ideas fails, due to the limitations in its narrative style, to maintain an even balance and structure.

During the fifties he set out on a general purge of his poetic style: he turned to the lyrical form, abandoning his narrative style. The first major sign that he had at last found the right direction for his talents was *The Boy Changed into a Stag Cries Out at the Gate of Secrets* (A szarvassá változott fiú kiáltozása a titkok kapujából, 1955), which was in part inspired by Bartók's *Cantata Profana*. This enormous poem describes the confrontation of two worlds: the essence of the ancient world, and the more complex world of today. Between them stands Man. The rather Surrealist but original word order and construction, which in the final analysis are dictated by grammar and logic, express the very same socialist ethic as is found in the work of Benjámin. Only occasionally do we notice an absence of discipline in the welter of words and images. From these ambitious verses emerges the face of an artist knowing that man is wrestling with the cosmic secrets of life and death, freedom and necessity, conscious and unconscious existence as in *The Love of the Universe* (A mindenség szerelme). Ancient incantations, folk songs and ballads all contribute to these long, tumbling lines, reminiscent of Whitman and Apollinaire. Simplicity and sophistication, crude disconnections and inspired ease entwine in his many poems, reminiscent at times of Dylan Thomas. Among them are *Power of the Flowers* (A virágok hatalma); *Four Voices: Non-maledictory, in Lament and Supplication* (Vers négy hangra, jajgatásra és könyörgésre); *Uncursed* (Átoktalanul).

Legends of the Holy Flood of Fire (A szent Tűzözön regéi, 1969), combined the monumental features of epic poetry and modern thinking, renewing the old manner of the narrative myth with clarity and feeling. A mankind threatening to destroy itself provides the theme. Juhász fears for mankind, aware that it is endangered by the coming to power of forces not yet wholly civilized to real human needs. His volume of poems *My Mother* (Anyám, 1969), partly echoes the twenty-years-earlier *My Father* (Apám): couched in its simple verse form, the viewpoint in the earlier poem somewhat changed, and interspersing the crudity of Villon with the serene voice of the medieval hymns to the Virgin Mary. *The King of the Dead* (A halottak királya, 1971), is also an example of lyricized epic poetry. In a highly modern form it gives the moral and philosophical questions lonely King Béla IV has to face after the Mongol Invasion of 1241.

There are also shorter poems, constricting the internal tensions into more rigid forms, and some of these are among his finest verses. There is *Thursday, Day of Superstition, When it is Hardest* (Babonák napja, csütörtök, amikor a legnehezebb),

493

in which he assesses his relationship with his love, with his nation, with the current social order, with existence in general, and with the catharsis he is experiencing in his innermost soul. Nor can one forget *Farm on the Great Plain* (Tanya az Alföldön), with its echo of Attila József's feeling for locality; or *The Last Photograph of Endre Ady* (Ady Endre utolsó fényképe), with its shocking portrait of the poet, his body and soul wrecked by death; or *Drinking Song from Rezi* (Rezi bordal), which faces the passing of time with bitter courage.

László Nagy (1925-1978)

The lyric poetry of László Nagy, of peasant origin, can be compared with this last-mentioned poem of Juhász's. Nagy was a poet with a constant wonder and love in the face of beauty, and who confronted tragedy with defiant insolence. Many of his images and forms are taken from heroic song: prancing horses, flashing sabres, goblets of wine drained to the last drop enliven even those poems dealing with contemporary life. His attitude is expressed in brusque rhythms, in the imagery and significance of his words, their associations and sounds, and their abundance and colour. First and foremost, like Ferenc Juhász, he proclaimed himself to be on the side of the poor in their struggle: a "lover of the same flag".

There is a certain similarity between the two poets, but the differences are no less significant. Although an intellectual approach is an important factor in Nagy's lyrics, he is not so exacting in this regard as Juhász. His poetry is clearer, more pointed, more polished. The titles of his poems give some idea of the atmosphere he evokes: *Terrible Dusk* (Félelmes alkonyat), *Silver Plain* (Ezüst lapály), *Ice Crushed my Green Years* (Zöld koromat jég tördelte), *Winter Vision* (Téli látomás), *Rainbow of Fire* (Tűz-szivárvány), *On Fairy-beautiful Faces You Fed* (Tündér-arcokkal dő-zsölő), *Prayer to the White Lady* (Himnusz minden időben), *In Vermilion Light* (Cinó-ber fényben), *The Music of Wings* (Szárnyak zenéje), *Bone-crushing Life, My Love* (Szerelmem, csonttörő élet), *Skirt of Pearl* (Gyöngyszoknya), *Love of the Scorching Wind* (A forró szél imádata).

Nagy is also well known for his adaptations of Bulgarian heroic songs and the poems of García Lorca. He was not a typical translator; he was not capable of the kind of poetic impersonation that characterizes the ideal translator. He only wanted to salvage "between his teeth" the essence of that more colourful and lively heroic era, and place it in modern European conditions.

His poetry is characterized by an uncompromising firmness, a readiness to act, to revolt (*Fire* — Tűz), and by moral scrupulousness (*Mother-picture* — Anyakép). He tried to transfer the worthy elements of the culture of ancient peasant community into the world of modern civilization (*My Mother Approaching* — Ha döng a föld;

494

Carrying Love — Ki viszi át a szerelmet?). His ideal is a synthesis of the purely intellectual and childish amazement (*Bartók and the Predators* — Bartók és a ragadozók; *József Attila*). His pictures are occasionally gloomy, like in *The Arms of the Town* (A város címere), sometimes they have a very colourful effect (*Pleasuring Sunday* — A Vasárnap gyönyöre), and in some poems both characteristics are present (*Rainbow Over the Snow* — Havon delelő szivárvány). Tenderness and energy, simple means and loftiness are mingled here in perfect synthesis. The dinamics of his poems is ensured by the unique rhythm combinations (*Beautiful Women's Sayings on Gabriel* — Szépasszonyok mondókái Gábrielre; *Drought* — Aszály; *Legend of Fire and a Hyacinth* — Rege a tűzről és a jácintról; *Szindbád; The Sorrow of Resurrection* — A föltámadás szomorúsága; *Martyr Arab Mare* — Vértanú arabs kanca). Even his prose is elevated to the heights of poetry. His output has been prolific, and includes rhymed couplets, as well as poems of hundreds of lines.

One of his main subjects is the tragic necessity of the transformation of the old peasant way of life (*The Green Angel* — A Zöld Angyal; *The Little Horse's Farewell* — Búcsúzik a lovacska; *Sky and Earth* — Ég és föld; *The Bells are Coming for Me* — Jönnek a harangok értem). *The Bells are Coming for Me,* a late work, is a modern epic poem about the beauty and misery of peasant life. In other late poems, bitter irony dominates (*The Message of Rot* — A bomlás üzenete), but in his greatest poems, irony is counterpointed by the expression of faith in his ideals (*Wedding* — Menyegző).

István Simon (1926-1975)

Also of peasant stock, Simon's poetry was greatly influenced by Illyés, but is imbued with contemporary attitudes and dealing with contemporary problems. He wrote, moreover, in a mood often more personal than his mentors. In some of his best poems he portrays figures like the two taciturn friends, lifelong workmates who cannot endure each other's absence (*Carpenters Trudging Along* — Ballagó ácsok); the stokers whose every movement is a revenge for the bitternesses of bygone years; the peasants continuing to scythe, even with only one arm, indissolubly bound to their tools (*Heat Wave* — Kánikula). Elsewhere he evokes his mother sifting flour, enlarging her figure to symbolic dimensions in the perspective of memory, or the movements of old people dancing to an unchanging rhythm and ignoring their aching limbs (*Old Folk Dancing* — Táncoló öregek).

Mihály Váci (1927-1970)

was also a realist, and in his poems, akin to Simon's, he stressed with greater vigour the will to act, to be actively involved in forwarding the desires of the people. Occasionally he followed in the footsteps of Petőfi in his "public" writings, or the more modern tones of Illyés, and occasionally took to an Expressionist style (*You Fool* — Te bolond). Inspired by the ideals of socialism, he sometimes quarrelled with socialist society as it was developing (*Worthy Power!* — Méltó hatalmat!), but more often with the influences still remaining from the past, and their regressive moral and social effect. He expressed his bitterness over the past, his impatience for the future, and his joy in the present in *From the East* (Kelet felől), *Tell Me, My Love, What is the Sea Like?* (Mondd, kedvesem, milyen a tenger?), *This! Here! Now!* (Ezt! Itt! Most!). Other poems which claim the reader's attention are those which give voice to his long battle with his illness, his passionate grip on life, or when he carves deep in our mind the image of one of the condemned in the TB sanatorium (*You Just Sit...* — Csak ülsz...).

János Pilinszky (1921-1981)

Váci, according to a poem which gave the title to one of his books, felt "everywhere at home". Pilinszky's sense of a world fundamentally alienated from humanity is the most salient characteristic of his poems. Horror of the fascist era permeates his few verses — *Harbach, 1944; On the Wall of a Concentration Camp* (Egy KZ-láger falára); *The Passion of Ravensbrück* (Ravensbrücki passió). The reiterated use of this theme indicates that he was unable to rid himself of the memories of those times. The icy silence of coldly clinking "empty light bulbs" rings through his lines, and from men's eyes, "like an ownerless twig, the perishing world hangs out". Sharp images, hardly logical in their connections, are surrealistically juxtaposed, yet a very ordered word construction and disciplined grammar weld them into a coherent whole.

Most of the poetry of today is imbued with socialist ideals, but Pilinszky was far removed from the current life of Hungarian society. He was a Christian humanist–existentialist, and his poetry calls for little social action, nor is it much aware of the colour and taste of the material world. His poems are mostly short, and in vigorously contrasted images, they describe fallible man in the grip of a merciless world, offering at best a passive protest, rising above his torments only in a moral sense. His other important works are: *Four Lines* (Négysoros), *On the Third Day* (Harmadnapon), *Apocalipsis Christiana,* and *Van Gogh.* In his last years his tragic poetic vision somewhat mellowed, while the structure of his poems lost some of its extraordinary tension.

Other Poets

All these writers have already each produced a considerable body of works, but a large number of new, talented poets have also made their appearance.

Of the older generation, *Zoltán Zelk* (1906–1981) was a poet whose work is dominated by socialist ideas. His poetry reached full maturity in the last ten years of his life, with some especially moving pieces on old age. *Seagull* (Sirály), a long and touching poem evoking the figure of his dead wife, is perhaps the most outstanding piece of his poetic output, rich in emotion and, at times, contradiction.

Imre Csanádi (b. 1920), who, like László Nagy, also came from peasant stock, proclaims the importance of fulfilling one's commitments; his poetry is, however, more sombre in tone. Before 1956, *Péter Kuczka* (b. 1923) wrote a politically active, propaganda-type poetry in the Mayakovski tradition, which later took on a meditative and brooding tone. Among the poets with a more intellectual approach *Sándor Rákos* (b. 1921), who is obsessed with questions of the limits of time and space and the laws of human existence, *György Somlyó* (b. 1920), who has also won fame with his translations, and has written a broad variety of works, and *Ágnes Nemes Nagy* (b. 1921) can be singled out. Ágnes Nemes Nagy is interested in the "meaning" of objects, natural phenomena, and of the relationship between two people, but social considerations have no place in her often sombre, dramatic verse. She has produced extraordinarily strong, sensitive and highly intellectual poems on the contradictory horrors and delights of existence.

Gábor Garai (b. 1929) created a varied intellectual poetry of high standard, and was much influenced by many of his predecessors. As one of the writers in the *Fire-dance* (Tűztánc) anthology, which was published in 1958, he played a considerable part in the rebirth of socialist poetry, which was able once again to express political views after 1956.

With *Sándor Csoóri* (b. 1930), the problems of private and public life, and the experiences of peasant life combine with intellectual sensitivity and a certain plastic sense of the picturesque.

Scholarliness and a contemplative tendency characterize the poetry of *András Fodor* (b. 1929).

Of those who began their career later, *Dezső Tandori* (b. 1938) followed Pilinszky's example; his poetry, however, is more intellectual, wry and varied, and its subject is frequently written communication itself.

Among the poets in the Hungarian-speaking regions of neighbouring countries, *Árpád Tőzsér* (b. 1935) in Czechoslovakia, *Vilmos Kovács* (1927–1977) in the Carpathian Ukraine, *Sándor Kányádi* (b. 1929), *Aladár Lászlóffy* (b. 1937), *Géza Páskándi* (b. 1933—settled in Hungary in the '70s), *Domokos Szilágyi* (1938–1976) in Rumania, and *Ottó Tolnai* (b. 1940) in Yugoslavia, have all produced admirable work.

József Lengyel (1896-1975)

It was only after 1945 that Lengyel brought his characteristic style to final maturity, although work of his had already been published at the time of the First World War. He began his career as an avant-garde poet under Kassák. He later moved out of Kassák's orbit to become a communist, when he stopped writing poetry and took to prose. After the fall of the 1919 Republic of Councils he was forced to emigrate to Vienna and Berlin, and finally to the Soviet Union. At the time of the forged trials in 1949, he was sent to a labour camp, and later lived in exile. In 1955 he returned to Hungary and took his place as a writer again.

Among his early work, *Visegrádi Street* (Visegrádi utca, 1930) describes the Revolution of 1919; and *The Troubled Life of Ferenc Prenn* (Prenn Ferenc hányatott élete, 1930, 1958) is a reworking of this story in novel, or at times adventure story form. His longer works (*How Much can Man Bear?*—Mit bír el az ember?, 1965) are more distinctly novels, but in other works the essayistic tendencies are present, as in *Three Bridge Builders* (Három hídépítő, 1960).

His best works are a collection of short stories, most of which appeared in a volume entitled *Enchanter* (Igéző) in 1961. They tell in part of the life endured by the inmates of the labour camp. Without any embellishment or attempt to heighten the effect, he paints the hell of suffering they underwent, yet searching above all for the humanity that had survived or been confirmed in it—*From Beginning to End* (Elejétől végig); *Little Angry Old Man* (Kicsi, mérges öregúr); *Yellow Poppies* (Sárga pipacsok). In the undramatic simplicity of these tales, and even more in his descriptions of his exile—*They are Building a Road* (Út épül); *From Morning till Night* (Reggeltől estig); *Forest Pictures* (Erdei képek); *Enchanter* (Igéző)—the experiences of a man watching life with the calmness of a Tolstoy are clothed in aesthetic form. In his short stories he gives us descriptions of man and nature breathing together in harmony, which nonetheless are devoid of any hint of "magical" pantheism. They are constructed of a mosaic which forms a structural whole. They are laconic, undramatic in style, with a profound intellectual content, yet they glint suddenly with flashes of lyric beauty. Put together, these qualities make József Lengyel one of the finest Hungarian short-story writers, and a master of Hungarian socialist realist prose.

József Darvas (1912-1973)

Of Great Plain peasant origin, he finished his education under conditions of great poverty and hardship. He joined the workers' movement very early, and his Marxist views prevented him—unlike many of his companions—from being affected by the romantic image of the peasant. Since the liberation he filled many important posts, several times served as a government minister, and was president of the Writers' Association.

In his first important novel, *From Twelfth Night to New Year's Eve* (Vízkereszttől szilveszterig, 1934), he preceded Péter Veres in demonstrating how sociology and literature could be combined. *The History of a Peasant Family* (Egy parasztcsalád története, 1939) is one of the most successful examples of village sociology. *City on the Swamp* (Város az ingoványon, 1946) represents a fusion of belles-lettres and documentary journalism. Meditating among the ruins of the bombed capital, among personal thoughts and memories, he asks himself why this city had to perish.

As the last work shows, after the liberation his work took an increasingly intellectual direction. This is especially true of *Drunken Rain* (Részeg eső, 1963), the most important work of his last period, which encompasses the problems of *City on the Swamp* (Város az ingoványon). The novel is unmistakably modern in form, theme, and in the questions it raises. The story is told in the first person by its hero, a film director, seeking the reason for the suicide of his friend, a man of peasant origin whose talent as a painter had promised great things back in the thirties when they had begun the world together. The work broadens out to search for the causes of the tragic events of 1956 and the moral questions they pose, which in turn involves not only the fate of a nation but the entire future of Europe in the modern age.

Many of Darvas's plays have also been successful. Peasant life between the two wars was the theme for *Abyss* (Szakadék, 1942); *Sooty Sky* (Kormos ég, 1960), and the dramatized version of *Drunken Rain* were important theatrical events.

Imre Sarkadi (1921-1961)

The career of Imre Sarkadi came to a tragic close, when he accidentally (or deliberately?) fell twenty metres from a window. He began as a village schoolteacher, but then worked as a journalist and reporter, living an unconventional, bohemian life.

The central theme of his stories and plays is the development of the individual personality. The first full-length novel, written after numerous short stories, was *János Gál's Way* (Gál János útja, 1950), displaying the strong influence of Móricz's *A Happy Man* (A boldog ember). Sarkadi's hero, however, is unambiguously a happy man. He gives us an intimate picture of a poor peasant whose life becomes gradually richer. He relates in the guileless words of his hero, how he progressed from servility to his first independent action and so along the road to a deeper knowledge of himself and the world.

In later books, his chief characters are people who fail to find the way to develop their talents and ambitions; they may be defiant of their fate, but their courage cannot face the everyday world; they cannot cope with day to day matters, and their moral strength is sapped or destroyed: *In a Storm* (Viharban), *The Fool and the Monster* (A bolond és a szörnyeteg), *The Coward* (A gyáva). From naive, gently lyrical but direct narrative, or even from his vigorous, strikingly drawn dramatic plots, again reminiscent of Móricz, Sarkadi moves to the construction of a more intellectual, more graphic style, sensitive to the slightest vibration.

Sarkadi was one of the best playwrights of his generation. One of his most successful plays, *September* (Szeptember, 1955), is gently poetic but realistic, a piece dealing with the changes in peasant life. In *Simon Stylite* (Oszlopos Simeon, 1961), he captures with perfect, though slightly bizarre fidelity, but without renouncing realism, the agony of man finally losing his footing. The chief character claims that "form is breaking up, and we have no right to stop it...", and that he must revenge himself by making worse a world that is already infinitely corrupt. Sarkadi feels his Simeon irrational and inhuman, and on the threshold of his death forces him to abandon this attitude, but the reversal is not convincing. *The Lost Paradise* (Az elveszett paradicsom, 1961) is an accomplished, well-integrated work, in which Sarkadi, although he understands the position of the fallen hero, yet pronounces judgement on him, while providing a glimpse of the road to salvation. Film-makers were also much indebted to Sarkadi: the enormously successful film *Roundabout* (Körhinta), a story of village life, was based on one of his works.

Ferenc Sánta (b. 1927)

The literary career of Sánta shows many similarities with both Sarkadi and Juhász. He was discovered by Pál Szabó in 1954, when he worked in a factory. His early writing echoed the magic of Áron Tamási's short stories, the childlike naiveté of Ferenc Móra's early memories, and the hard realism of Móricz. His first short story, *There Were Too Many of Us* (Sokan voltunk), relates with apparently effortless economy the tale of the aged grandfather whose existence was burdening the already hard-pressed family, and who follows some age-old custom, and kills himself in a gas-filled cavern. Sánta later broke away from these and other reminiscences to embark on a more complex and reflective style as in *Earth* (Föld), though without departing from the values which inspired his earlier work.

Twenty Hours (Húsz óra, 1964), is cast within the framework of investigative reportage: the action takes place at different times, and the central event is viewed from several angles, but the parts are combined to create a picture of the human dramas that accompanied the transformation in village life. In trying to find the reason for the shooting of a peasant in the autumn of 1956, the author contemplates on whether it is necessary for one poor man to destroy another. The question finally remains unanswered, but the novel gives a vivid picture of the decisive years of

1945 to 1960 in Hungarian village life. *Twenty Hours* was made into a film and was well received abroad.

Sympathetic portrayal of the lives of the poor and downtrodden and an ethical–philosophical approach are the two main characteristics that stand out in Sánta's work. *The Traitor* (Az áruló, 1966), is a historical novel built on a series of monologues and dialogues: the single chain of events flows dramatically along, illuminated from various angles. The four characters are the priest who believes only in the pleasures of life and the arts, the student whom the priest "converts" from the Hussite movement to join the Imperial ranks, the Hussite leader, who left the Imperial side at the student's persuasion, and finally the peasant, the victim of both sides in the war, maintaining his distance from both parties in order to survive, and who, when they have destroyed one another, buries them all in a common grave.

Other Prose Writers

At the end of the 1940s and in the early 1950s, it was still the writers of the previous period, Németh, Déry, Veres, who dominated the scene. Several authors of an earlier date produced their masterpieces during this time. One of them was *Kálmán Sándor* (1903–1962) who had been relegated to obscurity before the liberation on account of his leftist views. His short stories and novels, especially *Tree of Shame* (Szégyenfa, 1951), contain much that is socially significant.

Both *Géza Ottlik* (b. 1912) and *György Rónay* (1913–1978) belong to the third generation of *Nyugat* writers, and both produced important books in the '30s, but they wrote their best works during the '40s and '50s. Ottlik's books are few, and *School on the Border* (Iskola a határon, 1959), is his best. The book is written in a modern manner—it is based on the diary of a single character, and the memories of another; and the psychology of fascism is faithfully portrayed in the personality of the school inspector. György Rónay was also a poet, essayist and translator. The central theme of his novel *The Night Express* (Esti gyors, 1963), is the moral problem of a man who becomes an accessory to a crime due to his cowardice. Different time elements are cunningly welded together, and the various threads of the plot woven into a brilliantly coherent pattern. *The Panther and the Kidling* (A párduc és a gödölye, 1978), is the story of a judge who played part in the forged trials of the period. The novel raises the questions of moral responsibility, revenge and forgiveness.

Gábor Thurzó (1912–1979) wrote his most remarkable works after the liberation, dealing mainly with the moral problems of the educated sections of society. In addition to several fine short stories, his best novel, *The Saint* (A szent), the story of a canonization procedure during the years of the Second World War, is also centred around ethical problems.

István Örkény (1912–1979) occupies a place of his own. His tales, in taut and disciplined prose, are often grotesque, verging on Surrealism. He is stimulated by the tensions concealed in the peaceful externals of existence—*Circus* (Cirkusz), *Snowstorm* (Hóviharban) —and the potential tragedy hidden in insignificant everyday things, or even in comedy, as in his play *Cat's Play* (Macskajáték). In his "one-minute stories", a genre of his own which he particularly favoured, high fantasy springs quite naturally from the most commonplace or ordinary background. He is a distinctly intellectual writer, lucid and intelligible. *The Tót Family* (Tóték) is one of the best Hungarian novels produced in the '60s. It recounts the tragicomedy of the little man who surrenders to the powers of authority, and is the story of a family which endures all the agonies of living with, and submitting to the mad vagaries of an officer billeted with them, who is in fact suffering from a nervous breakdown, for the sake of their son still at the front, whose fate the officer might influence. Between the comic situations a horrible paradox emerges: the lengths of human self-sacrifice. Their middle-class zeal to please is ridiculed by the author, but the final tragedy has been indicated at the beginning: unknown to the parents, their son was already dead. *An Exhibition of Roses* (Rózsakiállítás, 1977) is the novel of facing death without illusions. It deals with the question of frankness and role-acting, of art and reality.

Satire and the bizarre both play a large role in the work of *Gábor Goda* (b. 1911) in, for instance, *The Wax-works* (Panoptikum, 1956), and satire and ridicule are again weapons frequently used by *Ferenc Karinthy* (b. 1921). The novels of *Magda Szabó* (b. 1917) deal with the former middle classes and the new morality, as in *Fresco* (Freskó, 1958), *The Deer* (Az őz, 1959), *Pilate* (Pilátus, 1963). *Old-fashioned Story* (Régimódi történet, 1977), is one of her most successful works of late.

Between 1960 and 1970, there was a considerable recrudescence of popular interest in the novel. József Darvas's *Drunken Rain* and Ferenc Sánta's *Twenty Hours* are products of this period, and are evidence of the novel's abandonment of traditional forms, repeated in *Scrapyard* (Rozsdatemető, 1962), by *Endre Fejes* (b. 1923). This novel initiated a vigorous debate and aroused great interest among professional writers as well as the reading public. It has seized with rare perceptivity upon the type of human being who remains essentially untouched by the events of history: wars, revolutions and counter-revolutions with their pitiless brutality reach into the life of the Hábetler family, but its purposeless, monotonous rhythm is unaltered. Only the son attempts to rebel, but he is unable to control his passions, and finally commits a senseless murder. The novel is deliberately low-keyed—it is influenced by behaviourism—in the manner of Lajos Nagy, but Fejes skates over details with ease.

Similar in technique to *Twenty Hours*, *Cold Days* (Hideg napok, 1965), by *Tibor Cseres* (b. 1915) is a mosaic of memories framed in vastly different viewpoints.

The novel is told in a series of spoken and silent dialogues and monologues between Hungarian soldiers involved in the massacre of Jews which took place in Yugoslavia in 1942, men who represented different personal and class values, and who are imprisoned together at the end of the war. Basically, this is a realist novel, but it firmly rejects the traditional realistic form. Its central theme is moral responsibility set against the historical events of the time.

These attempts to modernize the novel found expression in historically accurate and socially committed works. For certain writers, however, this "new wave" of Hungarian literature took the form of an abstract, symbolic reaction far removed from reality. The extremely economical, somewhat Surrealistic writings of *Iván Mándy* (b. 1918) are a case in point. His interest centres on those outside society, those reduced to life on the periphery, and the "magic" of their lives, sensing the unrelenting laws to which they conform. One of his best novels is *On the Touchlines* (A pálya szélén, 1963). The football field is the stage of life: the hero's football fanaticism overcomes his fury and despair at his total failure, and the working of an inner compulsion to accept life as it is is neatly indicated. Several of his works have been filmed. In his collection of short stories, *The Movie of Old Times* (Régi idők mozija, 1967), the banal filmscripts of the twenties are interwoven with the tragic fate of his characters. *Miklós Mészöly* (b. 1921) creates an equally formalized, almost Kafkaesque world, often depressing in its atmosphere but painted with remarkable skill and intelligence. *Death of an Athlete* (Az atléta halála, 1966) recounts the tale of a man who never fulfilled himself, his tortuous struggles and unexpected collapse. *Saulus* (1968) describes the phases of a complete reversal in attitude. *Accurate Stories Along the Way* (Pontos történetek útközben, 1970), is a short novel of objective preciseness. His short novel *Film* (1976) is an even more characteristic example of the influence of French *nouveau roman*.

Recent Developments

György Moldova (b. 1934) is the most individual of the newest generation. His short stories are peopled with characters living on the outskirts of society, or swept along by the whirlwind of social and political events, yet who are all somehow typical of our age; *Mandarin, the Famous Tough* (Mandarin, a híres vagány), *Ferdinand the Thief* (Tolvaj Ferdinánd), *Nights on the Square* (Esték a téren), etc. The compelling charm of his work is reminiscent of Endre Andor Gelléri. His novel *A Mill in Hell* (Malom a pokolban, 1968), is an attempt to recreate a "Julien Sorel" figure of the fifties. His satires (*The Cursed Office* — Az elátkozott hivatal, 1967) are of great interest, as are his documentary articles and literary reportage, e.g. *The Trains Must Run* (Akit a mozdony füstje megcsapott, 1976).

István Szabó (1928–1976) wrote short stories of peasant life, exposing the contradictions in the change of life-styles.

Erzsébet Galgóczi (b. 1930) is a writer interested in the ancient customs and conventions of village life, and the lives and tragedies of the young. Her novels and stories are stark and realist in character: *Only Snow There Too* (Ott is csak hó van, 1961), *Boy from the Mansion* (Fiú a kastélyból, 1968), *Whose Law Is It?* (Kinek a törvénye?, 1971). Of the many writings on the great social changes that took place between 1945 and 1960, *Sándor Somogyi Tóth* (b. 1923) with *You were a Prophet, my Love* (Próféta voltál, szívem, 1964), and *Gyula Fekete* (b. 1922) with *The Death of a Doctor* (Az orvos halála), 1963, rightfully earned the acclaim of the critics.

Previously known as a critic and scholar, *György Konrád's* (b. 1933) novel, *The Caseworker* (A látogató, 1969), was much discussed when it appeared. It deals with the struggles of a caseworker—the action is both factual and in the realm of the imagination—over the limitations of his official and private life, and is told with detached and dramatic simplicity. Also relatively late in beginning, *György G. Kardos* (b. 1925) leapt to success with both the critics and the public with his *The Seven Days of Avraham Bogatir* (Avraham Bogatir hét napja, 1968). The book concerns the tensions and enmities of the various communities in Palestine just after the Second World War. His realism, embroidered with humour, is humanist in its outlook. Together with *Where Have All the Soldiers Gone?* (Hová tűntek a katonák?, 1971), and *The End of the Story* (A történet vége, 1978), the three novels constitute a loosely constructed trilogy.

An interesting development in the last ten years has been the renewal of interest in literary reportage. Alongside the elder writers of this genre from the 1930s, such as *József Darvas, Ferenc Erdei, Géza Féja* and *János Kodolányi*, come the newer generation, the poet *Sándor Csoóri, Gábor Mocsár, György Moldova, Antal Végh* and others. Promising writers who first appeared in print in the sixties include, among others, *Lajos Galambos, István Gáll, Anna Jókai, Ákos Kertész, András Simonffy, Károly Szakonyi.*

The best representatives of the generation of the seventies are *József Balázs, Géza Bereményi, Péter Esterházy, Péter Lengyel* and *Péter Nádas.*

Of the new Hungarian-speaking generation in Rumania, *Tibor Bálint* (b. 1932), who combines the fantastic with the realistic in a unique manner, and *András Sütő* (b. 1927), who combines autobiography, literary reportage and a poetic view in his works (*Mother Promised Better Dreams* — Anyám könnyű álmot ígér), well merit the critical praise they have received. *István Szilágyi* (b. 1938) won recognition with his novel *A Stone's Fall into a Drying Well* (Kő hull apadó kútba), in which he sheds new light on life in *fin de siècle* Hungary, a subject much written of. He has learnt equally well from the strict psychological character-building of László Németh, the technique of shifting planes of time, and the masters of style. In Czechoslovakia

László Dobos (b. 1930) and *Gyula Duba* (b. 1930), and in Yugoslavia *Nándor Gion* (b. 1941) can be singled out among the Hungarian-speaking writers as particularly promising.

Drama

The plays written in the last thirty years devote considerably more attention to social questions. As in the other forms of literature, rigid political dogmatism prevailed in the first decade after the war, and affected the style of these pieces, but in later years the crudities of this type of play diminished, and gave way to a sounder, more honest reflection of the community, while at the same time artistic standards improved. Nonetheless, the best plays were still those written by the older generation of playwrights, such as László Németh and Gyula Illyés.

A large number of the new generation of writers, contemporary with and following *Imre Sarkadi,* have, however, also contributed to the development of the Hungarian theatre. The most important plays, while not unaffected by modern trends, continued nevertheless to follow traditional forms. Successful experiments have been carried out in the field of narrative drama, such as *People of Pest* (Pesti emberek), written by *Lajos Mesterházi* (1916–1979), already known for his numerous novels.

Miklós Hubay (b. 1918) and the poet *István Vas* together wrote the musical *Three Nights of a Romance* (Egy szerelem három éjszakája) around the lives, tragedies and tragicomedies of young people affected by war.

Miklós Mészöly's work, *The Window Cleaner* (Az ablakmosó) is by no means socialist in outlook, and is reminiscent of the theatre of the absurd. It deals with the effect of a merciless authority intervening in the lives of little people and poisoning their existence. His more recent play, *The Bunker* (A bunker) reveals similar artistic intentions. *László Gyurkó* (b. 1930) wrote *Electra, my Love* (Szerelmem, Elektra), which translated the ancient story of Electra into a modern vehicle for social and ethical problems.

A number of novels have been dramatized, and proved theatrical successes. Among them are *The Tót Family* (Tóték) and *Cat's Play* (Macskajáték) by István Örkény, Endre Fejes's *Scrapyard* (Rozsdatemető), and József Darvas's *Drunken Rain* (Részeg eső). *Pisti in a Shower of Blood* (Pisti a vérzivatarban) by Örkény is the story of the historical vicissitudes man-in-the-street has to go through. Modern playwrights have provided a great variety of themes and styles. The most interesting experiments have been made by István Csurka, Imre Dobozy, Miklós Gyárfás, Miklós Hubay, Ferenc Karinthy, László Kamondy, István Eörsi, Magda Szabó, Károly Szakonyi, Gábor Thurzó, and Endre Vészi.

Of the work of the Hungarian-speaking playwrights in Rumania, Géza Páskándi's

Visiting (Vendégség) stands out. Set in the Reformation of the seventeenth century, it deals with the conflict between crude pragmatism which respects no principle, and the faith which upholds purity in morals and beliefs. Páskándi moved to Hungary in the seventies and since then he is a prominent representative of Hungarian literature both as poet and playwright. The plays of András Sütő (*Star at the Stake —* Csillag a máglyán, 1975 and *The Palm Sunday of a Horse-dealer —* Egy lócsiszár virágvasárnapja, 1974) deal with the historical-philosophical questions of power, personal freedom and the building of society. János Székely's *Caligula* (1972) is about the tension between moral truth and political realism.

A mention should also be made of the plays of *Ferenc Deák,* a Yugoslav writer in the Hungarian tongue.

Criticism and the History of Literature

The last thirty-five years have shown a vigorous development in the study of literature and in literary criticism. Of the numerous literary scholars of the previous generation, János Horváth has added several important books to his œuvre, and György Lukács who worked with undiminished energy until his death, and wrote his masterpiece during this period. Although Lukács had already exerted an influence on Hungarian scholars and critics in earlier days, he only came into his own, like József Révai, after 1945. Returning from exile they both began to play an active role in the intellectual life of the period. Their early books and articles then became available, and became models for both the young and the more experienced critics and literary historians alike.

From the end of the 1940s on Marxist views and methods gained increasing support. In the first years of the new communist power they were over-simplified and applied too rigidly, yet in themselves they enriched literature: they directed attention to the connections between literature and society and, theoretical aesthetics, away from Positivism, entangled in detail, and the school of *Geistesgeschichte*, remote from reality. The distance between the study of the literature of the past and criticism of the literature of the present began to diminish. Due to the introduction of comparative studies in literature, Hungarian literature was beginning to shed its insularity.

An entirely new generation of historians and critics has grown up since the liberation, who treat Marxist theory with originality and perception. By the 1960s several schools of thought had developed, differing considerably in their methods and approach to literature, but united in their basic concepts. In 1963, the review *Kritika* was founded; it originally concerned itself with the theories of literary and art criticism, but in its revised form it has a more popular appeal.

The greatest advance, however, considering the size of the subject, was in the expansion of studies in the history of Hungarian literature. The organization of research and the training of specialists, the increase in the number of journals and series of literary studies, has produced numerous monographs of the great Hungarian writers as well as critical editions of their works. The culmination of all this work was the six-volume *History of the Hungarian Literature* (A magyar irodalom története, 1964–66), edited by István Sőtér, the most complete account of the subject to date. It is the work of a number of young and elder historians, and can be regarded as an authoritative contribution to the literature of the post-liberation era.

A history of Hungarian literature in French appeared in 1962, entitled *Histoire abrégée de la littérature hongroise.* This was the work of Tibor Klaniczay, József Szauder and Miklós Szabolcsi. A Russian translation appeared in the same year, a German version in 1963, an English version in 1964, and a Polish version in 1966. The book, if only for its stopgap nature, was generally well received by foreign critics, although unfavourable reviews were not lacking. Along with its virtues, the writers as well as the publishers were aware of its faults, especially as it had been written before the definitive six-volume history of Hungarian literature produced by the Department of Literary History in the Hungarian Academy of Sciences. This was the history previously referred to, which appeared between 1964 and 1966, prepared by no less than sixty literary experts. The publication of this work led to a number of reappraisals and conclusions which the writers of the *Histoire abrégée,* or, in the English version, *History of Hungarian Literature,* could not have included in their book. A new foreign-language history of Hungarian literature is therefore timely. The present book was prepared with the aid of the six-volume history, and the *Histoire abrégée,* and with an eye to the reviewers of that book.

Selected Bibliography

Compiled by Ildikó Tódor

Introduction

When compiling the *Selected Bibliography* our aim was, on one hand, to provide the reader with a brief survey of the most important works dealing with the history and literary history of Hungary and with Hungarian writers treated in detail in the volume, and, on the other, to give a selection of the English-language translations of Hungarian fiction.

The present bibliography contains individual works and monographs; the size of the book, however, did not permit to deal with essays, articles and critical works published in periodicals.

In the chapter *Interactions between Hungarian and World Literature* it is only the comprehensive works that are included; to publish material about the relations of individual foreign and Hungarian writers was, for the afore-mentioned reasons, also impossible.

In Chapter II, *On Individual Writers*, after the monographs the reader will often find—with the note **Cf.**—cross-references to works enlisted in the *General Part* or the chapter entitled: *Hungarian Literature in English Translation*. (The page number after the title refers to the bibliography.)

The bibliography contains works published up to July, 1981, and a few which were then in preparation. They are listed in the chronological order of the years of their publication. Exceptions are the chapters *Works on Certain Periods and Trends of Hungarian Literature, Essay Volumes, Hungarian Literature in English Translation: II) Individual Works*, where the authors' names or the titles of the works are arranged alphabetically.

List of Abbreviations

a.	and	Forew.	Foreword
Afterw.	Afterword	Hrsg.	Herausgegeben von
annot.	annotation	Id.	Idem
Bp.	Budapest	Intr.	Introduction
compil.	compilation	K.	Publishing House, Publishers
Cf.	confer	pl.	plate
ed.	edition	Pref.	Preface
rev. enl. ed.	revised and enlarged edition	Red.	redaction
Ed.	Editor	sel.	selection, seleited
Ed.-in-chief	Editor-in-chief	Transl.	Translation

A) On Hungarian History and Literature

I GENERAL PART

Introduction. On Hungarian history
Bibliographies
Monographs
On the history of Hungarian literature
Bibliographies
Writers' biographies, literary encyclopaedias
Literary histories in Hungarian
Hungarian literary histories in foreign languages
Works on certain periods and trends of Hungarian literature
Essay volumes
Works on the history of literary genres (drama, novel)
Literary language, style, verse, translation
Book, library, printing, journalism
Representative anthologies of Hungarian literature

Interactions between Hungarian and world literature
General works
American–Hungarian
Bulgarian–Hungarian
Czechoslovakian–Hungarian
Dutch–Hungarian
English–Hungarian
Finnish–Hungarian
French–Hungarian
German–Hungarian
Italian–Hungarian
Polish–Hungarian
Rumanian–Hungarian
Russian–Hungarian
Southern Slav–Hungarian
Swiss–Hungarian

II ON INDIVIDUAL WRITERS
(In alphabetic order)

B) Hungarian Literature in English Translation

I ANTHOLOGIES
(In chronological order)

II INDIVIDUAL WORKS
(In alphabetic order)

A) On Hungarian History and Literature

I GENERAL PART

Introduction. On Hungarian History

BIBLIOGRAPHIES

Magyar történeti bibliográfia 1825–1867 [Bibliography of Hungarian history *1825-1867*]. Vols. 1–3. Ed. I. Tóth Zoltán. Bp. *1950–1952*, Akadémiai K.
Vol. 1. Általános rész [General part]. Bp. 1950. 118 pp.
Vol. 2. Gazdaság [Economy]. Bp. 1952. 260 pp.
Vol. 3. Politika, jog, oktatás, iskolák, tudomány, művészet, sajtó, vallás, egyházak [Politics, law, education, schools, sciences, arts, press, religion, churches]. Bp. 1950. 407 pp.
Vol. 4. Nem magyar népek (nemzetiségek) [Non-Hungarian nations—Nationalities]. Ed. Kemény G. Gábor, Katus László. Bp. 1959. 675 pp.
Kosáry Domokos: *Bevezetés a magyar történelem forrásaiba és irodalmába* [Introduction to the sources and literature of Hungarian history]. Vols. 1–3. Bp. *1951–1958*.
Vol. 1. to 1711. Bp. 1951, Közoktatásügyi K. 480 pp.
Vol. 2. from 1711 to 1825. Bp. 1954, Művelt Nép. K. 638 pp.
Vol. 3. Kiegészítések és névmutató [Addenda and index]. Bp. 1958, Bibliotheca. 398 pp.
Kosáry Domokos: *Bevezetés Magyarország történetének forrásaiba és irodalmába* [Introduction to the sources and literature of the history of Hungary]. 1. [vol.] 1 General part I–II. Bp. *1970*, Tankönyvkiadó. 889 pp.
A magyar történettudomány válogatott bibliográfiája 1945–1968 [Selected bibliography of Hungarian historiography 1945-1968]. Ed. Niederhauser Emil, Makkai László [etc]. Bp. *1971*, Akadémiai K. 855 pp.

MONOGRAPHS

Hóman Bálint–Szekfű Gyula: *Magyar történet* [Hungarian history]. Vols. 1–8. Bp. *1928–1934* [?] — (6th ed.) Vols. 1–5. Bp. 1939, Egyetemi Nyomda.
Magyar művelődéstörténet [Hungarian cultural history]. Vols. 1–5. Ed. Domanovszky Sándor. Bp. *1939–1942*, Magyar Történelmi Társulat.
Vol. 1. Ősműveltség és középkori kultúra [Ancient civilization and medieval culture]. Bp. 1939. 636 pp.
Vol. 2. Magyar renaissance [Hungarian Renaissance]. Bp. 1939. 670 pp.
Vol. 3. A kereszténység védőbástyája [The stronghold of Christianity]. Bp. 1939. 664 pp.
Vol. 4. Barokk és felvilágosodás [Baroque and Enlightenment]. Ed. Wellmann Imre. Bp. 1941. 658 pp.
Vol. 5. Az új Magyarország [The new Hungary]. Ed. Szentpétery Imre, Balanyi György, Mályusz Elemér, Varjú Elemér. Bp. 1942. 684 pp. [From 1900 to 1910].
Sinor, Denis: *History of Hungary*. London *1959*, George Allen and Unwin Ltd. 310 pp.
Halász Zoltán: *Ungarn*. Bp. *1961*, Corvina. 476 pp. — 1967[3] — in English: *Hungary*. Bp. 1966, Corvina. 456 pp.
Information Hungary. Ed.-in-chief: Erdei, Ferenc Bp. *1968*, Akadémiai K. — Pergamon Press. 1144 pp. (Countries of the World 2.)
Magyarország története [History of Hungary] Ed. Molnár Erik, Pamlényi Ervin, Székely György. 3rd rev. enl. ed. Bp. *1971*, Gondolat K. 1376 pp.
Magyarország története képekben [History of Hungary in Pictures]. Ed. Kosáry Domokos,

PAMLÉNYI Ervin (etc.). Bp. *1971*, Gondolat K. 750 pp. — *1973*[2].

Istoriya Vengrii [History of Hungary]. [V 3 tomakh. Red. koll. T. M. ISLAMOV, A. I. PUSHKASH, V. P. SHUSHARIN.] Moscow, *1971–1972*, Izdat. "Nauka". 643, 598, 965 pp.

Die Geschichte Ungarns. [Hrsg.] PAMLÉNYI. Ervin Bp. *1971*, Corvina. 786 pp.

Histoire de la Hongrie. Publié sous la direction de PAMLÉNYI, Ervin. Bp.–Roanne *1974*, Corvina–Éditions Diffusion Horvath. 756 pp.

History of Hungary. [Ed. by] PAMLÉNYI, Ervin. Bp.–London *1974*, Corvina—Collet's Holding Ltd. 676 pp.

A Magyar Tudományos Akadémia másfél évszázada. 1825–1975 [150 years of the Hungarian Academy of Sciences. 1825–1975]. Ed. PACH Zsigmond Pál. Bp. *1975*, Akadémiai K. 547 pp.

Magyarország története [History of Hungary]. [In ten volumes. Edited by the Institute for Historiography of the Hungarian Academy of Sciences. Head of the editing committee: PACH Zsigmond Pál.] Bp. *1976–*, Akadémiai K. Vol. 5. Parts 1–2: 1790–1848. Ed.-in-chief: MÉREI Gyula. Ed. VÖRÖS Károly. Bp. 1980. 1456 pp.

Vol. 6. Parts 1–2: 1848–1890. Ed.-in-chief: KOVÁCS Endre. Ed. KATUS László. Bp. 1979. 1760 pp.

Vol. 7. Parts 1–2: 1890–1918. Ed.-in-chief: HANÁK Péter. Ed. MUCSI Ferenc. Bp. 1978. 1422 pp.

Vol. 8.: 1918–1919, 1919–1945. Ed.-in-chief: RÁNKI György. Ed.: HAJDÚ Tibor, TILKOVSZKY Lóránt. Bp. 1976. 1400 pp. — 1978[2].

On the History of Hungarian Literature

BIBLIOGRAPHIES

SZABÓ Károly [3rd vol. SZABÓ Károly–HELLEBRANT Árpád]: *Régi magyar könyvtár* [Old Hungarian library]. Bp. *1879–1898*.

Vol. 1. Az 1531–1711. megjelent magyar nyomtatványok könyvészeti kézikönyve [Bibliographical handbook of Hungarian works printed between 1531–1711]. Bp. 1879. XIV, 751 pp.

Vol. 2. Az 1473-tól 1711-ig megjelent nem magyar nyelvű hazai nyomtatványok könyvészeti kézikönyve [Bibliographical handbook of non-Hungarian works printed in Hungary between 1473–1711]. Bp. 1855. XI, 754 pp.

Vol. 3. Magyar szerzőktől külföldön 1480-tól 1711-ig megjelent nem magyar nyelvű nyomtatványok könyvészeti kézikönyve [Bibliographical handbook of works by Hungarian authors in non-Hungarian languages printed abroad between 1480–1711]. Parts 1–2. Bp. 1896–1898. VIII, 800; 943 pp.

SZTRIPSZKY Hiador: *Adalékok Szabó Károly Régi Magyar Könyvtár c. munkájának I–II. kötetéhez. Pótlások és igazítások. 1474–1711* [Addenda to Károly Szabó's Old Hungarian library, vols.

I–II. Complements and corrections. 1472–1711]. Bp. *1912* (12), 710 pp. — Id. Bp. 1967. (Bibliographia Hungariae. Series editionum stereotyparum.)

A magyar irodalom bibliográfiája [Bibliography of Hungarian literature]. Ed. KOZOCSA Sándor. Bp. *1950–*
1945–1949. Bp. 1950, Közoktatásügyi Kiadóvállalat, 232 pp.
1950. Bp. 1951, Közoktatásügyi Kiadóvállalat. 80 pp.
1951–1952. Bp. 1954, Művelt Nép K. 180 pp.
1953. Bp. 1954, Művelt Nép K. 208 pp.
1954. Bp. 1956, Művelt Nép K. 232 pp.
1955. Bp. 1959, Gondolat K. 334 pp.
1956–1957. Bp. 1961, Gondolat K. 717 pp.
1958. Bp. 1965, Gondolat K. 581 pp.
1959. Bp. 1966, Gondolat K. 637 pp.
1960. Bp. 1970, Gondolat K. 526 pp.
1961–1965. Bp. 1978, Gondolat K. Vols. 1–2, 542; 543–1123 pp.

Nyugat repertórium [The *Nyugat* Repertory]. Ed. GALAMBOS Ferenc, PÓK Lajos. Bp. *1959*. 571 pp.

A magyar kéziratos énekeskönyvek és versgyűjtemények bibliográfiája (1565–1840) [A bibliography of Hungarian song-books and verse collections in manuscript (1565–1840)]. Ed. STOLL Béla. Bp. *1963*, Akadémiai K. 537 pp.

TEZLA, Albert: *An Introductory Bibliography to the Study of Hungarian Literature*. Cambridge, Massachusetts *1964*, Harvard University Press. XXVI, 290 pp.

A csehszlovákiai magyar nyelvű szocialista sajtó irodalmi bibliográfiája (1919–1938) [A literary bibliography of the Hungarian-language socialist press in Czechoslovakia (1919–1938)]. Ed. BOTKA Ferenc. Bp. *1966*, Akadémiai K. 376 pp.

TEZLA, Albert: *Hungarian Authors. A Bibliographical Handbook.* Cambridge, Massachusetts, *1970*, The Belknap Press of Harvard University Press. XXVIII, 792 pp.

BORSA Gedeon–HERVAY Ferenc–HOLL Béla–KÄFER István–KELECSÉNYI Ákos: *Régi magyarországi nyomtatványok 1473–1600* [Old Hungarian printed works 1473–1600]. Res litteraria Hungariae vetus operum impressorum 1473–1600. Bp. *1971*, Akadémiai K. 928 pp., 42 pl.

A magyar sajtótörténet irodalmának válogatott bibliográfiája 1705–1945 [A selected bibliography of the literature of the history of Hungarian press 1705–1945]. Ed. JÓZSEF Farkas. Bp. *1972*. 428 pp.

VARGA Rózsa–PATYI Sándor: *A népi írók bibliográfiája. Művek, irodalom, mozgalom (1920–1960)* [Bibliography of the populist writers. Works, literature, movement (1920–1960)]. Bp. *1972*, Akadémiai K. 940 pp.

A magyar irodalomtörténet bibliográfiája [Bibliography of the history of Hungarian literature]. Ed.-in-chief: VARGHA Kálmán, V. WINDISCH Éva. Bp. *1972*-, Akadémiai K.
Vol. 1. (To 1772.) Ed. STOLL Béla, VARGA Imre, V. KOVÁCS Sándor. Bp. 1972. 638 pp.
Vol. 2. (1772–1849.) Ed. KÓKAY György. Bp. 1975. 925 pp.
Vol. 6. (1905–1945.) Személyi rész. A–K [Individual Writers. A–K]. Ed. BOTKA Ferenc, VARGHA Kálmán. Bp. 1982. 959 pp.

STAUD Géza: *Magyar színháztörténeti bibliográfia* [Bibliography of the history of the Hungarian theatre]. Vols. 1–2. Bp. *1975*, Magyar Színházi Intézet. 469, 403 pp.

A magyar irodalom és irodalomtudomány bibliográfiája... [Bibliography of Hungarian literature and library history]. Ed. LICHTMANN Tamás, NÉMETH S. Katalin. Bp. *1979*-, Országos Széchényi Könyvtár.
1976. Bp. 1979. 456 pp.
1977. Bp. 1980. 375 pp.
1978. Bp. 1982. 477. pp.

WRITERS' BIOGRAPHIES, LITERARY ENCYCLOPAEDIAS

SZINNYEI József: *Magyar írók élete és munkái* [The lives and works of Hungarian writers]. Vols. 1–14. Bp. *1891–1914*, Magyar Tudományos Akadémia.—Reprint. Vols. 1–14. Bp. 1980–1981, Magyar Könyvkiadók és Könyvterjesztők Egyesülése.

Magyar irodalmi lexikon [Encyclopaedia of Hungarian literature]. Ed. VÁNYI Ferenc. Bp. *1926*. VI, 880 pp.

Irodalmi lexikon [Encyclopaedia of literature]. Ed. BENEDEK Marcell. Bp. *1927*. 1224 pp.

GULYÁS Pál: *Magyar írók élete és munkái. Új sorozat* [A–D] [The lives and works of Hungarian writers. New series]. Vols. 1–6. Bp. *1939–1944*.

Hungária irodalmi lexikon ["Hungária" literary encyclopaedia]. Ed. RÉVAY József, KŐHALMI Béla. Bp. *1947*. 624 pp.

Magyar irodalmi lexikon [Encyclopaedia of Hungarian literature]. Ed.-in-chief: BENEDEK Marcell. Vols. 1–3. Bp. *1963–1965*, Akadémiai K. 728, 639, 614 pp.

Slovník spisovatelů. Maďarsko (Zpracoval kolektiv autorů za vedení Petra RÁKOSE). Prague *1971*, Odeon. 386 pp.

LITERARY HISTORIES IN HUNGARIAN

A magyar irodalom története [History of Hungarian literature]. Vols. 1–2. Ed. BEÖTHY Zsolt. Bp. *1896*, Athenaeum. 516, 840 pp. — 3rd rev. enl. ed. Ed. BADICS Ferenc. Bp. 1906–1907.

PINTÉR Jenő *magyar irodalomtörténete. Tudományos rendszerezés* [Jenő Pintér's history of Hungarian literature. A scholarly systematization]. Vols. 1–8. Bp. *1930–1941*. Magyar Irodalomtörténeti Társaság.

SZERB Antal: *Magyar irodalomtörténet* [A history

of Hungarian literature]. Vols. 1–2. Cluj–Kolozsvár *1934*, Erdélyi Szépmíves Céh. 342, 255 pp.–Bp. *1972*[10].

Féja Géza: [1] *A régi magyarság. A magyar irodalom története a legrégibb időktől 1772-ig* [The ancient Hungarians. The history of Hungarian literature from ancient times to 1772]. Bratislava–Pozsony [*1937*], Tátra. 197 pp. [Further rev. enl. ed. 1941, 1943] [2] *A felvilágosodástól a sötétedésig. A magyar irodalom története 1772-től 1867-ig* [From Enlightenment to darkness. The history of Hungarian literature from 1772 to 1867]. Bp. *1942*, Magyar Élet. 288 pp. – 1943[2]. [3] *Nagy vállalkozások kora. A magyar irodalom története 1867-től napjainkig* [The age of great undertakings. The history of Hungarian literature from 1867 to our time]. Bp. *1943*, Magyar Élet. 428 pp.

Keresztury Dezső: *A magyar irodalom képeskönyve* [An illustrated handbook of Hungarian literature]. Bp. *1956*, Magvető K. 343 pp.–1981[2].

A magyar irodalom története... [History of Hungarian literature...]. Bp. *1957–1967*, Bibliotheca–Gondolat K.

[Vol. 1]: 1849-ig [To 1849]. Ed. Bóka László, Pándi Pál. Bp. 1957. 492 pp. – 4th rev. ed. 1971. 542 pp.

[Vol. 2]: 1849–1905. Ed. Király István, Pándi Pál, Sőtér István. Bp. 1963. 492 pp. — 1971[3].

[Vol. 3]: 1905-től napjainkig [From 1905 to our day]. Ed. Béládi Miklós, Bodnár György. Bp. 1967. 878 pp. — 1971[2].

A magyar irodalom története [History of Hungarian literature]. Compiled in the Institute for Literary History of the Hungarian Academy of Sciences. Ed.-in-chief: Sőtér István. Vols. 1–6. Bp. *1964–1966*, Akadémiai K.

1 *A magyar irodalom története 1600-ig* [The history of Hungarian literature to the year 1600]. Ed. Klaniczay Tibor. Bp. 1964. 567 pp.

2 *A magyar irodalom története 1600-tól 1772-ig* [The history of Hungarian literature from 1600 to 1772]. Ed. Klaniczay Tibor. Bp. 1964, 646 pp.

3 *A magyar irodalom története 1772-től 1849-ig* [The history of Hungarian literature from 1772 to 1849]. Ed. Pándi Pál. Bp. 1965. 831 pp.

4 *A magyar irodalom története 1849-től 1905-ig*

[The history of Hungarian literature from 1849 to 1905]. Ed. Sőtér István. Bp. 1965. 1072 pp.

5 *A magyar irodalom története 1905-től 1919-ig* [The history of Hungarian literature from 1905 to 1919]. Ed. Szabolcsi Miklós. Bp. 1965. 543 pp.

6 *A magyar irodalom története 1919-től napjainkig* [The history of Hungarian literature from 1919 to our day]. Ed. Szabolcsi Miklós. Bp. 1966. 1106 pp.

A magyar irodalom története 1945–1975 [History of Hungarian literature 1945–1975]. Ed. Béládi Miklós, Bodnár György, Sőtér István, Szabolcsi Miklós. Bp. *1981–* , Akadémiai K.

[1] Irodalmi élet és irodalomkritika [Literary life and literary criticism]. Ed. Béládi Miklós. Bp. 1981. 527 pp.

[4] A határon túli magyar irodalom [Hungarian literature beyond the country's borders]. Ed. Béládi Miklós. Bp. 1982. 463 pp.

HUNGARIAN LITERARY HISTORIES IN FOREIGN LANGUAGES

Horváth C.–Kardos A.–Endrődy A.: *Histoire de la littérature hongroise*. Ouvrage adapté du hongrois par I. Kont. Bp.–Paris *1900*, Félix Alcan. XII, 420 pp.

Riedl, Frederick: *A History of Hungarian Literature*. London 1906, William Heinemann. 294 pp. — Id. Detroit 1968. 293 pp. [Reprint.]

Katona, Ludwig–Szinnyei, Franz: *Geschichte der ungarischen Literatur*. Leipzig *1911*, G. J. Göschen'sche Verlagsbuchhandlung. 152 pp. — Id. Berlin–Leipzig 1927. 166 pp.

Hankiss [János]–Juhász [Géza]: *Panorama de la littérature hongroise contemporaine*. Paris *1930*, Kra. 348 pp.

Farkas, Julius: *Die Entwicklung der ungarischen Literatur*. Berlin *1934*, Walter de Gruyter. 306 pp.

Hankiss, Giovanni: *Storia della letteratura ungherese*. Torino–Milano–etc. *1936*, G. B. Paravia e C. 356 pp.

Cushing, George Frederick: *Hungarian Prose and Verse*. London *1956*, Athlone Press. 197 pp.

Menczer, Béla: *A Commentary on Hungarian Literature*. Castrop–Rauxel, *1956*. 147 pp.

KLANICZAY, Tibor–SZAUDER, József–SZABOLCSI, Miklós: *Histoire abrégée de la littérature hongroise.* Bp. *1962,* Corvina. 300 pp.

— *Kratkaya istoria vengerskoi literaturi.* Bp. 1962, Corvina. 404 pp.

— *Geschichte der ungarischen Literatur.* Bp. 1963, Corvina. 353 pp.

— *History of Hungarian Literature.* Bp. 1964, Corvina. 361 pp.

— *Historia literatury węgierskiej.* Bp. 1966, Corvina. 365 pp.

— *Kratka istoria na ungarskata literatura.* Bp. 1975, Gondolat K. 335 pp.

RUZICSKA, Paolo: *Storia della letteratura ungherese.* Milano 1963, Nuova Accademia Editrice. 830 pp.

TEMPESTI, Folco: *La letteratura ungherese.* Firenze–Milano *1969,* Sansoni-Accademia. 290 pp. (La Letteratura del Mondo 25.)

[BÁN] BAN, Imre–BARTA, Janoš [János]–CINE [CZINE], Mihalj [Mihály]: *Istorija mađarske književnosti.* Novi Sad *1976,* Matica Srpska — Forum. 430 pp.

Handbuch der ungarischen Literatur. Von István NEMESKÜRTY, László OROSZ, Béla G. NÉMETH, Attila TAMÁS. Hrsg. von Tibor KLANICZAY. Bp. *1977,* Corvina. 658 pp.

Histoire de la littérature hongroise des origines à nous jours. (Publié sous la direction de Tibor KLANICZAY.) Bp. *1980,* Corvina. K. 585 pp.

WORKS ON CERTAIN PERIODS AND TRENDS OF HUNGARIAN LITERATURE

ANGYAL, Andreas: *Barock in Ungarn.* Bp.–Leipzig–Milano [1948], Danubia. 136 pp.

Arcképek a magyar szocialista irodalomból [Portraits from Hungarian socialist literature]. Ed. ILLÉS László. Bp. 1967, Kossuth K. 433 pp.

Le Baroque en Hongrie. Par un collectif de l'Académie Hongroise des Sciences sous la direction de Tibor KLANICZAY et Imre VARGA. Préf.: Pierre CHARPENTRAT. In: *Baroque.* Revue Internationale du C.O.S.I.B. Cahier 8. Montauban (France), 1976, Mostra. 149 pp.

BENEDEK Marcell: *A modern magyar irodalom* [Contemporary Hungarian literature]. Bp. 1924, Béta. 121 pp.

BITSKEY István: *Hitviták tüzében* [In the crossfire of religious disputes]. Bp. 1978, Gondolat K. 249 pp.

BODOLAY Géza: *Irodalmi diáktársaságok 1785–1848* [Students' literary associations 1785–1848]. Bp. 1963, Akadémiai K. 807 pp.

BORI Imre: *A jugoszláviai magyar irodalom története 1918-tól 1945-ig* [History of Hungarian literature in Yugoslavia from 1918 to 1945]. Novi Sad 1968, Forum. 286 pp.

BORI Imre: *A szecessziótól a dadáig. A magyar futurizmus, expresszionizmus és dadaizmus irodalma* [From the art nouveau to Dadaism. The literature of Hungarian Futurism, Expressionism and Dadaism]. Újvidék 1969, Forum. 322 pp.

BORI Imre: *A szürrealizmus ideje. A magyar szürrealizmus irodalma* [The period of Surrealism. The literature of Hungarian Surrealism]. Újvidék 1970, Forum. 302 pp.

BORI Imre: *Az avantgarde apostolai. Füst Milán és Kassák Lajos* [The apostles of avant-garde. Milán Füst and Lajos Kassák]. Újvidék 1971, Forum. 238 pp.

BORI Imre: *Irodalmunk évszázadai* [Centuries of our literature]. Újvidék 1975, Forum. 283 pp.

BUCSAY Mihály: *Geschichte des Protestantismus in Ungarn.* Stuttgart 1959. 227 pp.

CSANDA Sándor: *Első nemzedék. A csehszlovákiai magyar irodalom keletkezése és fejlődése* [The first generation. The birth and development of Hungarian literature in Czechoslovakia]. Bratislava 1968, Tatran. 305 pp.

CSÁSZÁR Elemér: *A magyar irodalmi kritika története a szabadságharcig* [Hungarian literary criticism up to the time of the War of Independence]. Bp. 1925, Pallas. 409 pp.

CSÓKA J. Lajos: *A latin nyelvű történeti irodalom kialakulása Magyarországon a XI–XIV. században* [The emergence of Latin-language historical literature in Hungary in the 11th–14th centuries]. Bp. 1967, Akadémiai K. 683 pp.

DÁN Róbert: *Humanizmus, reformáció, antitrinitarizmus és a héber nyelv Magyarországon* [Humanism, Reformation, Anti-trinitarianism and the Hebrew language in Hungary]. Bp. 1973, Akadémiai K. 272 pp.

515

DÁVID Gyula–MAROSI Péter–SZÁSZ János: *A romániai magyar irodalom története* [A history of Hungarian literature in Rumania]. Bucharest 1977, Editura Didactică şi Pedagogică. 331 pp.

Élő irodalom. Tanulmányok a felszabadulás utáni magyar irodalom köréből [Literature living. Studies on Hungarian literature after the liberation]. Ed. TÓTH Dezső. Bp. 1969. Akadémiai K. 551 pp.

Ez volt a Sarló. Tanulmányok, emlékezések, dokumentumok [The history of the "Sarló" movement. Essays, memoirs, documents]. Ed. SÁNDOR László. Bp.–Bratislava 1978, Kossuth K.–Madách K. 431 pp.

Feljegyzések és levelek a Nyugatról [Notes and letters about the *Nyugat*]. Ed. VEZÉR Erzsébet. Bp. 1975. Akadémiai K. 546 pp.

FENYŐ István: *Új arcok—új utak* [New faces—new paths]. Bp. 1961, Szépirodalmi K. 257 pp.

FENYŐ István: *Az irodalom respublikájáért.* Irodalomkritikai gondolkodásunk fejlődése 1817–1830 [For a republic of literature. The development of our literary critical thought between 1817–1830]. Bp. 1976, Akadémiai K. 493 pp.

FENYŐ Miksa: *Följegyzések a Nyugat folyóiratról és környékéről* [Notes on the review *Nyugat* and its circle]. Niagara Falls, Ontario (Canada), 1960. 205 pp.

Fiatal magyar költők 1969–1978 [Young Hungarian Poets 1969–1978]. Ed. VASY Géza. Bp. 1980, Akadémai K. 342 pp.

Fiatal magyar prózaírók 1965–1978 [Young Hungarian Prose-writers 1965–1978] Ed. KULIN Ferenc. Bp. 1980, Akadémiai K. 361 pp.

GERÉZDI Rabán: *A magyar világi líra kezdetei* [The beginnings of Hungarian secular poetry]. Bp. 1962, Akadémiai K. 325 pp.

GERÉZDI Rabán: *Janus Pannoniustól Balassi Bálintig.* Tanulmányok. [From Janus Pannonius to Bálint Balassi. Essays]. Bp. 1968, Akadémiai K. 534 pp.

GYÖRFFY György: *Krónikáink és a magyar őstörténet* [Our chronicles and Hungarian prehistory]. Bp. 1948. 189 pp.

A hetvenes évek magyar irodalmáról [Hungarian literature in the 70s]. Ed. AGÁRDI Péter. Bp. 1979. Kossuth K. 448 pp.

HORVÁTH János: *A magyar irodalmi népiesség Faluditól Petőfiig* [The populist trend in Hungarian literature from Faludi to Petőfi]. Bp. 1927, Magyar Tudományos Akadémia. 390 pp. — 2nd ed. (Postscript KOROMPAY H. János). Bp. 1978, Akadémiai K. 400 pp.

HORVÁTH János: *A magyar irodalmi műveltség kezdetei. Szent Istvántól Mohácsig* [The beginnings of Hungarian literature. From St. Stephen to Mohács]. Bp. 1931. 311 pp. — 1944².

HORVÁTH János: *Az irodalmi műveltség megoszlása. Magyar humanizmus* [The repartition of literary cultivation. Humanism in Hungary]. Bp. 1935. 307 pp. — 1944².

HORVÁTH János: *A reformáció jegyében. A Mohács utáni félszázad magyar irodalomtörténete* [In the spirit of Reformation. History of Hungarian literature in the fifty years after the Battle of Mohács]. Bp. 1953, Akadémiai K. 544 pp. — 1957².

HORVÁTH János: *A magyar irodalom fejlődéstörténete* [The evolution of Hungarian literature]. Intr. BARTA János. Bp. 1976, Akadémiai K. 372 pp.

HORVÁTH János [jr]: *Árpád kori latin nyelvű irodalmunk stílusproblémái* [Stylistic problems of our Latin-language literature in the age of the Árpád dynasty]. Bp. 1954, Akadémiai K. 400 pp.

HORVÁTH Zoltán: *Magyar századforduló. A második reformnemzedék története (1896–1914)* [Hungary at the turn of the century. The history of the second reform generation (1896–1914)]. Bp. 1961, Gondolat K. 647 pp.

HORVÁTH Zoltán: *Die Jahrhundertwende in Ungarn.* Bp.–Neuwied am Rhein 1966, Corvina–Luchterhand Verlag GmbH. 548 pp.

Irodalom és felelősség. Tíz év irodalmi kritikáiból [Literature and responsibility. From the literary criticism of ten years]. Ed. SZABOLCSI Miklós. Bp. 1955, Művelt Nép. 602 pp. [1945–1955].

Irodalom és felvilágosodás. Tanulmányok [Literature and Enlightenment. Essays]. Ed. SZAUDER József, TARNAI Andor. Bp. 1974, Akadémiai K. 990 pp.

JÓZSEF Farkas: „*Rohanunk a forradalomba*" — A magyar irodalom eszmélése 1914–1919. ["Heading for Revolution"—The awakening of Hungarian literature 1914–1919]. 2nd rev. enl. ed. Bp. 1969, Gondolat K. 287 pp.

KÁNTOR Lajos–LÁNG Gusztáv: *Romániai magyar irodalom 1944–1970* [Hungarian literature in Rumania 1944–1970]. 2nd rev. ed. Bucharest 1973, Kriterion. 498 pp.

KARÁTSON, André: *Le symbolisme en Hongrie. L'influence des poétiques françaises sur la poésie hongroise dans le premier quart du XXᵉ siècle.* Paris 1969, Presses Univ. de France. 498 pp.

KARDOS Tibor: *Középkori kultúra, középkori költészet.* A magyar irodalom keletkezése[Medieval culture, medieval poetry. The beginnings of Hungarian literature]. [Bp. 1941.] 290 pp.

KARDOS Tibor: *A magyarországi humanizmus kora* [The age of humanism in Hungary]. Bp. 1955, Akadémiai K. 462 pp.

KIRÁLY György: *A magyar ősköltészet* [Ancient Hungarian poetry]. Bp. 1921. 134 pp.

KOMLÓS Aladár: *Az új magyar líra* [New Hungarian poetry]. Bp. [1928]. 238 pp.

KOMLÓS Aladár: *A magyar költészet Petőfitől Adyig* [Hungarian poetry from Petőfi to Ady]. 2nd rev. ed. Bp. 1980, Gondolat K. 465 pp.

KOMLÓS Aladár: *A szimbolizmus és a magyar líra* [Symbolism and Hungarian poetry]. Bp. 1965, Akadémiai K. 98 pp.

KOMLÓS Aladár: *Gyulaitól a marxista kritikáig.* A magyar irodalmi kritika hét évtizede [From Gyulai to Marxist criticism. Seven decades of Hungarian literary criticism]. Bp. 1966, Akadémiai K. 306 pp.

KOMLÓS Aladár: *Problémák a Nyugat körül* [Problems around the review *Nyugat*]. Bp. 1978, Magvető K. 165 pp.

KOVÁCS József: *A szocialista magyar irodalom dokumentumai az amerikai magyar sajtóban. 1920–1945* [Documents of socialist Hungarian literature in the American Hungarian press. 1920–1945]. Bp. 1977, Akadémiai K. 438 pp.

KÖPECZI Béla: *A magyar kultúra harminc éve. 1945–1975* [Thirty years of culture in Hungary. 1945–1975]. 2nd rev. enl. ed. Bp. 1977, Kossuth K. 243 pp. — in German: *Kulturrevolution in Ungarn.* Bp. 1978, Corvina. 404 pp.

Középkori kútfőink kritikus kérdései [Problematic questions of our medieval sources]. Ed. HORVÁTH János [jr], SZÉKELY György. Bp. 1974, Akadémiai K. 384 pp.

MACARTNEY, C[arlile] A[ymler]: *The Medieval Hungarian Historians.* A critical and analytical guide. Cambridge 1953, Cambridge University Press. xvi, 190 pp.

A magyar kritika évszázadai [Hungarian criticism through the centuries]. Ed. SŐTÉR István. Bp. 1981– , Szépirodalmi K.
Vol. 1. Rendszerek. A kezdetektől a romantikáig [Systems. From the beginnings to Romanticism]. Ed. TARNAI Andor, CSETRI Lajos. (Forew. SŐTÉR István.) Bp. 1981. 545 pp.
Vol. 2–3. Irányok. I–II. Romantika, népiesség, pozitivizmus. [Trends. I–II. Romanticism, Populism, Positivism]. Written by FENYŐ István, SŐTÉR István, NÉMETH G. Béla. Ed. FENYŐ István. Bp. 1981. 620, 350 pp.

Mégis győztes, mégis új és magyar. Tanulmányok a *Nyugat* megjelenésének 70. évfordulójára ["Triumphant, new and Hungarian". Essays for the 70th anniversary of the foundation of *Nyugat*]. Ed. R. TAKÁCS Olga. Bp. 1980, Akadémiai K. 249 pp.

Mesterség és alkotás. Tanulmányok a felvilágosodás és a reformkor magyar irodalmáról [Craftsmanship and creation. Studies on the Hungarian literature of the Reform Era and Enlightenment]. Ed. MEZEI Márta, WÉBER Antal. Bp. 1972, Szépirodalmi K. 563 pp.

MEZEI László: *Irodalmi anyanyelvűségünk kezdetei az Árpád-kor végén. A középkori laikus nőmozgalom. Az Ó-magyar Mária-siralom és a Margit-legenda eredet kérdése* [The beginnings of literature in the vernacular at the end of the Árpád Age. Secular women's movement in the Middle Ages. Source problem of the Old Hungarian Lament of Mary and the Margaret Legend]. Bp. 1955, Akadémiai K. 133 pp.

MEZEI Márta: *Felvilágosodás kori líránk Csokonai előtt* [Hungarian poetry of the Enlightenment before Csokonai]. Bp. 1974, Akadémiai K. 293 pp.

Mű és érték. A csehszlovákiai magyar kritika 25 éve [Literature and value. 25 years of Hungarian criticism in Czechoslovakia]. Ed. and intr. SZEBERÉNYI Zoltán. Bibliography: ALABÁN Ferenc. Bratislava 1976, Madách. 531 pp.

K. NAGY Magda: *A Válasz*. Tanulmány [The *Answer*. An essay]. Bp. 1963, Szépirodalmi K. 379 pp.

NAGY Péter: *Új csapáson. Regényirodalmunk a szocialista realizmus útján. 1948-1954* [On a new path. The Hungarian novel on the road of socialist realism. 1948–1954]. Bp. 1956, Magvető K. 150 pp.

NEMESKÜRTY István: *A magyar népnek, ki ezt olvassa. Az anyanyelvű magyar reneszánsz és barokk irodalom története 1533–1712* ["To the Hungarian nation that reads this." The history of Renaissance and Baroque literature in the Hungarian vernacular]. Bp. 1975, Gondolat K. 525 pp.

NÉMETH G. Béla: *Tragikum és történetfelfogás. A századvégi tragikumvita* [The tragic and the concept of history. The debate about the tragic at the end of the century]. Bp. 1971, Akadémiai K. 126 pp.

NÉMETH G. Béla: *Türelmetlen és késlekedő félszázad. A romantika után* [Impatient and belated 50 years. After Romanticism]. Bp. 1971, Szépirodalmi K. 301 pp.

NÉMETH G. Béla: *A magyar irodalomkritikai gondolkodás a pozitivizmus korában. A kiegyezéstől a századfordulóig* [Hungarian literary criticism in the age of Positivism. From the *Ausgleich* to the turn of the century]. Bp. 1981, Akadémiai K. 428 pp.

50 éves a Korunk. Az 1976. május 20–21-i emlékülés alapján [50 years of the periodical *Korunk*. Based on a commemorative session held on May 20–21, 1976]. Ed. KABDEBÓ Lóránt. Bp. 1977, MTA Irodalomtudományi Intézete, Petőfi Irodalmi Múzeum és Népművelési Propaganda Intézet. 374 pp.

PÁNDI PÁL: *,,Kísértetjárás'' Magyarországon. Az utópista szocialista és kommunista eszmék jelentkezése a reformkorban* [Hungary "haunted". The appearance of utopistic socialist and communist ideas in the Reform Era]. Vols. 1–2. Bp. 1972, Magvető K. 569, 481 pp.

PIRNÁT, Antal: *Die Ideologie der Siebenbürger Antitrinitarier in den 1570er Jahren.* Bp. 1961, Akadémiai K. 217 pp.

POMOGÁTS Béla: *A tárgyias költészettől a mitologizmusig. A népi líra irányzatai a két világháború között* [From Objective Poetry to Mithologism. Trends in Populist Poetry between the Two World Wars]. Bp. 1981, Akadémiai K. 449 pp.

RÓNAY György: *Petőfi és Ady között. Az újabb magyar irodalom életrajza* (1849–1899) [Between Petőfi and Ady. The biography of recent Hungarian literature (1849–1899)]. 2nd ed. Bp. 1981, Magvető K. 340 pp.

RÓNAY György: *A nagy nemzedék* [The great generation]. Bp. 1971, Szépirodalmi K. 355 pp.

RÓNAY László: *Az Ezüstkor nemzedéke* [The generation of the Silver Age]. Bp. 1967, Akadémiai K. 222 pp.

ROSSIYANOV, O. K.: *Realizm v novoy vengerskoy proze 60-70-ye gody XX veka.* Moscow 1979, Izd. "Nauka". 150 pp.

ROTH, Erich: *Die Reformation in Siebenbürgen. Ihr Verhältnis zu Wittenberg und der Schweiz.* Vols. 1–2. Köln–Graz 1962–1964, Böhlau. XVI 224; XII 137 pp.

SHAKOVA, Kira: *Vengerskaya literatura 20-40-kh godov XIX-ogo veka.* Kiev 1973, Izd. "Vysha Shkola". 205 pp.

SCHÖPFLIN Aladár: *A magyar irodalom története a XX. században* [The history of 20th-century Hungarian literature]. Bp. 1937. 311 pp.

SIVIRSKY, Antal: *Die ungarische Literatur der Gegenwart.* Bern–München 1962, Franke. 109 pp.

SOMOGYI Sándor: *Gyulai és kortársai. Fejezetek egy negyedszázad irodalomtörténetéből* [Gyulai and his contemporaries. Chapters from the literary history of twenty-five years]. Ed. SZÖRÉNYI László. Bp, 1977, Akadémiai K. 541 pp.

SŐNI Pál: *A romániai magyar irodalom története* [History of Hungarian literature in Rumania]. Bucharest 1969, Editura Didactică și Pedagogică. 301 pp.

SŐTÉR István: *Nemzet és haladás. Irodalmunk Világos után* [Nation and progress. Hungarian literature after the surrender at Világos]. Bp. 1963, Akadémiai K. 781 pp. [With a summary in French.]

SZINNYEI Ferenc: [1] *Novella- és regényirodalmunk a szabadságharcig* [The Hungarian short story and novel before the War of Independence].

Vols. 1–2. Bp. 1925–1926, Magyar Tudományos Akadémia. 292, 370 pp. [2] *Novella- és regényirodalmunk az abszolutizmus korának elején* [The Hungarian short story and novel at the beginning of the era of absolutism]. Bp. 1929, Magyar Tudományos Akadémia. 132 pp. [3] *Novella- és regényirodalmunk a Bach-korszakban* [The Hungarian short story and novel in the Bach era]. Vols. 1–2. Bp. 1939–1941, Magyar Tudományos Akadémia. 611, 748 pp.

Tamás Aladár: *A 100%*. A KMP legális folyóirata 1927–1930 [*The* periodical *100%*. The legitimate periodical of the Hungarian Communist Party 1927–1930]. (Postscript: Szabolcsi Miklós.) [3rd ed.] Bp. 1977, Akadémiai K. 328 pp.

Tamás Attila: *Költői világképek fejlődése Arany Jánostól József Attiláig* [The development of poetic vision from János Arany to Attila József]. Bp. 1964, Akadémiai K. 166 pp.

Tanulmányok a magyar szocialista irodalom történetéből [Essays on the history of Hungarian socialist literature]. [Vols. 1–3] Ed. Szabolcsi Miklós, Illés László. [Vols. 4–5] Ed. Illés László, József Farkas. Bp. 1962–1975, Akadémiai K. [1] 1962. 676 pp. — 2nd enl. ed. 1963. [2] *"Jöjj el szabadság!"* ["Come, freedom!"]. 1967. 705 pp. [3] *"Meghallói a törvénynek"* ["Those who hear the law"]. 1973. 710 pp. [4] *"Vár egy új világ"* ["A new world is awaiting"]. 1975. 546 pp. [5] *"Az újnak tenni hitet"* ["To stand by the new"]. 1977. 649 pp.

Tolnai Gábor: *Régi magyar főurak. Életforma és műveltség az újkorban* [Old Hungarian noblemen. Life-style and culture in the modern age]. Bp. 1939, Magyar Történelmi Társulat. 176 pp.

Történelmi jelen idő. Beszélgetések a magyar irodalom legújabb fejezeteiről [Historical present. Talks on the most recent chapters of Hungarian literature]. Ed. Béládi Miklós, Kulcsár Katalin. Bp. 1981, RTV–Minerva. 339 pp.

Turczel Lajos: *Két kor mezsgyéjén. A magyar irodalom fejlődési feltételei és problémái Csehszlovákiában 1918 és 1938 között* [In the borderland of two epochs. The conditions of development and problems of Hungarian literature in Czechoslovakia between 1918 and 1938]. Bratislava 1967, Tatran. 311 pp.

Valóság és varázslat. Tanulmányok századunk magyar prózairodalmáról Krúdy Gyula és Móricz Zsigmond születésének 100. évfordulójára [Reality and magic. Essays on Hungarian fiction for the 100th anniversary of the birth of Gyula Krúdy and Zsigmond Móricz]. Ed. Kabdebó Lóránt. Bp. 1979, Petőfi Irodalmi Múzeum—NIP. 322 pp.

Várkonyi Nándor: *A modern magyar irodalom* [Modern Hungarian literature]. Pécs 1927, Danubia. 466 pp.

Várkonyi Nándor: *Az újabb magyar irodalom 1880–1940* [Recent Hungarian literature between 1880 and 1940]. Bp. 1942. 579 pp.

Vita a Nyugatról [Discussions about the periodical *Nyugat*]. Ed. from the material of the Nyugat Conference Apr. 27, 1972: Kabdebó Lóránt. Bp. 1973, Petőfi Irodalmi Múzeum—NIP. 278 pp.

Waldapfel József: *Ötven év Buda és Pest irodalmi életéből 1780–1830* [Fifty years of literary life in Buda and Pest 1780–1830]. Bp. 1935, Magyar Tudományos Akadémia. 368 pp.

Waldapfel József: *A magyar irodalom a felvilágosodás korában* [Hungarian literature in the age of Enlightenment]. 3rd rev. enl. ed. Bp. 1963, Akadémiai K. 349 pp.

Wéber Antal: *A magyar regény kezdetei. Fejezetek a magyar regény történetéből* [The beginnings of the Hungarian novel. Chapters from the history of the Hungarian novel]. Bp. 1959, Akadémiai K. 237 pp.

Wéber Antal: *Irodalmi irányok távlatból. Fejezetek a felvilágosodás és a reformkor irodalmának történetéből* [Literary trends from a distance. Chapters from the history of the Enlightenment and the Reform Era]. Bp. 1974, Szépirodalmi K. 389 pp.

"Wir stürmen in die Revolution" Studien zur Geschichte der ungarischen sozialistischen Literatur. Hrsg. von Miklós Szabolcsi, László Illés, Farkas József. Bp. 1977, Akadémiai K. 473 pp.

"Wir kämpften treu für die Revolution" Studien zur Geschichte der ungarischen sozialistischen

Literatur. Hrsg. von Miklós Szabolcsi, László Illés, Farkas József. Bp. 1979, Akadémiai K. 584 pp.

Život a dielo Sándora Petőfiho a Imre Madácha. Zborník z konferencie pri 150. výročí narodenia básnikov. Red.: Ctibor Tahy. Bratislava 1973, Osvetový ústav. 133 pp.

Zoványi Jenő: *A reformáció Magyarországon 1565-ig* [Reformation in Hungary till the year 1565]. Bp. [1921], Genius. 485 pp.

Zoványi Jenő: *A magyarországi protestantizmus 1565-től 1600-ig.* [Protestantism in Hungary from 1565 to 1600]. Bp. 1977, Akadémiai K. 461 pp. [With a summary in German].

ESSAY VOLUMES

Bán Imre: *Eszmék és stílusok* [Ideas and styles]. Bp. 1976, Akadémiai K. 275 pp.

Baróti Dezső: *Írók, érzelmek, stílusok* [Writers, sentiments, styles]. Bp. 1971, Magvető K. 505 pp.

Baróti Dezső: *Árnyékban éles fény.* Irodalmi tanulmányok [Sharp light in the shade. Essays on literature]. Bp. 1980, Gondolat K. 554 pp.

Barta János: *Költők és írók* [Poets and writers]. Bp. 1966. Akadémiai K. 274 pp.

Barta János: *Klasszikusok nyomában.* Esztétikai és irodalmi tanulmányok [In the wake of classics. Studies on esthetics and literature]. Bp. 1976, Akadémiai K. 495 pp.

Barta János: *Évfordulók.* Tanulmányok és megemlékezések [Anniversaries. Essays and Recollections]. Bp. 1981, Akadémiai K. 441 pp.

Bata Imre: *Ívelő pályák* [Rising careers]. Bp. 1964, Szépirodalmi K. 321 pp.

Bata Imre: *Képek és vonulatok* [Images and trends]. Bp. 1973, Magvető K. 405 pp.

Béládi Miklós: *Érintkezési pontok* [Points of contact]. Bp. 1974, Szépirodalmi K. 723 pp.

Bodnár György: *Törvénykeresők* [The lawseekers]. Bp. 1976, Szépirodalmi K. 624 pp.

Bóka László: *Arcképvázlatok és tanulmányok* [Portrait sketches and essays]. Bp. 1962, Akadémiai K. 543 pp.

Bóka László: *Válogatott tanulmányok* [Selected studies]. Ed. Sík Csaba. Bp. 1966, Magvető K. 1592 pp.

Bori Imre: *Eszmék és látomások* [Ideas and visions]. Novi Sad 1965, Forum. 231 pp.

Bori Imre: *Fridolin és testvérei* [Fridolin and his brothers]. Újvidék 1976, Forum. 372 pp.

Bori Imre: *Varázslók és mákvirágok* [Magicians and Bad Eggs]. Újvidék 1979, Forum K. 357 pp.

Czine Mihály: *Nép és irodalom* [Nation and literature]. Vols. 1–2. Bp. 1981, Szépirodalmi K. 557, 414 pp.

Csehi Gyula: *Felvilágosodástól felvilágosodásig.* Írások három évszázadról, négy évtizedből (1930–1971) [From enlightenment to enlightenment. Four decades' writings on three centuries (1930–1971)]. Bucharest 1972, Kriterion. 454 pp.

Diószegi András: *Megmozdult világban* [In a moving world]. Bp. 1967, Szépirodalmi K. 702 pp.

Fenyő István: *Két évtized* [Two decades]. Bp. 1968, Magvető K. 613 pp.

Fenyő István: *Nemzet, nép — irodalom.* Tanulmányok a magyar reformkor irodalmáról. [Nation, people—literature. Studies on the literature of the Reform Era in Hungary]. Bp. 1973, Magvető K. 405 pp.

Fenyő István: *Magyarság és emberi egyetemesség.* Irodalom- és művelődéstörténeti tanulmányok [The Hungarian and the universal. Studies in the history of literature and culture]. Bp. 1979, Szépirodalmi K. 838 pp.

Gyergyai Albert: *A Nyugat árnyékában* [In the shadow of the *Nyugat*]. Bp. 1968, Szépirodalmi K. 442 pp.

Gyergyai Albert: *Késői tallózás.* Tanulmányok, arcképek [Late gleanings. Essays, portraits]. Bp. 1975, Szépirodalmi K. 330 pp.

Halász Gábor: *Tiltakozó nemzedék.* Összegyüjtött írások [Protesting Generation. Collected Writings]. Ed. Véber Károly. Bp. 1981, Magvető K. 1193 pp.

Hatvany Lajos: *Harcoló betűk* [Militant Letters]. Ed. Hatvany Lajosné. Bibliográfia: Rozsics István. Bp. 1981, Gondolat. 518 pp.

Horváth János: *Tanulmányok* [Studies]. Bp. 1956, Akadémiai K. 638 pp.

Horváth Zoltán: *Irodalom és történelem* [Literature and history]. Bp. 1968, Szépirodalmi K. 353 pp.

ILLÉS Lajos: *Kezdet és kibontakozás* [Beginning and development]. Bp. 1974, Szépirodalmi K. 438 pp.

ILLÉS László: *Józanság és szenvedély.* Tanulmányok és kritikák [Soberness and passion. Studies and reviews]. Bp. 1966, Magvető K. 638 pp.

ILLYÉS Gyula: *Iránytűvel* [With compass]. Vols. 1–2. Bp. 1975, Szépirodalmi K. 776, 834 pp.

JAKÓ Zsigmond: *Írás, könyv, értelmiség.* Tanulmányok Erdély történelméhez [Writing, books, intelligentsia. Studies in Transylvanian history]. Bucharest 1976, Kriterion K. 373 pp.

JANCSÓ Elemér: *A felvilágosodástól a romantikáig* [From Enlightenment to Romanticism]. Bucharest 1966. 325 pp.

JANCSÓ Elemér: *Irodalomtörténet és időszerűség.* Irodalomtörténeti tanulmányok 1929–1970 [History of literature and actuality. Studies in literary history 1929–1970]. Intr. SZIGETI József. Bucharest 1972, Kriterion. 659 pp.

JORDÁKY Lajos: *A szocialista irodalom útján* [On the road of socialist literature]. Bp. 1973, Magvető K. 531 pp.

JÓZSEF Farkas: *Írók, eszmék, forradalmak.* Válogatott tanulmányok és kritikák [Writers, ideas, revolutions. Selected studies and reviews]. Bp. 1979, Szépirodalmi K. 482 pp.

JULOW Viktor: *Árkádia körül* [Around Arcadia]. Bp. 1975, Szépirodalmi K. 312 pp.

KABDEBÓ Lóránt: *Versek között.* Tanulmányok, kritikák [Among poems. Studies, reviews]. Bp. 1980. Magvető K. 540 pp.

KÁNTOR Lajos: *Korváltás* [Bordering Epochs]. Bucharest 1979, Kriterion K. 366 pp.

KÁNTOR Lajos: *Korunk: Avantgarde és népiség.* Irodalomtörténeti és kritikai portyázások [Our Age: Avant-garde and Populism. Forays into Literary History and Criticism]. Bp. 1980, Magvető K. 502 pp.

KARDOS László: *Író, írás, irodalom* [Writer, writing, literature]. Bp. 1973, Magvető K. 473 pp.

KARDOS Pál: *Irodalmi tanulmányok* [Studies in literature]. Ed. FÜLÖP László. Bp. 1979, Gondolat K. 373 pp.

KARDOS Tibor: *Élő humanizmus* [Living humanism]. Bp. 1972, Magvető K. 653 pp.

KARDOS Tibor: *Az emberség műhelyei* [The workshops of humanity]. Bp. 1973, Szépirodalmi K. 516 pp.

KENYERES Zoltán: *Gondolkodó irodalom* [Literature and thought]. Bp. 1974, Szépirodalmi K. 472 pp.

KERECSÉNYI Dezső *válogatott írásai* [Selected writings of]. Ed. PÁLMAI Kálmán. Bp. 1979. Akadémiai K. 302 pp.

KERESZTURY Dezső: *Örökség. Magyar író-arcképek* [Heritage. Portraits of Hungarian writers]. Bp. 1970, Magvető K. 543 pp.

KERESZTURY Dezső: *A szépség haszna* [The use of beauty]. Bp. 1973, Szépirodalmi K. 437 pp.

KIRÁLY György: *A filológus kalandozásai.* Tanulmányok [Adventures of a philologist. Studies]. Ed. KENYERES Ágnes. Bp. 1980, Szépirodalmi K. 530 pp.

KIRÁLY István: *Irodalom és társadalom.* Tanulmányok, cikkek, interjúk, kritikák. 1946–1975 [Literature and society. Essays, articles, interviews, reviews. 1946–1975]. Bp. 1976, Szépirodalmi K. 682 pp.

KIS PINTÉR Imre: *Helyzetjelentés* [Progress report]. Bp. 1979, Szépirodalmi K. 379 pp.

KISS Ferenc: *Művek közelről* [Works of art in close-up]. Bp. 1972, Magvető K. 345 pp.

KLANICZAY Tibor: *Reneszánsz és barokk.* Tanulmányok a régi magyar irodalomról [Renaissance and Baroque. Essays on old Hungarian literature]. Bp. 1961, Szépirodalmi K. 595 pp.

KLANICZAY Tibor: *A múlt nagy korszakai* [Great epochs of the past]. Bp. 1973, Szépirodalmi K. 528 pp.

KLANICZAY Tibor: *Hagyományok ébresztése* [Awakening traditions]. Bp. 1976, Szépirodalmi K. 579 pp.

KOMLÓS Aladár: *Tegnap és ma.* Irodalmi tanulmányok [Yesterday and today. Studies in literature]. Bp. 1956, Szépirodalmi K. 356 pp.

KOMLÓS Aladár: *Vereckétől Dévényig* [From Verecke to Dévény]. Bp. 1972, Szépirodalmi K. 429 pp.

KOMLÓS Aladár: *Költészet és bírálat* [Poetry and criticism]. Bp. 1973, Gondolat K. 343 pp.

KOMLÓS Aladár: *Kritikus számadás* [Critical account]. Bp. 1977, Szépirodalmi K. 662 pp.

KOVÁCS Kálmán: *Eszmék és irodalom* [Ideas and literature]. Bp. 1976, Szépirodalmi K. 427 pp.

Kovács Sándor Iván: *Pannoniából Európába*. Tanulmányok a régi magyar irodalomról [From Pannonia to Europe. Studies on old Hungarian literature]. Bp. 1975. Gondolat K. 331 pp.

Kovács Sándor Iván: *Jelenlévő múlt* [The presence of the past]. Bp. 1973, Szépirodalmi K. 513 pp.

Lukács György: *Írástudók felelőssége* [The responsibility of clerks]. 2nd ed. Bp. 1945, Szikra. 144 pp.

Lukács György: *Irodalom és demokrácia* [Literature and democracy]. Bp. 1947, Szikra. 192 pp. — 2nd rev. ed. Bp. 1948, Szikra. 188 pp.

Lukács György: *Új magyar kultúráért* [For a new Hungarian culture]. Bp. 1948, Szikra. 234 pp.

Lukács György *válogatott művei* [Selected works of]. Vol. 3 *Magyar irodalom — magyar kultúra*. Válogatott tanulmányok [Hungarian literature—Hungarian culture. Selected studies]. Bp. 1970, Gondolat K. 694 pp.

Martinkó András: *Teremtő idők* [Creative times]. Bp. 1977, Szépirodalmi K. 483 pp.

Mervyn, Jones D.: *Five Hungarian Writers*. [Zrínyi, Mikes, Vörösmarty, Eötvös, Petőfi]. Oxford 1966, Clarendon Press. 307 pp.

Nagy Péter: *Rosta* [Sifter]. Bp. 1965, Szépirodalmi K. 447 pp.

Nagy Péter: *Útjelző* [Sign-post]. Bp. 1976, Szépirodalmi K. 556 pp.

Nagy Péter: *Drámai arcélek*. Tanulmányok a huszadik századi magyar drámairodalom köréből [Dramatic profiles. Studies on twentieth-century Hungarian drama]. Bp. 1978, Szépirodalmi K. 246 pp.

Nagy Péter: *Olvasó* [Literary reader]. Bp. 1980, Szépirodalmi K. 408 pp.

Németh G. Béla: *Mű és személyiség*. Irodalmi tanulmányok [Writing and personality. Literary studies]. Bp. 1970, Magvető K. 750 pp.

Németh G. Béla: *Létharc és nemzetiség*. Irodalmi és művelődéstörténeti tanulmányok [Struggle for life and nationality. Studies in literary and cultural history]. Bp. 1976, Magvető K. 560 pp.

Németh G. Béla: *11 vers*. Verselemzések, versértelmezések [Eleven poems. Analyses and interpretation]. Bp. 1977, Tankönyvkiadó. 281 pp.

Németh G. Béla: *Küllő és kerék* [Spoke and wheel]. Bp. 1981, Magvető K. 650 pp.

Németh László: *Die Revolution der Qualität*. Studien zur Literatur. Nachw.: Karl Kerényi. Stuttgart 1962, Steingrüben. 350 pp.

Németh László: *Az én katedrám* [My classroom]. Bp. 1969, Magvető K.—Szépirodalmi K. 667 pp.

Németh László: *Két nemzedék* [Two generations]. Bp. 1970, Magvető K.—Szépirodalmi K. 756 pp.

Ortutay Gyula: *Írók, népek, századok* [Writers, nations, centuries]. Bp. 1970, Magvető K. 475 pp.

Ortutay Gyula: *Fényes, tiszta árnyak*. Tanulmányok, emlékezések, vázlatok [Bright, clear shades. Studies, memories, sketches]. Bp. 1973, Szépirodalmi K. 444 pp.

Pándi Pál: *Elsüllyedt irodalom?* [Sunken literature?]. Bp. 1963, Szépirodalmi K. 209 pp.

Pándi Pál: *Kritikus ponton*. Bírálatok és tanulmányok [A point of crisis. Criticism and studies]. Bp. 1972, Szépirodalmi K. 758 pp.

Pándi Pál: *Első aranykorunk*. Cikkek, tanulmányok a magyar felvilágosodás és reformkorszak irodalmából [Our first Golden Age. Articles and essays on the literature of the Hungarian Enlightenment and Reform Era]. Bp. 1976, Szépirodalmi K. 620 pp.

Pándi Pál: *A realizmus igényével*. A második következtetés [With recourse to realism. Second conclusion]. Bp. 1980, Kossuth K. 320 pp.

Pomogáts Béla: *Regénytükör*. Harminchárom új magyar regény [Survey of 33 new Hungarian novels]. Bp. 1977, Móra K. 313 pp.

Pomogáts Béla: *Sorsát kereső irodalom*. Tanulmányok [Literature in search of its fate. Studies]. Bp. 1979, Magvető K. 523 pp.

Pomogáts Béla: *Versek közelről*. Értelmezések és magyarázatok [Poems in close-up. Interpretations and explanations]. Bp. 1980, Kozmosz K. 293 pp.

Reményi, Joseph: *Hungarian Writers and Literature*. Modern novelists, critics and poets. Ed. and with an introduction by August J. Molnar. New Brunswick, New Jersey 1964, Rutgers University Press. 512 pp.

Révai József: *Válogatott irodalmi tanulmányok* [Selected studies in literature]. Ed. F. Majlát Auguszta, 2nd ed. Bp. 1968, Kossuth K. 458 pp.

Réz Pál: *Kulcsok és kérdőjelek*. Esszék, tanulmányok [Keys and question marks. Essays, studies]. Bp. 1973, Szépirodalmi K. 422 pp.

Rónay György: *Olvasás közben* [While reading]. Bp. 1971, Magvető K. 540 pp.

Rónay György: *Kutatás közben* [While researching]. Bp. 1974, Magvető K. 299 pp.

Rónay György: *Balassitól Adyig* [From Balassi to Ady]. Bp. 1978, Magvető K. 319 pp.

Rónay László: *Hűséges sáfárok* [Faithful stewards]. Bp. 1975, Szépirodalmi K. 481 pp.

Sinkó Ervin: *Magyar irodalom* [Hungarian literature]. Novi Sad 1963, Forum. 455 pp.

Somlyó György: *A költészet vérszerződése* [Poetry: a compact sealed in blood]. Bp. 1977, Szépirodalmi K. 604 pp.

Sőtér István: *Játék és valóság* [Play and reality]. Bp. 1946, Hungária. 158 pp.

Sőtér István: *Romantika és realizmus*. Válogatott irodalmi tanulmányok [Romanticism and realism. Selected literary studies]. Bp. 1956, Szépirodalmi K. 611 pp.

Sőtér István: *Tisztuló tükrök*. A magyar irodalom a két világháború között [Brightening mirrors. Hungarian literature between the two world wars]. Bp. 1966, Gondolat K. 515 pp.

Sőtér István: *Az ember és műve* [Man and his creation]. Bp. 1971, Akadémiai K. 383 pp.

Sőtér István: *Werthertől Szilveszterig* [From Werther to Szilveszter]. Bp. 1976, Szépirodalmi K. 573 pp.

Sőtér István: *Félkör*. Tanulmányok a XIX. századról [Semicircle. Studies on the 19th century]. Bp. 1979, Szépirodalmi K. 770 pp.

Sőtér István: *Gyűrűk*. Tanulmányok a XX. századról [Rings. Studies on the 20th century]. Bp. 1980, Szépirodalmi K. 698 pp.

Szabolcsi Miklós: *Költészet és korszerűség* [Poetry and modernity]. Bp. 1959, Magvető K. 266 pp.

Szabolcsi Miklós: *Elődök és kortársak* [Predecessors and contemporaries]. Bp. 1964, Szépirodalmi K. 315 pp.

Szabolcsi Miklós: *Változó világ — szocialista irodalom* [Changing world—socialist literature]. Bp. 1973, Magvető K. 503 pp.

Szauder József: *A romantika útján* [On the road to Romanticism]. Bp. 1961, Szépirodalmi K. 486 pp.

Szauder József: *Az estve és Az álom*. Felvilágosodás és klasszicizmus [The Evening and The Dream. Enlightenment and Classicism]. Bp. 1970, Szépirodalmi K. 555 pp.

Szauder József: *Tavaszi és őszi utazások*. Tanulmányok a XX. század magyar irodalmáról [Travels in spring and autumn. Studies on 20th-century Hungarian literature]. Ed. Szauder Mária. Bp. 1980, Szépirodalmi K. 384 pp.

Szegedy-Maszák Mihály: *Világkép és stílus*. Történeti-poétikai tanulmányok [Vision and style. Studies in history and poetics]. Bp. 1980, Magvető K. 582 pp.

Szerb Antal: *Gondolatok a könyvtárban* [Thoughts in the library]. Ed. and intr. Kardos László. Bp. [1946], Révai. 639 pp. — New ed. *Hétköznapok és csodák. A harmadik torony. "Író ne írj!"* [Weekdays and wonders. The third tower. "Writer, do not write!"]. Intr. Szabolcsi Miklós. Bp. 1971, Magvető K. 761 pp. — 3rd ed. Bp. 1981, Magvető K. 777 pp.

Szigeti József: *A mű és kora* [Literary work and its age]. Bucharest 1970, Kriterion. 493 pp.

Tamás Attila: *Irodalom és emberi teljesség* [Literature and human entity]. Bp. 1973, Szépirodalmi K. 398 pp.

Tolnai Gábor: *Végzetes esztendők* [Fatal years]. Bp. 1945, Anonymus. 130 pp.

Tolnai Gábor: *Évek — századok* [Years—centuries]. Bp. 1958, Magvető K. 319 pp.

Tolnai Gábor: *Tanulmányok* [Studies]. Bp. 1970, Akadémiai K. 437 pp.

Tolnai Gábor: *Örökség és örökösök*. Kazinczytól máig [Heritage and inheritors. From Kazinczy to the present]. Bp. 1974, Gondolat K. 426 pp.

Tolnai Gábor: *Nőnek az árnyak*. Tanulmányok, esszék, emlékezések [Growing shadows. Studies, essays, memoirs]. Bp. 1981, Szépirodalmi K. 412 pp.

Tóth Dezső: *Élő hagyomány — élő irodalom* [Living traditions—living literature]. Bp. 1977, Magvető K. 777 pp.

Turczel Lajos: *Portrék és fejlődésképek* [Portraits and developments]. Bratislava 1977, Madách. 278 pp.

Tüskés Tibor: *Mérték és mű* [Standard and the work of art]. [Bp.] 1980, Szépirodalmi K. 479 pp.

Vargha Kálmán: *Álom, szecesszió, valóság. Tanulmányok huszadik századi magyar prózaírókról* [Dream, art nouveau, reality. Essays on 20th-century Hungarian prose writers]. Bp. 1973, Magvető K. 346 pp.

Vas István: *Az ismeretlen isten. Tanulmányok 1934–1973* [The unknown god. Studies 1934–1973]. Bp. 1974, Szépirodalmi K. 1238 pp.

Veres András: *Mű, érték, műérték. Kísérletek az irodalmi alkotások megközelítésére* [Art, value and the value of art. Experiments in approaching literary works]. Bp. 1979, Magvető K. 554 pp.

Waldapfel József: *Irodalmi tanulmányok. Válogatott cikkek, előadások, glosszák* [Literary studies. Selected articles, lectures, commentaries]. Bp. 1957, Szépirodalmi K. 555 pp.

Waldapfel József: *Szocialista kultúra és irodalmi örökség. Tanulmányok, glosszák, kritikák* [Socialist culture and literary heritage. Studies, commentaries, reviews]. Bp. 1961, Akadémiai K. 385 pp.

WORKS ON THE HISTORY OF LITERARY GENRES (DRAMA, NOVEL)

Bayer József: *A nemzeti játékszín története* [History of the national theatre]. Vols. 1–2. Bp. 1887, Magyar Tudományos Akadémia. VIII, 642; VI, 495 pp.

Bayer József: *A magyar drámairodalom története. A legrégibb nyomokon 1867-ig* [The history of the Hungarian drama. From the beginnings to 1867]. Vols. 1–2. Bp. 1897, Magyar Tudományos Akadémia. XV, 541; VII, 494 pp.

Császár Elemér: *A magyar regény története* [History of the Hungarian novel]. Bp. 1922, Pantheon. 336 pp. — 2nd rev. enl. ed. Bp. 1939. 400 pp.

Pukánszkyné Kádár Jolán: *A Nemzeti Színház százéves története* [Hundred years of the National Theatre]. Vols. 1–2. 1938–1940. Magyar Történelmi Társulat. IX, 581; X, 878 pp.

Rónay György: *A regény és az élet. Bevezetés a XIX–XX. századi magyar regényirodalomba* [Novel and life. Introduction into the 19th–20th-century Hungarian novels]. Bp. 1947. 376 pp.

Magyar színháztörténet [History of the Hungarian theatre]. Ed. and intr. Hont Ferenc. Bp. 1962, Gondolat K. 332 pp.

Nemeskürty István: *A magyar széppróza születése. Tanulmány* [The birth of Hungarian belles-lettres. An essay]. Bp. 1963, Szépirodalmi K. 305 pp.

Hegedűs Géza–Kónya Judit: *A magyar dráma útja* [The development of Hungarian drama]. Bp. 1964, Gondolat K. 251 pp.

Vogl, Ferenc: *Theater in Ungarn 1945 — 1965.* Köln 1966, Verlag Wissenschaft und Politik. 198 pp.

Siklós Olga: *A magyar drámairodalom útja 1945–1957* [Hungarian drama between 1945–1957]. Bp. 1970, Magvető K. 514 pp.

Binal, Wolfgang: *Deutschsprachiges Theater in Budapest von den Anfängen bis zum Brand des Theaters in der Wollgasse (1889).* Wien 1972, Böhlau. 490 pp.

Kocsis Rózsa: *Igen és Nem. A magyar avantgard színjáték története* [Yes and No. The history of Hungarian avantgarde theatre]. Bp. 1973, Magvető K. 654 pp.

Mezei József: *A magyar regény* [The Hungarian novel]. Bp. 1973, Magvető K. 903 pp.

Kováts Miklós: *Magyar színjátszás és drámairodalom Csehszlovákiában. 1918–1938* [Hungarian theatre and drama in Czechoslovakia. 1918–1938]. Bratislava 1974, Madách K. 225 pp.

Lakatos István: *A kolozsvári magyar zenés színpad (1792–1973). Adatok az erdélyi magyar nyelvű színház történetéhez* [The Hungarian musical stage in Kolozsvár (1792–1973). Contribution to a history of the Hungarian theatre in Transylvania]. Forew. Benkő András. Bucharest 1977, Kriterion. 186 pp.

Magyar Bálint: *A Nemzeti Színház története a két világháború között (1917–1944)* [History of the National Theatre in the interwar period (1917–1944)]. Bp. 1977, Szépirodalmi K. 434 pp.

Staud, Géza: *Adelstheater in Ungarn (18. und 19. Jahrhundert).* Wien 1977, Verlag der Österreichischen Akademie der Wissenschaften. 393 pp. (Theatergeschichte Österreichs, Band X: Donaumonarchie, Heft 2).

MAGYAR Bálint: *A Vígszínház története. Alapításától az államosításig. 1896–1949* [The history of the Comedy Theatre. From the foundation to nationalization. 1896–1949]. Bp. *1979*, Szépirodalmi K. 545 pp.

LITERARY LANGUAGE, STYLE, VERSE, TRANSLATION

RADÓ Antal: *A fordítás művészete* [The art of translation]. Bp. *1909*, Franklin. 161 pp.

HORVÁTH János: *A magyar vers* [The Hungarian verse]. Bp. *1948*, Magyar Tudományos Akadémia. 314 pp.

HORVÁTH János: *Rendszeres magyar verstan* [The system of Hungarian prosody]. Bp. *1951*, Akadémiai K. 210 pp. — New ed.: Bp. 1969.

VARGYAS Lajos: *A magyar vers ritmusa* [The rhythm of Hungarian verse]. Bp. *1952*, Akadémiai K. 264 pp.

Nyelvünk a reformkorban [Our language in the Reform Era]. Ed. PAIS Dezső. Bp. *1955*, Akadémiai K. XVI, 683 pp.

ZOLNAI Béla: *Nyelv és stílus*. Tanulmányok [Language and style. Studies]. Bp. *1957*, Gondolat K. 351 pp.

FÓNAGY Iván: *A költői nyelv hangtanából* [On the phonetics of the language of poetry]. Bp. *1959*, Akadémiai K. 289 pp.

BENKŐ Loránd: *A magyar irodalmi írásbeliség a felvilágosodás korának első szakaszában* [Hungarian written literature in the first phase of Enlightenment]. Bp. *1960*, Akadémiai K. 548 pp.

Dolgozatok a magyar irodalmi nyelv és stílus történetéből [Essays on the history of Hungarian literary language and style]. Ed. PAIS Dezső. Bp. *1960*, Akadémiai K. 289 pp.

GÁLDI László: *Ismerjük meg a versformákat* [An introduction to verse forms]. Bp. *1961*, Gondolat K. 238 pp.

A magyar stilisztika útja [The development of Hungarian stylistics]. Ed. SZATHMÁRI István. Bp. *1961*, Gondolat K. XVI, 699 pp.

Stilisztikai tanulmányok [Studies on style]. Bp. *1961*, Gondolat K. 452 pp.

BÁRCZI Géza: *A magyar nyelv életrajza* [Biography of the Hungarian language]. Bp. *1963*, Gondolat K. 462 pp.

ZOLNAI Béla: *Nyelv és hangulat. A nyelv akusztikája* [Language and atmosphere. The acoustics of language]. Bp. *1964*, Gondolat K. 297 pp.

PÉCZELY László: *Tartalom és versforma* [Content and verse form]. Bp. *1965*, Akadémiai K. 233 pp.

RÁKOS, Petr: *Rhythm and metre in Hungarian verse.* Praha *1966*, Univ. Karlova. 102 pp. (Acta Univ. Carolinae. Philologica monographia 11.)

RÓNAY György: *Fordítás közben*. Tanulmányok [The act of translation. Studies]. Bp. *1968*, Magvető K. 421 pp.

SZABÓ Ede: *A műfordítás* [Translation]. Bp. *1968*, Gondolat K. 343 pp.

RÁBA György: *A szép hűtlenek.* Babits, Kosztolányi, Tóth Árpád versfordításai [The beautiful unfaithful. Verse translations of Babits, Kosztolányi and Árpád Tóth]. Bp. *1969*, Akadémiai K. 465 pp.

SZABÉDI László: *Kép és forma*. Esztétikai és verstani tanulmányok [Image and form. Studies in aesthetics and prosody]. Bucharest *1969*, Irodalmi K. 407 pp.

SZABÓ Zoltán: *Kis magyar stílustörténet* [A brief history of Hungarian style]. Bucharest *1970*, Kriterion. 317 pp.

Formateremtő elvek a költői alkotásban. Babits: Ősz és tavasz között. Kassák: A ló meghal, a madarak kirepülnek. Az MTA Stilisztikai és Verstani Munkabizottság verselemző vitaülésén… 1968. nov. 14–15. [Creative approaches to form in poetry. Babits: Between Autumn and Spring. Kassák: The Horse Dies, the Birds Fly out. A session of the Committee for Stylistics and Prosody of the Hungarian Academy of Sciences… 14–15 Nov. 1968]. Ed. HANKISS Elemér. Bp. *1971*, Akadémiai K. 652 pp.

A novellaelemzés új módszerei (A szegedi novellaelemző konferencia anyaga. 1970. ápr. 9–11.) [New methods in the analysis of the short story. The material of the conference for the analysis of the short story at Szeged, 8–11

Apr. 1970]. Ed. HANKISS Elemér. Bp. *1971,* Akadémiai K. 333 pp.

SZABOLCSI Bence: *Vers és dallam.* Tanulmányok a magyar irodalom köréből [Verse and melody. Studies in the field of Hungarian literature]. 2nd enl. ed. Bp. *1972,* Akadémiai K. 208 pp.

RÓNAY György: *Fordítók és fordítások* [Translators and translations]. Bp. *1973,* Magvető K. 309 pp.

Jelentés és stilisztika (Magyar nyelvészek nemzetközi kongresszusa. 2. Szeged, 1972. aug. 22–25.) [Meaning and style. International congress of Hungarian linguists. 2. Szeged, 22–25th Aug. 1972]. Ed. IMRE Samu, SZATHMÁRY István, SZÜTS László. Bp. *1974,* Akadémiai K. 685 pp.

Tanulmányok a magyar impresszionista stílusról [Studies on Hungarian Impressionist style]. Ed. SZABÓ Zoltán. Bucharest *1976,* Kriterion. 178 pp.

TOMPA József: *Anyanyelvi olvasókönyv.* Rendszer és mozgás mai nyelvünkben [A vernacular text-book. System and change in our present-day language]. Bp. *1976,* Gondolat K. 392 pp.

SZILÁGYI Ferenc: *A magyar szó költészete.* Kis magyar stilisztika [The poetry of Hungarian words. A short stylistic survey]. Bp. *1978,* Tankönyvkiadó. 241 pp.

Verstani párbeszédek [Dialogues on prosody]. Participants: KÁROLY S(ándor), KECSKÉS A(ndrás), SZEPES E(rika), SZERDAHELYI I(stván), SZILÁGYI P(éter), SZUROMI L(ajos). Debrecen *1978,* Kossuth Lajos Tudományegyetem Könyvtára. 235 pp.

BENKŐ László: *Az írói szótár.* A szépirodalmi nyelv és stílus lexikográfiai feldolgozása [The vocabulary of the writer. A lexicographical study of literary language and style]. Bp. *1979,* Akadémiai K. 275 pp.

A régi magyar vers [Old Hungarian poetry]. Ed. KOMLOVSZKI Tibor. Bp. *1979,* Akadémiai K. 455 pp.

SZEGEDY-MASZÁK Mihály: *"A regény, amint írja önmagát."* Elbeszélő művek vizsgálata ["The novel as it writes itself." A study of narrative works]. [Bp.] *1980,* Tankönyvkiadó. 237 pp.

A műfordítás ma. Tanulmányok [Translation Today. Essays]. Ed. BART István, RÁKOS Sándor. Bp. *1981,* Gondolat. 674 pp.

SZEPES Erika–SZERDAHELYI István: *Verstan* [Poetics]. Bp. *1981,* Gondolat K. 598 pp.

BOOK, LIBRARY, PRINTING, JOURNALISM

BALLAGI Aladár: *A magyar nyomdászat történelmi fejlődése 1472–1877* [The history of Hungarian printing from 1472 to 1877]. Bp. *1878,* Franklin. 248 pp.

FERENCZY József: *A magyar hírlapirodalom története 1780-tól 1867-ig* [A history of journalism in Hungary between 1780–1867]. Bp. *1887,* VIII, 510 pp.

STEINHOFER Károly: *A könyv története. 1. A magyar könyvnyomtatás és könyvkereskedelem rövid története a legrégibb időktől napjainkig. 2. A könyv történeti fejlődése* [History of the book. 1) Short history of Hungarian printing and book-selling from olden times to our day. 2) Historical development of the book]. Bp. *1915–1916.* 124, 94 pp.

ZUBER Marianne: *A hazai német nyelvű folyóiratok története 1810-ig* [History of German-language periodicals in Hungary till 1810]. Bp. *1915.* 121 pp.

GÁRDONYI Albert: *Magyarországi könyvnyomdászat és könyvkereskedelem a XVIII. században, különös tekintettel Budára és Pestre* [Printing and book-selling in 18th-century Hungary with special regard to Buda and Pest]. Bp. *1917.* 64 pp.

RÉVAY Mór: *Írók, könyvek, kiadók.* Egy magyar könyvkiadó emlékiratai [Writers, books, publishers. The memoirs of a Hungarian publisher]. Vols. 1–2. Bp. *1920.* 396, 458 pp.

GULYÁS Pál: *Könyvek és könyvtárak hajdan és most* [Books and libraries in times past and present]. Bp. *1924.* 76 pp.

IVÁNYI Béla–GÁRDONYI Albert: *A Királyi Magyar Egyetemi Nyomda története 1577–1927* [History of the Royal Hungarian University Press 1577–1927]. Bp. *1927.* 202 pp.

GULYÁS Pál: *A könyvnyomtatás Magyarországon a XV. és XVI. században* [Book-printing in Hungary in the 15th and 16th centuries]. Bp. *1931.* 262. LXVII pp.

Kner Izidor: *Félévszázad mezsgyéjén 1882–1932* [On the borderline of half a century 1882–1932]. Gyoma *1931*. 176 pp.

Szemző Piroska: *Német írók és pesti kiadóik a XIX. században 1812–1878* [German writers and their Hungarian publishers in the 19th century. 1812–1878]. Bp. *1931*. 154 pp.

Egy magyar könyvkiadó regénye [The story of a Hungarian publishing house]. Ed. Révay József, Schöpflin Aladár. Bp. *1938*. 216 pp. [About the Franklin publishing house].

Raichle, Walter: *Das ungarische Zeitungswesen. Seine Entwicklung bis zum Jahre 1938*. Berlin *1939*, Walter de Gruyter. 152 pp.

Nyomdászatunk 500 esztendeje. Emlékkönyv... [500 years of Hungarian printing. A memorial volume...]. Ed. Novák László. [Bp. *1940*.] 160 pp.

Fitz József: *A magyar nyomdászat. 1848–1849* [Hungarian printing in 1848–1849]. Bp. [*1948*]. 213 pp.

Dezsényi Béla–Nemes György: *A magyar sajtó 250 éve* [250 years of Hungarian press]. Vol. 1. Bp. 1954, Művelt Nép K. 287 pp.

Fitz József: *A magyar nyomdászat, könyvkiadás és könyvkereskedelem története. I) A mohácsi vész előtt. II) A reformáció korában* [History of Hungarian printing, publishing and book-selling. I) Before the battle of Mohács. II) In the age of the Reformation]. Bp. *1959*–1967, Akadémiai K. 258, 295 pp.

Kőhalmi Béla: *A Magyar Tanácsköztársaság könyvtárügye* [Library system of the Hungarian Republic of Councils]. Bp. *1959*, Gondolat K. 258 pp.

Gulyás Pál: *A könyv sorsa Magyarországon* [The book's fate in Hungary]. Part 1. Bp. *1961*. 209 pp.

A könyv és a könyvtár a magyar társadalom életében [The role of books and libraries in the life of Hungarian society]. [Vol. 1] *Az államalapítástól 1849-ig* [From the foundation of the state to 1849]. [Vol. 2] *1849-től 1945-ig* [From 1849 to 1945]. Ed. Kovács Máté. Bp. *1963*–1970. Gondolat K. 758, 722 pp.

Lengyel Géza: *Magyar újságmágnások* [Hungarian newspaper-magnates]. Bp. *1963*, Akadémiai K. 196 pp.

Dersi Tamás: *A rejtélyes doktor. Mikes Lajos és az Est-lapok* [The mysterious doctor. Lajos Mikes and the"Est"-papers]. Bp.*1965*, Szépirodalmi K. 520 pp.

Bibliotheca Corviniana. Ed. Csapodi Csaba, Csapodiné Gárdonyi Klára, Szántó Tibor. [Bp.] *1967*, Magyar Helikon. 386 pp.

Bánáti Ágnes–Sándor Dénes: *A százesztendős Athenaeum* [The 100-year-old Athenaeum Publishers]. Bp. *1968*, Akadémiai K. 270 pp.

József Farkas: *A Magyar Tanácsköztársaság sajtója* [The press during the Hungarian Republic of Councils]. Bp. *1969*, Tankönyvkiadó. 111pp.

Kókay György: *A magyar hírlap- és folyóiratirodalom kezdetei (1780–1795)* [The beginnings of Hungarian newspaper and periodical writing (1780–1795)]. Bp. *1970*, Akadémiai K. 513 pp.

Csapodi, Csaba: *The Corvinian Library*. History and stock. Bp. *1973*, Akadémiai K. 516 pp.

Dersi Tamás: *Századvégi üzenet*. Sajtótörténeti tanulmányok [A message from the *fin de siècle*. Essays on the history of the press]. Bp. *1973*, Szépirodalmi K. 525 pp.

Dersi Tamás: *A századvég katolikus sajtója* [Catholic press at the end of the century]. Bp. *1973*, Akadémiai K. 191 pp.

Käfer István: *Az Egyetemi Nyomda négyszáz éve (1577–1977)* [Four hundred years of the University Printing House (1577–1977)]. [Bp.] *1977*, Magyar Helikon, 247 pp.

Fülöp Géza: *A magyar olvasóközönség a felvilágosodás idején és a reformkorban* [Hungarian reading public in the Enlightenment and the Reform Era]. Bp. *1978*, Akadémiai K. 290 pp.

Pogány Péter: *A magyar ponyva tüköre* [Hungarian pulp fiction through the ages]. Bp. *1978*. Magyar Helikon. 411 pp.

A magyar sajtó története [A history of the Hungarian press]. Ed.-in-chief: Szabolcsi Miklós. Series ed.: Vásárhelyi Miklós. Vol. 1. 1705–1848. Ed. Kókay György. Bp. 1979, Akadémiai K. 831 pp.

Holl Béla: *Ferenczffy Lőrinc. Egy magyar könyvkiadó a XVII. században* [Lőrinc Ferenczffy. A Hungarian publisher in the 17th century]. Bp. *1980*, Magyar Helikon. 221 pp.

Kiss István: *Az Athenaeum Könyvkiadó története és szerepe a magyar irodalomban* [The history of the Athenaeum publishing house and its role in Hungarian literature]. Bp. *1980,* Akadémiai K. 263 pp.

M. Pásztor József: *,,Az író beleszól..."* Baloldali irodalmi folyóiratok az ellenforradalmi Magyarországon ["The writer has his say..." Left-wing literary journals in counter-revolutionary Hungary]. Bp. *1980,* Kossuth K. 463 pp.

REPRESENTATIVE ANTHOLOGIES OF HUNGARIAN LITERATURE

Magyar versek könyve [The book of Hungarian poems]. Ed. and intr. Horváth János. Bp. *[1937.]* Magyar Szemle. xxvi, 592 pp. — 2nd enl. ed. Bp. 1942. 784 pp.

Magvető. A magyar irodalom élő könyve [Disseminator. The living textbook of Hungarian literature]. Ed. Móricz Zsigmond. Bp. *1940,* Kelet Népe. 320 pp.—1942² — Kolozsvár 1945³. 413 pp.—Id. Bp. 1979, Magvető K. 320 pp. (facsimile)

A magyar próza könyve [The book of Hungarian fiction]. Ed. Bisztray Gyula, Kerecsényi Dezső. Vols. 1-2. Bp. *1942-1948.* Magyar Szemle. 605, 820 pp.

Magyar versek Aranytól napjainkig [Hungarian poems from Arany to our days]. Ed. Cs. Szabó László. Rome *1953,* Anonymus. 505 pp.

Magyar népköltészet [Hungarian folk poetry]. Ed. Ortutay Gyula. Vols. 1-3. Bp. *1955,* Szépirodalmi K.
  Vol. 1 *Népdalok* [Folk songs]. 503 pp.
  Vol. 2 *Népballadák* [Folk ballads]. 352 pp.
  Vol. 3 *Népmesék* [Folk-tales]. 646 pp.

,,Mindenki újakra készül..." Az 1918/19-es forradalmak irodalma (Szöveggyűjtemény) ["Everybody is preparing for the new..." Literature of the 1918–19 Revolutions (Textbook)]. Ed. József Farkas. Vols. 1-4. Bp. *1959-1967,* Akadémiai K.
  Vol. 1 *A polgári forradalom szépirodalma* [Literature during the bourgeois revolution]. Bp. 1959, 654 pp.
  Vol. 2 *A polgári forradalom publicisztikája és irodalmi élete* [Journalism and literary life during the bourgeois revolution]. Bp. 1962. 970 pp.
  Vol. 3 *A Tanácsköztársaság szépirodalma* [Literature during the Hungarian Republic of Councils]. Bp. 1960. 741 pp.
  Vol. 4 *A Tanácsköztársaság publicisztikája és irodalmi élete* [Journalism and literary life during the Hungarian Republic of Councils]. Bp. 1967. 1221 pp.

Magyar elbeszélők [Hungarian short-story writers]. Ed. Illés Endre. Vols. 1-4. Bp. *1961,* Szépirodalmi K. 1241, 1327, 981, 1145 pp.

(Magyar irodalmi szöveggyűjtemény) [A reader of Hungarian literature]. Bp. Tankönyvkiadó.
  Vol. 1 *Szöveggyűjtemény a régi magyar irodalomból* [Old Hungarian literary reader]. Ed. Barta János, Klaniczay Tibor. 2nd rev. enl. ed. Part 1. *Középkor és reneszánsz* [The Middle Ages and Renaissance]. Bp. *1963.* 859 pp. — Part 2. *Barokk* [Baroque]. Bp. *1966.* 861 pp.
  Vol. 2, Part 1. *Szöveggyűjtemény a felvilágosodás és nyelvújítás korának irodalmából* [A reader of the literature of Enlightenment and the language reform]. Ed. Waldapfel József. Bp. 1953². 847 pp. — Part 2. *Szöveggyűjtemény a reformkorszak irodalmából* [A reader of the literature of the Reform Era]. Ed. Szauder József, Tóth Dezső, Waldapfel József. Bp. 1955. 1127 pp.
  Vol. 3, Part 1. *Szöveggyűjtemény a forradalom és szabadságharc korának irodalmából* [A reader of the literature of the revolution and War of Independence]. Ed. Pándi Pál. Bp. 1962. 1050 pp. — Part 2. *Szöveggyűjtemény a XIX. század második felének irodalmából* [A reader of the literature in the second half of the 19th century]. Ed. Bóka László, Nagy Miklós, Németh G. Béla. Bp. 1961. 1078 pp.
  Vol. 4, Part 1. Books 1-2. *Szöveggyűjtemény a XX. század irodalmából. A Nyugat és Ady kora* [A reader of the literature of the 20th century. The age of the Nyugat and Ady]. Ed. Bessenyei György, Koczkás Sándor. Bp. 1963. 710, 626 pp.

Magyar novellák [Hungarian short stories]. Ed. Illés Endre. Vols. 1-2. Bp. *1963,* Szépirodalmi K. 545, 518 pp.

A magyar valóság versei. 1475–1945 [Poems of Hungarian reality. 1475–1945]. Ed. CSANÁDI Imre. Vols. 1–2. Bp. *1966,* Magvető K. 573, 630 pp.

1945–1970. Negyedszázad magyar verseiből [1945–1970. Twenty-five years of Hungarian poetry]. Ed. and intr. ILLÉS Lajos. Bp. *1970,* Szépirodalmi K. 718 pp.

Magyar humanisták levelei XV–XVI. század [Letters of Hungarian humanists. 15–16th centuries]. Ed. and intr. V. KOVÁCS Sándor. Bp. *1971,* Gondolat K. 711 pp.

"Amíg szívünk dobog..." Válogatás a szocialista irodalomból 1932–1944 ["To our last heartbeat..." Selection from socialist literature 1932–1944]. Ed. BENJÁMIN László, ILLÉS László, MARKOVITS Györgyi. Bp. *1975,* Magvető K. 612 pp.

Magyar elbeszélők. 19. század [Hungarian short-story writers. 19th century]. Ed. SZALAI Anna. Vols. 1–2. Bp. *1976,* Szépirodalmi K. 1182, 1262 pp.

Magyar elbeszélők. 20. század [Hungarian short-story writers. 20th century]. Ed. ILLÉS Endre. Vols 1–3. Bp. *1977,* Szépirodalmi K. 1022, 1075, 1061 pp.

Humanista történetírók [Humanist historians]. Ed. KULCSÁR Péter. Bp. *1977,* Szépirodalmi K. 1195 pp.

A kuruc küzdelmek költészete. II. Rákóczi Ferenc születésének 300. évfordulójára [Poetry of the kuruc struggles. On the 300th anniversary of the birth of Ferenc Rákóczi II]. Sel. and ed. VARGA Imre. Bp. *1977,* Akadémiai K. 897 pp.

Esszépanoráma. 1900–1944 [A panorama of essays. 1900–1944]. Ed. KENYERES Zoltán. Vols 1–3. Bp.*1978,* Szépirodalmi K. 1088, 1149, 1075 pp.

Hét évszázad magyar versei [Seven centuries of Hungarian poetry]. Ed. committee: KIRÁLY István, KLANICZAY Tibor, PÁNDI Pál, SZABOLCSI Miklós. Vols. 1–4. 5th rev. enl. ed. Bp. *1978–1979,* Szépirodalmi K. 1084, 947, 873, 806 pp.

Program és hivatás. Magyar folyóiratok programcikkeinek válogatott gyűjteménye [Programme and mission. A selection of articles on policy in Hungarian journals]. Intr. VARGHA

Kálmán. Ed. KÓKAY György, OLTVÁNYI Ambrus, VARGHA Kálmán. Bp. *1978,* Gondolat K. 821 pp.

Vom Besten der alten ungarischen Literatur. 11.–18. Jahrhundert. Hrsg. von Tibor KLANICZAY. Bp. *1978,* Corvina, 253 pp. In French: *Pages choisies de la littérature hongroise des origines au milieu du* XVIIIe *siècle.* Ed. Tibor KLANICZAY. Bp. 1981, Corvina. 253 pp.

Magyar gondolkodók. 17. század [Hungarian thinkers. 17th century]. Ed. TARNÓC Márton. Bp. *1979,* Szépirodalmi K. 1275 pp.

Megváltó viharban. Az 1918–1919-es magyar forradalmak irodalmából [In redeeming storm. From the literature of the 1918–1919 Hungarian Revolutions]. Ed. JÓZSEF Farkas. Bp. *1979,* Szépirodalmi K. 613 pp.

Szöveggyűjtemény a forradalom és szabadságharc korának irodalmából [A reader of the literature of the Revolution and War of Independence]. Ed. KERÉNYI Ferenc, TAMÁS Anna. Parts 1–2. Bp. *1980,* Tankönyvkiadó. 394, 467 pp.

Magyar drámaírók. 16–18. sz. [Hungarian playwrights. 16th–18th centuries]. Ed. NAGY Péter. Bp. *1981,* Szépirodalmi K. 1177 pp.

Régi magyar levelestár. 16–17. sz. [Collection of old Hungarian letters]. Ed. HARGITTAY Emil. Vols. 1–2. Bp. *1981,* Magvető K. 610, 592 pp.

Szöveggyűjtemény a reformkorszak irodalmából [An Anthology of the Literature of the Reform Period]. Ed. CSETRI Lajos, WÉBER Antal. Part 1–2. Bp. *1981,* Tankönyvkiadó. 477, 453 pp.

Vándorének. Nyugat-európai és tengerentúli magyar költők [Wanderers' Songs. Hungarian Poets in Western Europe and Overseas]. Ed. and Szépirodalmi K. postf. BÉLÁDI Miklós. Bp. *1981,* 402, [12] pp.

INTERACTIONS BETWEEN HUNGARIAN AND WORLD LITERATURE

GENERAL WORKS

HANKISS János: *Európa és a magyar irodalom* [Europe and Hungarian literature]. Bp. *1942,* 619 pp.

TURÓCZI-TROSTLER József: *Magyar irodalom — világirodalom.* Tanulmányok [Hungarian literature—world literature. Studies]. Vols. 1–2. Bp. *1961,* Akadémiai K. 622, 823 pp.

La littérature comparée en Europe Orientale. Conférence de Budapest, 26–29 Oct. 1962. Org.: Académie des Sciences de Hongrie. (Publié sous la direction de István Sőtér, Kálmán Bor, Tibor Klaniczay, György Mihály Vajda.) Bp. *1963,* Akadémiai K. 534 pp.

Littérature hongroise—littérature européenne. Études de littérature comparée publiées par l'Académie des Sciences de Hongrie à l'occasion du IVᵉ Congrès de l' Association Internationale de Littérature Comparée. (Publié sous la direction de István Sőtér, Ottó Süpek.) Bp. *1964,* Akadémiai K. 647 pp.

Sőtér, István: *Aspects et parallélismes de la littérature hongroise.* Bp. 1966, Akadémiai K. 291 pp.

Waldapfel, József: *A travers siècles et frontières.* Études sur la littérature hongroise et la littérature comparée. Bp. *1968,* Akadémiai K. 438 pp.

Les Lumières en Hongrie, en Europe Centrale et en Europe Orientale. Actes du [Premier] Colloque de Mátrafüred. 3–5 Nov. 1970 (Sous la présidence de Béla Köpeczi. Publié par Eduard Bene). Bp. *1971,* Akadémiai K. 125 pp.

Sőtér, István: *The dilemma of literary science.* Studies—Small Hungarian biographical dictionary. Bp. *1973,* Akadémiai K. 271 pp.

Sziklay László: *Szomszédainkról. A kelet-európai irodalom kérdései* [Our neighbours. Essays on Eastern European literature]. Bp. *1974,* Szépirodalmi K. 364 pp.

Les Lumières en Hongrie, en Europe Centrale et en Europe Orientale. Actes de Deuxième Colloque de Mátrafüred, 2–5 Oct. 1972 (Sous la présidence de Béla Köpeczi. Publié par Eduard Bene et Ilona Kovács). Bp. *1975,* Akadémiai K. 190 pp.

AMERICAN–HUNGARIAN

Gál István: *Magyarország, Anglia és Amerika különös tekintettel a szláv világra.* Vázlatok a nemzeti vonatkozások köréből [Hungary, Britain and America with special regard to the Slav world. Sketches on national aspects]. Bp. *1945,* Officina 327 pp.

Gergely, Emro J.: *Hungarian Drama in New York: American Adaptations, 1908–1940.* Philadelphia *1947,* University of Pennsylvania Press. 197 pp.

Bueno, Salvador: *Cinco siglos de relaciones entre Hungría y América Latina.* Bp. *1977,* Corvina. 325 pp. (Colección Corvina.)

BULGARIAN–HUNGARIAN

Tanulmányok a bolgár–magyar kapcsolatok köréből. A Bolgár Állam megalapításának 1300. évfordulójára [Studies on Bulgarian–Hungarian connections. For the 1300th anniversary of the foundation of the Bulgarian state]. Ed. Chavdar Dobrev, Juhász Péter, Petar Mijatev. Bp. *1981,* Akadémiai K. 550 pp.

CZECHOSLOVAKIAN–HUNGARIAN

Csanda Sándor: *Magyar–szlovák kulturális kapcsolatok* [Cultural relations between Hungary and Slovakia]. Bratislava *1959,* Slov. Pedagogické Nakl. 414 pp.

Tanulmányok a csehszlovák–magyar irodalmi kapcsolatok köréből [Studies on literary relations between Czechoslovakia and Hungary]. Ed. Zuzana Adamová, Karol Rosenbaum, Sziklay László. Bp. *1965,* Akadémiai K. 592 pp. — In Czech: *Dějiny a národy. Literárnehistorické studie o československo–maďarských vztazích.* (Vědecký red.: Julius Dolansky.) Praha 1965. Nákl. Československé Akad. Ved. 365 pp.

Csanda Sándor: *Szülőföld és irodalom* [Homeland and literature]. Bratislava *1977,* Madách. 259 pp.

Kemény G. Gábor: *Kapcsolatok vonzásában* (Attractive relationship]. Bratislava *1977,* Madách. 194 pp.

Sziklay László: *Visszhangok.* Tanulmányok, elemzések, értékelések [Echoes. Studies, analyses, appraisals]. Bratislava *1977,* Madách. 401 pp.

Chmel, Rudolf: *Két irodalom kapcsolatai* (Literatury v kontaktoch). Tanulmányok a szlovák–magyar irodalmi kapcsolatok köréből. [Relations between two literatures. Studies in Slovak–Hungarian literary relations]. Bratislava *1980,* Madách. 253 pp.

DUTCH–HUNGARIAN

Trencsényi-Waldapfel Imre: *Erasmus és magyar barátai* [Erasmus and his Hungarian friends]. Bp. *1941*. 110 pp.

Sivirsky Antal: *Magyarország a XIX. századi holland irodalom tükrében* [Hungary as reflected in 19th-century Dutch literature]. Bp. *1973*, Akadémiai K. 226 pp.

ENGLISH–HUNGARIAN

Császár Elemér: *Shakespeare és a magyar költészet* [Shakespeare and Hungarian poetry]. Bp. *1917*. 256 pp.

Fest Sándor: *Angol irodalmi hatások hazánkban Széchenyi István fellépéséig* [British literary influences in Hungary until the appearance of István Széchenyi]. Bp. *1917*, Magyar Tudományos Akadémia. 111 pp.

Varannai Aurél: *Angliai visszhang* [Echo in England]. Bp. *1974*, Magvető K. 192 pp.

Czigány Lóránt: *A magyar irodalom fogadtatása a viktoriánus Angliában 1830–1914* [The reception of Hungarian literature in Victorian England 1830–1914]. Bp. *1976*, Akadémiai K. 287 pp.

FINNISH–HUNGARIAN

Domokos Péter: *A finn irodalom fogadtatása Magyarországon* [The reception of Finnish literature in Hungary]. Bp. *1972*, Akadémiai K. 211 pp.

FRENCH–HUNGARIAN

Kont, Ignác: *Étude sur l'influencede la littérature française en Hongrie*. Paris *1902*, Ernest Le Roux. 509 pp.

Eckhardt Sándor: *A francia forradalom eszméi Magyarországon* [The ideas of the French Revolution in Hungary]. Bp. [*1924*], Franklin Társulat. 222 pp.

Sőtér István: *Magyar–francia kapcsolatok* [Hungarian–French relations]. Bp. *1946*. 255 pp.

Eszmei és irodalmi találkozások. Tanulmányok a magyar–francia irodalmi kapcsolatok történetéből [Encounters of ideas and literatures. Studies on the history of literary connections between France and Hungary]. Ed. Köpeczi Béla, Sőtér István. Bp. *1970*, Akadémiai K. 571 pp.

"Sorsotok előre nézzétek". A francia felvilágosodás és a magyar kultúra. Tanulmányok [Essays on the connections between French Enlightenment and Hungarian culture]. Ed. Köpeczi Béla, Sziklai László. Bp. *1975*, Akadémiai K. 447 pp.

GERMAN–HUNGARIAN

Pukánszky, Béla: *A magyarországi német irodalom története. A legrégibb időktől 1848-ig* [The history of German literature in Hungary. From olden times to 1848]. Bp. *1926*. 603 pp.

Pukánszky Béla: *Geschichte des deutschen Schrifttums in Ungarn*. Bd. 1. Von der ältesten Zeit bis um die Mitte des 18. Jh. Münster in Westfalen *1931*, Aschendorf. xx, 490 pp.

Studien zur Geschichte der deutsch–ungarischen literarischen Beziehungen. Hrsg. von Leopold Magon, Gerhard Steiner, Wolfgang Steinitz, Miklós Szabolcsi und György Mihály Vajda. Berlin *1969*, Akademie-Verlag. 512 pp.

Salyámosi Miklós: *Magyar irodalom Németországban 1913–1933* [Hungarian literature in Germany 1913–1933]. Bp. *1973*, Akadémiai K. 183 pp.

Mádl Antal: *Írók történelmi sorsfordulókon. Osztrák és német írók — magyar kapcsolatok* [Writers at the crossroads. Austrian and German writers—Hungarian connections]. Bp. *1979*, Akadémiai K. 259 pp.

Ritoók János: *Kettős tükör. A magyar-szász együttélés múltjából és a két világháború közötti irodalmi kapcsolatok történetéből* [Double Mirror. On the Past of Hungarian–Transylvanian Saxon Coexistence and the History of Literary Connections between the Two Word Wars]. Bucharest *1979*, Kriterion K. 256 pp.

ITALIAN–HUNGARIAN

Váradi, Emerico: *La letteratura italiana e la sua influenza in Ungheria*. Storie e bibliografia. Tom. 1–2. Roma *1933*–*1934*, Istituto per l'Europa Orientale.

Szauder József: *Olasz irodalom — magyar irodalom*. Tanulmányok [Italian literature—Hungarian literature. Studies]. Bp. *1963*, Európa K. 462 pp.

Italia ed Ungheria. Dieci secoli di rapporti letterari A cura di M. Horányi e T. Klaniczay. Bp. *1967*, Akadémiai K. 393 pp.

Venezia e Ungheria nel Rinascimento. A cura di Vittore BRANCA. (Atti del Convegno di studi promosso e organizzato dalla Fondazione Giorgio Cini, dall'Accademia Ungherese delle Scienze, dall'Istituto per le Relazioni Culturali di Budapest. Venezia, 11–14 giugno 1970). Firenze *1973,* Leo S. Olschki Ed. 498 pp.

Rapporti veneto–ungheresi all'epoca del Rinascimento. A cura di Tibor KLANICZAY. (Atti del II Convegno di Studi Italo–Ungheresi promosso e organizzato dall'Accademia Ungherese delle Scienze, dalla Fondazione Giorgio Cini, dall'Istituto per le Relazioni Culturali di Budapest. Budapest, 20–23 giugno 1973). Bp. *1975,* Akadémiai K. 437 pp.

Venezia e Ungheria. Nel contesto del barocco europeo. A cura di Vittore BRANCA (Atti del Convegno di Studi promosso e organizzato dalla Fondazione Giorgio Cini, dall'Accademia Ungherese delle Scienze, dall'Istituto per le Relazioni Culturali di Budapest. Venezia, 10–13 novembre 1976). Firenze *1979,* Leo S. Olschki Ed. 450 pp.

POLISH–HUNGARIAN

Tanulmányok a lengyel–magyar irodalmi kapcsolatok köréből [Studies on Polish–Hungarian literary connections]. Ed. CSAPLÁROS István, HOPP Lajos, Jan REYCHMAN, SZIKLAY László. Bp. *1969,* Akadémiai K. 659 pp. — in Polish: *Studia z dziejów polsko–węgierskich stosunków literackich i kulturalnych.* Wrocław–Warszawa–Kraków 1969, Zahł. im Ossolińskich Wydawnictwo. 528 pp.

HOPP Lajos: *A lengyel–magyar hagyományok újjászületése* [Renaissance in Polish–Hungarian traditions]. Bp. *1972,* Akadémiai K. 166 pp.

HOPP Lajos: *A Rákóczi-emigráció Lengyelországban* [The Rákóczi emigration in Poland]. Bp. *1973,* Akadémiai K. 230 pp.

CSAPLÁROS István: *A felvilágosodástól a felszabadulásig.* Tanulmányok a lengyel–magyar irodalmi kapcsolatok köréből[From Enlightenment to liberation. Studies on Polish–Hungarian literary connections]. Bp. *1977,* Magvető K. 287 pp.

Studia z dziejów polsko–węgierskich stosunków lit-erackich. Pod. red. Istvána CSAPLÁROSa. Warszawa *1978,* Wydawnictwa Uniwersytetu Warszawskiego. 328 pp.

Z dziejów polsko–węgierskich stosunków historycznych i literackich. Pod. red. Istvána CSAPLÁROSA i Andrzeja SIEROSZEWSKI ego. Warsawa *1979,* Wydawnictwa Uniwersytetu Warszawskiego. 267 pp.

RUMANIAN–HUNGARIAN

I. T ÓTH Zoltán: *Magyarok és románok.* Történelmi tanulmányok [Hungarians and Rumanians. Historical essays]. Ed. CSATÁRI Dániel. Bp. *1966,* Akadémiai K. 496 pp.

DÁVID Gyula: *Találkozások.* Tanulmányok a román–magyar irodalmi kapcsolatok múltjáról [Encounters. Studies on the past of Rumanian-Hungarian literary connections]. Kolozsvár-Napoca *1976,* Dacia. 261 pp.

RUSSIAN–HUNGARIAN

GYÖRGY Lajos: *A magyar és az orosz irodalom kapcsolatai* [Relations between Hungarian and Russian literature]. Kolozsvár *1946.* 121 pp.

REJTŐ István: *Az orosz irodalom fogadtatása Magyarországon* [Reception of Russian literature in Hungary]. Bp. *1958,* Akadémiai K. 115 pp.

Tanulmányok a magyar–orosz irodalmi kapcsolatok köréből [Essays on relations between Hungarian and Russian literature]. Ed. KEMÉNY G. Gábor. Vols. 1–3. Bp. *1961,* Akadémiai K. 595, 487, 485 pp. [With a summary in Russian.] — In Russian: *Vengersko–russkye literaturnye svyazi.* Red. koll.: I. I. ANISIMOV, I. SHETER [Sőtér] [etc.] Moscow 1964, Izdat. "Nauka". 280 pp.

LENGYEL Béla: *Szovjet irodalom Magyarországon 1919-1944* [Soviet literature in Hungary 1919–1944]. Bp. *1964,* Akadémiai K. 373 pp. [With a summary in Russian.]

VÁRADI-STERNBERG János: *Utak, találkozások, emberek.* Írások az orosz–magyar és ukrán-magyar kapcsolatokról [Roads, encounters, people. Writings on Russian–Hungarian and Ukrainian–Hungarian relations]. Uzhgorod-Bp. *1974.* Kárpáti K. — Gondolat K. 317 pp.

Irodalmunk barátsága. A magyar–orosz és magyar-ukrán irodalmi kapcsolatok történetéhez [Literary friendships. On the history of Hungarian–Russian and Hungarian–Ukrainian literary contacts]. Ed. FENYVESI István. Bp. *1977*, MSzBT. 381 pp.

Velikaja Oktjabr'szkaja szocialiszticseszkaja revolucija i vengerszkaja literatura. Red. koll.: M[iklós] SZABOLCSI, V. R. SCHERBINA [etc.] Moscow *1979*, Izdat. "Nauka". 300 pp.

SOUTHERN SLAV–HUNGARIAN

SZELI István: *Utak egymás felé* [Converging roads]. Újvidék *1969*, Forum. 275 pp.

BORI Imre: *Irodalmak—kölcsönhatások.* Kapcsolattörténeti tanulmányok [Literatures—interactions. Essays on the history of relations]. Újvidék *1971*, Forum. 159 pp.

Szomszédság és közösség. Délszláv–magyar irodalmi kapcsolatok. Tanulmányok [Neighbouring peoples and the sense of community. South Slav–Hungarian literary connections. Essays]. Ed. VUJICSICS D. Sztoján. Bp. *1972*, Akadémiai K. 550 pp.

DAVID, Andraš: *Mostovi uzajamnosti.* Poglavlja o jugoslovensko–madjarskim kulturnim i književnim vezama (A kölcsönösség hídjai. Fejezetek a jugoszláv–magyar kulturális és irodalmi kapcsolatokról) [The road to reciprocity. Chapter on Yugoslav–Hungarian cultural and literary connections]. Novi Sad *1977*, Radnički univerzitet "Radivoj Čirpanov". 349 pp.

FIED István: *A délszláv népköltészet recepciója a magyar irodalomban Kazinczytól Jókaiig* [The reception of South Slav folk poetry in Hungarian literature from Kazinczy to Jókai]. Bp. *1979*, Akadémiai K. 355 pp.

SWISS–HUNGARIAN

DEZSÉNYI Béla: *Magyarország és Svájc* [Hungary and Switzerland]. Bp. *1946*. 274 pp.

II ON INDIVIDUAL WRITERS

ADY, ENDRE

BÖLÖNI György: *Az igazi Ady* [The real Ady].
Bp. *1947*, Szikra. 403 pp. [New editions:
1955, 1974.]

FÖLDESSY Gyula: *Ady minden titkai.* Ady-kom-
mentárok [All of Ady's secrets. Studies]. Bp.
1949, Athenaeum, 318 pp. — [2nd ed.] Bp.
1962, Magvető K. 374 pp.

Emlékezések Ady Endréről [Remembering Ady].
Ed. KOVALOVSZKY Miklós. Vols. 1–2. Bp.
1961–1974, Akadémiai K. 659, 842 pp.

VARGA József: *Ady Endre.* Pályakép vázlat [Endre
Ady. A sketch of his career]. Bp. *1966*, Magvető K. 633 pp.

SCHWEITZER Pál: *Ember az embertelenségben.*
A háborús évek Ady-verseinek szimbolizmus
motívum-csoportjai [Man and the Inhuman.
Symbolist motifs in Ady's poems written
during the war]. Bp. *1969*, Akadémiai K.
191 pp.

VEZÉR Erzsébet: *Ady Endre. Élete és pályája*
[Endre Ady. His life and career]. Bp. *1969*,
Gondolat K. 474 pp.

KIRÁLY István: *Ady Endre.* Vols, 1–2. 2nd ed. Bp.
1972, Magvető K. 778, 788 pp.

HATVANY Lajos: *Ady.* Cikkek, emlékezések, levelek [Ady. Articles, memoirs, letters]. 2nd enl.
ed. Ed.: BELIA György. Bp. *1974*, Szépirodalmi
K. 846 pp.

JÉKEL Pál–PAPP Ferenc: *Ady Endre összes költői
műveinek fonémastatisztikája* [A statistical study
of phonemes in Endre Ady's poetical works].
Bp. *1974*. Akadémiai K. 179 pp.

Babits Adyról. Dokumentumgyűjtemény [Babits
on Ady. Collected documents]. Ed. and intr.:
GÁL István. Bp. *1975*, Magvető K. 280 pp.

Tegnapok és holnapok árján. Tanulmányo k Adyró
[In the stream of yesterdays and tom orrows
Essays on Ady]. Ed. LÁNG József. Bp. *1977*,
Petőfi Irodalmi Múzeum—Népművelési
Propaganda Iroda. 457 pp.

VARGA József: *Ady és kora* [Ady and his age].
Bp. *1977*, Kossuth K. 572 pp.

Endre Ady. 1877–1918. Materialy sesji naukowej
z organizowanej w dniu 27 pazdziernika 1977.
r. przez Katedre Filologii Węgierskiej UW
o raz Węgierski Instytut Kultury w Warsza-
wie. Red. István CSAPLÁROS. Warszawa *1978*,
Wydawnictwo Węgierskiego Instytutu Kultury. 183 pp.

,,*Akarom: tisztán lássatok.*'' Tudományos ülésszak
Ady Endre születésének 100. évfordulóján
["I want you to see me clearly". Scholarly
session held at the 100th anniversary of the
birth of Endre Ady]. Bp. *1980*, Akadémiai K.
269 pp.

SCHWEITZER Pál: *Szépség és totalitás.* A szép
fogalmának tartalma Ady utolsó alkotókor-
szakában. [Beauty and totality. The concept
of beauty in Ady's last creative period]. Bp.
1980, Akadémiai K. 296 pp.

Cf.: LUKÁCS György *válogatott művei.* Vol. 3.
Magyar irodalom — magyar kultúra (pp. 522)
BONNERJEA, René: Intr. In: *Ady, Endre:
Poems* (pp. 555.)
NYERGES, Anton N.: Endre Ady, the World of
Gog and God. [Intr.] In: *Poems of Endre Ady*
(pp. 555.)

AMBRUS, ZOLTÁN

KOREK Valéria: *Hangulat és valóság. Ambrus
Zoltánról* [Mood and reality. On Zoltán

534

Ambrus]. München *1976*, 195 pp. (Aurora Books)
Cf.: GYERGYAI Albert: *A Nyugat árnyékában* (pp. 520.)

ANONYMUS

CSAPODI Csaba: *Az Anonymus-kérdés története* [The history of the Anonymus problem]. Bp. *1978*, Magvető K. 162 pp.

APÁCAI CSERE, JÁNOS

BÁN Imre: *Apácai Csere János.* Bp. *1958*, Akadémiai K. 606 pp.
FÁBIÁN Ernő: *Apáczai Csere János.* Kismonográfia [Short monography]. Kolozsvár–Napoca *1975*, Dacia. 199 pp.
Cf.: SZIGETI József: *A mű és kora* (pp. 523.)

ARANY, JÁNOS

RIEDL Frigyes: *Arany János.* 4th partly rev. ed. Bp. *1920*, Pallas. 375 pp.
VOINOVICH Géza: *Arany János életrajza* [Biography of János Arany]. Vols 1–3. Bp. *1929–1938*, Magyar Tudományos Akadémia. 253, 416, 352 pp.
BARTA János: *Arany János.* Bp. *1953*, Művelt Nép. 188 pp.
KERESZTURY Dezső: *,,S mi vagyok én..." Arany János 1817–1856* ["And what am I...". János Arany 1817–1856]. Bp. *1967*, Szépirodalmi K. 365 pp.
KERESZTURY Dezső: *Arany János.* Bp. *1971*, Akadémiai K. 227 pp.
Az el nem ért bizonyosság. Elemzések Arany lírájának első szakaszából [Unattained certainty. Studies on the first period of Arany's poetry]. Ed. NÉMETH G. Béla. Bp. *1972*, Akadémiai K. 371 pp.
Arany János ma. 1817–1977 [János Arany today. 1817–1977]. Ed. MEZEI József. Az ELTE Bölcsészkar 19. századi Magyar Irodalomtörténeti Tanszéke 1977. okt. 5–6-án rendezett tudományos ülésszakának anyaga [Material of the symposium held on October 5–6, 1977, by the Department of Hungarian Literary History of the Loránd Eötvös University, Budapest]. Bp. *1980*, Tankönyvkiadó 163 pp.
Cf.: SŐTÉR István: *Nemzet és haladás* (pp. 518.)

TAMÁS Attila: *Költői világképek fejlődése Arany Jánostól József Attiláig* (pp. 519.)
KIRKCONNELL, Watson: Translator's preface. In: *Arany, János: The Death of King Buda* (pp. 555.)
NYERGES, Anton N.: Introduction: An epic journey. In: *Arany, János: Epics of the Hungarian Plain* (pp. 555.)

ARANY, LÁSZLÓ

SOMOGYI Sándor: *Arany László.* Bp. *1956*, Művelt Nép. 143 pp.
Cf.: KOMLÓS Aladár: *Tegnap és ma* (pp. 521.)
NÉMETH G. Béla: *Mű és személyiség* (pp. 522.)

BABITS, MIHÁLY

KISS Ferenc: *A beérkezés küszöbén.* Babits, Juhász és Kosztolányi ifjúkori barátsága [At the threshold of success. The friendship of the young Babits, Juhász and Kosztolányi]. Bp. *1962*, Akadémiai K. 153 pp.
PÓK Lajos: *Babits Mihály alkotásai és vallomásai tükrében* [Mihály Babits as reflected in his works and confessions]. Bp. *1967*, Szépirodalmi K. 215 pp.
BENEDEK Marcell: *Babits Mihály.* Bp. *1969*, Gondolat K. 136 pp.
KARDOS Pál: *Babits Mihály.* Bp. *1972*, Gondolat K. 668 pp.
SIPOS Lajos: *Babits Mihály és a forradalmak kora* [Mihály Babits and the age of revolutions]. Bp. *1976*, Akadémiai K. 152 pp.
RÁBA György: *Babits Mihály költészete 1903–1920* [The poetry of Mihály Babits. 1903–1920]. Bp. *1981*, Szépirodalmi K. 667 pp.
Cf.: *Formateremtő elvek a költői alkotásban.* Ed. HANKISS Elemér (pp. 525.)
RÁBA György: *A szép hűtlenek* (pp. 525.)

BAJZA, JÓZSEF

[BAJZA] Szücsi József: *Bajza József.* Bp. *1914*, Magyar Tudományos Akadémia. 497 pp.
Cf.: TÓTH Dezső: *Élő hagyomány—élő irodalom* (pp. 523.)

BALASSI, BÁLINT

ECKHARDT Sándor: *Balassi Bálint.* Bp. [1941], Franklin Társulat. 224 pp.

ECKHARDT Sándor: *Az ismeretlen Balassi Bálint* [The unknown Bálint Balassi]. Bp. *1943*, Magyar Szemle Társaság. 313 pp.

ECKHARDT Sándor: *Balassi-tanulmányok* [Studies on Balassi]. Ed. KOMLOVSZKI Tibor. Bp. *1972*, Akadémiai K. 439 pp.

CSANDA Sándor: *Balassi Bálint költészete és a közép-európai szláv reneszánsz stílus* [The poetry of Bálint Balassi and the Middle European Slav Renaissance style]. Bratislava *1973*, Madách. 356 pp.

NEMESKÜRTY István: *Balassi Bálint.* Bp. *1978*, Gondolat K. 278 pp.

Cf.: KLANICZAY Tibor: *Reneszánsz és barokk* (pp. 521.)

BALÁZS, BÉLA

LUKÁCS György: *Balázs Béla és akinek nem kell.* (Összegyűjtött tanulmányok) [Béla Balázs and those who have no need of him. (Collected studies)]. Gyoma *1918*, Kner. 121 pp. — Id. in: Lukács, György: *Magyar irodalom — magyar kultúra* [Hungarian literature—Hungarian culture]. Bp. *1970*, Gondolat K. pp. 68–136.

K. NAGY Magda: *Balázs Béla világa* [The world of Béla Balázs]. [Bp.] *1973*, Kossuth K. 404 pp.

Cf.: SZABOLCSI Miklós: *Elődök és kortársak* (pp. 523.)

BARTA, SÁNDOR

Cf.: ILLYÉS Gyula: *Iránytűvel.* 2nd vol. (pp. 521.)

BATSÁNYI, JÁNOS

SZINNYEI Ferenc: *Batsányi János. 1763–1845.* Bp. *1904*, Magyar Történelmi Társulat. 210 pp.

HORÁNSZKY Lajos: *Batsányi János és kora. Eredeti levelezések és egykorú források nyomán* [János Batsányi and his age. On the basis of original correspondences and contemporary sources]. Bp. *1907*. 535 pp.

Cf.: KERESZTURY Dezső: *Örökség* (pp. 521.)
SINKÓ Ervin: *Magyar irodalom* (pp. 523.)

BENJÁMIN, LÁSZLÓ

SIMON Zoltán: *Benjámin László.* Bp. *1972*, Akadémiai K. 159 pp.

Cf.: DIÓSZEGI András: *Megmozdult világban* (pp. 520.)

BERZSENYI, DÁNIEL

NÉMETH László: *Berzsenyi.* Bp. [1938], Franklin. 144 pp.

HORVÁTH János: *Berzsenyi és íróbarátai* [Berzsenyi and his writer friends]. Bp. *1960*, Akadémiai K. 293 pp.

MERÉNYI Oszkár: *Berzsenyi Dániel.* Bp. *1966*, Akadémiai K. 471 pp.

MERÉNYI Oszkár: *Újabb Berzsenyi-tanulmányok* [Further studies on Berzsenyi]. Bp. *1971*. 152 pp.

Berzsenyi emlékkönyv [Berzsenyi memorial volume]. Ed. MERÉNYI Oszkár. [Bp.] *1976*. 748 pp.

Berzsenyi Dániel versei (1808). [Poems of Dániel Berzsenyi 1808]. [An introductory essay]: MERÉNYI Oszkár: A collection of the poems of Dániel Berzsenyi published in 1808.] Bp. *1976*, Akadémiai K. 48 pp., 88 unnumbered letters, 1 supplement (a facsimile edition).

OROSZ László: *Berzsenyi Dániel.* Bp. *1976*, Gondolat K. 232 pp.

Cf.: MARTINKÓ András: *Teremtő idők* (pp. 522.)

BESSENYEI, GYÖRGY

GÁLOS Rezső: *Bessenyei György életrajza* [Biography of György Bessenyei]. Bp. *1951*, Közoktatásügyi Kiadóvállalat. 425 pp.

SZAUDER József: *Bessenyei.* Bp. *1953*, Művelt Nép. 155 pp.

BÍRÓ Ferenc: *A fiatal Bessenyei és íróbarátai* [The young Bessenyei and his writer friends]. Bp. *1976*, Akadémiai K. 351 pp.

BETHLEN, MIKLÓS

GYÁRFÁS Elemér: *Bethlen Miklós kancellár. 1642–1716* [Chancellor Miklós Bethlen. 1642–1716]. Dicsőszentmárton. *1924*. 226 pp.

Cf.: TOLNAI Gábor: *Tanulmányok* (pp. 523.)

BORNEMISZA, PÉTER

SCHULEK Tibor: *Bornemisza Péter 1535–1584.* Bp.–Győr–Sopron. *1939*. 452 pp.

NEMESKÜRTY István: *Bornemisza Péter, az ember és az író* [Péter Bornemisza the man and the writer]. Bp. *1959*, Akadémiai K. 558 pp.

BORZSÁK István: *Az antikvitás XVI. századi képe* (Bornemisza-tanulmányok) [The 16th-century image of the Antiquity. Studies on Bornemisza]. Bp. *1960*, Akadémiai K. 558 pp.

BRÓDY, SÁNDOR

FÖLDES Anna: *Bródy Sándor*. Bp. *1964*, Gondolat K. 187 pp.
JUHÁSZ Ferencné: *Bródy Sándor*. Bp. *1971*, Akadémiai K. 306 pp.
Cf.: NAGY Péter: *Drámai arcélek* (pp. 522.)

CSIKY, GERGELY

JANOVICS Jenő: *Csiky Gergely élete és művei* [Life and work of Gergely Csiky]. Vols. 1–2. Kolozsvár *1900*. 243 pp. — New ed. Bp. *1902*. 273 pp.
HEGEDŰS Géza: *Csiky Gergely*. Bp. *1953*, Művelt Nép. 113 pp.

CSOKONAI VITÉZ, MIHÁLY

HARASZTI Gyula: *Csokonai Vitéz Mihály*. Bp. *1880*. IX, 362 pp.
SINKÓ Ervin: *Csokonai életműve* [The life-work of Csokonai]. Novi Sad *1965*, Forum. 349 pp.
VARGHA Balázs: *Csokonai Vitéz Mihály alkotásai és vallomásai tükrében* [Mihály Csokonai Vitéz as reflected in his works and confessions]. Bp. *1974*, Szépirodalmi K. 366 pp.
JULOW Viktor: *Csokonai Vitéz Mihály*. Bp. *1975*, Gondolat K. 226 pp.
JUHÁSZ Géza: *Csokonai-tanulmányok* [Studies on Csokonai]. Ed. intr. and notes by JUHÁSZ Izabella. Bp. *1977*, Akadémiai K. 413 pp.
KATONA, Anna B.: *Mihály Vitéz Csokonai*. Boston *1980*, Twayne Publishers. 170 pp. (Twayne's World Authors Series.)
SZAUDER József: *Az éj és a csillagok*. Tanulmányok Csokonairól [The night and the stars. Studies on Csokonai]. Ed. and notes by SZAUDER Mária. Bp. *1980*, Akadémiai K. 386 pp.
SZILÁGYI Ferenc: *Csokonai művei nyomában*. Tanulmányok [In Search of Csokonai 's Works. Essays]. Bp. *1981*, Akadémiai K. 742 pp.

CZUCZOR, GERGELY

KOLTAI Virgil: *Czuczor Gergely élete és munkái* [Life and work of Cergely Czuczor]. Bp. *1885*. VII, 232 pp.

DARVAS, JÓZSEF

Cf.: *Arcképek a magyar szocialista irodalomból* (pp. 515.)
DIÓSZEGI András: *Megmozdult világban* (pp. 520.)
JORDÁKY Lajos: *A szocialista irodalom útján* (pp. 521.)
KOVÁCS Kálmán: *Eszmék és irodalom* (pp. 521.)

DÉRY, TIBOR

SZENESSY, Mario: *Tibor Déry*. Stuttgart–Berlin–Köln–Mainz. *1970*, Kohlhammer. 128 pp. (Sprache und Literatur 65.)
UNGVÁRI Tamás: *Déry Tibor alkotásai és vallomásai tükrében* [Tibor Déry as reflected in his works and confessions]. Bp. *1973*, Szépirodalmi K. 325 pp.
POMOGÁTS Béla: *Déry Tibor*. Bp. *1974*, Akadémiai K. 199 pp.
Cf.: BÉLÁDI Miklós: *Érintkezési pontok* (pp. 520.)
BORI Imre: *Eszmék és látomások* (pp. 520.)
LUKÁCS György *válogatott művei*. Vol. 3 *Magyar irodalom—magyar kultúra* (pp. 522.)

DUGONITS, ANDRÁS

PRÓNAI Antal: *Dugonits András életrajza* [Biography of András Dugonits]. Szeged, *1903*. II, 239 pp.
Cf.: SZAUDER József: *Az estve és Az álom* (pp. 523.)

EÖTVÖS, JÓZSEF

WEBER, Johann: *Eötvös und die ungarische Nationalitätenfrage*. München *1966*, Oldenburg. 154 pp.
SŐTÉR István: *Eötvös József*. 2nd rev. ed. Bp. *1967*, Akadémiai K. 347 pp.
VARDY, S. B.: *Baron J. Eötvös: the Political Profile of a Liberal Hungarian Thinker and Statesman*. Bloomington, Indianapolis *1969*. 327 pp.
BÖDY, Paul: *Joseph Eötvös and the Modernization of Hungary, 1840–1870*. Philadelphia *1972*. 134 pp.
Ábránd és valóság. Tanulmányok Eötvös Józsefről. [Day-dreaming and reailty. Studies on József Eötvös]. Ed. SZALAI Anna. Bp. *1973*, Szépirodalmi K. 319 pp.
Cf.: MERVYN, Jones D.: *Five Hungarian Writers* (pp. 522.)

EÖTVÖS, KÁROLY

HERCEG Matild: *Eötvös Károly*. Bp. *1928*. 46 pp.
NÉMETH Béla: *Emlékbeszéd Eötvös Károlyról* [Károly Eötvös, memorial speech]. Bp. *1943*. 32 pp.
LUKÁCSY Sándor: "Eötvös Károly helye irodalmunkban" [The place of Károly Eötvös in our literature]. [Intr.]. — In: EÖTVÖS, Károly: *Megakad a vármegye*. Bp. *1952*, Művelt Nép. pp. 5–34.

ERDÉLYI, JÁNOS

SCHÖNER Magda: *Erdélyi János élete és művei* [The life and work of János Erdélyi]. Bp. *1931*. 111 pp.
T. ERDÉLYI Ilona: *Erdélyi János*. Bp. *1981*. Akadémiai K. 214 pp.

FÁBRY, ZOLTÁN

KOVÁCS Győző: *Fábry Zoltán*. Bp. *1971*, Magvető K. 185 pp.
Fábry Zoltán kortársai szemével [Zoltán Fábry as seen by his contemporaries]. Ed. DUBA Gyula. Bratislava *1973*, Madách. 509 pp.
CSANDA Sándor: *Fábry Zoltán*. Bratislava *1980*, Madách. 177 pp.

FÁY, ANDRÁS

BADICS Ferenc: *Fáy András életrajza* [Biography of András Fáy]. Bp. *1890*, Magyar Tudományos Akadémia. VIII, 671 pp.
ERDÉLYI Pál: *Fáy András élete és művei* [The life and work of András Fáy]. Bp. *1890*, 352 pp.
Cf.: SZAUDER József: *Az estve és Az álom* (pp. 523.)

FAZEKAS, MIHÁLY

JULOW Viktor: *Fazekas Mihály*. 2nd rev. enl. ed. Bp. *1982*, Szépirodalmi K. 514 p.

FÜST, MILÁN

SOMLYÓ György: *Füst Milán. Emlékezés és tanulmány* [Milán Füst. Recollections and studies]. Bp. *1969*, Szépirodalmi K. 246 pp.
FÓNAGY Iván: *Öregség — dallamfejtés* [Old age—an analysis of melody]. Bp. *1974*, Akadémiai K. 220 pp. (with a record).
Cf.: BORI Imre: *Az avantgarde apostolai* (pp. 515.)
KIS PINTÉR Imre: *Helyzetjelentés* (pp. 521.)

GARAY, JÁNOS

FERENCZY József: *Garay János életrajza* [Biography of János Garay]. Bp. *1883*. 237 pp.

GÁRDONYI, GÉZA

KISPÉTER András: *Gárdonyi Géza*. Bp. *1970*, Gondolat K. 229 pp.
Z. SZALAI Sándor: *Gárdonyi műhelyében* [In the workshop of Gárdonyi]. Bp. *1970*, Magvető K. 327 pp.
Gárdonyi-emlékülés. Tudományos ülés az író halálának 50. évfordulóján. *1972*. okt. 22-én [Gárdonyi memorial session. Symposium on the 50th anniversary of the writer's death]. Eger *1973*. 142 pp.
Z. SZALAI Sándor: *Gárdonyi Géza alkotásai és vallomásai tükrében* [Géza Gárdonyi as reflected in his works and confessions]. Bp. *1977*, Szépirodalmi K. 289 pp.
Cf.: NAGY Péter: *Drámai arcélek* (pp. 522.)
AMBRUS, Viktor C.: *To the Reader.* (Foreword.) In: *Gárdonyi Géza: Slave of the Huns* (pp. 556.)

GELLÉRI, ANDOR ENDRE

VARGHA Kálmán: *Gelléri Andor Endre alkotásai és vallomásai tükrében* [Endre Andor Gelléri as reflected in his works and confessions]. Bp. *1973*, Szépirodalmi K. 295 pp.
NAGY SZ. Péter: *Az idilltől az abszurdig*. Gelléri Andor Endre pályaképe [From the idyllic to the absurd. The career of Endre Andor Gelléri]. Bp. *1981*, Akadémiai K. 111 pp.

GOZSDU, ELEK

LUKÁCSY Sándor: Gozsdu Elek (1848–1919). [Intr.]. In: *Gozsdu Elek: Nemes rozsda*. Válogatott elbeszélések [Selected short stories]. Bp. *1955*, Szépirodalmi K. pp. 5–19.
ÁCS Margit: Egy századvégi "magyar Tantulus" [A fin-de-siècle "Hungarian Tantulus"]. [Afterw.] In: *Gozsdu Elek: Köd* [Fog]. Bp. *1969*, Szépirodalmi K. pp. 565–580.

GVADÁNYI, JÓZSEF

SZÉCHY Károly: *Gróf Gvadányi József. 1725–1801* [Count József Gvadányi. 1725–1801]. Bp. *1894*, Magyar Történelmi Társulat. 320 pp.

CSORBA Zoltán: *Gvadányi József élete és munkái* [The life and work of József Gvadányi]. Miskolc *1975*. 78 pp.

JULOW Viktor: *Gvadányi József.* [Intr.] In: *Gvadányi József: Egy falusi nótáriusnak budai utazása. — Rontó Pál.* Bp. *1975*. Szépirodalmi K. pp. 5–71.

GYÖNGYÖSI, ISTVÁN

BADICS Ferenc: *Gyöngyösi István élete és költészete* [Life and poetry of István Gyöngyösi]. Bp. *1939*. 264 pp.

AGÁRDI Péter: *Rendiség és esztétikum. Gyöngyösi István költői világképe* [Feudalism and the aesthetic quality. The poetic vision of István Gyöngyösi]. Bp. *1972*, Akadémiai K. 238 pp.

GYULAI, PÁL

PAPP Ferenc: *Gyulai Pál.* Vols. 1–2. Bp. *1935–1941*, Magyar Tudományos Akadémia. 602, 728 pp.

KOVÁCS Kálmán: *Fejezetek a magyar kritika történetéből. Gyulai Pál irodalmi elveinek kialakulása, 1850–1860* [Chapters from the history of Hungarian criticism. The formation of Pál Gyulai's literary principles, 1850–1860]. Bp. *1963*, Akadémiai K. 304 pp.

Cf.: KOMLÓS Aladár: *Gyulaitól a marxista kritikáig* (pp. 517.)
SOMOGYI Sándor: *Gyulai és kortársai* (pp. 518.)

HELTAI, GÁSPÁR

BORBÉLY István: *Heltai Gáspár.* Bp. *1907*. 79 pp.

KŐSZEGHY Péter: *Heltai Gáspárról* [On Gáspár Heltai]. [Afterw.] In: *Háló. Válogatás Heltai Gáspár műveiből* [Net. Selected works of Gáspár Heltai]. Bp. *1979*, Magvető K. pp. 407-436.

HERCZEG, FERENC

HORVÁTH János: *Herczeg Ferenc.* Bp. *1925*. Pallas. 28 pp. — 1962².

Cf.: BARTA János: *Költők és írók* (pp. 520.)
NAGY Péter: *Drámai arcélek* (pp. 522.)

HORVÁTH, JÁNOS

Horváth Jánosról. Méltatások—Emlékezések [On János Horváth. Appraisals—Recollections]. Ed. PAIS Dezső. Bp. *1958*. 31 pp.

Cf.: GYERGYAI Albert: *A Nyugat árnyékában* (pp. 520.)
KERESZTURY Dezső: *Örökség* (pp. 521.)
NÉMETH G. Béla: *Küllő és kerék* (pp. 522.)
TÓTH Dezső: *Élő hagyomány — élő irodalom* (pp. 523.)

IGNOTUS (VEIGELSBERG, HUGO)

Cf.: BÓKA László: *Válogatott tanulmányok* (pp. 520.)
KOMLÓS Aladár: *Vereckétől Dévényig* (pp. 521.)

ILLÉS, BÉLA

DIÓSZEGI András: *Illés Béla alkotásai és vallomásai tükrében* [Béla Illés as reflected in his works and confessions]. Bp. *1966*, Szépirodalmi K. 201 pp.

ILLÉS, ENDRE

DERSI Tamás: *Illés Endre.* Bp. *1977*, Akadémiai K. 243 pp.

Cf.: GYERGYAI Albert: *Késői tallózás* (pp. 520.)

ILLYÉS, GYULA

GARA László: *Az ismeretlen Illyés* [Illyés the unknown]. Washington *1965*, Occidental Press. 178 pp.

Gyula Illyés. Choix de textes. Bibliographie, portraits, documents. Avant-propos par André FRENAUD. Présentation par Ladislas GARA. Paris *1966*, Seghers. 192 pp. (Poètes d'aujourd'hui 145)

A Tribute to Gyula Illyés. Ed. Thomas KABDEBO, Paul TABORI. Washington *1968*, Occidental Press. 148 pp.

Illyés Gyula. Tanulmányok a költőről [Gyula Illyés. Essays on the poet]. Ed. ILLÉS László. Bp. *1972* [Petőfi Irodalmi Múzeum — NIP]. 175 pp.

FODOR Ilona: *Szembesítés. Illyés Gyula életútja Párizsig* [Confrontation. Gyula Illyés's life until the Paris stay]. Bp. *1975*, Magvető K. 401 pp.

Cf.: BATA Imre: *Képek és vonulatok* (pp. 520.)
BÉLÁDI Miklós: *Érintkezési pontok* (pp. 520.)
KENYERES Zoltán: *Gondolkodó irodalom* (pp. 521)
KABDEBO, Thomas: Forew. In: *Illyés, Gyula: Selected Poems* (pp. 556.)

JANUS PANNONIUS

HUSZTI József: *Janus Pannonius*. Pécs *1931*. XIV, 448 pp.

Janus Pannonius. Tanulmányok [Studies]. Ed. KARDOS Tibor, V. KOVÁCS Sándor. Bp. *1975*, Akadémiai K. 600 pp.

CSAPODI Csaba: *A Janus Pannonius-szöveghagyomány* [Janus Pannonius's textual legacy]. Bp. *1981*, Akadémiai K. 108 pp.

Cf.: GERÉZDI Rabán: *Janus Pannoniustól Balassi Bálintig* (pp. 516.)

KARDOS Tibor: *Élő humanizmus* (pp. 521.)

JÓKAI, MÓR

SŐTÉR István: *Jókai Mór* [Bp. *1941*]. 178 pp.

NAGY Miklós: *Jókai. A regényíró útja 1868-ig* [Mór Jókai. The career of the novelist until 1868]. Bp. *1968*. Szépirodalmi K. 374 pp.

LENGYEL Dénes: *Jókai Mór*. 2nd ed. Bp. *1970*, Gondolat K. 199 pp.

NAGY Miklós: *Jókai Mór alkotásai és vallomásai tükrében* [Mór Jókai as reflected in his works and confessions]. Bp. *1975*, Szépirodalmi K. 261 pp.

Cf.: HEGEDŰS Géza: Intr. In: *Jókai, Mór: The Dark Diamonds* (pp. 556.)

JÓSIKA, MIKLÓS

DÉZSI Lajos: *Báró Jósika Miklós. 1794–1865* [Baron Miklós Jósika. 1794–1865]. Bp. *1916*, Magyar Történeti Társulat. 451 pp.

JÓZSEF, ATTILA

NÉMETH Andor: *József Attila*. Bp. *1942*. 222 pp.

Attila József. Sa vie, son œuvre. Avec une suite de poèmes adaptés du hongrois par Jean Rousselot d'après les traductions de Ladislas GARA. Paris *1958*, Médianes. 119 pp. (Les nouveaux cahiers de jeunesse.)

GYERTYÁN Ervin: *Költőnk és kora. József Attila költészete és esztétikája* [The poet and his age. Poetry and aesthetics of Attila József]. Bp. *1963*, Szépirodalmi K. 305 pp.

SZABOLCSI Miklós: *Fiatal életek indulója. József Attila pályakezdése* [The march of young lives. The beginning of Attila József's career]. Bp. *1963*, Akadémiai K. 634 pp.

SZABOLCSI Miklós: *A verselemzés kérdéseihez. József Attila: Eszmélet* [Some questions of poetry analysis. Attila József: Consciousness]. Bp. *1968*, Akadémiai K. 123 pp.

TÖRÖK Gábor: *A líra: logika. József Attila költői nyelve* [Poetry is logic. The poetic language of Attila József]. Bp. *1968*, Magvető K.—Tiszatáj. 292 pp.

BALOGH László: *József Attila*. 2nd ed. Bp. *1970*, Gondolat K. 220 pp.

GYERTYÁN Ervin: *József Attila alkotásai és vallomásai tükrében* [Attila József as reflected in his works and confessions]. 2nd ed. Bp. *1970*, Szépirodalmi K. 204 pp.

LEVENDEL Júlia–HORGAS Béla: *A szellem és a szerelem. (József Attila világképe)* [Intellect and love. The world view of Attila József]. Bp. *1970*, Gondolat K. 185 pp.

SZILÁGYI Péter: *József Attila időmértékes verselése*. [Metrical versification of Attila József]. Bp. *1971*, Akadémiai K. 317 pp.

TÖRÖK Gábor: *Költői rébuszok* [Poetic puzzles]. Bp. *1974*, Magvető K. 289 pp.

M. PÁSZTOR József: *József Attila műhelyei. Lapok, szellemi és irodalmi csoportosulások* [Attila József's workshops. Periodicals, intellectual and literary groups]. Bp. *1975*, Kossuth K. 351 pp.

TÖRÖK Gábor: *József Attila-kommentárok* [Comments on Attila József]. Bp. *1976*, Gondolat K. 388 pp.

SZABOLCSI Miklós: *Érik a fény. József Attila élete és pályája 1923–1927* [Mellowing light. Life and career of Attila József 1923–1927]. Bp. *1977*, Akadémiai K. 801 pp.

József Attila útjain. Tanulmányok [On the road with Attila József. Studies]. Ed. SZABOLCSI Miklós and ERDŐDY Edit. Bp. *1980*, Kossuth K. 463 pp.

SZÉLES Klára: *"... és minden szervem óra."* József Attila költői motívumrendszeréről ["... and all my organs clocks." On the system of motifs in Attila József's poetry]. Bp. *1980*, Magvető K. 203 pp.

SZABOLCSI Miklós: *Attila József*. Leben und Werk. Berlin *1981*, Akademie-Verlag. 199 pp.

Cf.: BÓKA László: *Válogatott tanulmányok* (pp. 520.)

BORI Imre: *Eszmék és látomások* (pp. 520.)
RÉVAI József: *Válogatott irodalmi tanulmányok* (pp. 523.)
SZABOLCSI Miklós: *Költészet és korszerűség* (pp. 523.)
SZABOLCSI Miklós: *Változó világ — szocialista társadalom* (pp. 523.)
GÖMÖRI, George: Intr. In.: *József Attila: Selected Poems and Texts* (pp. 557.)
NYERGES, Anton N.: Intr. In.: *[Poems of] Attila József* (pp. 557.)

JUHÁSZ, FERENC

BORI Imre: *Két költő* (Juhász Ferenc és Nagy László) [Two poets. Ferenc Juhász and László Nagy]. Novi Sad 1967, Forum. 286 pp.
Cf.: BATA Imre: *Képek és vonulatok* (pp. 520.)
BÉLÁDI Miklós: *Érintkezési pontok* (pp. 520.)
BODNÁR György: *Törvénykeresők* (pp. 520.)
DIÓSZEGI András: *Megmozdult világban* (pp. 520.)
ILLÉS Lajos: *Kezdet és kibontakozás* (pp. 521.)
KENYERES Zoltán: *Gondolkodó irodalom* (pp. 521.)
KISS Ferenc: *Művek közelről* (pp. 521.)
NAGY Péter: *Rosta* (pp. 522.)
SZABOLCSI Miklós: *Költészet és korszerűség* (pp. 523.)
SZABOLCSI Miklós: *Változó világ — szocialista irodalom* (pp. 523.)
McROBBIE, Kenneth: Intr. In: *Juhász, Ferenc: The Boy Changed into a Stag* (pp. 557.)
WEVILL, David: Intr. In: *Selected Poems [of] Sándor Weöres [and of] Ferenc Juhász* (pp. 557.)

JUHÁSZ, GYULA

KISPÉTER András: *Juhász Gyula.* Bp. 1956, Művelt Nép. 247 pp.
Juhász Gyula 1883–1937. Emlékkönyv [A memorial volume]. Ed. PAKU Imre. Bp. 1962, Magvető K. 719 pp.
PÉTER László: *Juhász Gyula a forradalmakban* [Gyula Juhász and the revolutions]. Bp. 1965, Akadémiai K. 340 pp.
VARGHA Kálmán: *Juhász Gyula.* Bp. 1968, Gondolat K. 191 pp.

Juhász Gyula költői nyelvének szótára [A dictionary of Gyula Juhász's poetical language]. Ed. BENKŐ László. Bp. 1972, Akadémiai K. 930 pp.
Cf.: KISS Ferenc: *A beérkezés küszöbén. Babits, Juhász és Kosztolányi ifjúkori barátsága* (pp. 535.)
SZABOLCSI Miklós: *Elődök és kortársak* (pp. 523.)
TOLNAI Gábor: *Tanulmányok* (pp. 523.)

KAFFKA, MARGIT

RADNÓTI Miklós: *Kaffka Margit művészi fejlődése* [The artistic development of Margit Kaffka]. 2nd ed. Szeged, 1934. 104 pp.
Cf.: BODNÁR György: *Törvénykeresők* (pp. 520.)
RÓNAY György: *A nagy nemzedék* (pp. 518.)

KARINTHY, FRIGYES

SZALAY Károly: *Karinthy Frigyes.* Bp. 1961, Gondolat K. 365 pp.
HALÁSZ László: *Karinthy Frigyes alkotásai és vallomásai tükrében* [Frigyes Karinthy as reflected in his works and confessions]. Bp. 1972, Szépirodalmi K. 267 pp.
Cf.: ILLÉS Endre: Forew.: Dream and reality. In: *Karinthy, Frigyes: Please Sir!* (pp. 557.)
SZALAY Károly: Frigyes Karinthy (1887–1938). [Afterw.] In: *Karinthy, Frigyes: Grave and Gay* (pp. 557.)
TABORI, Paul: Intr. In: *Karinthy, Frigyes: Voyage to Faremido—Capillaria* (pp. 557.)

KÁRMÁN, JÓZSEF

GÁLOS Rezső: *Kármán József.* Bp. 1954, Művelt Nép. 193 pp.
Cf.: SINKÓ Ervin: *Magyar irodalom* (pp. 523.)

KASSÁK, LAJOS

BORI Imre–KÖRNER Éva: *Kassák irodalma és festészete* [Kassák's literary works and paintings]. Bp. 1967, Magvető K. 234 pp.
RÓNAY György: *Kassák Lajos alkotásai és vallomásai tükrében* [Lajos Kassák as reflected in his works and confessions]. Bp. 1971, Szépirodalmi K. 282 pp.

PAŠIAKOVÁ, Jaroslava: *Lajos Kassák. Vývojové problémy a tendencie maďarskej avantgardy*. Bratislava *1973*. Univerzita Komenského. 244 pp. [Summaries in Russian and German].

Kortársak Kassák Lajosról [Contemporaries on Lajos Kassák]. Ed. ILLÉS Ilona, TAXNER Ernő. Bp. *1975*, Petőfi Irodalmi Múzeum—NIP. 255 pp.

Cf.: BÉLÁDI Miklós: *Érintkezési pontok* (pp. 520.)
BORI Imre: *Az avantgard apostolai* (pp. 515.)
Formateremtő elvek a költői alkotásban. Ed. HANKISS Elemér (pp. 525.)
JORDÁKY Lajos: *A szocialista irodalom útján* (pp. 521.)

KATONA, JÓZSEF

NÉMETH Antal: *Bánk bán (Katona József drámája) száz éve a színpadon* [Ban Bánk—József Katona's dramatic work—on stage for a hundred years]. Bp. *1935*. 279 pp.

WALDAPFEL József: *Katona József* [Bp. *1942*.] 200 pp.

GERSHKOVITCH, A[leksandr]: Jozhef Katona. Leningárad *1960*, Izd. „Nauka". 120 pp.

VÁZSONYI Gábor: *Grillparzers und Katonas Bearbeitungen des Bancbanus-Stoffes und ihre Vorläufer*. Diss. [Fribourg *1973*]. Fribourg Univ. 166 pp.

OROSZ László: *Katona József*. Bp. *1974*, Gondolat K. 239 pp.

PÁNDI Pál: *Bánk bán-kommentárok* [Ban Bánk—interpretations]. Vols. 1-2 .Bp. *1980*, Akadémiai K. 364, 254 pp.

KAZINCZY, FERENC

VÁCZY János: *Kazinczy Ferenc és kora* [Ferenc Kazinczy and his age]. Bp. *1915*, Magyar Tudományos Akadémia. 639 pp.

CZEIZEL János: *Kazinczy Ferenc élete és működése*. [Life and work of Ferenc Kazinczy]. Vol. 1. Bp. *1930*. 296 pp.

NÉGYESY László: *Kazinczy pályája* [Kazinczy's career]. Bp. *1931*, Magyar Tudományos Akadémia. 170 pp.

SZAUDER József: Kazinczy Ferenc élete és pályája [Life and career of Ferenc Kazinczy]. [Intr.] In: *Kazinczy Ferenc válogatott művei* [Selected works of Ferenc Kazinczy]. Vol. 1. Bp. *1960*, Szépirodalmi K. pp. VII-CXXVII.

MARTINS, Eva: *Studien zur Frage der linguistischen Interferenz*. Lehnprägungen in der Sprache von Franz von Kazinczy (1759-1831). Stockholm *1970*, Almqvist och Wiksell. 373 pp. (Acta Universitatis Stockholmiensis)

Cf.: SINKÓ Ervin: *Magyar irodalom* (pp. 523.)

KEMÉNY, ZSIGMOND

PAPP Ferenc: *Báró Kemény Zsigmond* [Baron Zsigmond Kemény]. Vols. 1-2. Bp. *1922-1923*. Magyar Tudományos Akadémia. 454, 585 pp.

NAGY Miklós: *Kemény Zsigmond*. Bp. *1972*, Gondolat K. 258 pp.

VERESS Dániel: *Szerettem a sötétet és szélzúgást*. Kemény Zsigmond élete és műve [I loved darkness and the roaring of wind. Life and work of Zsigmond Kemény]. Kolozsvár–Napoca *1978*, Dacia. 206 pp.

Cf.: MARTINKÓ András: *Teremtő idők* (pp. 522.)

KISFALUDY, KÁROLY

HORVÁTH János: *Kisfaludy Károly és íróbarátai* [Károly Kisfaludy and his writer friends]. Bp. *1955*, Művelt Nép K. 182 pp.

KISFALUDY, SÁNDOR

FENYŐ István: *Kisfaludy Sándor*. Bp. *1961*, Akadémiai K. 446 pp.

KISS, JÓZSEF

RUBINYI Mózes: *Kiss József élete és munkássága* [Life and work of József Kiss]. Bp. *1926*. 160 pp.

Cf.: DERSI Tamás: *Századvégi üzenet* (pp. 527.)

KODOLÁNYI, JÁNOS

TÜSKÉS Tibor: *Kodolányi János*. Bp. *1974*, Magvető K. 276 pp.

Cf.: BATA Imre: *Képek és vonulatok* (pp. 520.)
BODNÁR György: *Törvénykeresők* (pp. 520.)

KÖLCSEY, FERENC

JANCSÓ Benedek: *Kölcsey Ferenc élete és művei* [Life and work of Ferenc Kölcsey]. Bp. *1885*. 437 pp.

SZAUDER József: *Kölcsey Ferenc*. Bp. *1955*, Művelt Nép K. 263 pp.

ROHONYI Zoltán: *Kölcsey Ferenc életműve* [Lifework of Ferenc Kölcsey]. Kolozsvár–Napoca *1975*, Dacia. 200 pp.
Cf.: SZAUDER József: *Az estve és Az álom* (pp. 523.)

KOMJÁT, ALADÁR

KOMJÁT Irén: *Egy költői életmű gyökerei. Komját Aladár verseinek keletkezéstörténete* [Roots of a poetic œuvre. How Aladár Komját's poems were conceived]. Afterw.: SŐTÉR István. Bp. *1981*, Szépirodalmi K. 251 pp.
Cf.: KIRÁLY István: *Irodalom és társadalom* (pp. 521.)
WALDAPFEL József: *Szocialista kultúra és irodalmi örökség* (pp. 524.)

KOMJÁTHY, JENŐ

SIKABONYI Antal: *Komjáthy Jenő.* Bp. *1909.* 207 pp.
RIEDL Frigyes: *Vajda, Reviczky, Komjáthy.* Bp. *[1932?]* 140 pp.
Cf.: KOMLÓS Aladár: *Vereckétől Dévényig* (pp. 521.)

KOSSUTH, LAJOS

KOSÁRY Domokos: *Kossuth Lajos a reformkorban* [Lajos Kossuth in the Reform Age]. Bp. *1946.* 395 pp.
CUSHING, G. F.: *Széchenyi, Kossuth and National Classicism in Hungarian Literature* (Diss.) London *1952*, Univ. of London, School of Slavonic and East European Studies. x, 233 pp.
Emlékkönyv Kossuth Lajos születésének 150. évfordulójára [Memorial volume on the 150th anniversary of the birth of Lajos Kossuth]. Vols. 1–2. Bp. *1952*, Magyar Történelmi Társulat. 453, 488 pp.
CSABAI Tibor: *Kossuth Lajos és az irodalom.* [Lajos Kossuth and literature]. Bp. *1961*, Gondolat K. 317 pp.
KOVÁTS Endre: *A Kossuth-emigráció és az európai szabadságmozgalmak* [The Kossuth Emigration and the European Freedom Movements]. Bp. *1969*, Akadémiai K. 502 pp.

KOSZTOLÁNYI, DEZSŐ

KOSZTOLÁNYI Dezsőné: *Kosztolányi Dezső.* Bp. *1938.* 366 pp.
BENCZE Lóránt: *Pázmány Péter és Kosztolányi Dezső prózastílusa* [The prose style of Péter Pázmány and Dezső Kosztolányi]. Bp. *1973*, Eötvös Loránd Tudományegyetem. 103 pp.
RÓNAY László: *Kosztolányi Dezső.* Bp. 1977, Gondolat K. 307 pp.
KISS Ferenc: *Az érett Kosztolányi* [The mature Kosztolányi]. Bp. *1979*, Akadémiai K. 607 pp.
Cf.: BÓKA László: *Válogatott tanulmányok* (pp. 520.)
GYERGYAI Albert: *Késői tallózás* (pp. 520.)
KISS Ferenc: *A beérkezés küszöbén. Babits, Juhász és Kosztolányi ifjúkori barátsága* (pp. 535.)
A novellaelemzés új módszerei. Ed. HANKISS Elemér (pp. 525.)
RÁBA György: *A szép hűtlenek* (pp. 525.)
RÉZ Pál: *Kulcsok és kérdőjelek* (pp. 523.)
RÓNAY György: *A nagy nemzedék* (pp. 518.)
SZAUDER József: *A romantika útján* (pp. 523.)

KRÚDY, GYULA

Krúdy világa [Krúdy's world]. Ed. TÓBIÁS Áron. Bp. *1964.* 729 pp.
SZABÓ Ede: *Krúdy Gyula alkotásai és vallomásai tükrében* [Gyula Krúdy as reflected in his works and confessions]. Bp. 1970, Szépirodalmi K. 266 pp.
BORI Imre: *Krúdy Gyula.* Újvidék *1978*, Forum. 260 p.
Cf.: *A novellaelemzés új módszerei.* Ed. HANKISS Elemér. (pp. 525.)
SZAUDER József: *A romantika útján* (pp. 523.)
TABORI, Paul: Intr. In: *Krúdy, Gyula: The Crimson Coach* (pp. 557.)

LENGYEL, JÓZSEF

SZABÓ József: *Lengyel József alkotásai és vallomásai tükrében* [József Lengyel as reflected in his works and confessions]. Bp. *1966*, Szépirodalmi K. 178 pp.
Cf.: BÉLÁDI Miklós: *Érintkezési pontok* (pp. 520.)
DIÓSZEGI András: *Megmozdult világban* (pp. 520.)

LENGYEL, MENYHÉRT

Cf.: NAGY Péter: *Drámai arcélek* (pp. 522.)

LUKÁCS, GYÖRGY

Festschrift zum achtzigsten Geburtstag von Georg

Lukács. Hrsg. von Frank BENSELER. Neuwied–Berlin 1965, Luchterhand. 709 pp.

LICHTHEIM, George: *George Lukács.* New York 1970, Viking Press. 146 pp. — New ed.: München 1971.

Georg Lukács. The Man, his Work and his Ideas. Ed. by G. H. R. PARKINSON. London 1970, Weidenfeld and Nicholson. 254 pp. (Reading University studies on contemporary Europe 4.)

BOURDET, Yvon: *Figures de Lukacs.* Paris 1972, Éd. Anthropos. 220 pp.

"In memoriam György Lukács (1885–1971)." In: *The New Hungarian Quarterly* (Bp.) (Ed. Iván BOLDIZSÁR) Vol. XIII. No 47. Autumn 1972. 224 pp. (special edtion.)

"Georg Lukács." In: *Text + Kritik. Zeitschrift für Literatur.* Hrsg. H. L. ARNOLD. Heft 39/40. München, Oktober 1973, Richard Boorberg Verlag. 90 pp. (special edtion.)

HERMANN István: *Lukács György gondolatvilága. Tanulmány a XX. század emberi lehetőségeiről* [George Lukács—his world of ideas. An essay on human potentialities in the 20th century]. Bp. 1974, Magvető K. 415 pp.

Dialog und Kontroverse mit Georg Lukács. Der Methodenstreit deutscher sozialistischer Schriftsteller. Hrsg. Werner MITTENZWEI. Leipzig 1975, Reclam. 472 pp.

HELLENBART, Gyula: *Georg Lukács und die ungarische Literatur.* Diss. Univ. Hamburg 1975. 205 pp.

APITZSCH, Ursula: *Gesellschaftstheorie und Ästhetik bei Georg Lukács bis 1933.* Stuttgart 1977. 206 pp. (Problemata Fromann–Holzboog. 50.)

HERMANN István: *Die Gedankenwelt von Georg Lukács.* Bp. 1978, Akadémiai K. 402 pp.

"Lukács." = *Europe,* avril 1979. 193 pp. (special edition).

Cf.: KENYERES Zoltán: *Gondolkodó irodalom* (pp. 521.)

MADÁCH, IMRE

VOINOVICH Géza: *Madách Imre és Az ember tragédiája* [Imre Madách and The Tragedy of Man]. Bp. 2nd ed. 1922. 590 pp.

NÉMETH Antal: *"Az ember tragédiája" a színpadon.* [The Tragedy of Man on stage]. Bp. 1933. 159 pp.

BARTA János: *Madách Imre.* [Bp. 1942.] 187 pp.

SŐTÉR István: *Álom a történelemről. Madách Imre és Az ember tragédiája* [A dream about history. Imre Madách and The Tragedy of Man]. Bp. 1965, Akadémiai K. 101 pp. — New ed.: 1969.

KÁNTOR Lajos: *Százéves harc "Az ember tragédiájá"-ért* [A hundred years' fight for The Tragedy of Man]. Bp. 1966, Akadémiai K. 143 pp.

MEZEI József: *Madách. Az élet értelme. Monográfia.* [Madách. The sense of Life. A monograph]. Bp. 1977, Magvető K. 455 pp.

Madách-tanulmányok [Studies on Madách]. Ed. HORVÁTH Károly. Bp. 1978, Akadémiai K. 505 pp.

Cf.: NÉMETH G. Béla: *Létharc és nemzetiség* (pp. 522.)

SŐTÉR István: *Az ember és műve* (pp. 523.)

BENEDEK Marcell: Intr. In: *Madách, Imre: The Tragedy of Man* (1957[3], 1960[4], (pp. 558.)

HEVESI Sándor: Intr. In: *Madách, Imre: The Tragedy of Man* (1933) (pp. 558.)

HORNE, J. C. W.: Translator's intr. In: *Madách, Imre: The Tragedy of Man* (1963, 1973[5]) (pp. 558.)

KUNCZ, E. F.: Intr. In: *Madách, Imre: The Tragedy of Man* (1956) (pp. 558.)

MIKES, KELEMEN

GÁLOS Rezső: *Mikes Kelemen.* Bp. 1954, Művelt Nép. 139 pp.

HOPP Lajos: *Mikes és világa* [Mikes and his world]. Bucharest 1973, Kriterion. 559 pp. [Summaries in Rumanian and French].

Cf.: BARTA János: *Költők és írók* (pp. 520.)

MERVYN, Jones: *Five Hungarian Writers* (pp. 522.)

MIKSZÁTH, KÁLMÁN

RUBINYI Mózes: *Mikszáth Kálmán élete és művei. Az összes művek bibliográfiájával* [The life and works of Kálmán Mikszáth. With a bibliography of the complete works]. Bp. 1917, Révai. 129 pp.

RIEDL Frigyes: *Mikszáth Kálmán.* Ed. SOMOS Jenő [Bp. 1940.] 118 pp.

SCHÖPFLIN Aladár: *Mikszáth Kálmán* [Bp. *1941*] Franklin. 156 pp.

KIRÁLY István: *Mikszáth Kálmán*. 2nd ed. *1960*, Szépirodalmi K. 487 pp.

Mikszáth Kálmán. 1847–1910. Ed. BISZTRAY Gyula. Bp. *1961*, Magyar Helikon. 199 pp.

KOZMA Dezső: *Mikszáth Kálmán. Kismonográfia* [A short treatise]. Kolozsvár–Napoca *1977*, Dacia. 181 pp.

SCHEER, C. Steven: *Kálmán Mikszáth*. Boston *1977*, Twayne Publishers. 161 pp. (Twayne's World Authors Series 462. Hungary.)

Cf.: BARTA János: *Költők és írók* (pp. 520.)
KOVÁCS Kálmán: *Eszmék és irodalom* (pp. 521.)
SŐTÉR István: *Romantika és realizmus* (pp. 523.)

MOLNÁR, FERENC

VÉCSEI Irén: *Molnár Ferenc*. Bp. *1966*, Gondolat K. 150 pp.

GYÖRGYEY, Clara: *Ferenc Molnár*. Boston *1980*, Twayne Publishers. 196 pp. (Twayne's World Authors Series 574. Hungary.)

Cf.: NAGY Péter: *Drámai arcélek* (pp. 522.)
GLAZER, Benjamin F.: Intr. In: *Molnár, Ferenc: Liliom* (pp. 558.)
HELBURN, Therese: Forew.: Notes on the Theater Guild production of "The Guardsman". In: *Molnár, Ferenc: The Guardsman* (pp. 558.)
RITTENBERG, Louis: Ferenc Molnár. Intr. In: *All the Plays of Ferenc Molnár* (pp. 558.)
RITTENBERG, Louis: Ferenc Molnár. A portrait. [Intr.] In: *The Plays of Ferenc Molnár* (pp. 558.)

MÓRA, FERENC

FÖLDES Anna: *Móra Ferenc*. Bp. *1958*, Bibliotheca. 322 pp.

TÓTH Béla: *Móra Ferenc betűösvényein* [Exploring Ferenc Móra's works]. Bp. *1979*, Szeged Megyei Városi Tanács. 422 pp.

Cf.: FÖLDES Anna: Intr. In: *Móra, Ferenc: The Gold Coffin* (pp. 558.)

MÓRICZ, ZSIGMOND

FÉJA Géza: *Móricz Zsigmond*. [Bp. *1939*.] 188 pp.

NÉMETH László: *Móricz Zsigmond*. Bp. *1943*, 111 pp.

Kortársak Móricz Zsigmondról [Contemporaries on Zsigmond Móricz]. (Vol. 1.) Tanulmányok és kritikák 1900–1919 [Essays and reviews, 1900–1919]. Ed.: VARGHA Kálmán. Bp. *1958*, Akadémiai K. 500 pp.

CZINE Mihály: *Móricz Zsigmond útja a forradalmakig* [Zsigmond Móricz's road to the revolutions]. Bp. *1960*, Magvető K. 611 p.

VARGHA Kálmán: *Móricz Zsigmond és az irodalom* [Zsigmond Móricz and literature]. Bp. *1962*, Akadémiai K. 402. pp.

CZINE Mihály: *Móricz Zsigmond*. 2nd ed. Bp. *1970*, Gondolat K. 189 pp.

VARGHA Kálmán: *Móricz Zsigmond alkotásai és vallomásai tükrében* [Zsigmond Móricz as reflected in his works and confessions]. 2nd ed. *1971*, Szépirodalmi K. 213 pp.

NAGY Péter: *Móricz Zsigmond*. 3rd rev. ed. Bp. *1975*, Szépirodalmi K. 622 pp.

Móricz Zsigmond közöttünk [Zsigmond Móricz among us]. Ed. KÁNTOR Lajos. Bucharest *1979*, Kriterion K. 285 pp.

SCHÖPFLIN Aladár: *Móricz Zsigmondról* [On Zsigmond Móricz]. Ed. and intr.: RÉZ Pál. Bp. *1979*, Szépirodalmi K. 310 pp.

Cf.: *A novellaelemzés új módszerei*. Ed. HANKISS Elemér (pp. 525.)
NAGY Péter: *Drámai arcélek* (pp. 522.)
NAGY Péter: Intr. In: *Móricz Zsigmond: Be Faithful unto Death* (pp. 559.)

NAGY, LAJOS

KARDOS Pál: *Nagy Lajos élete és művei* [The life and work of Lajos Nagy]. Bp. *1958*, Bibliotheca. 416 pp.

KÓNYA Judit: *Nagy Lajos*. Bp. *1980*, Szépirodalmi K. 229 pp.

TARJÁN Tamás: *Nagy Lajos*. Bp. *1980*, Gondolat K. 254 pp.

Cf.: ILLÉS László: *Józanság és szenvedély* (pp. 521.)
A novellaelemzés új módszerei. Ed. HANKISS Elemér (pp. 525.)

NAGY, LÁSZLÓ

BORI Imre: *Két költő* (Juhász Ferenc, Nagy László)

[Two poets. Ferenc Juhász, László Nagy]. Novi Sad *1967*, Forum. 286 pp.
Cf.: Bata Imre: *Képek és vonulatok* (pp. 520.)
Illés Lajos: *Kezdet és kibontakozás* (pp. 521.)
Kis Pintér Imre: *Helyzetjelentés* (pp. 521.)
Kiss Ferenc: *Művek közelről* (pp. 521.)
Gömöri, George: Forew. In: *Nagy, László: Love of the Scorching Wind* (pp. 559.)

NÉMETH, LÁSZLÓ

Vekerdi László: *Németh László alkotásai és vallomásai tükrében* [László Németh as reflected in his works and confessions]. Bp. *1970*, Szépirodalmi K. 387 pp.
Grezsa Ferenc: *Németh László vásárhelyi korszaka* [The Vásárhely period of László Németh]. Bp. *1979*, Szépirodalmi K. 415 pp.
Cf.: Bata Imre: *Képek és vonulatok* (pp. 520.)
Béládi Miklós: *Érintkezési pontok* (pp. 520.)
Bori Imre: *Eszmék és látomások* (pp. 520.)

PAP, KÁROLY

Szabó József: [Bevezető]. In: *Pap, Károly: B. városban történt.* Összegyűjtött elbeszélések [Intr.]. In: [Pap, Károly: It all happened in the town of B. Collected short stories]. Ed.: Szabó József. Vol. 1. Bp. *1964*, Szépirodalmi K. pp. 5–41.
Lichtmann Tamás: *Pap Károly*. Bp. *1979*, Akadémiai K. 201 pp.
Cf.: Keresztury Dezső: *Örökség* (pp. 521.)
Németh László: *Két nemzedék* (pp. 522.)
Réz Pál: *Kulcsok és kérdőjelek* (pp. 523.)

PÁZMÁNY, PÉTER

Fraknói Vilmos: *Pázmány Péter. 1570–1637.* Bp. *1886*, Franklin–Társulat. 344 pp.
Sík Sándor: *Pázmány. Az ember és az író* [Pázmány. Man and writer]. Bp. *1939*. 449 pp.
Őry Miklós: *Pázmány Péter tanulmányi évei* [The student years of Péter Pázmány]. Eisenstadt *1970*, Prugg Verlag. 184 pp.
Bitskey István: *Humanista erudíció és barokk világkép. Pázmány Péter prédikációi* [Humanist erudition and Baroque world view. Péter Pázmány's sermons]. Bp. *1979*, Akadémiai K. 206 pp.

Cf.: Bencze Lóránt: *Pázmány Péter és Kosztolányi Dezső prózastílusa* (pp. 543.)

PETELEI, ISTVÁN

Kozma Dezső: *Egy erdélyi novellista: Petelei István* [A short-story writer from Transylvania: István Petelei]. Bucharest *1969*, Irodalmi K. 141 pp.

PÉTERFY, JENŐ

Zimándi P. István: *Péterfy Jenő élete és kora 1850–1899* [The life and age of Jenő Péterfy (1850–1899)]. Bp. *1972*, Akadémiai K. 562 pp.
Cf.: Németh G. Béla: *Mű és személyiség* (pp. 522.)

PETŐFI, SÁNDOR

Ferenczi Zoltán: *Petőfi életrajza* [A biography of Petőfi]. Vols. 1–3. Bp. *1896*. VIII, 390, 308, 411 pp.
Horváth János: *Petőfi Sándor*. Bp. *1922*, Pallas. 597 pp. — 1926².
Illyés Gyula: *Petőfi* [Bp. *1936*], Nyugat. 311 pp. Rev. enl. ed. Bp. *1963*, Szépirodalmi K. 681 pp. — Id. Bp. *1977*. 499 pp.
— in English: *Petőfi*. Transl.: G. F. Cushing. Bp. *1973*, Corvina. 590 pp.
— in French: *Vie de Petőfi*. Trad. et intr.: Jean Rousselot. Paris 1962, Gallimard. 335 pp.
— in German: *Sándor Petőfi. Ein Lebensbild.* Übers.: Johanna Till. Nachdichtungen: Martin Remané. Bp.–Berlin–Weimar 1971, Corvina–Aufbau. 438 pp.
— in Italian: *Petőfi*. Trad.: Nelly Vucetic, Umberto Albini. Milano 1960, Feltrinelli. 300 pp.
— in Russian: *Sándor Petőfi*. Perevod s vengerskogo E. Malyhinoy. Moscow 1972, Khudozhestvennaia Literatura. 496 pp.
Bettelsack und Freiheit. Leben und Werk Alexander Petőfis. Hrsg. René Schwachofer. Weimar 1954, Kiepenheuer. 243 pp. (pp. 7–85: Einführung—Das Leben Alexander Petőfis.—Petőfis Bedeutung für unsere Zeit).
Dienes András: *Petőfi a szabadságharcban* [Petőfi during the War of Independence]. Bp. *1958*, Akadémiai K. 643 pp.
Pándi Pál: *Petőfi. A költő útja 1844 végéig* [Petőfi.

The poet's career up to the end of 1844]. Bp. *1961*, Szépirodalmi K. 589 pp. — 2nd. rev. enl. ed. Bp. 1982, Szépirodalmi K. 578 pp.

Tanulmányok Petőfiről [Essays on Petőfi]. Ed.: PÁNDI Pál, TÓTH Dezső. Bp. *1962*, Akadémiai K. 509 pp.

MARTINKÓ András: *A prózaíró Petőfi és a magyar prózastílus fejlődése* [Petőfi the prose-writer and the development of Hungarian prose style]. Bp. *1965*, Akadémiai K. 634 pp.

HATVANY Lajos: *Így élt Petőfi* [The life of Petőfi]. 2nd rev. enl. ed. Ed.: KISS József, PÁNDI Pál. Vols. 1–2. Bp. *1967*, Akadémiai K. 939, 961 pp. — Id. Bp. 1980.

GERSHKOVITCH, A. A.: *Poeticheski teatr Petefi.* Moscow *1970*, Izd. "Nauka". 297 pp.

Petőfi és kora [Petőfi and his age]. Ed.: LUKÁCSY Sándor, VARGA János. Bp. *1970*, Akadémiai K. 705 pp.

FEKETE Sándor: *Petőfi romantikájának forrásai* [The sources of Petőfi's romanticism]. Bp. *1972*, Akadémiai K. 156 pp.

Petőfi tüze. Tanulmányok Petőfi Sándorról [Petőfi's fire. Essays on Sándor Petőfi]. Ed.: TAMÁS Anna, WÉBER Antal. Bp. *1972*, Kossuth K.— Zrínyi Katonai K. 577 pp.

SHACHOVA, K. A.: *Sándor Petőfi. Zhittya i tvorchist.* Kiev *1972*, Dnipro. 214 pp.

FEKETE Sándor: *Petőfi Sándor életrajza* [The biography of Sándor Petőfi]. Vol. 1. A költő gyermek- és ifjúkora [Childhood and youth]. Bp. *1973*. Akadémiai K. 363 pp.

L'irréconciliable. Petőfi, poète et révolutionnaire. Études et choix de poèmes publiés pour le 150e anniversaire de la naissance du poète. Préf.: Aurélien SAUVAGEOT. Dir. de publ.: LUKÁCSY Sándor. Bp. *1973*, Corvina. 205 pp.

Petőfi. 1823–1973. Tribute to Sándor Petőfi on the 150th anniversary of his birth—Homage à Sándor Petőfi à l'occasion du 150e anniversaire de sa naissance. By ILLYÉS Gyula, ACZÉL György etc. Bp. *1973*, Corvina. 144 pp.

Petőfi-szótár. Petőfi Sándor életművének szókészlete [A Petőfi dictionary. The vocabulary of Petőfi's life-work]. Ed.-in-chief: GÁLDI László. Ed.: J. SOLTÉSZ Katalin, SZABÓ Dénes, WACHA Imre. Bp. *1973–* , Akadémiai K.

Vol. 1. A–F. 1973. 1167 pp.
Vol. 2. G–M. 1978. 1349 pp.

PÁNDI Pál: *Petőfi és a nacionalizmus* (6 előadás) [Petőfi and nationalism—6 lectures]. Bp. *1974*, Akadémiai K. 307 pp.

TURÓCZI-TROSTLER József: *Petőfi belép a világirodalomba* [Petőfi entering world literature]. Ed.: KISS József. Bp. *1974*, Akadémiai K. 245 pp. [The first two chapters in German: "Petőfis Eintritt in die Weltliteratur." In: *Acta Litteraria* 1960, pp. 3–112, and 1961. pp. 23–182].

Petefi v mirovoi kulture [Materiali Konferentsii v Moskve 21 fevralya 1973 g.] Moscow *1975*, Izd. "Nauka". 155 pp. [pp. 143–152: Bibliography in German, English, French, Italian, Spanish, Russian and Ukrainian].

KOZMA Dezső: *Petőfi öröksége.* Két tanulmány [Petőfi's legacy. Two studies]. Bibliográfia: "Petőfi Sándor a romániai könyvkiadásban és a romániai magyar sajtóban. Könyvészeti válogatás, 1919–1974" [Bibliography: "Sándor Petőfi in the Rumanian book-publishing and the Rumanian Hungarian press. Selected bibliography, 1919–1974]. Ed. MÉSZÁROS József. Bucharest *1976*, Kriterion. 178 pp.

Petőfi állomásai. Versek és elemzések [Milestones in Petőfi's life. Poems and interpretations]. Ed., afterw.: PÁNDI Pál. Bp. *1976*, Magvető K. 702 pp.

CSUKÁS István: *Petőfi a szlovákoknál* [Petőfi and the Slovaks]. Bratislava *1979*, Madách. 248 pp.

GERSHKOVITCH, A. A.: *Az én Petőfim.* Cikkek, tamányok [My Petőfi. Articles, studies]. Bp. *1979*, Gondolat K. 257 pp.

MOLNÁR BASA, Enikő: *Sándor Petőfi.* Boston *1980*, Twayne Publishers. 190 pp. (Twayne's World Authors Series.)

Cf.: BLUMBERG, Henry d'A.: Petőfi, the Hungarian Burns. In: *Petőfi, Sándor: Prose and Poetry* (pp. 559.)

KÖPECZI Béla: Sándor Petőfi [Forew.] In: *Rebel or Revolutionary?* (pp. 559.)

MERVYN, Jones D.: *Five Hungarian Writers* (pp. 559.)

NYERGES, Anton N.: Intr. In: *Petőfi (Poems and Prose)* (pp. 522.)

Radó György: Intr. In: *Petőfi Sándor by himself* (pp. 559.)
Reményi, Joseph: Intr. In: *Petőfi Sándor: Sixty Poems* (pp. 559.)
Sík Csaba: Forew. In: *Petőfi, Sándor: The Apostle* (pp. 559.)

PILINSZKY, JÁNOS

Fülöp László: *Pilinszky János*. Bp. *1977*, Akadémiai K. 243 pp.
Radnóti Sándor: *A szenvedő misztikus. Misztika és líra összefüggése* [The suffering mystic. The inter-relationship of mysticism and poetry]. Bp. *1981*, Akadémiai K. 127 pp.
Cf.: Bata Imre: *Képek és vonulatok* (pp. 520.)
Béládi Miklós: *Érintkezési pontok* (pp. 520.)
Diószegi András: *Megmozdult világban* (pp. 520.)
Kovács Kálmán: *Eszmék és irodalom* (pp. 521.)
Hughes, Ted: Intr. In: *Pilinszky, János: Selected Poems* (pp. 559.)

RADNÓTI, MIKLÓS

Radnóti Miklós. 1909–1944. Ed.: Baróti Dezső. Intr.: Ortutay Gyula. Bp. *1959*, Magyar Helikon. 191 pp.
Bori Imre: *Radnóti Miklós költészete* [The poetry of Miklós Radnóti]. Novi Sad *1965*, Forum. 210 pp.
Baróti Dezső: *Kortárs útlevelére*. Radnóti Miklós 1909–1935 [On the passport of a contemporary. Miklós Radnóti 1909–1935]. Bp. *1977*, Szépirodalmi K. 504 pp.
Pomogáts Béla: *Radnóti Miklós*. Bp. *1977*, Gondolat K. 228 pp.
Nemes István: *Radnóti Miklós költői nyelve* [Radnóti's poetic language]. Bp. *1979*, Akadémiai K. 310 pp.
Cf.: Diószegi András: *Megmozdult világban* (pp. 520.)
Ortutay Gyula: *Fényes, tiszta árnyak* (pp. 522.)
Tolnai Gábor: *Tanulmányok* (pp. 523.)

RÁKÓCZI, FRANCIS II

Márki Sándor: *II. Rákóczi Ferenc*. Vols. 1–3. Bp. *1907*–1910, Magyar Történelmi Társulat. 646, 672, 736 pp.

Zolnai Béla: *II. Rákóczi Ferenc* [Bp. *1942*], Franklin. 224 pp.
Köpeczi Béla: *A Rákóczi-szabadságharc és Franciaország* [Rákóczi's War of Independence and France]. Bp. *1966*, Akadémiai K. 479 pp.
Rákóczi tükör. Naplók, jelentések, emlékiratok a szabadságharcból [The image of Rákóczi. Diaries, reports, memoirs from the War of Independence]. Ed.: Köpeczi Béla, R. Várkonyi Ágnes. Vols. 1–2. Bp. *1973*, Szépirodalmi K. 525, 587 pp.
Köpeczi Béla–R. Várkonyi Ágnes: *II. Rákóczi Ferenc*. 2nd rev. enl. ed. Bp. *1976*, Gondolat K. 533 pp.
Rákóczi-tanulmányok. A II. Rákóczi Ferenc születésének 300. évfordulója alkalmából rendezett tudományos ülésszak előadásai. ELTE Bölcsészettudományi Kar [Rákóczi studies. Papers of the conference held on the occasion of Ferenc Rákóczi's 300th anniversary. Arts Faculty of the Eötvös Loránd University]. Ed.: Sinkovics István, Gyenis Vilmos. Bp. *1978*, ELTE 204 pp.
Rákóczi-tanulmányok [Rákóczi studies]. Ed.: Köpeczi Béla, Hopp Lajos, R. Várkonyi Ágnes. Bp. *1980*, Akadémiai K. 778 pp.
Cf.: Kovács Sándor Iván: *Jelenlévő múlt* (pp. 522.)

RÉVAI, JÓZSEF

Cf.: Bodnár György: *Törvénykeresők* (pp. 520.)

REVICZKY, GYULA

Riedl Frigyes: *Vajda, Reviczky, Komjáthy*. Bp. [*1932?*]. 140 pp.
Komlós Aladár: *Reviczky Gyula*. Bp. *1955*, Művelt Nép K. 163 pp.
Mezei József: *A szimbolista élmény kialakulása. Reviczky Gyula* [The formation of the symbolist experience. Gyula Reviczky]. Bp. *1968*, Akadémiai K. 423 pp.
Széles Klára: *Reviczky Gyula poétikája és az új magyar líra* [The poetry of Gyula Reviczky and the new Hungarian lyric poetry]. Bp. *1976*, Akadémiai K. 258 pp.

RIMAI, JÁNOS

Ferenczi Zoltán: *Rimay János (1573–1631)*. Bp. *1911*, Magyar Történelmi Társulat. 264 pp.

SÁNTA, FERENC

VASY Géza: *Sánta Ferenc.* Bp. *1975,* Akadémiai K. 186 pp.
Cf.: BÉLÁDI Miklós: *Érintkezési pontok* (pp. 520.)
BORI Imre: *Eszmék és látomások* (pp. 520.)
FENYŐ István: *Két évtized* (pp. 520.)
ILLÉS Lajos: *Kezdet és kibontakozás* (pp. 521.)
TAMÁS Attila: *Irodalom és emberi teljesség* (p. 523.)

SARKADI, IMRE

KÓNYA Judit: *Sarkadi Imre alkotásai és vallomásai tükrében* [Imre Sarkadi as reflected in his works and confessions]. Bp. *1971,* Szépirodalmi K. 229 pp.
HAJDÚ Ráfis: *Sarkadi Imre.* Bp. *1973,* Akadémiai K. 171 pp.
Cf.: BATA Imre: *Ívelő pályák* (pp. 520.)
BÉLÁDI Miklós: *Érintkezési pontok* (pp. 520.)
SOMLYÓ György: The solution of the insoluble. About Imre Sarkadi [Afterw.] In: *Sarkadi, Imre: The Coward and Other Stories* (pp. 560.)

SÁROSI, GYULA

BISZTRAY Gyula: Sárosi Gyula költői pályája [The poetic career of Gyula Sárosi]. [Intr.] In: *Sárosi Gyula kisebb költeményei, prózai munkái és levelezése* [Minor poems, prose works and correspondence of Gyula Sárosi]. Ed.: BISZTRAY Gyula. Bp. *1954,* Akadémiai K. pp. 13–101.

SIMON, ISTVÁN

Cf.: ILLÉS Lajos: *Kezdet és kibontakozás* (pp. 521.)
SZAUDER József: *Tavaszi és őszi utazások* (pp. 523.)
TAMÁS Attila: *Irodalom és emberi teljesség* (pp. 523.)

SYLVESTER, JÁNOS

BALÁZS János: *Sylvester János és kora* [János Sylvester and his age]. Bp. *1958,* Tankönyvkiadó. 473 pp.

SZABÓ, DEZSŐ

NAGY Péter: *Szabó Dezső.* Bp. *1964,* Akadémiai K. 604 pp.

SZABÓ, LŐRINC

KABDEBÓ Lóránt: *Szabó Lőrinc lázadó évtizede* [Rebelling ten years of Lőrinc Szabó]. Bp. *1970,* Szépirodalmi K. 686 pp.
RÁBA György: *Szabó Lőrinc.* Bp. *1972,* Akadémiai K. 173 pp.
KABDEBÓ Lóránt: *Útkeresés és különbéke. Szabó Lőrinc 1929–1944* [Seeking ways and separate peace. Lőrinc Szabó 1929–1944]. Bp. *1974,* Szépirodalmi K. 415 pp.
KABDEBÓ Lóránt: *Az összegzés ideje. Szabó Lőrinc 1945–1957* [A time of reckoning. Lőrinc Szabó 1945–1957]. Bp. *1980,* Szépirodalmi K. 577 pp.
Cf.: ILLYÉS Gyula: *Iránytűvel.* Vol. 2 (pp. 521.)
SZABOLCSI Miklós: *Költészet és korszerűség* (pp. 523.)

SZABÓ, PÁL

CZINE Mihály: *Szabó Pál alkotásai és vallomásai tükrében* [Pál Szabó as reflected in his works and confessions]. Bp. *1971,* Szépirodalmi K. 306 pp.
Cf.: BATA Imre: *Képek és vonulatok* (pp. 520.)
BÉLÁDI Miklós: *Érintkezési pontok* (pp. 520.)

SZÉCHENYI, ISTVÁN

FRIEDREICH István: *Gróf Széchenyi István élete* [The life of Count István Széchenyi]. Vols. 1–2. Bp. *1914–1915.* VIII, 440; VII, 282 pp.
SPIRA György: *1848 Széchenyije és Széchenyi 1848-a* [The Széchenyi of 1848 and the 1848 of Széchenyi]. Bp. *1964,* Akadémiai K. 368 pp.
— In English: *A Hungarian Count in the Revolution of 1848.* Bp. 1974, Akadémiai K. 345 pp.
SILAGI, Denis: *Der grösste Ungar. Graf Stephan Széchenyi.* Wien–München *1967,* Verlag Herold. 150 pp.
BARANY, George: *Stephen Széchenyi and the Awakening of Hungarian Nationalism. 1791–1841.* Princeton, New Jersey *1968,* Princeton University Press. XVIII, 487 pp.
SPIRA György: *Széchenyi a negyvennyolcas forradalomban* [Széchenyi in the 1848 revolution]. Bp. *1979,* Akadémiai K. 266 pp.
Cf.: CUSHING, G. F.: *Széchenyi, Kossuth and National Classicism in Hungarian Literature* (pp. 543.)

SZENCZI MOLNÁR, ALBERT

Dézsi Lajos: *Szenczi Molnár Albert (1574–1633).* Bp. *1897,* Magyar Történelmi Társulat 243 pp.

Szenczi Molnár Albert és a magyar késő-reneszánsz [Albert Szenczi Molnár and the late Renaissance in Hungary]. Ed.: Csanda Sándor, Keserű Bálint. Szeged *1978,* József Attila Tudományegyetem I. sz. Magyar Irodalomtörténeti Tanszéke. 330 pp.

Cf.: Kovács Sándor Iván: *Pannoniából Európába* (pp. 522.)

Turóczi-Trostler József: *Magyar irodalom —világirodalom* (pp. 529.)

SZERB, ANTAL

Poszler György: *Szerb Antal.* Bp. *1973,* Akadémiai K. 451 pp.

Cf.: Bodnár György: *Törvénykeresők* (pp. 520.) Hegedűs Géza: Intr. In: *Szerb Antal: The Pendragon Legend* (pp. 560.)

SZIGLIGETI, EDE

Osváth Béla: *Szigligeti Ede.* Bp. *1955,* Művelt Nép K. 168 pp.

Cf.: *Magyar színháztörténet.* Ed.: Hont Ferenc (pp. 524.)

SZOMORY, DEZSŐ

Réz Pál: *Szomory Dezső alkotásai és vallomásai tükrében* [Dezső Szomory as reflected in his works and confessions]. Bp. *1971,* Szépirodalmi K. 291 pp.

Cf.: Vargha Kálmán: *Álom, szecesszió, valóság* (pp. 524.)

TAMÁSI, ÁRON

Féja Géza: *Tamási Áron alkotásai és vallomásai tükrében* [Áron Tamási as reflected in his works and confessions]. Bp. *1970.* Szépirodalmi K. 183 pp.

TERSÁNSZKY JÓZSI, JENŐ

Kerékgyártó István: *Tersánszky Józsi Jenő alkotásai és vallomásai tükrében* [Jenő Tersánszky Józsi as reflected in his works and confessions.] Bp. *1969,* Szépirodalmi K. 201 pp.

Cf.: Bodnár György: *Törvénykeresők* (pp. 520.)

Rónay György: *Jenő J. Tersánszky (b. 1888).* [Intr.] In: *Tersánszky Józsi, Jenő: Good-bye, my Dear. — The Harlot and the Virgin* (pp. 560.)

THURY, ZOLTÁN

Rejtő István: *Thury Zoltán.* Bp. *1963,* Szépirodalmi K. 419 pp.

TOLDY, FERENC

Greguss Ágost: *Toldy Ferenc félszázados irodalmi munkássága 1821–1871* [Fifty years of Ferenc Toldy's literary activity. 1821–1871]. Pest *1871.* 116 pp.

Kuncz Aladár: *Toldy Ferenc.* Bp. *1906.* 102 pp.

TOLNAI, LAJOS

Gergely Gergely: *Tolnai Lajos pályája. Egy fejezet a magyar regény történetéből* [The career of Lajos Tolnai. One chapter from the history of Hungarian novel]. Bp. *1964,* Akadémiai K. 454 pp.

TOMPA, MIHÁLY

Kéki Lajos: *Tompa Mihály.* Bp. *1912.* 192 pp.

Váczy János: *Tompa Mihály életrajza* [A Mihály Tompa biography]. Bp. *1913,* Magyar Tudományos Akadémia. IX, 303 pp.

TÓTFALUSI KIS, MIKLÓS

Dézsi Lajos: *Magyar író és könyvnyomtató a XVII. században. I. Misztótfalusi Kis Miklós. 1650–1702. II. Pápai Páriz Ferenc. 1649–1716* [Hungarian writer and printer in the 17th century. I. Miklós Misztótfalusi Kis 1650–1702. II. Ferenc Pápai Páriz 1649–1716]. Bp. *1898–1899.* 208, 332 pp.

Haiman György: *Tótfalusi Kis Miklós, a betűművész és tipográfus. Élete betűinek és nyomtatványainak tükrében* [Miklós Tótfalusi Kis the typographer. His life as reflected in his types and printings]. Bp. *1972,* Magyar Helikon — Európa K. 317 pp.

TÓTH, ÁRPÁD

Kardos László: *Tóth Árpád.* 2nd rev. ed. Bp. *1965,* Akadémiai K. 491 pp.

MAKAY Gusztáv: *Tóth Árpád*. Bp. *1967*, Gondolat K. 167 pp.
Cf.: RÁBA György: *A szép hűtlenek* (pp. 525.)

TÖMÖRKÉNY, ISTVÁN

ORTUTAY Gyula: *Tömörkény István*. 2nd ed. Szeged *1934*. 141 pp.
KISPÉTER András: *Tömörkény István*. Bp. *1964*, Akadémiai K. 299 pp.
Emlékkönyv Tömörkény István születésének centenáriumára [Memorial volume on the centenary of István Tömörkény's birth]. Ed.: KOVÁCS Sándor Iván, PÉTER László. Szeged *1966*. 471 pp.
Cf.: NAGY Péter: *Drámai arcélek* (pp. 522.)

VÁCI, MIHÁLY

KOVÁCS Sándor Iván: *Váci Mihály*. Bp. *1972*, Akadémiai K. 168 pp.
Cf.: KOVÁCS Sándor Iván: *Jelenlévő múlt* (pp. 522.)

VAJDA, JÁNOS

RIEDL Frigyes: *Vajda, Reviczky, Komjáthy*. Bp. *[1932?]*. 140 pp.
BÓKA László: *Vajda János*. [Bp. *1941*] 158 pp.
KOMLÓS Aladár: *Vajda János*. Bp. *1954*, Akadémiai K. 363 pp.
Cf.: BARTA János: *Költők és írók* (pp. 520.)
KOMLÓS Aladár: *A szimbolizmus és a magyar líra* (pp. 517.)

VAS, ISTVÁN

FENYŐ István: *Vas István*. Bp. *1976*, Akadémiai K. 282 pp.
Cf.: BÉLÁDI Miklós: *Érintkezési pontok* (pp. 520.)
KIS PINTÉR Imre: *Helyzetjelentés* (pp. 521.)
KOVÁCS Sándor Iván: *Jelenlévő múlt* (pp. 522.)
VARGHA Kálmán: *Álom, szecesszió, valóság* (pp. 524.)

VERES, PÉTER

BENKŐ László: *A szépirodalmi stílus elemzése. Veres Péter szókincse és mondatfűzése* [[Literary style analysis. The vocabulary and composition of Péter Veres]. Bp. *1962*, Akadémiai K. 135 pp.
Veres Péter koszorúja. Kortársak írásai, emlékezései
[A wreath to Péter Veres. Writings and memories of contemporaries]. Ed.: RÁDICS József. Bp. *1973*, Táncsics K. 483 pp.
NÁDASDI Péter: *A tölgyfa árnyékában. Vallomások apámról* [In the shade of the oak-tree. Confessions about my father]. Bp. *1974*, Móra K. 203 pp.
BATA Imre: *Veres Péter alkotásai és vallomásai tükrében* [Péter Veres as reflected in his works and confessions]. Bp. *1977*, Szépirodalmi K. 299 pp.
Cf.: BÉLÁDI Miklós: *Érintkezési pontok* (pp. 520.)

VERESMARTI, MIHÁLY

IPOLYI Arnold: *Veresmarti Mihály XVII. századi magyar író élete és munkái* [Life and work of Mihály Veresmarti, 17th-century Hungarian writer]. Bp. *1875*. 692 pp.

VÖRÖSMARTY, MIHÁLY

GYULAI Pál: *Vörösmarty Mihály életrajza* [Mihály Vörösmarty's life]. Pest *[1865]*, 1866. 216 pp. In: *Gyulai Pál válogatott művei* [Selected works of Pál Gyulai]. Vol. 2. Bp. 1956. pp. 234–414.
HORVÁTH Károly: *A klasszikából a romantikába. A két irodalmi irányzat Vörösmarty első költői korszakának tükrében* [From Classicism to Romanticism. The two literary trends in the first phase of Vörösmarty's poetry]. Bp. *1968*, Akadémiai K. 463 pp.
TÓTH Dezső: *Vörösmarty Mihály*. 2nd rev. enl. ed. Bp. *1974*, Akadémiai K. 577 pp.
„Ragyognak tettei…" Tanulmányok Vörösmartyról [Studies on Vörösmarty]. Ed.: HORVÁTH Károly, LUKÁCSY Sándor, SZÖRÉNYI László. Székesfehérvár *1975*. 430 pp.
Cf.: MARTINKÓ András: *Teremtő idők* (pp. 522.)
MERVYN, Jones D.: *Five Hungarian Writers* (pp. 522.)

WEÖRES, SÁNDOR

TAMÁS Attila: *Weöres Sándor*. Bp. *1978*, Akadémiai K. 263 pp.
BATA Imre: *Weöres Sándor közelében* [Sándor Weöres up close]. Bp. *1979*, Magvető K. 367 pp.

Cf.: BORI Imre: *Eszmék és látomások* (pp. 520.)
KARDOS Tibor: *Élő humanizmus* (pp. 521.)
KENYERES Zoltán: *Gondolkodó irodalom* (pp. 521.)
KOVÁCS Sándor Iván: *Jelenlevő múlt* (pp. 522.)
SZABOLCSI Miklós: *Költészet és korszerűség* (pp. 523.)
TAMÁS Attila: *Irodalom és emberi teljesség* (pp. 523.)
MORGAN, Edwin: Intr. In: *Selected Poems [of] Sándor Weöres [and of] Ferenc Juhász.* (pp. 560.)

ZRÍNYI, MIKLÓS

SÍK Sándor: *Zrínyi Miklós.* Bp. *1941.* 177 pp.
KLANICZAY Tibor: *Zrínyi Miklós.* 2nd rev. ed. Bp. *1964,* Akadémiai K. 852 pp.
PERJÉS Géza: *Zrínyi Miklós és kora* [Miklós Zrínyi and his age]. Bp. *1965,* Gondolat K. 390 pp.
KOVÁCS Sándor Iván: *Zrínyi-tanulmányok* [Studies on Zrínyi]. Bp. *1979,* Szépirodalmi K. 195 pp.
Cf.: MERVYN, Jones D.: *Five Hungarian Writers* (pp. 522.)

B) *Hungarian Literature in English Translation*

The present bibliography contains a selection from the latest possible English versions of Hungarian classics as well as contemporary. A useful addition to our bibliography, mainly as regards older translations, is Magda Czigány's *Hungarian literature in English translation published in Great Britain 1830-1968*. London 1969, Szepsi Csombor Literary Circle.

I ANTHOLOGIES

Magyar Poetry. Selections from Hungarian poets. Transl.: William N. Loew. New York *1908*, Amerikai Magyar Népszava. 510, XII pp.

Magyar Poems. Sel. and transl. from the Hungarian with biographical notes by Nora de Vállyi and Dorothy M. Stuart. London *1911*, Marlborough. 108 pp.

Modern Magyar Lyrics. Sel. gems from Alex[ander] Petőfi and other modern Hungarian poets. Ed., transl.: William N. Loew. (Pref.: Árpád Pásztor). Bp. *1926*, Wodianer F. 107 pp.

The Magyar Muse. An anthology of Hungarian poetry 1400-1932. Ed. and transl. [and intr.]: Watson Kirkconnell. Forew.: Francis Herczeg. Winnipeg (Manitoba) *1933*, Kanadai Magyar Újság Press. 222 pp.

Hungaria. An anthology of thirty short stories by contemporary Hungarian authors. Intr.: Alexander Korda. Transl.: Lawrence Wolfe. London–Bp. *1936*, Nicholson–Watson–Anthenaeum. XIV, 302 pp.

A Little Treasury of Hungarian Verse. Ed., transl.: Watson Kirkconnell. Washington *1947*, American–Hungarian Foundation. 56 pp. (American Hungarian Library 3.)

Hungarian Poetry. Sel. and ed.: Egon F. Kunz. Transl.: W[atson] Kirkconnell, Egon F. Kunz, etc. Sydney *1955*, Pannonia. 158 pp.

Hungarian Prose and Verse. Ed. George Frederick Cushing. London *1956*, Athlone Press. 197 pp.

Hungarian Folk-tales. Sel. (intr., annot.): Gyula Ortutay. Bp. *1962*, Corvina, 544 pp.

Hungarian Short Stories from the 19th and 20th centuries. [Ed.: László Pődör.] Transl.: István Farkas, Éva Rácz, etc. Intr.: István Sőtér. Bp. *1962*, Corvina, 391 pp. (Hungarian Library)

Hungarian Anthology. A collection of poems. Sel. and transl.: Joseph Grosz, W. Arthur Boggs. Munich *1963*, Greiff-Druck. 251 pp. — 2nd rev. enl. ed. Toronto 1966, Pannonia. 315 pp.

The Plough and the Pen. Writings from Hungary 1930–1956. Ed.: Ilona Duczyńska, Karl Polanyi. Forew.: W. H. Auden. London *1963*, Peter Owen. 231 pp. — Id. Toronto 1968, McClelland and Stewart. 231 pp.

Folk-tales of Hungary. Ed.: Linda Dégh. Transl.: Judit Halász. Chicago *1965*, Univ. of Chicago Press. 46. 381 pp. (Folk-tales of the world.) — Id. London *1965*, Routledge a. Kegan Paul. 46. 381 pp.

Landmark. Hungarian writers on thirty years of history. Ed.: Miklós Szabolcsi. Assisted by

Zoltán Kenyeres. Transl.: Earle Birney, Ilona Duczyńska etc. Intr.: József Bognár. Bp. *1965*, Corvina. 358 pp.

Arion. Nemzetközi költői almanach — Almanac International de Poésie. Publié par Somlyó, György. Bp. *1966*–1982, Corvina. Vols. 1–13.

The Literary Review. Hungary number IX, no. 3. *1966*, Spring. 493 pp.

Twenty-two Hungarian Short Stories (From the middle of the last century to the present day). Transl.: Gyula Gulyás, Paul Tabori, etc. Intr.: A[lfred] Alvarez. Bp.–London 1967–*[1966]*, Corvina–Oxford University Press. XVI, 432 pp.

Hungarian Short Stories. Transl.: Gyula Gulyás, Paul Tabori etc. Intr.: Alfred Alvarez. London etc. Bp. *1967*, Oxford University Press–Corvina. XVI, 432 pp. (The World's Classics 609.)

Hungarian Poetry. Poésie hongroise. 1848, 1919, 1945. Red.: Sándor Borbély. Transl.: Watson Kirkconnell, V. Levik, etc. Bp. *1968*, Youth Publishing House. 214 pp. (Poems in English, French, Russian and Spanish.)

New Writing of East Europe. Ed.: George Gömöri and Charles Newman. Chicago *1968*, Quadrangle Books. 263 pp.

Humana Hungarica. Hungarian poets and writers in the service of man. Compil. by László Pődör. Intr.: Máté Kovács. Published by The Society of Hungarian Bibliophiles. Bp. *1969*, 97 pp. (In English and French.)

Selected Hungarian Legends. Compil. from the coll. of Freda B. Kovács by Albert Wass. Transl.: Elizabeth M. Wass de Czege. Astor Park, Florida *1971*, Danubian Press. 87 pp. (Hungarian Heritage Books 3.)

Selected Hungarian Folk-tales. Compil.: Albert Wass. Transl.: Elizabeth M. Wass de Czege. Astor Park, Florida *1972*, Danubian Press. 135 pp. (Hungarian Heritage Books 4.)

Hundred Hungarian Poems. Ed., intr.: Thomas Kabdebo. Manchester *1976*, Albion Editions. 125 pp.

Modern Hungarian Poetry. Ed., intr.: Miklós Vajda. Forew.: William Jay Smith. Bp.–New York–Guildford, *1977*, Corvina–Columbia University Press. 286 pp.

[Forty-four] 44 Hungarian Short Stories. Ed.: Illés, Lajos. Intr.: C. P. Snow. Bp. *1979*, Corvina. 733 pp.

Ocean at the Window. Hungarian prose poetry since 1945. Ed. a. intr.: Albert Tezla. Minneapolis *1980*, University of Minnesota Press. 481 pp.

II INDIVIDUAL WORKS

ADY, ENDRE

The Explosive Country. A Selection of Articles and Studies 1898–1916. Intr., transl., annot.: G[eorge] F[rederick] Cushing. Sel.: Erzsébet Vezér. Bp. 1977, Corvina. 333 pp.

Poems. Transl. from the Hungarian and with an intr. by René Bonnerjea. Bp. 1941, Dr. Vajna & Bokor. 142 pp. — Id.: Forest Hills, New York 1947, Transatlantic. 142 pp.

Poems of—. Intr. and transl.: Anton N. Nyerges. Prepared for publication: Joseph M. Értavy-Baráth. Buffalo, New York 1969, Hungarian Cultural Foundation. 491 pp. (Program in Soviet and East Central European Studies 1.) — Id. 1977.

A Selection of Poems from the writings of—. Transl.: Antal Nyerges. Washington 1946, American Hungarian Federation. xiv, 54 pp.

ARANY, JÁNOS

The Death of King Buda. A Hungarian epic poem. Rendered into English verse by Watson Kirkconnell. Forew.: Géza Voinovich. Notes: Árpád Benczik. Cleveland, Ohio 1936. Benjamin Franklin Bibliophile Society. xviii, 159 pp. (The Hungarian Library.)

Epics of the Hungarian Plain. Death of Buda. A Hun legend.—Toldi.—Toldi's love.—[Selections.]—Toldi's Eve. Transl., intr.: Anton N. Nyerges. Cleveland, Ohio 1976, Classic Printing Corporation. 224 pp.

BABITS, MIHÁLY

The Nightmare [Novel]. Transl.: Éva Rácz. Bp. 1966, Corvina. 135 pp. (Hungarian Library.)

BALÁZS, BÉLA

The Mantle of Dreams (Stories). Transl. (from German): George Leitmann. Tokyo, etc. 1974, Kodansha. 123 pp.

Theory of the Film. Character and growth of a new-art (Studies). Transl.: Edith Bone. London 1952, Dobson. 291 pp. (International theatre and cinema.)

BÍRÓ, LAJOS

Gods and Kings (Six plays). London 1945, Allen and Unwin. 85 pp.

Patricia's Seven Houses.—School for Slavery (Plays). Pref.: Maurice Browne. London 1941, Faber and Faber. 239 pp.

BRÓDY, SÁNDOR

Rembrandt. A romance of divine love and art. Transl.: Louis Rittenberg. New York [1928], Globus Press, 257 pp.

CSÁTH, GÉZA

The Magician's Garden and Other Stories. Transl.: Jascha Kessler and Charlotte Rogers. New York 1980, Columbia University Press. 206 pp.

DÉRY, TIBOR

The Giant.—Behind the Brick Wall.—Love (Stories). Transl.: Kathleen Szász, Ilona Duczyńska. London 1964, Calder and Boyers. 139 pp.

Niki. The Story of a Dog (Novel). Transl.: Edward Hyams. London 1958, Secker and Warburg. 144 pp. — Id.: Harmondsworth 1961, Penguin. 123 pp. — London–Edinburgh 1965, Nelson. 115 pp. (Reading today.)

The Portuguese Princess and other Stories. Transl.: Kathleen Szász. London 1966, Calder and Boyars. 224 pp. — Id.: Chicago 1968, Quodrangle Books.

DOBOZY, IMRE

Village People (Reports). Bp. 1954, Hungarian Bulletin. 52 pp. (Not published in Hungarian.)

EÖTVÖS, JÓZSEF

The Village Notary. A romance of Hungarian life. Transl.: Otto Wenckstern. London 1850, Longman-Brown, etc. Vols. 1–3.

FEJES, ENDRE

Generation of Rust (Novel). Transl.: Sanford J. Greenburger. Teranece Brashear, New York, etc. 1970, McGraw-Hill. 215 pp.

GÁRDONYI, GÉZA

Slave of the Huns (Historical novel). Transl.: Andrew Feldmar. Forew.: Victor C. Ambrus. Bp. 1969, Corvina. 357 pp. — Id.: London 1969, Dent. 357 pp. — New ed. Harmondsworth 1972, Penguin Books.

HELTAI, JENŐ

The Silent Knight. A romantic comedy by Humbert Wolfe. London–Toronto [1937]. W. Heinemann. 91 pp.

HERNÁDI, GYULA

The Royal Hunt (Drama). Transl.: János Boris. (Publ. Centre Hongrois de l'I.I.T.) Bp. 1977, M. Színházi Intézet 126 pp.

ILLÉS, BÉLA

Carpathian Rhapsody (Novel). Transl.: Grace Blair Gárdos. Vols. 1–2. Bp. 1963, Corvina. 266, 284 pp. (Hungarian Library.)

ILLYÉS, GYULA

Matt the Gooseherd (An adaptation of the folktale Matyi Ludas). Transl.: Paul Tabori. Harmondsworth 1976, Penguin Books. Unnumbered pages.

Once Upon a Time. Forty Hungarian folk-tales. Transl.: Barna Balogh, Susan Kun. Bp. 1964, Corvina. 285 pp. (Hungarian Library.) — 2nd ed. 1970, 323 pp. (A selection from the author's Seventy-seven Hungarian folk-tales.)

People of the Puszta. Transl.: G. F. Cushing. Bp. 1967, Corvina. 307 pp. (Hungarian Library.) — Id.: London 1971, Chatto and Windus. 307 pp.

Selected Poems. Ed.: Thomas Kabdebo, Paul Tabori. Forew.: Thomas Kabdebo. (Transl.: Gavin Ewart, Michael Beevor, etc). London 1971, Chatto and Windus. 86 pp.

A Tribute to Gyula Illyés. Ed.: Thomas Kabdebo and Paul Tabori. Pref.: Jean Follain. (Poems transl.: Doreen Bell, John Brander, etc.) Washington 1968, Occidental Press. 148 pp.

JÓKAI, MÓR

The Baron's Sons. A romance of the Hungarian revolution of 1848. Transl.: Percy Favor Bicknell. Boston 1900, Page. VIII, 343 pp.

The Dark Diamonds (Novel). Intr.: Géza Hegedűs. Transl.: Frances Gerard. Bp. 1968, Corvina. 390 pp. (Hungarian Library.) — 2nd ed. 1978.

The Green Book or Freedom under the Snow (Novel). Transl.: Mrs. Vaugh (Ellis Wright). 8th ed. London [1906], Jarrold. 470 pp.

Halil to Pedlar. A Tale of Old Stambul. Transl.: R. Nisbet Bain. London 1901, Jarrold. 275 pp.

A Hungarian Nabob (Novel). Transl.: R. Nisbet Bain. New York 1899, Doubleday–Page. 358 pp. (Jókai, Maurus: Works. Hungarian ed.)

The Man with the Golden Touch (Novel). Transl.: Mrs. H[egan] Kennard. Bp. 1963, Corvina. 409 pp. (Hungarian Library.) —2nd ed. 1967— 3rd ed. 1975. 399 pp.

Menasseh. A Romance of Transylvania. Transl. (pref.): Percy Favor Bicknell. London 1901, Macqueen x, 328 pp.

The Poor Plutocrats. A romance. Transl.: Nisbet Bain. London 1900, Jarrold v, 423 pp.

The Strange Story of Rab Ráby (Romance). London [1909], Jarrold. XIII, 369 pp.

JÓZSEF, ATTILA

Poems. Ed.: Thomas Kabdebo. Transl.: Michel Beevor, Michael Hamburger, etc. London 1966, Danubia. 46 fols.

*Poems of—.*Transl., intr.: Anton N. Nyerges. Ed.: Joseph M. Értavy-Baráth. Buffalo, New York 1973, Hungarian Cultural Foundation. 224 pp. (Program in East European and Slavic studies 3.)

Selected Poems and Texts. Ed.: George Gömöri, James Atlas. Transl.: John Bátki. Intr.: George Gömöri. Cheadle 1973, Carcanet Press. 103 pp. (UNESCO collection of representative works. European series.)

A Selection of Poems. Transl.: R[ené] Bonnerjea. [Bp. 1965, British Embassy mimeograph.] 32 pp.

JUHÁSZ, FERENC

The Boy Changed into a Stag. Selected poems 1949–1967. Transl.: Kenneth McRobbie, Ilona Duczyńska. Intr.: Kenneth McRobbie. Toronto–New York–London, 1970 Oxford University Press. 158 pp.

Selected Poems [of] Sándor Weöres and [of] —. Transl., intr.: Edwin Morgan, David Wevill. Harmondsworth–Baltimore–Ringwood 1970, Penguin Books. 136 pp. (Penguin modern European poets.)

KARDOS, G. GYÖRGY

Avraham's Good Week (A novel about the formative years of Israel). Transl.: Ralph Manheim. Garden City, New York 1975, Doubleday. 284 pp.

KARINTHY, FERENC

Hot Air. (Play). Transl.: Jo. Ann Burbank, New York, 1969, French. 31 pp.

Spring Comes to Budapest (Novel). Transl.: István Farkas. Intr. Pál Réz. Bp. 1964, Corvina. 233 pp. (Hungarian Library.)

Steinway Grand (A play). Transl.: Matyas Eszterházy [Esterházy]. New York, etc. 1968, French. 34 pp.

KARINTHY, FRIGYES

Grave and Gay. Selections from his Work. (Sel. István Kerékgyártó. Afterw.: Károly Szalay.) [Bp.] 1973, Corvina. 246 pp. (Hungarian Library.)

A Journey round my Skull (Novel.) Transl.: Vernon Duckworth Barker. London 1939, Faber and Faber. 288 pp.

Please sir! (Humorous sketches.) Transl.: István Farkas. Forew.: Endre Illés. Bp. 1968, Corvina. 79 pp. (Hungarian Library.) (UNESCO collection of representative works. European series.)

Soliloquies in the Bath (Short stories). Transl.: Lawrence Wolfe. London–Edinburgh, etc. 1937, Hodge and Co. 222 pp.

Voyage to Faremido—Capillaria (Novels). Intr. and transl.: Paul Tabori. Bp. 1965, Corvina. XXI, 127 pp. (Hungarian Library.) — New ed.: London 1978, New English Library-Times Mirror. 124 pp.

KONRÁD, GYÖRGY

The Caseworker (Novel). Transl.: Paul Aston, New York 1974, Harcourt Brace Jovanovich. 173 pp. (A Helen and Kurt Wolff book.) — New ed.: London 1975, Hutchinson.

The City Builder (Novel). Transl.: Ivan Sanders. New York 1977, Harcourt Brace Jovanovich. 184 pp.

KOSZTOLÁNYI, DEZSŐ

The Bloody Poet. A book about Nero. With a prefatory letter by Thomas Mann. Transl.: Clifton P. Fadiman. New York 1927, Macy-Masius. 344 pp.

Nero (Novel). Transl.: Adam de Hegedűs. London 1947, Staples Press. 288 pp.

Wonder Maid (Novel). Transl.: Adam de Hegedűs. London 1947, Staples Press. 211 pp.

KRÚDY, GYULA

The Crimson Coach (Novel). Transl., intr.: Paul Tabori. Bp. 1967, Corvina. 214 pp. (Hungarian Library.)

KUNCZ, ALADÁR

Black Monastery (Novel). Transl.: Ralph Murray. London 1934, Chatto and Windus. 409 pp.

LENGYEL, JÓZSEF

Acta sanctorum and Other Tales (Stories). Transl.: Ilona Duczyńska. London 1970, Owen. 256 pp.

From Beginning to End.—The Spell (Novellas).

Transl.: Ilona Duczyńska. Delhi 1966, National Academy. 175 pp. — Id.: London 1966, Owen and Englewood Cliffs, N. Y. 1968, Prentice Hall. 138 pp.

The Judge's Chair (Novel). Transl.: Ilona Duczyńska. London 1968, Owen. 174 pp.

Prenn Drifting (Novel). Transl.: Ilona Duczyńska. London 1966, Owen. 293 pp. (UNESCO collection of contemporary writers.)

MADÁCH, IMRE

The Tragedy of Man. A dramatic poem in 15 scenes. From the original Hungarian by Charles Henry Meltzer and Paul Vajda. (Intr.: Sándor Hevesi.) Bp. 1933, Vajna. 180 pp. — 2nd ed. Bp. 1948, Vajna. 266 pp. — 3rd ed.: Intr.: Marcell Benedek. Bp. 1957, Corvina. 306 pp. 4th ed. 1960.

The Tragedy of Man. Transl.: C. P. Sanger. Intr.: E[gon] F. Kunz. 2. impr. Sydney 1956, Pannonia. 159 pp.

The Tragedy of Man (Dramatic poem). Transl. (and) intr.: J. C. W. Horne Bp. 1963, Corvina. XIX, 199 pp. — 2nd ed. 1964. — 3rd ed. 1967. — 4th ed. 1970. — 5th ed. 1973.

The Tragedy of Man. (Drama). Transl.: Joseph Grosz. Portland, Oreg 1965, Print. Taylor 204 pp. — manifold.

MIKSZÁTH, KÁLMÁN

S[ain]t Peter's Umbrella (Novel). Transl.: B. W. Worswick. Bp. 1962, Corvina. 188 pp. (Hungarian Library.)

S[ain]t Peter's Umbrella (Novel). Transl.: B. W. Worswick. London 1966, Folio Society. 218 pp.

A Strange Marriage (Novel). Transl.: István Farkas. Bp. 1964, Corvina. 361 pp. (Hungarian Library.) — 2nd ed.: 1969. 417 pp.

The Two Beggar Students. — *The Magic Caftan* (Novels). Transl.: Mari Kuttna. Bp. 1971, Corvina. 231 pp. (Hungarian Library.)

MOLDOVA, GYÖRGY

Dark Angel (Novel). Transl.: Ursula McLean. Bp. 1967, Corvina. 285 pp. (Hungarian Library.)

MOLNÁR, FERENC

All the Plays of —. (Forew.: David Belasco. Intr.: Louis Rittenberg.) New York 1937, Garden City Publishing Co. XXII. 823 pp.

The Captain of St. Margaret's. 25 chapters of memoirs (Story). Transl.: Barrows Mussey. (3rd ed.) New York 1945, Duell, Sloan and Pearce. 176 pp.

Captain Magnificent. (Story). Transl.: Barrows Mussey. London etc. 1946, Cassell. 160 pp.

Companion in Exile. Notes for an autobiography. Transl.: Barrows Mussey. New York 1950, Gaer Associates. 363 pp. — Id.: London [1951], Allen. 363 pp.

The Devil (Drama). Adapted by Oliver Herford. New York [1908], Kennerley. 167 pp.

Fashions for Men. — *The Swan.* (Plays). Transl.: Benjamin Glazer. New York 1922, Boni and Liveright. 309 pp. — Id.: New York [1930].

The Guardsman (Comedy). Transl.: Grace I. Colbron, Hans Bartsch. Acting version by Philip Moeller. Forew. by Theresa Helburn. 5th ed. New York 1929, Liveright. xv, 16–190 pp.

Liliom. A legend in seven scenes and a prologue. English text and intr.: Benjamin F. Glazer. New York 1931, Liveright. xvi, 4, 185 pp. — Id.: London 1945, Samuel French. 140 pp.

Plays of —. English texts and intr. by Benjamin F. Glazer. London [1927], Jarrolds. XXI, 23–312 pp.

The Plays of —. With a forew. by David Belasco. Intr:. Louis Rittenberg. New York 1929, The Vanguard Press. XXII, 823 pp.

Romantic Comedies (Eight plays). Transl.: Sydney Howard. New York 1952, Macy Masius. 331 pp.

Stories for Two (Stories in dialogue). New York 1950, Horizon Press. 351 pp.

The Wolf (A play). Transl.: Henric Hirsch, Frank Hauser. London etc. 1973, French. 91 pp. (French's acting edition.)

MÓRA, FERENC

The Gold Coffin (Historical novel). Transl.: Eva Rácz. Intr.: Anna Földes. Bp. 1964, Corvina. x, 417 pp. (Hungarian Library.)

Song of the Wheatfields (Novel). Transl.: Georg Halász. New York 1930, Brewer–Warren. 283 pp. — Id.: London 1931, Allan. 295 pp.

MÓRICZ, ZSIGMOND

Be Faithful unto Death (Novel). Transl.: Susan Kőrösi. Intr.: Péter Nagy. Bp. 1962, Corvina. 264 pp. (Hungarian Library.) — 2nd ed. 1969, 309 pp.

The Torch (Novel). Transl.: Emil Lengyel. New York 1931, Knopf. 276 pp.

NAGY, LÁSZLÓ

Love of the Scorching Wind. Selected poems 1953–1971. Transl.: Tony Connor, Kenneth McRobbie. (Ed.: George Gömöri, Gyula Kodolányi.) Forew.: George Gömöri. Bp.–London 1973, Corvina–Oxford Univ. Press. XIII, 84 pp.

NÉMETH, LÁSZLÓ

Guilt (Novel). Transl.: Gyula Gulyás. Bp.–London 1966, Corvina-Peter Owen. 439 pp.

Revulsion (Novel). Transl.: Kathleen Szász. London 1965, Eyre and Spottiswoode. 542 pp. — Id.: New York 1965, Grove. 542 pp.

OTTLIK, GÉZA

School at the Frontier. (Novel). Transl.: Kathleen Szász. New York 1966, Harcourt, Brace and World. 374 pp.

ÖRKÉNY, ISTVÁN

Catsplay (A tragi-comedy in two acts). Transl.: Clara Gyorgyey. New York 1976, Samuel French Inc. 83 pp.

PETŐFI, SÁNDOR

The Apostle (Epic poem). Transl.: Viktor Clement. Forew.: Csaba Sík. Bp. 1961, Corvina 98 pp.

His Entire Poetic Works. Transl.: Frank Szomy. (Boca Raton, Florida) 1972. XXVII, 747 pp.

Petőfi (Poems and prose). Selected works. Transl., intr.: Anton N. Nyerges. Ed.: Joseph M. Értavy–Baráth. Buffalo, New York 1973, Hungarian Cultural Foundation. 423 pp. (Program in East European and Slavic Studies 5.)

Petőfi Sándor by Himself. Selected works. Sel., intr.: György Radó. Transl.: G. F. Cushing, E. B. Pierce, etc. Bp. [1973], Pannonia. 41 pp. [On the cover: Petőfi. 1823–1973.]

Prose and Poetry, poems by Major Henry d'A. Blumberg, with a short introductory note on Petőfi, the Hungarian poet. Play, prose and poetry by Gustav d'A. Blumberg. Intr.: Rosa d'A. Blumberg. London 1934, Williams and Norgate. 221 pp.

Rebel or Revolutionary? Sándor Petőfi as revealed by his diary, letters, notes, pamphlets and poems. Sel., forew. and notes: Béla Köpeczi. Poems transl.: Edwin Morgan. Prose writings transl.: G. F. Cushing. Bp. 1974, Corvina. 332 pp.

Sixty Poems (1823–1849). Transl.: Eugénie Bayard Pierce, Emil Delmár. Intr.: Joseph Reményi. Bp. 1948, Petőfi Society. 78 pp.

PILINSZKY, JÁNOS

Crater (Poems 1974–75). Transl.: Peter Jay. London 1978, Anvil Press. 63 pp.

Selected Poems. Transl.: Ted Hughes, János Csokits. Intr.: Ted Hughes. Manchester 1976, Carcanet New Press, 67 pp.

RADNÓTI, MIKLÓS

Clouded Sky (Poems). Transl.: Steven Polgar, Stephen Berg, S. J. Marks. New York etc. 1972, Harper and Row. 113 pp.

The Complete Poetry. Ed. and transl.: Emery George. Ann Arbor Mich. 1980, Ardis. 400 pp.

Forced March (Selected poems). Transl.: Clive Wilmer and George Gömöri. Manchester 1979, Carcanet New Press, 62 pp.

Postcards (Poems). Transl.: Steven Polgar, Stephen Berg, S. J. Mark, West Brench, Io. 1969, Gummington Press [6]. (The translation of four of the author's "Razglednica".)

Subway Stops (Fifty poems). Transl., intr. and notes: Emery George. Ann Arbor, Mich. 1977, Ardis. 95 pp. (Ardis world poets in translation series 4.)

The Witness (Selected poems). Transl.: Thomas Ország. Market Drayton. 1977, Tern. Press. 59 pp.

SARKADI, IMRE

The Coward and Other Stories. Transl.: Barbara I. Scott, József Hatvany, etc. Afterw.: György Somlyó. Bp. 1967, Corvina. 143 pp. (Hungarian Library.)

SZABÓ, MAGDA

The Fawn (Novel). Transl.: Kathleen Szász. London 1963, Jonathan Cape. 215 pp.
Night of the Pig-killing (Novel). Transl.: Kathleen Szász. London 1965, Jonathan Cape. 224 pp. — New ed.: New York 1966, Knopf.
Tell Sally... (Novel). Transl.: Ursula McLean. Bp. 1963, Corvina. 286 pp. (Hungarian Library.)

SZABÓ, PÁL

People of the Plains (Novel). Transl.: George Halász. Boston 1932, Little–Brown. 287 pp.

SZERB, ANTAL

The Pendragon Legend (Novel). Transl.: Lili Halápy. Intr.: Géza Hegedűs. Bp. 1963, Corvina. 230 pp. (Hungarian Library.)

TAMÁSI, ÁRON

Abel Alone (Novel). Transl.: Mari Kuttna. Bp. 1966, Corvina. 168 pp. (Hungarian Library.) [The first part of the author's trilogy Abel.]

TERSÁNSZKY JÓZSI, JENŐ

Good-bye, my Dear.—The Harlot and the Virgin (Novels). Transl.: Barna Balogh. Intr.: György Rónay. Bp. 1965, Corvina. 165 pp. (Hungarian Library.)

WEÖRES, SÁNDOR

Selected Poems [of]—[and of] *Ferenc Juhász.* Transl., intr.: Edwin Morgan, David Wewill. Harmondsworth–Baltimore–Ringwood 1970, Penguin Books. 136 pp. (Penguin Modern European Poets.)

ZILAHY, LAJOS

The Angry Angel (Novel). Transl.: Thomas L. Harsner. Melbourne–London, etc. 1954, Heinemann. x, 384 pp. [The 3rd part of the novel The Dukays.]
Century in Scarlet (Novel). New York–Toronto, etc. 1965, McGraw-Hill, x, 411 pp. — Id.: London 1966, Heinemann. vii, 438 pp. [The lst part of the novel The Dukays.]
The Deserter (Novel). Transl.: George Halász. Garden City 1932, Doran. 6, 314 pp. — Id. London 1932, Nicholson and Watson. 286 pp.
The Dukays (Novel). Transl.: John Pauker. New York 1949, Prentice-Hall. 404 pp. — Id.: London etc. [1950], Heinemann. 687 pp. [The second part of the novel The Dukays.]
The Guns Look Back (Novel). Transl.: Lawrence Wolfe. London–Toronto [1938]. W Heinemann. 287 pp.
Two Prisoners (Novel). Harrisburg 1968, Giniger-Stackpole. 468 pp. (Great novels and memoirs of World War I. 4.)

Index of Names

561

Miklós Zrínyi

János Batsányi

Ferenc Kazinczy

Mihály Csokonai Vitéz

Dániel Berzsenyi

Károly Kisfaludy

József Katona

Ferenc Kölcsey

Mihály Vörösmarty

Sándor Petőfi

Mór Jókai

János Arany

Zsigmond Kemény

Kálmán Mikszáth

János Vajda

Imre Madách

József Eötvös

Endre Ady

Zsigmond Móricz

Mihály Babits

Dezső Kosztolányi

Margit Kaffka

Gyula Juhász

Árpád Tóth

Frigyes Karinthy

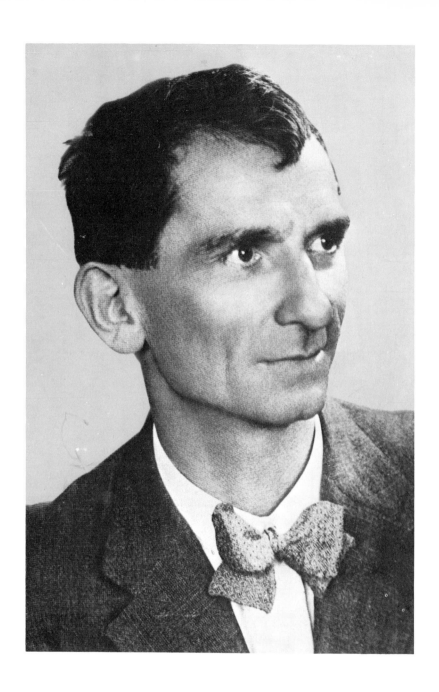

Jenő Tersánszky J.

Milán Füst

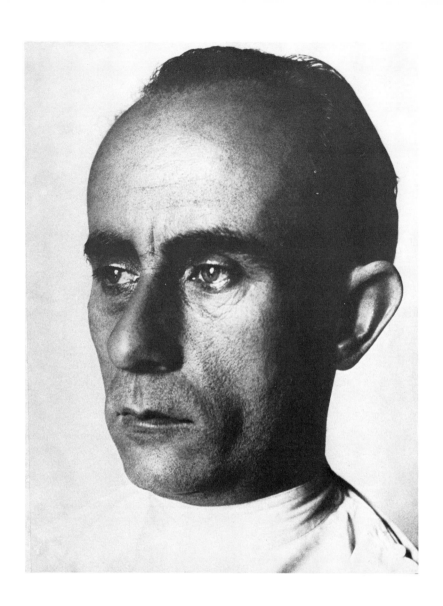

Lajos Kassák

Attila József

Miklós Radnóti

Sándor Weöres

Lajos Nagy

Áron Tamási

László Németh

Gyula Illyés

Tibor Déry

Ferenc Juhász

László Nagy

József Lengyel